The Russian-sponsored attack by the Shah of Persia on Herat was the latest move in the long-running tournament for predominant influence in Central Asia called the Great Game. Its proximity to India could not be tolerated as it threatened British designs for the expansion of trade along the Indus valley.

Urged on by hawkish secretaries, hoodwinked by the wily Maharaja of Punjab and prompted by his political masters in London, the ostensibly peaceful Governor-General of India, Lord Auckland, ordered the assembly of a vast army to counter the Persian move. The opportunity was also to be used to replace Shah Shuja back on his ancestral throne of Afghanistan.

At the eleventh hour, Persia withdrew from its failed attack and to many a sage observer, Lord Auckland should have ordered his army back to barracks. Instead, an army of 10,000 soldiers, 50,000 transport animals and 30,000 camp followers advanced in December 1839 for the single purpose of regime change. From the very first blare of bugles and the cracking of whips, this glorious army was to prove that the path to Hell is paved with good intentions.

In *Dust of Glory* the author explores the causes of the First Anglo-Afghan War and describes its course gleaned from a multitude of sources supported by seventeen sketch maps of key actions. No lessons were learnt as five more conflicts were to follow in this country that only produces fruit, nuts and opium.

The author was born in the Punjab, close to the border with Afghanistan. He left India with his parents after Partition. He finished his education at the Jesuit College of Mount St Mary's in Yorkshire. After National Service, he elected to proceed to the Royal Academy, Sandhurst and was commissioned into the Duke of Cornwall's Light Infantry. On completion of a course at the Staff College in Camberley, he was assigned to a staff appointment in Singapore. He was then seconded to the 10th Gurkha Rifles and served with them in Borneo. In 1969 he applied for early retirement and worked for a Chinese trading company in Taiwan for the next thirty years. He now lives with his wife in retirement in Gerrards Cross, Buckinghamshire. He is also the author of *Bright Eyes of Danger*, an account of the Anglo-Sikh wars, published by Helion in 2015.

DUST OF GLORY

The First Anglo-Afghan War 1839-1842, its Causes and Course

Bill Whitburn

Helion & Company

Dedicated to the 'Curry Club'

Helion & Company Limited
Unit 8 Amherst Business Centre
Budbrooke Road
Warwick
CV34 5WE
England
Tel. 01926 499 619
Email: info@helion.co.uk
Website: www.helion.co.uk
Twitter: @helionbooks
Visit our blog at blog.helion.co.uk

Published by Helion & Company 2021
Designed and typeset by Mach 3 Solutions Ltd (www.mach3solutions.co.uk)
Cover designed by Paul Hewitt, Battlefield Design (www.battlefield-design.co.uk)

Cover artwork: Shan Sujah's Horse Artillery, First Afghan War by David Rowlands.

ISBN 978-1-914059-33-9

British Library Cataloguing-in-Publication Data.
A catalogue record for this book is available from the British Library.

Contents

Appendices

List of Illustrations

List of Maps

Abbreviations

AAG	Assistant Adjutant General
ADC	Aide de Camp
BER	Bengal European Regiment
BomNI	Bombay Native Infantry
BNI	Bengal Native Infantry
Cav	Cavalry
CB	Companion of the Order of the Bath
CENTO	Central Treaty Organisation
Comm Dept	Commissariat Department
DAQMG	Deputy Assistant Quarter Master-General
DJAG	Deputy Judge Advocate General
HM	Her Majesty
Lt	Light
NAAFI	Naval Army and Air Force Institute
NATO	North Atlantic Treaty Organisation

Glossary

Atta	Wheat flour
Babu	Indian clerk
Bhais	Hindu priests
Bildar	Unskilled labourer
Buniers	Shopkeepers
Burra Tamasha	Big show or funfair
Burra Khana	Big dinner party
Batta	Out of Station allowance[1]
Buzhaski	A form of Polo, played with a goat's carcass
Chattie	Earthenware pots
Chalak	Cunning
Chowkidar	Watchman
Chuppow	Surprise attack
Chuprasi	Office orderly
Cooli	Porter
Cos	Length, approximately 2,000 yards
Cossids	Special messenger
Crores	100 Lakhs, written as 1,00,00,000
Dak	Post (letters)
Dangali	Liquid measure of three pints
Dewan	Governor
Dhoolie	A covered litter
Duck	A European of the Bombay establishment
Durbar	A royal court
Fakir	Literally a poor Sufi holy man
Feringhee	Foreigner
Ghat	A river crossing place
Golandoz	A native artilleryman[2]
Gora	Horse[3]

1 Forerunner of Local Overseas Allowance (LOA).
2 A Mughal word for 'gunner', bringer of round shot.
3 'Gora', a slang term used by natives for English soldiers, *Gora Log*.

Guddi	A Raja's throne
Howdah	Platform on elephant on which a VIP sits
Hakim	Indian doctor
Havildar	Indian Army native sergeant
Hazir-Bashee	King's Bodyguard
Ingrezi	English or English person
Jan Baz	Afghan cavalry
Jagir	A non-hereditiary territory given by a ruler to a chief
Jemadar	Indian Army native lieutenant
Jezails	A long-barrelled Afghan matchlock musket
Jehalchee	Afghan infantryman armed with a *jezail*
Jihad	Holy war
Kafila	A caravan
Khelat	A dress of honour
Khidmatgar	A major-domo
Khurbuddi	A five-a-side game of 'touch'
Koi Hai	European of the Bengal establishment (literally, 'Is anyone there?')
Kunwar	Crown Prince (Sikh)
Kushi	Easy
Lakh	One hundred thousand
Lal Khurthi	Redcoats
Lal Qila	Red Fort
Loya Jirga	National Assembly of Pashtun elders
Lungghar	Sepoy's dining hall
Mahout	Elephant driver or keeper
Maund	80 pounds (weight)[4]
Mohur	Gold coin worth 20 rupees or 30 shillings
Mooth	Lentils, gram
Muffussil	Countryside
Munchi	An Indian writer, private secretary or language teacher
Mull	An European of the Madras establishment
Mullah	Muslim priest
Musnad	Throne cushion
Mussuck	A water container made of goat skin
Mullah	A Muslim priest
Nawab	Lord (title)
Niak	Indian Army native corporal
Oot Wallah	Camel herder
Paltema	Flat-bottomed boat
Pugri	Turban
Puranna	Official order (instructions)

4 In the 1800s the weight value of the maund was different in the three Presidencies: in Bengal, a maund equalled 80 lb; in Madras, 25 lb; in Bombay, 28 lb. The Bengal equivalent is used in the text.

Rissaldar	A troop of Indian irregular cavalry
Sardar	Commander or nobleman (Sikh)
Sati	Hindu custom of widows' and slave girls' self-immolation
Seer	Weight measure of two and a half pounds
Sepoy	Indian Army native infantry private soldier
Shabash	Well done!
Shahzada	Crown Prince (Muslim)
Shashkas	Russian sword
Shroof	Moneylender
Sowar	Indian Army native cavalry trooper
Subadar	Indian Army native captain
Syce	Native groom
Syud	Holy man
Tiluk	A holy mark on forehead
Tulwar	Sword
Vakil	Ambassador, representative
Wazir	Chief minister
Wali	Supreme chief
Yaboo	Stout little horse[5]
Yaki	Mad
Zenana	Section of house reserved for women

5 This horse is capable of carrying 300 lbs with ease for 20 miles per day.

HM Regiments Mentioned in Text

3rd Light Dragoons
4th Light Dragoons
14th Light Dragoons
16th Lancers
2nd Foot. Queen's Royal (West Surrey)
3rd Foot. Buffs (East Kent)
9th Foot. Norfolk
13th Foot. Somerset
17th Foot. Leicestershire
21st Foot. Royal Scots
23rd Foot. Royal Welsh Fusiliers
26th Foot. Cameronians
28th Foot. Gloucestershire
31st Foot. Huntingdonshire. Later East Surrey
40th Foot. 2nd Somerset. Later South Lancashire
44th Foot. Essex
68th Foot. Lincolnshire

Preface

When Helion & Company kindly published my account of the Anglo-Sikh Wars, I was so enthused I felt I had to continue to occupy my retirement years writing a further account. The first hurdle was the selection of a subject of a Victorian war in the Indian subcontinent. While there are a number of such subjects to choose from, I selected the First Anglo-Afghan War as it was the very first of Queen Victoria's 'little wars' and also because many of the protagonists were also involved in the Anglo-Sikh Wars. I am very aware of the fact that hundreds of more eminent authors have written about the Afghan wars and, no doubt, many more will do so in the future for the simple fact that the Afghan issue is still with us, and my hope is that my account may prompt new comers to the subject to read more in depth histories of this particular war; a war waged in perceived justice and ending in humiliating disaster. I am vain enough to hope that despite the faults and imperfections that may be found in this account, it will not prove to be uninteresting to the general reader. Any errors in the text are entirely mine and I lay myself open to being corrected on points of fact; as regards opinions, I am prepared to defend them.

As with my first effort, I wanted to start my research with a personal reconnaissance of the theatre of operations, or at least some of it, both to get a feel of the distances involved, the feature of the terrain and to add some kudos to my planned account. This was my second hurdle. I wrote to the P.R. Department of the Ministry of Defence; this was before NATO pulled out in December 2014. To my surprise I was contacted by a very pleasant colonel, who told me that I would have to be sponsored by a group already operating in Afghanistan and based on my association with the Brigade of Gurkhas, I thought I would be able to square this away quite easily. However, the colonel's second condition was much more difficult, as he informed me that the venture would cost a minimum of £15,000. I asked him to kindly put my request on the back burner. Then a friend of ours suggested that I should write to a particular Member of Parliament who was known to have connections with Afghanistan. I wrote three times but never got a response. No doubt the Honourable Member is inundated with similar letters and his secretary files them all in File 13. I happened to mention my quest in our local Halal shop, and the immediate response from an Afghan working there was that for £1,500, cash down, he could get me safely to Kabul and back. The disparity between the two quotes compelled me to decline.

Then in early 2017, I came across a letter to the Editor of the *Daily Telegraph* dated 11 January and submitted by the UK Ambassador in Kabul. He wrote:

> SIR, Retracing, in 2017, the footsteps of those who fell in 1842 during the retreat from Kabul would be a foolish mistake. Afghanistan has made much progress but our travel

advice still clearly recommends against any tourism here. A holiday trek through Taliban-held territory would stand a good chance of repeating the events last August, when British tourists were among a group of travellers attacked after putting themselves in harm's way in Herat province.

The British Embassy, with the help of Afghan authorities and international allies, managed to ensure these nationals' safe return home. The next group may not be so lucky.

Dominic Jermey
Ambassador, British Embassy
Kabul, Afghanistan.

When my wife read this, any glimmer of hope to convince her of my intended travel plans, went up in smoke. Consequently, from the comfort of my armchair, my two eyes have scanned the campaign arena via the many excellent books and journals by authors who have been there; whilst my two fingers have travelled numerous miles across the keyboard of my computer. I have enjoyed the ride and only hope the reader of this reconnaissance enjoys the result.

I owe many 'thank yous' for the help I have received in completing this account. First and foremost, my thanks go to the authors of histories and journals listed in my bibliography without whom my project would never have got off the ground; in particular, Fakir Aijazuddin, *the* exponent on Maharaja Ranjit Singh's times, who I have quoted quite extensively in my Chapters 6 and 7 from his well-researched and excellent book, *The Resourceful Fakirs.* Secondly, I extend my sincere thanks to my publisher, Duncan Rogers of Helion & Company who was brave enough to take on the publication of my work. I am also deeply indebted to my editor, Christopher Brice, for his advice and assistance in polishing the text to an acceptable standard. My sincere thanks also go to Tom Mitford, who has been my mentor through the whole process of writing this account, and to my son Alexander for assisting me over my many computer hurdles. Finally, my wife, to whom I owe more than just thanks.

In my account I have employed a few innovations for the purpose of clarity and convention. At the start of each Chapter I have shown both the first and surname of the characters as they appear in the text, thereafter, I have only shown their surname, except in the cases of characters having the same surname, in which case I have shown both the first and surnames throughout the chapter. However, there were two officers who had the same first and surnames, Captain William Anderson, one man belonging to the Bengal Cavalry and the other to the Bengal Artillery. In this case I have left it to the text to indicate the identity. Captain William Anderson of the Bengal Artillery who was the commander of the Shah's Horse Artillery, is depicted in the painting on the cover of this book. Whenever an actual quote is given, I have kept the original spelling of place and people's names. Where pounds sterling are given I have, in brackets, shown today's equivalent value. I have done this by multiplying the original by 75. At Appendix VI, I have compiled a list of European Officers and civilians who were killed or died during the campaign. I believe it to be the single most comprehensive list ever published. I deliberately choose not to include European and native Other Ranks as all the despatches of that campaign do not name Other Ranks and due to amalgamations and computerisation, unless one knows the name of a soldier it is almost impossible to compile a list; in the case of native Other Ranks, it is impossible as the majority of the regiments were disbanded at the time of the Indian Mutiny and any records have since disappeared. Finally, in the case of gun sizes

I have resorted to the British Army's 'Staff Duties in the Field', in which gun sizes are shown as 6-pdr, etc.

In writing this account of the First Anglo-Afghan War, I concluded that the writing of military history is rather like mixing a cocktail; one part irrefutable fact, one part debatable conclusion with a dash of author's conjecture, stirred not shaken. I hope the reader enjoys my Afghan cocktail, which I have called 'Dust of Glory'.

Bill Whitburn

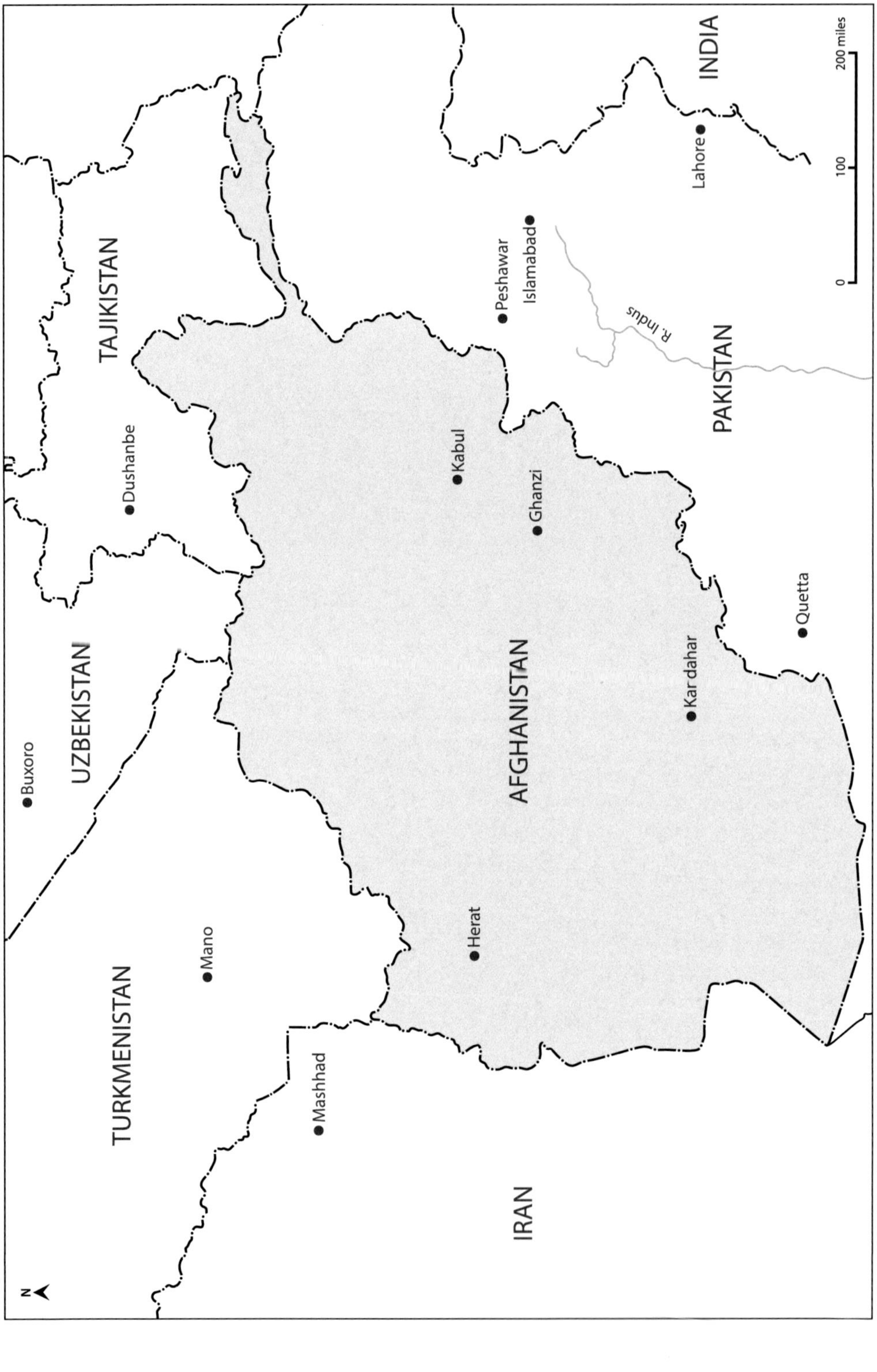

Map 1 Current Map of Afghanistan and neighbours.

1

From Out of the Hindu Kush[1]

It is said, when Allah finished creating the world he had a few rocks left over, and with these he made Afghanistan. In time, from these snow-capped rocks, streams flowed into the valleys and the resultant silt formed the earth for vegetation attracting diverse numbers of migrants to occupy these life-supporting valleys. They brought with them their various skills and customs and soon the families evolved into clans and then into tribes, each separated by ranges of rocks and each zealous of their acquired territory and adapting to it. The larger mud-brick dwellings were then fortified and each tribe preyed on the other for its existence. To these people the most important things in life were water to sustain life, women to procreate, and weapons to defend what little they had. Two thousand years later, the then Amir of Afghanistan was reported to have said, 'We have rocks and we have men, we have everything.'[2]

In ancient times this desolate and harsh geographical area was called Bactria and by 550 BC Cyrus the Great had added it to his vast Persian Empire. The Persian army had subdued the local tribes, gave them a language and a concept of currency. In each area Cyrus left a governor to maintain order with a garrison supplemented by local tribesmen. These local levies were eventually incorporated into the Persian army. One of these tribes could have been the Abdalis.[3]

Some 200 years later a young Philip II ascended the throne of Macedonia and in short order made it the most important Greek principality, in the process created an awesome army with which he planned to launch a crusade against the Persian Empire. However, on the eve of his crusade he was assassinated and his 20-year-old son, Alexander, eagerly hoisted on his breastplate to lead the crusade. His Persian opposite number at the time was Darius III, equally young and determined. Allied to the Persian army was a corps of 2,000 cavalry from Bactria.

Alexander the Great started his invasion in the spring of 334 BC. By the winter of 330 BC this young military genius had conquered the Persians, and Darius III was on the run with his Bactrian cavalry. For the next couple of years, Alexander chased Darius III through

1 Much of the chronology in this chapter is based on that given in Stephen Tanner's excellent book, *Afghanistan: A Military History from Alexander the Great to the War Against the Taliban* (Philadelphia: De Capo Press, 2002).
2 Amir Dost Mohammed Khan to Sir John Lawrence, in Peshawar at the signing of the Anglo-Afghan Treaty of 1855.
3 Tanner, *Afghanistan*, p.23.

Afghanistan and as far up north as Bokhara. His progress into this barren and strongly disputed land was methodical, securing supplies at each stop and reconnoitring ahead to check what they would come up against, making full use of the knowledge of the local collaborators. In the main Alexander left his 'camps' in the charge of local governors and garrisoned by his sick and wounded. The army moved with little baggage and of camp followers there were none; lean and mean, the key ingredients of speed and success. During this campaign Alexander's army could cover 260 miles in 11 days.[4] Over 2,000 years later the British Army, laden with baggage and hampered by a large multitude of camp followers, was to take 23 days to cover the same distance.

Alexander found Darius III at the southern tip of the Caspian Sea, dead. He had been murdered by disgruntled members of his meagre entourage. The quest of the Macedonian Army was now at an end, so it thought, and many of Alexander's soldiers wanted to return home carrying their accumulated loot with them. But Alexander had other ideas, he now wished to conquer the world, which in the era of a 'flat world' was at the other end of India. Meanwhile, one of the Persian governors had raised his head above the parapet and announced himself as the successor of Darius III, declaring his intention to oppose the young Alexander.

By now Alexander had moved his army south to Balkh, the legendary birthplace of Zoroaster and in an effort to ameliorate his soldiers' very long absence from home, he allowed them to take wives from the local population. At this time Alexander also enlisted the Bactrian cavalry into his army, partly to fill the gaps created by homeward bound soldiers and also to denude the area of potential aggressors. From Balkh the Macedonian Army spread out in columns to mop up the mountain fortresses that were still holding out. One of these was located at Sogdian Rock where the Persian governor was holding out with 1,000 men and plenty of supplies. This place was on an inaccessible precipice which gave strength to the governor's bravado. Undeterred, Alexander's men scaled the precipice and shocked the governor into surrendering. It was during this incident that Alexander noticed one of the governor's daughters, Roxane.[5] She was reputed to be the most beautiful woman in the world, so Alexander married her in the spring of 327 BC. That winter the Macedonian Army moved south to what was to become Charikar, at the mouth of the Parwan Valley and it was here that Alexander planned his invasion of India.

The Macedonian Army poured through the Khyber and onto the plains of the Punjab. At the River Jhelum, close to where 2,000 years later the British fought the Sikhs during the Second Anglo-Sikh War in a bloody battle neither side won, Alexander confronted King Porus and beat him in a lengthy battle. It is here that Alexander's famous horse, Bucephalus, was killed and buried with much ceremony. With no more opposition the Macedonian Army advanced to as far as the River Hyphasis, now the Bias. By now Alexander's men had had enough and were homesick. Reluctantly, Alexander agreed to withdraw but not before he had captured Multan where he was nearly killed. His army then proceeded north essentially along the route that the British 'Army of the Indus' took in its advance to Afghanistan in 1839. In this trek north, Alexander lost 70 percent of his exhausted army to heat, dehydration and hunger. The remnants of this once awesome army eventually reached Babylon, Alexander's favourite city, where a couple of years later he died at the very young age of 33.

4 Tanner, *Afghanistan*, p.31.
5 Tanner, *Afghanistan*, p.49.

Alexander the Great had had complete confidence in his own immortality and by dying so young he had failed to select and nurture a successor. When on his deathbed his generals asked him who his successor was to be, he replied, 'The strongest'.[6] His generals departed to the various corners of the vast Macedonian Empire to become the 'king-pins' in those corners. General Seleucus, from his base in Babylon, seized control of the centre and eastern territories. General Ptolemy took over Egypt, and Macedonia was held by his brother for Alexander's unborn son. Thus, Alexander's great empire disintegrated leaving, as in Bactria, garrison towns controlled by Persian governors.

A quarter of a century later a new force from India, led by Chandragupta Maurya, advanced north eliminating the Greek posts in the Punjab then traversed the Suleiman range of rocks to confront General Seleucus and beat him at Kandahar. In the peace settlement that followed, Chandragupta was given control of southern Afghanistan in exchange for 500 war elephants, which Seleucus successfully employed elsewhere. In the following 50 years the Mauryan Empire expanded to include Kandahar, Ghazni and Kabul up to the foothills of the awesome Hindu Kush rock pile. By 268 BC, Asoka, Chandragupta's grandson, had taken over the reins of the empire and is widely accepted as one of the greatest kings of India. After one of his more gruesome battles, Asoka was so struck with remorse that he converted to Buddhism. By the time of his death in 232 BC he had been instrumental in spreading Buddhism through the Punjab and into Afghanistan. After his death the Mauryan Empire began to crumble and at about the same time the Seleucids' grip on their territories was assailed by a surge south of Parthians, from east of the Caspian Sea, into the area of Herat. In the north, the Greek-Bactrian governor of Bactria asserted his independence by creating a kingdom in the centre of Afghanistan, which remained isolated and independent for the next 300 years.

In 209 BC, the Seleucids were blessed with a new, young and dynamic, king, Antiochus III. He pushed back the Parthians, recaptured Herat and Kandahar, scrambled over the awesome Hindu Kush and entered Bactria. Instead of the usual fight the Bactrians signed a mutual defence agreement with Antiochus, who withdrew back to Babylon to face a new emerging power in the Mediterranean, Rome. As he moved west so the Parthians filtered back to their previous strongholds.

In 190 BC, the Seleucids and the Romans clashed at the battle of Magnesia. The Romans disseminated the Seleucids who were now lost to history, and the Parthians moved into the wreckage and occupied Babylon. In time the Parthians were also to face the Romans but try as they did the Romans never made it into Afghanistan. Meanwhile back in Bactria, under its new warlord, Demetrius, its army marched south and captured Kandahar, then marched through the Bolan Pass onto the plains of the Punjab. At the height of its power this Graeco-Bactrian kingdom held sway from Merv in the north, through Afghanistan, to Taxila in the south. But they were also eventually overcome by a horde of nomadic tribes called the Kushans who occupied the Kabul valley. The Parthians having been pushed back concentrated on their territories in the west, leaving the new Kushan entrants to expand from the Caspian Sea to the Arabian Sea and into the Punjab.

In 125 AD, a man named Kanishka assumed the throne of Kushan. He extended his empire down to the River Ganges and to the Parthian territories in the west. He established Peshawar

6 Tanner, *Afghanistan*, p.53.

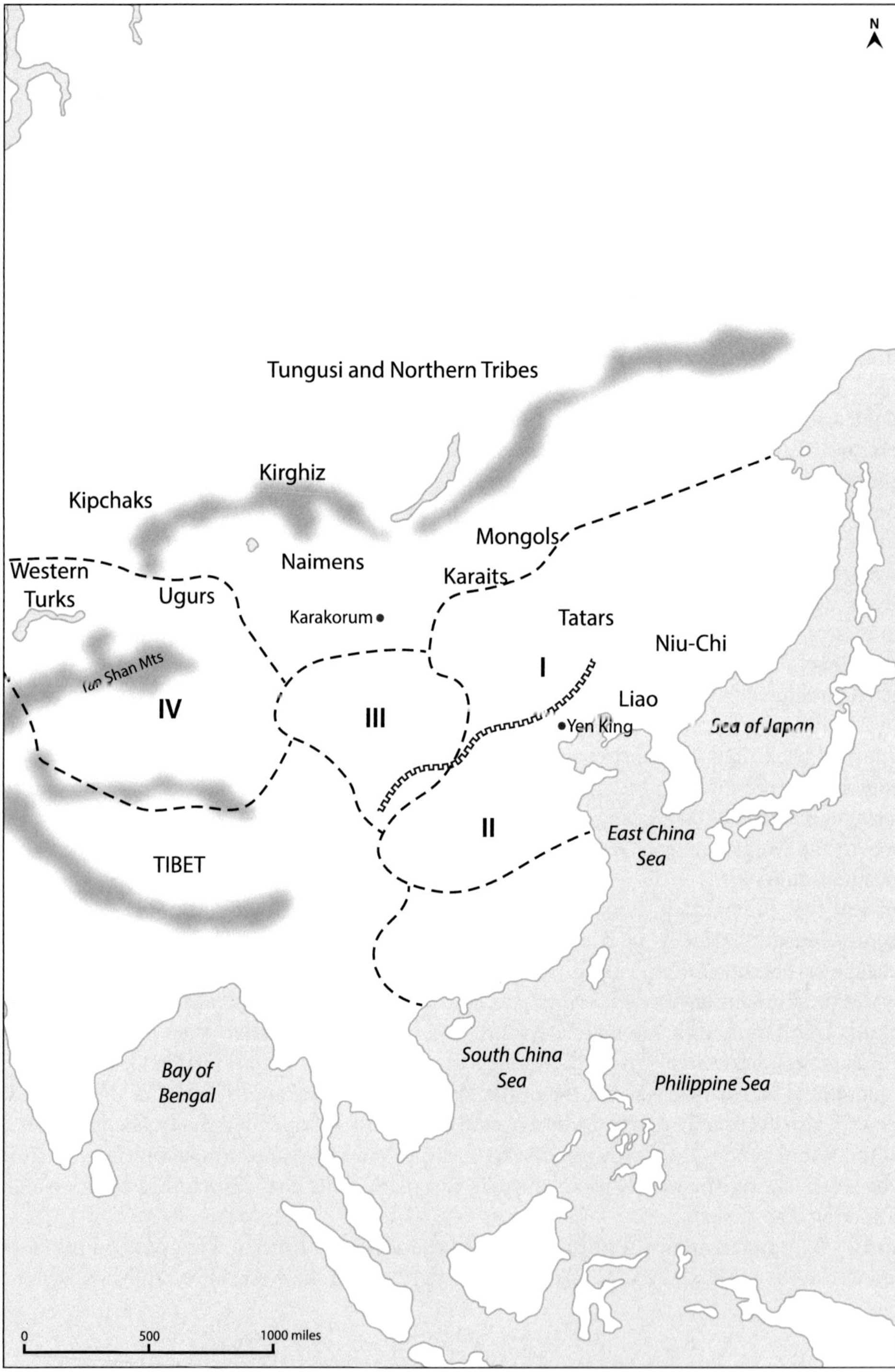

Map 2 Eastern Asia, at the end of the twelfth century.

as his winter capital while Bagram, now the site of Kabul International Airport, was his summer capital. Like Asoka before him, Kanishka converted to Buddhism and spread this religion even more extensively. He died in 150 AD and his empire, at the loss of so dynamic a character, gradually fell apart. By the time of his demise Afghanistan had been made witness to the great ancient civilisations of Persia, India, China and the Graeco-Roman. Now it was to return to the Persian fold as in 225 AD the Persian General Ardashir overran Afghanistan.

In 427 AD, Afghanistan experienced another invasion of conquerors, this time hordes of barbaric White Huns, who sprawled over Bactria into the Kabul valley and onto the Punjab plains. Theirs was a destructive invasion, devoid of culture resulting in much slaughter, particularly of Buddhists, but did not touch the huge carved statues of Buddha in Bamian. Within 100 years a counter-offensive by the Persians, assisted by local warlords, put paid to the White Hun regime. Remnants of these Huns remained to add to the mix of cultures in Afghanistan.

Halfway through the new century, another invasion, of the greatest significance, was launched. On the death of the Prophet Mohammed, a fanatical army of horsemen sprang forward to spread the word of the Prophet. The horsemen were essentially Arab and their mission was conversion, by force if necessary. Their first target were the Persians and by connection the Afghans. These horsemen, who in time evolved into *mullahs*, confined their activities to the valleys and towns. During this period Turkic-speaking nomads had carved out an empire in what was called Transoxiana with their capital at Bokhara. A Turkic slave named Alptigin, after an abortive coup, fled south over the Hindu Kush and established a centre of operations at Ghazni. These Turkic Ghaznavids became staunch followers of Islam and soon this religion spread across Afghanistan.

In 998 AD the third Ghaznavid king, Mahmud, succeeded to the throne. He was a warrior and a bigot, but also the first to establish an indigenous Islamic Afghan regime. Having established his control over Afghanistan, Mahmud pushed back the Hindus and focused his compass on the non-Islamic and ancient civilisation of India. He conducted a total of 17 brutal raids into India, sacking the cities and destroying the temples; in the process becoming exceedingly wealthy. One of his raids went as far south as Kathiawar where he seized the gates of Somnath and a stone carving of Shiva's penis. The former were to be the gates to his tomb and the latter the stepping-stone to it.

Mahmud of Ghazni died in 1030 AD and with his demise the empire started to falter, thus allowing another tribe called Ghorids to establish themselves as the new claimants of his empire. These people originally came out of the remote valleys of the Hindu Kush and established their capital at Herat. In 1040, the Ghorid king Alauddin attacked Ghazni and burnt it to the ground and expanded his control over the Ghaznavid Empire. But the Ghorid Empire was also to be short-lived as by 1205 the Turkics from Transoxiana attacked and defeated them thus establishing the new empire of Khorwasin, which in time was to become the most powerful Islamic state in the world. By 1215, the Khorwasin Army had completed its conquest of Afghanistan and Shah Mohammed II's son Jalaluddin was made governor. Jelalabad is named after him.

As strong as it was the Khorwasin Empire was unable to cope with the human avalanche that stormed in over the rocks of Afghanistan. This was the Mongol Army, led by its brilliant leader, Genghis Khan (Temujin). It was not the intention of the Mongols to conquer and hold, it was to destroy and loot. They were not just a horde of barbaric marauders; Genghis Khan's army was disciplined, organised and under excellent subordinates. The Mongols continued to expand long after Genghis Khan's death in 1227. At the height of their power they covered an area that included China into Mongolia, as far as Hungary and Baghdad in the west and down to Peshawar in the south. But by the end of the century the Mongol Empire began to fall apart. Kublai Khan, the grandson of Genghis Khan, remained in China, the north became the Kipchak Khanate, the conquered territories became the Il-Khanate, Transoxiana became the Jazatai Khanate and Afghanistan was left a 'no man's land' between the Il and Jazatai Khanates.

Then, out of what had been Transoxiana, there appeared another warlord, more ruthless and cruel than Genghis Khan by the name of Tamerlane. He was born in 1336 to a minor Mongol chief and by the age of 25 he had secured the control of the Jazatai Khanate and proceeded to successfully fight wars and battles all the way to Moscow and Damascus. Then, at the age of 62, he made a dramatic and unexpected raid through Afghanistan into India, going as far south as Delhi. On the way he plundered the countryside killing thousands of Hindus, and sacked Delhi. He then returned north to prepare for his new venture, China. This was not to be, as he died in 1405 aged 69. Interestingly, Tamerlane's tomb was discovered by Soviet archaeologists in 1941, but Genghis Khan's tomb, said to be somewhere in Mongolia, has yet to be discovered.

After Tamerlane, there were no more incursions into Afghanistan for the next 100 years. Instead the tribes fought each other for superiority and extension of their territories. One tribe, the Ghilzai, penetrated south, along Tamerlane's route to Delhi, and established the dynasty of Lodis there. Meanwhile, on the borders of Afghanistan, new empires were beginning to take shape. In Persia, a warrior named Shah Ismail Safari, who was later to give succour to Humayan, the second of the Mughal Emperors, consolidated his power and made Isfahan his capital. At about this time in the Jazatai Khanate was born a young ambitious warrior by the name of Zahiruddin Mohammed. He was better known as Babur, the first of the great Mughal emperors. He was a descendant on his father's side from Genghis Khan and on his mother's side from Tamerlane, the perfect DNA for a conqueror.

With a band of warriors, Babur attempted to become supreme in his own homeland and failed. So he ventured south, over the rocks of the Hindu Kush and tried his luck there. With relative ease and at the age of 21 he secured Kabul, his first victory and a place for which he always had a fondness, electing to be buried there. Babur kept a journal, known as the 'Baburnama' in which he described his adventures, the people and the places during the course of his lifetime. Not since the time of Alexander the Great, 1,800 years earlier, had the world been given a recorded history of Afghanistan. In his journal he also gave names to the more important Afghan tribes such as the Ghilzai, Yuzufzai, Afridi and Abdali. In his book *Places in Between*, Rory Stewart describes his own journey, on foot, along the same route that Babur took to Kabul, quoting from the 'Baburnama' at the appropriate stages.

In 1512 Babur pointed his compass towards India, and after some heavy going, bribing his way through the passes he arrived at Panipat to fight the first battle for India in April 1526 against the Afghan Lodi King Ibrahim. After a number of brutal battles against the Lodis and Rajputs, Babur consolidated his position becoming the first Mughal emperor of a dynasty which was to last for the next 300 years, until the British exiled the last emperor, Shah Zafar II, to Rangoon in 1858 and his two sons and grandson were cut down by an East India Company officer at the *Lal Qila* in Delhi in 1858.

Babur died in 1530 at Agra and was buried, in accordance with his wishes, in Kabul. His son Humayan took over, but was outmanœuvred by an Afghan named Sher Shah, who claimed the throne of Delhi. Humayan tried to get back to Kabul where his brother was governor, but this ungrateful sibling refused him succour, so the royal refugee sought and was given asylum by the

Shah of Persia, at the price of becoming a Shiite. During his travels the beggar emperor was blessed with a son, Akbar, born on a horse blanket in the Sindh desert, the greatest of all the Mughal emperors. At the age of 19 Akbar fought the second battle for India at Panipat and went on to rule India for the next 50 years. Having consolidated his position in India, Akbar sallied back north to reassert imperial control over his grandfather's legacy. He built a massive fort at Attock and the first road up the Khyber. He next conquered Kashmir and subdued the Afghan tribes along the Indus. By the time of Akbar's great-grandson, Aurangzeb, the Mughal Empire stretched from Balkh in the north down to Kandahar and the Arabian Sea, Kashmir and 90 percent of the Indian subcontinent. However, in Afghanistan, the Mughals were forever being pestered by Afghan tribes, particularly the Yuzufzais in the north and the Ghilzais in the south.

After Emperor Aurangzeb's death in 1707, the Mughal Empire began to lose its 'umph' while the tribes in Afghanistan were acquiring it. Herat, the seat of Tamerlane's empire, was essentially a Persian domain while Kandahar was a revolving door of claimants. During this period the southern valleys of the Hindu Kush evolved into an area of Pushtu-speaking people, who came to be known as Pushtuns or Pathans. Today, 90 percent of Afghans are Pathans speaking Pushtu.

In the 11th edition of *Encyclopaedia Britannica*, Colonel Sir Thomas Hungerford Holdich described the Afghans as:

> Inured to bloodshed from childhood, [they] are familiar with death, and are audacious in attack, but easily discouraged by failure; excessively turbulent and un-submissive to law and discipline; apparently frank and affable in manner, especially when they hope to gain some object, but capable of the grossest brutality when that hope ceases. They are unscrupulous in perjury, treacherous, vain and insatiable, passionate in vindictiveness, which they will satisfy at the cost of their own lives and in a most cruel manner. Nowhere is crime committed on such trifling grounds, or with such general impunity, though when it is punished the punishment is atrocious. Among themselves the Afghans are quarrelsome, intriguing and distrustful; estrangements and affrays are a constant occurrence; the traveller conceals or misrepresents the time and direction of his journey. The Afghan is by breed and nature a bird of prey. If from habit and tradition he respects a stranger within his threshold, he yet considers it legitimate to warn a neighbour of the prey that is afoot, or even to overtake and plunder his guest after he has quitted his roof. The repression of crime and the demand of taxation he regards alike as tyranny. The Afghans are eternally boasting of their lineage, their independence and their prowess. They look on the Afghans as the first of nations, and each man looks on himself as the equal of any Afghan.[7]

Next to appear on the Afghanistan canvas was a Persian adventurer by the name of Nadir Kuli Khan. He staged a coup against the Safavid regime, clashed with a combined force of Ghilzais and Abdalis, then incorporating the latter in his army, swept through Afghanistan, down the Khyber Pass, into the Punjab and descended on the imperial capital of Delhi. Such

7 Colonel Sir Thomas Hungerford-Holdich, KCMG, KCIE (British geographer and President of the Royal Geographical Society, Superintendent Frontier Surveys India. 1842–1929). He wrote many articles for Encyclopaedia Britannica. This quote is from his article, 'Afghanistan', in the 1911 edition under subsection 'Population'.

was the discipline of Nadir's army that for two days no outrage was committed; then a rumpus occurred in the famous Chandi Chowk bazaar when some of his men were killed. Nadir Shah, as he was then known, let slip the dogs of war with a vengeance. In a matter of six hours the slaughter that raged accounted for 110,000 slain. After a stay of 58 days, he retraced his steps back to Persia having demanded a subsidy of 20 *crores* of rupees, took, in marriage for his son, the granddaughter of Emperor Aurangzib, the Peacock throne, the *Koh-i-Noor* and the *Bhe-i-Noor* diamonds, 10,000 elephants, 7,000 horses, 10,000 camels and cart loads of treasure,[8] all protected by his elite Abdali bodyguard. Nadir Shah as a conqueror was very successful and this made him exceedingly arrogant and unbearable, so much so that he was murdered by his own officers; clearly, his elite bodyguard had been looking the other way. The commander of this guard was an Afghan named Ahmad Khan, who with his force of 4,000 cavalry was allowed to ride off into the sunset, taking with him the *Koh-i-Noor* diamond!

In October 1747, the Abdali tribe held a council or *loya jirga* at which they selected their next leader. With a 4,000-strong force behind him, the 25-year-old Ahmad Khan was the obvious choice and was duly proclaimed Ahmad Shah Duranni. This elevation was topped by a stroke of luck when a treasure-laden caravan, assigned to Ahmad Shah Duranni's previous boss, arrived in Kandahar and he claimed it for services rendered to his murdered boss. Ahmad Shah Duranni belonged to the Sadozai sub-clan of the Abdali tribe. Another sub-clan of the same tribe, which was to feature greatly in the history of Afghanistan, were the Barakzais. Having secured himself in the Kandahar area, Ahmad Shah ventured east to seize Ghazni and Kabul. Mission complete, he resolved to push south to claim for himself the lands ceded by the Mughal Emperpor to Nadir Shah. His first incursion into India was abruptly stopped by a Mughal force led by a brilliant young general and governor of Lahore, Mir Mannu. Ahmad Shah returned to the Punjab in the following year and succeeded in capturing Lahore. The 'fight' in the Mughals had deserted them and the Punjab was formerly ceded to the Afghan conqueror. Young Mir Mannu was left in Lahore to serve his new Afghan master.

On his return to Afghanistan, Ahmad Shah Duranni, now exceedingly wealthy, had no trouble persuading the other tribes to join him thus doubling the size of his army which he directed against Herat. This essentially Persian stronghold, succumbed after a nine-month siege. He then marched his huge army to the Persian capital of Isfahan. Based on his successes in the west, Ahmed turned his attention to the northern regions of Afghanistan and seized Balkh and Mazai-i-Sharif, thus establishing the northern boundaries of his empire.

In 1752, Ahmad Shah Duranni's young governor at Lahore switched allegiance back to the Mughals, and so angered the mighty Khan that he retraced his steps back to the Punjab. This time he not only repossessed Lahore but added Multan, Sindh and Kashmir to his empire, plus he collected an enormous amount in tax arrears. By the time of Ahmad Shah's fourth visit to India a new force had risen out of the wilds of the Deccan. This was the Maratha army, too strong for the Mughals and a potent enough threat to the Afghan conquerors' acquired Indian territories. So, in 1761 Ahmad Shah, at the head of a huge army, marched from Kandahar for the third battle for India at no less a place than Panipat. Both sides fought hard and the outcome was in the balance until a counter-attack, led by Ahmad Shah, broke the Maratha line followed

8 James Baillie Fraser, *The Persian Adventurer: Being the Sequel of 'The Kuzzilbash'* (London: H. Colburn and R. Bentley, 1830), p.363.

by the wholesale massacre of the mighty Marathas. Ahmad Shah then marched triumphantly into Delhi and had all his Indian acquisitions endorsed by Emperor Alamgir II. As part of the victory celebration, Ahmad Shah married one of the Emperor's daughters and bestowed another on his son Timur, whom he left behind in Delhi as Governor.

At the height of his power Ahmad Shah had carved out an Afghan empire which stretched from Herat and Meshed down to the Arabian Sea in the west, Balkh and Srinagar in the north and down to Lahore and Hyderabad in the south. At this juncture it can be said that at every turn of the pages of Afghanistan's history, the indigenous tribes had witnessed an endless series of invasions and occupations by a myriad of sometimes brutal conquerors, and in the chaos managed to keep their individualism. For the first time, with the advent of Ahmad Shah Duranni, there appears a purely Afghan state, albeit under a Duranni regime. To Ahmad Shah Duranni must surely go the title of *Ahmad Shah Baba*, Father of the Afghan Nation.

Ahmed Shah was to make a further three trips to India, essentially to cope with the increasing annoyances of a new aspiring military force called the Sikhs. At the beginning the Sikhs had been a passive religious movement which had been cruelly treated by Emperor Akbar's grandson and later by the Afghans. In order to survive, the Sikhs had donned their breastplates and unsheathed their *tulwars* and evolved into the implacable foes of the Afghans. They were masters of hit-and-run tactics and caused a great deal of damage to Ahmad Shah's army. In 1769 Ahmad Shah made his last trip to India. He died of skin cancer at Kandahar on 16 October 1772 at the young age of 50. His second son, Timur, ascended the Duranni throne.

The character of this prince differed greatly from that of his father. He was weak and fond of ease and when he felt himself secure in possession of the throne, he yielded to his natural disposition instead of endeavouring to consolidate his large empire. This inactivity encouraged the disaffected and inspired the conquered provinces with of regaining their independence. Although he continued to maintain the kingdom bequeathed him by his father without much apparent loss, he left it, at his death, in such a state as to be ready to fall to pieces upon the first shock. He reigned for 20 years and died in 1793 at Kabul, the city to which he had moved his capital. By the time of his death, he had failed to nominate any one of his numerous sons as his successor.

2

Brothers of Afghanistan

After a remarkably sedentary reign of 20 years, Timur Shah died in Kabul on 20 May 1793. He had not nominated a successor, and consequently the whole of the fabric of government fell to pieces as his 25 sons, by various wives, vied for a piece of the action if not the throne. Of these Sadozai brothers, seven were prominent in the chaos that followed. Timur Shah's eldest son, Humayun, logically the strongest claimant, was away in Kandahar; Mahmoud and his full brother Feroz were at Herat while Abbas was in Peshawar. Zaman and Shuja were conveniently in Kabul. The last two were the sons of Shah Timur's favourite wife who came from the influential Kuzzilbashe community in Kabul.

To add to this mix of princely ambitions, Pyndah Khan, the chief of the Barakzai clan and Shah Timur's trusty *Wazir*, was equally prolific with a string of 21 sons. These two clans, Sadozai and Barakzai, both of the Abdali tribe, were to dominate Afghan politics for the next 50 years. For the purpose of clarity, the names of the various brothers and their sons, will be suffixed in this chapter with the letter S (Sadozai) or B (Barakzai) to indicate to which clan they belonged.

A palace coup instigated by Shah Timur's Kuzzilbashe wife and executed by Pyndah Khan (B) placed Zaman (S), aged 28, on the throne as the new Shah. His first act was to put the other princes in Kabul at the time into prison, excluding his full brother Shuja (S). Shah Zaman's (S) next concern was the possible counteractions by his out-of-reach brothers, especially Humayun (S). An army was quickly organised to advance on Kandahar and snuff out this likely threat. It would appear that Humayun (S) was not very popular and when attacked by Shah Zaman's (S) army, led by Shuja (S), his troops deserted him and Humayun (S) was captured.

Apparently, according to Muslim custom, a blind man cannot be king, so Shah Zaman (S), in order to quash this threat forever, had his brother's eyes plucked out and the wretched Humayun (S) disappears from the pages of history. It is interesting to note that this law did not apparently apply to the blind Mughal emperor in Delhi, Shah Alam, who had his eyes gouged out in 1801 at the hands of an Afghan mercenary named Gholum Kadir.

Shah Zaman's (S) army then advanced on Herat, where Mahmoud (S) and Feroz (S) wisely surrendered and paid homage to the new Shah, but not for long.

During the first 18 months of his reign Shah Zaman (S) was busy putting down various rebellions and an incursion into Balkh by Morad Khan the Amir of Bokhara, plus a challenge from Mahmoud (S), who had declared his intention to replace his half-brother Shah Zaman (S). The two armies met on the Helmand River. It was a close fight with Shah Zaman (S) securing a victory as Mahmoud (S) scurried back to Herat.

Despite his paranoia about security on his home front, Shah Zaman (S) was determined to re-establish sovereignty over his grandfather's vast dominions in India. He was much encouraged in this desire by solicitations from all dissident Muslims in India, including Tippu Sultan, anxious to banish the English and subdue the Marathas, who were holding the Emperor, Shah Alam, prisoner. Both the English and the Marathas were greatly alarmed at the intelligence of the Afghan march on Delhi as this would throw the whole country into a state of disorder and anarchy. According to the governor general at the time, Lord Wellesley, the threatened Afghan invasion 'was creating the liveliest sensation throughout India'. The English response was to increase the East India Company's army not only to counter any Afghan threat but also to control the troublesome Marathas. Shah Zaman's (S) first invasion, made in the winter of 1795, only got as far as Rhotas on the River Jhelum. This massive fort, still inhabited, was built by Sher Khan in 1535 to keep invaders out; it was never used for that purpose and was last used, in a military context, by the fleeing Sikh army in 1849. On arrival at Rhotas, Shah Zaman (S) received the news that Agha Mohammed Khan, the eunuch Shah of Persia, had invaded the Afghan territories of Khorasan, so Shah Zaman (S) high-tailed it back to defend his kingdom. While the Shah of Persia was in Khorasan he had the bones of Nadir Shah dug up and taken to Teheran.

In November of the following year, Shah Zaman (S) assembled an army of 30,000 and marched into the Punjab creating a great deal of panic in all India. He advanced, unopposed, to Lahore when, yet again, he was forced to return home to contend with another challenge by Mahmoud (S). Shah Zaman (S) advanced to Kandahar and with bribes and promises he was able to get Mahmoud's (S) adherents to desert him, thus claiming mastership of Kandahar. Mahmoud (S) and his son Kamran (S) fled to Torskish.

For the third time, Shah Zaman (S) buckled on his sword belt for yet another invasion of India. He left Peshawar in October 1798 and advanced without opposition to Lahore. It was during this invasion that the young chief of the Sukerchakia clan of Sikhs, Ranjit Singh, paid homage to Shah Zaman (S). The Shah got no further than Lahore as, for the third time, news from the home front compelled him to retrace his steps. This time the new Shah of Persia, Fateh Ali Shah, had invaded Khorasan and he had done so at the behest of the English, who had sent a Muslim, Mehi Ali Khan from Bombay, well known at the Persian court, with a letter to the Persian Shah requesting his assistance to frustrate the Afghan shah's latest incursion into India. Before leaving Lahore, Shah Zaman (S) wrote to the Mughal emperor in Delhi reassuring him of his return in order to place him back on his throne and to make Muslims the paramount power in India.

On his way back to Afghanistan, during the winter of 1799, Shah Zaman (S) lost a number of his guns while crossing the River Chenab and his young friend Ranjit Singh undertook to dig the guns up and send them on to Afghanistan. The English were much concerned about this friendship and Lord Wellesley, the governor general, issued an instruction that 'a native agent appropriately qualified for the occasion should be immediately despatched to the Court of Maharaja Ranjit Singh with suitable instructions for impressing that young chief with a just sense of danger to which he would expose his interests and those of his nation by yielding to the insidious proposals of Shah Zaman (S)'.[1] The young Sikh chief did send some of the guns back, but he was never a friend of the Afghans.

1 Khushwant Singh, *A History of the Sikhs*, Vols 1 & 2 (Oxford: Oxford University Press, 1999), p.199.

As Shah Zaman (S) approached Herat the Shah of Persia moved his army back and Shah Zaman withdrew to Kandahar leaving his son Khyser (S) as governor of Herat. Shortly thereafter the dreaded Mahmud (S), with 10,000 men attacked but failed in his attempt to capture Herat. Then in the following spring, being promised assistance to grab the Afghan throne, Mahmoud (S) joined the Shah of Persia on his second invasion of Khorasan. The venture achieved little and Persian assistance proved to be more boastful than real. In despair, Mahmoud (S) moved off to Tubbas.

While Shah Zaman (S) was busy invading India and rushing back to protect his dominions he had left the administration of Afghanistan to his brother-in-law and *Wazir*, Wuffadar Khan. Shah Zaman's (S) brother Shuja (S) had also married one of the *Wazir*'s sisters. This choice of *Wazir* was most unfortunate as this gentleman used his ascendancy to overturn the power of Pyndar Khan (B) and all the great officers of the state particularly the Kuzzilbashe chiefs. About six of these chiefs, disgusted at the power and influence of Wuffadar Khan, conspired to have him killed, dispose of Shah Zaman (S) and place his brother Shuja (S) on the throne. On hearing of the conspiracy Wuffadar Khan duly informed Shah Zaman (S) and made a point of implicating old Pyndar Khan (B). The conspirators were apprehended and summarily beheaded. Shock and horror! As Pyndar Khan's (B) head fell to the ground the robust alliance that had existed between the Sadozai and the Barakzai clans, nurtured from the days of the great Ahmad Shah Duranni, was irreparably broken, and Shah Zaman's (S) fate was sealed.

Despite the rumblings of dissensions in Kabul, Shah Zaman (S) launched his fourth and final attempt at invading India in an effort to secure his throne by proving his worthiness to don the mantle of his illustrious grandfather. Meanwhile the eldest son of Pyndar Khan (B), Fateh Khan (B) bestirred himself from his fort at Girishk and approached the ever-envious Mahmoud (S) with a scheme to wrest the throne from his half-brother. Together they advanced on Kandahar with a large army and besieged the place for 42 days at which point the governor, Sydaul Khan, in customary treachery, handed over the city. Shah Zaman (S) had got as far as Peshawar when he was informed of this latest mischief. His reaction to this intelligence was rather extraordinary; instead of hurrying back to sort out the revolt in Kandahar, he sent part of his army to Kashmir to capture and torture the brother of Sydaul Khan, who was the governor of that province. He left his brother Shuja (S) in Peshawar with some men and with a somewhat depleted army advanced on Kandahar. Having secured Kabul the little army continued its advance to Kandahar. Then further treachery struck as the advance guard deserted causing Shah Zaman (S) to fall back on Kabul pursued by Fateh Khan (B). In Kabul Shah Zaman (S) found no support, so deserted and bedraggled the wretched Shah Zaman (S) wandered off and eventually sought asylum at the fort of *Mullah* Ashik.

This treacherous cleric, with an eye to a handsome reward, informed the gloating Mahmoud (S) of his guest, and Mahmoud (S) sent Assud Khan (B), accompanied by a *hakim* to gouge the eyes out of the hapless Shah Zaman (S). This happened in 1800 and so, after a rather disruptive reign of seven years, Zaman (S) was no longer shah, for ever more. He was bundled back to Kabul where he remained a prisoner during the reign of the new shah, Mahmoud Shah (S). The *Wazir*, Wuffadar Khan, was summarily executed.[2]

2 William Hough, *A Narrative of the March and Operations of the Army of the Indus* (n.p.: Elibron Classics Reprint, 2006), p.386.

It would appear that the great Ahmad Shah Duranni had so conditioned Afghan society of the day, that kingship belonged to his heirs and that a Sadozai had to rule, and there were many candidates.

Mahmoud Shah (S) proved to be unprincipled, indolent and timid, caring little about governing the country, which he left to his benefactor, Fateh Khan (B) and a gentleman named Akram Khan Alizye. As long as his own desires were met and his person was secure, the new king was indifferent to the conduct of his ministers, officials and the *Gholam-i-Shah*, the shah's bodyguard of Kuzzilbashes. Consequently, trouble started to erupt on all fronts. Shuja (S) in Peshawar had already proclaimed himself shah and was busy organising an army to make good his claim. Serious trouble erupted in Kabul itself, between the Sunni community and the Shia Kuzzilbashes,[3] while in the east the Ghilzais, never bosom pals of the Durannis, broke out in an insurrection proclaiming one of their own chiefs as their king.

In September 1801, Shuja (S) was on the road to Kabul with an army of 10,000 men. Halfway there he was met by an army of 3,000 men led by Fateh Khan (B), but the obvious victory eluded the unlucky Shuja (S) and he escaped back to the Khyber hills. During the following November a Ghilzai army of 20,000 threatened the regime and was soundly beaten off by the Durannis. Then in the following spring the Ghiljies were back in the field, this time with an army of 50,000 and were, once again, soundly beaten. The skulls of the beaten foe were piled in a pyramid to mark the victory.

Meanwhile, the hapless Shuja (S) was wandering round Baluchistan seeking help and living off the sale of family jewellery, which the prudent Zaman (S) had left behind in Peshawar with his brother. In the winter of 1802, his luck changed when given a tip-off that a rich caravan was travelling south. Shuja (S) and his cohorts surrounded the caravan and purloined its goods, worth three *lakhs* of rupees. With this Shuja (S) was able to assemble an army for an attack on Kandahar.

Back in Kabul quiet had been restored but the situation was grim. Many of the chiefs of outlying provinces refused to acknowledge Shah Mahmoud's (S) authority. Feroz Khan (S) at Herat while acknowledging the Shah's authority governed as if he was independent and a depleted treasury left Shah Mahmoud (S) with no options to strengthen his control.

Then the two great men of government, Fateh Khan (B) and Akram Khan Alizye had a big falling out. The latter, who was disgusted with the indolent behaviour of the Shah and favoured Shuja (S), fled from Kabul. This was on 8 July 1803. He was back in four days with Shuja (S) in tow. They found Mahmoud (S) besieged in the Bala Hissar, a great shapeless piece of power, by an uprising of the people. Akram Khan Alizye and Shuja (S) camped outside the city swelling their ranks to counter the advance of Fateh Khan (B). At first Fateh Khan (B) was winning the fight but then, in typical Afghan style, one of his chiefs declared for Shuja (S) and the battle was lost. Without any support, Fateh Khan's (B) only option was to flee to Kandahar, where Shah Mahmoud's (S) son, Kamran Khan (S) was then the governor.

Next morning, to the acclaim of the populace, Shah Shuja (S) entered the Bala Hissar, the Shah's palace in Kabul. He released his blind brother and put Mahmoud (S) into the cell that Zaman (S) had just vacated and in a rare instance of Afghan clemency, Shah Shuja (S) did not have Mahmoud (S) blinded. Shah Shuja's (S) next priority was to pay off, in cash or

3 Hough, *Narrative*, pp.384–5.

appointments, all the Duranni and Kuzzilbashe chiefs who had made his coronation possible after two years of trying. This largesse knocked a big hole in the budget and what remained came under the control of his appointed *Wazir* and benefactor Akram Khan Alizye, who made full use of his privileged position. Shah Shuja (S) next had the treacherous cleric, *Mullah* Ashik, apprehended and beheaded.

Having returned stability to the Kabul area, Shah Shuja (S) advanced on Kandahar where by means of a negotiated settlement Fateh Khan (B) offered his submission, while Kamran Khan (S) rode off to Herat and the Shah occupied the city of his grandfather. By his submission Fateh Khan (B) had hoped that the new Shah would revive the old custom of appointing a Barakzai as his *Wazir*, but this position was already held by Akram Khan Alizye, with whom Fateh Khan (B) had quarrelled. Frustrated in his designs, Fateh Khan (B) was allowed to slip away to his fort at Girishk, located on the road between Herat and Kandahar and commanding the summer ford of the Helmand. The government of Kandahar was now in the hands of Khyser Khan (S), the son of the blind Zaman (S), with a gentleman named Ahmed Khan Noszye as his councillor.

Unlike his predecessor, Shah Shuja (S) was disinclined to allow his *Wazir* a free hand in the administration of the country, consequently each endeavoured to build his own power base, which did not assist in the establishment of a robust administration capable of coping with the likes of Kamran Khan (S) and the arch conniver Fateh Khan (B), waiting in the wings to do mischief.

In the beginning things worked quite smoothly and with the west of the country stable, Shah Shuja (S) moved into the Sindh in 1804, to compel those chiefs to acknowledge his authority and to pay a subsidy of 17 *lakhs* of rupees. He then moved to his eastern frontier settling all the provinces enroute and arrived in Peshawar in April 1805. Here he was married to the daughter of Morad Khan, the Amir of Bokhara, thus solidifying the non-aggression pact made with his brother Zaman (S).

Meanwhile shenanigans broke out back in Kandahar. The ubiquitous Fateh Khan (B) had somehow persuaded Khyser Khan (S) to imprison his councillor and in retaliation this man's son opened the gates of the city to Kamran Khan (S), who in turn was booted out by the combined forces of Khyser Khan (S) and Fateh Khan (B). By this time Shah Shuja (S) had arrived on the scene and a contrite Khyser Khan (S) submitted to the mercy of his uncle the Shah. He was forgiven and reappointed to his post. Fateh Khan (B), with his newest designs shattered, moved to Herat to bend the ear of Feroz Khan (S) with ideas of claiming the throne. Feroz Khan (S), the younger brother of the Shah Shuja (S) advanced on Kandahar and the Shah sent Khyser Khan (S) to confront his uncle. In typical oriental fashion a truce was negotiated between uncle and nephew and the frustrated Fateh Khan (B) high-tailed it back to his fort in Girishk.

The scheming and tenacious chief at Girishk, Fateh Khan (B), still had a few tricks up his sleeve to tempt the rapacious Sadozai princes to bid for the throne and thereby make himself the *Wazir*. His next move was rather bizarre. He approached Kamran Khan (S) with a scheme to recover the throne of his imprisoned father, and this young prince duly advanced on Kandahar. Khyser Khan (S) was just about to capitulate when Fateh Khan (B) switched sides and renewed his plans to place Khyser Khan (S) on the throne. This act of treachery was not forgotten by the vengeful Kamran Khan (S).

This bizarre alliance between Khyser Khan (S) and Fateh Khan (B) was fraught with undertones of jealousy and suspicion. Fateh Khan (B) gave up the venture in disgust and audaciously approached Kamran Khan (S), whom he had just double-crossed, with new ideas of capturing Kandahar; a prelude to an advance on Kabul. The rapacious Kamran Khan (S) agreed and they marched on Kandahar. Khyser Khan (S) panicked and fled to Baluchistan leaving Kamran Khan (S) and Fateh Khan (B) masters of Kandahar.

At about this time Shah Shuja (S) was at his favourite place, Peshawar, organising an expedition to Kashmir, the only province still in rebellion. He sent Akram Khan Alizye, his *Wazir*, with a force of 10,000 to attack Abdullah Khan (B). The campaign was quite messy due to weather conditions and terrain. Eventually, by the spring of 1806, Abdullah Khan (B) had been killed and his Kashmiri army surrendered.

Shah Shuja (S), luxuriating in Peshawar, recalled his army from Kashmir and prepared for his advance on Kandahar, yet again. Close to Kandahar the two armies met and Kamran Khan's (S) army, having been reinforced from Herat by Kassim Khan (S) the son of Feroz Khan (S), got the better of the contest. Then, news arrived of a Persian threat to Herat and as one, the Duranni Shah and all the chiefs formed common cause to oppose the Persians. But the luckless Shah Shuja (S) could not accompany the chiefs as he had been informed that his *Wazir*, Akram Khan Alizye, had at last shown his hand by schemes of replacing the Shah with Abbas Khan (S), one of the imprisoned princes. While this particular scheme failed, Akram Khan Alizye next advocated the candidature of Khyser Khan (S). During all these strange goings on at Kabul the escape of the ex-Shah Mahmoud (S) was easily facilitated. Meanwhile, Shah Shuja (S) had withdrawn to Peshawar to await the advance of the combined forces of Akran Khan Alizye his *Wazir* and Khyser Khan (S), his nephew. After the customary negotiations failed the two opponents met for battle on 3 March 1808. The Shah's army was being worsted when, in a sudden twist of fate, Akram Khan Alizye made a reckless charge and was killed and his army fled. The Shah re-entered Peshawar triumphant with his ex-*Wazir*'s head on a spear. His nephew scurried up the Khyber Pass towards Kabul.

With Peshawar secure, Shah Shuja (S) had to contend with various rebellions; one in Kashmir, now under Atta Mohammed Khan, another in Kandahar, to which place the ex-Shah Mahmoud (S) had gone to join the conniving Fateh Khan (B) and another in Kabul, where the late Akram Khan Alizye's bosom pal, Meer Waez, along with Khyser Khan (S) was preparing to defend the city against the Shah's expected attack. However, by the time the Shah's army had approached Kabul, Meer Waez and Khyser Khan S had withdrawn to the Kohistan area where they remained in rebellion for some time. Eventually, Khyser Khan (S) submitted to his uncle, who once again forgave his nephew. The Shah now set his compass on Kandahar and after a battle with the combined forces of Mahmoud (S) and Fateh Khan (B) once again secured Kandahar.

Shah Shuja (S) then moved to Peshawar to counter the anticipated advance of Atta Mohammed Khan from Kashmir. It was while he was in Peshawar that the Shah entertained the large British Mission led by Mountstuart Elphinstone and signed a treaty of friendship with the understanding that the Afghan Shah would not allow 'the French tribe' into Afghanistan. The mission arrived on 8 February 1809 with loads of gifts for which the parsimonious Court of Directors were later to table a censure. Elphinstone's entourage included William Fraser, the Assistant Resident at Delhi, 13 officers, 4,000 cavalry and infantry, 600 camels, 13 elephants and his *munchi*, Pundit Budh Singh, who was to become the father of another 'Great Game' player named Mohan Lal.

No sooner than the ink had dried on the Anglo-Afghan treaty, Shah Shuja (S) was informed that Fateh Khan (B) was back in Kabul and had put Mahmoud (S) back on the throne. Everything

Taken from an early nineteenth engraving of 'Natives of Kabul Province'.

now depended on money with which to buy the support of the chiefs and the poor Shah had very little. By the sale of some of his jewellery, he was able by June to assemble an army of 14,000 and marched off to Kabul, while the Elphinstone mission crossed the River Indus back to India.

The situation in Kabul was reported to be unsatisfactory and the people were generally looking forward to the success of Shah Shuja (S). As his army marched through the mountain defiles it was attacked at Neemla by a relatively small force of 3,000 men under Fateh Khan (B). Quite unexpectedly the Shah's force was beaten and the Shah galloped back to Peshawar, where he regrouped his army and advanced on Kandahar, occupying the city without opposition. Not for long! Fateh Khan (B) was back on the road with a larger army. Thinking better of it, the Shah withdrew from Afghanistan and sought refuge in Rawalpindi. From there he sought asylum for his family from the Sikh Maharaja, Ranjit Singh, in Lahore and the family moved there along with the blind ex-Shah Zaman (S), once the conqueror of Lahore.

Back in Kashmir, Atta Mohammed Khan, fearing for his independence, sent his brother Jandar Khan to ex-Shah Shuja (S) with felicitations of support for the recovery of his throne in exchange for which Atta Mohammed Khan was to be given Attock. This huge fort, on the left bank of the Indus, was built by Emperor Akbar in 1535 and is still in use as a prison for political prisoners. Ex-Shah Shuja (S) happily went along with the scheme and joined Atta Mohammed Khan at Peshawar. No sooner had Shuja (S) arrived than he was instructed to disperse his army and hand over his artillery. Obviously, ex-Shah Shuja (S) objected to these terms causing his arrest and banishment to Moran in Kashmir, a prisoner.

Not surprisingly, Fateh Khan (B) had been appointed *Wazir* by the new king of Afghanistan, Shah Mahmoud (S), who continued in his indolent ways allowing his *Wazir* to rule the country. The Grand *Wazir*'s first concern was the recovery of Kashmir and as a prelude to this he sent his brother Azeem Khan (B) to remove Jandar Khan from Peshawar which he dutifully did allowing Shah Mahmoud (S) and his *Wazir* to move there in safety, while the ousted Jandar Khan slipped across the Indus to Attock. From Peshawar, the *Wazir*, the ruler of Afghanistan in all but title, solicited Maharaja Ranjit Singh's cooperation in a joint campaign against Atta Mohammed Khan in Kashmir. The Maharaja accepted with some alacrity, especially as he was to be handed 20 *lakhs* of rupees for providing an army, plus a share of the spoils. However, being a cunning man himself, the Maharaja saw in the grand *Wazir* an absolute *chalak*, so he positioned his troops accordingly. Meanwhile back in Lahore, Shuja's (S) favourite wife, Wuffa Begum, pleaded with Ranjit Singh to save her husband from the wrath of the *Wazir* and Shah Mahmoud (S). In exchange for her husband's safety and eyesight she promised to hand over the famous *Koh-i-Noor* diamond. After all, no diamond is worth a man's eyesight.

The ensuing campaign was anything but joint. The Maharaja had placed his forces on the River Jhelum while the Afghan *Wazir* made a speedy advance via Noushera into Kashmir and in quick order captured Atta Mohammed Khan. While the *Wazir*'s army was busy in Kashmir, he forestalled the payment of his promised fee, so the Maharaja 'negotiated' the entry of his army into Attock and sent his general, Mohan Chund, via the Pandal range, to secure the person of Shuja (S). As the *Wazir* had reneged on the agreed terms the Maharaja refused to give up both Attock and Shuja (S), who was escorted back to his grateful family in Lahore.[4]

It must be said that this version of Shuja's (S) 'rescue' is at variance with those accounts given by early historians, who state that Shuja (S) was rescued by Fateh Khan (B) and was given a free choice of either returning to Kabul to be reconciled with Shah Mahmoud (S) or proceeding to Lahore to join his family. This particular version of events was published by Alexander Burnes in the book of his travels through Afghanistan and was lapped up by early Victorian authors. Burnes had, no doubt, obtained this account from the brother of the *Wazir*, Dost Mohammed Khan (B). The version recorded by Khashwant Singh is the more plausible bearing in mind that the combination of Fateh Khan (B) and Shah Mahmoud (S) could hardly be described as a haven of compassion.

Once Shuja (S) was reunited with his grateful family in Lahore, the Sikh Maharaja went calling to collect his fee. Shuja (S) protested and some unsavoury haggling ensued. Wuffa Begum and the rest of his family were allowed to leave, while Shuja (S) was kept back under a form of 'house arrest' until he eventually handed over the coveted diamond.

Wuffa Begum was not the first Afghan royal to seek asylum with the British. In 1810, Colonel David Ochterlony, the British agent at Ludhiana, reported that the *Shahzada* Yunas (S), the eldest son of ex-Shah Zaman (S) had 'come with nine servants, distressed and fatigued, seeking asylum and wanting to go to Delhi'. The British authorities thought this too hot a potato to handle, as sanction of asylum could greatly annoy their neighbour Ranjit Singh. The reply to Colonel Ochterlony's application was the following instruction:

> Above all hold out no shadow of hope that the British Government will settle a pecuniary allowance upon him, because such hope, held out by you, would not only confirm him in his purpose, but might bring down others of the princes and even Shuja-ul-Mulk to our territories, which would be a most distressing and annoying circumstance.[5]

4 Hough, *Narrative*, p.396.
5 Records of the Ludhiana Agency, 1808–1815, p.228.

The British Government eventually relented and settled 15 rupees a day on the *Shahzada*. The young prince then informed the British authorities that his blind father, ex-Shah Zaman (S), recently the ogre of all non-Muslim India, wished to retire with his family to the British territories. The response to this request was, 'It is therefore the desire of His Excellency in Council that every effort should be employed to prevent the Shah from carrying his intention into effect.' This request was followed, two years later, by one from Wuffa Begum, the wife of ex-Shah Shuja (S), to which the British reaction was:

> The fulfilment of the intention of Wuffa Begum of seeking asylum would be an event so pregnant with inconvenience, embarrassment and probable expense that the Governor General in Council is extremely desirous that it should not take place. If she does, it will be incumbent on the humanity and generosity of the British Government to grant her the asylum she seeks and to receive her with every suitable mark of distinction and respect. Receiving her does not give claim for asylum to the male branch of the family.[6]

Then, on 19 December 1812, the British agent in Ludhiana received the inevitable request for asylum from ex-Shah Shuja (S) in order to join his family. This was received with a degree of embarrassment and consternation. After an exchange of much correspondence all the Afghan exiles were granted asylum, with pensions of 50,000 and 30,000 rupees being settled on Shuja (S) and Zaman (S) respectively. They were destined to remain in this state for the next 24 years.

As this generosity by the British could be misconstrued as an act of ill-will by the ever-suspicious Maharaja Ranjit Singh, the British agent was instructed to respond to any demand by the Maharaja for the return of the Afghan exiles with the following sentiments:

> The British Government will never give its countenance or support to the family or dependents of Shah Shuja in any design which may interfere with the views or wishes of Maharaja Ranjit Singh but recognises that the withdrawing from them the protection under which they have placed themselves would be inconsistent with the duties of humanity and character of the British nation, and so such can never be a fit object of solicitation.[7]

By this instruction it is clearly evident that the British were most anxious to ensure that nothing was done to upset their ally the Maharaja in Lahore, who was easily consoled over these particular issues; after all, he already had the diamond.

Back in Kashmir, Fateh Khan (B) appointed his brother Azeen Khan (B) the new governor and made preparations for the return of his army to Kabul. Before his departure he was informed of the Sikh acquisition of Attock, where for the consideration of one *lakh* of rupees the fort commandant had thrown open the gates to the Sikh army, who were now for the first time on the banks of the Indus. The *Wazir* resolved to attack the Sikhs in Attock, which is located at the main crossing point into India. His younger brother, Dost Mohammed Khan (B), led the attack with 2,000 men. The Sikhs were too well prepared and gave the attacking Afghans a really bloody nose as they scrambled back across the Indus into Afghanistan.

6 Records of the Ludhiana Agency, p.313.
7 Records of the Ludhiana Agency, p.425.

It was now 1814 and the Persians were demanding a tribute from Herat, a place they had always considered, with some justification, to be under Persian suzerainty. Feroz Khan (S), Shah Mahmoud's (S) full brother, still governed Herat and was advised to reject the Persians' demands, while the *Wazir* advanced to oppose them. Once the *Wazir* had arrived at Herat accompanied by his brother, Dost Mohammed Khan (B), ostensibly to give aid to the beleaguered Feroz Khan (S), he instead arrested the hapless Feroz on suspicion of duplicity and made himself master of all the governor's property and treasure. In the process of this rude assault Dost Mohammed Khan (B) is said to have violated the governor's harem and in particular defiled the person of Kamran Khan's (S) sister, an act brutally revenged. The *Wazir* attacked the Persians who withdrew back to their own territories.

By 1817 the kingdom of Afghanistan was relatively calm with the exception of the western front where the Persians continued to be a nuisance. Shah Mahmoud (S), rioting in debauchery, was quite happy to leave the running of affairs to his most capable *Wazir*. In quick order Fateh Khan (B), the *Wazir*, had filled all the key appointments of state with his 20 brothers, thus ensuring his own gravitas. However, not everyone was happy, least of all Crown Prince Kamran (S) who had good cause to be circumspect and jealous of the *Wazir*'s proceedings, which countered some of his own designs. So this prince resolved to remove his ex-collaborator by whatever means possible. He thus played on his debauched father's mind the notion that the *Wazir* had fulfilled his purpose and was now surplus to requirement and, if not cut down now, could in time replace the Shah. Based on the *Wazir*'s capacity for machinations this was not unlikely, so the father acquiesced with his son's notions.

It was about this time that the Grand *Wazir* had written to the British authorities to keep their hands off Kutch as he claimed that country for the sovereignty of Shah Mahmoud (S). Lord Hastings, the governor general at that time, apparently replied to the effect that, 'While the British Government did not wantonly misuse its strength by trespassing on its neighbour, it has never been attacked without destroying those who unjustly assailed it.'

In spring 1818, the *Wazir* and his trusty brother, Dost Mohammed Khan (B), launched an expedition into Khorasan in opposition to a Persian threat. They were accompanied by the rogue Sikh, Sardar Jai Singh Atariwalla. In 1848, it was this Sikh clan that opposed the British in the Second Anglo-Sikh War. The operation into Khorasan was a success and the Afghan army was returning back to Herat when the *Wazir*'s party was surrounded by some of the Crown Prince's cohorts. Dost Mohammed Khan (B) managed to escape, but the *Wazir* was apprehended and taken back to Herat a prisoner. There he was charged with a list of crimes against the royal family culminating in the order from the cruel prince to have the eyes of the Grand *Wazir* plucked out. The wretched Fateh Khan (B), the erstwhile ruler of Afghanistan, was shoved into a cell no darker, to him, than the rest of the universe.

The bulletin of this heinous deed ricocheted off all the rocks in Afghanistan. The 20 brothers of the erstwhile *Wazir* resolved as one to seek revenge, for him and their revered father Pyndah Khan (B). Their first and obvious move was to declare themselves independent of Shah Mahmoud (S). Thus Afghanistan was thrown into a state of chaos for the next decade, as the Barakzai brothers vied with each other to appoint their Sadozai candidate to the throne. Clearly, the ascendancy of a Sadozai to the throne was paramount at this time.

Meanwhile, Prince Kamran (S) made secure his western flank in a peace deal with Fateh Ali, the Shah of Persia, then, leaving his son Syf (S) and Yar Mohammed Khan in charge of Herat, departed for Kandahar with his father and the blind ex-*Wazir* Fateh Khan (B), where Sher

Dil Khan (B) had imprisoned the Sadozai governor, Mohammed Rahn (B). At the same time Jehangir (S), Shah Mahmoud's (S) grandson, went against Kabul with a large force to subdue the governor, Samad Khan, who had rebelled. On the approach of Jehangir (S), the governor quit the city allowing Jehangir (S) to enter unmolested.

When Azeem Khan (B), in Peshawar, heard about his brother's ordeal and Samad Khan's flight he proclaimed Sultan Ali (S) as the new Shah and proceeded post-haste to Kabul, leaving his brother, Dost Mohammed Khan (B) in charge of Peshawar. Back in Kabul the new *Wazir*, Ata Mohammed Khan (B), sent a message to Dost Mohammed (B) to the effect that if Dost Mohammed (B) advanced on Kabul with his troops, he would deliver Jehangir (S) into his hands. Dost Mohammed (B) left Peshawar and hurriedly joined his brother Azeem Khan (B) who was making his way to the city. Outside the city they met with their brother, the treacherous Ata Mohammed Khan (B). On hearing of the approach of the Barakzais, Jehangir (S) locked himself up in the safety of the Bala Hissar while the Barakzais occupied the city.

Shah Mahmoud (S) and his son Kamran (S) hastened, with a considerable force, to the relief of Kabul, taking the blind ex-*Wazir* with them. About 50 miles from Kabul at a place called Saidabad, Shah Mahmoud (S) called a halt to conduct a special interview with his prisoner. The blind ex-*Wazir* was asked to intercede with his brothers to quit their rebellion and return to the authority of the Shah. Fateh Khan (B), with great fortitude, refused, stating that, as he was blind, he had no further interest in the affairs of the state. A kangaroo court was assembled by Kamran (B) of a lynch mob of chiefs, who had harboured grudges against the ex-*Wazir*. In turn they proceeded to state their alleged grudge and then hack off a part of their victim's person, starting with his nose. They ravaged his body like a pack of hyenas, the Crown Prince providing the *coup de grace* by slicing off Fateh Khan's (B) head. Covered in blood the hyenas bundled up the body parts and sent them back to Ghazni where they were interred.

This cold-blooded murder of a sightless man was too much for even some Afghans, especially the Barakzai clan. The rebellion was carried forward and Afghanistan was plunged further into chaos during which it is estimated that 32,000 Afghans perished.

Dost Mohammed (B), taking his newly appointed sovereign Sultan Ali (S) with him, advanced from Kabul to oppose Shah Mahmoud (S). On this march many chiefs joined the Barakzai army and Shah Mahmoud (S) fearing a defeat retreated back to Ghazni and Dost Mohammed retraced his steps back to Kabul in triumph. While this was going on, Azeem Khan (B) left Kashmir in charge of his brother *Nawab* Jubbar Khan (B)[8] and proceeded to Peshawar. Along the way he met with Ayoob Khan (S), a candidate for the throne and negotiations took place resulting in Azeem Khan (B) proclaiming Ayoob as the new Shah.

Hearing of his brother's antics in Peshawar, Dost Mohammed (B) wrote to him suggesting that as he had already proclaimed Sultan Ali (S) as Shah, his brother should cancel his choice of Ayoob Khan (S). However, as Azeem Khan (B) was the elder, Dost Mohammed (B) was overruled and Ayoob Khan (S) was declared the Shah. As far as the Barakzais were concerned Ayoob Khan (S) was the perfect candidate for the job of Shah; all he desired was the title and trappings with the occasional feast thrown in and he would allow the Barakzais to rule as they

8 The title of *Nawab* was conferred on Jabbur Khan when he was the Afghan chief at Dera Ghuzi Khan. He was removed from there when charged with embezzlement by Fateh Khan who demanded a payment of 3 *lakhs* or loss of eyesight. The money was paid and Jabbur Khan was sent to Kabul from whence he escaped to join his more friendly brother in Kashmir.

Afghan warriors.

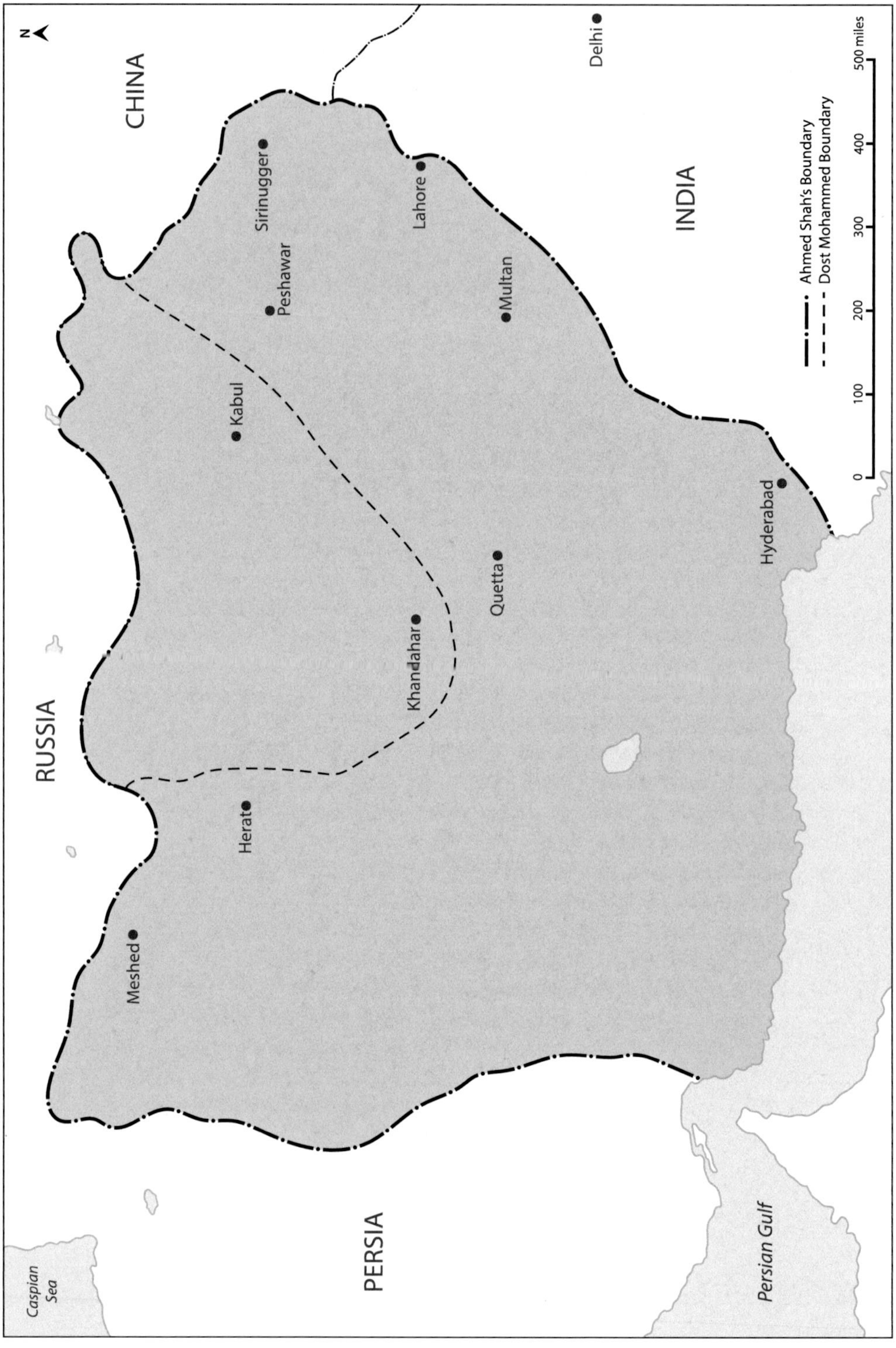

Map 3 Ahmed Shah's Empire versus Dost Mohammed Khan's domain.

wished. The very first task for the new Shah, at the behest of his benefactor, was the murder of his brother Sultan Ali (S). There appears to be no record of what happened to young Jehangir (S); no doubt, in the purge he was apprehended and killed.

The murder of Sultan Ali (S) was obviously not to the liking of Dost Mohammed (B) as with him on the throne Dost Mohammed (B) would have been the *Wazir*. It was this possibility that could have motivated Azeem Khan (B) to have Sultan Ali (S) murdered. Anyhow the two brothers agreed that hostilities between them could only lead to their own destruction so they came to terms by parcelling out the country; Dost Mohammed (B) went to Ghazni, Sher Dil Khan (B) remained in Kandahar and Sultan Mohammed Khan (B) was put in possession of Peshawar. Shah Mahmoud (S) with his son remained ensconced in Herat.

The chaos and preoccupation of the Afghan chiefs was good news for the wily Sikh Maharaja in Lahore, who helped himself to this excellent opportunity to invade Kashmir. *Nawab* Jabbar Khan (B) made a good showing with his much-depleted garrison, but the Sikhs got the better of him and forced him to retire to Peshawar from whence he went to Kabul.

During the apparent quiet on the home front, *Wazir* Azeem Khan (B) decided to kick the Sikh Maharaja, Ranjit Singh, out of Kashmir and by January 1823 his army had arrived at Naushera to give battle to the Sikhs. Unfortunately for the *Wazir*, the Sikhs were commanded by General Hari Singh Nalwa, the Sikh Maharaja's outstanding general, who completely destroyed the Afghan army, which fled back to Afghanistan. Along the way *Wazir* Azeem Khan (B) died of sickness or a broken heart and the Sikh Maharaja acquired suzerainty over Peshawar.

Back in Kabul Ayoob Khan (S) was still the nominal Shah, but had easily been shoved aside by Habidullah Khan (B), the erstwhile *Wazir*'s son, who had taken over as his father's acknowledged successor. The wretched Ayoob Khan (S) eventually pitched up in Lahore where he was granted a stipend by the kindly Maharaja and died there some 10 years later.

Habidullah Khan (B) did not have his father's guile or disposition and was soon aggressively opposed by his uncles, in particular Dost Mohammed (B). Like bees to honey the uncles assembled in Kabul to dispute their claims to the *wazirship*. A state of anarchy ensued and Dost Mohammed (B) finding himself at the short end of the straw wandered off a fugitive. Sometime later brotherly communications were resumed and a deal was struck whereby Dost Mohammed (B) was assigned Kandahar along with Sher Dil Khan (B) and Sultan Mohammed (B) assumed the *wazirship* in Kabul. This truce, like many others, did not last long. Sher Dil Khan (B) died of natural causes and the truce, which he had engineered, unravelled as Dost Mohammed renewed his claims to the *wazirship*.

It would appear that Sultan Mohammed (B) was too frightened to face his grasping brother, so withdrew to his former position in Peshawar and allowed Dost Mohammed (B) to take possession of the capital. All this took place in 1826 and from then on the supremacy between the Barakzai brothers was settled on Dost Mohammed (B). Much of his success was due to the fact that he was the full brother of the great Fateh Khan (B) and their mother Zainab Begum was from the very influential community of Kuzzilbashes.

Gradually, Dost Mohammed (B) extended his authority over what remained of Afghanistan. Kashmir was no longer part of the kingdom, the Amir of Bokhara had captured Balkh, and the Baluchis had stopped paying their tribute and were acting independently, while at Herat the Sadozai Shah Mahmoud (S) remained in complete authority. That left Peshawar, where Sultan Mohammed had surrendered suzerainty to the Sikhs, which could not be allowed to continue. If he could not have Kashmir, Dost Mohammed was adamant not to let the Sikhs lord it over

Peshawar. He assembled a huge army, declared a *jihad* and advanced to attack the Sikhs. At this point Maharaja Ranjit Singh deputed his very capable and astute minister, *Fakir* Azizuddin, and a mercenary employed by the Maharaja, Josiah Harlan,[9] to treat. Once in the Afghan camp the Sikh negotiators were arrested. However, the astute Azizuddin was able to create sufficient dissension among the Afghan chiefs and by liberal compensation, managed to get many of them to give up the cause and return home, much to the bitter resentment of Dost Mohammed (B).

By 1828, Dost Mohammed (B) came to the conclusion that to follow the tradition of having a Sadozai shah was fraught with difficulty, especially as one of these remained in Herat in opposition to the regime, so he declared himself Amir of Afghanistan. His regime was as just as could be expected among a rude and turbulent population: justice was fairly applied; the weak protected and real grievances were addressed. In so doing he trod on the sensitive toes of the old Duranni chiefs, who had previously, in great measure, monopolised all the power (wealth) of the government and were indignant at being controlled by an upstart and undoubtedly started to conspire against him. Many of the conspiracies involved ex-Shah Shuja, residing under British protection in Ludhiana, who in his desire to recover his throne gave credence to the effusive messages from these chiefs.

Based on these messages, and ever hopeful, ex-Shah Shuja resolved in 1833 that a successful return to Afghanistan was timely, but for the wherewithal he was much denuded, so some assistance was a prerequisite. He first approached Captain Claude Wade,[10] the British agent

9 Harlan was one of those strange characters who appear in the history of events and then fade into oblivion. He was a Quaker from Pennsylvania and first appeared on the scene in 1824 when he volunteered as a surgeon for the East India Company's war with Burma. He then trekked up to Afghanistan. During his time there he met up with Moorcroft and no doubt Charles Masson. He then turned up in Lahore and offered his services and knowledge of Afghanistan to Maharaja Ranjit Singh. It is in this capacity of advisor that he accompanied *Fakir* Azizuddin to negotiate with the Afghans. While in the employ of the Sikh Maharaja he had also offered his services to ex-Shah Shuja to raise a sort of 'Fifth Column' in Kabul to facilitate the ex-Shah's return. Harlan met Captain Wade in Lahore and informed him of Charles Masson's true identity, and with this knowledge Wade induced Masson to become his writer (spy) in Kabul. This eventually led to a Royal Pardon for Masson. By 1837 Harlan reappeared in Kabul as a sort of ADC to Amir Dost Mohammed Khan and in this capacity met Alexander Burnes.

10 Lieutenant Colonel Sir Claude Wade (1794–1861). Wade was the son of Lieutenant Colonel Joseph Wade of the Bengal Artillery and was born in Calcutta on 3 April 1794. He was sent to school in England and was awarded a cadetship in the Bengal service of the East India Company in 1809, and on arrival entered the Company's Seminar at Baraset. Six months later, having earned the Sword of Honour, he was commissioned into the 15th Bengal Native Infantry. In 1815 Wade was promoted to lieutenant and saw action in the Pindari Campaign. In 1823 he was appointed by the Governor General as political assistant to Captain Murray, the British agent at Ludhiana, and Wade was put in charge of Shah Shuja and his extended family. In 1825 Wade was promoted to captain and was now employed in conciliating with the Sikhs not to join the disaffected Raja of Bhurtpore, at a time when the British were preoccupied with troubles in Burma. On the death of Captain Murray, Wade took over the Agency of Ludhiana and became the main British contact with Maharaja Ranjit Singh. His influence and impact on the Anglo-Sikh 1834 relationship during the latter part of the Maharaja's reign has not been fully appreciated. Wade got to know the Sikhs better than any foreigner on the frontier and earned, in particular, the confidence of both the Maharaja and his esteemed foreign secretary, *Fakir* Azizuddin. While Wade worked for the benefit of British interests, by his personal character and influence he gave adaptation and flexibility to the rigid unsympathetic nature of a foreign and civilian supremacy. Such was Ranjit Singh's confidence in Wade that he gave him the

Colonel Sir Claude Martine Wade.

in Ludhiana, and duly received a reply from the governor general, Lord William Bentinck (Cavendish), stating:

> My friend I deem it my duty to appraise you distinctly that the British Government religiously abstains from intermingling with the affairs of its neighbours when this can be avoided. Your Majesty is of course master of your own actions (not under duress), but to afford you assistance for the purpose which you have in contemplation, would not concur with the neutrality which on such occasions is the rule of guidance adopted by the British Government.[11]

Cap in hand, ex-Shah Shuja swallowed his pride and approached his *bête noir* Maharaja Ranjit Singh. The wily Sikh chief, master in such matters, agreed to furnish the ex-Shah, when required, with an auxiliary force composed of Muslims and commanded by one of his principal officers to proceed as far as Kabul, on condition that the Sikh Maharaja was confirmed in possession of both Kashmir and Peshawar. Desperate, ex-Shah Shuja agreed and proceeded to make preparations for the great venture. But there was no evidence of the promised auxiliary force, so being thrown entirely on his own resources he managed to raise two *lakhs* of rupees and through the kind offices of Captain Wade secured an advance of four months of his and his brother's assigned pension, albeit the original condition of granting these pensions had been that they were not to be used for any purpose to reclaim the

dewani to collect taxes on his behalf from his Cis-Sutlej estates. This arrangement was a convenient way of smoothing out a complicated situation where the head of an independent state, on one side of the treaty river, was under British protection on the other side. There were many occasions when Wade, known as the 'Captain Sahib' had to sooth the anger of a furious Maharaja about perceived duplicity by the British. On the death of Maharaja Ranjit Singh, Wade's kudos with the Sikh Durbar diminished and his relationship with the Maharaja's grandson became acrimonious. In placating the grandson, the Governor General sidelined his worthy servant to the role of British Resident at Indore. Having served continuously since 1809, Wade retired to his house in the Isle of Weight in 1843 and in 1845, at the age of 51, he married 18-year-old Jane Salina, the daughter of his good friend Captain Thomas Nicholl, Bengal Horse Artillery, who was killed at Gandamuk. Wade died on 21 October 1861 at the age of 67 leaving one son, Claude Fitzroy, who became a barrister. Lieutenant Colonel Sir Claude Wade was described by Josiah Harlan as an expert diplomat, a master of finesse who wielded an expedient and peculiar policy with success.

11 Henry Beveridge, *A Comprehensive History of India*, Vol. 3 (Delhi: Atlantic Publishers, reprint 2003), p.363.

Afghan throne. With these limited means the ex-Shah left Ludhiana on 17 February 1833. By the following May he was at Shikarpore with 30,000 followers. After a battle with the Baluchis at Rohri, he induced them to increase his treasury and his army then advanced through the Bolan Pass on Kandahar, a journey he was to repeat six years later.

Amir Dost Mohammed, back in Kabul, summoned his army and that of his son Akbar Khan (B) from the eastern frontier. Together they marched on Kandahar to oppose the invasion of ex-Shah Shuja (S), who could possibly call on the assistance of the Sadozai Shah watching from Herat. By this time Shah Mahmoud (S) had died and his son Kamran Khan (S) was the shah and his *Wazir* was Yar Mohammed Khan; both declined to offer any assistance.

The two armies met outside Kandahar on 1 July 1834. At first ex-Shah Shuja's army commander, a Scots mercenary by the name of William Campbell, who had placed his troops on commanding ground, was winning the fight. Victory should have been theirs but for an inexplicable movement by the ex-Shah, Shuja, to the rear; his soldiers, thinking this was a retreat, panicked and fled. Campbell was taken prisoner and the ex-Shah was pursued to Kelat where the chief, Mehrab Khan, gave him refuge and refused to surrender him. After the customary negotiations the pursuers agreed to give up the pursuit and Mehrab Khan agreed to send his guest on his way. Defeated and disgraced, ex-Shah Shuja made his lonely way back to his family in Ludhiana. Meanwhile, as the opposing Afghan armies were fighting it out in the east of the country, Maharaja Ranjit Singh attacked and captured Peshawar, which was destined no longer to be Afghan. Sultan Mohammed Khan (B) was given a *jagir* worth four *lakhs* of rupees in the Kohat area and retired there with his family of 30 wives and concubines and 60 children.

3

Confetti of Treaties

Tsar Peter the Great (1682–1725) had long dreamed of expanding his Tsardom and did so thus creating an empire and emerging as a major European power. In 1717 he sent a force to Khiva under Prince Alexander Bekovitch, but this venture resulted in the slaughter of the Russians. On his deathbed, the great Tsar wished his heirs to continue his expansion plans and to possess India and Constantinople, the keys to world domination. Thereafter successive tsars had cast covetous eyes in the direction of the riches to the south and central Asia.

About the time when the great Ahmad Shah Duranni of Afghanistan was dying of skin cancer in Kandahar and Robert Clive was manœuvering around the *Nawab* Surajah Dowlah of Bengal, Tsar Peter III (1762) assembled an army of 20,000 Cossacks to invade India. Ahmed Shah Duranni eventually joined his ancestors in 1772; Clive won the Battle of Plassey (1757), more by chicanery than bayonets and Tsar Peter's Cossacks were destroyed crossing the River Volga, prompting one of his officers to put his hands around the Tsar's throat, strangling him.

Some years later, Prince Nassau Siegen presented Catherine the Great (1762–96) with a detailed proposal for marching an army through Bokhara and Kashmir into Bengal to drive the British out of India. While this particular proposal was not acted upon, it remained on the back burner as the desires of successive tsars to expand southwards burned ever brightly.

Back in Britain, the authorities were more concerned with the antics of France and the rebellion in their American colonies. Apart from a few intrepid adventurers no one had any knowledge of the lands of Central Asia and fewer still were concerned with developments there, least of all the East India Company, now established around Bombay, Madras and Calcutta. The few recorded British adventurers included a merchant, Anthony Jenkinson, who as early as 1558 had visited Bokhara and is reputed to have shown the Russians the way. Then in 1781 an East India Company officer on the Bengal establishment, Colonel Hartley, visited the ancient city of Bokhara on his overland journey to England. He was followed in 1783 by George Foster of the Madras establishment. As the new century dawned these few were to be followed by many more, some with the simple urge to see what was on the other side of the mountain, some to discover archaeological treasures but most to spy.

In 1779 a French artillery officer by the name of Napoleon Bonaparte led a *coup d'etat* and proclaimed himself First Consul of France. The ogre of 'Boney' quickly spread across Europe and beyond. In Calcutta, one of the finest of India's governor gnerals, Lord Wellesley (Richard), had just arrived in India as the French First Consul was invading Egypt. Lord Wellesley, not a great admirer of the French although his mistress of many years whom he later married was French, saw in the French occupation of Egypt a direct threat to the security of India, substantiated by reports of a proposed alliance between the First Consul of France and Tippu Sultan in Mysore. Lord Wellesley immediately ordered a force from Bombay, under General David Baird, to proceed to Egypt to contain the French threat.[1] Meanwhile he selected Captain John Malcolm,[2] a bright young officer of the Madras establishment and a Persian linguist, to proceed with haste to Persia on a diplomatic mission designed to keep the French out of Persia, thus further blocking any French designs on India, and also to counter any move into India by the Afghan, Shah Zaman. These moves were the first in what evolved as the Government in India's own foreign policy. At the beginning of the nineteenth century, the East India Company's interest in Persia was essentially commercial and it had representatives at Baghdad and Bushire. The representative at Baghdad was Harford Jones, who had trained as a jeweller and at the age of 20 decided to join the East India Company as a writer.

In this capacity he was sent to Baghdad as the assistant to the Company's representative there. While there he acquired an Armenian mistress, who bore him three children but he never married her. Later he fell ill and returned to England to recuperate. While in England, he was fortunate enough to meet the all-important president of the Board of Control, Henry Dundas, who took a liking to him and engineered his posting to Baghdad as the new Company representative there; hence his appellation, 'Baghdad Jones'.

These prudent measures were overtaken by events in the Mediterranean. On 1 August 1779, Admiral Horatio Nelson discovered the French fleet at Aboukir Bay, under the command of Admiral Brueys, and completely destroyed it.[3] The French First Consul was now stranded and his Egyptian venture a failure. The remnants of his army were eventually mopped up by General Baird's force, assisted by the Turkish army. In Persia, Captain Malcolm's mission had been a huge success. With the Shah of Persia, Fateh Ali Shah, he had concluded both political and commercial treaties and an exchange of representatives were agreed, after which the gallant captain returned to India in 1801. On his return he was appointed private secretary to the

1 General Baird, with a force of 6,400 British and *sepoy* troops, left Bombay at the end of December 1800, but only arrived at Kossir, on the coast of upper Egypt, on 8 June of the following year. In nine days this force traversed 140 miles of desert to the Nile and reached Cairo on 10 August. The united British and Turkish force then moved on to Alexandria where the French general capitulated on 31 August 1802. General Baird was later to be Sir John Moore's second in command at Corunna.

2 Sir John Malcolm (1769–1833). Born at Eskdale, Scotland. One of 17 children of an impoverished tenant farmer, George Malcolm. Through the good offices of the 'Scottish Mafia', John Malcolm obtained entry into the services of the East India Company and arrived in Madras in 1783, aged 14. For many years thereafter he was known as 'Boy Malcolm'. He served in the Madras Infantry as an ensign for 11 years and returned to Scotland for some well-earned leave. On his return to Madras in 1795, he was appointed military secretary to General Sir Alured Clarke. In 1800 he was selected by the governor general for a diplomatic mission to Persia and in 1812 returned to Scotland on furlough for five years, during which time he wrote his book on the history of Persia. On his return to India in 1817, he was employed as the governor general's agent in negotiations after the third and final Maratha War. In 1827 he was appointed governor of Bombay, finally returning to England in 1831 to become the MP for Launceston. John Malcolm died of a stroke in May 1833 and was buried at St James' Church, Piccadilly. During his time in England he was elected the first chairman of the Oriental Club.

3 Apparently Nelson's coffin was made from the planks of the French flagship *L'Orient*.

Governor General, who with the aid of his illustrious brother, Arthur Wellesley, put paid to Tippu Sultan's ambitions.

The Persian representative, Haji Khalil Khan, duly arrived in Bombay and was on his way to Calcutta to present his credentials to Lord Wellesley when a fight broke out between his personal attendants and the *sepoy* escort. As the Haji exited his tent to stop the fight he was accidentally shot by a *sepoy*. This was a massive *faux pas*, causing the greatest consternation in Calcutta, but not all that much in Tehran. In Calcutta all official functions were cancelled and flags were flown at half-mast. A letter of humble apology and sincere condolences was hurriedly despatched to Persia and Captain Malcolm was sent back to Teheran with personal messages of regret to the Persian court. Apart from the relatives of the Haji's unsuccessful appeal for compensation, the matter was forgotten.

Most regrettably, as was borne out by future developments, Lord Wellesley's Persian initiative and John Malcolm's treaties were largely ignored by the home authorities. This was, no doubt, due to the fact that the Court of Directors of the East India Company had become increasingly apprehensive about their 'Sultanised Englishman'[4] of a governor general and wished to exercise their prerogative of recall. Anticipating the storm, Lord Wellesley resigned and sailed back to England in 1805. He was replaced by a reluctant 65-year-old Lord Cornwallis (Charles), who had already served as governor general (1786–1793) and was ailing, in fact he died four months into his governorship and is buried at Ghazipur on the banks of the Ganges. On replacing Wellesley, Cornwallis immediately abrogated his predecessor's 'forward policy', establishing the River Jumna as the finite boundary of British expansion. Thus, any interest in the goings-on in Central Asia was kicked into the long grass. Prior to his departure for India, Lord Cornwallis had been sent to negotiate the Treaty of Amiens (1802) which was annulled a year later with war being declared on France, while the Russians were allowed to lay siege to Yerevan in Armenia, a Persian possession; Britain, despite Malcolm's treaty of 1809, did nothing about it.

At this time in India the three presidencies of the East India Company, Bengal, Madras and Bombay, whilst ostensibly under the overall authority of the governor general, conducted their affairs with a great deal of independence, primarily due to the restrictions of time and distance. Hence it was logical for the governor of Bombay and his officers to be the initiators and executors for affairs west of Bombay. For this reason, the Sindh, Persia, Mauritius and Aden came under their purview. As the Sindh gave access to the mighty River Indus, any development there was of great concern to the 'Ducks' of Bombay.[5]

Persia had for hundreds of years regarded the Sindh as a Persian dependency, then Mahmud of Ghazni added it to his many conquests. He was followed by Nadir Shah Afshar of Persia and Ahmad Shah Duranni of Afghanistan, both claiming Sindh as part of their kingdoms. Eventually, in 1786, one Fateh Ali Khan, a Talpur chief, assumed the sovereignty of the Sindh. This takeover was disputed and the matter subsequently settled on the basis that while Fateh Ali Khan would be recognised as the paramount chief, the country was divided into three districts. Amir Mir Sohral was assigned Khaiorpur, Amir Thora was assigned Mirpur and Amir Fateh

4 Lord Curzon, *British Government in India: The Story of the Viceroys and Government Houses*, Vol. II (London: Cassell & Co, 1925), p.173.

5 The Europeans in Bombay were nicknamed 'ducks', the ones in Madras were named 'mulls' and the ones at Calcutta 'koi-hais'.

Ali Khan kept Hyderabad and shared its sovereignty with his brothers Gholan Ali, Karam Ali and Murrad Ali.[6]

Always interested in grasping any opportunity for trade, the Bombay authorities had established a commercial resident at Tatta, about 80 miles south of Hyderabad, but their representative's life was made unbearable by the suspicious Amirs so not much was achieved. Then the Amirs became very concerned about the renewed designs of both Persia and Afghanistan and sent an envoy to Bombay seeking help. Captain David Seaton was duly despatched in 1803 to negotiate with the Amirs. However, this gentleman's brief was sufficiently vague to allow him to go beyond just a commercial trade agreement, concluding one of a defensive and aggressive alliance. Seaton was recalled and his alliance refuted and he was replaced by Captain Nicholas Smith. The enterprising Captain Seaton was later to become the resident at Dehli.

Affairs on the north-west frontier of the Company's Jumna boundary inevitably changed. The Marathas had risen again under Jaswant Rao Holkar and threatened Delhi. General Gerald Lake had successfully defeated the Marathas and chased Jaswant Rao up to the River Bias, where the Maratha had taken refuge with the young Sikh leader Ranjit Singh. General Lake demanded that the Sikh chief not make common cause with the Marathas. This was agreed and a treaty was signed with the Sikh chief in 1805, after which General Lake withdrew behind the Jumna and Jaswant Rao was allowed to return to his original possessions. A few years later Jaswant Rao went mad and died in 1811.

By now Napoleon Bonaparte had declared himself Emperor of France, and had instituted his 'Continental System', an attempt by changing the trading styles to shift the balance of power, through trade and commerce, in favour of France. However, with Admiral Nelson's victory at Trafalgar, 21 October 1805, the British navy ruled the waves while the French armies were pre-eminent on the Continent and had already taken on the Russians at Eylau and Friedland. It is not clear who won this contest which resulted in 50,000 casualties. Following this bloodbath, France and Russia signed the Treaty of Tilsit on 7 July 1807. A massive raft, on top of which a pavilion had been erected, was moored in the middle of the River Niemen at Tilsit, now called Sovetsk. Here, Alexander I, aged 29 and the grandson of Catherine the Great, sat down with Emperor Napoleon, aged 37, to review and sign this historic treaty. They undertook to join their two countries by bonds of 'unalterable confidence and friendship' and agreed to the precepts of the 'Continental System'. Despite stringent measures for security, a British spy was able to swim underwater and ensconce himself under the pavilion to hear the two great powers of Europe discuss a joint invasion of India.[7] One of the attendees at this meeting was Mirza Reza, the Persian Ambassador to France.

The shah of Persia, Fateh Ali Shah, had earlier written to Emperor Napoleon seeking an alliance which would afford the Persians some protection against the continued Russian annoyance. He had also sent a similar appeal to the British in Calcutta, but due to the British apathy at that time this appeal was put in the 'pending file'. Thus, Persia threw herself into the arms of France and General Gardanne was sent as ambassador to Teheran along with a cadre of French officers, to train the Persian army.

6 Beveridge, *A Comprehensive History of India*, vol. 3, p.1057.
7 Sir Henry Durand, *The First Afghan War and Its Causes* (London: Longman Green, 1879), p.10.

Napoleon greeting Czar Alexander I, Queen Louise of Prussia, and King Frederick William III of Prussia at Tilst, June 1807.

Having secured his eastern front with a treaty, the impetuous French emperor turned west to take care of Spain and Portugal. Four years later his 'unalterable friendship' with the Russians was conveniently brushed aside as his *Grande Armée* galloped into Russia. No doubt he would have then marched down the Khyber Pass into India, becoming the dominant power in the world, an ambition accomplished by neither Alexander the Great nor Julius Caesar. However, in considering the factors for his advance into Russia the great emperor had not taken into account the havoc that the Russian 'General Winter' could bring into play, and his *Grande Armée* trudged back to lick its wounds.

The intelligence from Tilsit must have come as a shot out of the blue for the Directors of the East India Company. They were shaken by the nightmarish thought of an unassailable French army storming down into their Indian possessions, especially as the British Navy would not be able to help. The president of the Board of Control sent an urgent instruction to the governor general, Lord Minto (Gilbert Elliot), to seek the co-operation of neighbouring countries. Acting on these instructions, the Governor General sent diplomatic missions to Persia, Afghanistan, Sindh and to the Sikh Maharaja, Ranjit Singh.

To Afghanistan he sent Mountstuart Elphinstone,to meet the King of that country, Shah Shuja-ul-Mulk, at Peshawar and concluded a treaty, which in part stipulated that, 'if the French or Persians, in pursuance of their confederacy, should move towards the King of Kabul's country in a hostile manner, the British State, endeavouring heartily to repel them, shall hold themselves liable to afford the expenses necessary for the above mentioned service, to the extent of their ability.' The Shah agreed and took the opportunity of this apparent British generosity to ask for a pecuniary grant to secure his shaky throne. This request, which was enthusiastically endorsed by Elphinstone, was as emphatically rejected by the Calcutta authorities. A bad mistake as a grateful Shah Shuja on a secured throne might have saved a great deal of trouble later. Elphinstone described Shah Shuja as 'a handsome man of about 30 years of age, of an olive complexion and with a thick black beard. The expression of his countenance was dignified and pleasing, his voice clear and his address princely.'

To the Sikh court, Lord Minto sent the very young and capable Charles Metcalfe,[8] who after being led a song and dance all over the Punjab eventually got the young Ranjit Singh to sign the Treaty of Amritsar in April 1809. Before this treaty was signed, Maharaja Ranjit Singh had made a number of successful incursions into the Malwa sector of the Punjab, which is the area south of the River Sutlej. The Sikh chiefs of the Malwa had in consequence implored the British to obstruct the takeover of their states by the rapacious Ranjit Singh, but these requests had been declined. Now with the change in policy, the British authorities left it to Charles Metcalfe to treat with an equally young and ambitious Ranjit Singh on the basis that the latter was to surrender any designs on the Malwa and at the same time conclude a friendship with the British and have nothing to do with the French. The young Sikh at first baulked at these arrogant terms. Fortunately, his team of advisors included a wise and prudent man by the name of *Fakir* Azizuddin,[9] who persuaded his young master that it was in his best interests to sign a friendly

8 Sir Charles Metcalfe, 1785–1846 He was born in Calcutta, the second son of Major Thomas Metcalfe, an officer in the Bengal Infantry. Charles and his brother were sent to England for their education, and on their return Charles was recruited into the Bengal Civil Service. In 1804 he was appointed as political assistant to General Lake, and in 1809 the governor general sent Metcalfe on his famous mission to the court of Maharaja Ranjit Singh. In 1811 he was appointed Resident at Delhi and in 1819 he was promoted to secretary of the Secret and Political Department. A year later he went as the Resident to the court of the Nizam of Hyderabad, a post he held for five years. In 1834 he was appointed governor of Agra, and on the departure of Lord Bentinck Metalfe became the acting governor general of India. On the arrival of Lord Auckland, Metcalfe was demoted to lieutenant governor of the North-Western Provinces. Having been rejected by the Court of Directors for the vacancy of the Madras governorship, Metcalfe returned to England for the final time. Less than six months later Sir Robert Peel sent Metcalfe to Jamaica as the governor, where he served for three years until his health required a return to England. After six months and fit again, Metcalfe was sent out on his last appointment as governor of Canada, a position he held for two and half years. On his return to England he was awarded a peerage for his services in Canada. Metcalfe died of cancer at Basingstoke in September 1846.

9 Fakir Azizuddin, 1780–1845. He was the eldest of three brothers, known to history as the 'Bokhara Brothers'. They were the sons of Ghulam Mohyuddin, a respected physician. All three started their careers as *hakims*. Azizuddin rose to become Maharaja Ranjit Singh's foreign secretary, while Imamuddin became the keeper of the Sikh Treasury at Gobindgarh and Nurauddin, the youngest, became the governor of Lahore. The brothers adopted the title *Fakir* as they knew this style of address was of the greatest protection in the intriguing and unscrupulous Sikh court. Azizuddin was renowned for having a way with words, and with his knowledge of Persian and Arabic, he was the perfect diplomat and an outstanding foreign secretary for, at times, an impetuous Maharaja; he was the genius behind many of the Maharaja's more astute policies. He built a good relationship with his British opposite number, Captain Claude Wade. His chief desire was the permanent establishment of a fruitful co-existence between the two remaining powers in India. He earned the adoration of all foreign officials who came into contact with him. Henry Lawrence was to say of him, 'He was the most honest, and perhaps the ablest of Ranjit Singh's advisers and well-wished of by both states.' After the death of Maharaja Ranjit Singh, his stature in the Sikh court declined and towards the end

treaty with what was then the paramount power in India, whose boundary had now advanced to the Sutlej. To his great credit, Maharaja Ranjit Singh upheld the terms of this treaty to his death in 1839.

In the Sindh, Fateh Ali Khan had died and the Amirs were now apprehensive about Sikh ambitions, so they readily agreed to another treaty with the British, which contained the following clauses, 'there is to be eternal friendship, enmity is never to appear between the states, there is to be an exchange of *Vakils* and the Sindh government is not to allow the establishment of the "tribe of French" in the Sindh'. At the same time an alliance was concluded with the grateful Khan of Bhawalpur, who was equally alarmed at Sikh ambitions.

As regards the mission to Persia, the British were about to embark on a very English 'bugger's muddle'. Lord Minto had selected the seasoned Colonel John Malcolm to proceed to Teheran to counter French influence and negotiate a treaty with the Persians. At the same time, the London authorities had decided to send their own representative, Sir Harford Jones. This gentleman was to proceed to Persia via St Petersburg, however the intelligence of the Tilsit affair deemed this an unwise route, so Jones along with his number two, Sir Gore Ouseley, sailed for Bombay instead. By the time they arrived, Colonel Malcolm, promoted to brigadier general, had already left on his mission, accompanied by his friend and secretary, Captain Paisley. Consequently, Sir Harford Jones was instructed to 'mark time' in Bombay and await the results of Malcolm's efforts.

Brigadier Malcolm arrived in Bushire in March 1808, loaded with gifts and 30 bags of potato seeds. Based on his previous experience and success he had high hopes of achieving his aim and success in the cultivation of potatoes. He sent Captain Paisley ahead to make the necessary preparations. At this juncture Malcolm sent a report to the Governor General informing him of his plans and clearly implying a successful conclusion. Unfortunately, the French had been more than assiduous in their protestations to the Persian court. So, instead of 'plain sailing' Brigadier Malcolm found obstacles and frigid indifference, with his mission being disregarded and Captain Paisley was almost thrown into prison. Chafed and indignant at the conduct of the Persian court, Malcolm decided to withdraw his mission and sailed from Bushire on 12 July, leaving Captain Paisley to hold the fort. On reflection it would appear that the Brigadier had been much too impetuous, no doubt caused by his huge disappointment and loss of face.

Meantime, based on Malcolm's first report, the Governor General had given permission for Sir Harford Jones to proceed to Persia. This permission was despatched on 10 August, and soon after, the Governor General was assailed with the distressing information of Malcolm's decision to withdraw his mission. On receipt of this 'bombshell', the Governor General sent another, urgent, despatch to Jones on 22 August cancelling his previous permission. However, Jones, a man of action, was already on his way to Bushire and arrived there on 14 October, with his military escort under Captain Henry Wilcock, by which time Brigadier Malcolm had arrived back in Calcutta to explain his actions.

While the Governor General was firing off messages to Jones to suspend his mission or his bills would not be honoured and his proceedings ignored, the Calcutta authorities had endorsed Malcolm's counter-plan to return to Persia with a force of 2,000 and take possession of Kharg

of his own life he tried his utmost to stop the Sikh Durbar from going to war against the British. He died a fortnight before the Sikhs crossed the Sutlej to ignite the First Anglo-Sikh War.

there to form 'an establishment', the modern equivalent of a bridgehead. The Calcutta authorities were absolutely certain that Jones' mission was bound to fail or be disgraced and thus become an embarrassment to both the home government and the East India Company, which still viewed Persia as their preserve. Jones, on the other hand, reckoned that as the representative of His Britannic Majesty, Calcutta had no authority over his proceedings albeit the Company would have to pay his bills. At this point it must be mentioned that Jones and Malcolm loathed each other, so the failure of one was an open invitation to the other to do better.

Fortunately for Jones, a change had taken place in the Persian court over its view of French promises, they were turning up duds. In particular the French had undertaken to secure the evacuation of Georgia, but still the Russian eagle was planted on Georgian soil and the Persian shah was beginning to have second thoughts about his French benefactors. Meanwhile, Jones bullied and blasphemed his way to Teheran. Meanwhile Malcolm, leaving his force to follow, had sailed from Bombay to sort out the inevitable mess into which Jones was bound to take the British. Of this rather stupid situation, Malcolm was to write, as many others have later felt: 'Will this lesson cure the fools at home of their mischievous propensity to interfere?'[10]

With both Jones and Malcolm now in Teheran a 'bun fight' erupted as both tried to outdo the other in gift-giving. In his desire to regain the lost gravitas for the Company, the Brigadier was the more magnanimous and Jones the more annoyed, making a formal complaint to Calcutta. On his return to India Malcolm was severely censored by his masters over his expenses.

The overabundance of gifts obviously did the trick, as despite a treaty with the French and a contretemps between Jones and the Persian *Wazir*, Mizar Shefee, the British delegation was welcomed by the Persian shah and the French embassy was forced to retire. Apparently, the Persian shah, Fateh Ali Shah, always had a soft spot for the British. A treaty was signed on 12 March 1809, and the Persians sent their ambassador to London. Article IV of this treaty stipulated:

> In case any European forces shall invade the territories of Persia, His Britannic Majesty will afford a force, or in lieu of it, a subsidy. That in case the dominions of His Britannic Majesty in India are attacked or invaded by the Afghans, or any other power, His Majesty the King of Persia shall afford a force for the protection of the said dominions.[11]

With the treaty signed and sealed, Sir Harford Jones sailed for England leaving Sir Gore Ouselay in Teheran as the British ambassador with Captain Wilcock as his private secretary, while Lord Minto sent Captain Charles Christie and Henry Pottinger, both of the Bombay establishment, to check out the terrain between India and Persia. While Christie headed for Herat, Pottinger travelled to Kerman in Persia, where he waited for Christie, who failed to show up; so he trekked up to Isfahan where he met his fellow spy. On his return to India, Pottinger was duly debriefed and appointed the Resident at Kutch. Much later, Henry Pottinger become the first governor of Hong Kong and then, in 1847, governor of Madras. Meanwhile the adventurous Christie appears to have attached himself to the Persian army and was killed in a night attack which was made by the Russians on the Persian camp at Asandozin in 1811.

10 Sir John Kaye, *History of the War in Afghanistan*, Vols 1 & 2 (n.p.: Forgotten Books, 2012), p.74.
11 Kaye, *History of the War in Afghanistan*, p.638.

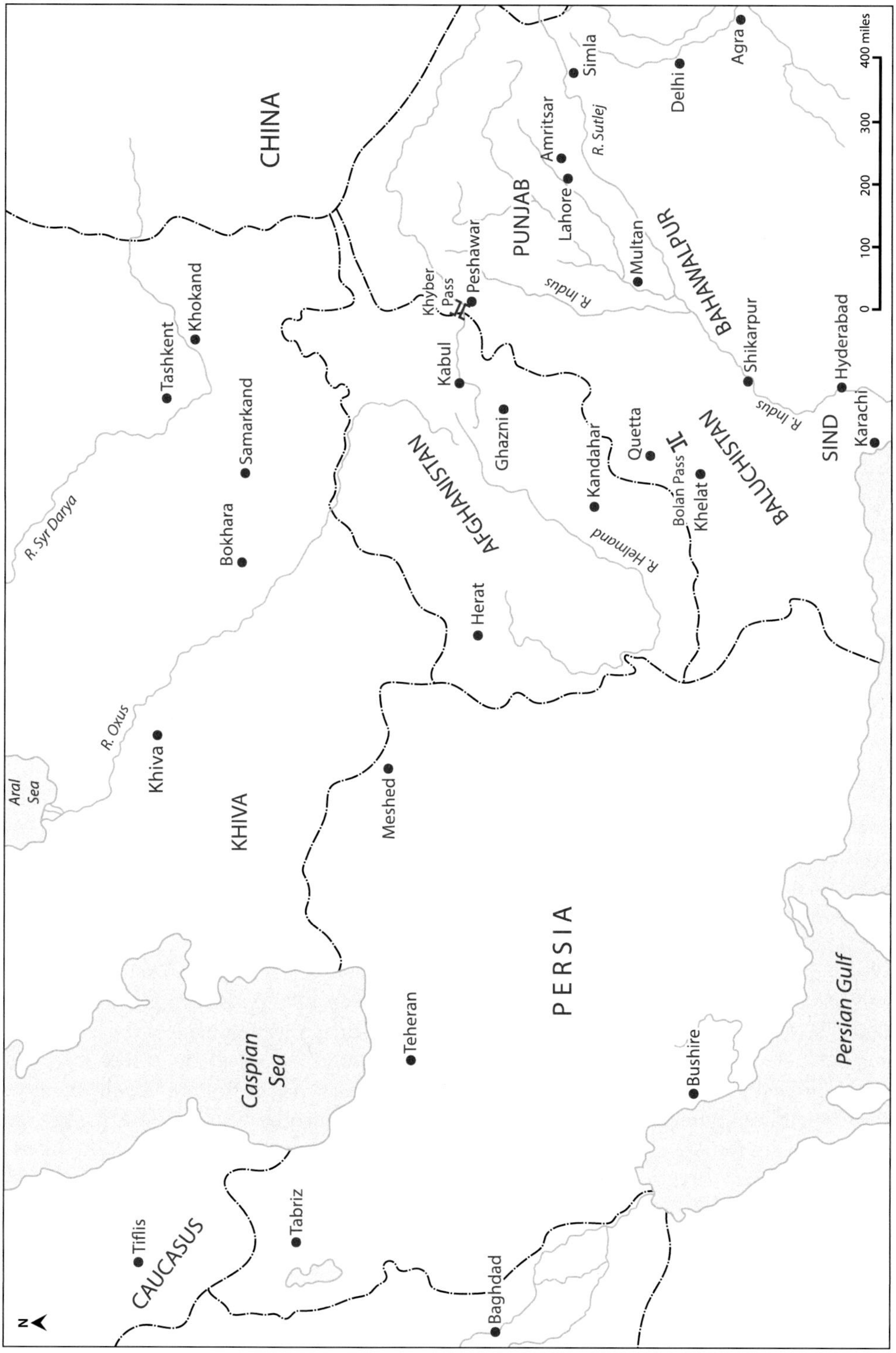

Map 4 The Arena of the 'Great Game'.

By their treaties with the Persians and Afghans the British had obtained Persian protection against the Afghans and Afghan protection against the Persians. At this time, the mention of Russia was loosely alluded to as 'any other power', as Britain and Russia were ostensibly on friendly terms and were to remain so for the next 20 years. While these two European powers were destined to clash in Central Asia, they did so by intrigue, not bayonets.

In June 1812, a French army of 60,000 invaded Russia, its 'unalterable friend'. It got horribly bogged down and was defeated, while on the Spanish peninsula a war of attrition was waged by Sir Arthur Wellesley against Napoleon's marshals, culminating in Napoleon's final destruction on a wet Sunday at Waterloo on 18 June 1815; Europe was parcelled up between the victors. Britain was at peace in Europe for the next 40 years. Also, by this time the East India Company had expelled French influence in India and had acquired the French island of Mauritius, Isle de France.

With Napoleon out of the way, Tsar Alexander I rekindled Russia's ancient desire for expansion southwards and sent General Kotliarovsky to annihilate the Persian army on the River Aras at the Battle of Aslanduz. By the consequent Treaty of Gulistan in 1814, the Persians were forced to surrender territories north of the Caucasus and the Russians obtained naval rights on the Caspian. Persia's ally, His Britannic Majesty, remained on the sidelines.

The phrase 'The Great Game' describes the power struggle over the mastery for influence in Central Asia. This phrase is attributed to Captain Arthur Conolly, an officer in the 6th Bengal Light Cavalry, who had travelled back to India in 1829 via Moscow, Persia and Herat, obviously on an intelligence mission, disguised as 'Ali Khan'. The words he actually used in writing to his friend, Captain Henry Rawlinson, were, 'If the British would only play the Grand Game'. The Russian foreign secretary, Count Karl Nesselrode, more appropriately referred to this struggle as a 'Tournament of Shadows', a secret war of illusions.[12] A hundred years later Stephen Potter might have called it 'One-Upmanship'.

During November of 1814, the British renegotiated their 1809 treaty with the Persians, which established the amount of payable subsidy at £400,000 (£30 million) a clear indication that the payment of a subsidy was the more prudent choice than 'afford a force' in the vast emptiness of Central Asia. Furthermore, in a greater effort to cross the Ts and dot the Is, the revised treaty included an additional clause which stipulated that in the event of the Persians being attacked by the Russians, the British Government would not interfere with either party unless its mediation, to effect a peace, was solicited by both parties.

At the time of this treaty revision with the Persians, Afghanistan, a natural barrier, was looked upon as necessarily opposed to British interests owing to the British accommodation with the Sikhs, so any approach to an unstable Afghanistan was regarded as too absurd to contemplate. Besides, at this time the governor general, Lord Hastings (Francis Rawdon), had his hands full with wars against both Nepal and Burma, it was not the time to launch an initiative in Afghanistan, which would undoubtedly be misconstrued by his suspicious friend, the Sikh Maharaja in Lahore. Colonel David Ochterlony, the British Representative at Ludhiana, writing after he had attended the wedding of the Maharaja's son, reported: 'Runjeet's ambition is as unbounded as is his rapacity. If Runjeet's opinions are decisively formed on any one subject they are on his utter inability to contend with British arms, but the more firm his belief the more

12 Karl Meyer and Blair Shareen, *Tournament of Shadows* (London: ABACUS, 1999), p.xviii.

he is inclined to doubt the pacific intentions of the British Government whose forbearance to him is incomprehensible.'[13]

Afghanistan in the meanwhile was a country in internal turmoil. Power was changing hands with alarming rapidity and the neighbouring Sikhs took great bites of it. It would not be too long before the Persians did the same, as it was the cherished dream of the Persian Crown Prince, Abbas Mirza, to repossess Herat, something he was unable to do while the Russians were biting into his own territories to the north.

In 1825 the Russians, under General Paskevitch, advanced into Persian territory and penetrated to the Kozat steppe between the Caspian and Aral seas. This was a step too far for the Persian Crown Prince so he launched his army against the Russians and in so doing invoked the assistance of his British ally. The British authorities declined, pointing out that the treaty did not include aggression by the Persians. Understandably, the Crown Prince was not happy and his son, Mohammed Mirza, even less so. After a two-year conflict and a crushing defeat at Tabriz, the Persians were compelled to sign the Treaty of Turkmanchai. It was in the crossfire of this war that Captain Charles Christie was shot, arguably the first British casualty of the Great Game. Back in England the Russophobic lobby tried to make an issue of this Russian provocation, however the political embarrassment was hushed up and as Lord Salisbury, a later foreign secretary, was to comment, 'All Englishmen have the right to be killed where so ever they wish.' By this treaty Russia established the line of the River Aras as their frontier with Persia and demanded a huge indemnity. In order to pay this indemnity, the Crown Prince gave his bond cancelling the British obligation to 'afford a force', provided the agreed subsidy of £400,000 (£30 million) was given to Persia to hand over to the Russians. This was confirmed by the old Shah in whose court the Russian star rose as that of the British waned. Writing in June 1828, Charles Metcalfe stated, 'The influence of Russia is that of a power the Persian Government fears and hates. If ever Russia is in a condition to set forth an army against India, Persia most probably will be under her banner.' He was of the opinion that any unnecessary interference in the affairs of Central Asia was to be avoided by all possible means, that the more Britain endeavoured to counteract supposed designs, the more certain it was to convert the remote into the proximate.[14] It would appear that by this time the British home authorities had reverted back to allowing the East India Company to take the lead with affairs in Persia via the president of the Board of Control.

Despite official complacency about faraway places, many individuals both British and others had the urge to explore the mysteries of 'no man's land'. In 1819, a Russian, Captain Nikolai Muravier, made a solo mission to the Khan of Khiva to evaluate the Khan's military power and to judge the plight of Russian slaves. Earlier, in 1812, William Moorcroft, a veterinary surgeon employed by the East India Company to superintend its stud farms, applied for permission to explore north of British possessions in order to seek out better breeding stock for the farms. At this time Charles Metcalfe, Maharaja Ranjit Singh's old friend, was the British Resident at Delhi, and gave his wholehearted support to Moorcroft's quest. Accompanied by Captain Hyder Young Hearsey, Gulam Hyder Khan, a horse trader and, significantly, a surveyor Pundit Harkh

13 F.S. Aijazuddin, *The Resourceful Fakirs: Three muslim brothers at the Sikh court of Lahore* (New Delhi: Three Rivers Publication, 2014), p.15.

14 Sir John Kaye, *The Life and Correspondence of Charles, Lord Metcalfe*, Vols 1 & 2 (London: Richard Bentley, 1854), p.197.

Dev, the party travelled through Nepal into Tibet as far as the sacred Lake of Manarasovar.[15] Here they discovered Russian presence in the form of Russian goods and dogs brought in by caravans all the way from Russia. They also learned that the greatest horse market in the world was at Bokhara. Moorcroft and his party eventually returned to India with lots of information, but no horses. His masters in Calcutta were not happy.

The journey had, however ,whetted Moorcroft's appetite for a more extensive trek to Bokhara. By 1819, Charles Metcalfe, Moorcroft's mentor was the head of the Company's Political and Secret Department and did not hesitate to strongly support Moorcroft's request to acquire the legendary Turcoman horses described by Marco Polo over 500 years earlier. He was supplied with a Gurkha escort by William Fraser, the Assistant Resident in Delhi, and was, no doubt, commissioned by Metcalfe to engage in secret military intelligence. Apparently on his way through Lahore Moorcroft inspected a contingent of Gurkha soldiers of the Sikh army which had been trained by a deserter *Niak* from the Bengal army. In Ladakh, Moorcroft blotted his copybook by engaging in a defensive treaty with the Raja of that country, who was more than apprehensive about Sikh designs on his domains. The authorities in Calcutta were furious, his 'engagement was repudiated' and his immediate return was demanded. Some 25 years later these same authorities were shocked to discover that General Zorawar Singh had conquered Ladakh for the Maharaja in Lahore. Moorcroft, undeterred, persisted in his quest without funds and eventually reached Bokhara in February 1826. Whilst the horse market there was disappointing, he discovered that the Russians had already established a trade link. That August Moorcroft died at Amu Darya and his Gurkha escort was forced into slavery. At the time it was rumoured that Moorcroft had been carrying a letter from Count Karl Nesselrode, the Russian foreign minister, to Maharaja Ranjit Singh.

Another intrepid traveller, of a disgraced background, was James Lewis, known to history as Charles Masson. He had joined the Bengal Artillery in 1820 and while stationed at Agra in 1827 deserted with his friend Richard Potter, alias John Brown. In those days the penalty for desertion was death by firing squad, so, the two friends changed their names and proceeded north via Rajistan out of British jurisdiction. At Dera Ghazi Khan they split up. While Charles Masson made his way, on foot, through the Khyber Pass to Kabul no more is known about John Brown.

During his lonely journey, Masson emerges as a pioneering archaeologist and numismatist and produced the first comprehensive archaeological record of early Afghanistan. He returned to the Punjab and from Karachi sailed to Bushire in Persia, where he palmed himself off to the British Resident, David Wilson, as an American from Kentucky. Wilson was so impressed by Masson's knowledge of Central Asia that he got his visitor to write a report, which he passed on to his boss in Teheran, Colonel Alexander Campbell. This gentleman hit on the idea of sending the 'American' back to Central Asia on a fully funded antiquarian research expedition, in other words to spy. While in Kabul in 1832, Masson was spotted by Captain Wade's news-writer, Karamat Ali, who had duly reported the arrival of a 'strange European'. Later Charles Masson was to play a chequered role in the Great Game.

In 1824 the Bombay authorities sent a surgeon by the name of John McNeill to Persia to join the British legation at Teheran. As this gentleman left Bombay a boy of 16 arrived with a

15 Mahatma Gandhi's ashes are said to have been scattered in this lake.

cadetship to the Bombay Native Infantry; both were destined to play key roles in the Victorian drama to follow.

The boy's name was Alexander Burnes, the third of four surviving sons of the Provost of Montrose in Scotland. Through a family friend, Joseph Hume, Alexander and his elder brother, James, obtained an introduction to Stanley Clerk, a member of the East India Company Court of Directors each of whom could exercise his power of patronage to the tune of 12 commissions a year. James was duly appointed assistant surgeon on the Bombay establishment, while Alexander was granted a commission in the infantry. The second brother, Adam, remained in Scotland to become a lawyer and the youngest, Charles, was later to join his brother Alexander, courtesy of Clerk. Ever since the days of Henry Dundas (Lord Melville), as the first president of the Board of Control, the Scottish 'mafia' had a significant hold on patronage, particularly to the Company's Political Department. Dundas 'nominated annually four times as many writers and cadets as an average director. This was the conduit through which he poured young Scots into India.'[16] Lord Rosebery (Archibald Primrose) was to call this influence 'the Scoticisation of India'.

Like hordes of others before and after him, Alexander Burnes arrived in Bombay with a sheaf of introductions, known in India as 'tickets for soup'. However, young Alexander's tickets were of some consequence as he was related to the great Scottish bard Robert Burns. This provenance did not escape the notice of the Scottish governor of Bombay, Sir John Malcolm.

From the outset young Alexander Burnes was fascinated by India and threw himself into learning the language and customs of the natives. At that time Persian was the official court language in India so Alexander learned this as well. Lord Bentinck ordered the official language of India to be changed to English in 1832.

By 1829, Lieutenant Alexander Burnes had wangled a transfer to the Political Department, more money, and was sent to Kutch as the assistant to Henry Pottinger, who, no doubt, related accounts of his own travels to Central Asia. In one of his letters home Alexander Burnes wrote, 'I have been tracing the magnanimous Alexander on his quixotic journey to these lands. My great ambition is to travel.' Meanwhile, back in Russia, Alexander I had died of typhus and his brother had been proclaimed Tsar Nicholas I.

In 1830, the Governor of Bombay received a letter from London informing him of a consignment of six dray horses to be presented to Maharaja Ranjit Singh, a present from His Britannic Majesty George IV. This was in reciprocation of the Maharaja's gift of a shawl tent which had been handed over to Lord Amherst (William) the governor general in 1827. The actual dates that these gifts were sent and received are not known, except that five of the dray horses were presented to the Maharaja on 17 July 1831, over a year after King George VI's death (26 June 1830). Consequently, the horses must have left England in the spring of 1830 and disembarked at Bombay by the end of that year; they were handed over as a gift from His Britannic Majesty King William VI, King George's brother.

Maharaja Ranjit Singh, an ace imperialist, was impatient to extend his domains and by 1827 his radar was focused on the Sindh, and the sea beyond. He was also a realist as any move in that direction would involve the Sutlej, the treaty river, so he sent a mission to meet the Governor

16 Raymond Callahan, *The East India Company and Army Reform, 1783–1798* (Cambridge, Mass.: Harvard Historical Monographs, 1972), p.17.

General, Lord Amherst, at Simla. Lord Amherst was the very first governor general to take residence at Simla. The purpose of the Maharaja's mission was to sound out the reaction of the paramount power to his contemplated plans. The mission included the Maharaja's outstanding diplomat *Fakir* Azizuddin and was headed by his trusted *Dewan*, Moti Ram. While the mission was graciously received and diplomatic pleasantries exchanged the Governor General avoided any direct reference to the Sindh, as being outside the British zone of concern.

Sir John Malcolm, the governor of Bombay, used this royal command as a subterfuge to cover a long-cherished desire to investigate the possibility of navigating the Indus. As the horses could be walked up to Lahore, he complemented the royal gift by having a carriage built, which of course would have to be conveyed by the rivers Indus, Sutlej, Chenab and the Ravi. As escort for the conveyance of the royal gift, the Governor chose his fellow Scotsman, 25-year-old Alexander Burnes.

Burnes sailed from Bombay on 21 January 1831 accompanied by Ensign John Leekie, Mohammed Ali a surveyor and an Indian doctor. No communication about this trip was sent to the Amirs of Sindh, Burnes and his party just turned up and arrogantly assumed that their royal purpose would ensure plain sailing. Not surprisingly the suspicious Amirs made him sweat for the next six weeks while they negotiated his onward movement. He eventually reached Hyderabad on 18 April and on 17 July 1831 arrived at Lahore.[17]

It was during this trip and his meeting with various traders that young Burnes developed an overwhelming desire to travel to the countries of Central Asia. In Lahore he met Captain Claude Wade and Dr Andrew Murray. The former was in Lahore to discuss preparations for the forthcoming historic event of the meeting of the Governor General with Maharaja Ranjit Singh, the first ever of such meetings. Dr Murray was there to attend to the Maharaja's medical condition.

Burnes obviously had immense charm and made full use of it in his audiences with 'the Lion of the Punjab', Ranjit Singh, who was more impressed by the young officer than the five dray horses, one of which had died during the journey. He is said to have called the horses 'small elephants'. In an official Sikh report of this visit, Burnes was described as 'the nightingale in the garden' no doubt a reference to his manner and speech. Oriental-type flattery came naturally to the suave Burnes. The carriage was passed on to General Ventura, the Maharaja's infantry commander, and was last used by Sir Henry Lawrence to convey his brother George's family to safety in Lahore after the Second Sikh War.

During Burnes' conversations with the Maharaja, he was asked what designs the British had on the Sindh, as obviously the Maharaja had not been taken in by the elaborate charade of 'gift delivery'. Burnes not being equipped to give an answer, promised to convey the Maharaja's query to the Governor General.

Burnes, accompanied by Captain Wade, left Lahore on 16 August and proceeded to Wade's sanctuary at Ludhiana, where he had an audience with the deposed kings of Afghanistan, Shah Shuja and his blind brother Shah Zaman. This was clearly not an amicable meeting as Burnes' charm made no impression on Shah Shuja's haughtiness. About this meeting, he was to write, 'I do not believe the Shah to possess sufficient energy to seat himself on the throne of Kabul and that if he did acquire it, he has not the tact to discharge the duties of so difficult a situation.' Rather an

17 Peter Hopkirk, *The Great Game* (London: John Murray, 2006), p.139.

insightful comment if not totally presumptuous as at this stage he had not visited Afghanistan and knew nothing of the Afghans. It is possible that the young officer based his assessment on what he had been told by Maharaja Ranjit Singh, who was recorded as saying of Shah Shuja, 'When I saw him for the first time, I felt assured that a crown was not intended for his brow.'

Captain Wade, then the British authority on the Sikhs and by extrapolation the Afghans, had been the East India Company's point man for Anglo-Sikh affairs since 1823 and much credit is due to him for nurturing the friendly state of affairs between the paramount power and the only independent native kingdom in India. Clearly, at this juncture, Wade's opinions reflected those of the British authorities and these were a strengthening of the Anglo-Sikh alliance by cultivating further ties through trade and allowing them to be the bulwark against any possible threat through Afghanistan, which was perceived to be highly unlikely due to the Afghans' inherent disunity. It would beggar belief that the ever-alert Captain Wade was not cognisant of the ex-Shah's renewed plans to reclaim his throne and whether any mention of such was not conveyed to Burnes. After 10 days of enjoying Wade's hospitality, he set off on the last leg of his journey to the cool of Simla where he submitted his report to the governor general, Lord William Bentinck, with special emphasis on the navigability of the Indus. Of this charade, Sir Charles Metcalfe, the doyen of the East India Company 'grey-heads', observed:

> The scheme of surveying the Indus under the pretence of sending a present to Ranjit Singh seems to me highly objectionable. It is a trick, in my opinion, unworthy of our government, which cannot fail, when detected, as most probably it will be, to excite the jealousy and indignation of the powers on whom we play it.[18]

The start of Russophobia in Britain could be attributed to Sir Robert Wilson, who published a pamphlet in 1817 entitled *On the Designs of Russia*. Wilson was a British general and a politician who in 1801, at the age of 24, had been expelled from Russia for spying. Then in 1812 he went back to Russia and seconded himself to the Russian army in its war with the French. Based on these experiences he seemed to be well qualified to expound on Russia's expansive designs in Central Asia.

By 1831, Lord Bentinck had become as Russophobic as most of his courtiers, and in his evaluation of the security of British India he began to see Russia as the main threat and the Company's unreliable native army as its main defence. Afghanistan, which had been a confederation of chiefs, was now more stable under Dost Mohammed, therefore a stable Afghanistan was in Britain's best interests, but His Lordship and his advisers knew very little about Afghanistan and they were keen to know more. During his conversations with the Governor General, Burnes took the opportunity to mention his desire to travel through Afghanistan to Central Asia. Fortune shone on him as he hit the right nerve, and writing to a friend he reported:

> The Home Government have got frightened at the designs of Russia and desire that some intelligence officer should be sent to acquire information in the countries bordering the Oxus and the Caspian, and I, knowing nothing of all this, came forward and volunteered precisely for what they want. Lord Bentinck jumped at it.[19]

18 Hopkirk, *The Great Game*, p.133.
19 Hopkirk, *The Great Game*, p.140.

Alexander Burnes was included in the Governor General's party to meet Maharaja Ranjit Singh at Rupar in October 1831. After this great event, Burnes moved to Delhi to await his instructions, which he received on 23 December. His brief was to check out the political conditions, commercial relationships and military and geographical features. His party included Dr James Gerrard, a surgeon and surveyor whose elder brother, Alexander Gerrard, had explored the passes between Simla and Tibet. James was to produce the first military map of Afghanistan. Also included in the party were Mohammed Ali the interpreter, Ghulam Hassan Burnes' servant and a 'Hindu lad' by the name of Mohan Lal. This individual had been recommended by Charles Trevelyan, the principal of the Delhi Indian College, founded in 1829. Mohan Lal was his star pupil and just happened to be the son of Mountstuart Elphinstone's *munshi* during his mission to Peshawar to sign a treaty with Shah Shuja in 1809.

The party proceeded north via Ludhiana and Lahore, up to Peshawar, through the Khyber Pass and on to Kabul. Burnes described Peshawar as delightful and Kabul as 'paradise'. Of Jalalabad he was most disparaging, calling it 'one of the filthiest places that I have seen in the East'. During this epic journey Burnes acquired the sobriquet of 'Sikander Burnes' and Mohan Lal was known as Hassan Jan.

In Kabul, Burnes was welcomed and wooed by the Amir, who clearly wished to impress the young representative of the paramount power in India. This charm offensive worked as Burnes saw in the Amir a more masterful occupant of the Afghan throne than the ex-Shah he had met in Ludhiana. What is not clear is whether Burnes was privy to the contemplated venture of Shah Shuja to reclaim his throne in 1833. After a very gratifying 10 days in Kabul, during which Burnes had been offered the command of the Amir's army, the party moved on to Bokhara. Based on this short visit, Burnes, condescendingly, considered the Afghans to be 'like little children'.

The group spent four weeks in Bokhara, but did not meet the murderous chief, Nusrullah Khan. From Bokhara, Dr Gerrard returned to India via Herat and Karachi and died soon afterwards, while Burnes and the rest of the group went onto Meshed where they met and dined with the Crown Prince of Persia, Abbas Mirza. From Meshed they proceeded to Teheran where they met up with the British envoy, Colonel Sir John Campbell, and his assistant John McNeill. No doubt they had much to discuss, particularly Afghanistan and Burnes' new friend, Dost Mohammed, in turn his hosts obviously related their take on Russian machinations regarding India.

Burnes and his group left Teheran via Bushire for Bombay in December 1832. From Bombay, he went on to Calcutta to present his report to the Governor General, who was so impressed with the young officer's accomplishment he sent him to London to personally present his report and lap up the glory and accolades of the intrepid traveller 'Bokhara Burnes', a Victorian version of Indiana Jones.

Meanwhile, Henry Pottinger had convinced the Amirs of Sindh to open up the Indus. The resulting treaty of 1832 contained clauses very different to the previous treaty. The rivers and roads of the Sindh were to be opened to the merchants and traders of Hindustan on payment of certain and proper dues. The Amirs had reluctantly agreed to sign after the insertion of a clause prohibiting any Englishman to settle in the Sindh and that the two parties bound themselves 'never to look with the eye of covetousness on the possessions of the other'. This treaty was again revised at the behest of the Amirs to prohibit the use of the rivers and roads by armed vehicles and military stores. The Maharaja in Lahore was quite perturbed by this British activity in the Sindh and Captain Wade was sent to smooth feathers, while at the suggestion of Colonel Campbell in Teheran, the Governor General sent a cadre of Persian-speaking British officers to Persia to train the Persian army. This group was headed by Colonel William Pasmore and included Captain Elliott D'Arcy Todd of the Bengal Horse Artillery, of whom more later.

Back in Russophobic England, British society was gripped by mad adulation for their hero 'Bokhara Burnes'. This young dashing adventurer of 28 had travelled the route of his namesake, Alexander the Great, braved daunting Asian mountains, had seen off murderous brigands, traversed the mysterious Hindu Kush, witnessed the plight of slaves, been offered the command of an Asian army and supped with the greatest of oriental potentates, all in the service of the Empire. Hostesses vied for the company of this most eligible bachelor. He was driven by coach to Brighton to meet His Majesty King William IV. In London he was installed as a member of the Royal Geographical Society, made a member of the Athenaeum Club and dined with the Prime Minister, Earl Grey (Charles), and with the Directors of the East India Company he also had occasion to meet Lord Ellenborough (Edward Law) at Holland House, the unofficial Whig court, where he met Lord Auckland (George Eden) – who, though it was unknown at the time, was to become the next governor general of India. It would appear that the one person Burnes did not meet was the new foreign secretary, Lord Palmerston (Henry Temple).

While in London, Burnes' book about his travels was published in three volumes. It was a literary sensation, selling 900 copies on the first day. Hostesses and their daughters read his book, the Prime Minister read it and so did the Russians. Captain Arthur Conolly's book, *Travels to North India*, was published at about the same time, but Burnes' fame completely overshadowed it, thus Conolly, who had returned to India as Burnes was setting off on his journey, received no acknowledgement for his achievements.

At dinner with the East India Company Court of Directors, his supreme masters, the ambitious young Burnes took the opportunity to suggest that the Company should place a representative in Kabul. No doubt he had himself in mind, however the Chairman, Henry Tucker, rejected the idea as he was 'perfectly assured that it must soon degenerate into a political agency and that we should, as a necessary consequence, be involved in the entanglement of Afghan politics'. Clearly Burnes' East India Company masters, who relished any opportunity for trade, were equally skittish about involvement in Afghan politics. There is little doubt that these sentiments flavoured decisions years later.

There was at least one individual who was not taken in by all the 'hoopla' and that was Lord Ellenborough, the ex-president of the Board of Control (1828–1830). He thought Burnes was 'intensely vain and self-sufficient and he had done that which he ought not to have done, acting as he was for a government [Whig] to which I am opposed in Parliament, he wrote to me from Kabul about affairs in Afghanistan.'

His Lordship obviously did not care for the young man's precociousness and does throw some light on the liberality in communications practised by some junior officers. In 1834 there was a change of government and Lord Ellenborough was back in his old appointment of president of the Board of Control. He offered Burnes the role of assistant in the British Legation in Teheran, which was declined by Burnes, who sailed back to India in September 1835 with his knapsack full of valuable and influential name cards thus crediting him with a potency way beyond his capacity. On his return he was posted back to his old slot as assistant to Colonel Henry Pottinger.

At about this time the old Shah of Persia was ailing and his son Crown Prince Abbas Mirza was effectively in charge. Quite suddenly in 1833 the Crown Prince died and this event was to cause a seismic shift in the accepted position of Persia in the Great Game. Hitherto, Britain had regarded a stable Persia as the first line of defence against Russian advancement in Central Asia. With the death of the Crown Prince, succession to the Persian throne was up for grabs by the Crown Prince's many brothers. Both Britain and Russia saw it in both their interests to avoid at all costs the inevitable chaos that would ensue at the death of the ailing Shah Fateh Ali. So, the two European powers saw to it that the late Crown Prince's son, Mohammed Mirza, was anointed the successor to Shah Fateh Ali. Then in November 1834 the old Shah died and Mohammed Mirza ascended the throne and soon manifested his desire for conquests, causing Lord Palmerston to write to Sir Henry Ellis in 1835 instructing him to 'especially warn the new Shah against allowing himself to be pushed on to wage war with Afghanistan'. According to Lord Palmerston, the foreign secretary, it was evident that 'Afghanistan must be ours or Russia's.'[20]

20 Diana Preston, *The Dark Defile: Britain's Catastrophic Invasion of Afghanistan, 1838–1842* (New York: Waller & Co., 2012), p.85.

4

Reform and Reflection

A pause is necessary in this narrative to focus on events in Britain, a period of rapid change and of political and economic development; also, to reflect on the governorship of Lord William Henry Cavendish-Bentinck (1828–35), both pivotal to the change of conditions in India.

In Britain, apart from a couple of years at the end of the eighteenth century, Tory prime ministers had directed policy for over 60 years. They had steered Britain through the contagion of the French Revolution, put paid to Emperor Napoleon's designs for world domination and elsewhere given free rein to the expansion of trade and the acquisition of empire. In Europe their policy had been the maintenance of the balance of power and at home they had been stalwarts against anything that challenged the status quo. However, with the hot blasts of the Industrial Revolution and the growth of the ill-represented northern cities, cries for reform challenged their cherished status quo, giving rise to a social consciousness which the Whigs embraced with rigour while the Tories viewed any reform as a prelude to revolution.

The disaffected, unemployed and underpaid workers were mustered by radical leaders in protest marches across the country and the landed gentry responded by raising private yeomanry to disband them. On 16 August 1819 at St Peter's Field in Manchester the local yeomanry attacked a mob of demonstrators, killing 18 and injuring hundreds of protestors. This incident was later called the Peterloo Massacre. Laws were introduced prohibiting unlawful assemblies. Then, as late as October 1831, a major riot broke out in Bristol. A mob of 6,000 burnt down many houses including the Bishop's Palace and Customs House; in addition, they attacked the prison and set free the prisoners. A troop of HM 14th Light Dragoons, under the command of Lieutenant Colonel Thomas Brereton, was ordered out to quell the riot, which resulted in the death of 11 protestors and the wounding of over 100 men, women and children. It was reported in the local press that Captain William Beckwith of HM 14th Dragoon Guards 'lobbed off a man's head'. It could have been worse had not the commander, Colonel Brereton, refused to open fire on the crowd. For this leniency he was court-martialled for disgraceful conduct and dereliction of duty. His court martial was held in January 1832 during which the gallant colonel honourably shot himself in the heart.[1] Civil war was openly talked of and the radicals poured on the pressure.

1 Antonia Fraser, *Perilous Question: the Drama of the Great Reform Bill 1832* (London: Phoenix, 2014), p.169.

Against all his political instincts, the Duke of Wellington's Government passed the Catholic Emancipation Act of 1829 allowing Catholics to become members of Parliament and to receive commissions in the armed forces; it also split the Tories. This Act was the bellringer for the more profound issue of the day, which was the reform of Parliament itself.

In June 1830 King George IV died and his less political brother, William, ascended the throne making it easier for the Whig party under Earl Grey (Charles Grey) to sweep into power, and by 1832 the momentous Reform Act was sanctioned. Wellington's reaction to the Reform Bill, when first tabled by Lord John Russell in March 1831, had been, 'I don't in general take a gloomy view of things, but I must confess that knowing all I do, I cannot see what is to save the Church or property, or colonies or union with Ireland, or eventually monarchy, if the Reform Bill passes.'[2] The Reform Act was designed to take effective measures for correcting the diverse abuses that had longed prevailed in the choice of members to serve in the House of Commons. It effectively eliminated what were known as 'pocket' and 'rotten' boroughs.

If all these concerns were not enough to engage the peoples of Britain, King George IV had brought spice to the table by his scandalous extravagance and relationship with his wife Queen Caroline of Brunswick. In their animosity towards the landed gentry, the large majority of Englishmen were in total sympathy with his repudiated Queen. The King's only liaison with the Queen produced a daughter named Charlotte, who married King Leopold of Belgium. She died in 1817 in childbirth. The baby girl was stillborn.

Lord Palmerston, who had previously declined the governorship of India, was appointed foreign secretary in Earl Grey's administration of 1832, at a time when the great powers of Europe were grappling with the problems of Belgian independence, rival contenders for the throne of Spain and the disintegration of the Ottoman Empire, known as the 'Eastern Question', which loomed when the Greeks claimed independence in 1821. Consequently, it is not surprising that with all the pressing problems in Europe and the social upheaval in Britain, the great Foreign Secretary comes across as being less concerned with the affairs of Central Asia, thus allowing his colleague the President of the Board of Control to take the lead in policy for this area.

After the Battle of Waterloo, the great powers of Europe were Britain, Prussia, Austria and Russia, who at the Congress of Vienna parcelled out Europe creating a *cordon sanitaire* around France. In so doing the great powers were anxious to produce a settlement that France itself would regard as just and would therefore be made to work. Thus, as an alternative to Emperor Napoleon they agreed to place the Bourbon Louis XVIII on the French throne. The overriding concern of the great powers was to maintain a balance of power so that no one nation could again dominate Europe. Unfortunately, Louis XVIII proved not to be a wise choice and a second French Revolution ushered in Louis Philippe to be known as the 'King of the French'.

Back in the Ottoman Empire, Sultan Mohamud II was being harassed on all fronts. In 1805 he had lost Egypt to one of his army commanders, Mehmet Ali Pasha, who proclaimed himself the *Wali* of Egypt, which had been part of the Ottoman Empire since 1517. In the north the Sultan faced his Greek subjects demanding independence. He requested British intervention which was declined as the sympathy of the great powers was in favour of the Greeks. So, the Sultan asked the *Wali* for assistance, which was readily agreed in exchange for Crete. Mehmet

2 Fraser, *Perilous Question*, p.122.

Ali Pasha sent his son Ibrahim with an army to help the Sultan; however, on his own initiative, Admiral Edward Codrington on board the *Asia*, built in Bombay, blasted the Egyptian navy out of the water at Navarino on 27 October 1827. Mehmet Ali Pasha's next move horrified all four powers as he sent his son's army against the Sultan in a bid for Syria. The Egyptian army got as far as Anatolia, much too close to Constantinople and a scramble for power ensued. Lord Palmerston did not totally trust the Russians and felt that while it was prudent to engage with them, this had to be done robustly. Joint British and Russian support of the Ottoman Empire was the best way to counter Mehmet Ali Pasha's French-backed advance into Syria. While Palmerston was distrustful of the Russians, he loathed the French. Russia sent a naval force to the Bosphorus to shore up the Sultan's position, while the British Cabinet, against the strong recommendation of Lord Palmerston, declined to get involved. Russia meanwhile signed a defensive treaty with the Sultan thereby securing greater influence in the area, while Britain ruefully looked on. Love Fifteen!

This was seen by the likes of Colonel De Lacy Evans, a Russophobic Member of Parliament, as a direct threat to British influence and access to its Indian empire. Eventually, the incursion of the *Wali* into Syria was settled at a meeting of the four great powers in London in July 1840 compelling the Egyptians to withdraw Ibrahim's army back to Egypt. However, the Russian initiative caused nothing more than a few eyebrows to be raised in the salons of stately homes of England. The vast majority of the population knew little of Central Asia and the Indian empire, and in view of all that was occurring in Britain, cared even less.

In India, short of the normal tenure of five years, Lord Amherst the governor general resigned in 1828 for undisclosed personal reasons. In his stead Lord William Henry Cavendish-Bentinck was nominated. Lord Bentinck was the third son of the Duke of Portland, a Whig and ex-prime minister (1793), and was also a lieutenant general in the British army having been commissioned into the Coldstream Guards in 1791. He had also been the governor of Madras, where in 1806 the Vellore Mutiny had occurred. This was a mutiny of East India Company *sepoys* in defiance of the army commander General John Craddock's order to have caste marks on the foreheads of Hindu *sepoys* removed and the beards of Muslim *sepoys* shaved. The mutineers attacked the only British regiment in the garrison, HM 69th Foot, killing 300 of them. The mutiny was eventually put down and horrific reprisals taken. Six mutineers were blown from cannons, five were shot, eight were hanged, five were transported and the remainder awarded 50 lashes, and the three Madras native regiments involved were disbanded:

> This incident caused quite a stir and the young Governor, Lord William, was held responsible and recalled by the Court of Directors, who declared that, although the zeal and integrity of the present Governor, Lord William Bentinck, are deserving of the Court's approbation; yet when they consider the unhappy events which have taken place at Vellore, and also other parts o's administration which have come before them, the Court are of the opinion that it is expedient, for the restoration of confidence in the Company's government, that Lord William Bentinck should be removed and he is hereby removed accordingly.[3]

3 Beveridge, *A Comprehensive History of India*, vol. 3, p.236.

Thereafter, during the course of some years, Lord Bentinck successfully pursued his case for exoneration claiming the recall to have been unjust. Then, on the sudden death of Lord Cornwallis, he applied to be appointed to the vacancy. His application was rejected and Lord Amherst was sent out instead. When Lord Amherst unexpectedly resigned, Bentinck applied again. This time the Court of Directors relented and Bentinck, aged 54, sailed for India in February 1828 with the blessing of the Duke of Wellington's government.

Bentinck was sworn in on 4 July 1828 and from the outset launched into a massive and rigorous economy drive, possibly to prove to his pusillanimous masters that he had been wronged by their Madras recall and was out to prove that he would now be their most outstanding acolyte. Officially, his principal concern was to turn around the loss-making Company in order to ensure that its charter would be renewed by the British Government, which was due to take place in 1834 and was not a foregone conclusion. The 'forward' policies of both Lord Wellesley and Lord Hastings had allowed the East India Company to gain sway of all India except the Punjab and Sindh. However, this was achieved at great expense, forcing the Company to petition Parliament for help. By the end of Lord Bentinck's seven-year governorship, brought to a close by ill health, India was at peace and the Company's finances in robust shape. This governor general was to wield power with scrupulous regard to existing treaties and the policy of non-intervention to an unprecedented extent. He was a reforming governor general determined to modernise and by implication westernise the Company's Indian empire.

His first target for economy and modernisation was the Company's army, which he thought was the least efficient and the most expensive in the world. One particular task assigned by the Court of Directors to their new governor general was the proper issue of *Batta*. This was an allowance issued to officers and *sepoys* to offset the higher cost of living while operating in the field where provisions were scarce. It was based on the basic rate of pay, but unlike basic pay could be modified or withdrawn. The system had come into being well before the time of Warren Hastings and its regular issue over many years came to be regarded as a right, especially as basic pay was considered to be too low. After the battle of Plassey, Mir Jafar the *Nawab* of Bengal paid an allowance of double *Batta* to the Bengal army, with the approval of the Court of Directors. However, with the demise of the *Nawab* this burden became the Company's liability. Hence, full *Batta* was issued while operating in the field, *moffussil*, within the Company's territories and double *Batta* while on operations outside the Company's territories. Then in 1801 an order was issued which required officers of the Bengal Army to find and pay for their own accommodation while in garrison. This gave rise to an awful uproar and to compensate for this additional burden, the governor general, Lord Wellesley, who was also the captain general, authorised the issue of full *Batta* whether in the field or not.

This arrangement had not been approved by the home authorities. Whether they would have done so was not the issue, what enraged the gentlemen sitting at Leadenhall Street was that they had not been asked! In 1814, the Court of Directors sent out instructions allowing for half *Batta*, but only in those garrisons that had not been established before the extensions of the Company's territories. This instruction was as unwelcome as it was fraught with difficulties, successive governors general were instructed to tackle this thorny problem and each had kicked it into the long grass.

As their best acolyte, Lord Bentinck pledged himself before leaving England that the issue of what became known as the 'half *Batta* order' would be one of his first measures of retrenchment. The half *Batta* order was issued within 200 days of his arrival to a huge uproar. The commander-in-chief, Lord Combermere, protested strongly and resigned rather than take any part in the order's execution. The order could not be disobeyed as this would constitute mutiny however, such was the excitement caused by the proclamation that meetings were held to consider what could be done. A petition to the Court of Directors was drawn up and subscription raised to send a senior officer to present the petition to the Directors, who backed their crusading governor general.

With the army still in his sights, Lord Bentinck next reduced the strengths of native regiments, and in an act of enlightenment abolished flogging. This latter measure was complete anathema to the ethos of armies of the day as flogging was the key to the maintenance of discipline. In addition, to remove this authority from officers commanding regiments was seen as emaciating the power and respect that commanding officers had in their regiments. As a contemporary observed:

> The service is exceeding unpopular with both officers and men. The former are great pecuniary losers and the latter have been alienated from their officers by Lord Bentinck's arrangements, that we no longer get the sons of respectful landowners but the poor and needy to keep whom in order the lash is absolutely necessary, but not to be used by his wise measure to give 'home popularity'. Lately every effort has been made to reduce the power of commanding officers and the Government has nearly succeeded.[4]

The abolition of flogging did not apply to His Majesty's regiments serving in India, which caused much resentment and acute embarrassment when a British soldier was flogged for an infraction of discipline, whereas the 'backward' native *sepoy*, for the same infraction, was not flogged. Some 10 years later flogging was reintroduced into the Company's army by Sir Henry Hardinge on the eve of the first Anglo-Sikh War, but was limited to 50 lashes. Despite being a serving officer, Lord Bentinck was decidedly unpopular with the Company's armies. On one occasion at Allahabad, after reviewing the 3rd Bengal Light Cavalry, His Lordship invited the officers to dinner, an invitation they all refused; Lord Bentinck was most put out and the officers were ordered to attend.

Lord Bentinck's economy drive, which he maintained throughout his stewardship, was at times quite ridiculous bordering on vandalism. Having sold the Moote Masjid in Agra, he next targeted the Taj Mahal for the sale of its marble. This spectacular mausoleum, of white marble, was built by Emperor Shah Jehan as a memorial to his beloved wife, Mumtaz Mahal. It took 20 years to build. Sadly, with the demise of the Mughal Empire, this edifice of Mughal splendour fell into a state of disrepair and decay. By Lord Bentinck's time it had become a ruin and the area overgrown and a haunt for vagabonds and criminals. Instead of allowing for a major clean-up, the pusillanimous Governor General sent out invitations to builders and contractors to remove the marble for a fee. Chief Justice Sir John Strachey protested vociferously at this act of vandalism, and His Lordship's invitations were withdrawn. Regrettably the huge Agra gun, known as the *Dhoon Hanee*, did not escape Lord Bentinck's economic axe. This gun had been cast in Emperor Akbar's time weighing 30 tons and 14 feet long. It was broken up and sold as scrap metal. For all such measures of economy Bentinck acquired the sobriquet 'the Clipping

4 Eldred Pottinger's letter to R. Haughton, Esq., 29 May 1842.

Dutchman', however the Court of Directors loved him; the Company was heir to the Mughals and their governor general the de facto emperor, who had a natural taste for simplicity, disliked ceremony and form and was resolved to widen the circle of Government House society and to extend an equal patronage to all. On the throne of the great Mughal His Lordship acted like a Pennsylvanian Quaker.[5]

Not all Lord Bentinck's schemes were devoted to the economy. He was a humanitarian full of liberal ideas characterised by the extended employment of native Indians. According to him, 'no native of the said territories, nor any natural born subject of His Majesty therein, shall by reason only of his religion, place of birth, descent, colour or any of these, be disabled from holding any place, office or employment under the Company'. In the case of Indian judges, the concept of equality was extended by allowing them to adjudicate in cases involving Europeans. This was far too liberal a measure for the old *Koi Hais* of Bengal and under a less resolute governor general would have failed.

In keeping with his masters' wishes, Lord Bentinck next took on the inhuman and quasi-religious Indian practices of his day. The Court of Directors had long been anxious to abolish the practice of *Sati* (widow burning) and as far back as 1824 had declared their conviction of the practicability of abolishing this practice, an extremely sensitive subject for Hindus. The Governor General must be given credit for his moral courage for pushing through banishment of this inhuman practice. By his order in 1829, *Sati* was banned in the Company's territories to the great distress of many high-placed Hindus and the apprehension of many high-placed civil servants A high-powered Hindu delegation was sent to London to have the ban repealed. The matter was discussed in Privy Council and the petition was dismissed. *Sati* was to continue in the Indian states until 1877. The other quasi-religious practice of *thugee* (ritualistic banditry) was also banned and eradicated to the approbation of many Indians.

It is probably true to say that Lord Bentinck's greatest legacy in India was the expansion of education, albeit limited to English. He and his contemporaries felt that while the peoples of India needed to be educated, this was not possible in their many mother tongues so English had to be taught, especially as they also felt that all the collected knowledge in Sanskrit was too steeped in superstition and was less valuable to the modern world.

The manner in which they intended to accomplish this massive task was to create a class of persons to be interpreters between the British and the millions they governed, Indian in blood and colour, but English in taste, in opinion, in morals and intellect. To kickstart this process, Lord Bentinck ordered the official court language to be changed from Persian to English. In the light of the Company's changing charter from that of trading and commerce to one of administering an empire on behalf of the Crown, he felt that the Company's primary role was now to offer the benefit of western education and religion to the suffering masses oppressed by native superstition and ignorance about spiritual and worldly affairs, and to this honourable task they eagerly applied themselves. These pioneers would be ecstatic to witness the fruits of their endeavours in today's global market.

The renewed Company Charter of 1813 had removed the monopoly in trade that the Company had enjoyed in India but allowed for the continuance of its monopoly of the tea trade from China, however this concession became the target for revision by the increasingly

5 Beveridge, *A Comprehensive History of India*, Vol. 3, p.220.

clamorous merchants in England. So, when the charter was renewed in 1834 for another 20 years, the Company's tea monopoly was cancelled. The Honourable Company of Merchants, at the stroke of the pen, were now the Honourable Company of bean-counters. However, although they no longer enjoyed a monopoly in trade, they retained the monopoly to tax it. Consequently, the Company's purpose was now to open up trade at every opportunity and by all means. In this endeavour, the dramatic development in steam navigation provided a huge impetus and the rivers of India beckoned to become the highways of trade.

As early as 1825 Moorcroft had reported his positive impression with the use that could be made of the Indus as a channel for British commerce and that the Indus was probably superior for navigation to the Ganges. Lord Bentinck eagerly adopted any scheme which could open up the Indus and its tributaries to the navigation of the world and set about to engineer opportunities to make this possible. Hence the Burnes trip in 1831 to deliver the King's gift to Maharaja Ranjit Singh. However, once the navigability of the rivers was established it was necessary to get the countries bordering these rivers to buy into the grandiose project. Furthermore, the use of the Indus route to transport British goods to Kabul would be the most effective way of undermining Russian influence in Central Asia. English goods, not English bayonets. His Lordship was spurred on by a secret despatch from the president of the Board of Control, Lord Ellenborough, directing him to open up navigation with the principal aim of repelling Russian commerce from Kabul and Bokhara; the secondary aim was to establish British influence in Central Asia. Hence the great minds of the day, with mercantile blood flowing in their veins, were dead set on the accomplishment of this most beneficial of schemes. It may not be too far-fetched to contemplate this cherished scheme as the curtain-raiser to British entanglement in Asian politics with unseemly results, and that the great pacifist and humanitarian, Lord Bentinck, qualifies as the surrogate of the events that followed.

In dealing with the Indian states within the Company's domain, Lord Bentinck's administration was wanting. The Company's agents in these states were directed to leave the native sovereigns alone and not to interfere with the management of their states unless absolutely necessary, which generally meant then too late and the necessary interference too dramatic. This policy of non-intervention necessarily involved, to some extent, the condoning of unsavoury practices within the states. Native princes were left a free hand to manage their states as they pleased as long as they discharged their treaty obligations to the Company. Some of these princes were excessively cruel, extravagant and despotic. Constructive interference at an early stage would have avoided a great deal of unpleasantness.

His Lordship's dealings with Bahadar Shah, the Mughal King of Delhi, were also peevish and not in keeping with the high standard of compassion and dignity associated with Englishmen. This descendant of the great Mughals had petitioned, justifiably, for an increase in his pension. Without much consideration being given to this imperial petition, it was rejected out of hand. Miffed at this unwarranted humiliation, Bahadar appealed directly to London and his mission sailed secretly to London headed by the celebrated unorthodox religious thinker, Rammohun Roy, who had been a strong advocate for the education and modernisation of India and by some people is acclaimed as the Father of India. The mission duly appeared before the gentlemen sitting at Leadenhall Street, who after much humming and hawing over this embarrassing predicament allowed for a modified appeal to stand. This partial success was no doubt due to the celebrity status of Rammohun Roy, who was much feted during his stay in England. Regrettably, he died in Bristol in 1833 so avoided the wrath of the Governor General, who in a

Maharaja Ranjit Singh.

childish display of spite had refused to visit the King of Delhi when on his grand tour to the upper provinces in April 1831. Subsequently, His Lordship had it conveyed to Bahadar Shah to bear in mind that he was a pensioner and that he had better shape up.

Maharaja Ranjit Singh had been informed by Captain Wade of the Governor General's intended visit to the upper provinces of British India and of his planned sojourn at Simla. The Maharaja grasped this opportunity to send a high-powered delegation to meet him at Simla. This delegation included *Dewan* Moti Ram, General Hari Singh Nalwa and the Maharaja's trusty confidant *Fakir* Azizuddin and met His Lordship on his arrival. At this time the fame of Ranjit Singh was at its highest. The Sikhs had taken Multan from the Afghans in 1818 followed by Kashmir a year later then they had seized Attock and subdued the Derajat. In 1822, to the displeasure of the British, the Maharaja had employed veterans of Emperor Napoleon's Grand Army to train and command Sikh regiments which had sallied into Peshawar forcing the Afghan governor to pay tribute. Sikh expansion then suffered a setback caused by the activities of a religious fanatic named Syad Ahmed who had mustered a vast following and had taken over Peshawar proclaiming himself the new caliph. At a place called Helakot[6] this troublesome gentleman felt the sharp edge of Prince Sher Singh's *tulwar* and was consigned to history. So, the British were not without suspicion that the Sikhs had great ambitions and there were rumours that they were in correspondence with the Russians. Hence a meeting with the delegation was an opportunity not to be missed; the delegation was given the red carpet treatment.

Maharaja Ranjit Singh was always cautious about two things. Firstly his ambivalent relationship with the British, he was never far from suspecting the paramount power in India of Machiavellian designs and had no wish to be their next victim; secondly, his rapacious army, which, while employed, was the font of his power, but sitting idle it could become his nemesis. The army had to be kept busy thus creating its own means of existence by demanding tributes.

6 According to J. Cunningham's *History of the Sikhs*, this place was called Belakot, whereas Fakir Aizajuddin, the renowned cartobibliographer, calls it Helakot in *The Resourceful Fakirs*. It is most likely the same place with slightly different spelling and the latter is probably the more correct.

Thus, further expansion of his domains was vital and the most logical direction was into the Sindh and the ocean beyond. But bearing in mind the recent British interest in the Sindh, the Maharaja felt inclined to check out British resolve and their long-term aims. He did this by probing questions at every opportunity, such as his desire to know what the British intended to do about the rumoured marriage of a Persian princess to the son of one of the Sindh Amirs and thereby its connotation of allowing in Russian influence. On the British side there was an equal amount of concern about Sikh expansion, as demonstrated by Charles Trevelyan's letter to the Governor General, 'In 1809 the rising power of the Sikhs was considered so formidable that it was necessary to place a check on its further progress. If therefore we open to the Sikhs the door of Sindh, this power must rise to an inconvenient height.' Captain Wade in his letter of 15 August 1831 to Henry Prinsep, secretary to the Governor General, countered with the argument that because of the marriage alliance Sindh might follow Persia and become subservient to Russia:

> In the event it might be a question for Govt. to consider whether its best line of policy would not consist in taking advantage of our connection with Maharaja Ranjit Singh to counteract Russian diplomacy. We possess the same ascendancy in the councils of His Highness that Russia does in those of Persia, and the power of establishing a paramount influence in Afghanistan and Sindh is as open through the agency of the Maharaja as to Russia through Persia.[7]

Such was the atmosphere when the Sikh delegation was entertained by Lord Bentinck in Simla and a meeting of the heads of this long alliance was deemed to be beneficial to both sides. However, the Governor General, as head of the paramount power, desired that the proposal for such a meeting should come from the Maharaja. Alluding to his purpose in desiring such a meeting, Lord Bentinck writing to Robert Campbell stated:

> I shall take the opportunity of considering the disposition of Ranjit Singh to discuss with us in opening a free navigation up the Indus, according to the spirit of the instructions recently received from the Secret Committee. The Amirs of Sindh are the only intervening power: and their unfriendly and disrespectful conduct with regard to the present of horses sent by the King to Ranjit Singh gives a fair opportunity to demand that the interruption shall not again take place. They can make no resistance to the united demands of our own government and to that of the Lahore chief. The countries west of the Indus are now principally supplied with Russian manufactures. We have lately obtained very correct information upon these points.[8]

Now the niceties of correct protocol were to be played out as the indefatigable Captain Wade hurried to and foe between Ludhiana and Lahore with an equally harried *Fakir* Azizuddin to bring this historic meeting of equal heads of state to fruition. An inkling of some of the types of niceties to be covered was given in Sir Charles Metcalfe's letter to the Governor General of 4 September 1831:

7 Aijazuddin, *The Resourceful Fakirs*, p.55.
8 Aijazuddin, *The Resourceful Fakirs*, p.64.

> I see that Ranjit Singh wishes to have some presents sent to him instead of waiting to receive them at a meeting. I think he is in the right. Sending presents and giving them at a meeting are distinct things. He has sent presents. If the compliment be not returned, it will make him appear in an inferior rank. It will look as if he were made to come as an inferior to receive presents. The compliment to him will not be complete unless presents are sent by a return mission. What he proposes as to the envoys, one of your Lordship's staff assisted by Captain Wade, would be quite sufficient. Afterwards at the interviews, whatever is done by one side might be done on the other, all would be equal, *comme il faut*.[9]

The key protocol hurdle was the matter of who was to officially request the meeting, the implication being that the requester would be viewed as inferior to the requestee. This hurdle was crossed on 23 September in a very subtle manner by *Fakir* Azizuddin when he reminded Captain Wade that Lord Bentinck had asked one of the Sikh delegation if he had a portrait of the Maharaja, so clearly indicating His Lordship's desire to see the original. Based on this Maharaja Ranjit Singh sent his formal request to meet the Governor General and attached the following conditions, thus maintaining a stance of equality:

- The interview was to be strictly between two states and not involve any contentious political subjects;
- The visit would be in the vicinity of Anandpur Makhowal, with each party camping on its own side of the river;
- Lord Bentinck was to make the first call;
- Ranjit Singh would send his heir *Kunwar* Kharak Singh to escort Lord Bentinck from his camp which was to be on the banks of the river Sutlej. He hoped that the Commander-in-Chief would accompany the Governor General;
- This interview should not be regarded as a precedent by future Governors General.[10]

The last point is rather curious except for the fact that the Maharaja was prone to be very superstitious and this meeting was regarded as unique, requiring the Sikh gurus to determine the most auspicious date and time. Consequently, such meetings were not to be regarded as *de rigueur* for future governors-general. After all, the great Maharaja had reigned through no less than seven stewardships of British governors general.

On 9 June 1831, Lord Bentinck responded to the Maharaja's conditions:

- By agreeing to the first point;
- To the second, the location, Bentinck told Wade he could not find Anandpur on the map. As he would be bringing infantry, cavalry, and artillery, he preferred Ludhiana instead;
- It would be impossible for him to call on Ranjit Singh first.
- The Commander-in-Chief was not well enough and therefore he would be accompanied by the Secretary to the Government in the Persian Department (William Macnaghten). And

9 Aijazuddin, *The Resourceful Fakirs*, p.73.
10 Aijazuddin, *The Resourceful Fakirs*, p.70.

if Kharak Singh could not accompany him, 'none would be more agreeable' to him than the members of the delegation who came to Simla;
- The meeting would not be treated as a precedent.[11]

The sticky matter of who was to visit whom first rattled around like a ball in a squash court. Eventually, at the last minute, it was decided that the venue for this historic meeting would be Rupar on the banks of the Sutlej and the auspicious day was to be Wednesday 26 October 1831. The no-frills Governor General was persuaded that the British delegation should display as much pomp as was expected from the Sikh side, which was reported to include 10,000 of the Maharaja's finest troops. Besides his normal bodyguard, the Governor General's contingent included HM 16th Lancers, HM 31st Foot, two regiments of Bengal Native Infantry, Skinner's Horse and two troops of Bengal Horse Artillery, of which he gave the Maharaja the guns and horses of the two troops of Horse Artillery, lock stock and barrel.

The meeting lasted for six days during which there were parades, reviews, receptions, dancing, present giving, and drinking. While the Sikhs impressed the visitors with their gold, diamonds, and horses, the British impressed on them the benefits of navigating the rivers of the Punjab.[12] On the sixth day the British delegation moved to Patiala, while the Maharaja withdrew to Amritsar. A detailed account of this great meeting is given in Chapter 5 of *Fakir* Aizajuddin's most excellent book, *The Resourceful Fakirs*. While the great meeting had given Ranjit Singh assurance of perpetual friendship and achieved His Lordship's aim of giving the world the impression of complete unanimity between the two powers in India, it was void of any strategic objectives or joint designs for the future. The meeting was important not for what was said, but for what was not said or was deflected. Asked whether the British had any plans to extend their domains into Sindh, 'No', replied the Governor General, albeit he had already directed Colonel Henry Pottinger to start negotiations with the Amirs of Sindh for the opening up of the lower portion of the Indus for trade. In his letter to Pottinger, Lord Bentinck indicates the nature of his discussions with Maharaja Ranjit Singh:

> Ranjit Singh is, I believe aware that something is on the carpet. He however asked no questions, but on two occasions, put forward the subject of the Sindh valley, as if to give an opening for any remarks. It was however done with apparent indifference and was met precisely in the same manner. He has not disguised his views on Shikarpur.[13]

A few months after the great meeting Captain Wade was sent to Lahore to explain, in person, the object of Colonel Pottinger's mission to Sindh and to propose the navigation of the Sutlej, and to assure the ever-suspicious Ranjit Singh that the extension of commerce did not mean the extension of British power. Having consulted with his Sikh chiefs, Ranjit Singh gave his assent to the common use of the Sutlej and Indus, and also to the residence of a British officer at Mithenkot to superintend the navigation. A commercial treaty was signed on 26 December 1832 setting out the toll on boats at 570 rupees from the Himalayas to the sea, of which the

11 Aijazuddin, *The Resourceful Fakirs*, p.71.
12 . K.Singh, *A History of the Sikhs*, vol. I, p.276.
13 Aijazuddin, *The Resourceful Fakirs*, p.99.

Lahore government was to get 155 rupees for territories on the right bank and 39 Rupees for those on the left bank.[14]

Lord Bentinck's commercial desires coupled with his policy of non-interference complicated things and were to be further complicated by the revived hopes of Shah Shuja in his third attempt at regaining his throne in Afghanistan, where Dost Mohammed held sway over Kabul, Ghazni and Jalalabad. In Kandahar his brothers hardly pretended to acknowledge his authority, and in Peshawar his brother Sultan Mohammed governed on behalf of the Sikh Maharaja, Ranjit Singh, who was holding one of his sons as hostage. Herat in the far west was ruled by a prince of the Sadozai dynasty.

In 1831, Shah Shuja was fed with reports of the Sindh Amir's dissatisfaction with the British envoys and their apprehension of possible British complicity with the dreaded Sikhs. Maintaining that Sindh had always been under Sadozai sovereignty, the Amirs encouraged him to make an attempt. Thus, the Shah opened up communications with the Lahore *durbar*, which was also out of humour with the British about Sindh. Maharaja Ranjit Singh viewed the Shah's request for aid as an excellent opportunity to expand his domain to include Shirkapore and thence to the ocean, but negotiations were fraught with difficulties as one of the conditions stipulated by the Maharaja was the prohibition of the slaughter of cows in Afghanistan, and he also made a strange demand for the gates of Somnath to be returned to their original temple. Then, in 1832 it was rumoured that the Persians planned to advance against Herat giving further encouragement to Shah Shuja, who now offered the Maharaja to waive his rights to Peshawar and the *Koh-i-Noor* diamond, which the Maharaja had taken from him. The Maharaja, ever mindful of what the British might think of this venture, impressed on the Shah that the British should be involved or at least he should obtain their blessing. The Shah duly approached the British and received the reply: 'Sorry. We do not wish to get involved.'

It was also about this time that the Afghans opened up communications with the British, expressing a desire for a closer relationship based on their fear of Persian designs and Sikh encroachment and their hope that British interest would provide stability between the contending powers. However, the strict policy of non-interference was applied as the British were not in the mood to get involved in any foreign entanglement, but when the Shah Shuja appealed for financial help, the Governor General authorised the advance issue of one third of the Shah's annual pension of £5,000 (£370,000) per year. Lord Bentinck was bent on economy and if Shah Shuja succeeded, his pension would revert to his state. This is apparent by the Shah's being made to understand that should he return he must not expect any pecuniary assistance. However, the advance of pension could not fail, in the east, to be construed into material aid and countenance of the Shah's designs, albeit the payslip did include a caveat that the money was not to be used to reclaim his throne, which fooled no one.

Shah Shuja left Ludhiana on 17 February 1833 and according to Captain Wade he had with him 2 *lakhs* of rupees and 3,000 armed followers. His progress and the result of the Shah's adventure has been covered in a previous chapter; suffice to say that amongst the Shah's captured baggage there were documents that indicated more than a mild interest by the British in this bizarre escapade. A much-dejected Shah was back in Ludhiana on the eve of Lord Bentinck's

14 To initiate this great project Ranjit Singh proposed to send the first two steamers down river with a cargo of opium, and for them to return from Bombay with armaments. Not exactly what the British had in mind.

departure from India. Ranjit Singh, having captured Peshawar on 6 May 1834, now had an army of 10,000 men deployed in the area restless for further action. This development gave the governor of Bombay, Lord Clare (John FitzGibbon) a good friend of Lord Byron, much cause to complain to Lord Bentinck about his concern over Sikh strength in the Indus valley and the apparent exclusion of Bombay in Sindh affairs, no doubt prompted by the appointment of a Bengal officer (Lieutenant Fredrick Mackeson) to Mithenkot:

> I distrust the Sikh chief and he has such good cause of complaint against the Amirs, he may I fancy overrun their country before 'we little folk in Bombay' may say Jack Robinson. My hope is that you and he understand each other, but Ventura's army of 10,000 men with an undisciplined host besides but ill accords with what Ranjit's vakil told you that he meant to move a few battalions towards Sindh.[15]

Maharaja Ranjit Singh's dislike of the Sindhis was no less than theirs of him, nevertheless, after their defeat by the Shah, the Sindhis confidence had much diminished and Noor Mohammed Khan of Hyderabad offered to surrender Shikarpore to the Sikhs on their guarantee against any further attempt by the Shah to take over Sindh.[16] Maharaja Ranjit Singh was sorely tempted to provide this guarantee but he hesitated in deference to the reactions of his British allies. For the same reason, he had earlier restrained his Governor of Multan, Sawan Mal, who had proposed to garrison Rojhan from where the predatory tribe of Mazaris were being troublesome.

In early January 1834, Maharaja Ranjit Singh fell seriously ill. This illness lingered through when Dr Murray was summoned from Ludhiana, conducted his diagnosis and reported to Captain Wade that the Maharaja had acute inflammation of the liver. By April, Dr Murray was able to report that his patient was 'in excellent spirit.' However, was this great man's recovery durable? A question on many minds both British and Sikh.

Later that same year a communiqué was received at the Lahore *durbar* from Dost Mohammed promising to sort out the Sikhs after he had taken care of the insufferable Shah Shuja at Kandahar. In another communication to the British, Dost Mohammed asked for their assistance, which, of course, was denied. Meanwhile in a display of unanimity with his British allies Ranjit Singh sent a mission to Calcutta with presents for King William IV. The Governor General was at that time wrapping up his affairs in preparation of his departure. He had requested to resign due to ill health. There is no question that Lord Bentinck had accomplished great and lasting change in India, but there remained two separate viewpoints as to his stewardship. According to his friend and renowned humanitarian Macaulay:

> During his seven years he ruled India with eminent prudence, integrity and benevolence, who placed at the head of a great empire, never laid aside the simplicity and moderation of a private citizen, who infused in oriental despotism the spirit of British freedom.[17]

15 Aijazuddin, *The Resourceful Fakirs*, p.98.
16 J.D. Cunningham, A *History of the Sikhs*, from the origin of the nation to the battles of the Sutlej (Calcutta: N. Roy, 1904), p.285.
17 Vincent A. Smith, *The Oxford History of India* (Oxford: Oxford University Press, 1919), p.657.

An opposite view was taken by Sir Edward Thornton, a Bengal civil servant and historian, who remarked:

> It remains only to state that he quitted India in 1835 having held the office of Governor General somewhat longer than the ordinary period but having done less for the interest of India and for his own reputation than any who had occupied his place since the commencement of the nineteenth century.[18]

Lord Bentinck's return to England in March 1835 was not unexpected as he had been ailing for some time and had been convalescing at Ootacamund in the Nilrigi Hills, the Simla of the south. It was here that he exercised the new rule that the Governor General in Council could meet anywhere within British territories, a rule that the next governor general was to make full use of. Lord Bentinck died in Paris 10 days earlier than Maharaja Ranjit Singh in Lahore (17 and 27 June, 1839 respectively). No doubt Sindh was on their celestial agenda. His Lordship had desired expansion of trade to gain influence, whilst His Highness had desired expansion of territory to gain tributes.

On Lord Bentinck's departure, Sir Charles Metcalfe became the pro tem governor general, as the wheels of appointing a new governor general were put in motion. The Court of Directors strenuously advocated that Sir Charles Metcalfe be confirmed in the role. However, the new administration of Sir Robert Peel and his president of the Board of Control had other ideas. This contretemps went on for some time until Sir Charles blotted his copybook with the Court of Directors by lifting the censorship ban on Indian newspapers and their support for his candidature fell apart. Had this not happened, Governor General Sir Charles Metcalfe would never have ventured into Afghanistan. Eventually, Sir Robert Peel recommended to King William IV the appointment of the Tory candidate, Lord Heytesbury (William à Court), lately the British ambassador to the Imperial Russian Court at St Petersburg.

Then in short order Sir Robert Peel's government fell and the Whigs were back in power with Charles Grant, later Lord Glenelg, as the president of the Board of Control and Lord Palmerston as the foreign secretary. These two gentlemen objected vociferously to the appointment of Lord Heytesbury, indicating that he was too close to the Russians and hence a flawed choice for the governorship of India. In addition, Charles Grant was equally negative about the Court of Directors' candidate, Charles Metcalfe. He felt that 'the one link [non-Company man] at least between the systems of India and the British Government ought, for the advantage of both to be invariably maintained.' Earlier Lord Cornwallis had put the kibosh on any Company man being appointed to the governorship of India when he stated that during his period of government, 'it was scarcely possible to find any old or eminent servant of the Company, who had not in some period of his career, practised or connived at the abuses and corruption which it would be one of his first duties to suppress.'

So, whilst Lord Heytesbury was being tailored for the fineries of governorship, Lord Palmerston and Charles Grant rummaged around looking for a suitable Whig candidate and the issue devolved into the cesspit of petty party politics. They eventually found their man in the person of George Eden, Lord Auckland, a 52-year-old bachelor, First Lord of the Admiralty,

18 Smith, *The Oxford History of India*, p.656.

an aristocrat of good manners and a party man who would do as he was told; a safe pair of hands even the Court of Directors could agree upon. At the time there was not one iota of suspicion that these safe hands were made of jelly, allowing the honour of England to be dragged into the dirt and expose India to the most grievous military disaster. George Eden was the second son of the first Lord Auckland, who had fathered six sons and eight daughters. As George's elder brother, William, died by drowning in the Thames, George succeeded to the title on his father's death. The Eden family were staunch Whigs, genteel, liberal and well connected. The Whig Prime Minister, Lord Melbourne (William Lamb), was said to be 'close' to Emily Eden, and Lord Melbourne's sister, Lady Cowper, was Lord Palmeston's mistress before he married her.

5

Peshawar: The Elephant in the Room (Phase I)

Lord Auckland arrived in Calcutta on 3 March 1836, after a five month voyage on the good ship *Jupiter* commanded by Captain Grey. The new Governor General, a bachelor, was accompanied by his two younger sisters Emily and Fanny (Frances), his nephew Captain the Honourable William Osborne of HM 26th Foot, six valets and maids and a French cook by the name of St Cloud. Captain Osborne, a nonchalant bachelor, had already served in India with his regiment in the Bharakpur campaign of 1826 and was returning in his new role as his uncle's military secretary and chaperone to his aunts; he brought with him a pack of six greyhounds and to this dog count was added Emily's pet spaniel, Chance.

Their actual arrival up the river from Diamond Point was attended by a combination of misfortunes. The *Jupiter* was being towed up the River Hooghli when it ran aground. Then in attempts to refloat her, the steamboat *Sonamukli* collided with the *Jupiter*. The Governor General's party was then forced to tranship to the steamer to continue their journey. They finally arrived at Chandpal Ghat at the uncivilised hour of 10:00 p.m.[1] Normally it was at this place that a new governor general was met by a bevy of high officials and escorted through the welcoming crowd to Government House, where he would be taken to the council chamber to take the oath and assume the reins of office. Instead, the bevy of high officials were seated at the welcoming dinner at Government House and the welcoming crowd had gone to bed. So, Lord Auckland was rushed off in a carriage to Government House, where on arrival he was hurriedly sworn in and escorted to the Banqueting Room to join Sir Charles Metcalfe and a party of 80 at dinner. Not a very auspicious beginning.

The next day, while their brother George was at a meeting with his new acolytes to be 'put in the picture' and the maids and valets were busy unpacking the vast number of trunks, Emily and Fanny were conducted around what was to be their abode for the next five years by the stern Captain David Bryce in his capacity of major-domo of Government House.

The new Government House was the brain-child of Lord Wellesley, one of the greatest of governor generals. At the start of his tenure in 1798 Lord Wellesley had determined to erect the finest residence for the representative of any sovereign in the world.[2] The building was completed

1 Curzon, *British Government in India*, Vol. I p.196.
2 Curzon, *British Government in India*, Vol. I, p.28.

by 1803 at a cost of £169,000 (£12.6 million). This expense was not to the liking of the pusillanimous Court of Directors back in London. According to them this was 'an extravagant and unauthorised outlay', by their 'Sultanised Englishman', their nickname for the Governor General. They had a paranoia about local officials 'going native', adopting Asiatic habits and indulgences.[3] Extravagant though it may have been, it was indeed justified as pointed out by Lord Valentia (George Annesley) in his book *Voyages and Travels in India*:

George Eden, 1st Earl of Auckland.

> The sum expended upon it has been considered extravagant by those who carry European ideas and European economy into Asia, but they ought to remember that India is a country of splendour, of extravagance and of outward appearance; that the head of a mighty Empire ought to conform himself to the prejudices of the country he rules over, and that the British, in particular, ought to emulate the splendid works of the Princes of the House of Timour, lest it should be supposed that we merit the reproach which our great rival, has ever cast upon us, of being alone influenced by a sordid mercantile spirit.

Lord Wellesley had selected Captain Charles Wyatt of the Bengal Engineers to be his architect and the design was based on Kedleston Hall in Derbyshire; it was made of brick and covered in plaster. 'The state rooms were for the first time lighted up', recalled Lord Valentia; 'at the upper end of the length was placed a very rich Persian carpet and at the centre of that a *musnud* of crimson and gold, formerly comprising part of the ornament of Tippu Sultan's throne'.[4] There were outhouses for kitchens, servants' quarters, stables and barracks for the Governor General's 300-strong bodyguard. To run this vast establishment, Captain Bryce had a force of 400 native servants, one of whom was now appointed 'dogsbody' to Chance, Fanny's little dog.

The sisters marvelled at what they saw, 'it was like something out of *Arabian Nights*'[5] except that by midday it was like living in an oven. Of the many introductions to their new home one

3 Tristram Hunt, *Ten Cities that Made an Empire* (London: Penguin Books, 2015), p.206.
4 Hunt, *Ten Cities*, p.182.
5 Janet Dunbar, *Golden Interlude: The Edens in India, 1836–1842* (London: John Murray, 1955), p.28.

of the more curious was the adjutant bird',[6] so called by British soldiers as from a distance it resembled a stern adjutant on parade.

It was reported that one old bird had mounted guard at Government House for 30 years. From all accounts the younger sister, Fanny, aged 35, was to enjoy her stay in India more. Emily, going on 40, was more detached and a greater influence on her brother. Later she was to write, 'He [George] could not have existed here alone, and, for want of other colleagues, I can see constantly that it is a great comfort to him to have me to talk over his bothers with.'[7]

His Lordship was briefed by his council on the first day of his governorship. They portrayed the situation as one of tranquillity, the army was in barracks, there were no schemes for extending borders and the treasury was in robust shape. These were ideal conditions for the Whig Governor General to pursue and expand on his predecessor's liberal reforms. Had he had the courage of his own convictions he might well have succeeded, but he was more cautious than courageous and this cautious man had two masters to serve, the Whig party in England and the East India Company Court of Directors; his immediate advisors, on the other hand, had but one, the Company's interests.

Before the Regulating Act of 1773, the English in India were merely representatives of a private trading concern whose object was to make money. This was the era of the 'Pagoda Tree' and many went out to shake it and returned as wealthy 'Nabobs'. This trading concern was administered by a court of 24 directors possessing £2,000 (£150,000) worth of stock and a court of proprietors possessing £500 (£37,500) worth of stock. Greed and ill-administration drove the Company close to bankruptcy compelling it to seek a British Government bailout of £1.4 million (£105 million), shades of Northern Rock some 250 years later. By William Pitt the Younger's India Act of 1784 the British Government became involved in the administration of the Company by the setting up of a Board of Control, a sort of permanent 'Company Voluntary Arrangement', to represent the government. This board consisted of the president and five other privy councillors, to include the lord chancellor and one secretary of state. This body was invested with great powers, it could approve, modify or amend the instructions of the Court of Directors, or issue independent orders on its own. In practice this was done through a secret committee of the Court consisting of three directors, who were empowered to transmit to India, in secret, any orders from the Board of Control. The Company's Court was thus reduced to a subordinate position to the Government; however, the Court retained the power of patronage, each director being allowed 12 nominations per annum. While the Court could nominate a governor general, the appointment had to have the sovereign's approbation, which in practice meant the governments of the day.

An account has been left by Sir John Kaye of the manner in which this dual form of administration worked in practice. Apparently, the despatches to India were first prepared by the

6 Adjutant birds. The greater adjutant is a member of the stork family, once found widely across southern Asia, but now only in Assam and Cambodia. They are currently included in the list of endangered species. This large stork, standing six foot seven inches, has a massive wedge-shaped bill, a bare head and a distinctive neck pouch. It is the tallest of all stork species and feeds mainly on carrion and offal. The name 'adjutant bird' is derived from their stiff military gait when walking on the ground, and when standing still, which they can do for hours on end, resembling an 'adjutant on parade'. Bearing in mind the lack of sanitation in the 1800s, these birds were much valued as scavengers and a fine of 50 rupees was imposed on anyone who killed them.

7 Dunbar, *Golden Interlude*, p.91.

Directors at Leadenhall Street and sent over to the Board of Control in Cannon Row, where they would be vetted, amended and substituted, resulting in something entirely different, so in all questions regarding peace, war or foreign affairs, the Directors were mere signatories. Of this system, Lord Curzon (George) was to write:

> Had a Committee been assembled from the padded chambers of Bedlam, they could hardly have devised anything more extravagant in its madness, or more mischievous in its operation. To it must be attributed many of the astounding errors and contradictions that characterised our India policy at that time.[8]

In those days, reports of events 6,000 miles away took 150 days to reach England and a further 150 days for the Indian authorities to react to their masters' dictum. To put this time lag into perspective, the news of the victory at Waterloo (18 June) was eventually received in Calcutta on 11 November. Consequently, most decisions had to be made by 'the man on the ground' holding to a broad concept set out by his masters. It was for this reason that the supreme authority in India lay with the 'governor general in council', as it was in this way that the almost inevitable ignorance of a ruler sent out from London could be guided and controlled by Indian experience from the precipitate or arbitrary exercise of a governor general's awesome powers. It could be said that Lord Auckland over-oiled this 'failsafe' mechanism by overdependence on his advisers' 'Indian experience'.

The 'council' consisted of five members with the commander-in-chief being opted in as an *ex officio* member. In earlier days the governor general had a casting vote, but this gave cause for much mischief, so before Lord Cornwallis went out as governor general, he had insisted on the constitutional power to overrule his council. This was granted by the Act of 1786 and was limited to cases of high importance. Then, by the Act of 1833, the governor general when many hundreds of miles away from his council in Calcutta was allowed to exercise the full powers of governor general in council. It was this rule which allowed Lord Auckland to administer the affairs of India, closeted by his 'Indian' advisers in the cool of Simla for a period of over two years, while his council remained in the oven of Calcutta.

Of the advisers three are significant to this history, all of whom started their service in India as officers in the Company's army and by being proficient in languages were transferred to the more lucrative Political Department.

William Hay Macnaghten. A Scotsman born in 1794. He was educated at Charterhouse and was sent to Madras on a cadetship in 1809 and was transferred to the Bengal Civil Service in 1816. He displayed a talent for languages and published several books on Indian religions and culture. In 1823 he married Frances Martyn, a widow of no high pedigree, but ambitious; they had no children. In 1830, he entered the diplomatic service when appointed secretary to the governor general, Lord Bentinck, and was with him at the meeting with Maharaja Ranjit Singh at Rupar in 1831 where he also met Captain Wade and Alexander Burnes. Returning in 1833 to Calcutta with his experience greatly enhanced during the Governor General's tour of the Upper Provinces and armed with his boss's recommendation, he was given charge of the Secret and

8 Curzon, *British Government in India*, Vol. 2, p.69.

Political Department and remained in that slot with the arrival of Lord Auckland. He and his wife were part of the Governor General's cavalcade to the north-west territories and into the pages of history. Emily Eden was to refer to him as 'Our Lord Palmerston, a dry sensible man, who wears an enormous pair of blue spectacles and speaks Persian, Arabic and Hindustani rather more fluently than English.'

Sir William Hay Macnaghten.

Henry Whitelock Torrens. Born in Canterbury in 1806, he was also educated at Charterhouse and Corpus Christi Oxford. He first joined the British Foreign Service and soon afterwards accepted a cadetship to the Bengal army and arrived in Calcutta in 1826. He was also an accomplished linguist and fairly rapidly came under the tutelage of his fellow scholar Macnaghten, as in 1835 he was recruited into the Secretariat as Macnaghten's deputy and in this capacity was included in the group that accompanied Lord Auckland on his lengthy tour of the Upper Provinces. Sir William Kaye says of him, 'His gaiety and vivacity made him a welcome addition to the Governor General's vice-regal court and perhaps not the least of his recommendations as a travelling champion was that he could amuse the ladies of Lord Auckland's family with as much felicity as he could assist the labours of that nobleman himself.'[9] Henry Torrens married Eliza Roberts in 1832; Emily Eden thought that Eliza played the harp beautifully and was a wasted talent in India. Henry Torrens died in Calcutta in 1852 of dysentery.

John Russell Colvin. Another Scotsman. He was the fourth child of an illustrious Anglo-Indian family and was born at Meerut in 1807. John Colvin was educated at the Company's college at Haileybury in England and arrived back in India on a cadetship in 1826 and was transferred to the Bengal Civil Service in 1830. Standing over six feet, John Colvin soon made a name for himself and in 1836 Lord Auckland personally selected him as his private secretary. John Colvin married, at the comparatively early age of 20, Miss Emma Sophia, the sister of Major Henry Sneyd the commander of the Governor General's bodyguard; they had 10 children. He was devoted to the Governor General during the ensuing six years, who had the greatest confidence in him. He was bound to Lord Auckland like a man of aspiring nature to one who had given him his first opportunity to distinguish himself. Theirs was a closer relationship than that of chief and subordinate, and as Lord Auckland was to say many years later, 'he worked with me not for me'. John Colvin returned to England with Lord Auckland in 1842, then, in September 1845 he was back in India to take over from Henry Lawrence as the

9 Kaye, *History of the War in Afghanistan*, Vol. 1, p.303.

British Resident in Kathmandu. In 1854 he was selected by Lord Dalhousie to be the lieutenant governor of the North-Western Provinces. He died in Agra in September 1857. In evidence of the reliance placed by Lord Auckland on his private secretary, Henry Prinsep recorded:

> He [Auckland] was considered to have yielded too much to his Private Secretary, who on occasions when the Governor General called his members of Council and others into private consultation with him, would take the whole initiative of the discussion, while his Lordship sat listening with his hands at the back of his head, and having thus thrown upon him he got the monogram of 'Lord Colvin among the younger civil servants'.[10]

At first the new governor general's proceedings justified the hopes of those who had recommended his appointment. He developed his predecessor's plans for the promotion of education in the belief that it was only through education, in English, that the native Indians could be helped to understand their own conditions and in time take over their own schools. Moreover, the new governor general was determined to leave behind him a significant contribution to the good and happiness of India. He was as evangelical in his ideas as his predecessor. However, as depicted by his biographer, L.J. Trotter, George Eden 'was eminently fitted by temperament and long experience to discharge the most exacting duties of "quiet times", but, as George Eden was to discover, there are no "quiet times" in India.'

Of the many welcoming letters to the Governor General, all wishing him great success in his appointment, was one from the Amir of Afghanistan, Dost Mohammed Khan, in which he invited Lord Auckland to 'communicate to me whatever may suggest itself to your wisdom for settlement of affairs of this country, that it may serve as a rule for my guidance. I hope that your Lordship will consider me and my country as your own.' He also took the opportunity to ask for advice on the best means of dealing with the 'conduct of the reckless and misguided Sikhs'. Lord Auckland replied, 'My friend you are aware that it is not the practice of the British Government to interfere with the affairs of other independent states', adding that he would be sending 'some gentleman to discuss commercial ties'.

In addition to all the welcoming messages and *nazars* there was a minute left by Lord Bentinck, in which he warned his successor of a possible threat from Russia, and the object of his minute was to review the resources which the Government of India had at its command in order to frustrate such an event:

> From the time of Peter the Great to the present time, the views of Russia have been turned to obtaining possession of that part of Central Asia which is watered by the Oxus and joins the eastern shore of the Caspian. This is the best line of operation against India, but it can only be considered at present as a very distant speculation.[11]

It had been the estimable British commercial policy and dogma that peace and industry be introduced to the wilderness of Sindh, Khorasan and Punjab, and in so doing fix the limits on newly founded feudal governments and impress moderation on further grasping of territories.

10 Curzon, *British Government in India*, Vol. 2, p.197.
11 Dunbar, *Golden Interlude*, p.40.

Dost Mohammed Khan.

It was hoped and desired that this could be achieved through the Indus navigation project and that once this was in full swing all concerned would feel secure in what they had, but incapable of obtaining more. This might have worked had the Russians not been credited with pushing their intrigues to the banks of the Indus.

While Lord Auckland was absorbing his predecessor's minute, the foreign secretary, Lord Palmerston, received a communication from the British representative in Teheran informing him that:

> The Shah of Persia lays claim to the sovereignty of Afghanistan as far as Ghazni and is fully determined to attempt the conquest of Herat in the spring. Unfortunately the conduct of Kamran [the Sadozai chief of Herat] in violating the engagements entered into with His Highness, the late Abbas Meerza, and his permitting his Wazir, Yar Mohammed, to occupy part of Seiston, has given the Shah full justification for commencing hostilities. The success of the Shah in this undertaking is anxiously wished for by the Russians and their minister here [Simonovich] does not fail to press it on to early execution.[12]

The Foreign Secretary duly replied to the effect that it was to be made abundantly clear to the Shah that his contemplated invasion of Afghanistan would be considered an unfriendly act by

12 Durand, *The First Afghan War and Its Causes*, p.27.

the British Government and would not be viewed with indifference. Later in the year the new Governor General received a very significant despatch from Sir John Hobhouse, the chairman of the Secret Committee (later Lord Broughton), dated 25 June, which laid the foundation of the proceedings that followed; it informed him:

> We have received from the Commissioner for the affairs of India, copies of two letters which the Right Honourable Henry Ellis addressed to Viscount Palmerston on February 25 and April 1 last – the former stating the particulars of an overture said to have been made by Dost Mohammed of Kabul to the Shah of Persia in view to the conquest and partition of the territories of Prince Kamran of Herat, and the latter mentioning that a similar overture had been received by the Shah from the Chiefs of Kandahar, and there was also a rumour of the Khan of Khiva having entered into an engagement with the Russian Government.
>
> As Mr Ellis does not state that he has communicated with your Lordship in Council on the subject of these despatches, copies of them are enclosed for your information.
>
> The facts above mentioned are clearly indicative of a disposition on the part of the rival Chiefs of Afghanistan to engage the Shah of Persia in their views of personal aggrandisement, and from the views which the Shah himself is known to entertain in respect of Herat there is reason to apprehend that he may be disposed to countenance any scheme which may facilitate the accomplishment of a favourite object of his ambition, encouraged as he doubtless will be by the Russians to extend his influence and through him their own, in the countries bordering upon our Indian possessions.
>
> Mr Ellis mentions in his letter of February 25, that he suggested to Haji Husain Ali, the Afghan nobleman from whom he received the particulars of Dost Mohammed's overture to the Shah of Persia, the propriety of Dost Mohammed himself opening a communication with the Governor General of India, and it is therefore probable that before this letter reaches you, you may be in possession of an overture from this chief which will enable you the better to judge as to what steps it may be proper and desirable for you to take to watch more closely than has hitherto been attempted, the progress of events in Afghanistan and to counteract the progress of Russian influence in a quarter which, from its proximity to our Indian possessions could not fail, if it were established, to act injuriously on the system of our Indian alliances, and possibly to interfere even with the tranquillity of our own territory.
>
> The mode of dealing with this very important question, whether by despatching a confidential agent to Dost Mohammed of Kabul merely to watch the progress of events, or to enter into relations with this chief, either of a political, or merely, in the first instance, of a commercial character, we confide to your discretion, as well as the adoption of any other measures that may appear to you desirable in order to counteract Russian advances in that quarter, should you be satisfied from the information received from your own agents on the frontier, or hereafter from Mr McNeill, on his arrival in Persia, that the time has arrived at which it would be right for you to interfere decidedly in the affairs of Afghanistan.
>
> Such an interference would doubtless be requisite, either to prevent the extension of Persian dominion in that quarter, or to raise a timely barrier against the impending encroachment of Russian influence.

> We shall transmit to Mr McNeill a copy of this despatch for his information and guidance, and you may expect to receive from his intelligence sufficiently full and accurate information to assist you in coming to a decision on the important question to which we wish to direct your immediate and most earnest attention.[13]

Sir John Cam Hobhouse, 1st Baron Broughton.

This important communication, strangely not mentioned by Sir John Kaye, clearly indicated the presumed threat and equally clearly, imparted the assumption that the responsibility for any counteraction was that of the governor general in council. If India was threatened, it was by India that it had to be met. The governor general was first to endeavour to enter into commercial or into political relations with Afghanistan and adopt any other measures which he thought desirable in order to counteract Russian influence in that country. It was quite clear that as far as Lord Palmerston, the foreign secretary, was concerned the treaty of 1814 calling on British aid in the defence of Persia against a European power was a dead letter, as in 1828 the Russians had made themselves the paramount influence in Persia: hence the cover for Persia no longer existed, and consequently the approaching crisis was not an English one but an Indian one.

While the storm clouds gathered 2,000 miles away, Lord Auckland had to sort out a number of problems closer to home. Raja Pratab Singh of Satara, in the Western Ghats, who had been put on the *guddi* by Lord Hastings in 1822 and had now 'given himself up to indolence and pursuits so childish and eccentric as to make his sanity more than questionable'. Regime change was called for, the Raja was pensioned off to Benares and his brother was put on the *guddi.* In the state of Oudh, the *Nawab* Nasiruddin Haidar had died and his widow Begum had illegally endeavoured to place her boy nominee on the vacant *guddi.* The tumult in Lucknow was eventually put down by Colonel Sir John Low, and Mohammed Ali, who had agreed to pay six *lakhs* rupees extra for an additional subsidiary force, was placed on the *guddi.* In a move to ensure that the King of Ava, in Burma, remained contented, Lord Auckland arranged to send him a white elephant that had just been born at Madras, which, Auckland hoped, 'should bind him to us forever'.

13 Auckland Colvin, *Rulers of India. John Russell Colvin: The Last Lieutenant Governor of the North West Under the Company* (n.p.: Kessinger Publishing, 2007), p.86.

Further away, in the sensitive area of the Indus valley, the Sikhs were on the verge of entering Sindh on the pretext of punishing the Mazari tribe and the Amirs who had provoked them to attack Sikh outposts south of Multan. In August 1836, the Sikh army marched down to Mithenkot on the banks of the Indus and then on to Rojhan further down the river. In the following October, the Mazaris were thrashed by the Sikhs who now occupied a fort called Ken. The next, inevitable, step was Shikarpore, a sitting duck and a long-cherished desire of Maharaja Ranjit Singh. The Maharaja was strongly advised by his generals to make the final push into Sindh, and for the first time Ranjit Singh hesitated. Was the ever-suspicious Maharaja aware of the small print in the British treaty with the Amirs of Sindh and in his old age fearful of attacking a party joined by treaty to his mighty ally, or was the still wily old ruler using the situation, probably staged, to negotiate a British understanding to acknowledge and thereby strengthen his claim to the territories he already held? Captain Wade was deputed to Lahore to persuade the Maharaja to give up his campaign for the Sindh. The crux of the diplomatic double-talk employed was whether the Sutlej, 'the stream of perpetual friendship', was a tributary of the Indus or vice versa. Ranjit Singh argued that the incursion was designed to punish the intriguers of the unprovoked Mazari attacks and that Shah Shuja had relinquished Shikarpore to him by treaty, and by treaty the British had promised not to interfere with Sikh affairs north of the Sutlej. The British conceded the first point but refused to acknowledge the second and on the last point the British maintained a diplomatic quibble stating that the territory in question was not north of the Sutlej, but north of the Indus which was not the same thing. Captain Wade, known by the Sikhs as the 'Captain Sahib', was directed to use every means, short of menace, to induce the Maharaja to abandon his designs against Shikarpore. Thus, the British involvement in Sindh became political, not just commercial. Due note was probably taken of this development by the equally wily Amir in Kabul, who, no doubt, may have calculated that if the British were capable of stemming Ranjit Singh's greed, they could be tempted into some advantageous negotiation in his favour.

The Sikh Sardars were furious at this apparent violation of a long-standing agreement of non-interference and recommended that the Noble Sarkar (Ranjit Singh) stand firm even if this meant war, an opinion strongly supported by his French generals. The Noble Sarkar reminded the chiefs of what had happened to the conquering Marathas and sent *Fakir* Azizuddin to conciliate with the 'Captain Sahib' to have Sindh declared a neutral zone, but this proposal was beyond the strict remit of no Sikh interference in Sindh. The Sikh *durbar* buckled under but refused to sign any treaty and although they withdrew from Fort Ken, the Maharaja refused to give up Rojhan. This episode did much to create an anti-British feeling in the young breast of Prince Naonihal Singh and his hatred of the 'Captain Sahib', egged on by the clearly anti-British Chief Minister, Dhian Singh, and his brother Raja Gulab Singh. There is no doubt that this brush with the Sikhs and the Maharaja's compliance with British wishes played much in Lord Auckland's resolve later to maintain the good Maharaja in his possessions, bearing in mind that a 'friendly' nation between British India and lawless Afghanistan was a much better choice than a dissatisfied Sikh nation on its border. Unfortunately, the Maharaja's health was causing concern, as by August 1836 fissures within Ranjit Singh's family became apparent when *Kunwar* Kharak Singh sent a secret message to the British requesting their support for his rightful succession and accusations about the Dogra rajas' anti-British sentiments. In reply, William Macnaghten of the Political Department asked Captain Wade, the 'Captain Sahib', to convey to the *Kunwar* that Hs Lordship in council must decline entering upon the consideration of any question affecting the succession to the dominion of its old and faithful ally Ranjit Singh, whose valuable life, it was hoped, would long be spared to his family and country.

Earlier, in reply to Sir Charles Metcalfe's concerns about developments, the Governor General had replied:

> I share with you the apprehension of our being at no distant date involved in political and possibly military operations upon our western frontier, and even since I have been here, more than one event has occurred, which led me to think that the period of disturbance is nearer than I had wished or expected. The constitutional restlessness of the old man of Lahore seems to increase with his age. His growing appetite for the treasures and jungles of the Sindh, the obvious impolicy of allowing him to extend his kingdom in that direction, the importance which is attached to the free navigation of the Indus, most justly, I think, and yet with perhaps some exaggeration, from its volume nothing having been tried, the advance of the Persians towards Herat, and the link which may in consequence be formed between Indian and European politics – all lead to fear, that the wish, which I had to confine my administration to objects of commerce and finance and improved institutions and domestic policy, will be far indeed from being accomplished.[14]

By his reference to the 'link' between Indian and European politics, Lord Auckland obviously desired the Home authorities to play an equal part in the defence of British interests. The only measure Auckland decided upon at this time was to give priority to the opening up of the Indus for commerce much favoured by his predecessor and his East India Company masters in London. In September 1836, Auckland selected Captain Alexander Burnes to be the 'gentleman' he promised the Amir in Kabul he would send to 'discuss commercial ties'; Burnes had been agitating for just such an opportunity. Auckland had asked the President of the Board of Control how Burnes could be best employed and was told do with him whatever the Governor General wished. Based on this young officer's experience of Afghanistan and on the reputed favourable impression he had made on the Amir of Kabul, the Governor General selected Burnes to head up the mission. While the new Governor General thought his choice most appropriate many others did not think so. Charles Masson, who was the British spy in Kabul at the time the Burnes mission was there recorded. 'The Government furnished no instructions, apparently confiding in the discretion of a man who had none. However, this selection did have the added advantage of being pleasing to the Governor of Bombay by having one of his officers lead the mission. This commercial mission would also, his Lordship hoped, help counter Russian influence.'

Captain Alexander Burnes' party included Lieutenant Robert Leech of the Bombay Engineers and Lieutenant John Wood of the Company's navy; later they were joined by Dr Perceval Lord of the Company's Medical Department and Mohan Lal. The party left Bombay by sea on 26 November 1836 for Hyderabad, then went up the river to Khairpur and on to Mithenkot, where it was to meet up with Captain Wade and Lieutenant Frederick Matheson, the Indus navigation superintendent there. Following this meeting they proceeded to Peshawar and thence up the Khyber Pass to Kabul. The official brief, compiled by William Macnaghten, directed

14 Beveridge, *A Comprehensive History of India*, Vol. 3, p.569.

that Captain Burnes was to conduct a commercial mission to the countries bordering on the Indus with a view to complete the reopening of the navigation of that river, on the basis of a treaty lately concluded with the powers possessing territories on its banks. Along the way this remit was altered by the Governor General and it was now to 'monitor the progress of events in Afghanistan with particular emphasis on the effectiveness of Russian attempts to influence Afghanistan foreign policy'.

The selection of Burnes for this delicate mission was later considered to have been inappropriate by Sir Henry Durrand, who had himself advanced with the British army into Afghanistan and was the young officer who blew up the gates of the fortress at Ghazni. His comment on Burnes' appointment may be a little biased, but nonetheless valid. He wrote:

> A man [Burnes] of inordinate ambition but of average ability and shallow acquirements, sanguine in temperament and wanting in self-control, Burnes was not possessed of qualifications essential to success. Lord Auckland and his advisers were misled by the reputation which Burnes' amusing but not accurate book of travels had obtained for the author and thought to reward merit and secure popularity by selecting him for the duty. Burnes was aware of the apprehension entertained by both Home and Indian Governments respecting the Persian schemes of conquest, saw with eager aspiration that his commercial mission was in fact quickly assuming the functions of a political mission, and, his imagination being already inflamed by McNeill's despatches before he reached Kabul, he entered that city on September 20, 1837, quixotically prepared to find, and to combat giants of Russian influence and Persian intrigues.[15]

Meanwhile, Lord Auckland and his sisters entertained their special guest, General Jean Francois Allard, Maharaja Ranjit Singh's favourite foreign general. He had just returned from France where he had been on leave of absence with his Kashmiri wife and four children. He had left them in St Tropez and had returned to resume his duties as the governor of Peshawar. As he danced with the Eden sisters at the ball given in his honour, he did not tell his host that in his pocket he was carrying his credentials as the French attaché to the Sikh *durbar*. While it was perfectly acceptable to dance with a foreign general in the employ of an ally, it was quite another matter to discover that the gentleman was the representative of the French King! Concerns were raised, questions asked and explanations demanded. It transpired that this piece of paper, 'acquired' by General Allard, was designed to provide him with diplomatic immunity in the event his position in the Sikh kingdom became dangerous. After some diplomatic shuttling between Paris and London, it was resolved that British recognition of the appointment would only be operable in the event the General's life was in danger. However, he died peacefully at Peshawar in January 1839, to the great regret of his boss, the Sikh Maharaja.

Back in Teheran, a new player in the Great Game was to make his entrance. He was another Scotsman, by the name of John McNeill, a 29-year-old surgeon of the Bombay Medical Department; he had been posted to the British Legation in Persia in 1824, and by 1835 had risen to the position of political assistant to the Envoy and was considered to be an authority on Persian affairs. During his furlough in Britain in 1835 he is reputed to have been the author of

15 Durand, *The First Afghan War and Its Causes*, p.34.

the anti-Russian pamphlet *Progress and Present Position of Russia in the East*. In this pamphlet the author maintained that the lack of European interest in the countries eastward of the Caspian had allowed Russia to advance her influence there to the detriment of British interests and security; and if Britain remained indifferent to this present danger, the situation could worsen to the point where the next peace treaty with Russia would be negotiated in Calcutta! Frightening stuff, yet it was McNeill whom Lord Palmerston selected in 1836 to take over from Sir Henry Ellis as the British envoy at the Persian court. He remained in this sensitive slot for the next eight years.

While there is no doubt that the now 40-year-old McNeill was a staunch advocate for the protection of British interests, he was also a scaremonger and his incessant cries of 'wolf at the door' caused more panic than the situation demanded and most assuredly influenced the decisions taken in Simla. McNeill was a long-time Russophobe and became increasingly so as he witnessed the growing influence of his Russian counterpart, Count Ivan Simonovich, on the young Shah of Persia. Had Count Simonovich not been recalled on the insistence of Lord Palmerston, it is not beyond the bounds of speculation that McNeill could have instigated the murder of the Count as he had done in 1829 with the murder of the then Russian ambassador, Alexander Griboyed. McNeill was married three times, and after a long and distinguished career died in France in 1883 at the ripe old age of 88.

In early January 1837, Maharaja Ranjit Singh sent out invitations to the wedding of his 15-year-old grandson, Naunihal Singh, to Nanaki the daughter of General Sham Singh Attariwala. This brave general was to be killed by a British musket ball nine years later at the Battle of Sobraon. The Maharaja was determined that the marriage was to be celebrated in great splendour. His long invitation list included the British Governor General, the Governor of Agra, Sir Charles Metcalfe an old friend of Ranjit Singh's, and the British commander-in-chief, General Sir Henry Fane. For sound diplomatic reasons the Governor General could not attend as this would create a precedent for him to attend all subsequent Indian state weddings, also the then governor general had not been invited to the wedding of the Maharaja's son, *Kunwar* Kharak Singh. Sir Charles Metcalfe for similar reasons declined, consequently only the Commander-in Chief and his group were able to attend.

General Sir Henry Fane's group, which included his son as ADC, Major William Garden the quartermaster-general or spy-master at Army Headquarters, Captain Claude Wade and a bevy of ladies, crossed the Sutlej on 3 March and were met by Prince Sher Singh, Ranjit Singh's second son. The group moved on to Amritsar where it was met by *Kunwar* Kharak Singh and the Sikh chief minister, Raja Dhian Singh. The following day, General Fane formally called on Maharaja Ranjit Singh, who on 7 March took all his guests to the actual wedding. Then on 12 March the group followed the Maharaja to Lahore. Fane, a cavalryman who had served as a brigade commander in Wellington's Peninsular campaign, took the opportunity to observe the military means and soldierly qualities of his host's army. At the conclusion of this visit he was to estimate that it would take a force of 67,000 soldiers two years to complete the subjugation of the Punjab. He further laid down, as a principle, that the Sutlej and the deserts of Rajputana and Sindh were the best boundaries which the British could have in the west. While Fane was doing his sums, Major Garden had a detailed map of the country compiled, which became the basis of all maps used by the British in their wars against the Sikhs.

In May 1837 Lord Auckland received some very disturbing news: the Sikh fortress at Jamrud had been attacked by an Afghan army on 30 April. This action had been provoked by the Sikh general Hari Singh Nalwa building of a string of forts along the Afghan foothills. The Amir in Kabul, thinking this a prelude to a Sikh invasion, sent his second son, Akbar Khan, at the head of an army to attack the Sikhs. His timing was well calculated as Prince Naunihal Singh had left for his wedding in Lahore and much of the Sikh garrison had left with him. It was touch and go, with the Sikh garrison the worse for it. However, General Nalwa, ill in Peshawar at the time of the attack, left his sickbed and rushed to Jamrud to rally his men. The fortress was saved but at the cost of the brave General's life. When news arrived in Lahore, Maharaja Ranjit Singh mustered his reserves and advanced north to reinforce his beleaguered garrison. Field guns were dragged up from Ramnugar, a distance of 200 miles, in six days across three main rivers. The invading Afghans, having failed to master Jamrud or Peshawar, engaged in plundering the Peshawar valley but on the arrival of the Sikh reinforcements the Afghan army high-tailed it back up the Khyber.

While the Sikh provocation may have been deliberate, it certainly put the kibosh on the cherished British schemes for the commercial navigation of the Indus. According to Lieutenant Joseph Cunningham, at that time on Captain Wade's staff:

> To the Government of India, the time seemed to have come when political interference would no longer be embarrassing, but, on the contrary, highly advantageous to schemes of peaceful trade and beneficial intercourse. It was made known that the British rulers would be glad to be the means of negotiating a peace honourable to both parties, yet the scales were turned in favour of the Afghan, by the simultaneous admission that Peshawar was a place to which Dost Mohammed could scarcely be expected to resign all claim.[16]

Up to now it had been the strict policy of Lord Auckland and his predecessors to leave the native states alone and to keep out of any entanglement with countries beyond the frontier. However, as the paramount power in India a continued policy of isolation was no longer a viable option. This slide into the political arena of independent states was acknowledged by Auckland in his communication with the president of the Board of Control in which he regretted that, 'I have departed from the extremely forbearing policy of my predecessor. We are henceforth, I conceive, irretrievably involved in the politics of the countries of the Indus.'

In June 1837, Auckland and his sisters having endured one boiling summer in Calcutta – described by sister Emily in a letter to a friend, 'It is so very HOT. I do not know how to spell it strong enough' – decided to travel to the cooler climes of the north-west. In his *exeat* application to Sir James Carnac, at the time chairman of the Court of Directors, observed:

> The hot season has this year been a trying one, and we have felt it more than we did last year. My appetite for going up country, so as to pass one summer in the hills, is growing upon me. It would be useful to me personally, to know the men upon whom I have most to depend; to compare modes of administration, and to see public works; and I shall not defer such experience until the period of my residence here shall be drawing to a close. I think too, my presence may have useful effect upon our neighbours on the North West Frontier,

16 Cunningham, *A History of the Sikhs*, p.299.

> and, possibly on the affairs of Oudh. It will be of advantage for me too, that for discussions military, I shall find the Commander-in-Chief in the north.[17]

Thus, began the grand tour of the Governor General to the northern domains of British India and on to the sanatorium of Simla. The Governor General and his party were to be away from his Council in Calcutta for the next two and a half years. William Macnaghten was selected to travel with the Governor General in the role of secretary to the Government of India and in many respects a very apt selection. As his deputy Macnaghten selected Henry Torrens, and John Colvin was included in his capacity of private secretary, as was Captain Osborne the Governor General's military secretary. Such were the men who were to form Lord Auckland's inner circle of advisors during his long absence from Calcutta. They were among the best and most accomplished in the country and were all more 'dovish' than 'hawkish'. However, they were all, like many able characters, also ambitious and this ambition would turn out to be perilous. Besides these fine gentlemen the party included Lord Auckland's sisters, the wives of Macnaghten, Torrens, and Colvin, Major General William Casement as the military member, Dr Andrew Drummond, Charles Wimberley the Chaplain and his wife, Miss Sneyd, Mrs Colvin's niece, Captain Francis Hawkins in charge of the commissariat and his flirtatious wife, Captain George MacGregor as ADC, Captain Robert Codrington as a sort of camp commandant, a military contingent consisting of the Governor General's bodyguard, an escort regiment of native infantry, a troop of horse artillery and a squadron of cavalry, plus 40 elephants, 850 camels, thousands of cattle and 5,000 servants and camp followers, a moving town the size of Reigate at the time.

As the preparations for this regal trip were in progress the Governor General received one sad and one distressing piece of news. An official communiqué was received in September reporting the death of King William IV on 20 June and that the new monarch was the young Queen Victoria. The other, disastrous, piece of news was that the young Shah of Persia and an army of 45,000 men and 22 guns had set off from Teheran on 23 July for their attack on Herat 600 miles away.

At about this time, a 26-year-old Bombay Artillery officer by the name of Lieutenant Eldred Pottinger who had joined his uncle Colonel Henry Pottinger at Hyderabad, was granted a year's leave to explore the lands between the Indus and Persia. His uncle had made a similar reconnaissance in 1806 under the auspices of Sir John Malcolm. Like his uncle, Eldred Pottinger travelled to Afghanistan via the Bolan Pass in the disguise of a Muslim holy man. It is not clear whether this young officer's leave of absence into a critical area had the sanction of the British Government or was an attempt by the Bombay establishment to play a bigger role in the emerging saga of Persian actions and Russian intrigues. This desire was clearly indicated by a previous communiqué from the Governor of Bombay; 'the little folk' in Bombay had not taken too kindly to the apparent usurpation by the Bengal establishment (the appointment of a Bengal officer to Mithenkot) of involvement in Sindh and Persian affairs which to date had been their preserve. Whichever, this 'shooting leave' was clearly a spy mission with no detectable Government involvement should it fail. Lieutenant Pottinger arrived in Herat in mid-September, just as the Heratis were returning from their campaign in Seiston, and he

17 Colvin, *Rulers of India*, p.65.

was to prove more useful to the Heratis and the British envoy in Persia than to the Bombay establishment.

As young Pottinger was trekking up north, another young officer was making his way down south, he was Captain Ivan Viktorovich Vitkevich. This officer was first spotted, in the middle of nowhere, by Captain Henry Rawlinson, who was on envoy John McNeill's staff and on his way to join the Shah of Persia's camp. The stranger declined to identify himself or disclose his purpose, however by the time this stranger reached Teheran, he was identified as a Russian Cossack officer on a mission to deliver a letter from the Tsar to Dost Mohammed Khan, no doubt the reply to the Dost's appeal for assistance sent in 1835. This news, conveyed to the Governor General by Lieutenant Colonel Charles Stoddart, vibrated like thunder announcing a massive storm, proof positive that the Russians were up to no good in Afghanistan. This British reaction of horror to the passage of one Russian is at odds with their *laissez-faire* attitude towards many more Englishmen doing the same thing, in fact regarding some of their excursions as heroic, at the same time considering it inconceivable that the Russians could hold similar sentiments.

On the morning of Saturday 21 October 1837, Lord Auckland and his sisters rose at five o'clock and came down for coffee and found the hall full of officials and notable locals. There were troops at the embarking place and a band playing marches. The Governor General's sisters watched as he inspected the guard of honour; he reached the place where his sisters were waiting, offered his arm to Emily, made a gesture of general goodbye to the crowd and boarded the vessel standing by for them. The guns fired, the gentlemen at the landing stage waved their hats, the soldiers saluted; then the boat moved off and they left Calcutta. Such was the scene as described by Janet Dunbar in her book *Golden Interlude*. As the crowds dispersed there was a general impression that some imminent danger was about to assail the British in the north-west and a feeling of alarm prevailed throughout India.

By the time the Governor General's party had reached Rajmahal he was in receipt of his first communication from Alexander Burnes, announcing his welcomed arrival in Kabul and his optimistic forecast for the success of his mission. At this juncture any meddling with the affairs of Afghanistan was furthest from His Lordship's thoughts as clearly indicated by his letter to Sir Charles Metcalfe his lieutenant governor in Agra:

> You are quite right in believing that I have not a thought of interference between the Afghans and the Sikhs. I should not be sorry to see a strong independent and commercial power established in Afghanistan, but short of Persian and Russian occupation; their present state is as unsatisfactory as possible, with national, family and religious feuds so inveterate as almost to make any one party ready to join any invader against another. It is out of the question that we can ever gain direct power or influence amongst them. All idea of a 'dominant influence' with powers so broken and disjointed as are those of Kabul and neighbouring countries, is of course, out of the question.[18]

Up to now, and ever since the first Anglo-Persian treaty of 1809, it had been the British aim to establish Persia as a buffer state against the advancement of any Russian influence, but it

18 Beveridge, *A Comprehensive History of India*, vol. 3, p.374.

was now quite clear that this policy had failed as the Russians had established an unassailable hegemony in that country. Far from being a buffer against an invasion of India, Persia was looming as the launch pad, and under her banner the dreaded Russians. In so far as this fear was justified, the blame must lie with Lord Palmerston, who had been dilatory in winning over Persia and more importantly in warning-off Russia, and also with the British Legation in Teheran, who probably exaggerated Russian influence to excuse their own lack of clout. A satirist could have made much of the fact that while the Russians and Persians were bent on replacing the Sadozai at Herat with a Barakzai, the British and Sikhs aimed to replace the Barakzai in Kabul with a Sadozai.

As the Governor General's canvas city wound its laborious way north, the tone of his correspondence from that direction became ever more disheartening, clamorous and foreboding with both McNeill and Burnes never ceasing, week by week, to pour in fervent warnings. Lord Auckland had earlier expanded Burnes' brief to include an assessment of Persian influence, and in particular that of the Kuzzilbashe community in Kabul, on Afghan affairs. He now received Burnes' findings and henceforth all Burnes' reports contained fewer and fewer commercial matters and more and more political ones. About the Persian influence Burnes reported:

> I have now the honour to report the result of my enquiries on the subject of Persian influence in Kabul and the exact power which the Kuzzilbashe, or Persian party resident in the city, exercise over the politics of Afghanistan. The Shah of Persia has not been slow in responding to Dost Mohammed Khan's desire for an alliance, an *elchee* has been sent with robes and presents in return, and is now in Kandahar, but he has appeared at a time most unfavourable to his master, when the attention of the British Government is directed to Afghanistan, which goes far to discredit him with all parties, and even to damp the hopes of the Kuzzilbashes. It is even doubtful he will advance to Kabul, and it is certain if he does so that any offers which he may make will never be placed in the balance against those of the British Government. The King of Persia desires to add Herat to his dominions, and the chiefs of Kandahar and Kabul might certainly aid him in his designs, but the probabilities of a return for such good offices are more than doubtful.[19]

During the five months which elapsed between 21 October and their arrival at Simla, news of events beyond the frontier were regularly received at the Governor General's camp, and those from his masters in England were now arriving much quicker, due to the deputation of Lieutenant Thomas Waghorn, Royal Navy, to Egypt to set up an overland route; this cut delivery time of five or six months to just two. This arrangement, known as the 'Suez Pony Express', was further expanded to include Aden as a refuelling station; after a dispute with the local sultan, Aden was captured by the British on 16 January 1839. Besides attending to the toxic stream of correspondence, Lord Auckland met with local dignitaries, frequently at elaborate *durbars*, visited Lord Cornwallis's tomb and at each garrison town attended gala balls given in his honour. By early December, the Governor General's party was at Allahabad and attended the wedding of Miss Sneyd to Mr Cecil Beaton, who happened to be the nephew of Lord Heytesbury, the 'could-have-been' governor general. In a telling aside about the relationship

19 Colvin, *Rulers of India*, p.94.

between the ladies of the Governor General's party, Janet Dunbar writes, 'Mrs Macnaghten thought that Allahabad was a nice and sociable-seeming place and that she would have liked to stay there for two months. Neither Emily nor Fanny would have wept if she could have been granted her wish.'[20]

By Christmas 1837 the regal cavalcade was at Cawnpore, which Miss Emily Eden thought was the ugliest of all the ugly Indian stations. At this place, Sir Charles Metcalfe presented himself and then promptly resigned from the Company's service. The reason for his resignation is not clear, but no doubt his unrewarded stint as Governor General had some bearing.

Two years were to elapse before a replacement was nominated, so during this interval Lord Auckland was also his own lieutenant governor of Agra. As the group approached Agra, the horrors of the famine littered their path. This famine was to kill 800,000 men, women and children, over a million cattle and at a cost of 38 *lakhs* of rupees. Equally horrific to Auckland was the news that the Russian Cossack, Captain Vitkevich, had arrived in Kabul. On receipt of this intelligence His Lordship sent a letter to Dost Mohammed warning him that should he entertain any dealings with the Russians, Britain would not feel under any obligation to restrain Ranjit Singh, clearly indicating that some type of 'understanding' existed that would 'oblige' the British to intervene.

By the beginning of February 1838, the party had arrived at Meerut, a big garrison town, where it stayed for two weeks enjoying the hospitality of the garrison and in particular that of HM 16th Lancers commanded by Lieutenant Colonel Robert Arnold. All the while news from the mission in Kabul was unwholesome and that from Persia unpalatable, compelling Lord Auckland to inform his masters in London that, 'This emergency in affairs may compel me to act without waiting for any intimation of your views.' A couple of days later His Lordship wrote a most telling letter to Sir John Hobhouse, president of the Board of Control:

> Burnes is well established in Kabul, with only this disadvantage, that he can hardly hope that Dost Mohammed will be satisfied with anything that would not be offensive to Maharaja Ranjit Singh; and yet he ought to be satisfied that he is allowed to remain at peace and is saved from actual invasion. But he is reckless and intriguing, and will be difficult to keep quiet, as are the other Afghans, and Sikhs, Heratees, Russians and Persians. It is a fine embroilo of diplomacy and intrigue, with more bluster than real strength anywhere. Yet it is impossible not to feel that East and West are drawing sensibly nearer to each other.[21]

The party then proceeded to Karnal via Delhi, where Mrs Colvin presented her husband with their fifth son. The Governor General's entourage eventually arrived in Simla on Tuesday 3 April 1838. As Emily was to write, 'Well, it really is worth all the trouble. Such a beautiful place. Views only too lovely, and the climate, no wonder I could not live down below.' Howver, during the next three months the idyll of Simla was to be rocked by the events in arid Afghanistan. No doubt this prompted Sir John Kaye to say of Simla that it has been the cradle of more political insanity than any place within the limits of Hindustan.

20 Dunbar, *Golden Interlude*, p.112.
21 Dunbar, *Golden Interlude*, p.143.

6

Peshawar: The Elephant in the Room (Phase II)

The mighty Persian army first laid siege to the fortress at Ghorian 40 miles from Herat, which was treacherously surrendered to the Persian shah on 15 November. By the beginning of December 1837, as the first flutters of snow fell to the ground, the Persians laid siege to Sadozai-held Herat. From the start this siege was a mismanaged affair, but its potency was felt throughout Central Asia and to the very southern tip of India. The *Calcutta Review* concluded that 'if Herat fell, Kandahar and Kabul would certainly make their submissions, and Russian influence would then have been brought to the threshold of India'. To this dire prediction the new British envoy in Teheran, John McNeill, added his own evaluation: 'The invasion of India by the Russians from their present positions is impracticable, but possessed of Herat, there will no longer be any insuperable impediment to the invasion of India.' Rumours of invasion were eagerly received and quickly spread by the vanquished princes of India as the whole country vibrated with hopes of the ascendancy of a power beyond the Hindu Kush. Furthermore, the greybeards of the British establishment questioned the fidelity of the Company's native regiments if push came to shove.

Herat at this time was tightly held by the Sadozai clan, the head of which was Shah Shuja's nephew, Prince Kamran, the worst of the clan who had a collection of murderous thugs about him, now old before his time, thick-set, and ugly. He left the affairs of the state to his *Wazir*, Yah Mohammed Khan, of whom Sir John Kaye wrote, 'of all the unscrupulous miscreants in Central Asia, Yah Mohammed was the most unscrupulous, avaricious, brutishly cruel and utterly treacherous'. The Barakzai Afghan chiefs at Kandahar and Kabul welcomed the Shah of Persia's intention to eliminate the Sadozai at Herat, the murderers of their esteemed brother Fateh Khan, and in a ploy to ensure the Shah would not press his invasion further, hurriedly proposed alliances with him. However, the Shah reckoned that he did not need their assistance and it was not his intention to stop at Herat. The Shah's siege of Herat was to last for 280 days and from start to finish was thoroughly ill-conducted, and the Herat defence, in reality not any better managed and owed its *éclat* to Persian ignorance and timidity. Despite laudable accounts later, Lieutenant Eldred Pottinger's advice was not often called for and less often taken by the defenders, who viewed his presence more as a political foil rather than a military asset, especially so after John McNeill appointed Lieutenant Pottinger the British Agent at Herat and British cash started rolling in.

Five hundred and twenty miles further east, the Amir of Kabul was playing the head of the British commercial mission there like a well-tuned violin. Amir Dost Mohammed had no great reserves of money, his brothers in Kandahar owed him little or no allegiance and in Kabul itself, according to Godfrey Vigne, a recent visitor there, 'was distracted by parties that were not unwilling to dethrone him, but could not agree as to whom they should place in his stead'.[1] By playing to Alexander Burnes' ambition Dost Mohammed hoped to secure a lifeline by association with the British thus boosting his hold on Afghanistan, scaring off the Persians, and have Peshawar restored to him. It had long been the Amir's desire to form a compact of friendship with the British, which he had sought in vain, but now the British had sent a mission to do just that, an opportunity not to be missed, and one he played to the full. Burnes was skilfully wooed by the Amir and soon announced that, 'Dost is our man. Now is the time to bind him to us.' The best description of 'our man' has been left to us by Godfrey Vigne:

> Dost Mohammed stands about five feet ten in height, of a spare and sinewy figure. The upper part of his face is handsome, the forehead high, but not prominent, the nose aquiline; eyebrows high and arched, the eyes large and very expressive. The worst part of his face is the mouth, which is large and course. His appearance altogether is very *distinguee. He* dresses in better taste than any man in the Durbar, and his address and manners are far superior to those of any Duranni. He usually sits in a small room in the Bala Hissar, which commanded a view of the city, the parade-ground and the peaks of the Hindu Kush.[2]

But, at the end of December 1837, all in Afghanistan expected the Persians to steamroll into the country and all the Barakzai chiefs rushed to ally themselves to Persia. Burnes, having tasted glory after his first trip saw, in the current situation an opportunity for more accolades by demonstrating his prowess and winning over the panicky chiefs. Writing to a friend, he reported:

> The chiefs in Kandahar have gone over to Persia. I have detached them and offered British protection and cash if they would recede and Persia attacks them. I have no authority to do so, but am I to stand by and see us ruined in Kandahar? I am off there with the Amir and his force and mean to pay the piper myself.[3]

Earlier, Burnes had sent Lieutenant John Wood and Dr Percival Lord on reconnaissance missions to the Oxus and Kunduz under the pretext of answering a call from Mohammed Beg, the psychopathic khan of Kunduz, for medical assistance for his ailing brother, he now sent Lieutenant Robert Leech to Kandahar to deliver the British offer of assistance to Kohin Dil Khan, the Barakzai chief there, and to assure him that if necessary Burnes himself would come to fight; 'Captain Marvel' to the rescue! However, this courageous show of bravado, designed to impress Dost Mohammed of Britain's honourable intentions, was not well received by the Governor General, who issued a diplomatic rap over the young officer's knuckles:

1 G.T. Vigne, *Personal Narrative of a Visit to Ghuzni, Kabul, and Afghanistan* (London: Whittaker, 1840; Cambridge: Cambridge University Press, reprint, 2012).
2 Vigne, *Personal Narrative*, p.375.
3 Beveridge, *A Comprehensive History of India*, Vol. 3, p.388.

> It is with great pain that his Lordship must next proceed to advert to the subject of the promises you have held out to the chiefs of Kandahar. These promises were entirely unauthorised by any part of your instructions. They are most unnecessarily made in unqualified terms, and they would, if supported, commit the Government on the gravest question of policy. His Lordship is compelled, therefore, most decidedly to disapprove them. He is only withheld from direct disavowal of these engagements to the chiefs of Kandahar, because such disavowal would carry with it the declaration of a difference between you and your government, and might weaken your personal influence, and because events might in the meantime have occurred which would render such a course unnecessary. But the rulers in Kandahar must not be allowed to rest in confidence upon the promises so given, and should affairs continue in the same uncertainty as that which prevailed at your last despatch, you will endeavour to set yourself right with the chiefs and will feel yourself bound in good faith to admit that you have exceeded your instructions and held out hopes which you find on communication with your government, cannot be realised.[4]

How Burnes sidestepped from his promise to the Kandahar chiefs is not recorded; in the event the chiefs, lacking the promised cash and with only a single officer as reinforcement, duly treated with the Shah of Persia and their agreement was guaranteed by the Russian Ambassador, Count Simonovich.

On a bitterly cold Tuesday 19 December, a stranger calling himself Osman Beg entered the city of Kabul. Once at the gates of the Bala Hissar he disclosed his true identity as Captain Ivan Vitkevich, an envoy from His Imperial Majesty, Tsar Nicholas, the emperor of Russia. In his saddlebag he was carrying a three-foot-long letter from the Tsar for delivery to the hand of Amir Dost Mohammed Khan of Afghanistan. His presence in Afghanistan was not altogether a surprise, but that did not deflect from the shock of his actual appearance in Kabul at this time. This event was to cause a sudden change in the tempo of negotiations and in the stance of the Afghans, who became inflated by the apparent importance of their position, and young Alexander Burnes was cast into a state of ludicrous excitement. Dost Mohammed and his court were almost as much astonished at the Russian's appearance as was the head of the British Mission. The Russian's credentials were shown to Burnes for his examination, who immediately pronounced them as genuine although he was entirely inexperienced in the official forms of Russian correspondence. Regarding this event, Major General Sir Henry Marion Durand states that in his father's private journal he found the following note written on 31 January 1839:

> We called on Mr Masson. He gave us a very amusing account of Burnes' rencontre with Captain Vicovich at Cabul. This Russian officer reached Cabul 'with a pair of black kid gloves, a French translation of Burnes' travels and a long Persian epistle, well powdered with gold leaf, purporting to be from the Emperor of Russia.' The Afghans, of whom Mr Masson speaks highly, laughed at this *soi-disant* envoy, and discredited him *in toto.* Had Burnes had the sense to laugh too, all would have gone well; but he took the thing seriously,

4 Patrick Macrory. *The Fierce Pawns* (the U.S. title of *Signal Catastrophe*) (Philadelphia: J.B. Lippincott Co, 1966), p.58.

> lost his head, and was the person who induced the Afghans to consider Captain Vicovich in the light of an accredited envoy.[5]

To learn more about the Cossack officer's purpose, Burnes invited him to Christmas dinner, describing him as 'a gentleman and an agreeable man of about 30, who spoke French, Turkish and Persian fluently'. To the Governor General Burnes wrote urging the adoption of more vigorous action to counteract Russian intrigues and to a friend he wrote, 'We are in a mess here. The Emperor of Russia has sent an envoy to Kabul with a blazing letter three feet long offering Dost money to fight Ranjit Singh. It is now a neck and neck race between the Russians and ourselves and if his Lordship would hear reason he would forthwith send agents to Bokhara, Kandahar and Kunduz not forgetting Sindh.' The Governor General's vigorous counteraction was to write to Dost Mohammed requesting him to abstain from all foreign alliance and to dismiss from his court his Russian visitor.

The crafty Amir was impatient for glory and triumph and encouraged by the fact that his friendship was now being sought by both major powers and his price would be Peshawar, his Jerusalem! In real terms the Amir probably calculated that while the Russians could provide unspecified amounts of desperately needed money, they were not in a position to deliver Peshawar to him; whereas with an association with the paramount power in India, his long-time preference, the restoration of Peshawar was feasible, provided British fear of Russia could be artfully engineered to out-balance the British attachment to Maharaja Ranjit Singh; and in Alexander Burnes he had a willing instrument. For the next three months *cossids* hurried back and forth with Burnes' suggestions as to how the Amir could be satisfied and His Lordship's responses to these. While in Kabul the patient Amir kept Captain Vitkevich on the back burner and Captain Burnes on his toes.

All Burnes' communications were channelled through Captain Wade in Ludhiana, the Sikh expert[6] and the standard bearer of the Anglo-Sikh alliance. Captain Wade was thus able to comment on Burnes' reports or to contradict them which lent a bias against the Amir. The siege of Herat by the Shah, the correspondence of Russian authorities with Kandahar and the arrival of Captain Vitkevich in Kabul still further disunited Lord Auckland from an accommodation with the Amir. Captain Wade, with his wealth of Sikh experience, held that a robust alliance with the Sikhs was a better barrier to any encroachment from the north, that the Afghans were at best impotent and at worst unreliable. However this analysis was totally dependent on the continued wellbeing of his friend Ranjit Singh. When this dominant figure was to succumb, the 'Captain Sahib' knew, better than most, that the Sikh kingdom could well fall apart and that it would be British India which was attacked not Afghanistan, therefore any action being contemplated regarding Afghanistan had to be undertaken without too much delay.

Lord Auckland, from the outset, was totally opposed to any deal with Dost Mohammed which risked upsetting the esteemed Maharaja. If a choice had to be made between the two it had to be Ranjit Singh, who had already been restrained from seizing part of the Sindh, and to

5 Durand, *The First Afghan War and Its Causes*, p.42.

6 In 1861 it came to light that some of Burnes' despatches from Kabul in 1838 had been altered, so as to convey opinions opposite to his. This matter was brought before Parliament on an application for an enquiry. However Lord Palmerston's Government resisted the motion, which was defeated on the grounds of the interval of time that had passed since the occasion.

try to persuade him to hand over Peshawar to his *bête noir*, Dost Mohammed, would be both futile and dangerous. In counter-argument both Burnes and McNeill held that a consolidated backing of Dost Mohammed was a better and more resilient bet. In desperation for his mission to succeed, Burnes at one point suggested that Dost Mohammed be secretly promised Peshawar on the death of Ranjit Singh.

When New Year's Day heralded in 1838, it was perfectly clear to even the most languid of observers that real trouble was brewing in Afghanistan. The unrest was largely created by panic-stricken politicos, who turned one Russian officer in Kabul into an army of Cossacks dragging guns. At this juncture, Lord Auckland's confidence on the ultimate success of Burnes' mission, was as strong as his conviction that any solution to the situation required the active participation of the Home government. A month later he was still inclined to anticipate the adherence of Dost Mohammed to British interests, but that the Russian mission in Kabul demanded the serious consideration of the Home authorities.

Whether Captain Vitkevich was a genuine envoy from the Tsar was never substantiated. When Count Nesselrode, the Russian foreign minister, was questioned on this matter he denied all knowledge of the young officer's actions and said that he had exceeded his orders and instructions. If this denial can be accepted, then the origin of this officer's appearance in Kabul could well have been part of Count Simonovich's schemes, in conjunction with the Governor of Orenburg, Count Petrovski whose ADC Captain Vitkevich had been, to muddy the waters for the known British Mission in Kabul. On his recall from Kabul the young Russian envoy, who had created such a stir in that city, burned all his personal papers and then committed suicide.

Early in the New Year, Captain Wade had been summoned to meet the Governor General who had by now reached Cawnpore and there he was to discuss the feasibility of a meeting with Maharaja Ranjit Singh, a meeting that the current situation demanded of the two allies. Captain Wade then conveyed Lord Auckland's long letter to the Maharaja. Quoted below are the relevant parts of this very long letter:

> I learn from Captain Wade that you are desirous of knowing when it may be convenient that an interview take place between Your Highness and myself … the wish nearest to my heart has been that I should have an opportunity of taking Your Highness by the hand and conversing face to face upon the interests of the two allied countries, but … I find it would on this occasion be impossible for me to proceed to meet Your Highness with all the state and ceremony which are due to the dignity of the two States and the intimate relation of friendship which subsists between them. … Should the gratification which I had anticipated be postponed to the end of the rains, I shall be consoled by the reflection that Your Highness feels the interests and wishes of both Governments to be identical and relying on Your Highness's disposition to act in concurrence with the views and wishes of the British Government that in the meantime no interruption to the existing tranquillity can be apprehended. I need not report to Your Highness the great satisfaction I should have felt in being able personally to disclose to you my views and sentiments on the present aspect of affairs, and in learning from your own mouth your opinion as to the best means of bringing to a final issue the differences which have unhappily interfered with the complete establishment of those relations of unanimity and concord under which alone commerce can be expected to flourish … Though I regret that any circumstances should render a personal interview with Your Highness so difficult at the present juncture, yet I entertain a confident hope that

> you will gratify me frequently by the receipt of your friendly letters and it has afforded me moreover satisfaction to think that the distance between us will be so small as to render the early interchange of our sentiments a matter of facility.[7]

The length of this letter and the skating around of a specific date for a meeting would indicate that while Lord Auckland was anxious to meet with the Maharaja, but it would serve no purpose to do so while his mission in Kabul was still a 'work in progress', and the anticipated intervention of the Home authorities in Persia was still wanting. In an accompanying instruction to Captain Wade, William Macnaghten, secretary to the Government of India, told him that as far as specific dates were concerned, Lord Auckland wished the meeting to take place at the latter end of October and beginning of November. No doubt His Lordship's advisers had calculated that by this time the Governor General would have spent the hot months in the cool of Simla and that by then the overall situation would be much clearer. However, the Maharaja was not too happy with the suspected ambiguity in His Lordship's letter and his continued suspicion of plots being conjured up with the crafty Amir in Kabul. After detailed questioning of all aspects of the letter, meanings analysed and nuances examined, the Maharaja sent his reply, camouflaging all his suspicions in laudable verbiage, which in part stated:

> The English nation are celebrated for their good faith, their exalted virtues and manly abilities; and a due regard for the obligations of their mutual relation of lasting amity according to established treaty has always been an object of paramount concern to the States; and I feel such no alteration in this state of perfect concord and amity will ever be contemplated – on this point my reliance is complete. The additional proof of your sincerity in what you had now written and declared to me, viz. 'I would guard the honour and rights of Your Highness with the same scrupulous care as I would those of the British nation', has given me the highest satisfaction. The words of brave men endure.[8]

There then followed what *Fakir* Aijazuddin has called, a period of nineteenth century-style 'ping-pong' diplomacy as the British explored all options for a settlement with Dost Mohammed and the establishment of peace between the Sikhs and Afghans, while the Maharaja portrayed the Afghans as unscrupulous and emphasised his priorities as the preservation of friendship with the British Government, the welfare and prosperity of his present domains, and if peace could be established on a firm basis he would have no objection.[9]

On 14 March 1838, John Colvin, Lord Auckland's private secretary, wrote to Burnes asking for clarification of Dost Mohammed's position:

> You will see that it is a principal object with the Governor General to ascertain what does not clearly appear from the papers yet before him, whether Dost Mohammed Khan intends to make under all circumstances a *sine quâ non* of possessing some share in the Peshawar territories. Apprised as you are now of his Lordship's fixed opinions, you will,

7 Aijazuddin, *The Resourceful Fakirs*, p.171.
8 Aijazuddin, *The Resourceful Fakirs*, p.177.
9 Aijazuddin, *The Resourceful Fakirs*, p.178.

> he is quite satisfied, use every endeavour to dissuade Dost Mohammed from persisting in such a resolution.
>
> The question is whether Dost Mohammed would prefer renouncing his connexion with us, that he may retain a barren claim to a portion of the Peshawar territory, to leaving the Sikhs in the immediate occupation of that country, under the continued exercise of our influence for his safety in his Kabul domains.
>
> If Dost Mohammed should wish his scheme of having a share in Peshawar to be freely discussed, though without making a *sine qua non* of it, this, I dare say, will readily be done.[10]

Prior to this communication, Lord Auckland had made it perfectly clear, in many previous messages, that before he could broach the matter of Peshawar with Ranjit Singh, Dost Mohammed would have to first disclaim all intentions of making a *sine qua non* of any restoration, whole or partial. This disclaimer Dost Mohammed never made, consequently his stubborn insistence that the cession of Peshawar be a precondition of his allegiance to British interests led inevitably to the actions that followed. In a final salvo to Dost Mohammed, a fraught Lord Auckland observed:

> You must desist from all communications with Persia and Russia, you must never receive agents from them or have ought to do with them without our sanction, you must dismiss Captain Vitkevich with courtesy and you must surrender all claims to Peshawar. In return for this I promise to recommend to the Government that it use its good offices with its ancient ally, Ranjit Singh, to remove present and future differences between the Sikhs and Afghans.[11]

With no hope of British support for his unconditional demand for Peshawar and with a Russian at his court promising the moon, Dost Mohammed, in desperation, summoned the Russian envoy to the Kabul *durbar* on 21 April. A much-dejected Burnes, his mission in tatters, had his last audience with the Amir on 25 April and on the following day rode out of Kabul as ignominiously as his entry had been grand. He left behind lieutenants Wood and Leech who were to follow him. These two gentlemen caught up with Burnes in Peshawar and were to report that 'the mass of the population was disconcerted by the Dost's flirtation with the Persians'. Of Burnes' discredited mission, Durand stated in his book:

> The conduct of the mission, official and private, had sunk into contempt, and the irascible vanity of Burnes, wounded by the proceedings of his own Government, by the countenance now open to Vicovich at Cabul, and by the neglect shown to himself, impelled him to a line of conduct hasty and injudicious, and which, wanting in truth, composure and dignity, exasperated the Amir. Negotiations, after some fruitless attempts for renewal by the wiser part of Dost Mohammed's advisers (*Nawab* Jubbar Khan), were broken off and, finally on April 26, Burnes quitted Cabul.[12]

10 Colvin, *Rulers of India*, p.98.

11 G. Buist, *Outline of the Operations of British Troops in Scinde and Afghanistan, betwixt Nov. 1838 and Nov. 1841; with remarks on the policy of war* (Bombay: Times Office, 1843; Ulan Press reprint, n.d.), p.64.

12 Durand, *The First Afghan War and Its Causes*, p.46.

Back in Herat, the Persian Shah had endured a frustrating winter outside the gates of the fortress, which had stubbornly defied all Persian efforts to reduce it. With the sprouting of spring the Shah's resolve to capture Herat was renewed, while Lieutenant Colonel Charles Stoddart, who had been deputed to the Shah's camp, did all he could to persuade the Shah to call off the operation. The more Stoddart projected his Government's abhorrence at the Shah's objective the more adamant the Shah became; this was manifested by undiplomatic actions such as the case of the violation of the person of accredited British messenger, Ali Mohammed Beg, by Persian forces.

Four months into the siege John McNeill, who had remained in Teheran, heard via Lieutenant Robert Leech in Kandahar that the Governor General had issued instructions for McNeill to proceed to the Shah's camp and to endeavour by every means in his power to induce the Shah to come to terms with the ruler of Herat. McNeill arrived at the camp on 13 April and was coldly received by the Shah, who had endeavoured to have him stopped at Ghorian. McNeill informed the Shah that an attack on Herat would be considered by the British as a violation of the 1814 treaty and an act of war. The Shah, in response, pointed out that Article 9 of the treaty precluded British intervention unless this was sought by both sides. Earlier, Lieutenant Eldred Pottinger had been sent out by the Heratis to treat with the Shah, but the Shah deemed Prince Kamran a treacherous liar and declared that he would not rest satisfied until he had planted a Persian garrison in the citadel of Herat. So ended these first negotiations for the suspension of hostilities.

McNeill, aware that the continued stalemate was wearing thin on the Shah's patience, continued to press him to allow the British to intervene and seek an acceptable settlement. By his discreet and conciliatory bearing, McNeill smoothed down the Shah's earlier irritation, who eventually consented to the mediation of a British mission and on 18 April Major D'Arcy Todd,[13] a Bengal Artillery officer, was sent as mediator to the beleaguered city. He entered the

13 Lieutenant Elliott D'Arcy Todd (1808-45). Born in London, the third and youngest son of a Yorkshire gentleman, he arrived in India in 1824 and was posted to the Bengal Artillery. Todd saw action at the siege of Bharakpore and in 1833 was selected for special duties in Persia with the local rank but not the pay of a major. He remained at these duties for five years. Then in 1837 he was appointed acting secretary to the British Legation in Teheran and in this capacity he accompanied Mr John McNeill to Herat; on the failure of this mission was sent to Simla with McNeill's report to the governor general. He was then appointed military secretary to Mr Macnaghten and accompanied him to Kandahar and was then sent to Herat at the head of a mission to secure a treaty with the Sadozai Shah Kamran. He was officially appointed political agent at Herat on 18 January 1841 aged 32 and was to find himself and his mission in a position of grave difficulty and positive danger in consequence of the intrigues, the insolence and the treachery of the *Wazir* Yah Mohammed. By February 1841 he felt himself compelled to withdraw his mission from Herat, as the only measure consistent with the honour and dignity of the government which he represented. Lord Auckland was 'exasperated and writhing with anger' and in bitterness, repudiated Todd's proceedings and removed him from political employment. On his return to India, Todd was posted to the Bengal Horse Artillery at Ambala. Here he married Marian, the daughter of the surgeon of HM 16th Lancers, on 22 August 1842. She was 20 and he was 34. Marian died at Ambala on 9 December 1845. On the following day, Major Todd led the 2nd Troop 3rd Bengal Horse Artillery to the First Anglo-Sikh War. At the first battle his troop had acquitted themselves with honour, and at sunrise on 21 December his troop was ordered, with cavalry, to advance against the enemy at Ferozeshah. He was in the process of giving his orders for the advance when a Sikh cannonball smashed into his head. He was buried in his tent on the battlefield.

city in full military regalia on 19 April and returned to the Shah's camp with assurances of Prince Kamran's desire to accept the mediation of the British.

On 21 April McNeill presented himself at the gates of Herat and was formally accredited by Prince Kamran to negotiate a settlement on the most favourable terms he could manage. However, the euphoria he must have felt on his journey back to the Shah's camp did not last long. While he had been away the Russian envoy, Count Ivan Simonovich, had arrived at the Shah's camp and in quick order changed the Shah's conciliatory mood to heights of bombast and belligerence. Count Simonovich gave the Shah a heap of much needed cash and promises of Russian military support. On the strength of these great offers the Shah now resolutely refused to submit to British arbitration, and instead demanded that either the whole peoples of Herat made their submission to him, or he would take the fortress by force. McNeill was mortified. Prince Kamran was not surprised, and said, 'The Kajars were noted for their want of faith ever since they had been heard of.' McNeill then instructed Major Todd to carry a full report of the situation to the Governor General in Simla, a journey of 1,200 miles accomplished in 60 days. Major Todd arrived in Simla on 20 July, the day after Macnaghten had returned from Lahore.

The situation in Herat had already attracted the attention of the Governor General, who had sent a letter to McNeill in early May informing him that as the situation was so critical, he had ordered a force to be sent to the Persian Gulf as essential aid to be held in readiness to maintain British interests in Persia. This force comprised five warships, which included the Company's steamers *Semirames* and *Hugh Lindsay*, conveying detachments of the 15th, 23rd and 24th Bombay Native Infantry and a battalion of the Company's marines, a total of 387 men. The force sailed from Bombay on 4 June and arrived at Bushire on 19 June.

Towards the end of April a Sikh delegation comprising of *Fakir* Azizuddin and *Sardars* Ajit Singh, Kamran Singh and Rai Gobind Jos set off from Lahore to deliver Maharaja Ranjit Singh's invitation to Lord Auckland. By the time the Sikh delegation had arrived, accompanied by Captain Wade, the British Mission in Kabul had been recalled. This development threw a totally different complexion on the situation and while the First Lady, Emily Eden, graciously played her part, the Governor General's advisers partook in 'off the record' enquiries of the guests as to how they saw the situation unfold. It was common knowledge at this time that there existed a treaty between the Sikhs and the ex-Shah Shuja. By the time the Sikh delegation left, Lord Auckland had made his decision to send his own delegation to Lahore for reasons beyond customary protocol and handed his letter for the Maharaja to the head of the Sikh delegation, which stated:

> My honoured and valued friend,
> I cannot permit Your Highness's Deputation to quit Simla without conveying to you by its hands an assurance of the cordial esteem and regard I entertain for Your Highness and the very great satisfaction which I have derived from my intercourse with Your Highness. In the selection of the personages to represent you, you have evinced the judgement and sagacity for which you have been so highly distinguished. The mission of such men as these is calculated if it were possible to draw more closely the bonds of amity and concord between the two States.
>
> These officers will explain to Your Highness how anxiously I desire to maintain the strict friendship which has so long and so happily endured between the two States and how

> ardently I wish for the arrival of the time when I shall have the happiness of making your personal acquaintance.
>
> I shall not further enlarge on these pleasing topics in this letter because I am now about to despatch a friendly mission to Your Highness, to the Head of which mission I have delivered a letter containing my sentiments more at large and to that Gentleman I must refer Your Highness for a more full explanation of my views and wishes.[14]

'Crunch time' had arrived for the band of Englishmen nesting in the eyrie of Simla, as firm decisions had to be made for the protection of the British domains in India. The withdrawal of the mission from Kabul had left the Russians free to further their intrigues in that country, while in India the failure of the mission fuelled the imagination of many that the Russians had outmanœuvred the British and that Herat would now fall, with an invasion more probable. The situation clearly demanded some bold action to thwart Russian intrigues and Persia's success at Herat. This bold action had to be an Indian affair with no material aid from the Home authorities, who were still, ostensibly, allies of both protagonists; the Governor General had already ordered a token force to the Persian Gulf to add support to the diplomatic effort there, but what was to be done with the intransigent, and Russia's new friend, the Amir in Kabul? Whatever form this action was to take, it had to keep both the Company Directors in London and the Maharaja in Lahore onside, as cheaply as possible and with the involvement of Ranjit Singh's resources.

Up to now, the British authorities in India had not given much consideration to Shah Shuja and his misfortunes; their principles and policy being of non-interference when it suited their interests and all kinds of intermeddling when it did. Shah Shuja was said to have many partisans in Kabul and it was supposed that by the British restoring him to his throne, he would be a faithful ally and a sort of bulwark and a first line of defence for British India. Lord Auckland was well acquainted with the opposing views as to the merits of Dost Mohammed to British interests as represented by Captains Burnes and Wade, however both these gentlemen were in unison in their belief that if ex-Shah Shuja was sent back to Kabul with a mere personal guard of British troops, he would be received with open arms. 'There is little doubt,' wrote Wade quoting Masson his news-writer in Kabul, 'but that if (on the occasion of the Shah's last attempt on Kabul) a single British officer had accompanied him, his simple appearance would have been sufficient to have procured the Shah's re-establishment.'[15] Interestingly, after the decision had been made to remove Dost Mohammed, but before the conclusion of any treaty, Burnes had written to a friend indicating his full support for regime change:

> As for Shah Shuja, the British Government have only to send him to Peshawar with an agent and two of its own regiments as an honorary escort, and an avowal to the Afghans that we have taken up his cause, to ensure his being fixed for ever on his throne.
>
> The present time is perhaps better than any previous to it, for the Afghans, as a nation, detest Persia, and Dost Mohammed Khan's having gone over to the court of Teheran, though he believed it to be from dire necessity, converts many a doubting Afghan into a

14 Aijazuddin, *The Resourceful Fakirs*, p.188.
15 Colvin, *Rulers of India*, p.114.

> bitter enemy. The Maharaja's permission has only to be asked for the ex-king's advance to Peshawar, granting him at the same time some four or five of his regiments, which have no Sikhs in their ranks, and Shah Shuja becomes King. He need not move from Peshawar, but address the Khaibaris, the Kohistanis of Kabul, and all the Afghans from that city, that he has the co-operation of the British and the Maharaja, and with but a little distribution of ready money, say two or three lakhs of rupees, he will find himself the real king of Afghanistan in a couple of months.[16]

On 12 May 1838, Lord Auckland, secluded in the comfort of Auckland Lodge, sat down to review the situation in which he considered the several courses open to him. These included the building of a 'rampart' (his word) of allied native states to replace the defunct alliance with Persia, the removal of Dost Mohammed to make such a rampart possible and the use of the agency of both Ranjit Singh and Shah Shuja to put it into effect. Only if all this failed did the Governor General visualise the implementation of direct military action. He then warned the Secret Committee that the emergency of affairs might compel him to make decisions without reference to it. To his Whig colleague, Sir John Hobhouse, he sent his appreciation of the situation:

> I would not commit myself now to any course of action. But we must prepare to meet the serious difficulty which is hanging over us with a promptitude adequate to the occasion, and it is well, therefore, to follow out the several plans which are open to us in some fullness of detail. If Persia should succeed against Herat, and advance upon Eastern Afghanistan, we have, as it appears to me, but three courses to follow: the first, to confine our defensive measures to the line of the Indus, and leave Afghanistan to its fate; the second, to attempt to save Afghanistan by granting succour to the existing Chiefships of Kabul and Kandahar; the third, to permit or encourage the advance of Ranjit Singh's armies upon Kabul under counsel and restriction, and (subsidiary to his advance) to organise an expedition headed by Shah Shuja-ul-Mulk, such as I have above explained. The first course would be absolute defeat and would leave a free opening to Russian and Persian intrigue upon our frontier. The second would be only to give power to those who feel greater animosity against the Sikhs than they do against the Persians, and who would probably use against the former the means placed at their disposal. And the third course which, even in the event of the successful resistance at Herat, would appear to be the most expedient, would, if that state were to fall into the hands of the Persians, have yet more to recommend it, and I cannot hesitate to say that the inclination of my opinion is, for the reasons which will be gathered from these papers, very strongly in favour of it.[17]

No doubt the Governor General's preference owed much to the fact that by Maharaja Ranjit Singh's dormant treaty with Shah Shuja, the latter had relinquished all claims on Peshawar, to date the sole obstacle to the formation of Lord Auckland's desired 'rampart', the elephant in the room would be no more.

16 Colvin, *Rulers of India*, p.103.
17 Colvin, *Rulers of India*, p.106.

The decision for a regime change having been made, a mission was deputed to the Maharaja in Lahore to invite His Highness to become party to the British contemplated actions. It was correctly assumed that Shah Shuja, who had enjoyed British hospitality for the past 20 years, would embrace this British initiative with much eagerness. This mission was made up of William Macnaghten, political secretary to the Government of India, Captain Claude Wade, political agent at Ludhiana, Captain the Honourable William Osborne, military secretary to the Governor General, Dr John Drummond, surgeon to the Governor General and Captain George MacGregor, ADC. The mission had an escort which consisted of two companies of 20th Bengal Native Infantry, two Bengal Horse Artillery guns and a squadron of irregular cavalry. The mission crossed the Sutlej at Rupar on 20 May and was met by *Sardars* Ajit Singh and Kamran Singh. The Sikh court at the time was at Adinanagar, the Maharaja's summer residence, the recorded temperature was 107°. Macnaghten had his first interview with the Maharaja on 31 May on which occasion he presented His Highness with Lord Auckland's letter.

Essentially the British plan was to encourage Ranjit Singh and Shah Shuja to implement their 1833 treaty with the sanction of the British Government, which would also finance the operation and appoint an accredited agent to accompany Shah Shuja with a certain number of British officers to direct the movements of his army. Macnaghten was also handed a brief by Henry Torrens, his deputy, which, no doubt, he himself had drafted, stating in part:

> You can then as you observe the disposition of the Maharaja, listen to all he has to say, or, in the event of his showing no disposition to commence the conference, you can state to him the views of your own government – that two courses of proceeding had occurred to his Lordship – the one that the treaty formally executed between His Highness and Shah Shuja should be recognised by the British Government – that whilst the Sikhs advanced cautiously on Caubul, accompanied by British agents, a demonstration should be made by a division of the British army occupying Shikarpore with Shah Shuja in their company, to whom the British Government would advance money to enable him to levy troops and purchase arms, and to whom also the services of British officers should be lent, that the same opportunity should be taken of securing to the Maharaja what it had been customary for him to receive from the Scindians, and that with regard to Shikarpur, the supplementary article in the treaty now proposed should be substituted for Article IV, in the former treaty – that in the event His Highness agreeing to this convention, the Governor General would be prepared to ratify it … You will at the same time propose the only other course of proceedings, which in the opinion of the Governor General the case admits of, which is to allow the Maharaja to take his own course against Dost Mohammed Khan without any reference to us. Should His Highness show a decided preference for this course, you are authorised to tell him at once that he is at liberty to follow it, but you should point out to him the possibility of defeat by the combined army of the Persians and Afghans … Of the relative advantages which may be derived from these two plans you will be better able to judge after you shall have fully opened them, with the consideration which each has to recommend it to the Maharaja. His Highness may possibly be unwilling to commit his troops in the passes of the Khyber, and he may strongly feel the difficulty which religious and natural animosity will oppose to any measure mainly resting on Sikh power and Sikh influence. He may not, therefore, reject the plan that stands first in this paper; and there

> can be little doubt of that. For ultimate efficiency, and for bringing greater weight and greater strength to bear in concert upon the objects in view, that this plan should have the preference; but it is cumbrous, and a considerable time may elapse before it can be set in motion; and if it might conciliate Afghan opinion on one hand, on the other it might impair with the Sikhs that cordiality which would be essential to the success of co-operation. His Lordship, on the whole, is disposed to think that the plan which is second in order is that which will be found most expedient.[18]

From the length of Macnaghten's brief it is quite clear that the British delegation to the ever-suspicious Maharaja did not expect a free ride, nor did they get one. After the customary sessions of gift-giving and exchange of salutations, the Governor General's letter was handed to the Maharaja. The Sikh court then moved to Lahore where the real business was conducted, and where the returning Captain Burnes joined the group along with Lieutenant Frederick Mackeson.[19] Here His Lordship's letter was thoroughly scrutinised.

By the time Macnaghten had arrived in Lahore he was of the strong opinion, shared by both Wade and Mackeson, that it would be highly impolitic to let Ranjit Singh take up the cause of Shah Shuja without British partnership. In his opinion there was no middle course, either the British Government act in a totally defensive mode, or take up arms against the perceived threat. To have Shah Shuja restored to his throne with Sikh bayonets was madness. Day by day he pressed the Governor General to allow him to tell Ranjit Singh that with or without his co-operation, the British would restore Shah Shuja to his rightful throne. But Lord Auckland was not to be hurried. Ever-cautious, he was not about to authorise a venture into the unknown 600 miles away, without exploring all options and waiting for information from his masters in England, which might relieve him of direct responsibility.

On 12 June Auckland wrote to his friend Sir John Hobhouse, informing him that owing to a lack of information about what was being contemplated in Europe about the affairs in Persia he

18 Kaye, *History of the War in Afghanistan*, Vol. 1, p.309.

19 Lieutenant Frederick Mackeson 1807–1853. He arrived in India in 1826 and was posted to the 14th BNI; with this regiment he went to Ludhiana and was present at the meeting between Lord Bentinck and Maharaja Ranjit Singh. In 1835 he was selected for the Political Department and sent to Mithenkote as the agent for the navigation of the Indus. In 1837 he was based in Peshawar and was employed in the preparation of the route from Ferozepore to Bahawalpur. He was then commissioned to raise a force of irregular levies and was involved in Wade's advance up the Khyber Pass. He returned to Peshawar with General Keane's force, and was then involved in many actions in and around the Khyber region. In 1842 he was with the force that recaptured Ali Masjid and accompanied General Pollock's force to Kabul. He rejoined his regiment in 1843. In 1846 he was appointed superintendent of the Sikh states in the Cis-Sutlej; he then joined Major General Sir Harry Smith's division for the First Anglo-Sikh War. For the Second Anglo-Sikh War, Mackeson was appointed by Lord Dalhousie, the governor general, as his political agent with General Lord Gough, the commander-in-chief. In 1850 he went to England on furlough, aged 40, having served in India for 24 years; at the behest of Lord Dalhousie, he carried with him the *Koh-i-Noor* diamond to be presented to Queen Victoria. He returned in 1852 and was appointed Commissioner of Peshawar by Lord Dalhousie. It was here on 10 September 1853 that he was attacked by a fanatic with a dagger while conducting a plea audience, and he died of his wounds on 14 September. Mackeson never married. Of this outstanding Company officer, Lord Dalhousie, not generally overgenerous with praise, recorded: 'In all the important political matters in which he had been employed, Major Mackeson's proceedings had been distinguished by ability, judgement, discretion and firmness.'

was not confident about the measures he should take. He felt as if 'he was playing in the dark, and with his hands tied, in a game requiring clear-sighted vigour'. The obscure responsibility of the Government of India in regard to Persian and European politics was the real cause of the Governor General's hesitation. 'The road to India through Persia having been thrown open by Teheran, to a European power, will not England acting from Europe, endeavour to replace the barrier of 1814?' Little wonder that he hesitated hoping for instructions from England, or information from Teheran, and he was quite prepared to pause for a fortnight to await such instructions before he would take any measure of such importance as making India the Foreign Secretary's stalking-horse. On the following day, the Governor General told Macnaghten that no plans would be made until he returned to Simla; he then penned another letter to Sir John Hobhouse:

> All that I am doing, or preparing to do, is well justified by the avowed policy of the Persian Court and by the hostile proceedings of the Russian agent; and you may assume it for next to certain that I shall go onwards, with many deep feelings of regret that I am not allowed to prosecute measures of peace and peaceful improvement, but with a perfect conviction that it is only by a bold front, and by strong exertion, that the aggressions and dangers with which we are threatened can be warded off. I can decide absolutely on nothing until Macnaghten's return, and I think that I shall then be able to see my way to all that is to be done, and with no fear of the result, though I shall be sorry for the money which it will cost.[20]

In a further interview with the Maharaja, envoy Macnaghten reviewed the situation in the north and the obvious threat to both Sikh and British interests. The wise old Maharaja could well see the portrayed threat, but he could also see the opportunity to bind the British to his interests and to squeeze as much as he could during this period of British anxiety. He asked Macnaghten what were the wishes of the British Government and in reply Macnaghten told him that as far as the British were concerned there were two courses open to the Maharaja, one was to act independently, an option favoured by his Chief Minister Raja Dhian Singh, and the other course was to act in concert with the British Government. The Maharaja opted for the latter, at which point the Envoy continued: 'Your Highness some time ago formed a treaty with Shah Shuja-ul-Mulk, do you think it would be still for your benefit that the treaty should stand good, and would it be agreeable to your wishes that the British Government should become party to that treaty?' 'That,' replied Ranjit Singh, 'would be like adding sugar to milk.'[21] Macnaghten then proceeded to inform the Maharaja of the outline of the British plan, which saw the Sikhs advancing up the Khyber Pass to Kabul, while Shah Shuja, with some British troops, advanced up the Bolan Pass to Kandahar.

In accordance with the first article of the original 1833 treaty between Ranjit Singh and Shah Shuja, the latter had given up all claim and title to those territories of the original Duranni Empire that the former had since acquired, which included Peshawar. But the British had not been party to this treaty. Now the paramount power in India was offering to bind itself to the

20 Colvin, *Rulers of India*, p.114.
21 Kaye, *A History of the War in Afghanistan*, Vol. 1, p.314.

treaty thus legitimising the Maharaja's territorial claims, an opportunity Ranjit Singh eagerly grasped, despite the urging of some of his anti-British advisers to go it alone, a course that Ranjit Singh calculated would leave Sikh claims, especially Peshawar, up for grabs as and when it suited the British.

What stuck in the Maharaja's craw was that the British plan excluded Shikarpore, thus sealing once and for all any ambition to extend into Sindh and to the sea beyond. The Maharaja felt that his imperial ambitions were being strangled in the embrace of British friendship. In exchange for the 'hands-off Shikarpore' Ranjit Singh made an outrageous demand for Jalalabad, then settled for an annual tribute from Shah Shuja of two *lakhs* of rupees. He also suggested that the Barakzai, Sultan Mohammed Khan, be appointed *Wazir* to Shah Shuja, which under the circumstances was not feasible but could well have been beneficial. The Maharaja then had misgivings about the success of the venture dependent on Shah Shuja's raw recruits and his Sikh troops, who, he knew, would be most reluctant to venture through the gauntlet of the Khyber Pass and proceed beyond Jamrud. The British commander-in-chief, General Sir Henry Fane, was later to have similar misgivings of a rag-tail army achieving any success.

While negotiations continued in Lahore, Macnaghten was informed of the dire reports received from Teheran which portrayed Herat about to fall and a Russian force of 12,000 marching down to help the Shah of Persia. After the Shah of Persia's volte-face, McNeill had remained in the Persian camp as he was determined not to abandon all hope of bringing about a satisfactory settlement. However, any influence that McNeill may have had was fast diminishing and he was giving serious consideration to his departure. On 3 June he addressed a letter to the foreign minister in the Persian camp announcing his departure. 'I feel myself called upon to inform you that, until the reparations and satisfaction I have demanded, for the indignities already offered, shall have been fully given, the Queen of England cannot receive at her Court any minister who may be sent thither by the Shah of Persia.' McNeill went on to demand the removal from office of the man who violated the person of Ali Mohammed Beg, and the Governor of Bushire for his insults to the British Resident there. The Persians met these demands and despite their pleas for the Envoy to remain, McNeill took his departure on 7 June, thus Persia was no longer, officially, an ally of Great Britain. Now under Russian direction the Persians continued to prosecute the siege with increased vigour. An assault was made on 13 June, which was gallantly repulsed by the Heratis. Then, at first light on Sunday 24 June, a massive barrage of Persian heavy guns broke the silence of the night and announced the advance of an all-out Persian attack led by a regiment of Russian mercenaries commanded by Major General Berowski. The fate of Herat was trembling in the balance; the struggle was brief but bloody with as many as 1,800 men killed or wounded on the Persian side including the dead Berowski. The defenders, with much encouragement from the young artilleryman Lieutenant Pottinger, put up a gallant defence and Herat was saved.

Back in Lahore, the Maharaja continued to nit-pick and demand all sorts of concessions and safeguards including an outrageous one to have his Barakzai friend, Sultan Mohammed Khan, appointed *Wazir* to Shah Shuja until on 23 June a very frustrated Macnaghten, not wishing for the whole project to blow up in his face, issued the Sikhs with an ultimatum that if the Maharaja was not satisfied with the proposed revised treaty he was at liberty to act independently, without offending the British, who would also be at liberty to take what course they deemed necessary to safeguard their interests, and he would be left out.[22] On Tuesday 23 June the revised treaty was signed by the Maharaja. Besides slight modifications to the original and the addition of four new articles, the treaty had undergone no big alterations.

The signed treaty was forthwith despatched to Simla for the Governor General to attach his signature, but Lord Auckland, rightly, refused to sign until it had been agreed and signed by Shah Shuja. With Maharaja Ranjit Singh's blessing the British Mission left Lahore on 13 July and were in Ludhiana two days later when, accompanied by Captain Wade and Lieutenant Mackeson, Macnaghten waited on Shah Shuja telling him that it had always been the British Government's desire to see Shah Shuja restored to his throne as it was with him that the treaty of 1809 had been signed. The ex-King of Afghanistan had dreamed of the opportunity to regain his throne for the past 20 years and to do so under the auspices of his generous hosts was indeed a fillip. However, to be perceived by his people as nothing more than a puppet of the British and the dreaded Sikhs was not worth the attempt. Hence, Shah Shuja insisted on some changes to the proposed treaty. Foremost, he deemed it essential that, firstly, no interference be exercised with his authority over those of his tribe, and secondly, he was to advance at the head of his own army, albeit recruited and financed by the British until such time as he was established on his throne. Thirdly, the stipulated tribute he was to pay Ranjit Singh implied a subservience to that monarch, so this had to be changed to a subsidy for the maintenance of a reserve of 10,000 Sikhs in a tribute from the Amirs of Sindh, historically due to the Shah. Additionally, the annual gift-giving to Ranjit Singh was to be reciprocal. Furthermore, the British agreed to pay Shah Shuja a special allowance of 25,000 rupees per month to meet essential expenses while in Ludhiana and 50,000 rupees per month on arrival at Shikarpore. In return for this monumental change in his fortunes, Shah Shuja was to keep his hands off Herat. All these issues were quickly resolved and the Shah gave his anticipated approval.

There is no better way to conclude this chapter than to quote from Chapter 11 of *Fakir* Aijazuddin's excellent *The Resourceful Fakirs*:

> At Simla, Lord Auckland and his staff were busy planning the campaign that would restore Shah Shuja to a precarious throne in Kabul.
>
> At Lahore, Runjit Singh purred with contentment at having converted a sterile agreement with a deposed ex-Amir, with a document binding the British Government as his guarantor in the last resort.
>
> And at Ludhiana, Wade delivered to Shah Shuja his copy of the Tripartite treaty. It was like assigning Hamlet the script to play the Prince of Denmark, or in this case the Amir of Afghanistan.

A British army to Kabul with the Sikhs cheering on the touchline. Lord Auckland had meant it to be the other way round.[23]

22 Cunningham, *A History of the Sikhs*, p.309.
23 Philip Woodruff, *The Men Who Ruled India 1: The Founders* (London: Jonathan Cape, 1953), p.389.

7

The Declaration (a.k.a. The Simla Manifesto)

The Tripartite Treaty (see Appendix I) was signed by Maharaja Ranjit Singh on 16 June 1838 and by Shah Shuja-ul-Mulk on 16 July; three days later the document was placed by William Macnaghten before Lord Auckland for his ratification. The only signatures not on this document were those of the Amirs of Sindh through whose country the allied army was to march, and from whom the allies were to gouge out 21 *lakhs* of rupees in compensation. Instead, the Amirs were sent a mission in June 1838, headed by Colonel Henry Pottinger, to sign a further treaty permitting the British free navigation of the Indus River with a Sindhi-instigated proviso that the river was not to be used for the transportation of military arms and materials. This proviso was either an oversight or an exercise in diplomatic chicanery, especially as British boots and empty stomachs were to be much in evidence a short time later.

The treaty was no secret, as even before the ink was dry on the document, Shah Shuja was writing to all his friends in Afghanistan calling for their support, and Indian contractors were rubbing their hands with glee as the bush telegraph buzzed with intelligence of troop movements and estimated commissary requirements. Also, the British authorities were not averse to news of their contemplated actions reaching the ears of the hitherto prophets of doom and those of the Shah of Persia. Army morale, which had taken a beating with the Bentinck reforms and 20 years of garrison boredom, shot up as officers strove to find ways of being included in the venture and its anticipated opportunities for extra cash, promotion and glory.

History has judged Lord Auckland's decision to invade Afghanistan as ill-conceived, disastrous and the brainchild of ambitious young advisers. A correspondent of a London daily paper was more explicit as to the sources of the plan of the campaign. 'Macnaghten was at once ambitious and unpopular, he wished to become an envoy and was wished out of the Secretariat to make room for Mr Torrens, whose wife, a fashionable and accomplished woman, was in great favour with the rulers of the ruler of India, the Honourable Miss Eden, the sister and manager of Lord Auckland.'[1] However, Lord Auckland was the exact opposite of a warmonger, his prime desire was to do the right thing and his prime role was the defence of India; and in mid May 1838 it was essential that some bold action be taken against a disunited Afghanistan, prone to Persian and Russian intrigues, hence ticking all the right boxes for securing the British position

1 Buist, *Outline of the Operations*, p.712.

in India and the opening up for trade along the Indus, a long-time cherished objective; plus, to the righteous Victorians, the restoration of a throne to a rightful king was both just and noble. Lord Auckland in a letter dated 14 August 1838 wrote. 'Of the justice of the course about to be perused there can exist no reasonable doubt. We owe it to our safety to assist the lawful sovereign of Afghanistan in the recovery of his throne.'[2] Besides, intelligence from the most reliable of current sources all indicated that Shah Shuja's return would be welcomed. Whatever the cause, the East India Company had for the past 20 years been anxious to establish itself west and north of the Indus and the Governor General's advisers, all Company men, were not about to let this opportunity slip. The record shows that Lord Auckland's decision has its history in the loss of British influence in Persia, the reluctance of the Home authorities to challenge Russian schemes of aggrandisement in Central Asia, the disunity within Afghanistan, the Kandahar chief's alliance with the Persian Shah, the Sikh/Afghan bust-up at Jamrud, the impossible conditions that Dost Mohammed had demanded for his alliance, Maharaja Ranjit Singh's reluctance to accept the burden of invading Kabul and the total lack of any confidence in Shah Shuja's capacity to levy sufficient troops in time to go it alone albeit with an open British cheque book. It was also quite evident that Lord Auckland agonised over his decision and desired nothing more than to be judged to have done the right thing. On 13 August he sent a long despatch to the Court of Directors vindicating his policy, and in part it stated, 'But I have felt, after the most anxious deliberation, that I could not otherwise rightly acquit myself of my trust.' As Lord Salisbury, a future foreign secretary, was to comment, 'You must either disbelieve altogether the existence of Russians, or you must believe they will be at Kandahar next year. Public opinion recognises no middle holding ground.' The British foreign secretary at the time, Lord Palmerston, obviously thought that Lord Auckland's decision was a perfect solution, when in a letter to Sir John Hobhouse in October of that year, he adds, 'By this vigorous decision of Auckland's will do us the utmost service in India, in Europe and at Home. We shall utterly defeat the Russian schemes in the East. That will tell upon Persia and probably establish our influence there; that will tell on Turkey and give us a good footing there.'

The matter was now placed in the hands of His Excellency, General Sir Henry Fane, the commander-in-chief, to give life to the plan of action. Sir Henry, a veteran of Waterloo, was lukewarm about the whole scheme and not too happy with the politicos display of confidence in what could be a very complicated military undertaking. He was adamant that any assembled military force had to be strong enough to guarantee success and that this force would be drawn mainly from the Bengal army, thus exposing the northern provinces to possible nuisances by disgruntled neighbours, which included the Sikhs, as and when the old Maharaja joined his ancestors. Additionally, as the Governor General had agreed to Ranjit Singh's stipulation that the advance of the British and Shah Shuja's forces be restricted to the left bank of the Sutlej, his line of communication to the objective was to be a long 1,200 miles through desolate country as opposed to 550 miles through the more verdant Punjab. General Fane warned the Governor General that, while he could assure the army getting to Afghanistan, maintaining it there was close to impossible. What he failed to add was that it would be costly, a factor that played hugely in the result.

2 Sir Algernon Law, *India Under Lord Ellenborough, March 1842–June 1844* (London: John Murray, 1926), p.19.

However, in India not all of the Company's hierarchy were ecstatic about the venture. John Low, a well established Company man and the Resident at Oudh wrote to the Chairman of the Court of Directors stating, 'The only thing I fear is the dreadful expense of sending so large an army to such a distance, and the future inconvenience that must follow extending our position so enormously as to take military occupation of Candahar, Cabool etc. on the other side of the Indus, for I suspect that we shall never be able to withdraw our troops from those countries.'[3]

On 28 July 1838 General Fane alerted the Bombay authorities to make ready a force of 5,000 and a reserve of another 3,000, to advance by sea to the Sindh when ordered. Sir Henry had calculated that as commander of the expedition his force would consist of two divisions of Bengal troops and a division, of brigade strength, of Bombay troops. The Bengal troops were to assemble at Karnaul, a garrison town, and both the Bengal and Bombay contingents were to meet at Quetta in Baluchistan. The two contingents were to operate with their own general staff and administrative back up.

Shah Shuja's force was to number 6,000 men, officered by East India Company British officers, recruited, trained, equipped and paid for by the East India Company; the British officers and NCOs were to have their salaries doubled. This force was to be supplemented by 200 native volunteers from 20 designated Bengal native regiments and the inducement for them to volunteer was promotion. The character of the volunteers was to be 'in no way objectionable', and the names were to be forwarded to Colonel Edward Simpson of 5th BNI at Ludhiana. The commissary requirements of this force were to be covered by the Bengal contingent. The plan was that this contingent would remain in Afghanistan, at the cost to the Calcutta treasury, until the formation of an Afghan national army. The Sikh contingent, all Mussulmans, was to advance from Peshawar to Kabul through the Khyber Pass. It was ostensibly under the command of *Shahzada* Timour, the Afghan Crown Prince, but in reality under the command of the recently promoted Lieutenant Colonel Wade and his small staff of British officers, all politicos. On 10 September a General Order was published announcing that:

> It being the intention of the Government to employ a force beyond the north-west frontier of India, and His Excellency General Sir Henry Fane, G.C.B. Commander-in-Chief in India, having acquiesced in the wish of the Right Honorable the Governor General, that he should take upon himself the command of the troops to be assembled on the occasion, His Lordship avails himself of his services; and His Excellency is accordingly requested to issue such orders for the organisation of the force as he may deem expedient.
>
> By order of the Right Honorable the Governor General.
> (Signed) W.H. Macnaghten
> Secretary to Government of India
> With the Governor General
> (Signed) W. Casement, Major General
> Secretary to Government of India, Military Department
> With the Governor General

3 Ferdinand Mount, *The Tears of The Rajas: Mutiny, Money and Marriage in India 1805–1905* (London: Simon & Schuster, 2015), p.307.

Appended to this order was a list of seven senior officers to be promoted to the rank of brigadier for the forthcoming operations. Prior to this the Commander-in-Chief had already selected his two divisional commanders for the Bengal contingent, they were Major General Sir Willoughby Cotton[4] and Major General Alexander Duncan. The Bombay commander-in-chief, Lieutenant General Sir John Keane, had nominated himself to lead the Bombay contingent. The above General Order also stated that:

1. The general officers named to command divisions will be pleased to take care, that good ground is early selected near Karnal, for the proper encampment of the several corps on their arrival; and that all necessary commissariat arrangements are completed.
2. For these purposes (to form brigades and allocate staff) the troops will halt six days at Karnal; after which they will march in four columns to Ferozepore (205 miles) where the army will be assembled.
3. The start date for this activity is to be 1 November 1838.

As previously mentioned, the bulk of Shah Shuja's force was mainly recruited from the districts of Kumaon, Grahwal and Simla. All these recruits were to be given the same rates of pay as regular native *sepoys*, excluding pensions. All were to assemble in Ludhiana under Major Thomas McSherry of 30th Bengal Native Infantry, the appointed recruiting officer. Significantly, a separate general order of 12 August 1838 was published calling for volunteers for two troops of Horse Artillery; all of these volunteers were Muslims and recruited from Meerut and Delhi and all were required to report to Captain William Anderson of the Bengal Horse Artillery, who was to command the two troops during the campaign. There were many volunteers for the infantry units so Major McSherry had no problem forming four regiments of infantry, each of eight companies of 100 men, one of which was designated 4th Gurkha Regiment. As these Gurkhas form a significant part of this account it would seem appropriate, at this point, to give a short background to the events that led to the employment of these marvellous soldiers by the British. Much of what follows is based on Major W.P. Northey's book *The Land of the Gurkhas*.

Nepal, a narrow stretch of country 500 miles long, lies along the Himalayan mountains on the northern border of India. It was a rugged unruly country comprising a score of kinglets. In 1769 the Chief of Gorkha, to the west of Katmandu, organised his people and proceeded to

4 Major General Sir Willoughby Cotton (1783–1860). The son of Admiral Sir Rowland Cotton, he was educated at Rugby School where, at the age of 14, he was the ringleader in the Great Rebellion of November 1797, for which he was expelled. He was commissioned, on purchase, into the Scots Guards in 1798. In 1809 he served as adjutant general in the Light Division under Brigadier Robert Crawford, and in 1811 he was promoted to lieutenant colonel in command of his regiment. He then returned to the Peninsula in April 1813 and served throughout the campaign. In 1814, while in command of the Light Division, he was taken prisoner but managed to escape by giving up his watch and all the money on him. He returned to England in April 1814 and in June 1815 went to France, arriving after the Battle of Waterloo. In 1824 he sailed for India and took part in the First Anglo-Burmese War, 1824-26. He was then posted to Jamaica as the garrison commander in 1831 and was involved in putting down the slave revolt of 1832. In 1837 he was back in India and in command of the First Bengal Division for the advance into Afghanistan. In 1847 he was appointed commander-in-chief of the Bombay Army. He returned to England in 1850 and died in bed on 4 May 1860. He married Lady Augusta Conentry in May 1806, and they had three children.

master the whole country. The chief of Katmandu asked for British help and a small force under Captain Kinlock was duly sent forth, however this force was overcome with malaria and had to retire.

Prithwi Narayan, the chief of Gorkha, died in 1771 and after a short reign of his eldest son, his infant son Rana Bahadar Sah came to the chieftainship in 1775, with his uncle Bahadar Sah acting as regent, who advanced the kingdom west as far as Kamaon and east as far as Sikkim. The move to the east resulted in the inclusion of the Rai, Limbu and Tamang tribes into the Gurkha army. The next move of this Gurkha army was to loot the Grand Lama's palace at Tashi-Lumpo; a wrong move as it brought down the wrath of the Chinese emperor in the form of a 70,000-strong army. A peace treaty was signed and the Gurkha regent accepted the suzerainty of China; he also appealed to the British for help. However, the governor general at the time, Lord Cornwallis, was unwilling to send troops and instead sent Colonel Kirkpatrick to take up residence in Katmandu. The Colonel only got as far as Nawaket and was forced to return as the Regent had baulked at the timidity of the British for sending one individual and not an army.

In 1795, Rana Bahadar Sah removed his uncle and there followed five years of misrule and violence till this despicable and unprincipled chief was forced to abdicate in favour of his infant son, and he retired to Benares, in the British territories, with his Brahmin wife Tripura Sundari. Before he left, he appointed one of his concubines as the regent and a man named Damodar Panre as the prime minister. This gentleman, fearing the possibility of the ex-chief mustering British support for his return, approached and signed a commercial treaty with the British and agreed to a permanent resident at Katmandu. Captain Knox was appointed resident and arrived at Katmandu in 1802, but conditions there were made unbearable for the Captain and he withdrew his mission in 1804. Rana Bahadar Sah apparently misbehaved himself in Benares and his wife successfully persuaded the Prime Minister to allow her to return to her rightful slot as regent to the infant king. Once back, Tripura Sundari engineered the return of her disgraced husband, who brought with him a young Rajput noble named Bhim Sen Thapa. There was the inevitable falling out between this noble and the Prime Minister, resulting in the latter being murdered by the former, plus the annihilation of the latter's entire family. During these murderous proceedings, Rana Bahadar Sah was cut down by his half-brother with a kukri.

Bhim Sen Thapa proceeded to appoint himself prime minister and was in that slot for the next 33 years. His father happened to be the renowned Gurkha general Amar Singh Thapa; he proceeded to extend the kingdom westward and besieged Kanga where the Raja, Sunwar Chand, only had a little army commanded by a British deserter by the name of O'Brien, ex-24th Dragoons. It was no match for the Gurkhas, so the Raja appealed to the British for help, but this was declined as action across the Sutlej would have been in violation of the 1809 treaty with Maharaja Ranjit Singh. Consequently, the Raja of Sunwar Chand was compelled to seek help from the Sikhs, which was agreed; the Sikhs saw off the Gurkha threat, but then claimed the place for themselves.

From 1804 to 1812 the Gurkhas, blocked in the north, east and west, steadily pushed southwards encroaching on the territories of petty hill rajas under British protection. By 1812 as many as 200 villages had been annexed, by which time British patience with these Gurkha antics came to a breaking point. A force under Major Bradshaw was sent to occupy the disputed ground, but with the coming of the rainy season the troops were replaced by native policemen. Then in the early hours of 29 May 1814 the Gurkhas attacked these police posts, and killed the policemen. British reaction was delayed to the end of the rainy season when on 1 November Lord Hastings, the governor general, declared war on Nepal.

At first the war went badly for the British. The Gurkhas were the toughest enemy they had yet met in India and the British suffered several resounding disasters. The strategy of Lord Hastings, who was also the commander-in-chief,[5] was faulty, the generals, with a few exceptions, were old and inefficient constantly breaking down in health and nerves and the troops thus handicapped were quite incapable of making any headway against the brave and tenacious Gurkhas; three out of the four British columns suffered reverses inflicted by a small number of these soldiers. Only in Kumaon to the west where Colonel David Ochterlony was operating independently, did the British meet with any success. It was during these operations in the Kumaon district that Mr William Fraser, acting as the political agent, was given a brief to 'recruit locals for an irregular force which would be highly effective in scouting operations and swift harassment of enemy supply lines in the difficult and hilly terrain'. Mr Fraser recruited 4,000 of these men,[6] who were commanded by Lieutenant Frederick Young. This was the very first time that Gurkhas were employed by the British. Earlier, Captain Hay, writing on 13 September 1813, informed his superiors:

> There is a class of men who I conceive to be particularly well suited for duties of light infantry and who voluntarily offer to be entertained to wear our uniform, carry the musket and submit to the necessary restraints of discipline. They are Rajputs originally the subjects of the Nepalese Government and who have fled. They are reputed to be excellent soldiers and bear their character and fidelity to their employer.

At the end of the Anglo-Nepalese War, Major General Ochterlony and General Amar Singh Thapa signed an agreement on 15 May 1815 permitting all troops in the service of Nepal to be at liberty to enter into the service of the British Government. It was from Lieutenant Young's irregular force that three battalions of eight companies each were formed. According to the Adjutant General's Circular No 77 of 9 January 1829, the uniform for these levies was stipulated as green tunics with blood facings and green trousers. Two of these battalions were named the Nassari and Sirmoor Battalions, the third was disbanded in 1830. At the time Major General Ochterlony declared, 'I shall with the sanction and approbation of His Excellency call it the "Nassari Pultan", and confirm myself its commandant.' These battalions were used to garrison Subathu, Raeengurh and Nahn. Interestingly, in accordance with General Orders of 28 April 1840, the commander-in-chief authorised volunteers from the Nassari and Sirmoor battalions to join the 4th Gurkha Regiment in Shah Shuja's force; six *Havildars* to be *Jemadars*, eight *Naiks*

5 Lord Hastings (1754-1826) accepted the governorship of India as a favour to his friend the Prince Regent (George IV). He came out in 1813 and served as governor general for 10 years, the longest period of any governor general. When he left in 1823 he was a broken man, much poorer than when he arrived, and was compelled to accept the governorship of Malta in 1824. On his return to England in 1826 he died at sea. When he was dying, he directed that his right hand be cut off and placed in the clasp of his wife when she followed him. This request was carried out, his hand was put in a small box and deposited in the family vault and when Lady Hastings died 14 years later the box was placed in her coffin.

6 Mildred Archer and Toby Falk, *The Passionate Quest: The Fraser Brothers in India* (London: Alfalak/ Scorpion Publishing, 1989), p.29.

to be *Havildars* and 12 *sepoys* to be *Naiks*. Gurkha troops were first used in combat by the British when the Sirmoor battalion was employed in the Bhurtpore campaign of 1825. Both battalions were then employed in the First Anglo-Sikh War in the battles of Aliwal and Sobraon in 1846. However, as the 4th Gurkha Regiment of Shah Shuja's force was officered, trained and paid for by the British, and reinforced with volunteers from the Nassari and Sirmoor battalions, there are reasonable grounds to claim that British Gurkhas were first used in actual combat in the First Afghan War, 1838. After the Second Anglo-Sikh War when the 66th Bengal Native Infantry mutinied and were disbanded by General Sir Charles Napier, he awarded that regiment's colours and designation to the Nassari Battalion, which thus became a regular part of the Bengal army.

After the Indian Mutiny of 1857, the regiments of the three East India Company's armies were all disbanded and new regiments were formed with the infantry adopting caste or territorial names and the cavalry territorial and in some cases the name of the officer who raised the regiment. In all cases the new regiments adopted various forms of dress and accoutrements, and all eventually became part of one single British Indian Army. Over the course of the next 75 years eight more regiments of Gurkhas were raised, numbering 1 to 10. Then, on the Independence of India in 1947, a Tripartite Agreement was signed by the British, Nepalese and Indian Governments, which allocated the 1st, 3rd, 4th, 5th, 8th and 9th Gurkha Rifles to the Indian Army, and the 2nd, 6th, 7th and 10th Gurkha Rifles to the British Army. John Masters, in his book *Bugles and a Tiger*, amusingly describes the British Gurkha officers as the 2nd idle, the 6th downtrodden, the 7th unshaven and the 10th alcoholic. All were marvellous regiments with the best soldiers in the world.

Prior to the independence of India, the Gurkha regiments were regarded and treated as being special, they were never billeted in the established garrison towns, instead, when not on active operations, they were billeted in the exclusive Gurkha regimental estates in the Kangra Hills, Dehra Dun or Almora, which were allotted to them as their private property by Royal warrants issued during Queen Victoria's reign.[7] They were also excluded from the scheme to 'Indianise' the services, in fact the British went to great lengths to ensure that their Gurkha regiments remained 'uncontaminated' by Indian influences. This special treatment continued well after Indian independence with the likes of rum ration and the complete overhaul of the lavatory arrangements of a 'British' barrack in order to accommodate an incoming Gurkha regiment's Asian custom of squatting.

While the commander-in-chief General Sir Henry Fane and his staff were frantically organising a force, to be called the Army of the Indus, Lord Auckland and his staff mulled over the multitude of political matters, policy and which ego to stroke, particularly that of the ailing Maharaja in Lahore with whom the forthcoming venture was a non-starter. The title 'Army of the Indus' was a clear indication of the true ambition of the British to hold sway over the Indus valley. The uppermost important appointment for consideration, at the time, was who should be the British envoy to the Court of Shah Shuja. According to some reports, Macnaghten is said to have volunteered his services for the occasion; he may have done so later, but on 26 May, while on his way to Lahore, he had strongly recommended to Lord Auckland that Colonel Henry

7 D.K. Palit, *Musings and Memories*, Vol. I (New Delhi: Palit & Palit in association with Lancer Publishers, 2004), p.241.

Pottinger, the British agent at Hyderabad, was the most suitable person for this role. Another person who fully expected to be given the role was Alexander Burnes, who was back in the corridors of power at Simla. Writing to his brother, he clearly indicates his expectation and adds a veiled threat in the event of being disappointed. 'What exact part I am to play I know not, but if full confidence and hourly consultation be any pledge, I am to be the chief. I can plainly tell them *aut Caesar aut nullus* [I'll be Caesar or nothing], and if I get not what I have a right to, you will soon see me enroute to England.'[8] Burnes was to be disappointed and duly applied for furlough, then withdrew his application on being offered a junior and semi-independent role, with heaven knows what other inducements. The matter was resolved on the basis of a letter dated 12 July from the Governor General's private secretary, John Colvin, to Macnaghten:

> It is right to let you know that a strong feeling is growing up here that it will be most desirable for the public interests, at whatever sacrifice to the daily ease and satisfaction of Lord Auckland's administration, that you should assume the diplomatic direction of Shah Shuja's expedition. This stake is so important that Lord Auckland feels that it may not become him to withhold his best card. Colonel Pottinger might in some respect do well, but (setting aside the possible objection on the score of his hard temper), he wants that general influence which is most essential. There must be free and confidential communication with the Government; and besides this, influence at Lahore, influence at Peshawar, over Wade, over Burnes, over every officer engaged, as well as cordiality in Lord Auckland's views regarding Sind. All this is not easy to see how to combine except in yourself. Think over this and let me be aware as fully as you like of your own inclinations and opinion.[9]

Obviously, Lord Auckland was concerned that if the superior political functions were to be separated from the military command, a person of higher rank, consequence, and official status than either Wade or Burnes must, if only out of courtesy, be placed in political control of the operation. Macnaghten, not lacking ambition and seeing the prospects of distinction and honour that would flow, accepted with alacrity. The Eden sisters, who were never attuned to Macnaghten's rather pedantic manner nor his wife's strumped-up airs, were quite pleased at the prospect of seeing the back of both.

As the British regiments arrived at Karnal they were brigaded under their newly appointed brigadiers. As was the practice in those days the appointed brigadier's own regiment was automatically part of his new brigade. It was also the practice to allow divisional commanders two aides-de-camp and brigadiers one.

Such gathering of regiments for campaigns was an excellent opportunity for young officers to be appointed to the staff with slightly higher salary and the chance to ride rather than march. Consequently, they many wrote home to have their relatives solicit important persons to write letters of introduction on behalf of the young officer. Typical of one of these is a letter from Lieutenant Edwin Utterton of HM 23rd Foot to his mother, on his arrival in India in September 1857. 'My Dearest Mamma, Gen Wilson is I see before Delhi. I wish you could get Mr Wilson

8 Kaye, *The History of the War in Afghanistan*, Vol. I, p.352.
9 Colvin, *Rulers of India*, p.133.

to write to for me against we go there. I am afraid I have no chance of getting on the staff. It would be a good thing for me if I could.'

The organisation of the two divisions was as follows:

Commander of the Army of the Indus: General Sir Henry Fane
First Infantry Division. Commander: Major General Sir Willoughby Cotton
First Brigade. Commander: Brigadier Robert Sale (HM 13th Foot)
HM 13th Foot
16th Bengal Native Infantry
48th Bengal Native Infantry
Second Brigade. Commander: Brigadier William Nott
31st Bengal Native Infantry
42nd Bengal Native Infantry
43rd Bengal Native Infantry
Third Brigade. Commander: Brigadier James Dennis
HM 3rd Foot
2nd Bengal Native Infantry
27th Bengal Native Infantry
One Company of Sappers
Second Infantry Division. Commander: Major General Alexander Duncan
Fourth Brigade. Commander: Brigadier Abraham Roberts
1st Bengal European Regiment
35th Bengal Native Infantry
37th Bengal Native Infantry
Fifth Brigade. Commander: Brigadier Thomas Worsley
5th Bengal Native Infantry
28th Bengal Native Infantry
53rd Bengal Native Infantry
One Company of Sappers
Cavalry Brigade. Commander: Brigadier Robert Arnold
HM 16th Lancers
2nd Bengal Light Cavalry
3rd Bengal Light Cavalry
Skinner's Horse Irregular Cavalry
Artillery Brigade. Commander: Brigadier Charles Graham
2nd Troop, 2nd Brigade Bengal Horse Artillery
3rd Troop, 2nd Brigade Bengal Horse Artillery
3rd Company, 2nd Battalion Bengal Artillery
4th Company, 2nd Battalion Bengal Artillery
2nd Company, 6th Battalion Bengal Artillery

Shah Shuja's force of 6,000, officered by 60 British commissioned officers and 14 volunteer non-commissioned officers, all from the Bengal establishment was assembled at Ludhiana. It was intended that this force would form the nucleus of the Shah's future army. Its organisation was to change during the course of the campaign, as officers left or were appointed to political roles. By the autumn of 1841 the force had been increased by additions of a further infantry regiment, a battalion of Sappers and Miners, a Mountain Train (3-pdr guns transported by mule) and more artillery.

Commander: Major	General Edward Simpson
ADC:	Captain John Griffin
Brigade Major:	Captain Thomas McSherry
1st Cavalry Regiment:	Captain John Christie
2nd Cavalry Regiment.	Captain William Anderson
Horse Artillery Battery:	Captain William Anderson
	Lieutenant George Cooper
	Lieutenant Frank Turner
1st Infantry Regiment:	Captain John Bean
	Lieutenant Peter Nicolson
	Sergeant Major W. Mathews
2nd Infantry Regiment:	Captain James Macan
	Lieutenant John Hoppe.
	Sergeant Major T. Smith
3rd Infantry Regiment:	Captain John Craigie
	Lieutenant Richard McKean
	Sergeant Major N. McDoudd
4th Gurkha Regiment:	Captain Isaac Handscomb
	Lieutenant T.H. Edgar Moorhouse
	Sergeant Major R. Young
5th Infantry Regiment:	Captain John Woodburn
	Lieutenant James Spense
	Sergeant Major W. Fitch
Commissariat Agent:	Captain Hugh Johnson

Medical Officers:
Surgeon John Forsyth
Assistant Surgeon George Rae
Assistant Surgeon Charles Mackinnon
Assistant Surgeon Paul Baddeley

Lord Auckland and his immediate advisers next laboured over the wording of a declaration which His Lordship was determined to publish, and in which he desired to lay out his reasons for the ousting of Dost Mohammed Khan for the whole world to see, as it did when his declaration was published in *The Times* of 22 December, 1838. He had tried without success to work in concert with the Home authorities, but the British Cabinet, through the Board of Control, had basically told him that it was entirely an Indian matter and he was to use his own discretion and resources. Having done so he wanted the world to know that viewed from his own 'Indian prospective' his intentions were just, logical and appropriate. However, as Lord Auckland was later to write, 'It would have been much more effective if I had not had the fear of Downing Street before my eyes.'[10] In this declaration the real motives which led to the war were studiously kept out of sight; there was to be no mention of Russia, no allusion to the instructions from England; and above all not a whisper of 25 June 1836 despatch from the Court of Directors (See Chapter 5). It was to be purely a matter between the British Government of India and the Amir of Afghanistan. Before the declaration was published, Lord Auckland had written to Sir John Hobhouse on his selection of Shah Shuja, saying, 'For desirable ends, no person appears so well adopted as Shah Shuja. He has already twice reigned, he is most popular in Afghanistan and under our auspices, his success would be prompt and certain, little or no blood would be shed, and he would be joined by all who are discontented with Barakzai rule.' The declaration, also known as the Simla Manifesto, was issued on 1 October 1838 (see Appendix II). This was 21 days after the Shah of Persia had abandoned his siege of Herat. This gem of intelligence was not known to the Governor General until 22 October, although Ranjit Singh was aware of it much earlier, another example of the effectiveness of the Indian bush telegraph. History was to tear Lord Auckland's document to bits albeit the chairman of the Court of Directors on receipt of a copy thought it 'an admirable document', as did John McNeill in Teheran.

Appended to the declaration was a list of eight political appointments. These were as follows:

1. Mr W.H. Macnaghten. Secretary to the Government to assume the functions of Envoy and Minister on the part of the Government of India at the Court of Shah Shuja-ul-Mulk. Mr Macnaghten will be assisted by the following officers.
2. Captain Alexander Burnes, of the Bombay Establishment, who will be employed under Mr Macnaghten's direction as Envoy to the Chief of Kelat, or other states.
3. Lieutenant E. D'Arcy Todd, of the Bengal Artillery, to be Political Assistant and Military Secretary to the Envoy and Minister.
4. Lieutenant Eldred Pottinger, of the Bombay Engineers, to be Political Assistant to the Envoy and Minister.
5. Lieutenant Robert Leech, of the Bombay Engineers, to be Political Assistant to the Envoy and Minister.
6. Doctor Percival Lord, of the Bombay Medical Establishment, to be Political Assistant to the Envoy and Minister.
7. Lieutenant E.B. Conolly, of 6th Bengal Cavalry, to command the escort of the Envoy and Minister, and to be Military Assistant. (This officer also happened to be Mr Macnaghten's nephew).
8. 8. Doctor George Berwick, of the Bengal Medical Establishment, to be Surgeon to the Envoy and Minister.

On 15 October, a further seven officers were added to the growing list of politicos eventually totalling, over the whole escapade, 120.

10 Colvin, *Rulers of India*, p.120.

The two Bengal divisions, numbering 15,000 men, set off for Ferozepore in brigade groups along three routes. Routes had to be different to ensure that enough feed could be foraged for the hundreds of animals involved. They covered the 205 miles in 14 marches, and by 22 November they were all assembled in one huge camp outside and to the south-west of the small town of Ferozepore. Shah Shuja's force of 6,000 left Ludhiana on 15 November and covered the distance of 81 miles in eight days. The Commander-in-Chief and his staff arrived on 25 November and the Governor General and his entourage, which included the wives of his senior staff, arrived on 27 November having left Simla on 7 November. The reason for this big gathering at Ferozepore was that it had been agreed that further *éclat* was to be given to the opening of the campaign with a ceremonial meeting between the Governor General and the Maharaja, Ranjit Singh, who arrived with an army of 10,000 Sikhs on 20 November. Significantly, Shah Shuja was not included in the party, probably because he had to be seen leading his own army and not part of the British force. The assembly of 20,000 troops, not including the Sikhs, in the arid surrounds of Ferozepore, comprised elephants in the hundreds, horses and camels in the thousands and camp followers in the tens of thousands, clearly a logistics nightmare made worse by the necessary trappings for a *bhurra tamasha*; with Ranjit Singh around, this was to be a bacchanalian affair. Some idea of the commissary needs for the Bengal contingent alone is given by *Fakir* Aijazuddin in his book *The Resourceful Fakirs*, in which he has calculated 100,000 fowls, 20,000 *maunds* of wheat, 60,000 *maunds* of *mooth*, 40,000 *maunds* of fuel, 15,000 eggs per day, 4,000 chickens per day and 3,000 *dangalis* of milk. These requisitions made on the Sikhs by Lieutenant Colonel Wade were calculated to cost 300,000 rupees.

During the preparations for the big jamboree *Fakir* Aizizuddin had informed Ranjit Singh that generals Allard and Avitabile had reported from Peshawar that Dost Mohammed had kindled up fires of fighting and war and they had recommended an immediate counter-attack. The Maharaja instructed *Fakir* Azizuddin to sound out the 'Captain Sahib's advice, which was that any pre-emptive action at this point would be premature. This report by the two generals was possibly baseless, but it did demonstrate to the British the Sikhs' eagerness and readiness to assume operations.

As the troops pitched their tents and smartened up for the inevitable parades and inspections, they were informed by General Order that the siege of Herat had been raised and that although the expedition across the Indus was not to be abandoned, many of them would now be surplus to requirements:

ORDERS BY THE RIGHT HONOURABLE THE GOVERNOR GENERAL OF INDIA 8 NOVEMBER 1838

The Right Honourable the Governor General of India is pleased to publish, for general information, the subjoined extract of a letter from Lieutenant Colonel Stoddart, dated Herat the 10th September, and addressed to the Secretary to the Government of India.

I have the honour, by direction of Her Britannic Majesty's Envoy Extraordinary and Minister Plenipotentiary, and the Honourable East India Company's Envoy at the Court of Persia, to acquaint you, for the information of the Right Honourable the Governor General of India in Council, that His Majesty the Shah of Persia yesterday raised the siege of this city, and with the whole of the royal camp marched to Songbust, about twelve miles, on his return to his own domains. His Majesty proceeds without delay, by Torrbut Sheki Jaum and Meshid to Teheran.

This is in fulfilment of His Majesty's compliance with the demands of the British Government, which I had the honour of delivering on 12 inst, and of the whole of which His Majesty announced his acceptance on the 14th August.

His Majesty Shah Kamran and his Vuzeer Yah Mahomed Khan, and the whole city, feel sensible of the sincerity of the friendship of the British Government, and Mr Pottinger and myself fully participate in their gratitude to Providence for the happy event I have now the honour to report.'

In giving publicity to this important intelligence, the Governor General deems it proper at the same time to notify, that while he regards the relinquishment by the Shah of Persia of his hostile designs upon Herat as a just cause of congratulation to the Government of British India and its allies, he will continue to prosecute with vigour the measures which have been announced, with a view to the substitution of a friendly for a hostile power in the eastern provinces of Afghanistan, and to the establishment of a permanent barrier against schemes of aggression upon our northwest frontier.

The Right Honourable the Governor General is pleased to appoint Lieutenant Eldred Pottinger, of the Bombay Artillery to be Political Agent at Herat, subject to the orders of the Envoy and Minister at the Court of Shah Shuja-ool-Moolk. This appointment is to have effect from 9th September last, the date on which the siege of Herat was raised by the Shah of Persia.

In conferring the above appointment upon Lieutenant Pottinger, the Governor General is glad of the opportunity afforded him of bestowing the high applause which is due to the singular merits of that officer, who was present in Herat during the whole period of the protracted siege, and who, under circumstances of peculiar danger and difficulty, has, by his fortitude, ability and judgement, honourably sustained the reputation and interests of his country.

By order of the Right Honourable, the Governor General of India.
(Signed) W.H. Macnaghten.
Secretary to the Government of India,
With the Governor General.

The report received by the Governor General gave him a much fuller account of what had occurred at Herat. No doubt, the Shah of Persia must have been influenced in his decision to raise the siege by the failure of his abortive attack on 24 June, the lack of promised Russian material support, and the implied threat of the Tripartite Treaty. The likelihood of having to face British troops advancing from Kandahar, with a British force already in his rear at Khang was a gamble he wisely declined to take, and he chose to retire gracefully to his domains with dignity.

While the latter part of this General Order is a textbook citation for a Distinguished Service Order (DSO) for the luckily placed Lieutenant Pottinger, the fourth paragraph proved to be a self-inflicted wound. His decision to continue with British participation in the operation, clearly prompted by his immediate expert 'Indian' advisers, was justly attacked by Sir John Kaye and others. In his book *History of the War in Afghanistan*, Sir John maintained that once the siege of Herat had been raised it cut from under the feet of Lord Auckland all grounds for justification of the British expedition across the Indus; that the Tripartite Treaty did not pledge the British Government to send a single soldier beyond the frontier; that the despatch of the British army into the heart of Afghanistan (described by Ranjit Singh as adding sugar to milk), was no part of the covenant either with Ranjit Singh or Shah Shuja; that the British Government had only pledged to raise, pay for and officer a force for Shah Shuja, who had himself expressed an eager hope that he would be allowed to advance as an independent prince, not as a mere British puppet.

However, Kaye was not there; those on the spot, without the value of hindsight, obviously had a perplexing situation on their hands and all decisions in politico-warfare run the risk of being wrong, these decisions are all based on the best intelligence available at the time, and it is the interpretation of this intelligence, even in today's world of instant communication, which allows human frailties and bias to creep in. On the one hand, thankfully, the Persian threat had been removed, but that still left Herat exposed to menaces by the Barakzais (Dost Mohammed Khan did eventually take Herat in 1863), and the Amir in Kabul, plied with enough Russian cash, could still make a grab for Peshawar as he had done in 1836, causing the whole of the Indus valley to erupt in chaos, thus presenting the awesome likelihood of a clash of *sepoy* and cossack on the Sutlej. Besides, Lord Auckland's desired 'rampart' had very little chance of success if left solely to an army of raw recruits led by the luckless Shah Shuja. With these 'worst case scenarios' in mind, Lord Auckland felt compelled to continue with his bold strike, and at the start it had a good measure of success.

The Commander-in-Chief calculated that as the Russian-backed Persian threat had been removed and the prospect of Russian *shashkas* and British bayonets clashing reduced, the size of the British force could also be reduced; but as the Bombay contingent had already sailed, this reduction was to be made from the Bengal contingent. He also issued an order stating that, under the altered circumstances, command of the Bengal contingent was to be assumed by Major General Sir Willoughby Cotton, the Second Division under Major General Alexander Duncan was to remain near the Sutlej with its headquarters at Ferozepore, and the Fifth Brigade plus a troop of horse artillery would be moved to Ludhiana. The other brigade and field batteries were to remain at Ferozepore. This reduced the Bengal contingent to 9,500 men. This was a huge disappointment to the 'stay behind' subalterns hungering for a chance at 'glory'. To decide who these unfortunates were, the extraordinary measure of drawing lots was used, consequently regiments at full strength, HM 3rd Foot were to stand down while HM 13th Foot, plagued by sickness and way understrength, was selected for the advance. Of the seven newly appointed brigadiers, Graham, Dennis and Worsley were ordered to stand down, and logically also the regiments they had recently been commanding. In regard to Brigadier Graham, he was made to remain behind as Brigadier Thomas Stevenson of the Bombay Artillery, being senior to him, would assume command of the artillery of the Army of the Indus. The command of the Army of the Indus was to be assumed by Lieutenant General Sir John Keane once the two contingents joined up in the Sindh. General Sir Henry Fane, not in the best of health and not too happy of being placed under the direction of the Envoy, took the opportunity to submit his resignation once he had handed over the Army of the Indus to Lieutenant General Keane. After the changes the final order of battle for the Bengal contingent was as follows:

Commander: Major General Sir Willoughby Cotton

First Infantry Brigade: Commander: Brigadier R.H. Sale

	HM 13th Foot 16th Bengal Native Infantry 48th Bengal Native Infantry
Second Infantry Brigade:	Commander: Brigadier W. Nott 31st Bengal Native Infantry 42nd Bengal Native Infantry 43rd Bengal Native Infantry
Fourth Infantry Brigade:	Commander: Brigadier A. Roberts 1st Bengal European Regiment 35th Bengal Native Infantry 37th Bengal Native Infantry
Bengal Artillery:	Commander: Major Peter Pew 2nd Troop, 2nd Bengal Horse Artillery 4th Company, 2nd Battalion Artillery 2nd Company, 6th Battalion Artillery[11]
Cavalry Brigade:	Commander: Brigadier R. Arnold[12] HM 16th Lancers 2nd Bengal Light Cavalry 3rd Bengal Light Cavalry 4th Local Horse
Sappers & Miners:	Commander: Captain Edward. Sanders 2nd Company 3rd Company

The Bombay contingent left Bombay by sea on 21 November and comprised the under listed. They arrived at the mouth of the Indus on 27 November and because the move was by sea they did not have any camels nor the ubiquitous crowd of camp followers, consequently they had to rely on the Bengal contingent for much of their commissary needs, much to the irritation of the latter.

Commander:	Lieutenant General Sir John Keane
Divisional Commander:	Major General Thomas Willshire
Infantry Brigade:	Commander: Brigadier John Baumgradt

11 This was an experimental camel battery, which was left in Ferozepore.

12 Brigadier Arnold was not a well man. He had recently taken command of his fine regiment and was determined lead it into this war. He was a veteran of Waterloo where he had been shot in the lungs and miraculously survived. Just before the assembly of the Army of the Indus, at a dinner party with Major General Cotton, Arnold was just about to take wine with the General when he burst a blood vessel and almost choked.

	HM 2nd Foot
	HM 17th Foot
	19th Bombay Native Infantry
	Sappers & Miners
Cavalry Brigade:	Commander: Major General Joseph Thackwell.[13]
	Lieutenant Colonel J. Scott
	Wing of 14th Light Dragoons
	1st Bombay Light Cavalry
	Poona Local Horse
Artillery Commander:	Brigadier Thomas Stevenson
	3rd Troop Horse Artillery
	4th Troop Artillery
	Horse field battery

Despite recently suffering a stroke, Ranjit Singh put his heart and soul into the preparations for this historic meeting with the Governor General of the paramount power in India, and the first ever encounter of the two armies. It was to be like a royal tournament over eight days interwoven with interviews, discussions, parades, inspections, feasting and dancing. This spectacle was only to be surpassed by the Great Delhi *durbar* staged by Lord Curzon 40 years later. The stage managers of the Ferozepore carnival were the indefatigable Captain Wade and *Fakir* Azizuddin.

Ranjit Singh's camp was located on the right bank of the Sutlej and he had a bridge of boats built across the river strong enough to take two elephants at any one time. He had *Fakir* Azizuddin prepare a list of Sikh VIPs who were to accompany him at his meeting with the British, these included: *Kunwar* Kharak Singh his heir, Raja Sher Singh also his son, Raja Gulab Singh later described by Sir Henry Hardinge as 'the biggest scoundrel in the Punjab', the Raja's brother the dashing Raja Suchet Singh, Raja Hira Singh the son of the Maharaja's chief minister, Jamadar Khushal Singh the Maharaja's old confidant and all-purpose Jeeves, Attar Singh, Ajit Singh, Lehna Singh all of the Sandhanwalia clan and distant relations of the Maharaja, and Nihal Singh Ahluwalia the son of the deceased Fateh Singh Ahluwalia, the Maharaja's brother-in-arms. They were all to wear brocade or *kimkhab* and 'whosoever would be wearing white clothes would be debarred from meeting the Sarkar'.[14]

On Wednesday 28 November *Kunwar* Kharak Singh paid a welcome call on the Governor General. He was met by John Colvin and escorted to Lord Auckland's huge tent. The next day

13 On 16 November, the Commander-in-Chief had written to Major General J. Thackwell stating, 'I have persuaded the Government that the Army of the Indus should have a chief; and I have therefore named you, and an order goes to you today to join us as soon as you can. P.S. I think that you may bring up an Aide-de-Camp if desirable.' Thackwell selected Cornet Edmund Roche of HM 3rd Light Dragoons, his wife's brother. Major General Thackwell joined the Army of the Indus on 19 December.

14 Aijazuddin, *The Resourceful Fakirs*, p.219.

Major General Cotton returned the compliment by calling on the Maharaja and 'came back very tipsy', according to Emily Eden.

On Thursday 29 November the stage was set for the meeting of the two heads of state. The Maharaja crossed the river seated in the *howdah* on his favourite elephant, Raja. Lord Auckland, seated in the *howdah* of his elephant, met the Maharaja on the British side of the river. In a symbolic gesture, Ranjit Singh left his sword, dagger and other arms in his own *howdah* and joined Lord Auckland in his. Sir John Kaye describes this event rather disparagingly as, 'Lord Auckland, in his uniform of diplomatic blue, was seen to take a bundle of crimson cloth out of the Sikh *howdah*, and it was known that the Lion of the Punjab was then seated on the elephant of the English rule.' He goes on to write 'Then the huge phalanx of elephants was set in motion again. There was a rush towards the Durbar tent – the English and Sikh cortege were mixed up together in one great mass of animal life. Such was the crush – such was the struggle – that many of the attendant Sikhs believed that there was a design to destroy their old decrepit chief and began to blow their matches and grasp their weapons with an air of mingled distrust and ferocity.'[15] A more balanced view of this rush into the *durbar* tent has been given by Emily, Lord Auckland's sister. 'The Sikhs were very unmanageable and they rushed in on all sides, and the European officers were rather worse.'[16] It was on this occasion that Ranjit Singh was presented with a portrait of Queen Victoria, painted by Emily; she was also to describe Ranjit Singh as 'a little grey mouse with whiskers'. Interestingly, according to Chinese mythology Ranjit Singh was born in the year of the Rat. It was during this event that Emily Eden drew a sketch of the Maharaja, which according to Joseph Cunningham, who was well acquainted with the Maharaja, wrote that the sketch was a 'true likeness'.[17]

On the following day, Lord Auckland paid his return visit to the Maharaja. Reciprocating Ranjit Singh's gesture, Auckland shifted from his *howdah* to that of his host and they both then went to the Sikh camp. Kaye described this event as, 'In a scene of oriental splendour, difficult to describe or imagine, the Sikh King received the representative of the British nation.' The splendid costumes of the Sikh Sardars – the gorgeous trappings of their horses – the glittering steel casques and corslets of chain armour – the scarlet and yellow dresses – the tents of crimson and gold – made up a show of Eastern magnificence equally grand and picturesque.[18] Another observer was to comment, 'The Sikhs shone down the English.' Then, again, Kaye in the censorious tone of Victorians:

> The evening entertainments were still less decorous. It was a melancholy thing to see the open exhibition, even on this great public occasion, of all those low vices which were destroying the life, and damning the reputation of a man, in whom were some of the elements of heroism who, indeed, but for these degrading sensualities, would have been one of the greatest, as he was one of the most remarkable, men of modern times.

At three o'clock in the afternoon on the Saturday, Lord Auckland called on the Maharaja, this time to specifically discuss matters of policy, but the old fellow did not talk much business, leaving such issues in the capable hands of *Fakir* Azizuddin and Macnaghten. Quite clearly,

15 Kaye, *The History of the War in Afghanistan*, Vol. I, p.374.
16 Aijazuddin, *The Resourceful Fakirs*, p.220.
17 Cunningham, *A History of the Sikhs*, p.314.
18 Kaye, *The History of the War in Afghanistan*, Vol. 1, p.375.

Ranjit Singh had no desire to be put on the spot by any awkward inquiry. Instead, on the Sunday while the British were busy attending church services and sky-racing,[19] Ranjit Singh had *Fakir* Azizuddin deliver a memorandum about the return of the British army through Sikh territory. He was seeking British assurances that the troops would avoid killing kine, that such passage would not be taken as a precedent, that the route was to be stipulated by the Sikh *durbar* and that the troops would respect the local authorities and pass through without delay. Apart from the issue of the route, the British agreed to all the points, and also to the Maharaja's request for two 24-pdr howitzers, 'ready for field service'; these eventually arrived in Lahore on 19 February 1839 commanded by a bespectacled Lieutenant William Barr of the Bengal Artillery. The British on their part requested the Maharaja's acquiescence to the establishment of garrisons at Ferozepore and Shikarpore, that he should overtly support Shah Shuja and that a British resident be appointed at Lahore. The Maharaja was to agree to the first two points, but to the appointment of a resident he was adamantly opposed, that would have been worse than having his mother-in-law, Sada Kaur,[20] back in the fold. However, under totally different circumstances, there was to be a resident in Lahore within 10 years.

On the following Monday, after the thick mist had risen, Maharaja Ranjit Singh arrived to inspect the three-mile line of British troops, then to receive the salute of each regiment as it marched past the Maharaja and the Governor General mounted on their horses. This parade was probably not much different to the Trooping of the Colour, a glorious display of military precision and a marvellous spectacle. The rest of the day was spent in continued discussions and negotiations. The following morning, the Maharaja attended a demonstration by the Bengal Artillery to show off its awesome firepower. Unfortunately, Lord Auckland thought that they had put on 'a very poor show'. It was during the inspection of the guns that the Maharaja stumbled and fell flat on his face; he was not hurt, but the omen of falling in front of British guns was considered an unlucky one.

On Wednesday 5 December it was the turn of the Sikhs to show off their prowess and Ranjit Singh made sure there was to be no slip-up at this opportunity to impress his British allies; he was not to be disappointed. According to Fanny Eden, 'All our people are in astonishment at the state of his discipline, and the very superior way in which they performed their manoeuvres. Our review was a remarkably poor piece of business compared to theirs.'[21] Her sister Emily was also of the same opinion, who wrote the next day:

> All the gentlemen went at daybreak yesterday to Ranjit's review and came back rather discomfited. He had as many troops out as Sir G.R. [Fane] had, they quite as well disciplined, rather better dressed, repeated the same military movements, and several others much more complicated and, in short, nobody knows what to say about it, so they say nothing except that they are sure the Sikhs would run away in a real fight. It is a sad blow to our vanities.[22]

19 'Sky-Racing', a euphemism for a daytime snooze known as 'Egyptian P.T.'

20 Sada Kaur was the mother of Ranjit Singh's first wife, and the grandmother of Sher Singh and his twin Tara Singh. At the beginning of his career, Ranjit Singh got a great deal of vital support from this lady, but once at the top he seems to have sidelined her. She nagged him incessantly for support for her grandsons until she and Ranjit Singh had a major falling-out. She died in seclusion in 1823.

21 Aijazuddin, *The Resourceful Fakirs*, p.227.

22 Aijazuddin, *The Resourceful Fakirs*, p.227.

On 6 December Maharaja Ranjit Singh decamped and moved to Amritsar, the soul of Sikhism. Lord Auckland and his party then struck camp and accompanied by Raja Sher Singh followed the Maharaja to Amritsar, a distance of 150 miles, and arrived on 12 December. Meanwhile, Major General Cotton's division, accompanied by the Commander-in-Chief, struck camp and marched out on their long haul to Afghanistan, leaving the dejected 'Buffs', at full strength, to retrace their steps back to their barracks in Meerut. The Governor General's party were in Amritsar for seven days: they were given a tour of this important Sikh city, including a tour of the celebrated Golden Temple, the Rambagh Gardens and the Gobindgarh Fort which housed Ranjit's treasure and bullion and was under the protection of *Fakir* Imamuddin, Azizuddin's younger brother. While on the road to Amritsar Lord Auckland had written to Sir John Hobhouse confirming his satisfaction with proceedings so far:

> Runjeet Singh observed that we are two brothers, the two nations are but one, the armies of the one are the armies of the other. We discussed Cabul and Herat. Some understanding upon the plan of the campaign was arrived at, so that there may not be too costly a collision between the Sikhs and the Afghans, or if possible, no collision at all, and lastly, a return of our army from Cabul through his territories.[23]

Sadly, the last point in Lord Auckland's letter, albeit verbally agreed by the Maharaja was never reduced to writing,[24] a vital point overlooked by newly promoted Lieutenant Colonel Wade and Macnaghten, much to the cost of the former.

Having 'done' Amritsar, the Governor General's party followed the Maharaja to Lahore, the seat of the Sikh government, They covered the distance of 26 miles in two marches arriving on 19 December (Auckland Colvin in his book says that they arrived on 21 December, whereas *Fakir* Aijazuddin gives the date used in this account). In Lahore Lord Auckland was to be the honoured guest of the Lion of the Punjab. He was the very first governor general to visit Lahore, the second most important city of Moghul India. The next governor general to visit was Sir Henry Hardinge, Lord Auckland's successor, but he arrived as the victor of the First Anglo-Sikh War, eight years later.

There was much to do and see in this imperial city, besides more inspections of the Maharaja's troops, attendance at numerous feasts and continued consultations about the joint campaign. Lieutenant Colonel Wade bore the brunt of diplomatic activity, as Macnaghten had remained in Ferozepore to accompany Shah Shuja in his march on Afghanistan and Captain Burnes had been sent in advance to smooth the passage of the following army by negotiating sources of supply and buying-off sources of mischief, neither of which he did all that well. Macnaghten's previous role as secretary to the Government was handed over to Mr Thomas Maddock.

During the Governor General's time in Lahore, the Maharaja again fell ill and there was some question as to whether the visit should continue. However, there were still a number of issues that still required clarification and confirmation in writing. Maharaja Ranjit Singh had been most concerned about the role the British envisaged for their representative at the Maharaja's camp. Clearly, he would have preferred that these officers were 'under command',

23 Aijazuddin, *The Resourceful Fakirs*, p.222.
24 Aijazuddin, *The Resourceful Fakirs*, p.240.

whereas the British in a communiqué dated 10 December, sent by Mr Colvin, opted for the more strident role of 'in support' and 'in command':

> Fakir Axeeezoodeen [*sic*: Azizuddin] mentioned that His Highness wished to know what duties were to be performed by the British officers deputed to His Highness's Camp and what relation they were to bear towards the officers of His Highness's army.
>
> In answer it is stated that the British officers referred to will attend to any orders that they may receive from the Maharaja provided they are deemed unobjectionable by Major Wade, who not only enjoys the full confidence and esteem of the Governor General but is an old and esteemed friend of the Maharaja, and the Governor General is satisfied that His Highness will pay close attention to the counsels of that officer.
>
> The officers in question may if Major Wade thinks fit be employed to assist him in the duties of his office, or may be sent on mission, or may be employed in disciplining the troops who may join the Shahzada.
>
> It will be in the recollection of the Maharaja that when Mr Macnaghten was deputed at Lahore it was agreed that if the *Shahzada* Timoor should join the Maharaja's Camp he should be treated with the greatest esteem.
>
> The object of the above understanding is that the designs of the two high Powers should be accomplished in the most easy and expeditious manner possible without difficulty and fighting, with view to the same object.[25]

Ranjit Singh had also been agitating for a written agreement to consummate the Governor General's visit to the Sikh Kingdom; ever suspicious, he was probably concerned as to what may happen after he had left the stage. The Governor General said that it would be done and on the last day of his historic visit a memorandum was handed to *Fakir* Azizuddin to be given to the Maharaja. This much sought after document included the reaffirmation of British recognition of the Maharaja's control and authority over his dominions, 'generation after generation'.

On the eve of his departure, Lord Auckland sent a farewell message to Ranjit Singh by hand of *Fakir* Azizuddin stating that he had left greatly pleased with the meeting and was very grateful to the Sarkar for the respect, regard, hospitality and treatment and courtesy shown to him. In a much longer letter to his friend Sir John Hobhouse, Lord Auckland wrote:

> The old man's illness threw a languor over the last days of my visit, for all were in some degree uneasy about him. I have left him with a strong impression of his sagacity and shrewdness, and at the same time, of his suspicious habits and uncertainty of opinion, combined with a great firmness of purpose.
>
> Yet a plan of operation in the ensuing campaign for the Sikh army was decided – it was a delicate matter to insist that nothing should be done by a Sikh soldier except with the advice and instance of a British political agent. Yet this, and all else that was asked for was cheerfully acquiesced in, and if well adhered to, it will be of great importance, for we are generally promised co-operation by the hill chieftains of Afghanistan on the side of Peshawar, unless the Sikh army should advance, and then main difficulty with which we

25 Aijazuddin, *The Resourceful Fakirs*, p.230.

> may have to contend will be that of remaining at once friends both with the Sikhs and the Afghans, whose natural feelings are keenly alive with mutual hatred most bitter.[26]

On his departure, the Governor General also said his farewell to Lieutenant Colonel Wade, and no doubt pressed on him the importance of his role with the Sikh army and the confidence he had of a successful outcome. As His Lordship made his way south, the 'Captain Sahib' headed north towards Peshawar. Lieutenant Colonel Wade was replaced in Ludhiana by Mr George Clerk, who had been the political agent at Ambala, a man of no mean talent, extremely well connected, but no reader of the Sikh mind.

Maharaja Ranjit Singh, lying on his sickbed and being attended to by his doctors and his faithful *Fakir* Azizuddin, must have felt very pleased with himself and also concerned at what the 'party' had cost and how much this joint venture was to bleed his treasury. At one point he had asked the 'Captain Sahib' how much the operation into Afghanistan would cost, to which Wade had replied, '20 *crores* of rupees'.[27] It was to cost a great deal more, not including the priceless reputation of the invincibility of the British Army.

26 Aijazuddin, *The Resourceful Fakirs*, p.241.
27 Aijazuddin, *The Resourceful Fakirs*, p.219.

8

Advance to Afghanistan – The Promenade

According to the old adage, the path to hell is paved with good intentions; the advance on Afghanistan was, likewise, paved with as many good intentions as there were miles, but these good intentions were marred by the fact that it had never been made clear to the participants whether the advance was a heavily escorted diplomatic mission commissioned to place a rightful and popular king on the throne of his ancestors, or a military invasion of an independent country to effect a regime change. According to Richard Kennedy, the Indian Parsi entrepreneur in Bombay, Jamsetji Jeejeebhoy, who was a key supplier of provisions for the army, declared the venture as the conquest of Afghanistan.[1] While the politicians clung to the euphoria of the former, the local inhabitants concluded it to be the latter and the military baulked at the political restrictions imposed on it. As the army advanced, conditions became further confused by petty jealousies, inflated egos, bad intelligence, a paucity of carriage and young political officers galloping around the country in wild attempts to enhance their reputations, confoundedly impressed with their own importance and with no idea of the army's role in the campaign. In the book containing Lieutenant Colonel William Dennie's personal narrative it is stated that a letter in *The Times*, signed by H. Fane, stated that the Commander-in-Chief had submitted his resignation 'disgusted with the intermeddling of the officials in military matters'. In addition, much to the displeasure of the Commander-in-Chief, Lord Auckland had given the task of organising provisions and animals for the advancing army to Macnaghten and his political officers. As Henry Durand was to write, 'The attempt to separate the conduct of political affairs in a military expedition from that of the army is futile. The two are essentially co-joined and do not admit severance, because one is styled envoy and the other commander.'[2]

The route selected for the advance of the Bengal Division and Shah Shuja's force was along the left bank of the Sutlej, through the territories of Bahawalpur, then across the Indus at Sukkur passing through Shikarpore, Bhag and Dadur at the mouth of the Bolan Pass; through that Pass to Quetta then on through the Khojak Pass to Kandahar; thence to Kabul via Ghazni. A long logistic nightmare of 1,200 miles, through mostly desert, as opposed to a more direct route of half that distance through a verdant Punjab via Peshawar and the Khyber Pass. The selection of this

1 Richard Kennedy, *Narrative of the Campaign of the Army of the Indus in Sind and Kaubool in 1838-9* (London: Bentley, 1840; ULAN Press reprint, n.d.), p.186.
2 Durand, *The First Afghan War and Its Causes*, p.196.

route had its origin in the 1834 treaty between Ranjit Singh and Shah Shuja, according to which the Shah was to advance via the Sindh in order to subjugate the Sindhis and have them pay him his rightful tributes, while Ranjit Singh was to advance from Peshawar up the Khyber Pass and on to Kabul. This scheme remained in the tripartite Treaty of 1838; consequently, the Bengal Column was required to follow the same route as the Shah and to assist him in collecting his due tributes, much to the chagrin of the Commander-in-Chief. Another, equally important, reason for the selection of the route was that Maharaja Ranjit Singh was adamantly opposed to British boots on his side of the treaty river. While it took the Bengal Column 35 days on 'Shanks's pony' to reach the Sindh, the Bombay Column was on its shores in eight days, courtesy of requisitioned ships.

The first 230 miles from Ferozepore to Bahawalpur was a relatively easy hike made up of 18 marches. The Bengal Column left Ferozepore on 10 December and marched in five columns proceeded by the engineers, sappers and miners. Shah Shuja's force had left three days earlier and passed through Ferozepore on 2 December; Major Todd, the Envoy's military secretary, accompanied Shah Shuja while the Envoy advanced with the main column.

The Shah's earlier start was designed to give him the precedence which he most anxiously claimed. Ostensibly this force was under the military command of Major General Edward Simpson, who laboured under the political authority of the envoy and British minister at the court of Shah Shuja-ul-Mulk, William Macnaghten.

The army advanced with 30 days' supplies of all kinds loaded on 14,235 camels moving at a rate of two miles per hour. If lined up head to tail, the camels would have stretched the length of a marathon. The camel was the main mode of conveyance for an army in India, and according to John Masters, 'the camel wears a conceited and abominably supercilious look because, it was into a camel's ear that the Prophet Mohammed whispered the hundredth name of God'. Much of these supplies could have been sent down the river in barges, but there were only enough boats to carry the sick, a field hospital and 10 barges for General Sir Henry Fane and his entourage. In addition to this vast number of supply camels, the army had two and a half months worth of slaughter cattle, on the hoof, plus horses and camels belonging to the cavalry and horse artillery, and the private hire of such animals by the officers who could afford them; a massive herd of about 30,000 animals, and topping this count there were 13 elephants, two for the exclusive use of the Envoy. This vast array of four-legged creatures was accompanied by the ubiquitous, two-legged, camp followers amounting to 38,000 men, women, and children. Despite orders from the Commander-in-Chief to keep baggage down to the basic minimum, with an official allocation of five camels for lieutenant colonels, two for each subaltern and one between seven soldiers totalling 200 for each Queen's regiment and 150 for each native regiment, a good many officers saw fit to equip themselves with creature comforts far in excess of essential campaign needs, thus causing this army advance to be referred to later in the House of Commons, as a 'picnic'. Brigadier Robert Arnold was credited with having 80 camels to carry his baggage and 'goodies', two of which were loaded with his cigars and snuff. There is no record of how many were assigned to carry his campaign wine cellar, however these must have been quite a few judging by the reported amounts available for auction after his untimely death, of a liver complaint. He is also said to have taken 60 servants with him,[3] while Major General

3 Ben Macintyre, *The Man Who Would Be King: The First American in Afghanistan* (New York: Farrar Straus & Giroux, 2004), p.241.

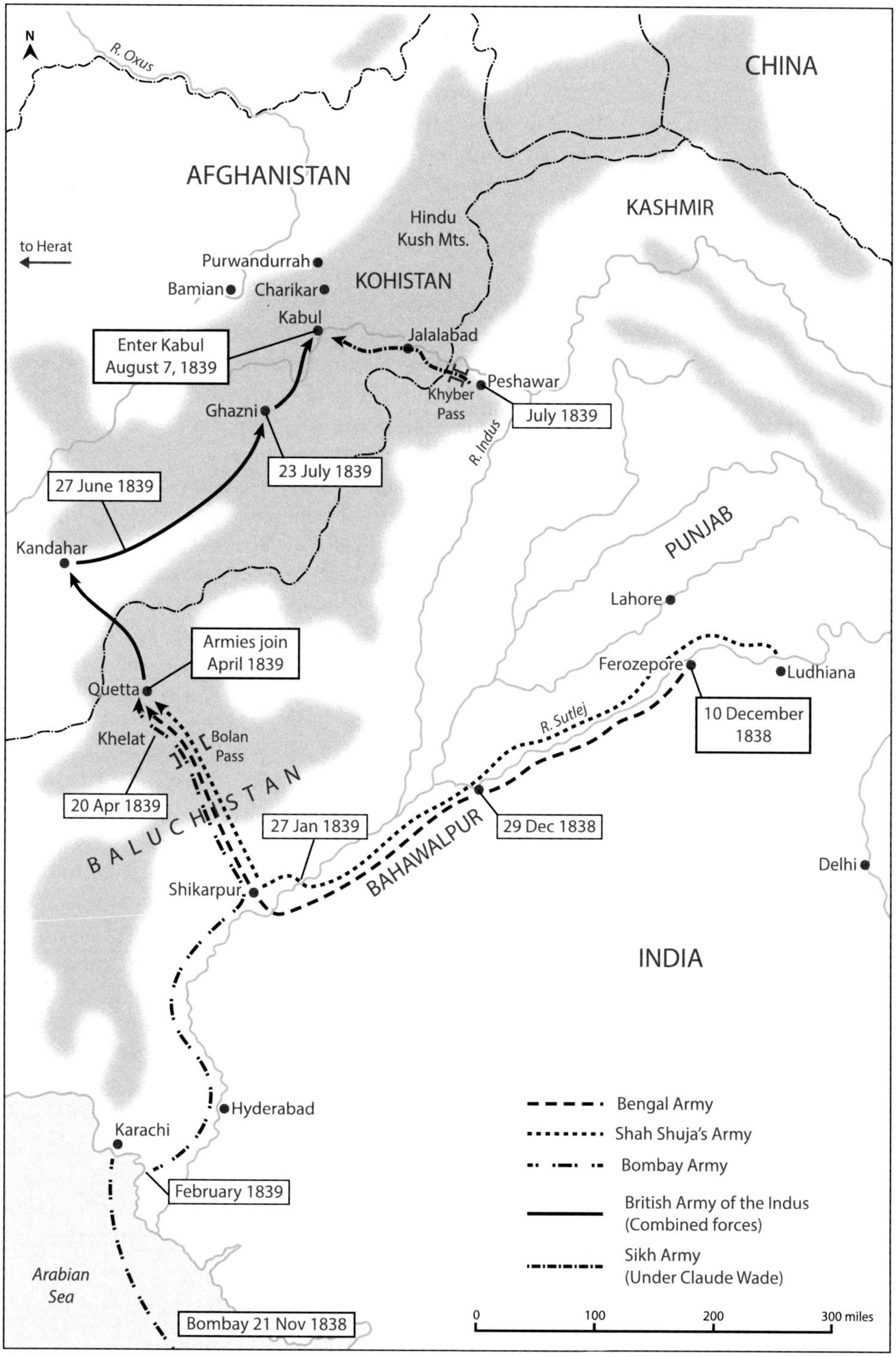

Map 5 Army of the Indus routes for the invasion of Afghanistan.

Cotton is credited as having only 20 camels. No doubt these gentlemen adhered to the old army school of thought that any damn fool can be uncomfortable. To ensure they were not deprived of their regular sport, the officers of HM 16th Lancers took their pack of greyhounds with them.

All these camp followers, comprising *dhooli* bearers, *oot wallahs* (camel herders), cooks, grass cutters, sweepers and servants, plus all the animals, formed the 'baggage train', which came under the control of the Commissariat Department. A good pictorial idea of what a baggage train looked like in those days can be gained from the long scroll painted by Henry and John Crealock which can be viewed at the National Army Museum.[4] As an Afghan once remarked to Captain George Lawrence, 'You are an army of tents and camels, ours of men and horses.'[5] In modern times the Afghan horses have been replaced by Honda 50cc motorbikes.

The baggage animals were hired from local contractors, and besides the hire charge they were compensated for a dead animal if they could produce the ears and tail, but nothing for an animal that was lost or stolen. This gave rise to a very lucrative line of business. A rich merchant, Jeytt Singh, bought in Shikarpore 'lost' camels at 20 rupees and sold them on to the Commissariat Department for 50 rupees; however, a stop was put to this by the novel idea of branding the animals. A dead or lost camel equated to loss of carriage of one days ration for 160 men. As the column advanced these losses increased, as did the cost of replacement. In those days modern financial facilities did not exist, there was no paper money and no machinery for extended credit. Each campaign had to be financed with chests full of coins, closely guarded and carried in bullock carts, and the Bengal Column had a 'treasure chest' of 25 *lakhs* of rupees. William Hough in his book, *A Narrative of the March and Operations of the Army of the Indus*, calculated that the loss of animals during the advance came to a staggering 11,000 camels, 1,350 horses, 620 bullocks and three elephants, costing 16 *lakhs* of rupees, equivalent to £11.8 million in today's money.

The infantry were organised in regiments of eight companies each of 100 soldiers. The soldiers were armed with the muzzle-loading 'Brown Bess' and its 16-inch bayonet. The 'Brown Bess' had a range of 300 yards, but was only accurate at 100, and an experienced soldier could fire two rounds per minute. Percussion caps had replaced the flintlock in 1835, thus reducing the number of misfires, and allowed the weapon to be fired in wet and damp conditions without the need to keep the firing pan dry. The soldiers were uniformed in red coats, black leather cross belts, close-fitting grey trousers, black leather stocks and a shako. Interestingly, the Indian bazaars that sprang up in the close vicinity to garrisoned troops were called *Lal Khurthi* (red coats) bazaars, and many such bazaars have retained this name to this day, such as in Rawalpindi.

The soldier carried 60 rounds of ammunition in a pack, a water bottle and a haversack and with his musket the total weight he carried was 70 lbs; boots were in three sizes and the same shape for both feet. The shako was made of wicker covered by a black cloth on which was the metal regiment badge. The only piece of equipment the British soldier hated was the leather stock, designed to keep his head up, and in the heat of the Indian climate his morale down. On religious grounds, the native *sepoy* was not required to wear the dreaded stock.

A total of 32 guns of various calibres were hauled to Afghanistan by the Bengal column by soldiers in the employ of the Company. No Royal Artillery units or men were employed in India

4 Ref. 6809-15 (29272).

5 Sir George Lawrence, *Reminiscences of Forty-Three Years in India* (London: J. Murray, 1874; Sang-i-Meel Publications, reprint 1969), p.12.

Shan Sujah's Horse Artillery, First Afghan War by David Rowlands.

until after the Indian Mutiny. Each presidency of the East India Company had one regiment of artillery and service in these was restricted to Europeans, although each included some natives who were known as *Golandaz*, employed mainly as labour and never allowed to work or fire the guns. Depending on the armament, these regiments were divided into brigades, companies, batteries and troops. All the officers were European graduates of the Company's seminary at Addiscombe in Surrey. The cadets sent to Addiscombe were generally the brightest and destined for the Company's artillery or engineer units, and the majority of these young officers went on to have brilliant careers.

Each artillery regiment had its own elite corps of horse artillery. The dress of these artillerymen resembled that of the Royal Horse Artillery (RHA) except for their headgear; instead of the Hussar Busby, the Company's horse artillerymen wore the 'pillbox' cap and the officers a Roman helmet like that of the French cuirassier with its long red mane. The trumpeters in each troop were dressed in reverse colours to the blue jackets with red facings and were mounted on grey or piebald horses. In a General Order of 1838, two troops of horse artillery were formed under the command of Captain William Anderson, for service with Shah Shuja's force. Both troops distinguished themselves during the Afghan Campaign and afterwards were amalgamated into the 5th Troop of the 1st Brigade of the Bengal Horse Artillery, and in 1861 were absorbed into the Royal Horse Artillery.

The armaments of the Company's artillery were divided into four categories, as shown below, along with the normal means of carriage.

Category	**Armament**	**Carriage**
Horse	6-pdr and 12-pdr howitzer	Horses
Field	9-pdr and 24-pdr howitzer	Bullocks
Heavy	18-pdr and 8 inch mortar	Elephants
Mountain	3-pdr	Mules

Four regiments of cavalry rode to Afghanistan with the Bengal Column. In India at that time both Queen's and Company were employed, the very first Queen's regiment being sent out in the eighteenth century and the very first Company regiment being raised in 1726. Queen's regiments generally served in India for a period of nine years; there were exceptions like HM 16th Lancers who served for a total of 16 years before being replaced by HM 9th Lancers. All the Queen's cavalry regiments sent to India were classified as 'light cavalry', each commanded by a lieutenant colonel, with two squadrons commanded by majors, each of two troops commanded by captains, a total of 600 cavalrymen armed with a curved sword or lance and a pistol.

The Company's cavalry were all classified as 'light cavalry' and comprised 10 regiments in the Bengal army, eight in the Madras army and three in the Bombay army. In addition to these there were about 18 'irregular' cavalry regiments. Each of the 'light' regiments consisted of six troops totalling 400 native *sowars* and 24 European officers, armed with swords, pistols and some carbines. The 'irregular' regiments were so named because the cavalrymen had to provide their own horses and care for them. They wore a *pugri* instead of the normal shako and each in an array of colourful uniforms. They were generally named after the officer who initially raised them, for example 'Skinner's Horse'. Besides the commander, there were no more than three other European officers in these 'irregular' regiments, the adjutant, the quartermaster and one other. The horsemen of 'local cavalry' had no recognisable uniform, hence were indistinguishable during clashes with the enemy.

The cavalry have forever been regarded by the infantry as a '*kushi* number' and an old story has it that a Bengal infantry officer named his cat 'Indian Cavalry', because all it did was eat, play, sleep, and fornicate.

On 29 December 1838 the Bengal Column arrived at Bahawalpur, halfway to the Indus. The column was headed by Major General Cotton in his horse-drawn carriage; the commander-in-chief, General Sir Henry Fane, preceded him by a day on his more comfortable boat, on which he remained, while Sir Willoughby quartered himself in the house built by the Khan of Bahawalpur earlier for Lieutenant Frederick Mackeson, the erstwhile superintendent for the navigation of the Indus. The army was encamped to the west of this shabby mud-built town of some 4,000 houses with a population of 20,000.

The next day was a Sunday, and after a short service of prayers the Khan of Bahawalpur was received in *durbar* by the Commander-in-Chief. While the Khan was obviously appreciative of the honour bestowed on him by his British allies, he was equally apprehensive that his guests were about to eat him out of house and home, especially as he had already fed, watered and reinforced Shah Shuja's contingent with 600 recruits. Although he had agreed with Dr Archibald Gordon, the political agent, to make grain and victuals available, he now started to make excuses, causing his allies to remonstrate with him. This was the first indication that despite all the efforts of political agents to pave the path of the advance with assurances of essential supplies, it was not to be, and the consequent deficiency was to cause this 'picnic' to be anything but. Normally the procurement of supplies was the job of the Commissariat Department and its designated contractors. However, as this advance was into areas where the Government of India had no sway, it was considered politically sensitive and therefore the commissariat transactions would be better handled by the assigned 'politicos'. A good idea on paper and quite the opposite on the ground as the inexperienced and gullible 'politicos' charged around making dubious deals and not always in concert with each other, thus making the life of the soldier very uncomfortable in a country which was already pretty uncomfortable.

On the following Monday, amidst bugle calls and gun salutes, the Commander-in-Chief and Major General Cotton returned the Khan's visit. Also on this day, Lieutenant Mackeson arrived from Peshawar on a special mission to recruit levies for the advance up the Khyber Pass, and sadly Lieutenant Colonel Adam Duffin, the Commanding Officer of the 2nd Bengal Light Cavalry, died of exhaustion making him the first casualty in the Bengal Column. The dubious honour of being the very first casualty of the campaign goes to Lieutenant Francis Fyers of HM 4th Light Dragoons, who blew his brains out at Bominacote 20 days earlier. On 3 January the Bengal Column struck camp and advanced to the Sindh, where the British Government had managed, by its arrogance, to stir up a hornet's nest thus placing the grand promenade in jeopardy.

As indicated earlier, it had been the long-time desire of the East India Company to develop the navigation of the Indus for trade, and a prerequisite for this was to keep the reluctant three Amirs of Sindh on side, which the long-serving political agent, Colonel Henry Pottinger, had managed to do by making much of the British action in keeping Maharaja Ranjit Singh out of Shikarpore. However, the Colonel had also created a great deal of negativity by overdramatising the Amirs' friendly communications with the Persian Shah, who was at the time besieging Herat, consequently, in the lexicon of political faithfulness, the Amirs were classified as unreliable. The wretched Amirs found themselves in a tremendous quandary. On the one hand there was no guarantee that the Persian Shah would not sweep into the Sindh after his universally predicted success at Herat; and on the other hand they were most apprehensive about what they regarded as the grasping policies of the British, albeit a British attachment guaranteed to keep the more loathsome Sikhs out of the Sindh. In April 1838, the Sindhis signed a treaty with the British allowing a resident to reside at the Court in Hyderabad and on the insistence of the Amirs the treaty included a clause prohibiting the use of the Indus for military purposes. Then five months later, almost the first-fruit of Colonel Pottinger's new role as resident, he was ordered to convey to the Amirs Lord Auckland's wishes and intentions:

> Their Highnesses have, of course, long heard of the unsettled state of Khorassan and Afghanistan; and, in the opinion of the Governor General, a crisis has now arrived in those countries which imperiously demands the interference of the British Government, both with regard to the settlement and well-being of the countries in question, and also for the tranquillity and security of Hindustan and the states adjoining it.
>
> His Lordship is further of the opinion that it is now necessary that the real friends of the British Government should unequivocally stand forward to evince their friendly feelings by assisting in the measures which the Governor General may consider requisite to frustrate and render null the combination which the governments to the westward of India are known to have formed, with the object of disturbing and injuring the possessions of the British Government, and with them those of its allies and tributaries.
>
> A treaty was made about five years ago between his Majesty Shah Shooja-ool-Moolk and the Maharaja Ranjit Singh, consisting of fourteen articles. In the fourth article of the treaty was written: 'Regarding Shikarpore and the territory of Scinde lying on the right bank of the Indus, the Shah will agree to abide by whatever may be settled as right and proper, in conformity with the happy relations of friendship subsisting between the British Government and the Maharaja, through Captain Wade.
>
> The said treaty was not, for certain reasons, acted on at the time it was first written, but at present it has been resolved to bring it into execution; and the Governor General of India has agreed to become a party to it, with the addition of four articles. One of these articles provides for Maharaja Ranjit Singh receiving annually two lakhs of rupees from the Shah, in consideration of which his Highness is always to keep 5,000 Mussulman troops ready at Peshawur for the king's service when required. Another article stipulates that when Shah Shooja-ool-Moolk shall have established his authority over Cabul, &c, his Majesty is not to make any demands upon or to molest Kamran Shah of Herat. A third article provides for the Shah entering into no negotiations or treaties with any foreign powers without the knowledge and consent of the British and Lahore governments. And a fourth article is to the following effect:
>
> Shah Shooja-ool-Moolk agrees to relinquish for himself, his heirs and successors, all claims of supremacy and arrears of tribute over the country now held by the Ameers of Scinde, which will continue to belong to the Ameers and their successors in perpetuity, on condition of the payment to him by the Ameers of such a sum as may be determined under the mediation of the British Government; 1,500,000 of rupees of such payment being made over by him to Maharaja Ranjit Singh. On these payments being completed, article 6 of the treaty of March 12, 1833, will be considered cancelled, and the customary interchange

> of letters and suitable presents between the Maharaja and the Ameers of Scinde shall be maintained as heretofore.
>
> For the purpose of giving full and perfect effect to the said treaty, Shah Shooja-ool-Moolk has been furnished by the British Government with money, arms, and other necessary means for raising and equipping an army, which is to march, under his Majesty's personal command, by route of Bhawulpore and Shikarpore into Afghanistan; whilst another army, belonging to Maharaja Ranjit Singh, is to march with the king's eldest son from Peshawur by direct road to Cabul. With the object of supporting, in case it should be requisite to do so, the king's own army, a British force is also to take the same route by Shikarpore, and both these armies may be expected to reach the Indus about the beginning of the month of Sheval (December 19), and cross at Sukkur, or in that neighbourhood. They will thence move by the route of Shikarpore on Candahar; and the Governor General of India relies on the friendship and goodwill of the Government of Scinde to render every assistance, by ordering boats to be collected for crossing the river, and camel and grain to be also furnished as far as may be required. The hire and price of all boats, camels, grain &c, will be punctually paid agreeably to the custom of the British Government in friendly countries.
>
> The Governor General confidently trusts that the Ameers of Scinde will see the magnitude of the benefit which they will derive by being secured, by the payment of a moderate sum of money, from all future claims, either as to the tribute payable to the monarchs of Cabul or the undoubted pretensions of the latter to Shikarpore. His Lordship also believes and thinks that their Highnesses, as sincere friends and near neighbours, will be happy and ready to take this opportunity of meeting the views and assisting in the great objects of the British Government, from which the Ameers have already derived such essential relief and advantage by its mediation with Maharaja Ranjit Singh, and which has not, in the arrangements now in progress, forgotten or overlooked their interests and well-being, as is clearly demonstrated by the article of the treaty above quoted.[6]

This was not an invitation to become a party to the grand design, it was more a demand to conform, with a sting in the tail of having to pay a huge indemnity to Shah Shuja from whom, according to the Amirs, they already had signed receipts for the payments he had received in 1833. To the miserly Amirs this new demand was nothing short of shameless extortion and evidence of the British Government's grasping policy. Colonel Pottinger might have been able to convince the Amirs of the long-term benefits if he had had the time, but of time there was none. Instead, he was advised to seek out the more agreeable candidates and to replace any of the Amirs who were hostile, a procedure the British were becoming quite adept at, and one which Lieutenant Colonel Sir Alexander Burnes was already attempting in the Upper Sindh with Amir Mir Rustam. Based on his long experience with Sindh affairs, Colonel Pottinger knew that the course of British policy could only be achieved, in the timeframe envisaged, by a threat of military intervention, so he applied to the Bombay Government to hold troops in readiness to move to the Sindh upon his request. Reacting to this application, the British Government decided that it would be prudent to have the Bombay force of 5,000 despatched as soon as

6 Durand, *The First Afghan War and Its Causes*, p.71.

possible for the occupation of Shikarpore or such other places of Sindh as might be deemed essential in facilitating operations beyond the Indus and for giving full effect to the provisions of the tripartite treaty. It is for this reason that the Bombay Column was in the Sindh even before the Bengal Column had started its advance.

In the meantime, the premier Amir in Hyderabad, Noor Mohammed Khan, sounded the rallying call for all Sindhis to frustrate the designs of the *feringhees* and asked their wild neighbours, the Baluchis, to come and help. He also wrote to Shah Shuja to tell him that he would not be welcome in Sindh.

The Bombay Column commanded by Lieutenant General Sir John Keane, the designated commander of the Army of the Indus, left Bombay on 21 November in 10 requisitioned and overcrowded ships. This force landed at Vikkur on the Sindh coast on 29 November having lost three landing craft called *pattamers*; two carrying 15 artillery horses and one carrying 'officers' supplies' to the value of £100 (£7,500 in modern money), which had been sent on speculation by an eminent Parsee firm. This particular enterprise could possibly lay claim to being the very first NAAFI.[7]

Aside from horses, the Bombay column had sailed without camels and the usual host of camp followers. It had been assured that sufficient camels would be available on arrival to carry all the tents and supplies. The column, with neither a field hospital nor a medical depot, was now stranded for want of camels and faced decidedly unfriendly hosts. It was rumoured that the Sindhis were mustering a force of 10,000 to take the field against what they perceived as a British invasion. Captain James Outram of 21st Bombay NI, in his role as extra ADC, was sent forward to Hyderabad to find out what was going on. He reported that the Sindhis were acting in a decidedly unfriendly manner so the column was put in a state of combat readiness with troops being issued with 60 rounds of ammunition and picquets deployed forward. Lieutenant General Sir John Keane also called forward his reserve brigade from Bombay. By Christmas Day 1838, the Bombay Column had managed to advance, in two columns, to the town of Tatta where, unfortunately, a sentry shot a respected townsman believing him to be a thief.[8] This sad event exasperated the already tense situation as much as it did the temper of the irascible British commander, who continued to stand fast at Tatta awaiting the results of Colonel Pottinger's negotiations with the premier Amir, Noor Mohammed Khan of Hyderabad, and also the collection of much-needed camels to further his advance; officers were issued an advance of three months' pay to enable them to acquire the animals they needed. At this time the cost of a donkey was four rupees and a local horse cost 170 rupees.

Baulked by the ignominious recall of his 1836 mission to Kabul, and sore at William Macnaghten's selection as the Envoy to Shah Shuja's court, Alexander Burnes was given the quasi-independent role of envoy to the Khan of Kalat and was to proceed, in advance of the army, to Upper Sindh to arrange with the Amir of Khairpur, Mir Rustam, for the passage of the army across the Indus at Sukkur and the temporary cession of that place while the campaign lasted. In a further effort to stroke the ruffled feathers of this peacock, Lord Auckland had managed to wangle an elevation to a knighthood and promotion to lieutenant colonel for the young 33-year-old Captain Burnes. Whether these honours were bestowed on the young gentleman for his

7 William Taylor, *Scenes and Adventures in Afghanistan* (London: T.C. Newby, 1842; Naval & Military Press reprint, n.d.), p 9.

8 Taylor, *Scenes and Adventures in Afghanistan*, p.19.

Sir Alexander Burnes.

abilities, or for his capacity at penmanship to reach influential Whigs at home, remains unclear, but it certainly caused resentment in the senior officer ranks of the Company's army where promotion was strictly a matter of seniority. A knighthood for a mere captain in the Company's army would certainly have ruffled many more senior feathers. To overcome this source of potential embarrassment, Burnes was appointed acting lieutenant colonel on the British *The Army List* whilst remaining a captain on the Indian Army Register (the Indian Army had no provision for 'local' ranks). Lieutenant Colonel Sir Alexander Burnes arrived at Khairpur on 18 October 1839, a good month before any British troops were to, unexpectedly, land on Sindh soil.

When the decision was made for the British army to cross the Indus at Sukkur, the sanction of the Amirs, with whom the British had concluded a treaty five months earlier, had neither been asked for nor obtained, and now in accordance with the Governor General's policy, Sir Alexander Burnes commenced negotiations with Amir Mir Rustam on the basis that he was not there to solicit the Amir's co-operation, rather to compel him into a lopsided treaty which could enable the stronger party to disregard inconvenient treaty provisions at will. While his negotiations with the Amir were in concert with the Governor General's aims, they were not in tandem with the more difficult negotiations being conducted by the British resident in Sindh, Colonel Henry Pottinger, with the premier Amir, Noor Mohammed Khan of Hyderabad, who was in open revolt.

When Burnes arrived in Khairpur, Amir Mir Rustam was already aware that the Persian Shah had given up his quest for Herat and hence probably calculated that as this removed the main cause of the British contemplated advance it would preserve the Upper Sindh from passage and occupation by the British; consequently, Burnes' reception was one of compliments and gushing friendship. It did not take long for the representative of British might to disabuse his host of any such hope. The poor old Amir was in a cleft stick: his brother Amir in Hyderabad was calling for a *jihad* against the *feringhees* while his guest was implying that the jungles of Upper Sindh would be on fire if British wishes were not met. The Amir adopted a mode of conciliation and laid on the charm, and as proof of his sentiments he made the naïve Burnes privy to a letter he had sent to the premier Amir in Hyderabad whom he knew was not in the same conciliatory mood:

> Captain Burnes is here in Khyrpore. In the first meeting I have only welcomed him and learnt from his expressions that both he and Colonel Pottinger have been appointed by the

> Governor General of India to manage the affairs of Scinde. You know that the English possess India and many other extensive countries; notwithstanding the Sikhs are so aspiring, still they lean towards the English with extreme friendship, harmony and mutual concord, as if they were one party. In such a case it is but foresight to make friendship with them, and advisable to act according to Colonel Pottinger's inclinations, that he may not be offended, for he is ambassador and guest.[9]

Burnes was clearly deceived by what he deemed the sincere friendship of Amir Mir Rustam and his devotion to British aims, but down in Hyderabad Colonel Pottinger was not taken in by the young man's enthusiastic admiration of the conduct of Amir Mir Rustam and rejected the draft treaty that Burnes had sent him for approval having also sent a copy to the Governor General. This draft treaty overlooked the fact that the Sindh was a confederacy of Amirs of which Noor Mohammed Khan was the paramount chief; singling out the Amir of Khairpur as the sole party to the proposed treaty, guaranteeing the independence of Khairpur, the appointment of a British Resident and exempting Amir Mir Rustam from payment of any subsidy. This was not an arrangement that would sit well with the other Amirs and would cause untimely disruption. Colonel Pottinger warned Burnes that the time for a separate treaty had not arrived and that when it did it had to be upheld with troops on the ground and in concert with a similar treaty with the Amir of Hyderabad. Unfortunately the Governor General, not taking his lead from the more experienced colonel, had directly authorised Burnes to proceed with the proposed treaty with Amir Mir Rustam of Khairpur, with the proviso that he was to adopt the utmost secrecy in his communications with Amir Mir Rustam regarding the guaranteed independence of his domains. Thus, at the same time as the British resident to Sindh, responsible for the political affairs with Sindh, was issuing one set of instructions to his subordinate in Khairpur, the Governor General 600 miles away not only issued contrary instructions but empowered a subordinate to act in independence of his principal. Lieutenant Colonel Sir Alexander Burnes, cock-a-hoop with the Governor General's sanction of his proposed treaty, wasted no time in discussions with the Amir of Khairpur, oblivious or careless of the fact that whatever was discussed was blown with the wind to the anxious ears of Noor Mohammed Khan in Hyderabad, the paramount chief of the Sindh Confederacy.

Lieutenant General Sir John Keane was, at this time, in Tatta, eight marches from Hyderabad and in a precarious position, acutely short of carriage, 600 miles from half his army at Bahawalpur, his Bombay reserve not expected for at least another month and his hosts becoming uglier by the day. Not a robust position to be in, nor one that allowed him to attack the fortified stronghold of Hyderabad. The designated commander of the Army of the Indus was forced to bide his time and sincerely hope the Sindhis and their Baluchi brothers did not grasp the initiative to give battle; nor did the situation in the Upper Sindh make the General feel any safer.

Meanwhile, General Sir Henry Fane and the Bengal Column had arrived at Khanpur on 8 January on the frontier of the Khan of Bahawalpur's territory. Here they stopped for a couple of days to replace the camels, which were dying off faster than the grain was consumed. Replacements were hard to procure as the owners did not like the notion of crossing the Indus which was now four marches away. On 14 January 1839 General Fane and the Bengal Column

9 Durand, *The First Afghan War and Its Causes*, p.98.

entered Sindh territory at a place called Subzul-ka-Cote, 18 miles from the Indus, and here Lieutenant Colonel Sir Alexander Burnes presented himself to the Commander-in-Chief assuring him that grain had been collected and that arrangements were under control for the passage of the army across the Indus and through the Upper Sindh. Of the situation in Lower Sindh, Burnes was either ignorant or aloof. On Thursday 24 January, the Bengal Column was on the banks of the Indus at Rohri. Shah Shuja's force and Envoy Macnaghten had arrived seven days earlier and had crossed the river, without their artillery, in seven days at a *ghat* about seven miles north of Rohri and were now on their way to Shikarpore two marches further on.

The Engineers had been sent forward to build the bridge of boats required for the crossing of the river by the army and its camels. This was a major undertaking as there were not enough boats and the Engineers had to build many from scratch. According to the young engineer, Lieutenant James Broadfoot, 'The bridge was the largest military bridge ever built in India.' On the afternoon of their arrival, General Sir Henry Fane held a *durbar* to receive the son of Amir Mir Rustam. The young man and his attendants were scared stiff of the *Ingrezi* soldiers and alarmed about how this subordination to British might would play back in anti-British Hyderabad.

It was arranged that Amir Mir Rustam was to pay his respects to the British Commander at 7:00 a.m. on 27 January. He did not show up, instead he sent his minister to ask the General to call on him. Clearly, the Amir was having second thoughts about his earlier conciliation with British aims and also the reactions of his fellow Amirs. The minister was sent packing and a much-dejected Mir Rustam made his appearance three hours later. At about this time, the proposed treaty with the Amir of Khairpur, having been signed by the Governor General, had arrived. It had been correctly addressed to Colonel Pottinger, but no doubt to save time, delivered directly to Sir Alexander Burnes. By this new treaty, Amir Mir Rustam was to deliver up the fort at Sukkur, situated on an island in the middle of the Indus near the town of Rohri. The Amir was clearly unhappy about the concessions demanded and implied that he would have to await the approbation of the premier Amir in Hyderabad before he could proceed with matters. At this juncture General Fane, not in the best of moods as he had just received information that his request to resign had been rejected, undiplomatically declared, 'I have wasted enough time treating, I will now march down and attack him, and if you like I will show you the troops I will send to do it.'[10] The General then issued orders for the Cavalry Brigade and two infantry brigades, under the command of Major General Cotton, to move west along the left bank of the river, to Hyderabad; morale immediately rose at the prospect of battle, loot or prize money. This advance was delayed until the treaty with Amir Rustam had been signed and the fort, built in the time of Alexander the Great, surrendered to the British. This was done on 29 January and the fort placed under the command of Lieutenant Colonel Thomas Monteath, the commanding officer of the 35th Bengal Native Infantry.

Back in Hyderabad Colonel Pottinger, by now *persona non grata* at the Hyderabad court, sent a draft treaty to Amir Noor Mohammed Khan on 18 January for his acceptance. He also had to inform the Amir of the Governor General's latest ruling that, 'while the present emergency lasts the Amirs are to be apprised, that the article of the treaty prohibiting the use of the Indus for the conveyance of military stores, must necessarily be suspended during the course of the operations undertaken for the permanent establishment of security for all those who are a party

10 Hough, *Narrative*, p.16.

to the treaty.'[11] Colonel Pottinger had calculated that with a British force now in Upper Sindh and another easing up towards Hyderabad, the Amir and his advisers would be ready to treat for some favourable accommodation. Instead, but not unexpectedly, the Amir rejected the proffered treaty, thus charging the atmosphere with the inevitability of war. By 25 January Lieutenant General Sir John Keane, with his Bombay Column, was at Jerruck, only two marches from Hyderabad, an objective which, in his opinion, his force alone could not engage successfully. Had the Sindhis and their Baluchi friends attacked at this time and not adopted the oriental fashion of warfare of blustering bravado, rattling of spears and the making of unholy noise, General Keane might well have found himself embroiled in a schemozzle that could well have unhinged the whole of the Governor General's grand strategy. He sent an urgent despatch to the Commander-in-Chief for assistance.

Keane's request for assistance crossed with the intelligence that the Commander-in-Chief had already ordered a force to advance on Hyderabad and that he had also ordered Major General Edward Simpson, commanding Shah Shuja's force, to advance on Larkana. This apparent deflection from the main purpose of advancing on Afghanistan irritated the envoy, William Macnaghten, who reckoned it to be 'a wild goose chase', thus failing to appreciate the military axiom of securing one's lines of communication. He advocated that the advance be continued and that the Sindhis be left to the mercy of 20,000 of Maharaja Ranjit Singh's troops who could march down from Peshawar in quick order. It is not stated, but quite obviously General Fane had no high regard for the Envoy, considering him to be an interfering 'popinjay'. Macnaghten wrote to John Colvin, his friend and private secretary to the Governor General, about his frustration:

> I grieve to say that I have no consolation to afford you. Our accounts from every quarter as to what is really passing are most unsatisfactory, and Sir Willoughby Cotton is clearly going on a wild goose chase. He cannot possibly, I think, be at Hyderabad under twenty-five days from this date, and he seems to be travelling by a route which has no roads. He will soon, I fear, find himself in the jungle. If this goes on as it is now doing, what is to become of our Afghan expedition?[12]

Moreover, Macnaghten was cognisant of the fact that it was not within the plan of the campaign that Hyderabad should be taken. Lord Auckland had been quite specific on this point, and nothing short of an attack on British troops or the positive refusal of the Amirs to come to terms, would have justified the Commander-in-Chief in using force by attacking Hyderabad, it being thought that a consequence of such an attack would retard the whole operation.

The force, under the command of Cotton, left Rohri on 30 January in two columns and was at Naushera by 6 February. Meanwhile, Major General Edward Simpson and his force had completed the 52-mile advance from Shikarpore to Larkana, along the right bank of the river, and taken that town by 4 February, while on the same day Lieutenant General Sir John Keane had managed to push his force to Kotra, just across the river from Hyderabad.

In addition to the activity along both banks of the Indus, the Bombay Reserve had arrived at Karachi on Sunday 3 February, on a flotilla of warships under the command of Rear Admiral

11 Kaye, *History of the War in Afghanistan*, vol. I, p.382.
12 Kaye, *History of the War in Afghanistan*, p.400.

Sir Francis Maitland on his flagship HMS *Wellesley*. He was welcomed by a shot across his bow from the old fort of Manora, built of mud and straw in 1797. The Admiral responded with a broadside from his 74-gun frigate, reducing the fort to rubble, silencing the 11 guns and putting to flight the garrison of 13 men. The Reserve, of brigade strength, disembarked and advanced to join Lieutenant General Sir John Keane at Kotri. While this brigade enhanced General Keane's battle capacity, it ate a big chunk out of his logistics capacity. The brigade, 3,050 strong, consisted of:

Commander: Brigadier Thomas Valiant
HM 40th Foot
HM 2nd Foot
22nd Bombay Native Infantry
26th Bombay Native Infantry
3rd Company Bombay Artillery

News of the arrival of this force at Karachi and the intelligence of a considerable force advancing along both banks of the river caused Amir Noor Mohammed Khan and his advisers to double-check their options. It did not take them long to wake up to the fact that faced with a combined force of 20,000 troops, their only unpalatable option was to treat with the mighty *Ingrezis*. The Amir handed the signed treaty to Colonel Pottinger on 5 February 1839 with his acceptance of the payment of 21 *lakhs* of rupees once the British had determined the validity of this claim. In his book, Henry Durand was to comment:

> Thus, was concluded the overthrow of independent rulers, our allies by treaty, whom we professed to befriend and secure at the time that we sanctioned and instigated an absolute demand for tribute preferred against them by a puppet king of our own raising and unscrupulously subjugated their country, on the plea that it was an integral part of Hindustan, and that its occupation was essential for the defence of our frontier and the peace and security of India.[13]

Regarding the payment of the 21 *lakhs* of rupees, the British Government had undertaken to be the mediators between the Amirs and Shah Shuja and had pledged itself to impartially adjudicate the claims and impose the correct amount to be paid. When the Amirs produced verified releases showing that the alleged had been paid in full, Colonel Pottinger saw the injustice of the demand for tribute and wrote to the supreme government:

> The question of money payment by the Amirs of Sindh to Shah Shuja is, in my humble opinion, rendered very puzzling by two releases written in Korans and sealed and signed by His Majesty, which they have produced. Their argument now is that they are sure the Governor General does not intend to make them pay again for what they have already bought and obtained, in the most binding way, a receipt in full.[14]

13 Durand, *The First Afghan War and Its Causes*, p.117.
14 Kaye, *History of the War in Afghanistan*, Vol. I, p.381.

To this, the supreme council in Simla replied:

> Admitting the documents produced to be genuine, and that they imply a relinquishment of all claims to tribute, they would hardly appear to be applicable to present circumstances. Whatever may be the real facts of the case the question is one that concerns the contracting parties and it is not incumbent on the British Government to enter into any formal investigation of the plea addressed by the Amirs.[15]

The tribute was paid by the Amirs in three instalments and the British Government congratulated itself on the settlement made in Sindh, without bloodshed. The confederacy of Amirs had been dissolved, the Sindh was formally placed under British protection and navigation of the Indus from the sea to the northern point of Sindh was free of toll. These were undoubtedly great advantages, but when the Governor General congratulated the Secret Committee on their attainment 'without bloodshed', he was unable to add, without fraud, extortion and intimidation. As one old wag was to comment, 'Never thought to see the might of British soldiery embark on an invasion for no better reason than to secure the supply of fruit.' Dr Richard Kennedy reckoned that the tribute found its way back to the Sindhi treasury by way of the exorbitant prices obtained from the British for the provision of essential supplies.

Upon the successful conclusion of negotiations with the Amir of Hyderabad, orders were despatched to major generals Cotton and Simpson to halt their advance, and on 9 February further orders directed them to retrace their steps back to their starting points. The troops trudged back, morale was low as their knapsacks were weighted down by the disappointment of missing out on an action that could have resulted in huge prize money, as the Amirs were known to be weak and rumoured to be very wealthy. The troops arrived back at their starting points by 16 February and orders were issued for the Bengal Column to cross the mighty Indus, the first Europeans to do so since Alexander the Great. The bridge of boats consisted of 74 boats, which stretched for 500 yards over the river. J.H. Stocqueler, the editor of the *Bombay Times*, who was accompanying the army in a private capacity and could well claim to be the very first war correspondent, published the following account of the crossing:

> The passage across the river was the first interesting event of the campaign. It was truly a beautiful sight to see the different corps with their bands playing, followed by long strings of camels and camp followers, winding their way over the bridge. The glittering of their arms in the sun, the fort of Sukkur with its picturesque battlements fronting over the bridge, the ancient towns of Rohri and Sukkur overhanging the mighty stream, formed together a delightful picture.[16]

The entire column was across the river by 18 February and General Sir Henry Fane took the opportunity to bid his farewell to the Bengal troops. An order was issued stating that, 'His Excellency desires that the officers of all ranks and departments will accept the expressions of his approbation of the zeal and good example they have set.' These sentiments, no doubt,

15 Beveridge, *A Comprehensive History of India*, vol. 3, p.432.
16 J.H. Stocqueler, *Memorials of Afghanistan: Being state papers, official documents, dispatches, authentic narratives, etc.* (Calcutta: Ostell & Lepage, 1843; Bishop's College Press, reprint, 2010), p.21.

excluded Sir Willoughby Cotton, of whom His Excellency is reported as saying, 'I don't think Cotton has a mind that carries away much of verbal instructions.'[17] To the regret of all ranks the General then set off down the river on his boat to Sehwan where he halted for his interview with Lieutenant General Sir John Keane and to hand over the Army of the Indus to him. General Fane, a no-half-measure Tory with strong views regarding the general shabbiness of all Whig doings, then proceeded to Bombay where he set up his headquarters. While in Bombay General Fane's health failed, and he was allowed to resign. Handing over to General Sir Jasper Nicolls, he sailed for home in March 1840 on the Company ship *Malabar* and died at sea near the Azores.

Keane's[18] assumption of Army of the Indus command occasioned the following arrangements all of which were expected: the cavalry formed a division under the command of Major General Joseph Thackwell,[19] the entire artillery now came under the command of Brigadier Thomas Stevenson, and the Bengal Column became the 1st Infantry Division under Major General Cotton, whilat the Bombay infantry regiments became the 2nd Infantry Division under Major General Thomas Willshire. Captain George Thomson was appointed Chief Engineer and Major James Parsons was directed to assume general control of the commissariat of both Bengal and Bombay troops. It was also directed that the native troops of both Presidencies were to be placed on the same footing of equality as regards pay and allowances. The Bengal troops knew very little about their new commander, what little they did know did not fill them with any great desire to place themselves under his command. All these command changes were not put in force until the whole army had assembled at Quetta.

17 George Bruce, *Retreat from Kabul* (London: Mayflower-Dell, 1967), p.34.

18 Lieutenant General Lord Keane, GCB, GCH (Baron Keane of Ghazni and of Cappoquin in the County of Waterford), 1781–1844. He was born in Belmar, Ireland and was commissioned into the British army in 1792 as an ensign aged 11. In 1794 He was appointed captain in HM 124th Foot just before this regiment was broken up, and the young captain was placed on half pay. In 1799 he was brought on to full pay and posted HM 44th Foot, then at Gibraltar. Keane then obtained a majority in HM 60th Foot and shortly afterwards a colonelcy in HM 13th Foot. In April 1813 he joined Wellington's army and commanded a brigade during the Peninsular Campaign. He was promoted to major general in 1814 and sent to America. In 1823 he was appointed commander of British troops in Jamaica and remained there for several years. On being promoted to lieutenant general in 1833, he was appointed commander-in-chief of the Bombay Army and held that post until he returned to England in October 1839. He was first married to Grace, the daughter of General Sir John Smith, and they had four sons and two daughters; Grace died in Bombay on the eve of the Afghan Campaign. Keane's second marriage was to Charlotte, the youngest daughter of Colonel Boland. Keane died of dropsy on 26 August 1844 at Burton Lodge, Hampshire.

19 Lieutenant General Sir Joseph Thackwell, GCB, KH (1781–1858). He was commissioned as a cornet in the Worcester Fencible Cavalry in 1798 and served with this regiment until it was disbanded in 1800. In April of that year he purchased a commission in the 15th Hussars. This regiment formed part of Lord Paget's brigade, which was employed under General Sir John Moore in the Peninsula. The regiment was back in the Peninsula under the Duke of Wellington and took part in many of his battles. At the Battle of Waterloo Thackwell's regiment served under General Grant's brigade; Thackwell had two horses shot from under him and he lost his left arm. Despite this, he charged the enemy with his sword in his right hand and the reins of his horse in his teeth. In 1819, HM 15th Hussars were involved in what became known as the Peterloo Massacre. Thackwell took command of his regiment in 1830 and was put on half pay in 1832. Then in 1837, when he heard that the 3rd Light Dragoons was being sent to India, he exchanged command for a fee of £4,000 (£300,000 at today's value). He was promoted to major general and given command of the cavalry division in the Army of the Indus. After a short break in England Thackwell returned to India and took a prominent part in the Second Sikh War. He married Maria Roche in 1825 and they had four sons and three daughters. Lieutenant General Thackwell died in County Cork in 1858.

9

Advance to Kandahar – The Gauntlet

Having crossed the River Indus, Major General Sir Willoughby Cotton advanced his column to Shikarpore where he met Shah Shuja and William Macnaghten, in the meantime Lieutenant General Sir John Keane and the Bombay Column had moved up the river to Sehwan. Lieutenant Colonel Thomas Monteath, commanding the 35th Bengal Native Infantry, was directed to stand fast at the Sukkur fort until arrangements were made for his relief. The bridge of boats was put under the command of Lieutenant John Wood of the Company's navy and was to remain intact until all the artillery had crossed, after which the bridge was to be broken up and the boats used for conveyance of supplies.

The Bengal Column arrived in Shikarpore on 20 February. This dirty town of 30,000 inhabitants, described by Lieutenant Thomas Holdsworth of HM 2nd Foot as 'one of the hottest places in existence', was now awash with 15,000 British and Hindu soldiers plus a horde of camp followers. The local traders were delighted as they jacked up their prices, thus giving the local people more reason to hate the invading *feringhees*.

Rumours, not altogether unbelievable, were rife about Afghans rushing down the Bolan Pass to challenge the further advance of Shah Shuja and his British masters. Macnaghten, already annoyed about the loss of time occasioned by the movement against Hyderabad, was all for pushing on as quickly as possible to secure the pass, while Major James Parsons, the head of the Commissariat, pleaded for a halt at Shikarpore for at least 20 days in order for enough supplies and grain to be collected for the estimated 32 marches to Kandahar.

At this time the commander of the Army of the Indus was with the Bombay Column at Larkana 15 marches behind and in dire need of camels necessitating a halt of nine days at that place. Instead of moving forward with a suitable escort to head-up the advance of his army, the commander elected to remain with the Bombay troops and ordered the Bengal Commissariat to send down both supplies and camels for the Bombay troops. It was estimated by Major William Hough, the DJAG of the Bengal Division, that during the whole campaign the Bengal Commissariat supplied a total of 6,800 camels to Bombay troops.

Macnaghten's anxiety about the security of the Bolan Pass was further exacerbated by the intelligence that Shah Kamran of Herat had ordered both Lieutenant Colonel Charles Stoddart and Lieutenant Eldred Pottinger to leave the city, despite the fact that Lieutenant Pottinger, the British representative, had granted bills upon the credit of the British Government and had continued to do so even after the Shah of Persia had lifted his siege of Herat. However, when the two British officers discovered that Shah Kamran and his *Wazir*, Yah Mohammed Khan, had returned to their old activity of slave trading the two British officers strongly remonstrated against this practice and so became obnoxious to the Herati chiefs, who ordered them to quit the city. Lieutenant Colonel Stoddart did so and proceeded on his fateful journey to Bokhara. In 1839 Bokhara was ruled by Amir Nasrullah Khan, who had ascended to the throne in 1826 having murdered his father and elder brother, and for good measure his three younger brothers. Colonel Stoddart was sent to Bokhara by John McNeill to convince Amir Nasrullah Khan that he had nothing to fear from the British advance into Afghanistan. The Herati chiefs then became alarmed at the length to which matters had proceeded and begged Lieutenant Pottinger to delay his departure. In the meantime John McNeill, the British envoy at Teheran, continued to write in alarming tones to Sir Alexander Burnes, on the distinct possibility of the Shah of Persia renewing his operations against Herat, and Burnes added fuel to the flames by insinuating that Captain Ivan Vitkevich was accompanying the Kandahar chiefs on an advance on Herat in concert with the Persians.

Envoy Macnaghten had written to the army commander on 18 February pressing him to sanction an immediate advance, but General Keane was at the time grappling with the real problems of supply and was not overly concerned with the civilian envoy's anxiety. However, a couple of days later, Macnaghten had a meeting with Major General Sir Willoughby Cotton. This was after the two had had a major row over a demand the Envoy had made for supplies and camels to be transferred to the Shah's force. This episode was reported in a letter Macnaghten wrote on 24 February to John Colvin:

> Sir Willoughby made his appearance in camp yesterday morning. He is evidently disposed to look upon His Majesty and his disciplined troops and myself as mere ciphers. Any hint from me, however quietly and modestly given, was received with hauteur; and I was distinctly told that I wanted to assume command of the army; that he, Sir Willoughby, knew no superior but Sir John Keane. All this rose out of my requesting 1000 camels for the use of the Shah and his force. Sir Willoughby was ably backed by the Commissariat officers. My arguments were urged throughout in the most mild and conciliatory tone. I was determined on no account to lose my temper; and we parted at a late hour last night very good friends. I told him I was the last man in the world who would presume to interfere with his military arrangements; but I found it requisite to tell him, during one of our conversations, that if he thought it good for the service to leave Shah Shuja in the lurch, without the means of moving, I should esteem it my duty, as a political officer, to protest most strongly against the arrangement, and that the Governor General would determine which of us was right.[1]

It was the general feeling of many senior officers in the Bengal Division, that it was militarily imprudent to withdraw carriage and supplies from two disciplined armies of united action, simply for the sake of keeping a body of raw levies in the vain hope of giving plausibility to the fiction that the Shah was entering his dominion surrounded by his own people, of whom not one was an Afghan. This feeling was conveyed by Lieutenant Colonel Dennie to Lieutenant

1 Kaye, *History of the War in Afghanistan*, Vol.1, p.404.

Colonel Ranald MacDonald, the Army Commander's military secretary, which was to earn Dennie no 'brownie points'.

This was not the first nor the last time Macnaghten was to clash with his, ostensibly, military subordinates and he was very conscious of his unkind reputation in the army. On 5 March the sensitive envoy was to write:

> I foretold that endeavours would be made by a certain great man to poison Sir John's mind against me and the result has verified my prediction. I have had it from the best authority, that Sir John was told that I was the most assuming personage on earth, that I was constantly in the habit of meddling with military matters and that I take every opportunity of appearing with epaulettes and sword.[2]

After their flaming row Major General Cotton, now in a more conciliatory mood, acquiesced to Macnaghten's notion, with the concurrence of Sir Alexander Burnes, that an immediate advance to secure the pass was vital to the accomplishment of the overall aim of the campaign. At this meeting, the General pointed out that if the advance was expected to be opposed in the pass it would be militarily prudent to have the British army lead the advance and not Shah Shuja's untried force. Macnaghten agreed, but clearly had a problem selling the idea to the Shah, whom he was now finding to be 'unmanageable'. It would appear that the army commander, Lieutenant General Sir John Keane, 52 miles away, was not party to these decisions, and as it turned out no opposition was encountered in the pass except for the annoying and debilitating plundering by local marauders and the politicos' irritating conciliatory responses to their crimes. According to the *Boorhani Katia*, a celebrated Persian dictionary, 'the Baluchie's chief employment was in fighting and shedding blood, thieving and robbery on the roads. If it at any time happens that they cannot find strangers, they murder each other.'[3]

The Bengal troops, after a halt of two days at Shikarpore, left that place in eight columns, the last leaving on 28 February, with one and a half month's supplies and rum for three months. Before their departure the troops were paraded in review order for inspection by Shah Shuja-ul-Mulk, who was by now known to the British soldier as 'Sugar an' Milk'. Major Parsons of the Commissariat had been led to believe, by the political officers, that 10 days' supply would be available at Dadur, at the mouth of the pass, and a further 20 days' supply at Quetta, 18 marches further on. As the troops were to discover, these expectations were way off the mark.

The Governor General had directed at the very start of the campaign that the political agents were to make arrangements for as many as 45,000 camels to be made available for the conveyance of supplies, forage and baggage. Nothing like this number was collected, so there was a running squabble for the few that were collected. As mentioned earlier, Lieutenant Colonel William Dennie of HM 13th Foot complained to Keane's military secretary, Lieutenant Colonel MacDonald, achieving again the displeasure of the commander for which he was later to suffer.

As early as August 1838 Captain Robert Leech, who had accompanied Sir Alexander Burnes on his earlier mission to Kabul, had been in negotiations with the Khan of Kelat, the chief of the Baluchis, Mehrab Khan, for his cooperation in the collection of grain and sheep. This was

2 British Library, MSS Eur F332, Macnaghten correspondence.
3 James Atkinson, *The Expedition into Afghanistan* (London: W.H. Allen, 1841), p.90.

the chief who gave Shah Shuja safe harbour when he was being chased out of Afghanistan in 1833, so it was reckoned he would be amicable to British needs. But Mehrab Khan, by whose domain the British army was to pass, threw every impediment in the way of collection of grain, and Captain Leech withdrew to take up the appointment of political adviser to Major General Cotton. Prior to the advance on Dadur, Captain Leech, in his role of political adviser, issued detailed instructions for the behaviour of troops regarding local inhabitants and their places of worship. This instruction also gave authority to brigade commanders to flog any camp follower who failed to do his duty, and an award of five rupees to any Baluchi who brought in a deserter. This was only two rupees short of a *sepoy*'s monthly pay.

The distance between Shikarpore and Dadur is 146 miles, half of which was desert with the odd scrub and scarcely any water. As Captain Henry Havelock, of HM 13th Foot, second ADC to Major General Sir Willoughby Cotton, was to record, 'The path extended over unbroken level of sandy desert, in which there is not only neither well, spring, stream, nor puddle, but not a tree, and scarcely a bush, an herb, or blade of grass.' In addition to this topographical misery, troops fell by the wayside sick (mainly with dysentery) or exhausted and the *oot wallahs* started to desert rather than be caught and murdered by the marauding Baluchis. In those days there were no Compo or K rations, the army lived off the land, but there was little to live off and the camels that carried what little there was suffered badly on the rocky paths. As the army advanced from Shikarpore in driblets, cracks began to appear in the grand strategy as the dust from the many trampling boots got up the noses of the troops. At one point the heat was so great (137° Fahrenheit) that the commanding officer of 31st Bengal Native Infantry, Lieutenant Colonel James Thomson, died of apoplexy. One of the stops made was at the desolate little village of Khangarh some 50 miles from Shirkapore. This little village was later named Jacobabad after Brigadier General John Jacob.[4]

The Bengal troops arrived at Bhag on 6 March. Here water was found in abundance and grain in sufficient quantity to service immediate needs and for the remainder of the advance to Dadur. Meanwhile, Lieutenant General Sir John Keane and the Bombay Column had arrived at Larkana on 4 March; the advance to Larkana had been supported by supplies ferried up the river. The column halted at Larkana for nine days in order to collect enough camels for its further advance inland. While there, Keane decided to advance directly to Gandava and from there explore the possibility of proceeding through the Gandava Pass to Kalat, thus avoiding the Bolan Pass. It was probably for this reason that the Lieutenant General elected to remain with the Bombay troops instead of advancing forward and assuming active command of his army. This decision did little to coordinate the needs and objectives of the Army of the Indus. At Gandava, the Bombay Column halted for a further 10 days during which time Keane sent Captain Sidney Powell, his interpreter, to reconnoitre the Gandava Pass and to report whether it

4 Brigadier General John Jacob, CB (1812-58). John Jacob was born in Somerset. He was commissioned into the Bombay Artillery and arrived in Bombay about the same time as Sir Alexander Burnes. He saw action with the Army of the Indus and in 1847 was given command of the Sindh Irregular Cavalry, and in this command was involved in the Sindh War under General Sir Charles Napier. Later Jacob raised another cavalry regiment which was known as 'Jacob's Horse'. He chose the village of Khangrah as his base and developed it into a town, it thus becoming the centre of the Upper Sindh District over which he presided. In the due course of time permission was given to change the name of the town to Jacobabad. Brigadier General John Jacob died at his beloved Jacobabad in 1858.

was suitable for the passage of artillery. Powell returned with a negative report and the General changed his mind about an advance to Kalat and hurried forward to join the main body at Dadur.

On 14 March, the leading column of the Bengal Army troops, comprising of 13th Foot (Somerset), 2nd Bengal Light Cavalry, 48th Bengal Native Infantry, plus a troop of Bengal Horse Artillery, entered the Bolan Pass, a terrible chasm of 70 miles. This column included Sir Alexander Burnes, who on arrival at Quetta was to proceed to Kelat, accompanied by Lieutenant Richard Pattison, to renew negotiations with the chief, Mehrab Khan, for supplies and his cooperation. The Bolan Pass provided the only practical entrance into Afghanistan from the south-east. It was a deep continuous ravine traversed by a river the channel of which, covered with boulders and pebbles, was the only road; on both sides the mountains, which at the highest were nearly 5,700 feet above sea level, were in some places only 60 to 80 feet apart. At these points the concealed caves in the mountains provided excellent cover and protection to the marauders, who lay in wait to plunder. Prior to the advance into the pass, William Macnaghten and his band of politicos had arranged for a liberal distribution of money to the tribes to smooth the way of the advance through, but to many of the military officers this was considered a waste of money as no confidence could be placed in these wild tribes who had little regard for western ideas of integrity. Macnaghten had also authorised the raising of a local levy of 800 men, named the Bolan Rangers, on the premise of turning poachers into gamekeepers. This levy was raised and commanded by Lieutenant Frederick Bosanquet of 16th Bengal Native Infantry. During the course of the campaign many more such levies were to be raised with a view to forming them into an army for Shah Shuja as the Hindu element of his current force was replaced. A very few of these levies proved to be worthy or loyal.

On 24 March, a much exhausted Bengal Column emerged into the valley of Shawl, three more marches from Quetta. It had dragged its guns through the pass and had been pestered all the way by Baluchi marauders, who whenever caught were handed a rupee to 'go home', and, no doubt, tried again. The pass had been a veritable gauntlet with the marauders cutting off couriers, murdering stragglers and carrying off baggage and cattle; its path was now strewn with dead soldiers, horses and camels, all in various degrees of putrefaction to the greater horror of the troops who were to follow. A young officer of 3rd Bombay Light Cavalry came across the corpses of a pair of camp followers near Kandahar, one of the woman's breasts had been cut off and placed in her husband's mouth, while his penis had been removed and placed in her mouth.[5] The Baluchis had robbed and plundered with such audacity that a retreat was openly talked about. Richard Kennedy, a doctor with the Bombay Division, was of the opinion that the Baluchis were thieves by profession and from birth, and if hanging would prevent the robberies, then the whole population of the country would have to be hanged.

After a brisk march the column arrived at Quetta on 27 March, a town of some 500 houses. Thirty years later, Quetta was to become the site of the Indian Army's Staff College, where in the early 1930s the then lieutenant colonel Bernard Montgomery was the chief instructor. On arrival, guards were posted at each of the gates and strict orders were issued preventing all troops and camp followers from entering the bazaar. Of Quetta, Major William Hough was to write, 'A most miserable mud town, with a small castle on a mound, on which there was a small

5 Lawrence James, *Raj: The Making and Unmaking of British India* (London: Abacus, 2009), p.93.

gun on a rickety carriage.'[6] As for the expected 20 days' supply, the troops were soon to discover that this was a mirage. Major General Cotton now had a problem. He had just enough supplies and carriage to enable him to possibly advance through the Khojak Pass and on to Kandahar, but from all accounts this advance would be actively challenged by the Kandahar chiefs, who were reported to be riding down south en masse. However, the decision was made for him by a direct order from Keane that he was to stand fast in Quetta until the complete army had assembled there. Cotton stood fast in Quetta while his troops ate up 11 days of precious rations. Yet, while doing so no attempt was made to use this period to send out a reconnaissance party to check out the Khojak pass only 52 miles further on; instead, the Major General sent his deputy adjutant general, Major Patrick Craigie, with an escort back through the Bolan Pass to guide Keane through it, a round trip of 150 miles; the army commander could well have followed the markers of dead bodies left behind.

Quetta was in the domain of the Baluchi chief Mehrab Khan, with whom Sir Alexander Burnes was now to conclude a treaty, sweetened by a *lakh* and a half of rupees, to supply grain and sheep, to instruct his followers not to hinder the advance and to pay homage to the rightful King of Afghanistan, Shah Shuja-ul-Mulk. The Khan pocketed the money and before retiring to bed gave his British guest a few home truths. He told Sir Alexander Burnes that while the British would be able to restore Shah Shuja to the throne, they would not be able to maintain him there, and that the whole operation would be a failure. The Khan reckoned that Shah Shuja should have trusted the Afghans to restore him instead of deluging the country with Hindustanis, an insult to the Afghan people who would never forgive him. Burnes returned to Quetta with his treaty, but as it was to transpire, no supplies of grain or sheep were collected, the Baluchi marauders continued their brutal annoyance, and then, there was no treaty as it had been stolen from Sir Alexander's tent. Writing to Henry Torrens on 9 April, Macnaghten reported:

> The Khan of Khelat is our implacable enemy and Sir John is burning with revenge. There never was such treatment inflicted on human beings as we have been subjected to on our progress through the Khan's country. I will say nothing about Burnes' negotiations. His instructions were to conciliate, but I think he adhered too strictly to the letter of them. The Commander-in-Chief is very angry.[7]

According to Henry Havelock, Burnes had on behalf of the Government guaranteed Mehrab Khan the sovereignty of Baluchistan and full command of its revenues, which poses the question, was this treaty stolen or buried?

The camp followers with the Bengal Column had already been on half rations and on 23 March they were put on quarter rations, while native and European troops were put on half rations as were the cavalry and artillery horses, and the poor camels were left to forage for what was available. Major General Cotton in his order announcing these restrictions appealed to the military spirit of his soldiers and asked for their understanding of the situation and willingness to overcome the difficulty which he reckoned would be for a short duration. This short

6 Hough, *Narrative*, p.61.
7 Kaye, *History of the War in Afghanistan*, Vol. 1, p.419.

duration was to last well into their stay at Kandahar. Meanwhile, Brigadier Abraham Roberts expressed his concerns over the plight of the camp followers to his dear friend General Sir William Casement, the military member of the Governor General's Council: 'You will, I think, admit that it is a great hardship to bring camp followers so great a distance and then deprive them of the only chance of buying grain, bought by the Commissariat.'

Keane arrived at Dadur on 28 March, where he met envoy William Macnaghten and Shah Shuja. They were eight marches behind the Bengal Column at Quetta.

On 31 March the Bengal troops became involved in the 'Battle of Cockatoo', named such by the British troops after a hill called Takatoo. On this day Baluchi marauders came down from the hills and drove off 200 camels, sufficient carriage of rations for a regiment of troops for 10 days. Captain Leech, the column's political adviser, had earlier, with a generous contribution, commissioned the Baluchi chief of Quetta to post his men to protect the gorge of a pass some six miles to the north-west of Quetta. This worked for a couple of days, then the posted men disappeared, as did the chief, and the marauders came in. A pursuit party hurriedly came together and rode out to retrieve the camels and apprehend the robbers. Officers of various regiments joined the party. They found a group of 12 robbers and managed to dislodge them from the hill. The party returned in the evening with no prisoners or camels. The only casualty they had suffered was the hat of Lieutenant Christopher Hasell, 48th Bengal Native Regiment, which had been holed by an enemy bullet. This pursuit by a motley crew was to prompt Major General Cotton to issue a strict order that when a party was detached or called out, no officer except those belonging to it was to proceed with it as he might be wanted by his own corps. The General also issued an order that his troops were at liberty to act against marauders, which Sir Alexander Burnes characterised as 'bloodthirsty and calculated to bring on a blood feud'. Meanwhile a pursuit party of the Bombay Column under the command of Major Francis Daly of HM 4th Light Dragoons had captured 11 marauders and General Keane had ordered them to be shot. The Duke of Wellington, in a letter to Colonel James Murray of the Bombay Army. had this to say on the subject:

> However, I think the Bheels, and people of that description, whose profession is plunder, and who come armed into the camp for that purpose, ought not to be considered and treated as common robbers. They are public enemies and rebels against authority, and I recommend that when one of these is caught in the camp, whether it be situated in the Company's territories or in those of the Raja, he may be shot by the nearest rear guard if he is taken in the act of robbing. If something of this kind be not done, the robberies and outrages of the Bheels, will reduce the troops to the greatest distress.[8]

On Thursday 4 April, Cotton rode out of Quetta with his principal staff officers and escort to meet the Army Commander at Sir-i-Ab where the Shah and Envoy had also arrived. There Keane was given a 19-gun salute and the group then proceeded to Quetta where the exalted party arrived on 6 April and Shah Shuja-ul-Mulk was honoured with a 21-gun salute. After congratulating the army for the admirable manner in which they had conducted themselves, Keane put into effect the command changes made earlier, by which the army was to consist

8 Hough, *Narrative*, p.75.

of two divisions commanded by Cotton and Major General Willshire, with the two cavalry brigades under Major General Thackwell. The appointment of Willshire to the command of the 2nd Division greatly annoyed Welshman, Major General William Nott, who was now to command the 4th Brigade of Cotton's 1st Division and this Brigade was to be left behind to garrison Quetta, so missing out on any action in Afghanistan. The reason for Nott's resentment was that being senior to both Cotton and Willshire he should have been given command of the 2nd Division, and in a stormy interview with the Army Commander implied that the only reason for his being passed over was because Willshire was a Queen's commissioned officer which reflected badly on him and on the Company's Army. Keane, not known for smooth handling of ugly situations, rejected Nott's plea and adding salt to the wound, directed him to pay back the 9,000 Rupees he had drawn while acting as a Divisional Commander in the Bengal Column. Keane ended the interview by shouting, 'Sir, I will never forgive your conduct as long as I live.'[9] Nor did he. Brigadier Abraham Roberts, another long-serving Company officer, must have had some sympathy for his brother officer, but only made his feelings known in a letter to his wife. 'Unfortunately, we are commanded by Queen's officers who know nothing of the country or the language.' This sad episode was but a reflection of the long-standing jealousy between Queen's and Company's officers, the latter being officially designated junior in corresponding rank regardless of length of service. This especially irked the Company officers as their promotion was based on length of service whereas the Queen's officer could purchase it, allowing at times for much younger and inexperienced Queen's officers to be senior to Company officers. This system was changed after the Indian Mutiny.

At about this time, Captain Henry Stockley was en route to Dadur, with much needed supplies, when he was attacked by a gang of Baluchis and forced to take shelter in a fort close by. On receipt of this information Lieutenant Colonel Dennie, at Shikarpore, hastily put a force together of 200 *sepoys* of 42nd BNI and forced marched it over 150 miles of desert, to the rescue of Captain Stockley and his valuable cargo. At Dadur, Dennie received orders to join his regiment at Quetta. Captain William Anderson with two troops of Shah Shuja's Horse Artillery was about to set off from Dadur to join the army by the same route and asked Lieutenant Colonel Dennie for infantry protection. The march commenced under burning sun and the troops suffered all the way with temperatures to 120°. Attached to the artillery under Captain Anderson were several bullock carts; noting the poor state of the animals, Dennie warned Anderson that the bullocks were too unfit to proceed, but nevertheless, they were included. On the last day of their passage through the Bolan Pass, Dennie had ordered that all baggage was to be sent in advance for security reasons, however for some reason, Captain Anderson forgot about his 'dead beat' bullock carts, which were left in the rear. When nearly through the Pass, it was reported that the bullocks had stopped moving and were now being fired upon by the Baluchis. Naturally, many of the animals and a good deal of the baggage were lost. For this Lieutenant Colonel Dennie received the undeserved reproof from the Army Commander for 'faulty arrangements'.

While at Quetta, Shah Shuja was assailed with reports of Mehrab Khan's disgraceful behaviour and refusal to come in and pay homage. The Shah made his feelings known, as reported by Mr Macnaghten in his letter to the Governor General:

9 Bruce, *Retreat from Kabul*, p.52.

The Shah's horse artillery crossing the Lora River.

> His opinion of Afghans and nation is, I regret to say, very low. He declares that they are a pack of dogs, one and all, and as for the Barakzais, it is utterly impossible that he can place the slightest confidence on any one of that accursed race. We must try and bring him gradually round to entertain a more favourable opinion of his subjects.[10]

Major General Cotton's 1st Division had now been in Quetta on short rations for 11 days, awaiting the arrival of the Army Commander, who correctly decided that there was no reason for any further delay and ordered the advance to proceed the very next day. The 4th Brigade under the command of Major General Nott was duly left behind to garrison Quetta, and Captain John Bean of 23rd Bengal Native Infantry was appointed political agent of that place.

By now rumours were circulating that the Kandahar chiefs, after an unaccountable delay, were at last mustering for an encounter and the British troops braced themselves for the possibility of a real fight. Shortly after the advance guard had left their camp they heard repeated firing which, sadly, turned out to be the shooting of 60 cavalry horses judged to be too weak to proceed any further; Major General Thackwell was mortified and the erstwhile cavalrymen were now required to advance on two feet! At about this time, Mr Macnaghten wrote two letters to the Governor General which were significant and worth quoting:

> 6 April. Notwithstanding all the croaking about Shah Shuja's want of popularity, I feel certain that my prediction will be verified, and that His Majesty will be cordially welcomed by all classes of the people.
>
> 9 April. 'The whole of the force, from Sir W. Cotton downwards, are infected with exaggerated fears relating to the character of the King and the prospects of the campaign. They fancy that they see an enemy in every bush.[11]

By 12 April the army had reached the mouth of the Khojak Pass and Keane rode forward to take a look. The traversing of this pass was to be more difficult than the Bolan. As the troops approached the entrance they had to climb a steep ascent with hills on either side no more than 100 feet apart and after an ascent of 800 feet a descent, equally steep, with a precipice on one side of the narrow path, then another ascent and descent and so on all the way. The narrow slippery path consisted of many sharp turns around which it was impossible for the drag animals to pull the guns, so the guns had to be manhandled by European troops. This task was assigned to Lieutenant Colonel Joseph Orchard's 1st Bengal European Regiment. Regarding this arduous task, Brigadier Roberts had this to say:

> For four whole days working from sunrise to sunset the Regiment pulled at drag ropes. On the first day they only succeeded in getting one 18-pounder and a mortar through the Pass. Still they struggled, the officers working side by side with their men in the back-breaking work. Many baggage animals had dropped dead in the Pass and as a result orders were

10 Beveridge, *A Comprehensive History of India*, Vol. 3, p.442.
11 Kaye, *History of the War in Afghanistan*, Vol. 1, p.421.

> issued for the destruction of more than 27,000 rounds of musket ammunition and fourteen barrels of powder for there was no method of transporting it any further.[12]

At this juncture it would be of interest to give a short account of the East India Company's policy for the handling of guns and gunpowder. First of all and prior to the Indian Mutiny, no Royal Artillery units were employed in India. All artillery units and arsenals were manned by East India Company personnel, and apart from those employed in *cooli wallah* work all the personnel were Europeans, and non-Catholics. This latter qualification was, no doubt, a hang-up from the days of Guy Fawkes, and the fact that the Catholic penal laws had only been repealed in 1829.

In the early morning of 20 April a tribal chief by the name of Haji Khan Kakar, who had been commissioned by the Kandahar chiefs to harass the British advance, entered the British camp at the head of 100 of his horsemen, and tendered his submission to Shah Shuja. This was only one of a series of treacheries committed by this renegade chief for a bribe of 10,000 rupees. It was now widely rumoured that Kohan Dil Khan, the principal chief at Kandahar, upon the defection of Haji Khan Kakar and fearful of more defections had decided that a more prudent course of action was to flee the city. Based on this intelligence, William Macnaghten deemed it important that Shah Shuja be brought forward to resume the lead of the advance to Kandahar, and the Shah made his entrance into the city on Thursday 25 April with the Army of the Indus. The grand army of the Ferozepore parade ground now staged into Kandahar resembling a rabble. According to Lieutenant John Haughton of 31st BNI, '[the] Army arrived in a state of starvation, camel loads of the best Manillas (cigars) and not a drop of beer'.

Macnaghten's account of the Shah's entry into the city, no doubt viewed through his rose-tinted spectacles, informed the Governor General that, 'We have, I think, been fortunate everyway. The Shah made a grand public entry into the city this morning and was received with feelings nearly amounting to adoration.' This view was not corroborated by Henry Havelock of HM 13th Foot who wrote, 'Unless I have been deceived, all the national enthusiasm of the scene was entirely confined to His Majesty's immediate retainers.' In his communication envoy Macnaghten gives the Governor General the first indication that this venture would be long-drawn-out and expensive as he goes on to say, 'Of one thing I am certain, that we must be prepared to look upon Afghanistan for some years as an outwork yielding nothing, but requiring much expenditure to keep it in repair.'[13] According to some other accounts the welcome had definitely been bought by a lavish distribution of money from the Calcutta treasury. Of this expenditure Sir John Kaye was most critical:

> Early in the campaign, Macnaghten had encouraged the conviction that the allegiance of the Afghan was to be bought; that the Afghan cupidity would not be proof against British gold. So he opened the treasure chest, scattered abroad its contents with an ungrudging hand; and commenced a system of corruption which, though seemingly successful at the outset, wrought, at the end, the utter ruin of the policy he had reared.[14]

12 Lieutenant Colonel Ivor Edwards-Stuart, *A John Company General* (Bognor Regis: New Horizon, 1883), p.67.
13 Kaye, *History of the War in Afghanistan*, vol. 1, p.424.
14 Kaye, *History of the War in Afghanistan*, p.426.

As the troops arrived, the soldiers weakened by days of half rations and the cavalry wholly ineffective both from actual wear and the emaciated state of the horses, and the camp followers in a pitiful state, they were allotted their camping sites outside the city. There was to be no looting of the city as according to the unwritten rules of warfare the citizens had welcomed the invaders, and of course the city now belonged to the Shah. He pressed for the immediate pursuit of the fleeing Barakzai chiefs, who had fled to Girishk, the old-bolt hole of the Barakzai Grand *Wazir* Fateh Khan; however, instead, overtures were made to these chiefs to surrender and be banished to India, which overtures were rejected, and the British army was incapable of any immediate pursuit. Of Kandahar and its citizens Captain James Douglas of 53rd BNI records his feelings and, no doubt those of many others:

> Kandahar is a dirty place and so are the people, a miserable lot of bloody barbarians, the most dispiriting race I have seen in my travels. They are cunning, avaricious, proud and filthy notwithstanding all the romantic descriptions of Burnes, Conolly and Company.[15]

During the last days of April the 2nd Division started to arrive, equally exhausted, and the Army of the Indus was complete at Kandahar on 4 May 1839. The very first order, issued by army commander Keane, was to move the responsibility of supply procurement from the politicos back to the Commissariat.

On Wednesday 8 May the Army of the Indus was drawn up in front of the city with a platform raised at the centre of the line. The guns in the city announced the departure of Shah Shuja from the city and he was met at the Herat Gate by Keane, envoy Macnaghten in full court dress and Sir Alexander Burnes in a suit. Shah Shuja was then escorted by this delegation to the platform while the British guns fired a royal salute. Keane and Macnaghten presented His Majesty with a *nazar* of 101 gold *mohurs* on behalf of the British Government; this was followed with further presentations by friendly chiefs and native officers of his force. The parade ended with a march-past of the whole army with the Shah taking the salute. It was estimated that as many as 4,000 Afghans had come to witness this *tamasha* signifying the re-crowning of Shah Shuja-ul-Mulk.

As conditions in Kandahar were not great, a body of camp followers 300 strong decided to up sticks and return to India. When a *kafila* arrived on its way to India, its members placed themselves under the care of the *kafila* chief. A big mistake as besides the few exceptions who had returned to Kandahar, all were slaughtered at Marosf. Captain James Outram was sent out with a strong escort to deliver a sharp lesson. He destroyed the fort and killed all the able-bodied men.

After a fortnight of 'R and R', military minds thought it now appropriate to send out a pursuit force to apprehend the fleeing Barakzai chiefs, who had earlier refused the terms of submission. Brigadier Robert Sale, 'Fighting Bob',[16] was selected to command the force which was mainly

15 British Library, MSS Eur C 181, Captain Douglas correspondence.

16 Major General Sir Robert Sale (1782-1845). Born at Velore, the son of Colonel Robert Sale of the Madras Army. In 1795 he was commissioned into HM 36th Foot (Herefordshire) at the time stationed at Trichinopoly. In 1797 the regiment returned to England, and Sale, desirous of remaining in India, transferred to HM 12th Foot (East Suffolk) and joined the regiment at Fort St George in Madras. He served with the regiment for 19 years and was involved in the Mysore Campaign, the

composed of Shah Shuja's troops. The force marched to the Helmand River and found the fort at Girishk deserted and the Kandahar chiefs reported to have fled to Seiston. The Brigadier left a company of the Shah's force at Girishk and retraced his steps back to Kandahar on 29 May. He brought back with him the incompetent political officer who had been sent out by Macnaghten.

Major General Sir Robert Sale.

The Army of the Indus was destined to remain at Kandahar for a long 60 days recuperating and replenishing stocks, which was no easy task as crops were not ready to harvest and feeding an army in a country where people only grow enough for their own needs is very difficult. During its long stay in Kandahar the Army of the Indus dispensed with 30 *lakhs* of rupees and nearly starved the local inhabitants. The campsites were plagued by robbers driving off the animals, and supply convoys from Shikarpore were subjected to running the gauntlet of the two passes. In one case a convoy of 2,000 camels carrying a load of 8,000 *maunds* of grain eventually arrived at Kandahar, 1,600 camels short. However, there was still enough rum to allow an issue to officers, on payment, who had lost their wine and an extra allowance to European troops on the occasion of His Majesty's birthday celebrated on 24 May. These celebrations were followed by the distressing news that Assistant Surgeon John Hallaran, Lieutenant

taking of Mauritius, duties in Ireland and eventually in the occupation of France, by which point he had attained the rank of major. Upon HM 12th being disbanded in 1818, Sale transferred to HM 13th Foot (Somerset), the regiment with which he is chiefly associated. In 1823 the regiment embarked for Calcutta. In April 1824 the regiment, with Sale in command, sailed for Burma. He served throughout the campaign (1824-25) taking a distinguished part in a long series of arduous operations including the capture of Rangoon. On the conclusion of the campaign, the regiment returned to India and was stationed variously at Dinapore, Berhampore, Agra and Karnaul. Upon the formation of the Army of the Indus, Sale was appointed to the command of First Brigade. For his eminent services during the campaign, he was advanced to the dignity of GCB. He returned with the regiment to Kasauli and a year later went to England for a spot of leave. He returned to India in January 1845 as the quartermaster general of HM forces in India and in this capacity accompanied the commander-in-chief to the First Anglo-Sikh War. In the very first engagement at Mudki on 18 December 1845 he fell dangerously wounded; his left thigh had been shattered by grape shot. He lingered for three days and on 21 December at the little fort at Mudki, he succumbed and was buried at Ferozepore. In May 1805, at Mangalore, Robert Sale married Florentia Wynch and they had one daughter. After Sale's death, Lady Sale remained in India on a pension of £500 and in 1853 went to South Africa for health reasons but died there.

John Chalmers, Ensign Stuart Beaufort, Conductor Havilland and a Mr Jervis of Frith & Co., had all expired in the tremendous heat while accompanying the 23rd Bombay Native Infantry convoy bringing up supplies and desperately needed treasure from Shirkapore.

Brigadier Sale's Pursuit Force returned on 28 May empty-handed but with the knowledge that had it been despatched earlier it would have returned crowned with success. It was also on this day that a group of officers had ventured out on a fishing expedition armed with rods and walking sticks. On returning, two of the party, lieutenants David Inverarity and William Wilmer, both of HM 16th Lancers, were savagely mutilated by a predatory gang of Ghilzis in the vicinity. They were rescued by a platoon of the 4th Gurkha Regiment, but sadly Lieutenant Inverarity died of his wounds a short time later. Shah Shuja on being informed of this atrocity exclaimed, 'O Gentlemen, you must be more cautious here, remember you are not in Hindustan.' A week later four robbers were caught and tried by native general courts martial for having stolen and carried away 23 camels, which apparently belonged to army commander Keane. All were sentenced to be blown from cannons[17] at the very spot where Lieutenant Inverarity had died. The Shah intervened and claimed the robbers as his subjects and had a court of Afghans convened to hear the evidence, upon which the Shah proclaimed them not guilty. Macnaghten was now to console an irate Keane on the premise that it was essential that the Shah was perceived to be magnanimous to his people, whereas the military officers all felt that the robbers, incited by the Ghilzi chiefs to plunder, had to be taught a lesson, otherwise not having the fear of death behind them they would continue to plunder, and so they did; three days later 80 camels were driven off.

It was quite clear by now that the Shah of Persia had given up all designs on Herat thus negating the need to send a British force to that place. However Macnaghten, the envoy, deemed it essential that a friendly mission be despatched to make sure that Shah Kamran and his *Wazir*, Yar Mohammed Khan, were kept onside and to assist in the repairs of the fort. The opportunity was also to be taken to relieve Lieutenant Eldred Pottinger, who had been there for a year and his expenditure had been lavish and unwise. A General Order of 26 May designated the composition of this friendly mission:

Major Elliot D'Arcy Todd, designated political agent
Captain Edward Sanders, mission commander
Captain James Abbott
Lieutenant Richmond Shakespeare
Lieutenant Charles North
Dr John Login[18]
Dr David Ritchie
One European sergeant and 25 Native sappers
One *Naik* and 10 *Golandozs*

17 Being blown from cannons was an old Mughal form of execution adopted by the British for the execution of mutineers. Reportedly this form of execution is still being used, as related by the *Daily Telegraph* on 14 May 2015, in its report of the execution of the North Korean defence minister, General Hyon Yong-chol, by anti-aircraft gun.

18 Sir John Login. After the Second Anglo-Sikh War, Login was appointed guardian to Maharaja Dulip Singh and accompanied the young boy to England. For this service he was knighted.

This friendly mission left Kandahar on 21 June with two *lakhs* of rupees to be used in improving the fortifications at Herat. It was also to draw Shah Kamran to a closer and more cordial alliance by negotiating a treaty, which included a clause banning correspondence with foreign powers and to be compensated (bribed) for this. The mission arrived there on 25 July, whereupon Lieutenant Pottinger, who had been quite liberal in his appeasement of Afghan appetite for gold, returned to India where he was to submit his report to an admiring Governor General. Macnaghten had originally intended to send Sir Alexander Burnes as head of mission, but this gentleman declined as, no doubt, he had no desire at this juncture to be sidelined from the main event. Clearly Macnaghten did not wish to have Burnes under his feet, as on another occasion he suggested that Burnes be sent to Kandahar, before settling on Captain Henry Rawlinson.

In mid-June it was reported that a Lohane caravan of 4,000 camels with 20,000 *maunds* of supplies, sufficient for an army on half rations for a month, was on its way to Afghanistan. It was also reported that a large party of Ghilzis was planning to subvert the caravan's arrival in Kandahar. A *rissaldar* (troop) of the 4th Bengal Local Horse, under the command of *Jemadar* Uzeem Khan, was sent out to gain intelligence of this caravan. Largely thanks to this officer's efforts, the chief of the caravan, Surwar Khan, was persuaded to proceed to Kandahar and not Kabul. Lieutenant Colonel Hugh Wheeler[19] was then sent out with a strong force to protect the caravan approach from Ghilzi attack. The caravan arrived in Kandahar on 24 June to the great joy of the army. But the mood was to change as the caravan chief declared that his men would not proceed to Kabul with their camels for fear of reprisals by Amir Dost Mohammed against their families in Kabul. The chief was quite prepared to sell the camels but his men would not go with them. As the treasure chest was nearly empty and camels without their *oot wallahs* would be a nightmare, they were left behind at Kandahar and the Army advanced on half rations.

On Thursday 27 June 1839, at the crack of dawn, the regimental bands struck up stirring martial music to herald the advance to Kabul. The music could not be heard at Lahore where the solemnity of silence had descended on the assembled *Sardars* and *Bhais* witnessing the heart of the Lion of the Punjab splutter to its end. Maharaja Ranjit Singh was dead.

19 Lieutenant Colonel Hugh Wheeler. Wheeler was in command of the Cawnpore Garrison when it was attacked by the rebels at the start of the Indian Mutiny, and the whole garrison was slaughtered.

10

The Fractured Sikh Advance

News of the Maharaja Ranjit Singh's death was received in Peshawar on 2 July and the Sikh army there was ordered into 12 days of mourning. The 'Captain Sahib', Lieutenant Colonel Claude Wade, was much saddened by this long-feared news as he had now lost a respected monarch with whom he had cultivated an enviable rapport, and without whom he was to be grossly handicapped in his preparations for the advance to Kabul.

In accordance with the Tripartite Treaty, a demonstration was to be made from Peshawar of an army consisting of *Shahzada* Timour's troops and an auxiliary Sikh force of 5,000 comprising Mussulmans. This demonstration was designed to draw away a portion of Amir Dost Mohammed's army from the main thrust to be made by Shah Shuja's force and the Army of the Indus via the Bolan Pass, and the advance up the Khyber Pass was to be in concert with the one from Kandahar. The time spent in preparation at Peshawar was also to be used to provide an opportunity for Afghan chiefs, in the vicinity, to render their allegiance to the interests of Shah Shuja and so facilitate his son's advance through the pass. All to be financed by the Calcutta treasury.

On the last day of 1838, Lord Auckland's historic visit to the capital of the Sikh Kingdom came to its end. As His Lordship departed, full of righteous resolve, the only cloud on the horizon was the speculation of the dangerous state of the Maharaja's health, who had taken to his bed too ill to personally bid farewell to his exalted guest. Ranjit Singh had reached the summit of his ambitions; his had been the genius that had given energy to every Sikh undertaking and the direction of all affairs was 'on the tongue of His Highness'.[1] On 3 January 1839 Ranjit Singh suffered another stroke, and as his speech became more impaired so too did his grip on affairs as his ministers gave to his orders their own interpretation coinciding with their various and divergent agendas. 'Authority forgets a dying king', wrote Alfred Lord Tennyson.[2]

1 Shahamat Ali, *The Sikhs and Afghans, in Connexion with India and Persia, Immediately Before and After the Death … of Ranjeet Singh* (London: J. Murray, 1846; Elibron Classics reprint, 2005), p.14. Shahamat Ali styled himself as 'the Persian Secretary with the Mission of Lieutenant Colonel Claude Wade'. He was a graduate of the English College in Delhi, as was the more famous Mohan Lal Kashmiri. Shahamat Ali had been selected in 1832 to join Wade's staff at Ludhiana and accompanied this officer to Peshawar and Kabul. When Lieutenant Colonel Wade returned to India in 1839, Shahamat Ali was sent as the Mir Munshi to the political resident at Malwa.

2 The *Morte D'Arthur*.

Lieutenant Colonel Wade, the appointed British representative responsible for the coordination of the joint advance through the Khyber Pass, left Lahore on 12 January with a small cadre of British officers, *Shahzada* Timour and his father's old *Wazir*, Mullah Shukore, Sultan Mohammed Khan the erstwhile Barakzai Governor of Peshawar and Khan Mohammed Khan the son of the Sadozai *Wazir* in Herat. Both these last named gentlemen had recently declared their support for Shah Shuja. Lieutenant Colonel Wade had intended to wait in Lahore for the arrival of the two 24-pdr howitzers, fully equipped for service and promised to the Maharaja by the Governor General. However, due to an administrative hiccup the departure of these guns from Delhi was delayed. Rather than waste any more time at Lahore, Colonel Wade decided to set off for Peshawar, the base of his imminent operations, and have the guns follow with a Sikh escort. Colonel Wade sent on ahead Lieutenant Frederick Mackeson with his cousin Mr Mackeson, a volunteer, and Dr Percival Lord with his friend Mr Carron,[3] also a volunteer, with 50,000 rupees each to conciliate chiefs and raise levies for *Shazada* Timour's force.

The howitzers, under the command of Lieutenant William Barr, accompanied by two companies of 20th Bengal Native Infantry, the escort for a treasure chest of 2.5 *lakhs* of rupees and commanded by Captain Joseph Ferris, reached Lahore on 19 February and left four days later. When this group reached Attock, on the Indus, its crossing of the river was thwarted by the silly antics of Prince Peshwara Singh, a reputed son of the Maharaja. His unseemly behaviour was duly reported to Wade, who in turn informed the Maharaja and the young man was given a royal rap over the knuckles. Barr with his howitzers and Ferris with the treasure eventually reached Peshawar on 27 March; the same day as the Army of the Indus was entering Quetta.

Shahzada Timour and Wade had been in Peshawar since 16 March. On entering the city they had been met by General Pablo de Bartolomea Avitabile,[4] the relatively new Governor of Peshawar. He had replaced General Jean-Francois Allard, the Maharaja's favourite of all his

3 Carron is mentioned only in Shahamat Ali's book (p.326.) It is possible that Shahamat Ali also spelt the name wrong and his 'Carron' could be Assistant Surgeon Patrick Cannon of the Bombay Medical Department, as was Dr Perceval Lord, hence the connection and the reason why he was included on Wade's mission. There was an Assistant Surgeon Cannan, who was with HM 2nd Foot at the storming of Ghazni.

4 General Pablo de Bartolomea Avitabile (1791–1850), was an artillery officer. On the disbandment of this army, Avitabile found employment in Persia where he met up with generals Allard and Ventura. In 1826 General Ventura suggested that he seek employment with Ranjit Singh and in 1827 he was introduced to the Maharaja, who duly employed him and sent him to Wazirabad as the governor; in spite of a lot of opposition, Avitabile proved to be very effective. On the death of General Allard, Avitabile was sent to troublesome Peshawar, which he ruthlessly tamed. Avitabile had all the extrovert characteristics of an Italian. Colin Mackenzie, who became quite a friend of his, describes the General as 'evidently a man of great talent and dauntless determination, but capacious, somewhat cruel and most unscrupulous in increasing his already large fortune. He is very hospitable to the English and popular accordingly. His appearance is rather *outré*, a tall burly man, ordinarily apparelled in a magnificently laced Horse Artillery jacket, wide crimson Turkish trousers drawn at the ankle, a golden girdle, and a very handsome sabre, his large Jewish features and bronzed countenance adorned with fierce mustachios, which look like twisted bayonets, and a thick grey beard; the whole mounted by a gold-laced forage cap, which he never takes off.' After the assassination of Maharaja Sher Singh in September 1843, he saw the writing on the wall, cashed in all his assets and slipped out of Punjab history. He returned to his villa in Castelmare, where his greedy family cajoled him into marrying his niece and appointing her paramour his lawyer and financial adviser. He died a mysterious death in 1850.

foreign officers, who had died at Peshawar in early January. News of his death had been kept from the sick Maharaja for some time as it was feared that the sudden loss of his friend might cause another stroke. When the Maharaja was eventually given the news, he was told that the General had 'bade farewell to the material world and packed up the baggage of his existence'.[5]

Based on assurances given in Lahore, Lieutenant Colonel Wade had expected the Sikh army at Peshawar, 10,000 strong and under the command of *Sardar* Sham Singh Attriwalla, to have started preparations for the joint advance and in particular to have secured the fortress at Ali Masjid at the mouth of the Khyber Pass. But, he was horrified to discover that nothing had been done, and worse, no orders had been given to the Sikh troops; furthermore Wade's efforts to get things moving were thwarted at every turn. Being an old hand at the workings of the Sikh *durbar*, the 'Captain Sahib' bombarded it with pleas to comply with its treaty obligations. In his correspondence, he drew attention to the urgency of designating the 5,000 Mussulman troops for the Sikh auxiliary force which was to accompany the *Shahzada* to Kabul. It is of interest to note that in his communications Wade assiduously avoided using the anti-British chief minister, Raja Dhian Singh, as the medium of communicating with the Maharaja. Wade knew from experience that no amount of correspondence could be as effective as the physical presence of a British representative at the *durbar*, but this could only happen under the guise of a diplomatic mission which he strongly advocated but was not to take place until well after Kabul had been taken. After a vexatious month in Peshawar, Wade was writing to the Governor General about his woes:

> I do not doubt the sincerity of the Maharaja in his professed wish to fulfil his engagement, but his promises convey no assurance that they will be fulfilled. His increasing infirmity has generally impaired the vigour of his Government, and to obey his orders or not greatly depend on the views and prejudices of his officers.[6]

On the arrival of Captain Ferris and Lieutenant Barr, the head of the British Mission hosted a welcome dinner for all his officers in his *kuss-kuss tattied* tent.[7] As William Barr was to write, 'They sat down to an elegantly spread table covered with silver and furnished with a profusion of delicate viands that would have suited the taste of the most fastidious epicure.'[8] The British Mission at this time was made up of the following persons:

Lieutenant Colonel Claude Wade, political agent and head of mission
Captain Joseph Ferris, commander of two companies of 20th BNI
Captain Charles Farmer, commander of two companies of 21st BNI
Lieutenant Richard Maule, acting ADC to *Shahzada* Timour
Lieutenant Ralph Dawson, 5th BNI, assigned to raise levies

5 Aijazuddin, *The Resourceful Fakirs*, p.243.
6 Aijazuddin, *The Resourceful Fakirs*, p.250.
7 A panel made up of roots of the kuss kuss plant to fit a window or door. When water is thrown onto the panel from outside, the warm breeze is cooled passing through the matted panel. It is as good as modern air conditioning.
8 William Barr, *Journal of a March from Delhi to Peshawar and thence to Cabul* (London: J. Madden, 1844), p.125.

Lieutenant William Hillerston, 53rd BNI, assigned to raise levies
Lieutenant Alfred Corfield, 62nd BNI, adjutant to Captain Farmer
Lieutenant Joseph Cunningham, Bengal Engineers, assisting Colonel Wade
Lieutenant Charles Rattray, 20th BNI, adjutant to Captain Ferris
Lieutenant William Barr, Bengal Artillery, commander howitzer detachment
Dr Alexander Reid, Bengal Medical Department, mission doctor
Munshi Shahamat Ali, Persian interpreter
Lieutenant Frederick Mackeson. 14th BNI. On special assignment
Mr Mackeson, accompanying Lieutenant Mackeson
Dr Percival Lord, Bombay Medical Department, on special assignment
Mr Patrick Cannon, on special assignment at Bajour
Captain Augusto de la Font, seconded from Sikh service as liaison officer

The only pleasing aspects of conditions in Peshawar were the unstinting support given to the British Mission by the Maharaja's foreign officers, in particular General Avitabile, and the increasing number of Afghans who were arriving in the *Shahzada*'s camp to tender their allegiance to the cause of Shah Shuja. The latter, in accordance with custom, expected to be honoured with a *khelat* plus the appropriate amount of cash commensurate with the rank of the individual. While General Avitabile's generosity and attentiveness to the British Mission's need for fuel and forage, given at times in contradiction to official orders, was most welcome, the influx of Afghans to the banner of the *Shahzada* became an embarrassment about which Shahamat Ali had this to say:

> It is customary with these people (Afghans) when they offer their services, to advance extravagant claims. Being so avaricious, no present is sufficient to satisfy them. We are exceedingly plagued by their greedy demands. Many of them come with no other view than to make money. It is difficult to draw a distinction between the good and bad. They all solemnly declare their fidelity, by oath, yet think nothing of betraying their master. Some of the Afridis who joined us at Rawalpindi, later deserted the camp after they had filled their pockets.[9]

According to Shahamat Ali, and for the purpose of this narrative, there were three main tribes in and around Peshawar and the Khyber Pass. These were the Usafzais, the Khataks and the Afridis. The Usafzais were the largest and occupied both banks of the Indus and the area to the north-east of Peshawar. They were warlike, independent and never missed an opportunity to harass the Sikhs. The Khataks occupied the banks of the River Kabul up to Lalpur at the head of the pass. They likewise did not care for the Sikhs. The Afridis occupied the Khyber Pass and were the wildest, strongest and the most formidable of the lot, allying themselves to whichever power paid them for their neutrality. All these tribes were subdivided into many clans, each with its own chief and each invariably at odds with its neighbour. Of the Usafzais, two chiefs, Fateh Khan and Paendesh Khan, were described as 'desperate characters' and were totally faithless. The other chiefs of this tribe were of a more amenable nature. Of the Khataks, the main

9 Ali, *The Sikhs and Afghans*, p.215.

clan was the Momands who occupied two distinct tracts, Lalpur at the head of the pass and the other around the town of Muchnee. The chief at Lalpur was Sadat Khan who was related to Mohammed Akbar Khan by marriage and was a staunch opponent of Shah Shuja. This man had achieved the chieftainship by killing his cousin who was the chief and driving his son, Turabaz Khan, out of the area. The chief at Muchnee was Karim Khan who was open to negotiations to the interests of Shah Shuja. The Afridis of the Khyber Pass were divided into five clans. The Khuki Khail at the mouth of the pass, the Sinwari at the head, the Sipa at the centre with the Malikdia Khail and Zada Khail on either side of the Sipas. Of all these clans the Khuki Khail, at the mouth of the pass was the most important as it held the fort at Ali Masjid. Its chief was a gentleman by the name of Abduraman Khan. It is said that the people of the Khyber call the region 'Yaghestan': the land of rebellion.

Aside from their rapaciousness all these tribes shared a common loathing of the prospect of Sikh troops entering Afghanistan under the banner of Shah Shuja. This possibility would be met with 'jihadish' vigour. Lieutenant Colonel Wade, acutely aware of these sentiments, spent a great deal of his time persuading the chiefs that the Sikh auxiliary force accompanying the *Shahzada* would comprise only Muslims and that these would leave once Shah Shuja was back on the Kabul throne. Letters to this effect were sent to all the chiefs, many of whom had also received letters from Amir Dost Mohammed urging them to oppose the march of the 'infidels'. A good deal of money and solicitations were expended on these chiefs with no tangible means to test their avowed fidelity. Wade called a meeting of all the chiefs, especially the Afridis, for them to prove their fidelity and devotion to the cause of Shah Shuja. The Colonel inferred that they could prove their faith by clearing the pass of any opposition and he would provide each chief with the means (cash) to employ 1,000 men for the task. These wild chiefs, who perceived the British to be rolling in wealth, upped the ante. The Colonel sent them home and resolved to deal with them individually at the appropriate time. During the course of his advance up the pass, Wade was to disperse a great deal of money in bribes to the local chiefs to keep it open.

On 11 April General Jean-Baptiste Ventura arrived in Peshawar at the head of a Sikh army which he had left camped at Attock. This army had been sent by the Maharaja to be the Sikh reserve stipulated by the treaty. General Ventura, gentlemanly in appearance and haughty of manner, was one of the Maharaja's trusted senior foreign officers and in charge of his infantry. The General was also a friend of the 'Captain Sahib' and on his arrival Wade expected Sikh preparations to be given some vigour. However, General Ventura did not deem it appropriate, in his current position, to be as forthcoming as the Governor of Peshawar, General Avitabile, probably because he knew that his new commander-in-chief was about to join him.

Three days later, trouble erupted in Peshawar. The Nujeeb Regiment, earmarked to be part of the Sikh auxiliary force, mutinied because it had not been paid for three months and the troops held their commanding officer, Colonel Jacob Thomas, responsible. Colonel Thomas was the mixed race son of the celebrated soldier of fortune George Thomas, but nothing like his swash-buckling father. Jacob Thomas was described as 'a dull and heavy man'.[10] He and his adjutant were thrown out of their camp and their tents levelled to the ground with the mutinous troops declaring that they 'wanted nothing to do with them'. Wade, much irritated by this incident, intervened, resolved the issue and charged the expense to the Sikh treasury.

10 Barr, *Journal of a March*, p.128.

A week later, a roar of cannon fire announced the arrival of Prince Naunihal Singh, the 18-year-old Sikh commander-in-chief and grandson of the Maharaja. This young man, popular with both the army and the Sikh *Sardars*, had all the makings of another Ranjit Singh. Had he lived as long as his grandfather, the course of British proceedings in India could well have been widely different. Prince Naunihal Singh resembled a nineteenth-century Sikh edition of 'Harry Hotspur', but not as wily as his revered grandfather Ranjit Singh. In his youthful arrogance, Naunihal Singh felt that he could expand on his grandfather's achievements and in this vein was opposed to his grandfather's apparent subservience to British interests and also to the power of the Dogra rajas in the Sikh *durbar*. To this 'overconfident prince' the 'Captain Sahib' represented the conduit through which British influence had flowed and thus he alienated himself from his grandfather's English friend. In turn, the 'Captain Sahib' made no great effort at conciliation, instead he treated the young prince rather like a discerning uncle and felt that his young 'nephew' was more concerned with winning unsavoury friends for Lahore than promoting the aims of the Tripartite Treaty.

Prince Naunihal Singh's group included Raja Gulab Singh Dogra, *Sardars* Attar Singh Sandhanwalia and Lehna Singh Majithia and Jemadar Khushal Singh, who remained at Akola in command of the Sikh troops camped there. At this time the strength of the Sikh army in the vicinity of Peshawar was estimated at three regiments of cavalry, 14 battalions of infantry and about 50 guns. This increase of Sikh force, at the entrance of the Khyber Pass, and the long halt of the British army at Kandahar, caused the Amir in Kabul to think that the plan was to proceed to Herat and that the real threat to Kabul was to come via the Khyber Pass, so, in a state of panic he despatched his warrior son, Mohammed Akbar Khan, with an army to Jalalabad to block this threat from the east. The Amir was hopeful that any threat from the Bolan Pass would be effectively challenged by his Barakzai brothers in Kandahar to whom he offered to send assistance. As further insurance to block the threat from the west he sent another son, Gulam Hyder Khan, to fortify the city of Ghazni.

The news of the unopposed entry of Shah Shuja into Kandahar was received in Lahore on 6 May and no doubt gave the ailing Maharaja a 'moment of distant triumph – a spark of gunpowder'[11] to his frail constitution and vindication of his participation in the British-inspired treaty. However, Shah Shuja had succeeded in entering Kandahar once before and had then stumbled, so, as the halt of the Army of the Indus lengthened, the delay may have served to cheer the dying Maharaja's vexed spirit with the hope that the English would yet be baffled.[12] In Peshawar the temperature had risen to 110° and the majority of Wade's officers fell sick, thus causing preparations to drag. On 9 May Wade, from his sickbed, sent Shahamat Ali to ask Prince Naunihal Singh for a decision regarding the nomination of a commander for the Sikh force. At first the Prince suggested General Ventura to be the commander while at the same time imposing a restriction on the Sikh advance to as far as Takal. Wade rejected this as implying no advance at all and the nomination of Ventura designed to cause embarrassment to the overall command structure.

During one of his more lucid moments, Ranjit Singh convened a meeting of all his principal *Sardars* and advisers and formally invested his eldest son, Kharak Singh, as his successor. He then

11 Aijazuddin, *The Resourceful Fakirs*, p.249.
12 Cunningham. *History of the Sikhs*, p.312.

placed his son's hand in that of his chief minister, Raja Dhian Singh Dogra, thus making over to him the charge of his son and heir. When the last moments of Maharaja Ranjit Singh arrived, a reported 22 *lakhs* of rupees were distributed in alms among the poor, much to the dismay of his son, who was alarmed at the disposal of his inheritance. Ranjit Singh also wanted to give the *Koh-i-Noor* diamond to the temple at Jagannath, but this order was not complied with.

Ranjit Singh suffered his final stroke on 24 June. He was totally disabled and his speech was slurred and hardly audible. Chief Minister Raja Dhian Singh and *Fakir* Azizuddin never left his side, and through them the old Lion's last instructions were made known. As they laid the Maharaja on Mother Earth and the gathered *Bhais* invoked the will of God, Ranjit Singh breathed his last on 27 June 1839, one of the greatest monarchs ever to have reigned in India. His unification of the Punjab was itself a phenomenal achievement only to be surpassed by his turning of the tide of history in stopping the flow of conquerors from the Hindu Kush, forever. Among his subjects, a mixture of Sikhs, Muslims and Hindus, Ranjit Singh had been revered as a kind and generous master; from the time he became Maharaja he never had anyone put to death, even for the most heinous crime, and yet he managed to keep his wild people in perfect subjugation. So personal had been his rule, and so absolute his authority, that the institution of sovereignty and government, through which his successor might establish himself, hardly existed. As rival factions gave support to their preferred candidates, authority was to eventually drain back to its source, the army.

There may be no fuller description of the cremation of Maharaja Ranjit Singh than that given by Syed Muhammad Latif in his 'History of the Punjab', from which the following extract is taken.

> The Maharaja's body, having been bathed with fragrant waters and embalmed, was dressed in rich clothes and decorated with ornaments as in life. Four of the Maharaja's Ranis and seven of his slave-girls prepared to burn themselves along with the body of their lord and master. According to the tenets of the Hindu religion only childless wives burn themselves alive on the funeral pile of their husbands, and they undergo the horrid ceremony apparently in the hope of getting in the next world what they have been denied in this.
>
> The Maharaja's body was placed on a decorated bier and placed on a board on which the body of the Maharaja lay and was carried by a number of men. Thousands of people accompanied the funeral and the procession from the interior of the fortress towards the funeral pile.
>
> For the first time in their lives, the Ranis of the Maharaja came out unveiled from the harem and meekly followed the corpse barefooted. They were dressed in pure white silk and wore no ornaments as they had distributed all their jewels and valuables among the poor before leaving the harem. In front of each Rani, at a distance of two or three paces walked a man with his face turned towards her and moving backwards. He held a looking glass before the Rani so that she might see that her features were unaltered, and that her resolution to sacrifice her life had no effect on her appearance.
>
> After the Ranis, followed the seven slave-girls were barefooted. Some of them appeared to be only fourteen or fifteen years of age. All seemed quite indifferent to the awful fate which awaited them.
>
> The drums beat mournfully, the musicians sang melancholy dirges, and the sound of their instruments spread gloom and sorrow throughout the whole assembly. This,

> combined with the murmuring of a vast mourning crowd, whose anxious faces bore testimony to the grief and affliction inwardly felt by them, and to their love of their departed master, whom they adored, and who had loved them, gave the whole scene a most melancholy aspect. The funeral pile was constructed of sandalwood and aloe, in the form of a square six feet high. Upon it were strewn inflammable substances, such as cotton seeds. The bier having been brought close to it, its valuable ornaments and costly covering were given away to the mob. The Brahmins and the Gurus then recited passages from their holy books and offered prayers for the benefit of the departed soul of the Maharaja. This occupied about half an hour. The ascent to the funeral pile was by a ladder. The ministers and the sardars first ascended and helped in gently removing the royal body from the bier and respectfully placing it in the middle of the pile, together with the board on which it lay. The four Ranis, with death-despising intrepidity, then ascended the fatal ladder, one by one, according to their rank, and occupied a place at the head of their royal husband, holding the head with their hands. The slave-girls, with equal courage and contempt for death, then ascended the ladder and placed themselves at the foot of their lord. The *sattis*, having thus seated themselves round the royal corpse, were covered with reed mats, on which oil had been profusely poured. A strong thick mat of reeds was then brought and saturated with oil, with which all were covered. The Minister, Raja Dhian Singh, and the sardars then came down. The Raja seemed the most affected, and grief had so much overpowered him that he felt his own life a burden, and insisted on being burnt with the Ranis.
>
> Twice or thrice he even attempted to force his way forward; and it was with some difficulty that he was persuaded to refrain from sharing the fate of the *sattis.* Oil, otto and ghee were then profusely thrown on the pile. This being done, Prince Kharak Singh lighted the pile at each corner, and in a moment the whole was ablaze, the flames of which ascended to a prodigious height. In almost the twinkling of an eye the unfortunate creatures who had been covered with the mats, had ceased to exist, and in a short time the whole mass was reduced to ashes. The burning of the pile occupied two days.

Both contemporary accounts and historians have labelled *Kunwar* Kharak Singh as being an imbecile. This feeble man was further disadvantaged by having a dynamic dominating father, an ambitious impatient son, a reputed half-brother who disputed his succession, a chief minister foisted on him whom he feared, and, if that was not enough, a wife who was promiscuous and horrid. Yet he was now the legitimate successor to the great Ranjit Singh, anointed as such by the late Maharaja on his deathbed. Of what was probably of greater impact was the immediate acknowledgement of the British Government of Kharak Singh as the new monarch. There can be no doubt that without this predominating influence of British authority, the succession would have resulted in bloody civil commotion. Writing about the succession, Captain William Osborne, the Governor General's military secretary who also viewed Kharak Singh as an imbecile, had this to say:

> Upon the death of Ranjit Singh, Kharak Singh was immediately acknowledged by the British Government and he is (for the present at least) seated upon the throne of his father. But there can be no doubt that he owes his peaceful accession to the predominating influence of British authority and to the course of events that occasioned the presence of a British

> army north of the Sutlej at the moment of Ranjit Singh's death. This alone prevented those civil commotions and rival contests which would otherwise have infallibly taken place.[13]

Writing to John Hobhouse on 28 June, Lord Auckland, oblivious of Ranjit Singh's death the day before, gave his friend his assessment of the situation:

> I look upon the death of the Maharaja as now very near, and it may have an effect on our operations on the side of Peshawar. Kharak Singh will quietly succeed so long as his own son Naunihal Singh and the Minister Dheen Singh can bring themselves to act together, but this is not likely to last long. Sher Singh has estates on this side of the river [Sutlej] upon which he would probably take up his residence and bide his time. He is clever and bold, but he is wild and unprincipled and has at present little influence.[14]

His Lordship's reference to Sher Singh being 'unprincipled' was no doubt prompted by Sher Singh's earlier request for British support for his claim to the Sikh *guddi*, which the high-minded Governor General had rejected and the applicant was admonished and told to accept his new master.

It was only natural for the unfortunate Maharaja Kharak Singh to find solace in a collection of sycophants, in particular one Chet Singh Balwa, who had been the manager of his estates. This gentleman made much of his association with the new Maharaja to the acute irritation of many in the Sikh *durbar* especially Chief Minister Raja Dhian Singh, who saw in the machinations of this upstart a threat to his exalted position. Had Chet Singh Balwa been more subtle and patient he might well have achieved his ambition of replacing the Chief Minister to the gratification of his master, but he was neither; instead he became obnoxious to many and a prime target for speedy elimination. However, Raja Dhian Singh, more crafty than most, knew that any such measure would require the concurrence of Prince Naunihal Singh and the approbation of the despised British, so he worked his charm on both and struck 100 days later.

On 26 June Lieutenant Colonel Wade had written to Prince Naunihal Singh informing him of the imminent advance of the Army of the Indus to Kabul, and hence the immediate need for the force from Peshawar to be assembled, advance and capture the fort at Ali Masjid. Earlier, the small Afghan force at Ali Masjid had been offered employment in the *Shahzada*'s contingent at 10 rupees per month and a bounty of 20 rupees on presenting themselves, but this more than generous deal was rejected, thus Ali Masjid had to be taken in the face of deadly Afghan *jezails*.[15] The Prince and his advisers, which included Raja Gulab Singh Dogra, were less than enthusiastic about the British initiative of placing the ill-fated Shah Shuja on the throne of Afghanistan as, once there, the British could stifle any further Sikh ambitions for expansion. Sikh involvement in the scheme had been acquiesced to by the dying Maharaja and they had now to look to the future without him. The continued vacillation of the Sikh high command was becoming unbearable to the normally cool and calm 'Captain Sahib', who in a fit of choking frustration accused the young Prince of intriguing with the Afghans and deliberately sabotaging

13 W.G. Osborne, *Ranjit Singh: the Lion of the Punjab* (Calcutta: Susil Gupta, 1952; New Delhi: Rupa & Co. reprint, n.d.), p.25.
14 Aijazuddin, *The Resourceful Fakirs*, p.250.
15 Ali, *The Sikhs and Afghans*, p.406.

the Sikh role in the Tripartite Treaty. The Prince bitterly resented this slur by the man who had held such sway over his grandfather. The Dogra rajas lost no time in fuelling the Prince's animosity, thus the Prince and Dogras found common cause to eliminate both the 'Captain Sahib' and the dreaded Chet Singh Balwa.

At the end of July 1839 a British Commissariat officer, Captain William Nuthall, turned up in Lahore. His purpose was to establish a supply depot at Rawalpindi for the returning Army of the Indus through the Punjab. For this purpose he had with him 2 *lakhs* of rupees. The timing of this officer's arrival, two weeks before the Army had reached its objective, Kabul, was clearly a deliberate ploy by the British to force the issue of right of passage of the British army through the Punjab. This had been discussed between Ranjit Singh and Lord Auckland during the latter's visit to Lahore; although there had been no disagreement the matter had not been officially sanctioned, and the British were hell-bent in settling the matter with the new and decidedly pro-British Maharaja, Kharak Singh. However, the Sikhs in general including the late Maharaja were horrified at the thought of British boots on Sikh soil, which it was universally held 'would never leave'. The Sikh authorities were profuse in welcoming Captain Nuthall and allowed him to go on his way, but at the same time placed impediments on his ability to purchase the necessary supplies. The issue was to bubble along through August and was only resolved after the British Mission was sent to Lahore in September. It is somewhat surprising that the British negotiator of the Tripartite Treaty overlooked this vital factor in the treaty.

A month earlier, Naunihal Singh, now *Kunwar*, returned to Lahore with a good portion of his army and in tow Raja Gulab Singh and General Ventura, the latter very keen to hurry back and safeguard his interests in Lahore. Before his departure *Kunwar* Naunihal Singh had nominated Colonel Shaikh Bassawan as the commander of the Sikh auxiliary force to accompany *Shahzada* Timour to Kabul. Obviously, with the capture of Kandahar unopposed, it would not be too long before Shah Shuja and the Army of the Indus would be ensconced in Kabul. Hence, it would now be prudent for the Sikhs to be seen to be more enthusiastic about their treaty obligations. In the meantime Lieutenant Mackeson had arrived at Kohat with 300 Multani levies and Dr Lord had returned from Bajour having secured the district with loads of cash and leaving Mr Cannon there as the British agent; and in Peshawar a force of 5,000 had been cobbled together under the banner of the *Shazada*. This force comprised the following:

Two companies of 21st BNI, under command of Captain Farmer	160
Regular cavalry	400
Irregular cavalry	600
Jehalees (armed with jezails)	320
Infantry (armed with matchlocks)	2,860
Afghan levies	100
Pioneers	200
Artillerymen	40
Total	4,680

Guns: 2 24-pdr howitzers and 20 × swivel guns

The accompanying Sikh force was made up of the following:

Commander: Colonel Shaikh Bassawan (Sikh Artillery)	
Regular cavalry (French legion)	174
Irregular cavalry	893
Regular infantry	1,868
Irregular Infantry[16]	3,000
Artillerymen 100	100
Total	6,035
Guns: 1 × howitzer, 1 × mortar, 8 × 6-pdr and 2 × 9-pdr	

The two contingents comprising some 10,000 soldiers, 3,000 animals including elephants plus a motley crew of camp followers advanced to Jamrud on 20 July and were immediately involved in a fracas at this Sikh-held fort. Apparently, Mackeson's Multani levies had brought some meat with them, which the Sikhs identified as beef. The killing of cows and consumption of beef is anathema to the Hindu Sikhs and an almighty, religion-fuelled row broke out with an exchange of musket fire, which the Sikh commander was either reluctant or incapable of bringing under control. Eventually Lieutenant Mackeson, at the risk of being fired at, forced the enraged Sikhs to come to their senses and agreed to have his Multani levies camp outside the fort. This ugly situation could well have caused the death knell of the entire campaign.

Not surprisingly the British officers harboured some concerns about the success of the advance, through a defile infested with faithless Afghans and with the ostensible support of a boisterous Sikh force. In his book *Journal of a March from Delhi to Peshawar and from thence to Cabul*, Lieutenant William Barr expresses these concerns as follows:

> The co-operation to be expected from these allies [Sikhs] is not of the most cordial description, for it is well known that the Sikhs, as a nation, are extremely jealous of the British power, and nothing would afford them greater pleasure than to see it met with a reverse. Strong, however, as the Khalsa's dislike for us, I believe their hatred to the Khyberies to be tenfold more bitter, and therefore we have at least the passion to work on our side. Of the Afghan levies it is most difficult to speak. Some amongst them have no doubt been led to espouse the Shahzada's side out of love to his cause, but the majority, it is to be feared, have done so purely for the desire of gain.[17]

The following day Lieutenant Colonel Wade joined his army for its advance, in three columns, into the Khyber Pass. For more than 2,000 years Persians, Greeks, Tartars, Moguls and Afghans had encroached the plains of India through the impressive defiles of the pass, 28 miles of rock, boulders and craggy hills hostile to both change and authority. Now, for the first time, a European led army was to traverse it in the reverse direction. Seven miles into this dragon's mouth, on a rocky isolated hill, lies the fortified position of Ali Masjid with the approach to it

16 This number included two battalions of Nujeeb troops who disgraced themselves during the advance by retreating during one of the actions.

17 Barr, *Journal of a March*, p.183.

overlooked on either side by perpendicular hills from which the Khyberis effectively fired on the advancing troops as they trudged along the rocky bottom. The fort contained a considerable number of wild Afridis and Wade fully expected to be opposed by a force of 2,500 Afghans, as it was reported that the chiefs at Ali Masjid had implored Mohammed Akbar Khan to send part of his army down to help. However, news of Shah Shuja's advance from Kandahar had forced the Amir in Kabul to recall his son from his position at the head of the Khyber for the defence of Kabul, hence the Afridis were left to manage on their own.

Prior to the advance, Wade had taken the precaution of buying over the Khyberis between Peshawar and the entrance to the pass while Shah Shuja's emissaries had secured the neutrality if not the support of the tribes beyond Ali Masjid. It was largely due to Wade's actions at this time that the chiefs of faraway Kohistan, to the north of Kabul, had also declared for the returning Shah. Despite the very generous terms offered, the chiefs at Ali Masjid were resolved to oppose the advance of the *Shahzada*, thus a fight for this stronghold became inevitable. From Jamrud there were two routes into the pass; while Wade advanced along the Jabaghi route, Lieutenant Mackeson's column took the Shade Bagiar route. By 24 July the allied force was within striking distance of the Afridi stronghold, taking up positions from which to make the final attack. A strenuous effort was made by the Afridis to dislodge Mackeson from his position. The Nujeeb regiment of this column, unreliable as ever, fled when attacked leaving their families to the mercy of the Afridis. Fortunately, Mackeson's Multani levies stood firm and with the support of the Sikhs' 6-pdr guns were able to drive off their attackers.

On the following morning the allied force dislodged the enemy from a commanding height on which they had barricaded themselves. Then on 26 July the force moved forward to the immediate investment of the Ali Masjid fortress and after some judicious employment of artillery the allies drove the enemy from one stockade to another until they were forced to seek refuge. Lieutenant Colonel Wade ordered the destruction of the fortifications and a halt of six days. This break was used to send Captain Ferris back to Peshawar with the wounded and to replace the rations that had been plundered by the Afghans, and to rest his exhausted troops. The allied casualties at Ali Masjid were 27 killed and 130 wounded. The time was also used to continue negotiations with the Afghan chiefs further up the pass, in particular Sadat Khan at Lalpur.

On 2 August, the advance continued leaving a small detachment at Ali Masjid under the command of Lieutenant Dawson. Some officers who had taken ill were carried forward; in the case of Lieutenant Barr all the way to Kabul. At one stage he was kindly allowed to use the *howdah* on the *Shahzada*'s elephant. Of the *Shahzada* Barr was to write in his journal, 'The Prince is kind in the extreme. It is a pity he is so deficient in energy as his whole nature is replete with the milk of human kindness, and without it, he will never be able to control the tumultuous passion of the turbulent Afghans, should it ever be his lot to rule over them.'[18]

Four days later, after the continued harassment of plundering, changing the course of water supply and the incessant firing by long range *jezails*, the allied force arrived at Dakka. By this time Kabul was under threat, Mohammed Akbar Khan's army had dispersed and the chiefs at Jalalabad had declared their allegiance to the cause of Shah Shuja. The sole exception was the truculent chief Sadat Khan, at Lalpur, which lay across the river from Dakka. An emissary

18 Barr, *Journal of a March*, p.206.

Entrance of Shah Shuja into Kabul.

was sent to this gentleman assuring him of indemnity on his declaring for Shah Shuja. This he refused, declaring instead his intention to fight to the death. He was obviously not prepared to die too quickly, as on the advance of the allies across the river he fled to Bajour. Lalpur was easily taken and the chieftainship conferred on Turabaz Khan, who remained faithful to the British while their Sikh allies remained doubtful. From Jalalabad, Wade wrote to Mr Torrens:

> I have received a report from Peshawar that the Sikhs are employing the agency of Pir Mahhamed Khan to incline the people of Swat and Bunnu to their Government in the same manner as they are attempting through Sultan Mohhamed Khan to extend their influence in other directions. I have accordingly advised the Shahzada to address letters to all the chiefs of these plains which are not included in treaty with Ranjit Singh informing them of the restoration of the Shah to the throne of Kabul and deciding their allegiance to him as their rightful sovereign.[19]

Jalalabad was the Shah's choice for his winter residence, but in the summer this place became the most unhealthy of locations. According to Lieutenant Barr's notes in his journal, 'In addition

19 Turabaz Khan stood by the British when all the Afghan chiefs had deserted them. He was the medium of communication between the beleaguered British garrison at Jalalabad and the Peshawar authorities and above all it was Turabaz Khan who escorted the supplies of grain, ammunition and money to the garrison at Jalalabad when they were in great need. Regrettably, upon the British evacuation Turabaz Khan was abandoned to his fate.

to one third of several regiments and detachments being on sick report, numbers were daily swelling the list. At noon the temperature never stood lower than 120° Fahrenheit and a hot wind blew all day, but at night it became so cold that counterpanes and blankets were absolutely necessary.'

Another irritant to the British was the presence of the Nepalese general, Matabar Singh, at the Lahore *durbar*, which under the prevailing atmosphere did not allay British suspicions of Sikh intrigue.

While at Lalpur, and in recognition of its success in forcing the Khyber Pass, Lieutenant Colonel Wade distributed a donation of 5,000 rupees given by *Kunwar* Naunihal Singh for the *Shahzada*'s force, and on behalf of the British Government the Colonel distributed a similar amount to the Sikh auxiliary force. It was at Lalpur that Wade heard of the successful storming of Ghazni and the fact that the Army of the Indus was now within a few miles of Kabul. With this heartening news, Wade's army left Lalpur on 13 August for its final objective having left a small garrison at Jalalabad with Lieutenant Mackeson as the political agent. Consequently on the withdrawal of Mohammed Akbar Khan and the flight of Sadat Khan, the remainder of the advance to Kabul was unopposed.

By 23 August the allied force was at the soon-to-be infamous town of Gandamak and by 26 August it was at Jagdalak. On 3 September the *Shahzada*, accompanied by Wade and Colonel Shaikh Bassawan entered the city of Kabul. Their passage was lined by British troops presenting arms to the accompaniment of stirring music played by the regimental bands. At this juncture there was a total of 25,000 allied troops in Kabul. On the morning of 6 September a military review was held, at which Shah Shuja took the salute and Bassawan had the honour of hoisting the Sikh flag on the Bala Hissar. To this worthy gentleman, Lord Auckland sent a sword as a token of his appreciation.

Besides conducting the allied force through the Khyber Pass, Lieutenant Colonel Wade brought with him seedlings of potatoes, thus introducing this vegetable to Afghanistan.

11

The Final Push

The Army of the Indus had been in Kandahar for a long nine weeks recuperating and replenishing. The rumoured renewal of a Persian advance on Herat had proved false and the Kandahar chiefs had vanished along with their army, so all attention was now given to the advance on Kabul, concluding the honourable mission of restoring Shah Shuja-ul-Mulk back on the throne of his ancestors. Enough time had already been lost to the Amir, Dost Mohammed Khan, allowing him to strengthen his defences and muster an army to oppose the Shah and his infidel allies; in fact a report had already come in to the effect that the Amir's son, Ufzul Khan, was advancing on Kandahar with a force of 1,000 infantry, 500 cavalry and four guns. It was militarily important and politically essential that the 318 miles to Kabul, a minimum of 30 marches, be undertaken with some expediency. However, the British army commander Lieutenant General John Keane had a huge problem: an acute lack of carriage for the supplies and forage of his army of 10,400 troops, 25,000 camp followers, 3,450 horses, 480 bullocks and 11,200 camels to carry 44,000 *maunds* (1,500 tons) of supplies for one month. Consequently he made the decision to advance on half rations, and on the advice of his overconfident politicos and the chief artillery officer, to leave his 'battering train' in Kandahar, a decision that could have caused him great embarrassment and no accolades. The European troops were to suffer further as the Commissariat had run out of rum and they were only to receive their next issue at Kabul. Some ultra-Evangelical officers credited this particular deficiency with the apparent good behaviour of the European troops in the conquest of Ghazni.

At 3:00 a.m. on Thursday 27 June, the first of three columns departed Kandahar headed by Keane, the second followed on 29 June, and Major General Thomas Willshire,[1] commanded the

1 Major General Sir Thomas Willshire (1789–1862). He was born at Halifax, Novia Scotia and was commissioned into HM 38th Foot (Staffordshire) in 1795 and joined the regiment in the West Indies. Later he was involved in the Peninsular War and was at Corruna and was back in the Peninsular in 1812 commanding the Light Brigade in the assault on San Sabastian. It was during this affair that his brother was killed. In 1815 the regiment was sent to the Netherlands, but it arrived too late for the Battle of Waterloo; in 1818 it was sent to South Africa, and while Willshire was there he wrote the first drill book for the army. Willshire was a strict disciplinarian and was to earn the sobriquet of 'Tiger Tom'. He arrived in Calcutta with his regiment in 1822 and was then transferred to HM 2nd Foot (Queen's Own), which was stationed at Poona. He served with this regiment for 10 years. Sir Lionel Smith, inspecting the regiment in 1830, said that 'He had never yet met so perfect

third column which left on 1 July. A garrison commanded by Lieutenant Colonel John Herring and consisting of 37th BNI, 3rd Infantry Regiment and a troop of horse artillery from Shah Shuja's force, a *Rissaldar* of Anderson's Horse and 12 guns under the command of Lieutenant Francis Hawkins, were left in Kandahar where Captain Robert Leech was appointed political agent and Captain John Ripley[2] the fort adjutant and postmaster. In view of the shortage of carriage, envoy William Macnaghten had suggested leaving the Bombay Division at Kandahar as he was convinced that no opposition would be encountered on the advance to Kabul.

The route to Kabul lay through wild and mountainous country. The roads were rocky, difficult and at times almost impossible for the passage of the guns. This part of the country was populated by the western Ghilzais, fanatical and the boldest of the Afghan mounted troops. Of these men, William Taylor, a troop sergeant major of HM 4th Light Dragoons, observed:

> I have no hesitation in saying that Afghan cavalry are a most effective body of men. They may not be equal to ours in the field, but for a harassing system of mountainous warfare when they are required to make sudden descents upon infantry hemmed in between defiles and embarrassed by ignorance of the country, no body of troops can be better adopted. Their horses are light-limbed but strong and wiry and are capable of undergoing incredible fatigue which the trooper himself practised from infancy in management of the animal, can ride him over places where no European horseman would venture. Had these wild mountaineers but the advantage of discipline and proper organisation this country would be inaccessible to any troops in the world.[3]

Five days into the advance, Keane was given information, said to be reliable, that the Ghilzais were assembling in great force at Kelat-i-Ghilzai and enemy *chuppaos* and raids on the baggage train were to be expected. Due precautions were taken and the advance slowed down. In the event, there was no opposition at Kelat-i-Ghilzai where the first column was halted for a day allowing Shah Shuja's contingent to join it. It was assumed that the 3,000 strong Ghilzais, who, obviously hostile, had been stalking the flanks of the army, were waiting to be joined by Dost Mohammed Khan before making a determined attack. On the twentieth day of the advance at a village called Mukoor, the Ghilzai chief, Abdul Raman, with 1,000 horse, attacked the flank of Shah Shuja's force. This was resoundingly beaten off by the Shah's 4th Gurkha Regiment, who followed the Ghilzai horse up the hill, killing and wounding many. The Gurkha loss was one man killed and two wounded. Apart from this affair and the continuous raids on the baggage

a commanding officer'. In 1837 Willshire was promoted to brigadier in command of the Poona Garrison, and the following year was made a major general in command of the Bombay Division of the Army of the Indus. After the disbandment of the army at the conclusion of the campaign, Major General Willshire returned to England. In 1848 he married Annette Maxwell, by whom he had two sons and three daughters. He died at Hill House, near Windsor, in May 1862.

2 Captain John Ripley (1801–1857). At the time of the Indian Mutiny, May 1857, Ripley was in command of 54th BNI at Delhi. When the mutiny broke out he led his regiment to the Kashmir Gate to restore order. Regrettably, the *sepoys* of his regiment turned and joined the rebels. Ripley was hacked to bits receiving 17 wounds and was left for dead. Later he was taken back to the garrison, and when this place also came under attack, Ripley was put in a *dhooli* and sent to Kaunal for safety. He never arrived and was never seen again.

3 Taylor, *Scenes and Adventures in Afghanistan*, p.89.

train the Ghilzais remained on the flanks awaiting the arrival of Dost Mohammed, or if he failed, to come in and declare their allegiance to the Shah as some had already done.

Lieutenant John Hall of HM 40th Foot wrote one of the only accounts of the routine at the end of a day's march, a valuable contribution to knowledge of the life of a Victorian soldier on the march in enemy territory:

> The main body reaches the ground, and each corps marches at once to its quarters. The individual to the site of his palace for the day. Shortly comes the numerous train of baggage, carried by camels, elephants, mules, horses. Asses, bullocks carts etc etc, many thousands in number, and followers far exceeding the number of troops. The followers attached to the various portions of baggage proceed at once to their spots of ground. The tent and its baggage arrive together, and all is prepared to 'Pitch Camp.' A signal is given, and as if it were by magic, a town, a fort and a stronghold is formed, guards mounted, pickets arranged and sentries placed, and all is quiet and settled for the day. The Commissariat proceeds to kill the cattle and issue the provisions. The baggage cattle are all sent out to graze under strong guards. The bazaars (one to each corps) open their stores of merchandise and, and expose it for sale, at an enormous and extortionate profit. The authorities at the head are engaged in the arrangement of the objects in view; emissaries are sent out; chiefs are received and negotiated with for the supply of provisions; the weary soldier, after smoothing down for his domestic comfort his parlour of twenty-one inches by six feet, lulled by the aid of that refreshing genius, sleep, beguiles the long dreary hours of the day, filled with anxiety and overpowered oftentimes with the intense heat, rendered more so by the trifling protection under canvass. At length comes the night, and every precaution having been taken, all is prepared for a fresh start, the cattle are placed in front of their tomorrow's load, each soul devolves unto that earthy heaven, which soon relieves the mind from the world's anxiety and care; at the dead of night is heard the trampling of the patrols carefully visiting the guards and pickets and the reliefs cautiously challenged by the watching sentries. And shortly after midnight are heard the shrill trumpets and bugles arousing the tired soldier from the midst of perhaps dreams of the happy hours of boyhood and home. The sound carries with it a volume of directions; and in a few minutes all is again confusion – yet regularity is there; all a tip-toe of bustle – yet all is steady and each at his place. The camp appears as one blaze of fire from the darkness of the night, and the bushes or piles of brushwood collected, being fired to give light to enable the packing and loading to be carried on, and should you stray a dozen yards perchance it will take you half an hour to find your place again. Long ere the day dawns, all are again on the march.[4]

At each of the halts by the army, it was the practice of officers to mooch off on shooting expeditions, no doubt to supplement their rations regardless of the fact that they could become victims to enemy raiding parties, and many were to be killed in this manner. With the prospect of an imminent attack by the ever-watchful Ghilzais, Keane felt it imperative to issue a General

4 J.H.W. Hall, *Scenes in a Soldier's Life: Being a Connected Narrative of the Principal Military Events in Scinde, Beeloochistan and Affghanistan, during 1839, 1840, 1841, 1842 and 1843, under Generals Lord Keane, Brooks, Sir R. Sale, Wiltshire, Pollock, Nott, England, M'Caskill and Sir C. Napier* (Montreal: R. and C. Chalmers, New York: Berford, 1848; Facsimile Publishers reprint, n.d.), p.112.

Order calling the attention of all officers to the 'impropriety in the present position of the army, of officers quitting camp on shooting parties'. While this order may be considered a mild reprimand, discipline in the ranks was most strict and severe. In his journal William Taylor writes, 'At Chesgow, two marches from Ghazni, a soldier of the 2nd Light Cavalry was caught thieving and was shot dead by a staff officer. The extreme severity of this punishment and its informal nature were bitterly conversed amongst the native troops.'[5] This incident may have had a bearing on this regiment's behaviour later in the campaign.

On 20 July, the first two columns of the army arrived at the village of Nanni some 10 miles from Ghazni at an elevation of 7,700 feet above sea level and a temperature of 95°, a bit cooler than the 103° at Kandahar and 3,000 feet higher. From here the minarets of Ghazni were just visible. Keane called a halt and sent out his DQMG, Major William Garden of 36th BNI, with an escort of 30 troopers to reconnoitre the fortress of Ghazni. Major Garden approached within 500 yards of its massive walls and was to report that he had seen no armed men and that there was nothing to indicate that the place was occupied in force, it looked as if it had been deserted, was very weak and was completely commanded from the hills to the north. This intelligence substantiated the earlier assessment given by Sir Alexander Burnes. Based on this reassuring information envoy Macnaghten, on behalf of an impatient Shah, pressed for the advance to continue bypassing this 'insignificant fortress'. Keane, considering the security of his lines of communication, and influenced by the information he had been given, decided to attack and capture the fortress, much to the displeasure of the Shah who had, at Macnaghten's instigation, sent a letter to Dost Mohammed in which he said he was prepared to bury all feelings of animosity which had long subsisted between the two families and that the British Government would guarantee his personal safety, honourable treatment and suitable provision for his wife and family and dependents in the number not exceeding 100, provided that he immediately disbanded his armed retainers and agreed to retire to such place in Hindustan as determined by the British Government. Not surprisingly, there was no answer.

The third column, under Major General Willshire, arrived that night and orders were issued for the advance on Ghazni in three columns. The army, 10,400 strong, moved forward at 4:30 a.m. on 21 July. The country over which it moved was undulating but open and although it had to cross a number of water courses, there was nothing to impede its movement or disrupt its formation. The route was nearly in a direct line all the way except the last three miles when it turned to the left and the fortress of Ghazni burst into view:

And this is Ghizni! This the imperial town
Which once the mighty Mahmood called his own;
Where suppliant princes bowed to him, and high
The banners waved of Eastern chivalry.
James Atkinson

From here the route followed the course of the River Turnuk, which skirted round the north side of the fortress. To the soldiers approaching it the fortress looked massive and formidable, but strangely lifeless. As the soldiers continued to march forward, the customary noise of tramping

5 Taylor, *Scenes and Adventures in Afghanistan*, p.151.

boots, rattling of gun carriages and the ubiquitous dust would have clearly indicated to any occupant of the fortress that it was about to be assailed. Yet there was no sign of any panic or readiness until a mile from its walls. Then, from the gardens and dwellings that lay outside the walls, shots were fired signalling the fact that the Afghans were prepared and ready to fight for Ghazni, the historic capital of Afghanistan.

Now began a firefight to dislodge the Afghans from the gardens and dwellings in front of the fortress. It was during this action that Captain Harry Graves and Lieutenant Fredrick Mullin of 16th BNI were severely wounded. While these preliminary actions were in progress, Keane had ridden up to within artillery range of the fortress to direct operations which were bogging down as his troops got closer to the 35-foot–high walls. Captain George Lawrence of 2nd Bengal Light Cavalry was later to write, 'We were out of range watching the fun when down came a 54-pdr shot, fired from the great gun called "Zubbir Jang" (Lord of War), and by our men "Long Tom", falling in the midst of us killing one man and took off a horse's leg.'[6] As 'Long Tom's' shot whizzed over his head it was very clear to army commander Keane that Ghazni was to be a far tougher nut to crack than he had been led to believe. As he was later to write in his despatch (Appendix IV), 'It is a place of great strength, both by nature and art, far more so than I had reason to suppose from any description I had received of it, although some are from officers in our own service, who had seen it in their travels.' To besiege the fortress was totally impractical as this would take too long with his own forces starving before the besieged surrendered. Breeching was equally impossible due to the strategic error, or incompetence, of the battering train being left in Kandahar 230 miles away. These 18-pdr guns were the only guns capable of blasting a way through the thick walls of the fortress. The only option open to the army commander was the storming of this 'impregnable' fortress.

The army commander ordered his troops to withdraw out of range of enemy artillery and despatched HM 4th Light Dragoons to the rear to forestall an expected attack from Ufzul Khan on the baggage train. He then ordered his chief artillery officer, Brigadier Thomas Stevenson, to have the artillery play on the fortress in order to draw enemy fire thus revealing their gun positions, and the Afghans duly obliged. Finally, Keane instructed his chief engineer, Captain George Thomson, to carry out a detailed reconnaissance of the fortress to determine the weakest spot at which he could direct his storming of it. The fortress was built on a scarped mound about 35 feet high with a high rampart in good repair. It was flanked by numerous towers and surrounded by a *fausse-braye* and a wet ditch. In addition, the towers at the angles were enlarged, screen walls had been built before the gates, the ditch cleared out and filled with water, apparently unfordable, and an outwork had been built on the right bank of the river bend to command the bed of it.

That evening, a deserter from the Afghan garrison in Ghazni came in to the British lines having made contact with Sir Alexander Burnes' *munchi*, Mohan Lal, whom he had known when the latter was in Kabul with Burnes' mission. As Sir John Kaye was to comment, 'The *munchi* seems to have been endowed with a genius for traitor-making, the lustre of which remained undimmed to the end of the war.'[7] The deserter's name was Abdul Rashid Khan, a cousin of Dost Mohammed who said he had defected because of ill treatment. Burnes introduced

6 Lawrence, *Reminiscences*, p.16.
7 Kaye, *History of the War in Afghanistan*, Vol. 1, p.443.

Abdul Rashid Khan to the chief engineer, to whom he revealed that of the three gates into the fortress, the Kabul Gate was the only one that had not been blocked up and was kept open for the expected reinforcements from Kabul. In his later report the chief engineer made a fleeting reference to this valuable piece of information and Keane made none. About his reconnaissance, the chief engineer wrote:

> The fortifications were found equally strong all round, the only tangible point observed being the Cabul gateway, which offered the following advantages for a *coup-de-main*. The road to the gate was clear, the bridge over the ditch unbroken, there were good positions for the artillery within 300 yards of the walls on both sides of the road, and we had information that the gateway was not built up, as reinforcement from Cabul being expected.[8]

Captain Thomson reported his findings to Keane and informed him that should he decide on an immediate attack, the only option was to blow the Kabul Gate open with bags of gunpowder and this during the hours of darkness. This the General resolved to do and the next morning he conducted his own reconnaissance of the point of attack and ordered the repositioning of his troops for the storming of Ghazni. Keane, being no great admirer of the Company's army, determined to make his storming of Ghazni a purely European affair, as can be seen from the composition of this force.

> *Explosion Party*
> Captain Alexander Peat, lieutenants Henry Durand and Norman MacLeod, three engineer sergeants and 18 sappers carrying 100 pounds of explosives in sandbags and a 72-foot hose; all of the Bengal Engineers. Escort of six soldiers of HM 13th Foot.
>
> *Entry Party*
> Light Companies of HM 2nd Foot, HM 13th Foot, HM 17th Foot and 1st BER commanded by 54-year-old Lieutenant Colonel William Dennie. Lieutenant John Sturt, Bengal Engineers, accompanied the group as a guide.
>
> *Storming Party*
> HM 2nd Foot, HM 13 Foot, HM 17th Foot and 1st BER. All under the command of Brigadier Robert Sale.
>
> *Reserve*
> 16th, 35th and 48th Bengal native regiments. All under the command of Brigadier Abraham Roberts.

The Cavalry Brigade, under the command of Major General Joseph Thackwell, was ordered to position itself across the Kabul road a couple of miles from the gate, to oppose any reinforcements from Kabul and also to pursue any retreating Afghans. The chief artillery officer was ordered to arrange for the placement of his guns 300 yards from the walls and on either side of

8 Stocqueler, *Memorials of Afghanistan*, p.38.

the road in order to give the assault immediate support and once entry had been made to switch his fire to the citadel. Finally, a part of Shah Shuja's force was detailed to launch a diversionary attack on the north face of the fortress in order to mask the activity of the explosion party.

While these movements were being arranged, Ufzul Khan suddenly appeared with a force of 3,000 Ghilzais upon the ridge of the hill immediately in the rear of Shah Shuja's camp, clearly intending to attack the Shah and his infidel troops. As they rushed down the slope they were met by the prompt appearance of the Shah's troops with two guns and a troop of cavalry, which diverted what could have developed into a very ugly situation. After the course of an hour, with kukri-armed Gurkhas scrambling over the hillside in pursuit of the enemy and Lieutenant Peter Nicholson's cavalry troop charging into the enemy's horse, Ufzul Khan's fanatics were on the run with the loss of 100 killed and wounded. One of the dead was the father-in-law of Dost Mohammed. Several prisoners were taken, but after they had declared that they had been forced to attack, they were released by the Shah on the recommendation of Macnaghten. However, later on another 38 prisoners were brought in and this group were more belligerent. Shah Shuja wanted them all to be beheaded on the spot, but the Envoy intervened and suggested that the execution be limited to the worst of the bunch. Apparently, the British were bound by treaty not to interfere between the Shah and his subjects, so the decision was left to the Shah who decided to have all the prisoners, except for two, beheaded and they were 'hacked to death with wanton barbarity by the knives of his executioners'.[9] Later, this event was to be described by the liberal press as the 'massacre of the Ghilzais' and there was a great deal of controversy as to whether Keane had been made aware of the Shah's decision before or after the fact. According to Macnaghten, he had been informed before the slaughter and Keane had been of the opinion that 'the most summary example be made of all such dastardly ruffians.' On the other hand an 'officer of rank' on Keane's confidential staff (presumably Lieutenant Colonel Ranald MacDonald) asserted that Keane was only made aware after the fact and was recorded as saying, 'the murderers and treacherous rascals deserved it'.[10]

By 3:00 a.m. on 23 July the artillery and cavalry had taken up their positions and the diversionary force of 35th BNI under the command of Captain John Hay launched its attack on the fortress, effectively distracting the Afghans from the Kabul Gate. The explosion party, led by Captain Peat, moved down to the gateway and under cover of the artillery barrage arrived at the ditch when it came under heavy fire from the ramparts. Taking what cover they could, the explosion party advanced to the gateway where Lieutenant Durand, assisted by Sergeant Robertson, placed 100 pounds of gunpowder and laid the hose fuse. Returning to adequate cover, the fuse was lit and at 4:15 a.m. the gate was blown The explosion concussed Captain Peat and shocked the occupants. Despite his condition and as the officer-in-charge, Peat rushed up to the gate to ascertain the success of the explosion. The fog of war had now descended and pandemonium ensued. The scene is best described from the pen of a participant:

> These events produced a short delay, and Peat, fearing that Durand and his sergeant had been slain before they could lay and fire the hose, quitted the lower sally-port, and, ascending towards the gate, came within the sphere of the explosion. He was violently thrown to the ground, and for a time, stunned; but being a calm brave soldier he no sooner recovered his

9 Kaye, *History of the War in Afghanistan*, Vol. 1, p.445.
10 Durand, *The First Afghan War and Its Causes*, p.180.

senses than he went up and into the gate to ascertain whether there was a clear passage for the assaulting column. Failing to see the sky through the back of the domed entrance, and swordsmen showing themselves, he was forced to retire. In the meantime the engineer who had fired the train had lain down in a position from whence he could see the flame and smoke followed by a dull heavy report proved that the charge was sprung. He waited, therefore, two or three minutes anxiously expecting the advance to be sounded; but Peat's bugler had been shot through the head; and Durand, concluding by the delay that some casualty had occurred to Peat, sought to obtain a bugler from the nearest party of infantry. The fire from the battlements was at the moment heavy, and to repeated demands for a bugler he met with the reply not to draw fire on the men by speaking, while the officer with the party, instead of furnishing the bugler required, with misplaced punctilio referred the engineer to the field officer without being able to say where the field officer was to be found. Foiled in his endeavours to have the advance sounded, Durand was forced to hasten back towards the column. He was met by Lieutenant James Broadfoot of the Bengal Engineers, who had been sent forward by the Chief Engineer to ascertain the cause of the delay; and reported, in answer to the question whether the attack was a failure, that all was right, but that the advance must be sounded without loss of time. This being at length done on went Dennie with his four companies, and after him Sale with the main column.

Peat, much shaken by the explosion, had on retiring from the gate been unable to reach the head of the column, and had been forced to lie down at the roadside, where he was observed by the Chief Engineer as the column was advancing. To an enquiry from Thomson, Peat replied that he had not been able to see through the gateway, though he had been onto it. Sale overheard the hasty dialogue, and his bugler sounded the retreat, the bugles of his column in rapid succession repeated the fatal sound; and Keane, who was watching from the heights in the rear of his artillery the progress of the assault despatched his aide-de-camp to learn what had happened. Before he could descend the hill and reach the position of the guns the mistake had been rectified; for the Chief Engineer had ascertained that Dennie with his four companies was effecting his passage through the gateway;[11] and the bugles of Sale's column sounded, while Dennie's men, already in part in the town, were cheering loudly and firing heavily.

Dennie had been enjoined to occupy the ramparts right and left of the gateway in order to secure the command of this all-important point, but, with intermingled rolls of musketry and bursts of cheering, his party pushed on into the town, and neglected the precaution enjoined.

The head of the main column under Sale, led by the Chief Engineer, was slowly making way in close support of Dennie through the dark debris-encumbered gateway, when a few Afghan swordsmen, dashing boldly down from the ramparts, fell sword in hand upon the leading section, bore down on Sale and the Chief Engineer, and for a moment checked and pressed back the head of the column But it was already well jammed into the narrow passage, and the rear, answering the cheers of Dennie's men, and ignorant of what was taking place in the jaws of the gateway, pushed eagerly onwards, and thus the few swordsmen were overborne by weight of numbers, and finally thrust back into the place. This hand-to-hand combat was for a moment critical, and the sword seemed on the point of

11 The gateway was reported to be 150 feet long and 20 feet wide.

> sweeping back the bayonet, but the effort being only that of a few brave men unsupported, and the column passing through the gate, the loud hurrahs of our men and the storm of musketry told Keane that Ghuznee had been won.[12]

As Brigadier 'Fighting Bob' Sale, leading the storming party, dashed through the mangled gateway and into a mass of bloodied bayonets, he was brought down by a sabre slash across his face; to avoid a fatal blow by his assailant he grabbed the sabre and damaged his hand; he was on the ground at the mercy of his assailant and called out for help. Captain James Kershaw of HM 13th Foot was close at hand and swiftly despatched the assailant to his ancestors. Despite his wounds 'Fighting Bob' led his storming party in the mad hand-to-hand fighting, moving into the town, up the ramparts and thence to the citadel where Ensign Richard Frere[13] of HM 13th Foot planted the regimental colour. To quote Sir John Kaye:

> There was horrible confusion and much carnage. Some Afghans in their frantic efforts to escape by the gateway, stumbled over the burning timbers, wounded and exhausted and were slowly burnt to death. Some were bayoneted on the ground. Others were pursued and hunted into corners and shot down like mad dogs. Many an Afghan sold his life dearly, and, though wounded and stricken down, still cut out at the hated enemy, but when resistance was over, mercy smiled down upon him. The appeals of the helpless were never disregarded by the victors in their hour of triumph.[14]

At approximately 8:00 a.m., the European troops were withdrawn and Brigadier Roberts assumed command of the fortress with his reserve force. His task was now to secure the place, corral all the prisoners and preserve the captured property, which included 30 guns of various calibres. This latter involved the collection of loot by the prize agents, in this case Captain George Lawrence and Captain John Swanston, the paymaster of the Bombay Division, assisted by the army commander's son and ADC, Lieutenant Edward Keane. This was not a very popular procedure as many soldiers and officers much preferred to keep what they found and were loath to give up their treasures. Once collected the loot was auctioned and the procedures were eventually parcelled out to all ranks involved in the operation on a pro rata basis as prize money. For example, in 1825 after Bhurtpore had been attacked and looted the prize money allocations were £60,000 (£4.5 million) to the Commander, Lord Combermere, down to £2.14s (£202) for the private soldier. The Ghazni prize money was paid out 10 years later. According to the old rules of war a fortress that did not surrender laid itself open to looting. William Taylor recounted an amusing scene about how a Scotsman in his regiment, James Hamilton, an inveterate snuff-taker, was found in a tobacco shop surrounded by *chatties* of the stuff.'[15] William Taylor does not say whether the young officer was sorely tempted! In another case a soldier of HM 13th Foot found gold pieces worth £600 (£45,000), which the prize agent duly took off him.

12 Durand, *The First Afghan War and Its Causes*, p.180.
13 Ensign Richard Frere. This able and gallant young officer, having served throughout the Afghan campaign, died of high fever at Rawalpindi during the final march from Afghanistan. He was probably the last casualty of the war.
14 Kaye, *History of the War in Afghanistan*, vol. 1, p.449.
15 Taylor, *Scenes and Adventures in Afghanistan*, p.138.

British troops storming the fortress of Ghazni, 23 July 1839.

Inside view of Ghazni gateway during the battle.

The 17th (Leicestershire) Regiment of Foot on the walls of the Ghanzi citadel.

Thereafter, Brigadier Roberts arranged guards for the 1,500 prisoners and protection for the women and children. One of those captured was Ghul Mohammed Khan who had been paid by Sir Alexander Burnes to provide provisions at Quetta, which he failed to do. He was sentenced to be bowstringed, but somehow managed to escape. Brigadier Roberts now directed his efforts at finding the chief of Ghazni, Gulam Hyder Khan, who was rumoured to have also made his escape, but Captain Arthur Taylor of 1st BER told the Brigadier that he had been assured that the Afghan chief had not escaped and was in hiding in the vicinity of the Kandahar Gate. At that juncture the Brigadier saw a fine-looking horse, richly caparisoned with a handsome brace of pistols in the holsters, outside a building, clearly made ready for a quick getaway. The Brigadier ordered Captain Taylor and Captain George Macgregor, an assistant to envoy Macnaghten, to make a thorough search of the building. They did so and found Gulam Hyder Khan huddled in a corner, sword in hand, ready to fight to the death. The two officers giving the young chief their solemn guarantee for his safety and that of his family, Gulam Hyder Khan surrendered. He was then escorted to Keane who, during their interview, took possession of the Sword of Ghazni from his stout young 21-year-old prisoner. Keane claimed this sword, valued at 14,000 rupees, as his by right. However, there were rumblings in the ranks questioning this right and declaring that the sword should be part of the collected loot. The rumblings continued and when these morphed into acute embarrassment a General Order was published stating that the sword, as part of the Ghazni loot, was to be auctioned, whereupon the new Lord Keane of Ghazni submitted the highest bid of £425 (£32,000) and became the rightful owner of the sword, but the Chinese whispers continued, prompting Lord Keane to sell the sword to the Directors of the East India Company for £105 (£7,875).

After his interview with Keane, Gulam Hyder Khan was taken and introduced to Shah Shuja, who, as advised by Macnaghten, pardoned the young chief. Meanwhile the wife of Gulam Hyder Khan and the other women of his *zenana* were conducted by Captain John Conolly to a house in the town and put under the superintendence of *munchi* Mohan Lal, while Gulam Hyder Khan was placed under the charge of Sir Alexander Burnes. According to Major William Hough, the DJAG, the British casualties amounted to six Europeans and 11 natives killed, 18 officers, 117 European other ranks and 30 natives wounded. Of the Afghans, it was estimated that 1,200 were killed and 300 wounded, plus 1,500 prisoners most of whom were eventually released. Nine guns and a sizeable quantity of supplies were also captured. All the horses, camels and bullocks found in the area, amounting to 500 animals, were collected and picketed in the 2nd Bengal Light Cavalry lines until they were allocated to regiments or sold.

On the night of 23 July Gulam Hyder Khan's brother, Ufzul Khan, with a force of 3,000, was miles away from the fortress listening to the firing and explosion and waiting for daylight to see the state of affairs. When at first light he saw the British flag, he knew that the fate of Ghazni had been sealed and made his way to Kabul as fast as possible, leaving his baggage and elephants behind. At Kabul, a disappointed and angry father refused to see his cowardly son.

The fall of Ghazni was a staggering blow to the Amir Dost Mohammed Khan. At the beginning of the campaign, Dost Mohammed believed that the main threat would come in concert with the Sikhs from the Khyber Pass, consequently he had despatched his warrior son Akbar Khan in that direction with a large part of his army and was obliged to recall him when it became clear that it was from Kandahar that he was to be assailed. The flight of his brothers in Kandahar had been a disappointment and the defection of Haji Khan Kakar was a bitter pill to swallow. Now, with the fall of Ghazni, rebellion in Kohistan to the north, threatened by Wade

Afghan prisoners at Ghazni under guard by men of the 19th Bombay Native Infantry.

The prison of Gulan Hyder Khan after the fall of Ghazni. The guard appears to be a mix of British Native infantry and Afghans.

and the dreaded Sikhs from the east and Keane and the loathsome Shah from the west, there was vain hope that any effective resistance could be offered. Negotiations, therefore, seemed the Dost's only recourse and his brother, *Nawab* Jubbar Khan, pro-British, was despatched to the British camp for the purpose of ascertaining the kind of terms that might be expected.

Nawab Jubbar Khan, 'a slight man, his nose a huge beak on his little face', rode into the British camp at noon on 28 July with a small escort. He was met by his friend Sir Alexander Burnes and taken to see the envoy, William Macnaghten. The *Nawab*'s proposal was that in acknowledging Shah Shuja as king of Afghanistan, Dost Mohammed was to be made his *Wazir* and he also demanded the immediate release of his nephew, Gulam Hyder Khan. The *Nawab* was then taken for an interview with Shah Shuja who received him with courtesy and offered to confirm the *Nawab* in any possessions he had and to confer honours on him. The *Nawab* said that he wanted nothing for himself and that he had come on behalf of his brother. The Shah informed him that Dost Mohammed Khan, if he agreed, would receive a pension of one *lakh* rupees per year and that he would have to reside in India under British surveillance. The release of Gulam Hyder Khan was refused as was the *Nawab*'s requested interview with his nephew. Empty-handed, the *Nawab* rode back to Kabul the next morning. Before leaving, the said to Macnaghten that his brother would not on any terms consent to reside in India, and 'if Shah Shuja is really a king and come to the kingdom of his ancestors, what is the use of your army and name? You have brought him by your money and arms into Afghanistan. Leave him now with us Afghans and let him rule if he can.'[16]

Keane did not embroil himself in the negotiations with the *Nawab*, instead he busied himself in the writing of the obligatory despatch to the Governor General (Appendix V). This despatch was to attract much criticism, particularly as the action was brought on by bringing his army into a position where there was no choice and in deciding to burst open the Kabul Gate he did not so much exercise his judgement as yield to necessity. The General's assertion that the action was 'one of the most brilliant acts' was considered by many to be overcharged especially from the pen of a Waterloo veteran. While the despatch mentioned a number of officers who had played no key role in the drama, it slurred over the actions of real heroes and there was no mention of Sergeant Robertson. According to Charles Nash:

> The chief achievement at Ghazni was Thomson's, who conceived the daring plan, but its success was due to Dennie who, at the head of his gallant party, rushed into the imminent death breach and was in possession of the fort before any help arrived. The part played by Keane was subordinate, but he received a peerage and £2,000 [£150,000] pension. But whatever merit Keane was entitled to was tarnished by his subsequent ill-treatment of the main actor Dennie. The report said that Sale led the leading column, Dennie only mentioned and his brilliant gallantry slurred over with a list of others.[17]

Having spent a week at Ghazni, the Army of the Indus proceeded to cover the last 90 miles to Kabul in two columns at 4:15 a.m. on 30 July. The army commander left his sick and wounded at Ghazni along with a small garrison under the command of Major James MacLaren of 16th

16 Kaye, *History of the War in Afghanistan*, Vol. 1, p.453.

17 Charles Nash, *History of the War in Afghanistan, from its Commencement to its Close* (London: Thomas Brooks, 1843; Kessinger Legacy reprint), p.108.

Dost Mohammed Khan.

BNI. Of the sick and wounded, 54 were to die at Ghazni. The main road to Kabul lay over a succession of low hills and ravines climbing in the first eight miles to 9,000 feet above sea level, 1,200 feet higher than Ghazni. Six miles further on the lead column reached Shaiydabad, a cluster of villages and a small mud fort. Here Keane, called a halt, so allowing the second column to close up. It was here that a *cossid* brought the news of Maharaja Ranjit Singh's death.

Back in Kabul, Dost Mohammed Khan, being appraised of the failure of his brother's negotiations with the British, was now in total despair. He summoned his council and declared his intention to make an all-out bid to stop the infidels in their track, but the fall of Ghazni, rapid and unexpected, had shaken the confidence of many of his followers and the council of war showed him that no reliance could be placed on the continued support of his followers; his previous support by the Kuzzilbashe fell away. In any event, he managed to muster a force of 13,000 with 30 guns and marched out to meet the foe. By the time he reached Urgundeh, 25 miles from Kabul, a number of his chiefs had given up the quest and sought accommodation with Shah Shuja. To whatever side he looked, Dost Mohammed Khan saw reluctance and even treachery, and giving a formal discharge to all whom he knew to be longing for it, he fled in the direction of Bamian on 2 August.

Some 24 hours later, Keane was informed of the Dost's flight in the direction of Bamian. In order not to repeat the failure to pursue the Kandahar chiefs, he ordered the formation of a small force, under the command of his ADC, Captain James Outram, to pursue and bring back as prisoner the man who had been the main target of the campaign. This small force amounted to 800 horsemen from various regiments and included 12 officers, all volunteers. To supplement this small force, it was decided, unwisely, that Haji Khan Kakar's force of 2,000 horsemen be included, thus making the pursuit force strong enough for the task, and the whole was placed under the charge of William Macnaghten. This course of action was probably recommended by Macnaghten and Sir Alexander Burnes, as at one time Haji Khan Kakar had been the governor of the Bamian district, knew it well and could probably solicit the help of the local inhabitants in the speedy capture of the fugitive. Another small cavalry group under the command of Major Robert Cureton of HM 16th Lancers was despatched to Urgundeh, to capture the guns and baggage left behind by Dost Mohammed Khan.

The pursuit force was ordered to assemble outside the Envoy's tent at noon on 3 August, but due to the delay caused by Haji Khan Kakar's contingent, it did not assemble until last light. This was not to be the last of Haji-instigated delays and frustrations during the course of the pursuit. As his was the larger contingent and more knowledgeable of the ground being covered, the British officers and their gung-ho commander, while impelled to rely on the Afghan's expertise, were acutely frustrated at what was increasingly perceived to be deliberate actions designed to impede the pursuit; which ultimately failed and Captain Outram was not slow in blaming the failure on Haji Khan Kakar's treacherous behaviour. When the force eventually arrived in Kabul on 18 August Haji Khan Kakar, who had earlier been honoured by Shah Shuja with the title of 'Defender of the State' (*Nusser-ool-Doulah*), was now made 'Prisoner of State'. In his frustration at the failure of this extremely important venture, Keane, referring to the volunteer officers, was said to have commented, 'He had not supposed there were 13 such asses in the whole of his force.'[18] It would appear that the General was unconscious of his own role as the jack!

The Army of the Indus, with Shah Shuja to the fore, continued its advance on Kabul on Wednesday 7 August 1839 with no further interruptions. The Shah, mounted on a richly caparisoned charger made a triumphant entry into his capital, accompanied by Macnaghten, Keane, Sir Alexander Burnes, general officers and staff. The exuberant Shah entered the Bala Hissar, aged 60 and after 30 years of exile. While the Shah's rule was about to begin, the Army of the Indus's mission was complete. In replying to a despatch sent to him, Lord Auckland, expressing his gratitude, wrote, 'It is to be hoped that the measure which has been accomplished of restoring this prince to the throne of his ancestors, will be productive of peace and prosperity over the country in which he rules, and will confirm the just influence of the British Government in the region of Central Asia.'

Lord Auckland's nephew, William, in writing to a friend about this worthy result that his uncle had achieved, probably expressed the feelings of many compassionate Christians by pointing out that 'it must be satisfactory to the lovers of legitimacy to know that Shah Shuja is the rightful king and that his defeated competitor, Dost Mohammed was only a usurper and has not even any blood royal in his veins.'[19] On the news of the capture of Kabul being received in Calcutta, the royal salute was fired from the ramparts of Fort William. The Court of Directors, who had been acrimoniously divided on Lord Auckland's 'forward policy' for some time, now sent its congratulations, and Sir John Hobhouse and the Secret Committee 'were in great glee'.[20]

Now little more remained than to fulfil the promise of the Simla Manifesto by the withdrawal of British troops. Great was the sense of achievement and boisterous were the celebrations for this glorious feat. However, five time zones away, the more sombre mind of His Grace

18 Lawrence, *Reminiscences*, p.24.
19 Osborne, *Ranjit Singh*, p.16.
20 Dunbar, *Golden Interlude*, p.191.

the Duke of Wellington predicted that when Kabul was reached the most difficult part of the task that the Indian Government had undertaken would only begin. Later this axiom would become known as the 'exit strategy' and would nearly always be tarnished. It was quite apparent to many, at the time, that the success of the undertaking had been achieved by British bayonets and only with these bayonets could the regime change be maintained, because, against all prostrations, the regime was far from popular.

12

Restoration or Occupation

Caubul, proud Afghan city! Change and crime
Have been thy stigma, from remotest time;
Dark, bloody thy career, to treason prone,
Thou'st banished sons and brothers from the throne.
James Atkinson

Kabul lay in a triangular gorge about 6,000 yards long. The town was encompassed by hills upon three sides having a narrow entrance between them, which completely overlooked the city. The town was about a mile long east to west and about half a mile broad. East of the town, and separated from it by a ditch, was the fortress of Bala Hissar, built by the Mughals, with a circumference of a mile and a quarter. On the slope of the acclivity was situated the Shah's palace and gardens; and above the fortress, the Barakzais had built a fort called the *Koolah-i-Feeringee* (later used as a hospital by HM 13th Foot). The River Kabul flowed eastwards along the edge of the city of dirty, narrow and irregular streets and houses mostly of mud with flat roofs. The famous *Char-Chouk* bazaar lay in the north with its alphabetical array of fruits from apples to water melons and nuts from almonds to walnuts. The Kuzzilbashe quarter, surrounded by high walls, of some 20,000 souls called the *Chandoul* occupied the west of this city of 60,000 people.

After the triumphal entry of the Shah the day before, the morning of Thursday 8 August was indeed glorious. The temperature was a comfortable 72°, and after a long slog of 1,525 miles over a devilish obstacle course with nearly half that distance on half rations, there were no more parades, marches, forts to be stormed nor gauntlets of deadly *jezails* to hurry through; 12,500 British troops had arrived at the fabled city, hitherto only visited by a handful of renowned travellers. There can be little doubt that a great feeling of achievement permeated the atmosphere as officers and men mingled about checking on friends, exchanging tales, cleaning their equipment, writing boastful letters home and generally relieved that their glorious mission had been accomplished, but as William Taylor, of HM 4th Light Dragoons, lamented, 'We had seen little of fighting and promotions had been consequently few.' However, they had all now 'Been there, done that, bought the T-Shirt' and were ready for home. All that remained was for the British high command in Kabul to work out its exit strategy.

The basis of this strategy had already been given in the Governor General's manifesto promising that, 'Once he [Shah Shuja] shall be secured in power, and the independence and integrity of Afghanistan established, the British army will be withdrawn.' At that time it was the firm conviction of the Governor General, his advisers and the Whig Government in England that the Afghan venture had been just, that the restoration of a friendly government with every prospect of establishing tranquillity and prosperity in Afghanistan could not fail to render the kingdom an efficient barrier against the invasion of India, and the regeneration of the British North-West Frontier could not fail to convince the people of the area that the inevitable changes that would be brought about would be for their general benefit.

But what was it going to cost and how long was it going to take? Once the corks of the celebratory bottles of champagne had popped and their contents consumed, these questions began to dominate. The army that had just dared to enter Afghanistan now dared not leave. For the Government of India there were other compelling reasons for the return of the army to India. First and foremost, and of great concern to the new commander-in-chief, General Sir Jasper Nicolls, was that the number of troops employed in Afghanistan was greater than the number that India could sustain for any length of time. Next, with near anarchy in the Punjab after Ranjit Singh's death and rumblings of trouble breaking out in both Burma and Nepal, Nicolls needed the bulk of his army in India and not hundreds of miles away at the end of an insecure line of communication.

After a Sadozai absence of 30 years many Afghan chiefs had known nothing except Barakzai rule. The sudden regime change was sponsored by British bayonets and cash, and in a wild country like Afghanistan it was clearly going to take some time before it could be said that Shah Shuja was established and secured in power; no matter how frequently Macnaghten was to extol the popularity of the restored king, during this unspecified period British bayonets and cash were essential. The previous ruler, Dost Mohammed Khan, had been the Amir since 1826; his intimate knowledge of the internal feuds and divisions and his unscrupulous actions allowed him to maintain control. The restored monarch, on the other hand, only had the authority of British bayonets and while these instruments of authority remained, his reign over a lawless and savage community would be shackled by the superintendence of an envoy determined to enforce the principles of a civilised government. As this epic unfolded, it might have occurred to some that had Britain removed her bayonets and left the Shah with his special force to impose his authority in the rough ways of his ancestors, as recommended by Henry Elphinstone 30 years earlier, the result might have been better and certainly not have cost as much. Macnaghten in his letter on entering Kandahar had already anticipated that the process would take longer than expected despite his protestations that the Shah had been welcomed by the Afghans with feelings nearly amounting to adoration. He was now to decide on how many bayonets and for how long. Macnaghten was not a stupid man, he had been the chief nursemaid for this grand Afghan strategy and was not about to allow it to fail. So, while at the same time as he acclaimed the popularity of the Shah, he magnified the external threats that could derail this honourable cause. The Governor General was of the opinion that a strong brigade would suffice to hold Afghanistan in conjunction with the Shah's contingent, and he added, 'I indulge the hope that, unless new events should occur, all or nearly all the remainder may be returned to India when the routes shall be open in the next spring.'[1]

1 Kaye, *History of the War in Afghanistan*, Vol. 1.

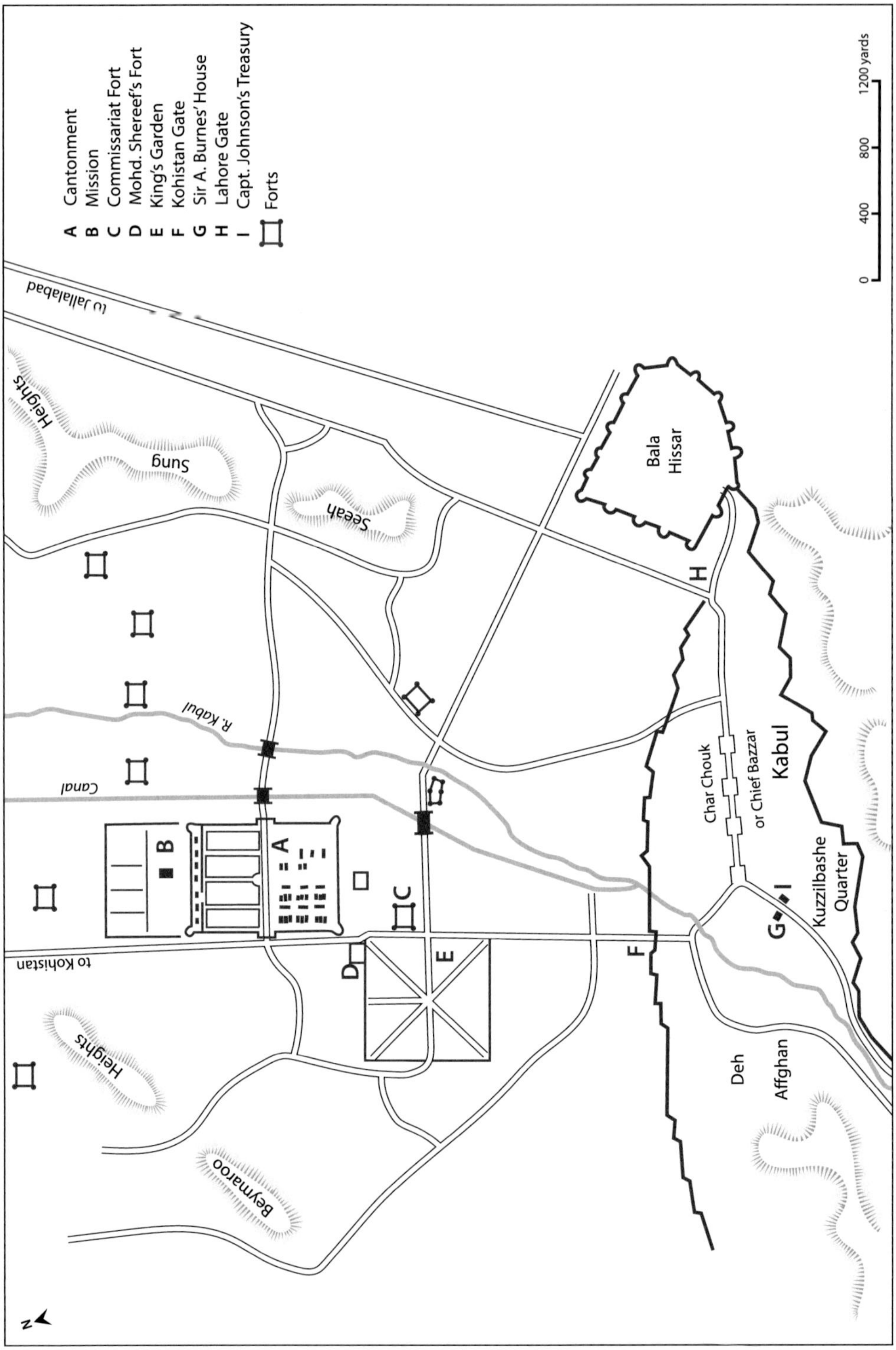

Map 7 Plan of the cantonment and surrounding countryside, Kabul 1839.

Mr Macnaghten's task was indeed a difficult one, as a similar task was to be some 170 years later. Up to now the Afghan venture had essentially been a military affair complicated by supply problems. Now it was to take on a more political aspect as Macnaghten, the supreme head of British interests in Afghanistan, embarked on a recruiting campaign of appointing Company officers as politicos in order to maintain his exercise of general supervision; Queen's officers, many in command of divisions and brigades, were debarred from the exercise of political functions. By the end of 1840, there were no less than 32 Company officers in political slots across Afghanistan and Sindh. Apart from two civilians they were all Company army officers, not one of whom had attained the rank of major. There were 10 captains and 20 lieutenants, all given the authority to call upon the army to enforce the Envoy's orders. Not all of these appointees were suited to the role they were given and nearly all were to clash with their respective military commanders on the ground. They were awarded very generous salaries (see Appendix VIII), which gave them an air of being special and in most cases the projection of this feeling was unbearable arrogance. For the Envoy, failure was not an option and success depended on British boots on the ground, the Shah's capacity to take charge, and also the unstinting and continued support of the Governor General. Accordingly, Macnaghten mulled over the situation and gave much consideration to any 'new events' that could occur. In this regard and within a couple of days of the glorious entry into Kabul, he received a report via the British Envoy in Teheran to the effect that a Russian force was destined for Khiva and that Colonel Charles Stoddart was still held prisoner at Bokhara. Then on 17 August Captain Outram returned from his abortive pursuit of Dost Mohammed Khan, which in the minds of both Macnaghten and the Shah conjured up the horror of the renegade Amir stirring up the Uzbeks in rebellion against the Shah and his infidel supporters:

> It had earlier been frequently asserted in camp that the Envoy had earnestly entreated Sir John Keane to send a large British force with Captain Outram Pursuit Party but his advice was ineffectual. It is quite clear that one of the most important objects of the campaign (the capture of Dost Mohammed) was defeated through the inadequacy of the means resorted to secure it.[2]

Besides, further west at Herat the situation was not all that satisfactory. Yah Mohammed, the sinister *Wazir* of Herat, made a treaty with the British under which Herat was bound not to enter into negotiations with any other state without the knowledge and consent of the British Resident. In return, *lakhs* of rupees were showered upon Herat. But nothing seemed to satisfy the Heratis, as shortly after signing the treaty it was discovered that Yah Mohammed was secretly negotiating with the Persians.

Although Shah Kamran and the people of Herat had been living off the generosity of the British Government, Shah Kamran had been alarmed at the British advance in Afghanistan with his uncle, who could on the slightest pretext take off his head. Suspicious of British intentions (throughout Asia the British were credited with duplicity), Kamran's *Wazir*, Yar Mohammed Khan had made overtures to the Persian court and to the chiefs at Kandahar to form a coalition against Shah Shuja and his British allies. The Persians at that time could not have been less

2 Nash, *History of the War in Afghanistan*, p.199.

interested and the Kandahar chiefs were now impecunious fugitives. So, the wily *Wazir* had sent a mission to the British in Kandahar to congratulate Shah Shuja and to ask the British for more money as a sort of guarantee for good behaviour.

But now, Major Elliot Todd, who had been sent to Herat and had replaced Lieutenant Pottinger, was reporting that Shah Kamran and his *Wazir* were not being totally cooperative, and Macnaghten began to think that it would be no bad thing if Herat was to be restored to Shah Shuja's domains. However, this idea was not to the liking of the Governor General, who had in the spring of 1839 received a clear directive from the president of the Board of Control, Sir John Hobhouse, informing the Governor General that, 'It is of the utmost importance not only so far as India, but as Europe is concerned, that there should be no appearance of any intention on our part to acquire any permanent possessions beyond the frontier.'[3] Lieutenant Pottinger arrived in Kabul on 10 November on his way back to Calcutta where he was to be debriefed by the Governor General.

The Army of the Indus was accommodated in tented camps outside the city of Kabul while Macnaghten ensconced himself in the Bala Hissar and senior officers requisitioned the houses of absent chiefs. Sir Alexander Burnes lost no time in taking over the house he had stayed in during his 1837 mission, and Mohal Lal quartered himself in the Kuzzilbashe compound. Burnes' house, a large courtyarded mansion in the city, was designated the Residency. Two other officers had houses on the same street, Captain Robert Warburton and Captain Hugh Johnson, the latter the paymaster of Shah Shuja's force. From their tents, officers and men wandered into the city to behold its mysteries and buy souvenirs. Some of the old and bold soon sniffed out the liquor shops causing a General Order to be issued as early as 12 August, restricting entry into the city without an official pass, which was only to be granted to persons 'on whose sobriety and steadiness dependence could be placed'. But this did not entirely stop the misbehaviour of both officers and men throughout their time in Kabul who, many reports indicate, 'whored their way round the city', much to the annoyance of the local inhabitants. Sir John Kaye, in his *History of the War in Afghanistan*, places the blame for any sexual license on the loose women of Kabul, who were more accommodating. In saying so he was no doubt influenced by an old Persian proverb, 'A Caubal wife in boorka cover, was never known without a lover', or as one historian noted, 'necessity is the mother of invention and the father of the Eurasian'.

On 20 August HM 16th Lancers lost their popular brigadier, Robert Arnold. This 60-year-old cavalryman, a Waterloo veteran, who had been carried sick all the way from Kandahar to Kabul, died of a liver complaint and was buried in the Armenian Cemetery south-west of the city with full military honours. The next day his property was auctioned. His cigars went for two shillings and sixpence each, snuff for 10 shillings an ounce and wine for four pounds a bottle. These high bids at auction for a dead officer's property were the genteel way of giving donations to the family of the deceased person. The higher the bid the greater the esteem in which the person was held.

Five days later Dr Percival Lord rode into Kabul in advance of the *Shahzada* Timour, who arrived on 3 September along with Lieutenant Colonel Wade and Colonel Shaikh Bassowan. Major General Sir Willoughby Cotton and Sir Alexander Burnes went out to meet the *Shahzada* and marched in with him. A guard of honour was formed on the approach of the Prince, a Royal

3 Bruce, *Retreat from Kabul*, p.99.

Salute was fired by the artillery and the Prince was escorted to the Bala Hissar to meet his father.

Macnaghten was never far in his mind from Russian machinations, and the combined horror of Russian battalions advancing on Khiva and occupying both banks of the Oxus and of Dost Mohammed rallying a rebel force, caused him to write a reasoned communication to the Governor General in which he gave his requirement for the distribution of troops. Earlier, the Envoy had sent out 32-year-old Dr Percival Lord on a mission to the Khan of Kunduz to convince him not to make common cause with the fugitive, Dost Mohammed. However, Lord had not gone 30 miles from Kabul when he had hurried back in a panic with misinformation, fed to him by his Afghan escort, that the country ahead was in full rebellion.

Macnaghten's letter to the Governor General had the Bombay troops returning to India via Kalat, a move he knew was much favoured by army commander Keane; a brigade of Bengal troops was to garrison Kabul, and on the advice of a panic-stricken Dr Percival Lord, a brigade was to move to Syghan in order to prevent Dost Mohammed making common cause with the Khan of Kunduz, while also to possibly influence the Khan at Bokhara to release his captive; another force was to move against Bokhara. This latter move was to be done without the sanction of the Governor General due to the lateness of the season and the urgency to cover the Russian advance. But, as far as Keane was concerned, he had done his job and was loath to get involved in any protracted grandiose scheme. Before its despatch, Macnaghten sent the communication to Keane fully expecting his approval and support. The General's good sense caused this dreamy venture to be abandoned, but the Envoy, prompted by his fear of Dost Mohammed and loath to forego an expedition which would flatten Russian designs, resolved on making some sort of demonstration to the westward. On 11 September he instructed Major General Edward Simpson to send the 4th Gurkha Regiment, a Horse Artillery troop and some Afghan cavalry to Bamian, under the direction of Dr Percival Lord; his idea was to threaten the ruler of Kunduz, Murad Beg, with reprisals should he offer any assistance to Dost Mohammed. This move was the start of the Envoy's policy of sending forth valuable troops in penny-packets to inaccessible areas, unsupportable, and eventually, due to the paucity of troops not reinforceable. Of this policy Sir John Kaye was to write, 'I believe that the system of placing small detachments in isolated positions was one of the great errors which marked our military occupation of Afghanistan.'[4]

As Captain Isaac Handscombe had elected to return to India with Lieutenant General Keane, Captain William Hay of 1st BER was appointed to the command of 4th Gurkha Regiment. This regiment and a small supporting force left Kabul on 12 September for Bamian, 100 miles north-west of Kabul which involved the crossing of the Koh-i-Baba range 12,000 feet above sea level. They toiled for a month to cover the exceedingly difficult route of 100 miles to their objective. Prior to leaving, Captain Hay had requested that a survey be made for the best route for his accompanying 6-pdr guns; this request was denied by Macnaghten, who did not take kindly to unnecessary difficulties thwarting his plans. Consequently, right from the start of this mission, Captain Hay left an indelible impression of being troublesome. The events at Bamian will be covered in the following chapter.

4 Kaye, *History of the War in Afghanistan*, Vol. 1, p.473.

At the end of August, the mangled body of Lieutenant Colonel John Herring was brought into the city. He, with his regiment, the 37th BNI, had been escorting much-needed treasure from Kandahar to Kabul and while camped at Hyder Khail some 45 miles from Kabul, Herring with two of his officers, Lieutenants Hugh Rind and Charles Carlyon and a couple of NCOs went out, unarmed, for an evening stroll. About a mile from their camp, they were set upon by Afghan ruffians with rocks and sling shots. The Colonel fell while his companions managed to make their escape and sound the alarm back in camp. An armed rescue party was immediately sent out which soon discovered the butchered body of their colonel, but no sign of his murderers. Hyder Khail was the site of the cruel murder of *Wazir* Fateh Khan 20 years earlier. Colonel Herring was buried on 5 September with full military honours in the Armenian cemetery in Kabul, as was Captain George Fothergill of HM 13th Foot, who had died from diarrhoea the day before, and Captain Henry Timings of the Bengal Artillery, who had died from utter exhaustion and was buried on 12 September. On the morning of his fatal evening stroll, Colonel Herring had received a letter from the Envoy offering him command of the Shah's forces in place of Major General Edward Simpson, who had elected to return to India. Colonel Herring's murderers were later traced and shot. A couple of days later, Captain John Barstow at the head of 37th BNI brought in 13 *lakhs* of the much needed treasure. This officer had earlier received a severe gunshot wound while passing through the Bolan Pass; he would have been hacked to death had he not been rescued by *Havildar* Lachman Singh.

Just before Colonel Herring's body had been brought in, Macnaghten had requested the services of Captain Outram as his political assistant and commissioned the indefatigable Outram to lead a force against the Ghilzai chiefs; if possible he was to arrest them and replace them with more friendly ones, thus securing the important lines of communication between Kandahar and Kabul. He was also to search out and punish the perpetrators of the Herring atrocity. The force placed under Outram's command consisted of the Shah's 1st Cavalry, the Shah's 3rd Infantry Regiment Regiment, a battery of 9-pdr guns and a troop of the Shah's Horse Artillery, plus 1,000 Afghan cavalry under the command of one Mohammed Osman Khan, said to be an uncle of Shah Shuja. This latter contingent was included to induce the local populace into believing that the Shah was using his own people to establish order in the country. Captain Outram's force was to move out on 7 September, but the Afghan cavalry was not ready, and based on his previous experience Captain Outram started out without them. A few days later the Shah was able to cajole some of his cavalry to leave Kabul and catch up with Outram, and on 21 October the force was reinforced by a wing of 16th BNI under the command of Major James McLaren which had been sent out by Major General Nott.[5] The force attacked the Ghilzais at every opportunity, destroyed their forts, recovered many of the army's looted camels and captured many prisoners including the murderers of Colonel Herring. Of the prisoners, 64 of the most ferocious were selected and sent to Kabul under an escort commanded by Lieutenant Peter Nicolson, there to be executed by beheading. This action was to keep the area quiet until the following spring. On completion of his task, Captain Outram joined Major General Willshire at his headquarters on 8 November, at which time Outram's political powers ceased.

5 Major James McLaren (1789–1846). At the last battle of the First Anglo-Sikh War he was in command of the 4th Brigade; he was shot in the knee during the assault and obliged to undergo amputation from which he did not recover. He died 12 days later at Ferozepore. It later transpired that on the day he died he had been appointed Honorary ADC to the Queen.

On the day Colonel Herring was being buried at Kabul, 500 miles away at Lahore Mr George Clerk, the acting political agent at Ludhiana, and Captain the Honourable William Osborne, the Governor General's military secretary, were making their entry into the Sikh *durbar* at Lahore on the long-awaited 'condolence and congratulatory mission' to the new Maharaja, Kharak Singh. In fact the real purpose was to thrash out a firm agreement with the Sikh *durbar* for the unfettered return of the Army of the Indus through the Punjab and thereafter the passage of convoys, escorts and traders. While this requirement had been verbally agreed with the late Maharaja Ranjit Singh there was nothing in writing nor was there any official declaration by the Sikh *durbar*. The Sikhs, ever suspicious of British intentions, were understandably apprehensive that an army that had just conquered Afghanistan, once allowed into the kingdom, would stay and the current unsettled state of the kingdom could well cause this stay to become permanent. In fact, the Sikh apprehension was not that far wrong, as within the year both Macnaghten and Mr George Clerk were contemplating the division of the kingdom and the occupation of the Punjab with 12,000 troops. On 14 September, Clerk wrote to Herbert Maddock, the political secretary to the Government of India about the Sikh attitude:

> They regard it as a matter of deep importance. They seem to feel it is to be any time a hazardous experiment, but just at present, when they know not but tomorrow may see the Punjab rent by dissension, their apprehension is a natural one that the Supreme Government of India might avail itself of the presence of its overwhelming army, in the heart of a distracted country, to restore order and protect its people, and all experience teaches this must terminate this country's independence.[6]

The Sikhs took the opportunity of this visit and the new British representative's sympathetic ear to also broach the subject of Maharaja Kharak Singh's capacity to rule and the ascendancy of Chet Singh Balwa over the weak mind of the Maharaja. Mr Clerk was to report, 'Every party has separately consulted me on this subject even the Fukeer [Azizuddin] himself, whom nobody can pronounce as yet belonging to any party, whispering when we were alone, his sense of the absolute necessity of some measure.'[7] Clearly, Clerk was not adverse to the Sikhs' desired change in authority as it was quite clear that the government of the nation could not remain in the hands of the new Maharaja. It is also probable that he viewed the desired change in authority as not very dissimilar to the British Act of Regency in 1810. At a later date Clerk did admit to his complicity in the scheme when writing in November of that year:

> It was lately in contemplation to shoot or sabre the favourite, they consulted me and I advised an impressive remonstration on all their parts, to the Maharaja and in the advent of his not consenting to cast off the wretches, to do everything possible to get rid of Bajwa short of doing injury to his person as this would bring disgrace to the Durbar.[8]

On the evening of 7 October, seven prominent Sikhs rendezvoused at Raja Dhian Singh's house in Lahore City with murderous intent. The party included the Raja's two brothers, Rajas Gulab

6 Aijazuddin, *The Resourceful Fakirs*, p.273.
7 Aijazuddin, *The Resourceful Fakirs*, p.275.
8 Singh, *A History of the Sikhs*, vol. 2, p.9.

and Suchet Singh, and most significantly *Kunwar* Naunihal Singh. Once the group had assembled, confirmed their grisly intent and attired themselves in ordinary clothing they left Raja Dhian Singh's house at four o'clock in the morning of 8 October, entered the fort and made their way to the Maharaja's chambers. The conspirators on approaching were challenged by the guard, who after identifying Raja Dhian Singh by his six-fingered left hand, allowed the group to enter the chamber. There, the surprised Maharaja was seized and bound while they searched for their target, Chet Singh. He was soon found in a dark corner in the rear of the Maharaja's bedchamber. He was dragged into the presence of Raja Dhian Singh, who instantly thrust his *tulwar* into the breast of the cringing Chet Singh, his body then cut to pieces by the other assassins. This brutal murder was followed by a declaration of the Sikh regency to the terrified Maharaja Kharak Singh, who was told that while he would remain the nominal king, the nation would henceforth be ruled by his son, *Kunwar* Naunihal Singh. It is possible that had *Kunwar* Naunihal Singh not been there, the Maharaja would also have been eliminated. As much as the young Naunihal Singh was an avowed enemy of his father, he could not have ruled with the blood of his father on his hands, and of much greater significance was the dread of the paramount power's reaction to a situation that they would consider as anarchy.

The matter of the British army's access through the Punjab remained unresolved as Clerk returned to his base at Ludhiana and the Governor General, impatient for a solution, wrote to Sir John Hobhouse, 'If they [Sikhs] wish to support the Tripartite Treaty, they cannot but accede to the demand. If they refuse, it must be absolutely insisted on and we are collecting a force in consequence.'[9]

While the elimination of Chet Singh admirably suited Raja Dhian Singh's designs, the young *Kunwar* and regent was apprehensive about the increased anti-British influence this had given to the Dogra rajas in the Sikh *durbar*. He decided to counterbalance the Dogra influence by a *rapprochement* with the British, but in return he needed a favour. On a reciprocal visit later that month to Simla, the Sikh delegation gave consent to the passage of British troops through the Punjab, with conditions and 'whispering' that in the way of an appreciation the removal of the 'Captain Sahib' would be more than adequate. In reporting this to his friend Sir John Hobhouse, Lord Auckland observed:

> Wade has unhappily given offence to some of the Principal Chiefs and secret applications have been made to me to substitute another officer, and letters on the subject have been sent to me which I thought inexpedient to acknowledge. And in the meantime Wade's agency has not been recognised, his letters were not answered, and the passports and facilities for his convoy were not provided. Serious differences, resting upon personal quarrel have arisen at a time when important interests are at stake. My recourse was that Wade should accept the Residency at Indore.[10]

In conquered Kabul it did not take long before more competitive and organised activities were arranged. Within a couple of days of their arrival the cavalry had marked out a racecourse, HM 16th Lancers had taken their greyhounds out to hunt jackals, polo matches were played and

9 Aijazuddin, *The Resourceful Fakirs*, p.309.
10 Aijazuddin, *The Resourceful Fakirs*, p.293.

regimental bands played in the evenings. Inter-regimental cricket matches were arranged and the Afghans put on displays of *Khurbuddi and Buzhaski.* The highlight of the racing calendar was the 'Kabul Stakes' which took place on 14 September. There was an entry of about 20 riders over a course of a mile and a half and the event was graced by the attendance of His Majesty, Shah Shuja. The race was won by Major Francis Daly of HM 4th Light Dragoons, to whom His Majesty presented a very handsome Afghan sword.

The restored monarch genuinely felt obligated to thank his 'restorers' in some special way. Caught up with the pageantry of reviews and parades, Shah Shuja, persuaded by his British carers, established an order of knighthood and held a grand *durbar* at 5:00 p.m. on 17 September at which the Order of the Duranni Empire (*Nishan-Dar-Durani*) was awarded to British officers and politicos, in three classes, for their services to the restored Duranni Empire. Queen Elizabeth I would never have allowed her sheep to be stained by another's mark! Nor did Queen Victoria. There were six fairly obvious nominations for the First Class and these were selected by Shah Shuja. They were Lord Auckland, Lieutenant General Sir John Keane, Mr William Macnaghten, Major General Sir Willoughby Cotton, Lieutenant Colonel Sir Alexander Burnes and Lieutenant Colonel Claude Wade. The nominations for the 14 Second Class awards and the 36 Third Class awards were decided by Keane for officers of the Army of the Indus and by Macnaghten for the officers of Shah Shuja's force. Very significantly Shah Shuja did not include the representative of his Sikh ally, Colonel Shaikh Bassowan. As with all such awards there were glaring anomalies. The Second Class recipients comprised mostly staff officers and pointedly did not include Lieutenant Colonel William Dennie, who had bravely led the 'storming party' into Ghazni, but did include Brigadier Robert Arnold who was *hors de combat* from the time the army left Kandahar. Clearly the army commander, who had threatened 'never to forget' Dennie, had chosen to do so on this occasion. Another senior officer missing from the list was Major General William Nott, the officer Keane had sworn 'never to forgive'. Also missing from the list was Captain James Outram because, no doubt, Keane was still annoyed with his failure to capture the fleeing Dost Mohammed Khan. No one below the rank of captain was listed. No doubt this omission gave vent to the man who blew up the Ghazni gate to comment that the award was instituted to gratify the vanity of British envoys and commanders. Back in Bombay, the 'Ducks' were not best pleased at the omission of Colonel Pottinger's name.

Lieutenant Colonel Dennie had been nominated for the Third Class award, but he was aggrieved by this apparent snub and wrote to Keane declining the award, which only drew on him Keane's increased animosity, who characterised the letter as 'remarkable for its rude and insulting tone and the coarseness of its insinuations'.[11] At a later stage, after his successful operations in Bamian, Dennie was offered the Second Class award, which he also felt compelled to decline. In the case of Captain James Outram, his status was corrected when Macnaghten, writing from Jalalabad on 7 January 1840, informed that officer that Shah Shuja desired him to be awarded the Second Class Order of the Duranni Empire. A long time after the great venture into Afghanistan had turned to dust, the wearing of Shah Shuja's award was banned and all the medals were recalled. Not surprisingly some were not returned, so equally unsurprisingly one of these could well show up in a future Antiques Roadshow.

To ensure that the native troops were not totally sidelined, Keane ordered the formation of a committee to record the claims of native officers and men for the Indian Order of Merit.

11 Nash, *History of the Campaign in Afghanistan*, p.203.

Apart from the sombre visits to the cemetery, the month of September passed pleasantly, the fine climate, the strange scenery and the delicious fruits of Kabul were enjoyed by all, and all were happy in the belief that they were all soon to turn their backs on Afghanistan forever. No doubt Captain James Douglas of 53rd BNI looked forward to leaving as he found the city to be 'beastly dirty and so are the people, they are cunning, avaricious, proud and filthy'. After the grand investiture of the day before, the Bombay Division, under the command of Major General Thomas Willshire, commenced its march back to India. The Division was to proceed via the Khojak and Bolan Passes bypassing Kandahar, and on the way Major General Willshire was to inflict a signal punishment on Mehrab Khan of Kelat for the perfidious conduct he had pursued during the passage of the Army of the Indus through his domains, which were now to be incorporated into the Duranni Empire. This animosity towards Mehrab Khan was undoubtedly fuelled by Sir Alexander Burnes who had lost much prestige with his defunct treaty with the Khan, and now recommended him for castigation.[12] It was believed that a large portion of the Bengal Division would also trace their way back to India via the Khyber Pass recently cleared by Colonel Wade.

Soon rumours started to fly around that the plans for mass exodus of the Bengal Division had been abandoned and a general feeling of disappointment prevailed. The official order designating the 'stay-behinds' appeared on 2 October which stated that the whole of the 1st Bengal Infantry Division, 2nd Bengal Cavalry Brigade and 6th Bengal Light Field Battery were to remain in Afghanistan under the command of Major General Sir Willoughby Cotton. Cotton had earlier been scheduled to leave Afghanistan with Keane and was to be replaced by Major General John Lumley, at the time adjutant general of the Bengal Army. This officer declined the appointment on medical grounds and the next senior Bengal officer was Major General William Nott. But this officer was totally unacceptable to Macnaghten as he had made it quite clear that he would not tolerate any interference from the Envoy or his politicos. Consequently, Macnaghten convinced Cotton to extend his stay in Kabul as army commander until such time as a suitable Queen's officer could replace him. No doubt his eventual replacement by Major General William Elphinstone had much to do with Macnaghten's desire to have a more compliant army commander. The remaining British troops were, in addition to the Shah's Force, now numbering about 8,000 troops and commanded by Brigadier Abraham Roberts.[13] Earlier, Roberts had applied for the lucrative vacancy left by the departing Major General Simpson. Initially both Cotton and Macnaghten were against Roberts' selection. In

12 Kaye, *History of the War in Afghanistan*, Vol. 2, p.29.

13 General Sir Abraham Roberts (1784–1873). In 1801 he became an ensign in the Waterford Militia and two years later was commissioned into HM 49th Foot (Hertfordshire). In 1805 he transferred to the East India Company and on arrival at Calcutta was assigned to 1st BER. With this regiment he served in the Second Maratha War and many other smaller campaigns. In 1813 he was assigned to the Public Works Department and was one of the founders of the hill station at Simla. Apart from active service during the Nepalese War, he remained in the Public Works Department until 1832 when he took command of 1st BER and at the start of the Afghan campaign he was made commander of the 4th Brigade. After his tour in Afghanistan he returned to India to command 15th BNI. In 1844 he went to England on furlough and on his return was appointed Commander of the Punjab Division; his son, Frederick, joined him as his ADC. Fredrick was later to become Field Marshal Lord Roberts. At the age of 72, Roberts retired due to ill health, and returned to England. He was promoted to lieutenant general in 1857 and to general in 1864. He died nine years later.

addition, the Envoy proposed that the command of the Shah's forces be split into two brigades, one based in Kabul and the other at Kandahar. Both Cotton and Governor General Lord Auckland rejected this idea, and the Governor General approved of Roberts' nomination. Clearly, His Lordship's decision was based on the advice from his council's military member, General Sir William Casement, who happened to be a good friend of Roberts. Confidence in the selection of Roberts was further confirmed by a personal letter from Captain William Osborn, the Governor General's military secretary, stating that 'Lord Auckland has every confidence in your zeal and activity and trusts that this proof of it will induce you to continue the same course.' Thus began the unhappy partnership between Roberts and Macnaghten. The former was the epitome of an Indian army officer with a fine service record, who was very conscious of his position and authority, which had now been boosted by the Governor General's confidence in him; while the latter had tasted the joy of being able to order the Shah's force here and there at whim, a power he was not prepared to give away and one he was to exercise through his cortege of political agents.

On 13 October Captain John Hay of 35th Bengal Native Infantry died of sheer exhaustion and duly joined his fallen brother officers in the Armenian Cemetery. Captain Hay was the commander of the diversionary force at the storming of Ghazni. A month prior to his death he had attended the *durbar* at which he had been honoured by the award of the Order of the Duranni Empire Third Class.

The Bengal troops who were to return to India via the Khyber Pass, under the command of Major General Sir John Keane, were HM 16th Lancers, 3rd Bengal Light Cavalry, 4th Bengal Local Horse and one company each from 20th, 21st and 27th BNI. This group left Kabul in two columns with the first leaving on 15 October, under the command of Keane and the second column on 17 October under Major General Joseph Thackwell. With this latter column were the two state prisoners Hyder Khan and Haji Khan Kakur under the escort of Major Thomas Sherry. Also included in this column was Josiah Harlan, the American Quaker who had originally gone to Kabul to spy for the British, but had been sidelined by the then Captain Wade, as he had overreached himself and had recommended that no further communication be held with him. Lieutenant Colonel Wade and Colonel Shaikh Bassowan had departed 10 days earlier on 5 October, with Wade being given the unenviable task of informing the Khyberi chiefs that the subsidy promised by Shah Shuja would not be forthcoming. Prior to the exit of these two columns Captain Perin Hopkins, with two companies of 27th BNI under his command, arrived in Kabul on 8 October, with a much needed 13 *lakhs* of rupees.

On 9 October, a General Order was issued stipulating the disposition of troops for the occupation of Afghanistan. They were as follows:

Kabul. HM 13th Foot, 35th BNI, Shah's 1st Cavalry, Shah's 2nd Infantry Regiment, artillery detachment. Commander, Brigadier Robert Sale.

Jelalabad. 1st BER, 48th BNI, 2nd Bengal Cavalry, *Rissaldar* of Skinner's Horse, artillery detachment. Commander, Lieutenant Colonel Joseph Orchard.

Ghazni. 16th BNI, *Rissaldar* Skinner's Horse, artillery detachment. Commander, Major James MacLaren.

Kandahar. 42nd BNI, 43rd BNI, 4th Local Horse, Shah's 3rd Infantry Regiment, artillery detachment, which included the four 18-pdr guns. Commander, Major General William Nott.

Bamian. Shah's 4th (Gurkha) Regiment, troop of horse artillery under Lieutenant Murray Mackenzie and a detachment of Afghan horse under Captain Hubert Garbett. Commander, Captain William Hay.

It should be noted that this order for the disposition of troops in Afghanistan did not include those troops, mainly from the Bombay Army, required to protect Quetta, Bolan Pass, Dada, Shirkapore and Karachi, at that time the only viable line of communication. Also, as time went on there were many changes and additions to this initial disposition of troops and the command structure.

As winter of 1839 was approaching, a winter clothing allocation of two pairs of worsted stockings, a pair of gloves and a *poshteen*[14] were issued to the troops, while the cavalry horses were issued with a blanket, and to warm the hearts of the European troops, permission was given for wives to join their husbands. Macnaghten sent his nephew, Captain Edward Conolly, back to India to escort the ladies to glorious Kabul. The other big need before winter set in was proper accommodation. The garrison engineer, Lieutenant Henry Durand, and Mohan Lal first inspected the forts that had been recommended by Sir Alexander Burnes as being suitable. These were rejected on the grounds that they were located several miles from Kabul, and lacked sufficient space and available water. Durand reported that the only suitable and defensible place was the Bala Hissar, which could easily be adapted to accommodate all troops, however the Envoy, yielding to the Shah's objections, vetoed the idea. Brigadier Sale appealed to Macnaghten on the basis that the Bala Hissar was the only secure military alternative, but yet again the Envoy bowed to the Shah's objections. Eventually, a hotchpotch solution was adopted whereby the stables of the Bala Hissar and part of the Shah's gardens were used. On his departure, Lieutenant Durand handed over to Lieutenant John Sturt of the Bengal Engineers.

The columns returning to India did not have an easy ride, as the Khyberis were up in arms at the cancellation of their subsidy and resorted to what they always did which was to attack and harass the convoys proceeding through the Khyber Pass. On 25 October they attacked Captain Joseph Ferris' garrison of *Jezailchees* at Ali Masjid. The fort at Ali Masjid lies on a steep hill some 300 feet above a mountain torrent at the bottom of the gorge. This was the position occupied by Captain Ferris and his garrison, and despite attacks by the Khyberis and much sickness in the fort, the garrison had held out. Close by, a Sikh detachment of 800 had built a stockade to provide the fort with mutual support. This stockade was attacked by 2,000 Khyberis; the Sikhs held out until all their ammunition was expended, and then tried to withdraw to the safety of the fort, but the majority were killed in the process and the stockade was destroyed. Captain Ferris' garrison was able to hold on, and on hearing of the approach of Keane's force the Khyberis withdrew to bide their time. On 8 November the returning Bengal army reached Peshawar and Keane immediately sent out a force escorting supplies and reinforcements for Ali Masjid. On their return to Peshawar the escort was ferociously attacked by the Khyberis. The Sikh contingent beat a hasty retreat and the remainder escaped with a loss of some men, all their baggage and 500 precious camels. Lieutenant Colonel Hugh Wheeler with 37th and 48th BNI under his command was sent out from Jalalabad to punish the Khyberis and make safe

14 Poshteen. According to John Masters this garment is a frontier coat reaching to the knees or lower, made of untanned goatskin with the hair innermost. The yellow hide is decorated in strange patterns in red and black thread. The whole has a strong smell of goat.

the Khyber Pass. At the same time, Captain Frederick Mackeson started negotiating with the troublesome chiefs, eventually striking a deal by which the Khyberi chiefs were given an annual contribution of £8,000 (£600,000) in exchange for no attacks on British convoys, however these tribes, reckless of promises and treaties, continued to rob, harass and commit violence whenever the opportunity presented itself.

Having left the hostile environment of the Khyber and the hospitable welcome of General Avitabile, the Governor of Peshawar, the returning British army left Peshawar on 20 November and were now in the territories of their Tripartite ally the Sikhs, whose subjects however could not be wholly trusted, causing an order to all commanding officers:

> [to] remind their men that they were passing through the territories of an ally, and that as the soldiers of that Prince, from not possessing the same degree of discipline of which the British army can boast, may be more ready to enter into quarrels, and to make use of offensive expressions; it will be the duty of all, to keep a guard on their temper, and to be careful not to allow themselves to be forced into collision with those whom the Governor requires that they shall look upon as friends.

It was at Jhelum that the Hero of Herat, Lieutenant Eldred Pottinger, caught up with the returning column on 13 December. Pottinger was on his way to Calcutta to submit his report to the Governor General. Regrettably, the column was afflicted by one last disaster. The crossing of the Jhelum was difficult and HM 16th Lancers lost Captain William Hilton, a heavy man and a non-swimmer, plus nine men, who drowned trying to cross. The bodies of Hilton and five troopers were eventually found and buried in one grave. Apart from this unfortunate disaster, Keane led his army across the River Sutlej and arrived safely at Ferozepore on New Year's Day, 1840, where he disbanded the Army of the Indus. Of General Keane, Charles Nash wrote:

> He is a man of fair average capacity, and much firmness and decision of character. This may fairly be conceded to him, but more he cannot claim, and his own opinion of the exploit which raised him to the position he occupies, may be gathered from his having described Ghuznee as 'but a rotten hole after all.' The other side of his character cannot be regarded without aversion. He is almost universally disliked by the army, both officers and men, for his proud, irascible and arbitrary character, and one of his favourite means of revenging himself upon his officers when they offend him, was to suppress in his despatches, as in the case of Colonel Dennie, all mention of the way in which they have distinguished themselves.[15]

At about this time news arrived of the British awards for the successful campaign in Afghanistan. In the London *Gazette* of 11 December 1839 it was reported that:

> the Queen has been pleased to direct "Letters Patent" to be passed under the great seal, granting the dignitaries of Baron and Earl of the United Kingdom of Great Britain and Ireland, unto the Right Honourable George Auckland, G.C.B., and the heirs male of his

15 Nash, *The History of the Campaign in Afghanistan*, p.219.

> body lawfully begotten, by the names, styles and title of Baron Eden of Norwood in the county of Surrey, and Earl Auckland.

In the same *Gazette*, Lieutenant General Sir John Keane was created Baron Keane of Ghazni in Afghanistan and of Cappoquin in the county of Waterford. Knighthoods were awarded to Mr William Macnaghten, Colonel Henry Pottinger and Lieutenant Colonel Claude Wade. On 13 December a further London *Gazette* gave a list of brevet promotions by which Brigadier Robert Sale was promoted to major general, 17 majors were promoted to lieutenant colonels and 19 captains to majors. In addition, major generals Cotton and Thackwell were made Knight Commanders of the Order of the Bath, GCB, and 14 officers were given CBs (Companion of the Order of the Bath). Surprisingly, there was no honour for Captain James Outram.

On 4 November Shah Shuja, envoy Macnaghten, Major General Cotton (army commander), Brigadier Roberts, and their entourages left Kabul to escape the rigours of the approaching winter for the more temperate climate of Jalalabad; while it snowed in Kabul oranges were being harvested in Jalalabad. Sir Alexander Burnes was left in charge of an apparently tranquil Kabul. Burnes obviously enjoyed his time of being in charge and was quoted as saying, 'I lead a very pleasant life'. His weekly dinner party was the high point of the Kabul social calendar. He boasted, 'I can place before my friends champagne, hock, Madeira, sherry, port, claret, sauterne not forgetting a glass of curaçao and maraschino, and the hermetically sealed salmon and hotch-potch.'[16] Served, no doubt, by handsome Afghan ladies.

Also in November, Sir William Macnaghten's boss in Simla had decided to quit that place and was on his way back to Calcutta, during which trip he intended to spend close to a year in Agra to learn more about the country and what good works to initiate. The Governor General's entourage arrived in Agra just after Christmas, but before two weeks had elapsed, he received an urgent message requiring his presence in Calcutta as the Chinese governor of Canton was refusing to allow the importation of opium into China, a key revenue source for the East India Company. The Governor General and his sisters were back in Calcutta on 1 March and his nephew, Captain William Osborne, had wangled a place on the expedition to China.

At Christmas in Kabul, while the provost marshal's troops patrolled the town to arrest disorderly soldiery, Sir Alexander Burnes hosted a grand Christmas dinner party for his admiring young officers. Lieutenant Neville Chamberlain later described the scene: 'We had a very merry party though we had nothing to drink but brandy and gin.' When Sir Alexander's health was drunk, he got up and said, 'This day two years ago I was eating my Christmas Dinner in this very room, but instead of being the guest of a British regiment, I was entertaining a Russian agent.'[17] Young Ensign Granville Chetwynd-Stapylton of HM 13th Foot was to record, 'The more I see of Kabul, the more I like it. For my part I should like to stay here.' Adding, 'Sir Alexander Burnes lives in the city and anyone who wishes to see him goes to breakfast with him, he is a very good fellow.'[18]

16 Macintyre, *The Man Who Would Be King*, p.252.

17 Sir G.W. Forrest, *Life of Field-Marshal Sir Neville Chamberlain* (Edinburgh: Blackwood, 1909) p.53. Lieutenant Chamberlain ended his service as a Field Marshal and was also the person who devised the game of snooker.

18 Ensign G. Chetwynd-Stapylton, *Diary and Related Documents*. (Privately Printed) p.8.

13

Mission Creep

As the envoy, Mr William Macnaghten, made his way to Jalalabad accompanying His Majesty Shah Shuja, he had time to contemplate on the apparent success of the campaign and the measures now necessary to establish Shah Shuja in firm control of Afghanistan. At this stage, the Envoy had two options: he could either have the British troops withdrawn at a favourable juncture with honour and leave Shah Shuja with a contingent force on whose fidelity he could rely and thus establish his authority; or, mistrusting the Shah's ability to maintain himself, continue the military occupation of Afghanistan and govern in the Shah's name on the plea that the expedition was not only to place the Shah on his throne, but also to secure his power and establish the independence and the integrity of Afghanistan. Isolated pockets of resentment were to be expected and all of these could be sorted out with the troops currently on the ground. Macnaghten was content with the overall general situation and made plans to address the top priority tasks ahead which were the reorganisation of the Afghan state and its finances. In devising his schemes, he was compelled to acknowledge that although Shah Shuja was ostensibly an independent monarch, this 'independence' would remain a contradiction in terms as long as British-officered troops studded the countryside thus projecting the real powers of sovereignty held by the British envoy. While Shah Shuja was to be allowed to control the administration of justice, collection of revenue and the appointment of ministers in accordance with the treaty, the Envoy retained control of external policy, deployment of all troops, and measures to counteract any dissension. This division of control was clearly based on the model the British had successfully employed with the Princely States in India. In regard to the external policy, Macnaghten was paranoid in his perceived machinations of the Russians and hence the necessity for extending the Shah's influence beyond the districts of Kabul, Jalalabad, Ghazni and Kandahar, and in so doing subjugating outlying provinces to Shah Shuja's authority. It was also his view that Balkh, the crucial bridgehead on the Oxus, should be seized in the coming May when the passes would be clear; and from there a quick and effective blow could be struck against Bokhara. Thus, as the various contingencies were to emerge, Macnaghten found himself inextricably dragged into option two.

From the Russian point of view, the British invasion of Afghanistan had put them in a difficult position. They had backed off in Persia to avoid provoking exactly this kind of reaction. All Asia knew that the British and Russians were in confrontation and the Russians had come out looking like losers. The British invasion of Afghanistan almost demanded some kind of response, but the Russians were powerless to intervene directly there. However, a campaign against Khiva would have the desired result of restoring Russian prestige without further antagonising the British, especially as Khiva was the centre of the slave trade, a business equally abhorred by the British. Hence, the advance of General Peroffski's force on Khiva which left Orenburg in early January. His force comprised infantry, cavalry and artillery numbering 5,200 troops and a baggage train of 10,000 camels. The Afghan winter was to cause havoc with the Russian General's force as many of his soldiers died and he lost half his camels. On 1 February, Peroffski issued his orders for the withdrawal of his force and by early May his dead-beat soldiers staggered back into Orenburg.

While General Peroffski was advancing on Khiva, Macnaghten, still fretting over possible Russian machinations, approved the despatch of a one-man mission to try to forestall the Russian initiative. On Christmas Eve Captain James Abbott,[1] with a small escort, left Herat on this most dangerous and demanding mission to Khiva; a journey of 500 miles over snow-covered mountains, populated by barbaric raiders and slave traders. Abbott's mission was to convince the Khan of Khiva to surrender his Russian slaves, thereby negating the ostensive reason for the Russian advance by General Peroffski. Abbott was also to ascertain what difficulties the Russian advance might face. After a great deal of hardship and clashes with the local tribesmen, the gallant Captain persevered and eventually managed to obtain the Khan's agreement to release his Russian slaves. During the course of his negotiations with the Khan, Abbott informed him that he was the representative of 'the greatest and most powerful country in the world', whereupon the Khan signed a treaty allowing for a British representative at Khiva and requested Abbott to mediate on his behalf with the Russians. Captain Abbott set off, without the slaves, on his journey to St Petersburg, via Moscow, in his dual capacity as the British envoy and mediator. He was to return to duty two years later minus two fingers lost during a fight with raiders and for which he was granted a pension of £50 (£3,750).

Four months after Captain Abbott had left Herat, Major Elliott Todd sent out another one of his officers, Lieutenant Richmond Shakespeare, to follow up on Abbott's progress and to ensure that all was well. The groundwork having been laid, Shakespeare was greeted by the Khan with open arms and after a short interval continued his journey, along with 400 freed Russian slaves. For this act of humanity, Shakespeare received a glorious welcome in England and was awarded a knighthood. When asked about this change in fortunes, Captain Abbott remarked, 'All the suffering fell to my lot, all the laurels to his.' Whether it was due to the good offices of these two officers or not, the Russians did conclude a treaty with the Khan of Khiva in the late summer of 1840.

Macnaghten, given the authority by the Governor General to control affairs in Afghanistan, had to exercise this control in the name of the ostensibly independent, and, according to him, the popular King of Afghanistan, Shah Shuja; no mean task especially as the main character defects of this 62-year-old monarch were his unbridled haughtiness and extreme arrogance. As the direct descendant of the mighty Ahmad Shah Duranni, Shah Shuja insisted on abject servility from his ministers and people. He was a product of the old system which he had perpetuated in his tattered court during his long exile in Ludhiana and was not about to change.

1 Captain James Abbott. He later took part in both the Anglo-Sikh Wars. The town of Abbottabad is named after him.

The Durannis clustered round the throne and clambered for compensation for their pretended forbearance and put forward the most extravagant claims for the reinstatement of old privileges they had previously enjoyed. In this vein, he appointed many unworthy sycophants to key posts including Mullah Shikore as his chief minister. This individual had served his master faithfully during all his trials and tribulations despite suffering numerous indignities such as having his ears cut off for a minor infraction. Mullah Shikore, slightly older than his master, had by now lost his memory but retained sufficient faculty to hate the British, oppose the people, to be corrupt and venal beyond all conception and to appoint subordinates as flagitious as himself. Not long afterwards, this decrepit gentleman was to seize all the granaries around Kabul, and the grain sold at the prices fixed by him. As Sir Alexander Burnes was to comment, 'Bad ministers are in every government solid grounds for unpopularity, and I doubt if ever a king had a worse set than has Shah Shuja.' Several of the Shah's sons had been given official posts. One of them, Suftar Jung, was appointed governor of Kandahar Province on a salary of £140 (£10,500), which he swiftly increased to £10,000 (£750,000) by the crudest of extortions.

On the arrival of the royal court at Jalalabad all the local chiefs came in to pay their allegiance to Shah Shuja with the exception of the Sultan of Bajour. It was at this time that Macnaghten was given the distressing news that Dost Mohammed had joined his brother-in-law, Nasrullah Khan of Bokhara. This information only made him more determined that the Shah's sphere of influence had to be extended. Macnaghten left the Shah at Jalalabad while he followed in the footsteps of Major General Thackwell's column down the Khyber Pass to Peshawar, where he sanctioned the deals made by Lieutenant Mackeson with the Khyberi chiefs and awaited the arrival of his wife Fanny. It was during a sumptuous dinner party for 58 officers, hosted by General Pablo Avitabile, that the heartening news of the capture of Kalat by Major General Thomas Willshire was received and duly celebrated by three cheers and gallons of champagne. Macnaghten was not much taken by the rough justice employed by General Avitabile to control his subjects, which was a pity as he may have done better in his handling of the Afghans had he adopted the Italian's *modus operandi* described by Colin Mackenzie as, 'Spoken by the Afghan population with the admiration of a troop of jackals for a tiger.' However, he was alarmed at the General's views and negative projection of the state of the Sikh kingdom and hints that he was planning on leaving the Sikh service. This added to Macnaghten's concerns about the Sikhs and their continued intransigent stand over the matter of British free access through the Punjab. According to a number of historians, envoy Macnaghten would have rushed into war with the Sikhs for the purpose of compelling them to give free passage at all times for British troops to cross their borders. Macnaghten, with his wife, along with her maid, chandeliers and cat, left Peshawar for Jalalabad on 15 December accompanied by Dr George Berwick and Captain Edward Conolly, one of the Envoy's three nephews.

Major General Willshire and his Bombay Division, joined by Captain James Outram, had arrived at Quetta on 29 October 1839. Here he had been informed by the Political Agent, Captain John Bean, that Mehrab Khan the chief of Kelat, who had in the past made overtures to come to favourable terms, had been told that nothing short of his complete surrender was acceptable. Shocked by Shah Shuja's ingratitude, the Khan had chosen to fight and die rather than surrender. Captain Bean also gave Major General Willshire to understand that that the taking of Kelat would be a pushover. Consequently, the General had split his force with one brigade under Brigadier John Scott continuing its march through the Bolan Pass to India, while the other brigade, under Brigadier John Baumgardt, consisting of HM 2nd Foot and HM 17th

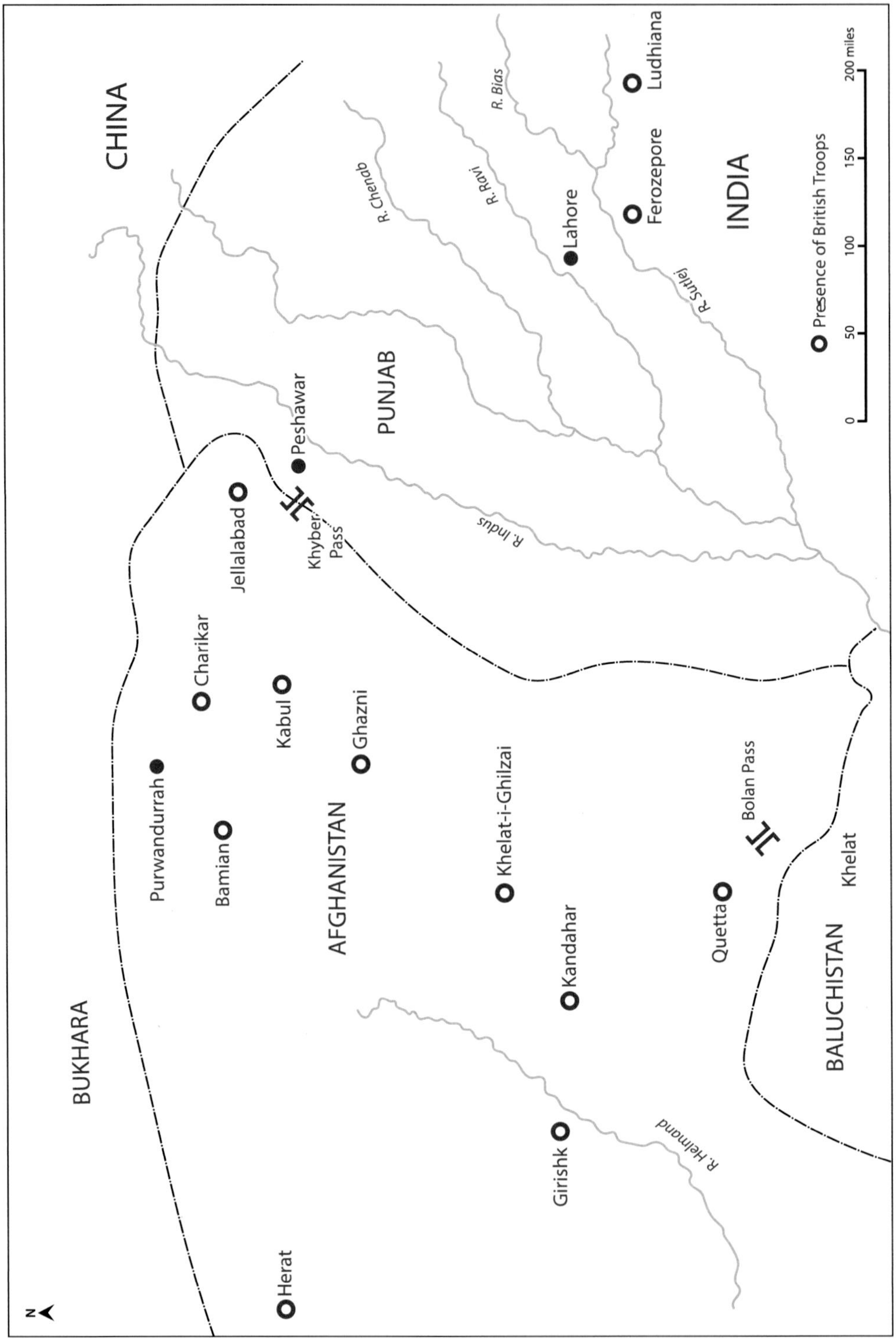

Map 8 Disposition of British troops at the end of 1839.

Foot and 31st BNI, left Quetta on 3 November to capture Kelat, 85 miles to the south-west of Quetta.

At the very last minute the General, not trusting Captain Bean's or civil servant Mr Andrew Ross Bell's assessments of the task, decided to join the attacking force, which arrived at its destination on 13 November. Sir John Kaye in his *History of the War in Afghanistan*, describes the scene as follows:

> Khelat is a place of commanding strength. On the north-west of the fort were three heights, which the Khan had covered with his infantry supported by five guns. The Engineer officer [Captain Peat] reported that until the heights were carried, it would be impossible to proceed against the fortress. Orders were given for the attack. It was Willshire's hope that the enemy might be driven down to the gates of the fortress, and that our stormers might rush in with them. Gradually the hills were carried, gradually the guns were captured. The infantry advanced under heavy fire from the British artillery. The Belooche footmen fled towards the walls of the fortress and our infantry pushed hotly after them. But not in time were they to secure an entrance, the gate was closed against their advance.
>
> The artillery was now brought into play. The infantry, compelled to protect themselves against the heavy fire, poured in from the rocks and sheltered themselves behind some ruined buildings, whilst our batteries, planted on the height, opened upon the gate. Two of Cooper's guns were brought within a distance of 200 yards, and whilst the gunners fell under the matchlock fire of the enemy, played full upon the gate. At last it gave way. Pointing his hand towards the gate, Willshire rode down to show the infantry that an entrance was ready for them. Rising at once from their cover, they rushed in with a loud hurrah. Pennycuick[2] and his men were the first to enter. The other companies soon followed, until the whole of the storming column were within the walls of Khelat. Onward they struggled manfully towards the citadel. Every inch of ground was obstinately disputed. But at last the citadel was won. There was a desparate resistance. Sword in hand, Mehrab Khan and some of his principal chiefs stood there to give us battle.[3]

Mehrab Khan was shot dead by Private Maxwell of HM 2nd Foot.[4] Besides the Khan and 13 of his principal chiefs, 2,000 Baluchis were killed, while on the British side the casualties were 39 killed including one officer, Captain Thomas Gravatt of HM 2nd Foot, and 107 Other

2 Lieutenant Colonel John Pennycuick (1789–1849). He was commissioned into HM 78th Foot (Ross-shire Buffs) in 1807 and served in Java where he was wounded. He was promoted to captain in 1821, exchanged into HM 47th Foot (Lancashire) in 1815 and fought in the First Anglo-Burmese War. In 1834 he was promoted to major, joined HM 17th Foot (Leicestershire) and served with the regiment in Afghanistan. Pennycuick married Sarah Farrell in 1820 and they had five sons and six daughters. In 1848 Pennycuick exchanged for the last time into HM 24th Foot (2nd Warwickshire). He joined the regiment in India along with his son, 17-year-old Alexander. Both he and his son were killed at the Battle of Chillianwala, 13 January 1848.

3 Kaye, *History of the War in Afghanistan*, Vol. 2, p.26.

4 Thomas Holdsworth, *The Campaign of the Indus in A Series of Letters from an Officer of the Bombay Division* (London: 1840). Reprinted as *Experiences of a British Officer of the 2nd (Queen's Royal) Regiment in the Campaign to Place Shah Shuja on the throne of Afghanistan 1838–1840* (Driffield: Leonaur Ltd reprint, 2007), p.127.

Ranks wounded. It was rumoured that Mehrab Khan had managed to send away his harem and family just before the appearance of the British, but some of his other chiefs had not been so fortunate and these chiefs had deliberately cut the throats of all females belonging to their establishments, including wives, mothers and daughters, rather than have them suffer at the hands of the infidels. Mehrab Khan's son, 15-year-old Nusser Khan, and a widow by the name of Bibi Gunjani were not at Kelat at this time and no effort was made to hunt them down. Both the widow, who was a woman of courage and talent, and the son were to cause the British a great deal of trouble during the following 18 months. As planned, Kelat was incorporated into Shah Shuja's kingdom and an old pretender to the chieftainship, Shah Newaz Khan, who had for some time been hanging on to the skirt-tails of Shah Shuja and his allies, was appointed chief. On completion of the operation, Captain Outram was sent with the General Willshire's despatch to convey the glorious news to the Governor of Bombay. While no medal was awarded for the capture of Kelat, the prize money amounting to £10,000 (£750,000) was applicable as the enemy had fired first, and much of this consisted of jewellery, which was entrusted to HM 17th Foot for safekeeping. The jewels and 300 men of the regiment boarded the transport ship *Hannah* for Bombay and were shipwrecked at the mouth of the Indus on St Patrick's Day 1840. No lives were lost and the jewels were saved by Major John Pennycuick, who carried them on his back a considerable way through the surf and marsh. The jewels were sold in Bombay in the following July for £6,000 (£450,000), but the salesman's premises were robbed and he was declared bankrupt, so the Bombay Government only received a small fraction of the sale price. Major General Willshire left the designated political agent, Lieutenant William Lovejoy of 27th BNI, in Kelat with an escort of 30 *sepoys*. Mehrab Khan's alleged treachery was, on subsequent inquiry, not confirmed.[5]

In the meantime Brigadier Scott, who had advanced through the Bolan Pass, had on his arrival at Dadur been ordered to halt until further notice. At the time it was falsely rumoured that the Bombay Division would be required for operations at Herat. The true reason was that it was imperative that the Sindh be held, thereby securing the only viable lines of communication. On 24 December the Governor General ordered Major General Sir Thomas Willshire to disband his division, and Sindh was put under the jurisdiction of the Bombay Army with Major General George Brookes in command of the troops and Mr Ross Bell the political supremo.

After a sombre Christmas at Jalalabad and with the new army commander, Major General Sir Willoughby Cotton, on hand, Sir William Macnaghten used the opportunity to chastise the Sultan of Bajour, *Syud* Mosteen, for his refusal to declare his allegiance to the Shah. It was decided to send out a force commanded by Lieutenant Colonel Joseph Orchard against the Sultan's fort at Pashat in the mountain country some 50 miles to the eastward of Jalalabad. It was made clear to the commander that he was to act under the political direction of his accompanying Political Officer, Captain George MacGregor. Besides his own regiment, 1st BER, Lieutenant Colonel Orchard's force comprised a troop of 2nd Bengal Light Cavalry, a company of 37th BNI, the Shah's 3rd Infantry Regiment, the Shah's cavalry of 700 horse, 3 x 6-pdr Horse Artillery guns and a detachment of 20 sappers led by Lieutenant Robert Pigou. Apparently Brigadier Roberts, who was at Jalalabad at the time, was not consulted about this

5 General Sir John Ayde, *Indian Frontier Policy: An Historical Sketch* (London: Smith, Elder & Co., 1897. Kessinger Publishing reprint, n.d.), p.6.

A scene from the storming of Kelat, depicting both British Infantry and horse artillery.

British troops outside Zenana during the storming of Kelat.

operation despite the fact that Colonel Orchard's force included a good portion of the Shah's force. The force left Jalalabad early on 5 January 1840 and arrived in the vicinity of Pashat at 5:00 a. m. on 18 January. It had been raining for several days. On arrival the guns were deployed and for the next couple of hours fired on the fort, resulting in two possible breaches on either side of the main gate. Lieutenant Pigou, with his party of sappers and an escort from 1st BER, advanced to examine the possible breaches. Colonel Orchard's bugler, on seeing the sappers appearing to enter a breach, sounded the advance and the whole column moved forward only to be caught under heavy enemy fire, causing the troops to fall back to a ravine close by. Two attempts were made to blow up the gate with gunpowder, but the rain had begun to fall rather heavily, putting a complete damper on Lieutenant Pigou's gallant attempts to fire the charge. Failure to blow up the gate, and failed attempts to scale the walls, drenched with rain and exposed to continuous enemy fire, led Orchard to call off the attack at noon. The enemy, reckoning that the infidels would continue to harass them and eventually win, took the opportunity to collect all their valuables and desert the fort, leaving the infidels to advance on an empty objective. The British casualties in the engagement were 69 men killed or wounded. Lieutenant William Collinson and Ensign William Hicks, both of 1st BER, were severely wounded, and the former died of his wounds shortly afterwards. During the battle and in an act worthy of a Victoria Cross, Private Dobbin saved the life of Lieutenant William Pattle; for his bravery Private Dobbin was promoted tocorporal and later Lieutenant Pattle's family presented him with a watch. While the battle at Pashat may be classified as a failure, it did achieve the overall aim in that a couple of weeks later, Sultan *Syud* Mosteen came in of his own accord to submit to Shah Shuja. This was the last action of the 1st BER involvement in the Afghan campaign. This fine regiment, nicknamed the 'Dirty Shirts' and later to be incorporated into the Queen's army as the Royal Munster Regiment, had been at the forefront of all the events in the British advance into Afghanistan. On its return to India it was replaced by HM 44th Foot.

A few days after the Pushut affair, Brigadier Roberts received a long and personal letter from the Governor General dated 29 December 1839. The letter was sent from Agra on the Governor General's route back to Calcutta. This letter is not mentioned in Sir John Kaye's prestigious history of the campaign, and because of its importance is quoted in full here. It clearly indicates the Governor General's overriding concern of having an efficient Shah's army up and running as soon as possible, thus allowing the Company's army to withdraw and thereby reduce the spiralling cost of his Afghan initiative. He also appears to be conscious of the fact that while speed was essential its efficiency was of paramount importance:

> My dear Sir,
> You will before you receive this letter have been some time in charge of the Shah's contingent and I am anxious as soon as you shall have become fully acquainted with its present condition, that you should provide me with a detailed report of your views upon it, and where its wants and its prospects are and all the measures which may be necessary for bringing it into efficiency. I have noticed with some of our officers and authorities a tone of impatience in regard to it, which I am not inclined to adopt. At the same time I am strongly impressed with the great importance of this force, I think after the withdrawal of our regular troops it may greatly conduce to the stability and quiet confirmation of the Shah's power and I would omit no exertion to have it on the footing on which it ought to be placed. It has hitherto not had fair play. Some of the men had had, before commencement

of the campaign, scarcely any opportunity of being drilled, none of them had been enlisted except for a very short period and with the major part of them their time has been spent on detachment and desultory duties, harassing to the men and by no means tending to their discipline and to their formation into good military corps. I trust that a few months repose from such service is at length open to them and that time may be afforded for the sick and harassed to recover and for all to improve. The calls of duty performed up to this time have been such as to make the service popular neither with the officers or men but if they have some rest and should be carefully attended to for some months I think that it will be more favourably regarded. It is beginning to be so already, I think, by our officers and will be so, I have no doubt presently by the men, but I do not think that you will be able with facility to obtain recruits from Hindustan, until your soldiers shall fully understand and appreciate with favour their present position – when political events will allow of it they might then be annually, in small proportions, allowed a furlough, and might with the promise of a modest bounty be induced to bring back recruits with them – such recruits being subject to inspection by an officer at Ludhiana or Kurnal. I should very much prefer this system to the establishment of a depot at which the men should be previously drilled, and which I fear would subject us to heavier losses by desertion – but the time has not yet come when such a system can be brought into operation, and in the meantime we must do for you here and you must do for yourselves what can most conveniently be done. I have seen Captain Gerrard of the European Regiment who has proposed to enlist Gurkhas for you and I have other schemes in view, but in a few days Major McSherry[6] will, I think, have crossed the Sutlej, and I shall have the benefit of his advice – and have ordered him for the purpose to join me here. In the meantime you must keep your ranks as full as you can, and you will judge whether you can safely admit into them any of the men of the country in which you are. The two Cavalry regiments are I know very much decried and they are maintained at an enormous expense, and it has been reported to me, that some detachments have on some occasions behaved exceedingly ill – but others again have done well and the observations I have made upon the manner in which the infantry has been collected and brought into the campaign apply yet more strongly to the cavalry. The regiment in particular which has been stationed at Candahar has been hardly worked, and the want of forage, and of rest and the consequent sickness and loss of horses and of men have been exceedingly discouraging to it – all this I trust is now in the way of being repaired and I hope that the officers in command of the regular troops will cooperate with you in carefully attending to the wants of this Corps. It has, I know, been suggested that the services of the two Cavalry Corps might be with advantage altogether dispensed with.[7] I am of the opinion that they should be reduced in numbers and would not have them higher even at present than 800 men each – but whether this reduction should immediately be carried forward, it will be up to you and Mr Macnaghten to consider. I am satisfied that with care they may be much improved, if other cavalry could not properly be substituted for them. I am inclined to think therefore that they must be maintained for some time, and I have authorised, in the uncertainty of what may be determined, Captain Anderson to take back with him clothing for 1,600

6 This was the officer who was in charge of the initial recruiting of the Shah's contingent.
7 The plan was to replace the Company's cavalry units with Afghan units called *Jan-Baz*.

> men and a few additional horsemen connected with men already in his regiment. In the meantime you will probably weed these corps of their worst men and as other schemes shall be matured they may be further diminished. Captain Codrington's regiment must be by this time in Candahar. I do not know how strong it is in numbers but though it was in the first instance composed of the worst men of the contingent and has been stationed in a severe climate, it has had some opportunities of being drilled and he is an excellent officer and his regiment should be effective. The 5th Regiment will I fear, have been greatly crippled at Girishk and will more than any other require rest and renovation, but I will not with my imperfect information endeavour to follow into detail the condition of this force and will, with interest for information and suggestions from you after you shall have communicated on all points with Mr Macnaghten. We are sending you a small mountain train under Captain Backhouse.[8] I know nothing of Captain Anderson's artillery but should think, looking to the Shah's long train of guns, that some reduction may be made in it, so as to keep down the very heavy expense to which the contingent must at all events be subject.[9] I should like your equipments to be as much as possible provided in Afghanistan either by contract from private merchants or from the bazaars of the country. The most convenient mode as regards the Government will be that of sending you stores and clothing by normal convoys and escorts and you will know better than I do the degree in which clothing, arms, equipment and ammunition can be provided in Afghanistan. The facilities of obtaining them there will I trust every day become greater. You will be pleased to write to me upon all these points and upon many others which may occur to you.[10]

The Governor General's letter also appeared to solicit reliable information of the progress being made. At this time many of the Company's officers were sending running commentaries to the local newspapers, while others were sending copious reports to influential acquaintances, and not all this verbiage was to the liking of Lord Auckland. His point man, at the centre of affairs, never failed to project the positive, and his conviction remained that the Shah was indeed popular, calling all doubters 'croakers'.

Brigadier Roberts, a stickler for military etiquette and the establishment of a robust command structure, had now been given the responsibility of organising an efficient army for the Shah, and was soon to discover he was not given the authority to implement such; this remained in the hands of his political master, who not being a soldier was either ignorant of military ethos or hostile to any idea contrary to his own. This difference of opinion was to develop into a clash between the two key representatives of the Company in Afghanistan and undoubtedly sowed the seeds of disunity between the politicos and the military to the detriment of overall morale. The *contretemps* revolved around two aspects of Brigadier Roberts' task. Firstly, what units were covered under the Brigadier's assigned task, and secondly, who was to be the ultimate authority in the selection of troops for deployment. Envoy Macnaghten held that the Brigadier's command was limited to those Hindustani troops recruited and designated by the

8 The mountain battery was armed with 3-pdr guns which were packed on teams of mules, thus better for mountain warfare, but useless on the plains and against forts.

9 The Shah's contingent, by mid-1841, was costing £300,000 (£22.5 million) per year. Buist, *Outline of the Operations*, p.97.

10 Edwards-Stuart, *A John Company General*, p.86.

Tripartite Treaty (see Chapter 7). Consequently, the levies now being raised to eventually form the Afghan army were directly answerable to the Shah, and while financed by the British were, by extrapolation, under the authority of the Envoy over whom, the Brigadier was not to have any jurisdiction. At this juncture it should be noted that the Shah had around him a small force under the command of Colonel Campbell, who had been with the Shah during his abortive attempt to regain his throne in 1834. This 'bodyguard' also included some artillery to which command Lieutenant Robert Warburton had been assigned. Brigadier Roberts accepted that the bodyguard was outside his jurisdiction. As a military person, Brigadier Roberts was horrified at this division in command structure especially in a country of troublesome and warlike people. The situation was further exacerbated by some officers, in efforts to maintain their independence of command, making full use of their ability to do so and appealing to the Envoy for his ruling. Macnaghten's overriding concern, apparently at the behest of the Shah, was that the newly raised levies, the embryos of a Royal Afghan Army, were seen to be Afghani in composition, formation and under the direct orders of the Shah. Brigadier Roberts on the other hand, although he accepted the fact that the Envoy was his superior, insisted on correct military form and he was not prepared to forego any of the authority and responsibility which had been given to him by the Governor General.

After its winter sojourn in Jalalabad the Shah's entourage, which included the recently elevated Sir William and Lady Macnaghten, Major General Sir Willoughby Cotton and Brigadier Roberts, left on 30 April and were back in Kabul on 3 May. In Kabul the troops had had a dreadful winter with temperatures as low as minus 10°, causing a good many of the troops to succumb. Lieutenant Colonel Dennie wrote in his journal:

> The casualties among the soldiers and my own regiment, 13th Foot, have been very great and the 13th have scarcely 200 effective men left. The 35th Native Regiment and some black artillery, being Indian you may conclude, have suffered equally from the cold. All my camels are dead. And one of my horses, an Arab, was frozen to death the other night, many of our poor camp followers and servants have suffered, I regret to say the same fate.[11]

Due to this poor condition of his regiment, Dennie submitted a report, backed by the medical advice of Assistant Surgeon Peter Robertson, to the effect that HM 13th Foot, the only remaining Queen's regiment, was no longer fit for military duty. This caused a hiatus with the astonished political and military authorities. Dennie was accused of being a troublemaker for not discussing the matter before submitting his report. No inquiry was held as the issue was allowed to improve as the weather improved. The one consolation was that the hard winter had also kept the Afghans indoors.

On his arrival back in Kabul, Brigadier Roberts took issue with Captain Hugh Johnson of 26th BNI, who was the officer in charge of his contingent's treasury. This officer, at the time of the initial occupation of Kabul, had been allowed by Major General Simpson to maintain the treasury in the house he had acquired in Kabul city on the same street as Sir Alexander Burnes. Brigadier Roberts now ordered Captain Johnson to move the treasury to a more secure place. The

11 Edmund Yorke, *Playing the Great Game: Britain, War and Politics in Afghanistan Since 1839* (London: Robert Hale, 2012), p.68.

Captain felt that this would be most inconvenient and applied directly to the Envoy for his decision, who ruled that 'Captain Johnson could place his treasury wherever he wanted.' The Brigadier exploded; not so much for the Captain's refusal to obey, as for the Captain's not submitting his appeal through the proper channels. One can easily understand the Brigadier's disappointment and the apparent rebuff. No doubt Captain Johnson enjoyed his moment of sly satisfaction.

While the snows melted and the green sprouts of vegetation shot up, so had the eastern Ghilzais despite the thrashing they had been given by Captain James Outram's mission the previous autumn. The whole of the Ghilzai country had risen in a state of insurrection. A small party of cavalry, under Captain Arthur Taylor and Captain Thomas Walker of 4th Local Horse, were sent out to apprehend Sultan Mohammed Khan, the chief who had been replaced by Captain Outram and who was now back heading up the rebels. This was the first of many deployments of the Shah's contingent made by Macnaghten without reference to Brigadier Roberts. Initially, on the advance of this cavalry force, the rebels had withdrawn to their mountain hideaways, but soon returned, on the attack, in vast numbers, forcing the British force to fall back on Khelat-i-Ghilzai. There, it was reinforced by a column of 200 infantry and 150 cavalry which had been proceeding to Kabul under Captain Christopher Codrington.

On receipt of the information regarding this situation, Major General William Nott despatched a larger force, of infantry, cavalry and guns, under Captain William Anderson, to tranquilise the Ghilzais and force a junction with Captains Taylor and Walker. This was done on 14 April. A couple of days later, Captain Anderson with his force advanced against a Ghilzai force of 2,000, which after a sharp action was destroyed and dispersed. On 22 May, another force under Lieutenant Colonel Newton Wallace, who had just arrived in Kabul with 2nd BNI, 4,000 camp followers, 2,000 camels and a treasure chest of £210,000 (£15.5 million), was sent out from Kabul to join up with Captain Anderson and to systematically subdue the Ghilzais. The despatch of this force was authorised by army commander Major General Cotton, who had asked Brigadier Roberts for his views; while flattered to be asked, the Brigadier told him he was not authorised to comment as everything official must as a matter of course come through the Envoy. He then went on to suggest that a larger and more efficient body of infantry be sent. This combined force, nearly 3,000 strong, proceeded to destroy the forts of the malcontents and captured a good number of the chiefs, some of whom were beheaded on the spot. On completion of this witch-hunt, Lieutenant Colonel Wallace occupied Ghazni while Captain John Woodburn, with the Shah's 5th Infantry Regiment and 300 Horse Artillery, garrisoned Khelat-i-Ghilzai.

There was, at the time, a good deal of evidence that the dispersed Ghilzais and their chiefs had made their way over the mountains to the safe haven provided by Dost Mohammed's brother, Sultan Mohammed Khan, at his Sikh-allocated *jagir* of Kohat, not far from Peshawar, and no doubt with Sikh cognisance. It had already been established that the Sikhs were in surreptitious communication with various Afghan chiefs to thwart British progress in Afghanistan. The British, who had quibbled over their treaty obligations with the Persians and broken their treaty promises to the Sindhis, were now outraged at the apparent duplicity of the Sikhs, their Tripartite Treaty partners, and were in a state of perplexity as to how strongly they could remonstrate, especially as their line of communication through the Punjab was of vital importance for their extended operations in Afghanistan. The Sikh attitude at the time was quite understandable; even in the days of the old Maharaja, the Sikhs had been ever-suspicious of British designs and now they were really apprehensive. Egged on by his anti-British Chief Minister, Raja Dhian Singh, *Kunwar* Naunihal Singh remembered that the Sikh initiative into

Sindh had been thwarted by the British and it was now occupied by the British, there was a British army in Afghanistan and a huge reserve at Ferozepore not 50 miles from Lahore. How long would it be, they reckoned, before they were squeezed out of Peshawar and the Derajat, and even Kashmir. For their own long-term safety the Sikhs felt they had to thwart British progress in Afghanistan, but without any overt act. This view of the situation may appear convoluted, but in those times convolution was second nature to many.

Major General Sir William Nott.

Richard Kennedy, a surgeon with the Bombay Division during the campaign, had this to say about the possible course of events resulting from British policy, which does suggest some clues for the Sikh attitude. His summary of the policy was clearly influenced by the views of his good friend Sir Alexander Burnes:

> The districts of Peshawar and the Derajat, on the west bank of the Indus, which were wrested by Ranjit Singh from Dost Mohammed are as valuable and important to the Duranni empire as they were to the ex-ruler, and our future position at Kabul will see the incessant renewal of those claims at every opportunity; and eventually, at no long interval, we shall have foreign intrigue offering influence and money to regain by force what we refuse to obtain in any way, and these suggestions will be listened to, and our treaty with Kabul, which debars the king of the Duranni empire from any political relation with any foreign power, save through British mediation, will be treated with ridicule by any foreign power to whom it is not politically inconvenient to declare war against us.
>
> Our policy is clear and imperative, to work through what has been begun, let it be distinctly understood that Lord Auckland's policy is not the end, but a beginning only. Herat must be subdued and annexed to Kabul for its own security, and our hold on Kabul must be, after compelling or bribing Ranjit Singh's successor to restore Peshawar and the Derajat, the maintenance of such a frontier force as shall show the Kabul Government that the first moment of a rupture with the British Government will be the certain loss of those valuable districts on the banks of the Indus, accessible at once to, and utterly indefensible from, British hostility. But Herat is not yet annexed to Kabul, and the Sikh Government still holds Peshawar and the Derajat; and the strife and the outlay yet to be prepared for are neither trifling, nor in what may result from them.[12]

12 Kennedy, *Narrative*, p.188.

Ten years later, during the Second Anglo-Sikh War, *Sardar* Chattar Singh, the leader of the Sikh insurrection, offered Peshawar to Dost Mohammed in exchange for Afghan assistance and Dost Mohammed sent 3,000 cavalry under his son Akram Khan. However, at the Battle of Gujarat the Sikhs were defeated, the Punjab was annexed and Akram Khan high-tailed it back to Kabul.

While at Jalalabad, Sir William Macnaghten, in consultation with the army commander and Shah Shuja, decided that in view of the Shah's reluctance to the occupation of the Bala Hissar and the pressing need for permanent accommodation for the troops, a cantonment had to be built. The task of erecting this from the ground up was given to the chief engineer of the Shah's contingent, Lieutenant John Sturt, who had taken over from Lieutenant Henry Durand. It would appear that the commandant of the Shah's contingent, Brigadier Roberts, who had a wealth of experience in public works projects, was not consulted. Upon the Brigadier's arrival back in Kabul, he wrote to Lieutenant Sturt to enquire whether the Shah's contingent was included in the accommodation being built, and if so, he listed a number of recommendations concerning security and configuration. His subordinate replied to the effect that there was no plan to include the Shah's contingent and that it was too late to make any changes as the foundations had already been laid.

The cantonment was erected on a flat plain about a mile from Kabul city's Kohistan Gate and between the Kabul River and the main road to Kohistan. The area occupied was a rectangle about 1,200 yards by 600 yards surrounded by a low parapet over which a man could easily vault, and a shallow ditch over which a mounted Afghan could easily jump. The cantonment area was surrounded by orchards, which although pleasant for officers' early morning rides provided no 'fields of fire' in the event of an attack. Worse, the whole of the cantonment area was vulnerable to and overlooked by half a dozen small forts, none of which were occupied or demolished, and all within range of the Afghan *jezail*. During its construction Sergeant Deane, Lieutenant Sturt's NCO, was rebuked by his officer for pointing out the ineligibility of the cantonment location and configuration, but the sense of security in which the British had been lulled, in the very grasp of a warlike people, saw nothing wrong in establishing a comfortable cantonment as opposed to a secure stronghold. The cantonment was completed in August 1840 and in his history of the campaign Sir John Kaye wrote:

> There stood the great indefensible cantonments, overawed on every side, a mountain of madness which Providence for its own end had permitted to cloud and bewilder the intelligence of the greatest military nation in the world! There it stood, a humiliating spectacle, but except for newcomers, who stood in amazement before the great folly, little account was taken of it. Men's eyes had become accustomed to the blot.[13]

The officers sent for their wives to settle down in their bungalows. Lady Macnaghten in the spacious mission residence presided over the social events of the cantonment. There were the 'coffee houses' after the morning rides, the gathering round the bandstand in the evenings, the impromptu dances, the *burra-khanas* in the larger houses, and marriages. Lieutenant Sturt married 20-year-old Alexandrina, the only daughter of Major General Robert Sale, who had

13 Kaye, *History of the War in Afghanistan*, Vol. 1, p.141.

Colonel Stoddart and Captain Conolly in captivity at Bokhara

arrived in Kabul with her famous mother, Florentina. Lieutenant Robert Warburton married a niece of Dost Mohammed Khan, which was witnessed by both Sir William Macnaghten and Sir Alexander Burnes, and Sergeant Deane married a beautiful Afghan girl. The British army in Kabul was not in occupation as much as in garrison. Outside this haven of Britishness were the all-important Commissariat, Treasury, and the Residence where Sir Alexander Burnes held court with his cortege of admiring young officers.

In June, one of Colonel Charles Stoddart's servants, Rujub Beg, arrived in Kabul to say that his master, held prisoner at Bokhara by the fiend Nasrullah Khan, had been circumcised and forced to convert to the Muslim faith. A furious Sir William Macnaghten immediately resolved to rescue the unfortunate Colonel and return him to the Christian faith. In Kabul, at that time, was his nephew Captain Arthur Conolly, a zealous Bengal Cavalry officer, whose passion was Central Asia, hell-bent on visiting Khiva and Bokhara to win them to the British cause and obtain the release of Colonel Stoddart. Sir William obtained permission to send his nephew into Central Asia, excluding Bokhara, it being understood that should Captain Conolly venture to the forbidden place, it would be at his own risk and expense and against the Government's wishes. Sir Alexander Burnes scoffed at the idea and reckoned that all the gallant Captain would achieve would be to keep Colonel Stoddart company in his cell. Captain Conolly duly arrived in Bokhara on 10 November 1841 and was unceremoniously bundled into Stoddart's cell. Both officers were beheaded on 17 June 1842. The Calcutta authorities later declared that Captain Conolly had not been authorised to go to Bokhara and in all probability owed his misfortune to his direct transgression of Government instructions.

By midsummer the relationship between Brigadier Roberts and envoy Macnaghten had become more distant. Apart from their weekly audience with the Shah, communications between the two were conducted through copious letters, a clear indication of the distrust and need to keep records of what transpired between them; many of the Envoy's replies were conveyed by his military secretary, and none too politely. Meanwhile and as requested, the Brigadier continued to write to the Governor General of his many concerns, which were, in the main, the impolicy of numerous units being spread all over the country, free from military control and with no reference to himself. He felt that as Commandant he was being rendered quite useless with no authority, with all deployment being kept secret and managed by the Political Department with little judgement and scant military experience. In particular, the Brigadier took issue over the situation of the Mountain Train. This experimental unit, under the command of Captain Julian Backhouse of the Bengal Artillery, had been recruited and equipped in Meerut and sent up to Kabul where it should rightly have formed part of the Contingent's artillery, under Captain William Anderson. But, due to some strange and unmilitary undertaking, Captain Backhouse was not to be interfered with until he had brought the unit up to a fit state for military service, and until then Captain Backhouse was independent of all military authority and particularly of the commandant of the Shah's contingent, who considered this to be highly prejudicial to discipline. The Envoy's stance was that the Mountain Train while in its embryo state was to remain independent of military control and under his political direction; and only when it was deemed to be fit for military service would this unit form part of the Shah's contingent. In the interim it was to be paid, fed, housed and maintained by the contingent's resources.

Brigadier Roberts' observations and recommendations were compiled in a communication which he sent via the Envoy for the Governor General. The Envoy listed his rebuttals and forwarded his troublesome Brigadier's 'blunt' report and instructed him not to communicate with His Lordship until the Governor General's views were known. The Governor General in Council replied on 6 July from Fort William, Calcutta, its reply arriving at the end of July:

> I have to acknowledge the receipt of your letter of the 2nd June last, including one from Brigadier Roberts of the 30th May and conveying observations from you upon the requests made by that officer in regards to his position in Afghanistan.
>
> In these observations His Lordship in Council is disposed very generally to concur. It might be a hazardous experiment, and one which could scarcely fail to give offence to His Majesty the Shah, if an attempt were made to put the National Troops on the same footing and under the same control as the Hindustani contingent.
>
> It may however, I am directed to remark, be of advantage to both the service as well as to the public finances, if, in cases in which such corps are commanded by British officers and paid by your Treasury deference were upon very many points to the opinion of Brigadier Roberts, so that at least in supplies and clothing and in allowances and control of accounts and even in general regulations there should be as much uniformity as is consistent with national habit and feeling, and with a perfect admission of the King's authority. And His Majesty would, no doubt, readily admit the understanding that in cases in which corps of the two services shall be in camp or on duty together, there should be a common subordination to the Officer in Command.
>
> His Lordship in CI [Council] has a strong desire, in which he looks for your concurrence, to uphold the military position of Brigadier Roberts. Whenever the regular forces

> shall be withdrawn from Afghanistan he will be your first military authority and every British officer employed in that country should be led to look up to him. But for the reasons which have been given His Lordship in CI though he would be glad to know that he is frequently consulted by you and by the Shah would not have him directly interfere with the organisation and internal management of the Corps which are not attached to the Contingent.
>
> With regard to the Mountain Train, it was raised and trained in Hindustan, it was at one time the opinion of His Lordship that it should be incorporated with Captain Anderson's Artillery and it was the understanding and the intention of His Lordship in Council that it should form part of the Contingent.[14]

This clear vindication of Brigadier Roberts' views did not please Macnaghten, who felt that the Brigadier's report had been an affront to his dignity and position and he wrote to his friend, John Colvin, Lord Auckland's private secretary, with the complaint that:

> I do not receive that support to which the overwhelming difficulties of my position entitles me. In deciding upon a controversy thrust upon me by Brigadier Roberts the Government convey to me an implied censure for not supporting his military position, though the justice of my views is admitted; and take the occasion of conveying a compliment to Brigadier Roberts, though he had written to me a most disrespectful letter.[15]

It is inconceivable that the army commander, Major General Sir Willoughby Cotton, could have been oblivious to the 'tittle-tattle' between the two most senior servants of the East India Company. One must assume that the General kept out of the fray on the basis that being a Queen's officer it had nothing to do with him, and he clearly did not want to get involved in a fracas which could delay his much desired and imminent departure, so he kept aloof, hence the erection of an insecure cantonment with its only military contribution being a vivid signal to the Afghan chiefs that the British were there to stay! Meanwhile envoy Macnaghten, full of his own self-importance and loathing to delegate, continued to sideline Brigadier Roberts thus prompting his band of 'politicos' to do likewise. This incongruity between the politicians and the military underlay the sequence of events that built up to the eventual disaster. Whilst the Envoy busied himself with the issues around Kabul and continued to declare the popularity of the Shah, his expedition to Bamian was not progressing as well as he had hoped.

14 Edwards-Stuart, *A John Company General*, p.116.
15 Edwards-Stuart, *A John Company General*, p.124.

14

The Bamian Salient

The detachment sent to Bamian on 12 September 1839 arrived there on 5 October after a gruelling march of 100 miles into the mountains of Koh-i-Babar, 12,000 feet high. Dr Percival Lord, the assigned political agent, joined it a few days later. The detachment, which included the Shah's 4th Gurkha Regiment, was under the command of Captain William Hay, an officer of the Bengal Infantry with 17 years of service.

Whilst Captain Hay was the ostensible military commander, it soon became apparent that under the mantle of superior political authority the 32-year-old Dr Lord, a 'Duck'[1] and a civilian at that, was making all the decisions and not all these to the advantage of maintaining an effect military force, virtually cut off from all assistance. These shortcomings and the desperate conditions in which the troops laboured were duly reported, in a stream of letters by Captain Hay to his military superior, Brigadier Roberts, who passed them on to the Envoy with his own comments for effective action. It seems that the fraught Roberts–Macnaghten relationship was to be replicated by that of Hay–Lord at the Bamian salient.

On arrival at Bamian with winter fast approaching, a bargain was struck with the owners for the use of three neighbouring forts. These forts, made of sun-baked mud, had walls about 20 to 30 feet high, enclosing an area of about 300 square yards. Two of these forts were allotted to the infantry, and the third, slightly better built, to the artillery. However, this was not enough to accommodate all, so it became necessary to send back to Kabul 100 Horse Artillerymen and 300 Afghan horsemen, the latter also being suspected of being in seditious correspondence with Dost Mohammed Khan, so it was better to get rid of them.

Soon after the arrival of the British, news was received that trouble was brewing in the Syghan valley. A young Uzbek, by the name of Khilish Beg, claimed superiority over the valley and the principal fort of Sar-i-Sang. To assist him in his quest, he had asked the *Wali* of Kholoom, Murad Beg, for a force to help him. The *Wali*, who at the time was playing host to the ex-Amir Dost Mohammed, jumped at the opportunity of extending his influence and sent a force of 700

1 'Duck' was the nickname given to officers of the Bombay establishment. In the 1800s there was a great deal of professional jealousy between the officers of the three Presidencies. The officers of the Bengal Presidency looked down on members of the other two and the Bombay officers (Ducks) were reckoned to be arrogant and spoilt. As a Bengal officer said during the campaign, while referring to an officer in the Bombay Army, 'He's rather a good fellow, despite the fact he is a Duck.'

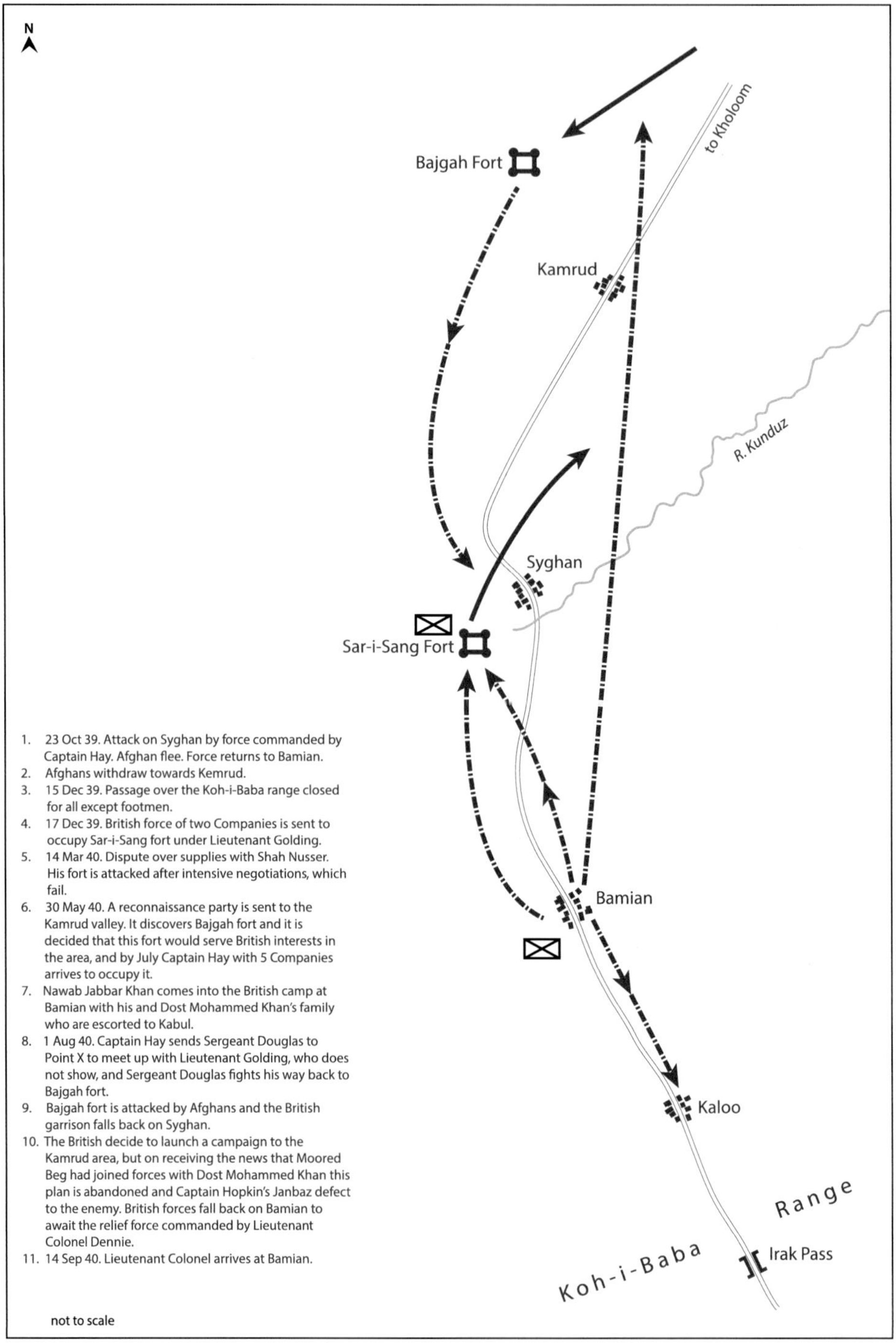

Map 9 Sketch Map of Operations in the Bamian sector, prior to the arrival of Lieutenant Colonel Dennie's force, 14 September 1840.

horsemen under the command of his son Ghulam Beg. The combined forces of Khilish Beg and Ghulam Beg began to besiege the Sar-i-Sang fort, held by the old Hazari chief of the Syghan valley, Mohammed Ali Beg. The old chief sent his agent to the British post at Bamian to solicit Dr Lord's help to rid him of the Uzbek threat, in exchange for which he promised to submit his allegiance to Shah Shuja. Dr Lord, a person of ambition and touched by expansionist megalomania, could not, in all good faith, decline this plea as it presented an excellent opportunity to impress the local population of British superiority and in so doing extend the authority of Shah Shuja; especially as the old chief was being attacked by a force harbouring the renegade, Dost Mohammed Khan.

Dr Lord sent the agent back with a message for Ghulam Beg to the effect that unless he called off the siege of Sar-i-Sang by 30 October he would be visited by a British force. Meanwhile he directed Captain Hay to lead a small force to surprise the besiegers. The Syghan valley runs parallel with the Bamian valley with a range of mountains 10,000 feet high separating them. Captain Hay's force consisted of 100 Gurkha troops, mounted on *yaboos* under the command of Lieutenant William Broadfoot, 60 horse artillerymen, with explosives but no guns, under the command of Lieutenant Murray Mackenzie, and 60 Afghan horsemen under the command of Lieutenant Charles Rattray, Dr Lord's assistant. Later Captain Hay was to complain to Brigadier Roberts that the force was too small for the task assigned as Dr Lord had grossly underestimated the strength of the combined Usbek force. After a laboriously weary march and bitterly cold nights, the British force came into view of the Sar-i-Sang fort perched on the summit of a large rock. On the British approach, and to their great surprise, the besiegers scattered up the neighbouring hills with the British now caught in the crossfire. The operations evolved into pursuits of the various groups of Usbeks. Ghulam Beg managed to escape and young Khilish Beg was cornered and submitted to the British. The British force, less three dead, returned to Bamian to take up winter quarters. As winter set in many more of the troops were to succumb to the bitter conditions, and for the next six months the detachment was isolated without supplies or reinforcements. Of this particular disposition, Henry Durand rather sarcastically wrote, 'A journey undertaken to lodge an excellent battery of Horse Artillery in a position where it would be of no use.'[2]

The failure of the Uzbek attack on Sar-i-Sang was bitter news for Dost Mohammed Khan because any bright vision that success might have conjured up dimmed, and his future seemed bleak. His funds were fast failing and he was unable to care for all his followers who now started to desert him. As a last resort he gave heed to the invitation from Nusrullah Khan of Bokhara. This gentleman had offered Dost Mohammed Khan one of his daughters in marriage and a force of 12,000 horsemen to assist him in getting rid of the British at Bamian. But the Bokhara chief was not renowned for keeping his word, so the cautious Dost Mohammed went to Bokhara with two of his sons and a small retinue leaving his vast family under the care of his older brother, *Nawab* Jabbar Khan. As history relates, Nusrullah Khan, not best pleased with Dost Mohammed Khan leaving his family behind thus out of his clutches, placed his guest into a dungeon. Meanwhile, Dr Lord sent messages to *Nawab* Jabbar Khan to come in with both his and his brother's family to be given British protection. The *Nawab* hesitated for many weeks as the tyrant at Bokhara made it known that should the families go over to the British

2 Durand, *The First Afghan War and Its Causes*, p.220.

and not him, he would cut off the head of Dost Mohammed Khan. However, *Nawab* Jabbar Khan eventually sought British protection and on 3 July came in with both families which were escorted to Ghazni.

By 15 December 1839, the passes over the Hindu Kush were closed against all except men on foot, communication with Kabul made difficult and supplies impossible. As winter set in so firewood and forage became increasingly more expensive and pleas for more allowances were made to Kabul. As the British detachment, about 700 strong, was thrown upon its own resources, it was determined to construct embattlements for better protection. In so doing the area of defence was greatly extended thus impinging on the availability of enough troops to man the outposts, especially as the whole area was overlooked and commanded by the neighbouring hills on either side of the forts. For this reason Dr Lord, dissatisfied with the position at Bamian, resolved on seeking a more favourable advance post in the valley of Syghan and thus wished to garrison the fort at Sar-i-Sang. A party consisting of two companies of the Shah's 4th Gurkha Regiment and 25 horse artillerymen with two mortars and a 3-pdr gun was despatched from Bamian on 17 December. On completion of this reconnaissance the party returned to Bamian, leaving in situ the two Gurkha companies under the command of Lieutenant William Golding. This disposition, ostensibly for the purpose of strengthening the deployment of the troops, was the more remarkable for the fact that the Sar-i-Sang fort was effectively dominated by the hills well within *jezail* range and that this separation of troops weakened the overall deployment. These measures were duly reported to Brigadier Roberts by Captain Hay, causing Dr Lord to look for an opportunity of getting rid of Captain Hay who was obviously a thorn in his side with his accurate intelligence and assessment of the situation.

As winter tightened its grip on all movement, it was not possible to start any new works and the detachment confined themselves to its winter quarters. Meanwhile, Dr Lord received many of the local chiefs who came in to submit their allegiance, but there was one exception, Baba Beg, the chief of Banuck, who stubbornly resisted all arguments of British power and greatness despite the fact that it was now reported that Dost Mohammed Khan was held prisoner by the chief of Bokhara.

By mid-January 1840, there were frequent falls of snow and the frost increased in intensity with temperatures falling to minus 12°. It was difficult to keep the quarters warm, night sentries were reduced and essential fuels became even more scarce and expensive. The works on the embattlements continued intermittently, most of the manual work being done by 200 Hazaris who were glad for the employment. These Hazaris were later to form part of the corps of sappers and miners that was raised by Lieutenant William Broadfoot and eventually handed over to his brother George.

In the following March, though the winter had not yet ended, snow had disappeared from the valley and morale rose with the temperature; but all was not rosy as a political storm was about to break in the Bamian valley. Ever since the arrival of the detachment in the valley, the locals had freely sold fuel and forage at very profitable prices. However, as these supplies were not inexhaustible, the Commissariat was forced to go further afield for them, and in order to combat price rises the Commissariat would buy in bulk, carry away the immediate needs and return in due course for the balance. It was to the fort of Shah Nusser that the Commissariat arrived on 14 March to collect the balance of the supplies already purchased. The Commissariat was refused entry and a squabble started between the two parties during which some harsh and strong language was exchanged; Shah Nusser refused both entry and the release of the supplies.

Dr Lord immediately sent a messenger to ascertain the cause of the row, but to no avail. He then solicited the good offices of Mir Moheb, the senior chief, to convince Shah Nusser to come in with his complaint for just arbitration by Dr Lord. But even this had no effect on the stubborn Shah Nusser. Dr Lord then sent a *puranna* in the name of Shah Shuja, demanding the chief's acceptance of British arbitration. Still the chief persisted in dogged silence, simply refusing to accept British interference and challenging Dr Lord's authority. Dr Lord now feared that this show of one chief's defiance, if not extinguished at once, could rapidly spread and increase to a dangerous level. He therefore ordered a force under the command of Captain Hubert Garbett, consisting of four companies of the 4th Gurkha Regiment, two guns and 60 cavalry troopers, to march against Shah Nusser. This demonstration of strength did not expect to meet with any opposition, but, on their approach to the fort, it was clear that the inmates were in a very warlike temper. Lieutenant Rattray was sent forward to the gate to parlay with the inmates, who refused to open the gate nor did they send a representative to confer with Rattray. After a fruitless time, Lieutenant Rattray returned to report his failure to Dr Lord. At this juncture, Dr Lord ordered the military attack on Shah Nusser's fort. Despite a stout defence, the skirmish did not last long, but its end deflected from any claim to glory. Some of the Hazari defenders had ascended through a trap door to the upper level of the fort and had pulled up the ladder after them. Unable to get them out to get them to surrender, a fire was lit to smoke them out. The cornered Hazaris refused to give in and all were smothered to death.

After this sad affair of imposing submission, the Hazaris were given time to reconcile themselves to the *fait accompli* and in the course of a few weeks Nusser Shah came in to submit to the authority of Shah Shuja. However, behind the overt signs of civility and normality, there was great resentment against the neighbourhood bullies.

At the end of May a reconnaissance party, mainly of cavalry, was sent northwards under Captain Garbett to examine the Pass beyond Kamrud which led to Kholoon. A short distance beyond Kamrud the reconnaissance party came upon the fort at Bajgah, which to Captain Garbett's great surprise was vacant, and he was still more surprised to be informed by the owner, Syud Mohammed, that he had purposely cleared it for the British to use as a post. In Captain Garbett's opinion, endorsed by his accompanying political agent, Lieutenant Rattray, this vacated fort ticked all the boxes of a good defensible position and this was duly reported to Dr Lord back in Bamian. Leaving a Gurkha detachment at the fort, the party moved on but its progress was interrupted by an increasing amount of hostility, so the party returned to Bamian. As soon as Dr Lord heard about the offer to use the fort at Bajgah, he immediately wrote to Macnaghten with his strong recommendation to occupy it.

Captain Hay, the commander of 4th Gurkha Regiment, was most distressed by this recommendation to further spread his hard-worked infantry in penny-packets around the Bamian salient and sent his complaint to Brigadier Roberts, who had not been consulted on the matter and had himself complained about the deployment of troops in small numbers with scant support and sitting targets for attacks. He wrote to the Envoy accordingly, who replied to the effect that the matter would be discussed with Dr Lord who was due in for consultations. However, these consultations, to which the Brigadier was not invited, resulted in permission to occupy the Bajgah fort with a contingent of Gurkhas.

In June, the garrison at Bamian was reinforced by 300 soldiers of Captain Perin Hopkins' newly raised Afghan *Jan-Baz*, a sort of irregular cavalry, and immediately afterwards Captain Hay marched out with four companies of Gurkhas to man the fort at Bajgah, leaving one company at Bamian under the command of Lieutenant Broadfoot. This fine regiment of Gurkhas was now spread out over four posts miles apart from each other in total disregard of any military principles of mutual support. After Captain Hay and his troops had settled into their new post they were visited by Lieutenant John Sturt, the chief engineer of the Shah's contingent, who had been sent out by Macnaghten to evaluate the various passes. Sturt totally condemned the suitability of the Bajgah fort as a suitable position. While the engineer declared the fort indefensible, the locals regarded its occupation as offensive; the friendly feeling that existed at Bamian was totally absent at Bajgah, although Captain Hay and his men endeavoured to develop a more friendly intercourse.

Each day brought more decided signs of hostility, gathering of armed men in the vicinity of the fort and groups of horsemen on the neighbouring hills watching the movements in the small garrison. In the second half of July there were many more sightings of armed bodies of men clearly not there simply to watch, and it was also reported that a strong body of armed men under Baba Beg had gathered in the valley between Kamrud and the Gurkha post at Bajgah. Captain Hay was at this time suffering from sickness and was confined to his bed. He had no officer with him and as the situation was clearly edging towards open hostilities, he sent an urgent message to lieutenants Rattray and Golding at the Sar-i-Sang fort to have Lieutenant Golding come up to join him, indicating the route he should take. As the Sar-i-Sang troops came under the command of Captain Garbett at Syghan, the request was referred to him and was duly authorised with confirmation being passed on to the sick and anxious Captain Hay. However, in the interim, Lieutenant Rattray received intelligence to the effect that the reported armed group of Hazaris between Kamrud and Bajgah had dispersed, so he calculated that there was no longer any great urgency to go to the assistance of Captain Hay, and sent another message to inform Captain Hay that Lieutenant Golding and his Gurkha escort would not be coming.

For some unknown reason or folly, Captain Hay did not receive this last communication and rightly assumed that Lieutenant Golding was on his way. On 1 August, Hay sent out a company of Gurkhas under the command of his senior British NCO Sergeant Douglas, to proceed towards Kamrud for the purpose of meeting and escorting back to Bajgah the expected Lieutenant Golding. Sergeant Douglas arrived at Kamrud without too much trouble, and with the permission of Sula Beg, who now purported to be friendly, was allowed to establish his bivouac for the night close under the walls of one of Sula Beg's forts. The friendly Sula Beg, treacherous as ever he had been, while at the same time smiling and being friendly, sent a message to Baba Beg to come and help himself to a victory over the unsuspecting British force.

On the morning of 1 August Sergeant Douglas made ready to welcome Lieutenant Golding, but as he had failed to arrive after a few hours of waiting Sergeant Douglas reckoned that he was either not coming or had taken a different route, so he decided to return to Bajgah. Suddenly, without the slightest suspicion of any danger, firing rained on the Gurkhas from all directions, then a body of Uzbek horsemen charged down upon them and the deadly Afghan *jezails* played down on them from inside the fort. Sergeant Douglas ordered a hasty withdrawal through the neighbouring orchards with the Uzbeks up within range with their deadly fire. As they retreated, many a brave Gurkha fell, and his weapon picked up by another in the running duel back to Bajgah. Sergeant Douglas's force was running out of ammunition and the prospect of a last stand and eventual elimination loomed high. Fortunately, news of this disaster had got back to Bajgah where, as luck would have it, Lieutenant Sturt had returned from his survey of the passes. This officer volunteered his services to Captain Hay and was immediately sent off, with a company of Gurkhas, to the assistance of Sergeant Douglas. On seeing this relief force the baying of the *jezails* ceased and the men behind them fled. The Gurkha detachment suffered 30 dead in this military fiasco.

Encouraged by their success in driving off a British contingent, the Uzbeks took courage and gathering their forces together they positioned themselves to attack the Bajgan post on 31 August. That morning the hills around the fort were covered by 300 Uzbek footmen and 500 horsemen. The Gurkhas reacted by climbing up the hills and driving off the footmen, while Lieutenant Rattray, who had since come up to Bajgan, charged the Uzbeks at the head of 200 Afghan horsemen. These efforts were crowned with success with the Uzbeks losing 15 killed or wounded and the same number of prisoners.

At the same period as their attack on Bajgah, the Uzbeks had also attacked the fort of a friendly chief at Heibuck causing the chief to flee. At this juncture a most unwelcome piece of information was received: the ex-Amir, Dost Mohammed Khan, had made his escape from Bokhara, was gathering a force behind him and was joined by the *Wali* of Kunduz in the joint aim of driving the British from Bamian. Their first target was to be Bajgah. In view of these new developments Lieutenant Rattray, concluding that Bajgah fort was no longer a tenable position, resolved to vacate it and fall back on Syghan while such a move could be made with a degree of safety. The withdrawal went well and the force bivouacked in the vicinity of Sar-i-Sang. The next day the Gurkhas were reinforced by Captain Hopkins' corps and two 6-pdr guns of Captain Thomas Hart's Horse Artillery. It was now, for some inexplicable reason, decided that the fort at Kamrud had to be attacked before the arrival of Dost Mohammed's expected advance, and that the Sar-i-Sang fort be handed back to its friendly owner. On the approach of the British, further bad news arrived that Mir Moheb had also joined the ex-Amir. This intelligence rendered all prospect of any success at Kamrud hopeless, so it was decided to fall back on Syghan. At this point, rather than turn back, half of Captain Perin Hopkins' *Jan-Baz* abandoned the British and joined the advancing Dost Mohammed. Weakened by this desertion, it was resolved that the most prudent course of action would be for the whole force to return to Bamian.

Meanwhile, back in Kabul, news of the problems at Bamian spurred Macnaghten into action, who, with the approval of Major General Sir Willoughby Cotton, sent Lieutenant Colonel William Dennie to Bamian at the head of a force consisting of 35th BNI and 200 cavalry. This force arrived at Bamian on 14 September, and with a Gurkha guard standing by Dennie immediately disarmed the remaining *Jan-Baz* and then made his plans for the advance on Syghan where, it was reported, the enemy had gathered in force. On 18 September he set off with one third of the British force at Bamian, plus one 6-pdr gun and a howitzer. This he considered was sufficient for the task, based on the intelligence he had been given of the enemy's strength by Dr Lord. In his despatch, Dennie was to report:

> I confess I was taken by surprise, after driving in what proved to be only their advance party, to find an army in my front. To have sent back for reinforcements would have caused delay and given confidence to the enemy. It would have checked the forward feeling that animated the party with me and gave assurance of success.
>
> The enemy had got possession of the chain of forts before us reaching to the mouth of the defile. They drew up and attempted to make a stand at each, with the main body, while the wings covered the heights on either side. In dislodging these from the latter, I am sorry to

> say the Goorkahs suffered. After four or five vollies, seeing our steady and rapid advance, the whole force appeared to us to lose heart fled in a confusion of men to the gorge of the Pass. I now ordered the whole of the Cavalry in pursuit, who drove them four miles up the defile, cutting down great numbers and scattering them in all directions, many throwing away their arms and escaping up the hills.[3]

Interestingly, in his despatch, Lieutenant Colonel Dennie commends two officers who had volunteered to take part in the action: they were Captain Arthur Conolly and Lieutenant Rattray. The former had been on his way to Bokhara and had accompanied Dennie to Bamian. In his report, Dennie also stated his opinion on the mode of transport used in the campaign, describing the *yaboo* as the only animal to be depended on through a mountainous, destitute and inclement country. The Indian camel, he reckoned, was worse than useless on the steep ascents and descents.

Immediately after Lieutenant Colonel Dennie's success at Syghan, Dr Lord sent messages to Dost Mohammed offering terms for his surrender, especially in view of the fact that his family were now in British protection. The ex-Amir replied to the effect that he had no family and that he was determined to expel the British or die in the attempt. Based on this refusal, Dennie advanced on Syghan with six companies of 35th BNI, six companies of 4th Gurkha Regiment and four 6-pdr guns. But he had not gone far when news arrived that Dost Mohammed and his allies had retreated from Syghan leaving a garrison at Sar-i-Sang. On 24 September Dennie's force entered the valley of Syghan and immediately destroyed the Sar-i-Sang fort, thus putting it beyond further use by the enemy. The next day news came in that the *Wali* of Kunduz wanted to treat with the British. Lieutenant Rattray was sent to the *Wali*, who concluded a treaty with that officer. In accordance with the treaty, Syghan was to be ceded to the British and Heibuck to the *Wali*, and both the *Wali* and Baba Beg engaged not to harbour Dost Mohammed or any of his family. On hearing of this desertion by his allies, Dost Mohammed fled to Nijrow valley with his son Afzul Khan. At this juncture, Dennie's force was ordered back to Kabul and arrived there on 18 October. For his brilliant actions in this expedition he received the sincere thanks of the Governor General and was offered the award of the Duranni Medal, Second Class, which the Colonel had great pleasure in refusing.

Meanwhile, Captain Hay withdrew to Bamian to recuperate and handed over command of 4th Gurkha Regiment to Captain Christopher Codrington on the apparently clear understanding that this would be for the duration of the time of Captain Hay's convalescence. However, in a letter dated 4 August, Brigadier Roberts informed the unfortunate Captain Hay that he had been relieved of his command and that he was to return to Kabul to answer a charge for the disgraceful employment of troops in the Kamrud affair and for his accounts not being in order at handover.

Captain Hay was aghast at this stab in the back but knew that the fingerprints on the dagger were those of Dr Lord, who had taken his revenge. In order to defend his honour and combat this slur on his character, Captain Hay wrote a long letter to the Brigadier telling him of all that had occurred and requested a court of inquiry. In his long very letter, the distraught Captain vehemently refuted the charges made against him, declared his utter surprise at being

3 Sergeant Douglas later rejoined his regiment, 1st BER, and was later drowned in the Kabul River.

double-crossed by his brother officers and in particular by the political agents including Sir William Macnaghten, and after 18 years of exemplary service felt that it was intolerable to have a charge of disobedience hanging over him.[4]

The finding of the court of inquiry, comprising Captain John Craigie as president and captains Julian Backhouse and William Anderson as members, completely vindicated Captain Hay. Miffed by this result, the Envoy vetoed the return of Captain Hay to his command and removed him from the lucrative employment in Shah Shuja's force.

4 Edwards-Stuart, *A John Company General*, p.126.

15

Kabul 1840

In the summer of 1840 two new players in the Afghan saga were about to enter the scene. They were Captain Colin Mackenzie and Captain George Broadfoot, both of the Madras Native Infantry. The former had just returned to India and was the brother-in-law of Mr H.T. Prinsep, a member of the Supreme Council; the latter was the older brother of William and James already employed in Afghanistan. Mackenzie and Broadfoot met in Calcutta and travelled together to Delhi. Here Captain Mackenzie attached himself to Lieutenant Colonel John Shelton and HM 44th Foot (Essex) for the journey up to Kabul. Captain Broadfoot remained in Delhi to recruit and train a corps of sappers and miners for service with Shah Shuja's force. A General Order had been published on 20 August calling for volunteers to form the nucleus of this corps, the inducement being promotion; one sergeant to be sergeant major (British), two corporals to be sergeants (British), four *Jemadars* to be *Subadars*, four *Havildars* to be *Jemadars*, 20 *Niaks* to be *Havildars* and 20 *Sepoys* to be *Niaks*. These volunteers were ordered to report to Captain George Broadfoot on his arrival at Delhi and then to assist him in the formation of a corps 400 strong, the majority being Gurkhas.

To envoy Sir William Macnaghten, back in Kabul with his wife, the overall situation was tranquil and he was satisfied with the success of the venture to date. At this time and well into 1841 he had convinced himself that the Afghan initiative and the security of Afghanistan would not be complete until the strategic designs of Russia were addressed, the glaring perfidy of Yar Mohammed resolved and the obstreperous Sikhs put in their place. Sir William now put forward his solution to these issues in his letter to the Governor General of 20 July 1840:

> We have a beautiful game on our hands, if we have the means and inclination to play it properly. It appears to me the time for accomplishing the great work which your Lordship has commenced, and of effectively frustrating the designs of Russia. Herat should now be taken possession of in the name of Shah Shooja. To leave it in the hands of its present possessors, after the fresh proof of treachery and enmity towards us which they have displayed, would, in my humble opinion, be most dangerous. Herat may be said to be the pivot of all operations affecting the safety of our possessions and our interests in the East, and thence Balkh and Bokhara would be at all times accessible. The Sikhs should no longer be suffered to throw unreasonable obstacles in the way of our just and necessary objects, and if they really feel (as they are bound by treaty to do) an interest in the success of our

> operations, they should not object to the passage of our troops, or even their location in the Punjab, should such a measure be deemed conducive to the welfare of us both. Your Lordship will, I feel assured, forgive the freedom of these remarks. I am convinced that one grand effort will place the safety of our interests on a firm and solid basis. I shall only add, that should offensive operations against Herat be undertaken, I should not entertain the smallest doubt of their complete and speedy success, especially as we should have many friends in the country.[1]

To this plea for a robust and forward-thinking strategy the Governor General was totally averse, never was it in his mind to expand his Afghan venture into a jousting match with the Russians until and when Shah Shuja was totally secure on his throne and in control of his country. Unfortunately, a few weeks later the tranquil situation changed for the worse and Sir William's demeanour changed with it; Kelat had fallen, Dost Mohammed Khan, the author of all his woes, had raised his head above the parapet in the north, and on top of all this Sir William had perceived a lack of confidence in his proceedings, and it was quite clear to most that the fidelity of the newly raised Afghan levies could not be relied upon. Army commander Major General Cotton, who was equally aware of the low standard of morale and of his resources being stretched to breaking point, wrote to Sir William saying, 'I really think the time has come for you and I to tell Lord Auckland, *totidem verbis*, that circumstances have proved incontestably that there is no Afghan army and that unless the Bengal troops are instantly strengthened, we cannot hold the country.'[2] Sir William duly wrote to the Governor General. 'My Lord I am much fatigued, having been severely worked the whole day; but I write these few lines just to appraise your Lordship that affairs in this quarter have the worst possible appearance.'[3] To Major Henry Rawlinson, his man at Kandahar, he was even more despondent:

> We are in a stew here, perhaps greater than the occasion warrants, but our situation is far from comfortable. It is reported that the whole country, on this side of the Oxus is up in favour of the Dost who with the Wallee is certainly advancing in great strength, so much so, our troops have been obliged to fall back on Bameen, whilst we have a considerable band of conspirators in the city and Kohistan is ripe for revolt. We are stretched with having only three infantry regiments including one of the Shah's.

In a subsequent letter to the same addressee, he wrote: 'The town is in a great fermented state. Some people are shutting up their shops, others sending their families away, and some active measure must be taken for stopping the panic.'[4]

The Governor General, now in Calcutta, was distressed to receive his envoy's gloomy report,as to date he had been the most exuberant of His Lordship's correspondents. The claim for more troops was put to the new commander-in-chief, General Sir Jasper Nicolls who, with Burma about to erupt into another war and Nepal possibly waiting for an opportunity to do the same,

1 Kaye, *History of the War in Afghanistan*, Vol. 2, p.56.
2 Kaye, *History of the War in Afghanistan*, Vol. 2, p.82.
3 Kaye, *History of the War in Afghanistan*, Vol. 2, p.82.
4 Kaye, *History of the War in Afghanistan*, Vol. 2, p.80.

declined the Envoy's indent for five more regiments as his resources were already stretched to the limit.

Such was the situation that Macnaghten thought it might be a good idea to put a price on the Dost's head. He certainly was not going to show any mercy. Shah Shuja had long been keen to 'hang the dog' and reminded the Envoy that he had for some time expressed a mean opinion of his own countrymen; he placed in the hands of the Envoy an intercepted letter from his blind brother, Shah Zaman, to the Sikh stooge Sultan Mohammed at Kohat, proposing that with his aid and that of the Sikhs, Shah Zaman could replace Shah Shuja on the throne as the latter had made over the country to the infidels. According to Sir John Kaye, the turning point of British fortunes in Afghanistan came on 18 September when the Envoy wrote to Lord Auckland, 'Never was the aspect of affairs more threatening. At no time of my life do I remember having been so much harassed in body and mind as during the past month. Nor is my uneasiness yet much lessened. The Afghans are gunpowder and the Dost is the lighted match. Of his whereabouts we are woefully ignorant.'[5]

Despite all this gloom and doom, Macnaghten still reckoned that the implementation of his grand strategy of annexing Herat and the subjugation of the Punjab would culminate with the total success of the Afghan venture; and he chafed under Lord Auckland's passive restraints. Writing to a friend, he moaned:

> I had a letter from Lord Auckland yesterday and from that I gather that His Lordship's intentions are essentially pacific, both as regards Herat and the Punjab. Oh! for a Wellesley or a Hastings (who had been advocates of a 'Forward' policy). This drivelling is beneath contempt.[6]

Then, to his great surprise and relief, the Envoy received the news of Lieutenant Colonel Dennie's victory over the Dost at Bamian. Taking up his pen, he wrote to Major Rawlinson:

> Before I close this, I may be able to tell you of some of the consequences of this glorious success. It has enabled me, in the meantime, to breathe a little more freely. I can assure you I was beginning to be very nervous and I entertained great apprehension that Afghanistan was about to be convulsed from one end to the other.[7]

After his defeat at Bamian, Dost Mohammed Khan with his son Afzul Khan and about 50 followers moved to the area of Nijrow where in a fairly short time he had collected a considerable number of adherents. Reports of his activities were received by Sir Alexander Burnes, who advised the now confident envoy that a show of force had to be made in order to stem a general uprising in Kohistan. At first the Kohistan chiefs were called in to Kabul to affirm their allegiance to Shah Shuja. They came and did so, then returned to their forts and banded together to intrigue for the banishment of their puppet king. Neither Macnaghten nor Shah Shuja were blinded by the readiness of the chiefs to declare their allegiance and letters were produced to prove their treachery. As a consequence, Major General Robert Sale was directed to move to

5 Kaye, *History of the War in Afghanistan*, Vol. 2, p.83.
6 Macrory, *The Fierce Pawns*, p.135.
7 Edwards-Stuart, *A John Company General*, p.132.

Tutundurra and there to destroy any resistance to the authority of Shah Shuja. General Sale marched out on 29 September with a force consisting of six companies of HM 13th Foot, two companies of 27th BNI, one company of the 37th BNI, the Shah's 2nd Cavalry Regiment under Captain William Anderson, two squadrons of 2nd Bengal Light Cavalry under Captain James Fraser and two 6-pdr guns. On this mission Major General Sale was accompanied by Sir Alexander Burnes, the first of any overt employment of this highly paid panjandrum. In the meantime, Lieutenant Colonel Dennie's force had been ordered back to Kabul.

While Macnaghten hoped that Sale would be fortunate enough to secure the person of Dost Mohammed so that Shah Shuja could execute him, Brigadier Roberts was not happy about this further distribution of limited forces and took up his pen, yet again, to the Governor General on 30 September; apologising for intruding on His Lordship's valuable time, he proceeded to give a litany of complaints, all of them poignant. This letter, which he sent via the Envoy, included the following statement:

> It grieves me my Lord, to see the manner in which military matters are carried on in regard to the whole of the Shah's troops. At Lucknow, I am told, although the Resident is a military man, he is too happy to leave all matters relating to the contingent to the Brigadier commanding, and unless I am placed on the same footing, I trust your Lordship will see the justice of relieving me from all responsibility in case of failure, and yet to hold the situation on such terms would be most painful to my feelings.[8]

The comparison the Brigadier makes here is a strong indication that he like many others viewed the British aim in Afghanistan as establishing a 'Princely State' based on the model successfully used in India. Clearly, this was also what Macnaghten had in mind, however, for this idea to succeed two conditions were essential: firstly, there was a popular or acceptable chief, and secondly, there was a self-sufficient state. While the Envoy held steadfastly to the popularity of Shah Shuja, the state collection of taxes at the point of British bayonets made the Shah abhorrent to his wild people.

In his covering letter to Sir William, the Brigadier included the most telling comment of this disconnect at the very top of British governance in Afghanistan:

> It has been a source of the deepest regret ever since I joined the Force that there has not existed that confidence and free intercourse between us essentially necessary for the good of the service and which I feel satisfied in my own mind might have prevented some of the disasters that have occurred.[9]

Naturally Macnaghten, in passing on the Brigadier's letter, attached his own list of rebuttals.

The Brigadier in Kabul was not the Envoy's only 'troublesome' soldier; the Major General at Kandahar was equally so but for a different reason in that he could not tolerate the 'mamby-pamby' stance taken by the politicos in regard to the royal family and chiefs. This was, of course, completely the reverse of Macnaghten huge efforts to project the popularity of the royal

8 Edwards-Stuart, *A John Company General*, p.134.
9 Edwards-Stuart, *A John Company General*, p.135.

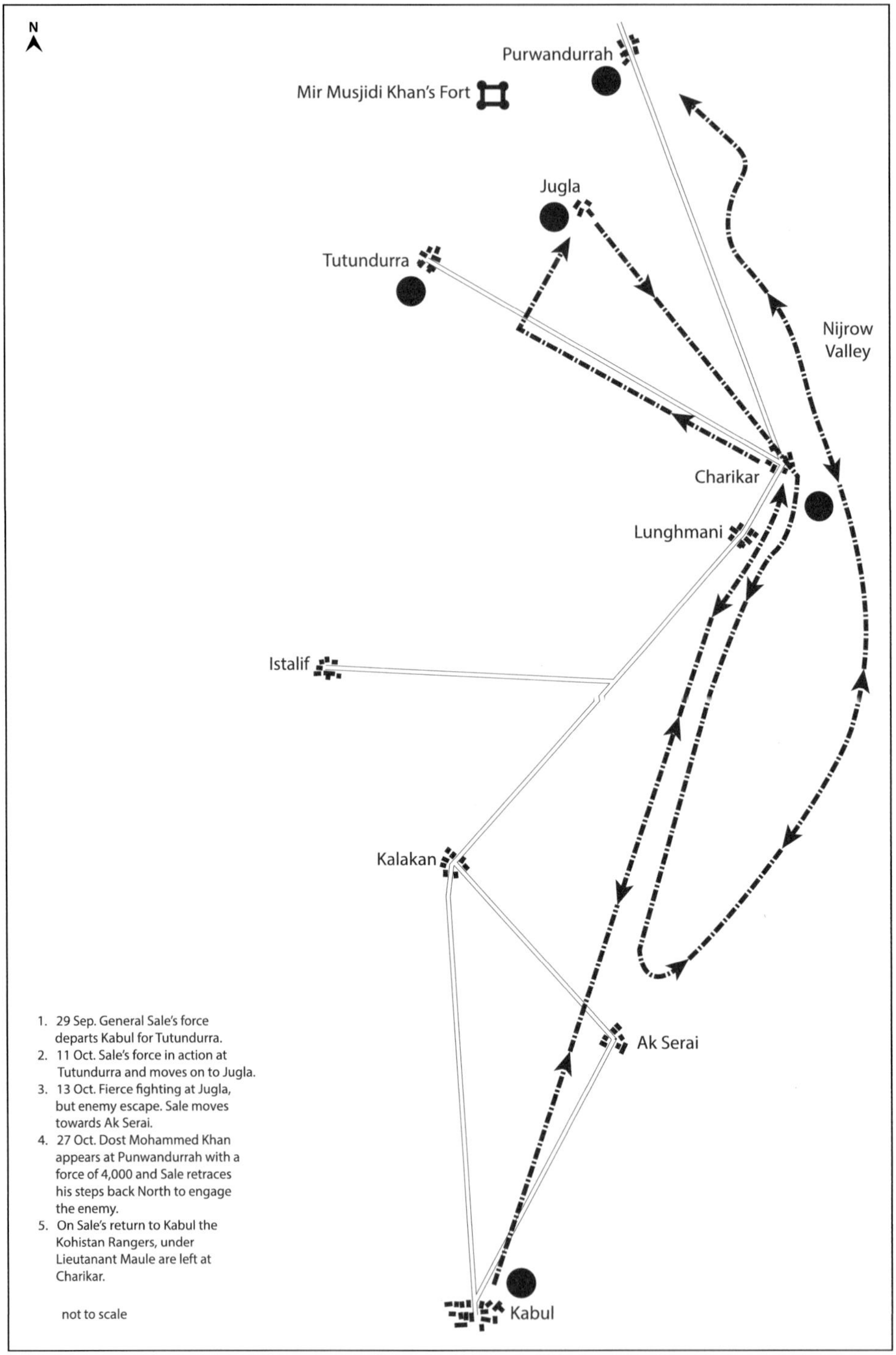

Map 10 General Sal's campaign in the Kohistan area.

household. Major General Nott was greatly annoyed at the way the servants of *Shahzada* and particularly those of his brother Suftar Jung were enriching themselves by their plundering, robbery and oppression of the local people, and, being a man of action, Nott resolved to correct the situation. He told the *Shahzada* and the political agent, Captain Peter Nicholson, that if they did not punish the offenders he would. In a letter to his two daughters he wrote:

> The politicals blustered in the name of the Prince. My answer was short. 'You are in possession of my determination which I will carry into effect at sunset unless you send your people to punish the marauders in my presence as an example to all.' Well sunset came, when I had the fellows tied up and flogged.[10]

Naturally, this event was reported to the Envoy, who in turn blustered to the army commander, Major General Sir Willoughby Cotton:

> I need now dwell on the anxiety of the Governor General in Council, that in the difficult and perilous position we occupy in this country, the greatest possible respect and tenderness should be shown for the honour and feelings of His Majesty, and should you concur with me in thinking that. In the act which has proved so offensive to the Prince, Major General Nott has deviated from those principles. I have to request that you will be good enough to convey to him your opinion in such terms as may effect to prevent his falling into a similar error in the future.[11]

Major General Nott received a mild rap over the knuckles and resolved to stay clear of political matters unless they impinged on military ones, when he would continue to apply his military justice, even over civilians as sanctioned by the Commander-in-Chief. Major General Nott was never an admirer of political officers albeit he had a good working relationship with both Henry Rawlinson and James Outram. It is of interest to note that while Cotton censured Nott's actions, he was clearly sympathetic with his sentiments when recording his views on politicos:

> Some check must be imposed, or the whole system must be altered as regards young political Officers sent to accompany regular troops. Much disgust has risen from this and it is absurd that old experienced military men should be under the orders of lieutenants merely because they place after their name, Acting Assistant Political Agent.[12]

On reaching Tutundurra, Major General Sale discovered that his objective was strongly defended, as were the outlying forts and surrounding hills. So his first action was to clear the hills and the outlying forts. These manœuvres were successful as the rebels were pushed back at all points. The British casualties were few but included Captain Edward Conolly, the first of three brothers to be killed during the Afghan campaign. Conolly had been commanding the Envoy's bodyguard and had volunteered to join Sale's expedition. A great deal of 'volunteering'

10 Beveridge, *A Comprehensive History of India*, Vol. 3, p.463.
11 Beveridge, *A Comprehensive History of India*, vol. 3, p.464.
12 Bruce, *Retreat from Kabul*, p.128.

occurred in the British Army, then and now; the 'volunteers' being usually employed as extra ADCs or liaison officers.

After the success at Tutundurra, the British force moved on to Jugla where it was reported that a number of rebel chiefs had taken refuge. To forestall any further withdrawal by the renegade chiefs, Major General Sale sent his cavalry forward to prevent any further escape until his infantry and artillery arrived, which they did on 3 October. After a fairly heavy barrage of artillery had played on the enemy position, lasting a couple of hours, it was decided that a sufficient breach had been made to launch the storming party commanded by Lieutenant Colonel Edward Tronson of 13th Foot. Desperate and brave, the enemy fought back, pouring down a deadly blanket of fire which compelled the storming party to fall back into an adjoining ravine. During this lull in fighting, the rebels managed to withdraw despite the precautionary measures taken earlier. However, one fort remained manned and heavily defended and negotiations were set in motion so to avoid further casualties, but these were fruitless as the rebels were determined to fight to the death. On 21 October Major General Sale moved his force forward in three columns for the assault, and yet again the erstwhile defiant rebels fled to the hills. The fort was set on fire and burned to the ground.

On the advice of Sir Alexander Burnes, Major General Sale now moved his force down to Ak-Serai in order to be closer to Kabul in the event of the situation there worsening. The ex-Amir's agents in Kabul were already working to raise the country to pronounce in favour of him and as Macnaghten looked around he found no evidence for the support of the Shah's authority apart from British guns and bayonets.

Then, on 27 October, Dost Mohammed broke ground and was reported as being encamped at Mir Musjidi's fort with a force of 4,000. Upon receipt of this information Sale moved his force up to challenge the Dost's new army and Dr Lord joined the party in expectation of action. A strong reconnaissance party under the command of Lieutenant Colonel Henry Salter was sent forward, and reported that the rebels were at Purwandurra evacuating the forts and moving up into the hills. Dr Lord was with this group, and on his suggestion Salter sent the Shah's cavalry, commanded by Captain Clement Macan, to the left and the 2nd Bengal Light Cavalry, commanded by Captain James Fraser, to the right, in order to cut off the rebels' escape. The infantry and artillery were about a mile to the rear due to the difficulty of the terrain. As Captain Fraser's group approached the hills they came upon a body of rebels headed by Dost Mohammed Khan who, reacting to the closeness of the British cavalry, turned to face them. Captain Fraser formed up his *Sowars* to meet this threat, at which point he received orders to withdraw, no doubt to allow the infantry and artillery to smash this rebel advance. Meanwhile Dr Lord, seeing the development of real action and an opportunity for glory, dug his spurs into his horse and galloped off to join the fight. The rebels, taking courage from the static state of the cavalry, came on faster leaving Captain Fraser no option but to order the charge. Forward rode the officers, the riding master and *Havildar Major* Bhawan Singh, but the bulk of 2nd Bengal Light Cavalry did a 'threes about' and fell back ignominiously. Three of the officers were killed, Dr Lord and lieutenants James Broadfoot and Lieutenant George Crispin. Of Lord's demise, Heathcote wrote, 'Among the dead was Assistant Surgeon Percival Lord. His restless spirit and thirst for adventure had put him in the forefront of a cavalry battle where neither his medical profession or diplomatic calling required him to be.'[13] Captain George Ponsonby,

13 T.A. Heathcote, *The Afghan Wars 1839–1919* (Staplehurst: Spellmount, 2007), p.50.

severely wounded and the reins of his horse cut, was guided out of the melee by riding master John Bolton.[14] Captain Fraser, six feet seven inches tall, covered in blood from various wounds and his sword arm cut,[15] calmly reported the destruction of his two squadrons to Major General Sale. On 11 February 1841 a General Order was published, disbanding 2nd Bengal Light Cavalry (see Appendix V).

After this action the rebels withdrew in the face of the oncoming infantry and artillery, and,on the strong recommendation of Sir Alexander Burnes, Major General Sale took his force back to Kabul. One of the on-side chiefs was appointed governor of the region and Lieutenant Richard Maule, commanding the Kohistan Rangers, was left at Charikar while Lieutenant Charles Rattray with an escort moved into Mir Musjidi's fort at Lughmani as the political agent. However, Dost Mohammed, the author of all Macnaghten's woes, was still at large.

It was with a heavy heart that Sir William Macnaghten left his residence on the morning of 3 November 1840 for his usual early morning ride. He was accompanied by his military secretary, Captain George Lawrence, who recorded what happened next:

> Just as we were approaching the Residency, we were surprised by a horseman suddenly riding up, who pushing his horse between the Envoy and myself, asked me 'if that was the Lord Sahib', on my saying yes, he caught hold of Sir William's bridle, exclaiming 'The Amir, the Amir'! The Envoy surprised and agitated, called out, 'Who, who, Where, where'. Looking behind me on that instant, I saw another horseman close to us, who riding up, threw himself off his horse, and seized hold of the Envoy's stirrup-leather and then his hand which he put to his forehead and his lips as a sign of submission. Sir William instantly dismounted, and said to the Amir, 'You are welcome, you are welcome', and then led him through the Residency garden into his own room. Dost Mohammed on entering, prostrated himself in Oriental fashion and taking off his turban, touched the ground with his forehead. On rising, he delivered up his sword in a token of surrender, saying he had no more use for it.[16]

Naturally, Macnaghten was delighted with this turn of events. The Dost, while under the strict supervision of Captain George Lawrence, was treated like an honoured guest and many officers

14 John Bolton (1798–1852). He joined the Russian Army in 1812 and was a lieutenant in the 1st Cossack Regiment. Four years later he left and enlisted into HM 23rd Light Dragoons. He then returned to the Russian Army in 1819, and in 1822 left again and enlisted into HM 16th Lancers. He arrived in India in 1823 and served with the regiment at the siege of Bharatpore. In November 1827, by special permission, he was allowed to join the 2nd Bengal Light Cavalry as quartermaster sergeant and in 1833 he was appointed riding master of the regiment, in which capacity he went to Afghanistan. At Purwandurra he was instrumental in saving the life of Captain Ponsonby, who gifted him with a handsome sword. On the disbandment of 2nd Bengal Light Cavalry, Bolton was posted to 8th Bengal Light Cavalry and served with this regiment until 1847 when he was promoted to ensign and transferred to the Veteran's establishment. He died at Ambala in 1852.

15 His damaged arm was not amputated and remained useless. After the affair at Purwandurra Captain Fraser convalesced in Kabul, then accompanied Major General Sale to Jalalabad. On the return of British forces from Afghanistan, he was sent to England with a gift from Maharaja Sher Singh to Queen Victoria, the Government paying his passage. For his wound he was granted a year's salary. On his return to India he was appointed honorary ADC to the governor general.

16 Lawrence, *Reminiscences*, p.49.

came to visit him, more so than ever went to pay their *salaams* to the Shah, who refused to see the prisoner. Writing to the Governor General with the great news and in a classic political somersault, the Envoy said about 'the author of all his woes':

> The Dost should be treated more handsomely than was Shah Shuja, that we had no hand in depriving Shah Shuja of his kingdom, whereas we ejected the Dost who never offended us, in support of our policy, of which he was the victim.[17]

Dost Mohammed remained in Kabul for 10 days during which time he wrote to his sons advising them to make their submissions. Afzul Khan came in while Akbar Khan remained at large. The Dost was assured that he would not be sent to England, the prospect of which he dreaded, but would be housed in secure accommodation in India. On selection, Captain Peter Nicholson, the erstwhile political agent at Kandahar, was appointed escort commander for the ex-Amir and remained so for the duration of his time in British custody. Meanwhile Sir Alexander Burnes claimed that the reason for Dost Mohammed's surrender was because he had written to the Dost promising good treatment in exile and a generous pension.[18]

On 12 November a detachment of troops left Kabul for India and the Dost and his escort marched with it; so did the army commander, Major Cotton, whose health had deteriorated, and as the situation was perceived to have improved with the surrender of Dost Mohammed, felt that the time of his departure had arrived. The chief medical officer, Dr James Atkinson, joined the General's party. At Peshawar, the Dost was joined by his family including the remainder of his sons except for Akbar Khan. His brother, *Nawab* Jubbar Khan, elected to remain in Afghanistan. Captain Nicholson with his charge, now amounting to 381 souls, proceeded to Ludhiana where the Dost and his family were housed in the same quarters recently vacated by Shah Shuja. The Governor General granted the Dost a pension of two *lakhs* of rupees and the following June the Dost was received as a guest of the Governor General at Barrackpore. Whilst at Peshawar Dost Mohammed, conversing with his captors, warned:

> The Sadozai have never been accustomed to obey and never would they, and by their intrigues under the anomalous sovereignty of Shah Shuja we should be involved in perpetual embarrassment. You will also find, the very courtiers about the Shah, who have for years been fattening on your bounty, the most forward in plotting against you.[19]

With the departure of Major General Cotton, command of the army in Kabul temporarily devolved on Major General Sale and the process of appointing a new army commander began. The majority of those concerned with matters in Afghanistan expected and advocated the selection of Major General William Nott, a pretty obvious choice and one supported by the commander-in-chief, General Sir Jasper Nicolls. However, Lord Auckland and his advisors, being privy to the fraught relationship between Macnaghten and his two senior Company officers, were apprehensive about appointing Major General Nott, whose negative views on politicos were well

17 Kaye, *History of the War in Afghanistan*, Vol. 2, p.98.
18 John H. Waller, *Beyond the Khyber Pass: the Road to British Disaster in the First Afghan War* (New York: Random House, 1990), p.186.
19 Nash, *History of the War in Affghanistan*, p.259.

established and could therefore be more of a disruptive factor in a situation which had so dramatically changed, allowing their envoy to accomplish his task unharried by a general 'with superfluous opinions'. Also, as Queen's troops were involved, it was customary for the commander to be a Queen's officer and there was one such senior Queen's officer in India at the time: he was 60-year-old Major General William Elphinstone, then commanding Benares District.

Major General Elphinstone, an intelligent and amiable man and a friend of Lord Auckland's, had secured a posting to India to a 'soft' command to save some money for his imminent retirement. He was also a sick man suffering from chronic rheumatic gout. Elphinstone was born in Scotland in 1782 and was commissioned into the army in 1802. He saw service throughout the Napoleonic Wars and commanded the 33rd Foot at the Battle of Waterloo. He was promoted to colonel in 1825 and to major general in 1837 and arrived in India in 1839. He did not want the Kabul Command and pleaded with his friend, the Governor General, not to appoint him, but bigger fish were at play. Lord Auckland was informed that Lieutenant General Sir Fitzroy Somerset, the Duke of Wellington's military secretary, had let it be known that the Horse Guards' choice was Elphinstone who was already in India. Thereupon, Lord Auckland convinced his sick friend to accept the appointment. It is possible to conjure that the General's friend gave him to understand that he would only be required to officiate in wholly military matters as the Envoy would take care of the rest. As the unfortunate Elphinstone was to discover, all matters in Kabul were political and he was no better than the 'Constable to the Lord Lieutenant'. One of the more scurrilous English language newspapers, no doubt an advocate for a Nott candidacy, opined that Elphinstone was 'the most incompetent soldier that was to be found amongst the officers of required rank'.

Whilst the state of affairs in Kabul seemed to be on an even keel, matters in the Sikh kingdom had taken an ugly turn. In the autumn of that year Maharaja Kharak Singh became ill and died of dysentery on 5 November, although many believed he had been poisoned. There was no question that his son, *Kunwar* Naonihal Singh, would succeed him. The Sikh army was 100 percent in support of the *Kunwar* and the British readily accepted his legitimacy.

The full Sikh *durbar* assembled around the late Maharaja's pyre as Rani Isur Kaur and three slave girls climbed onto the pile to be consumed by the flames lit by his son. The Maharaja's senior wife, Rani Chand Kaur, escaped committing *sati*, being the mother of the new maharaja. However, then the elephant carrying Maharaja Naunihal Singh back to the palace to be anointed as Maharaja, while passing through the *Roshnai* Gate, brushed against one of the wooden beams bringing down the whole gate. Maharaja Naunihal Singh was struck on the head and some hours later died of a fractured skull. The news of the death of the young maharaja was withheld by the chief minister to avoid instant panic and also to allow time in which to resolve the issue of succession.

The chief minister, Raja Dhian Singh, and the majority of the other *Sardars* agreed that the most suitable candidate to succeed was Prince Sher Singh, the reputed son of Ranjit Singh by his first wife. Prince Sher Singh was undoubtedly best qualified to fill this sudden vacancy as he was both popular with the army and friendly with the British. Any chance of orderly succession depended on the acquiescence of both these bodies. Unfortunately, by the time the Prince arrived on the scene, the throne had been claimed by Rani Chand Kaur, who had declared herself regent on the basis of being the widow of Maharaja Kharak Singh, the mother of Maharaja Naunihal Singh and, the grandmother of the child being carried by the widow of Maharaja Naunihal Singh. Intensive negotiations ensued, even the proposal of a marriage between the two protagonists. Rani Chand Kaur exploited the sympathy that the tragedy had generated and called for Raja Gulab Singh from Jammu as a counterpoint to the influence of his brother Raja Dhian Singh, the chief minister. Negotiations having failed, both the Prince and the chief minister quit Lahore, leaving the administration of the kingdom to Rani Chand Kaur and cohorts, the Sandhawalia *Sardars*. Sadly, the moderating influence of the eminent *Fakir* Azizuddin was no longer involved in the *durbar* affairs. Rani Chand Kaur's regime was both corrupt and chaotic, causing great concern for the British authorities who were fearful that the Sikh army would disintegrate into a rabble and proceed to general plunder. This nervous tension as to what might occur lasted for the rest of the year, necessitating the strengthening of the base in Ferozepore.

Back in Kabul, Shah Shuja felt that it was safe enough to move his court to Jalalabad for the winter. The royal court, accompanied by Sir William and Lady Macnaghten, their entourage and Brigadier Roberts, moved out on 4 December. After a day's march they arrived at Tezeen where Sir William received a letter from the Governor General dated 9 November and signed by the political secretary, Mr Herbert Maddock, referring to the Envoy's letter of 9 November:

> In reply I am desired to state for your information and that of Brigadier Roberts that His Lordship can only regard the expression made use of by the Brigadier in the concluding paragraph of his letter as a tender of resignation of his appointment as Commanding HM Shah Shuja's Forces and understanding it as such and considering the tone and purport of his letter as entirely unbecoming of his position, His Lordship is pleased to accept the resignation due intimation of which will be made to the military authorities.[20]

In the same letter, Mr Maddock informed the Envoy that Brigadier Thomas Anquetil had been selected to succeed Brigadier Roberts. *Fait accompli*, the Envoy had won. Had the Governor General been a Wellesley or Dalhousie, both Roberts and Macnaghten would have been removed.

Macnaghten expressed his belief that the tranquillity of the country would now allow him time to devote his attention to the affairs of the state. Blindly believing that the Shah was popular, the Envoy saw as his main task the self-sufficiency of the country. Writing to a friend, he clearly indicates that this was not going to be an easy task, made no easier by the appointment of corrupt Afghan agents and the parsimonious Directors back in London.

> By-and-by His Majesty will, I hope, be able to make both ends meet. At present pecuniary assistance to a considerable extent will be indispensable. As I said when we first reached Candahar, the country must be looked upon as an outwork, requiring large expenditure to keep it in repair. You are a little too sanguine, I think, in your hope of a speedy and universal reform in this country. For thirty years the inhabitants of most of the districts have never paid a fraction of the revenue, until they were coerced into payment by the presence of troops. The habit has grown into second nature with them, and we cannot expect them to subside at once into the condition of cheerful tax-payers.[21]

20 Edwards-Stuart, *A John Company General*, p.156.
21 Kaye, *History of the War in Afghanistan*, Vol. 2, p.100.

As the year closed not all was as tranquil as the Envoy had hoped. Trouble had already broken out in Baluchistan and was also about to do so at Kandahar. During the course of the year, Baluchistan had been a hotbed of rebellion, the son of Mehrab Khan, Nuseer Khan, had still not made his submission and the *Wazir* at Herat had not given up his intrigues and perfidy. The following chapters cover the events in Baluchistan, post the capture of Kelat, and the developing situation in the Kandahar sector.

16

The Baluchistan Enclave

On the break-up of the Army of the Indus and the new structure for the occupation of Afghanistan, the Sindh and Baluchistan evolved into separate zones of influence, albeit Sir William Macnaghten remaining the political supremeo in his role as the envoy to the Court of Shah Shuja for whom tribute had to be collected. Besides, by the time Macnaghten had returned to Kabul in April 1840, he discovered that he had a great deal more on his Afghan plate and a degree of devolution of power was both necessary and prudent. It is for this reason that the chronology of this account is interrupted in this chapter which covers the events in the Sindh and Baluchistan up to the close of 1841.

In December 1839 Colonel Sir Henry Pottinger, having been knighted for his services in the Sindh, had handed over his charge to Andrew Ross Bell, a 30-year-old civil servant of the Bengal Presidency. In many respects Ross Bell, another Scotsman, was the exact opposite number to 'our man' at Kabul. He was a man of vigour and determination who felt that the niceties of common behaviour could be dispensed with in transactions with local chiefs. He did not cling to Macnaghten's dream that the restoration of Shah Shuja was either popular or beneficial and that the chiefs of Baluchistan, who owed no allegiance to Shah Shuja, would have to be subdued into submission if only to secure the British army's main line of supply. By mid 1840 Ross Bell had set himself up as the sole political authority in Sindh and such areas and situations of Baluchistan that relied on support from Sindh. It was he who had ordered Brigadier John Scott to halt at Dadur until further notice, in the supposed expectation of a Russian advance from Khiva and an attack on Kandahar from Herat. According to a number of accounts, this action was not authorised by the Governor General nor was it in accordance with his policy concerning Herat, which was basically not to stir-up the hornet's nest. Major General William Nott had been moved to the command of Kandahar Garrison, being made responsible also for the northern region of Baluchistan, and Major General George Brooks, of the Bombay Army, was appointed the military commander of the Sindh.

Having installed their puppet, Shah Nawaz Khan, on the *musnad* of Kelat, the British authorities considered it sufficient to leave him there with a handout of £5,000 (£375,000) and the appointment of young Lieutenant William Loveday as the political agent with an escort of 30 *sepoys*. From this precarious base, Shah Nawaz Khan, who was made to transfer to Shah Shuja the most fertile areas of the Shal valley. He was also expected to make his acquired authority felt over those remaining domains of the ex-chief Mehrab Khan, and to contribute a good portion of the revenues collected to the coffers of his new master, Shah Shuja. However, it quickly became apparent that Shah Nawaz Khan, despite being of royal blood, was abhorrent to many of the chiefs, who regarded him as being the puppet of the 'murderers' of Mehrab Khan, an event not easily obliterated from the minds of the people in whom revenge was a powerful principle. This animosity towards the British-installed Shah Nawaz Khan, attracted a growing support base for the son of the ex-chief, Nusser Khan and his widow, Bibi Gunjani, who had escaped into the mountains to become beacons of resentment towards the hated infidels. It was of no great surprise that the tribes were to take the first opportunity to attack small isolated posts and plunder at whim.

Just before the close of the triumphant year of 1839, a force of 200 bayonets under Captain Charles Raitt of 5th BNI was sent from Lehree to take possession of Kahan, the capital of the warlike Murrees of the mountain region stretching eastwards from the Bolan Pass; another force, acting in conjunction with Captain Raitt and under the command of Major Thomas Billamore of 1st BomNI, proceeded to Dera, the capital of the neighbouring tribe of Bhoogtis. The purpose of these manoeuvres, at the instigation of Mr Ross Bell, was to compel these tribes to pay tribute to Shah Nawaz Khan.

On arrival at Kahan, Captain Raitt found the town occupied by about 400 warriors with many more in the surrounding area. The chief, enquiring after the purpose of Captain Raitt's visit, gave warning that there would be much blood shed should the Captain try to occupy the place. Captain Raitt reckoning that the place was too strong to attack and as the Murrees appeared friendly, left a small detachment of 100 men under Lieutenant Christopher Peacock of 1st BomNI a mile from the town and returned to join Major Billamore.

Twenty miles from Dera, Major Billamore had been met by the son of the Bhoogti chief. The man turned out to be friendly and escorted the Major to meet his father. The father also professed friendship and expressed his surprise at the small size of Major Billamore's force, which was completely outnumbered by the warriors the chief had at his fort, however, provisions from the town were readily available but at exorbitant rates. After a couple of days, Major Billamore noticed that many of the warriors had left town; he further learnt that a plan was afoot for the tribes to collect on the neighbouring hills and to attack the puny British force. This attack came on 3 January 1840 and was successfully repelled by the British force which then moved into the town, where the chief still remained. A few days later Major Billamore sent out a foraging party to collect provisions; once the camels had loaded up, the party was attacked by Bhoogtis who rushed down from the hills. They were defeated leaving behind about a quarter of their numbers dead and wounded. By now the detachment that had been left behind at Kahan by Captain Raitt had joined Major Billamore at Dera. On 15 January, the old Bhoogti chief was apprehended and sent under guard down the Indus to Sukkur. Before his departure, the locals were warned that any attempt at his rescue would result in his immediate shooting. The chief was imprisoned for the next eight months in the fortress at Sukkur. The town of Dera and everything in it, down to the last donkey, became prize money. Major Billamore left a small garrison under Captain Raitt at Dera and returned to the plains via Kahan.

At Kahan, Major Billamore discovered that the town had been completely deserted. Messages sent to the old chief received insolent replies. For his route back to Phulji, Major Billamore had selected a footpath across the mountain known as the Nufoosk Pass and he sent Lieutenant John Jacob of the Bombay Artillery to survey the pass and make it adequately suitable for the passage of accompanying guns and baggage. Apparently, the Major had selected this route not only to

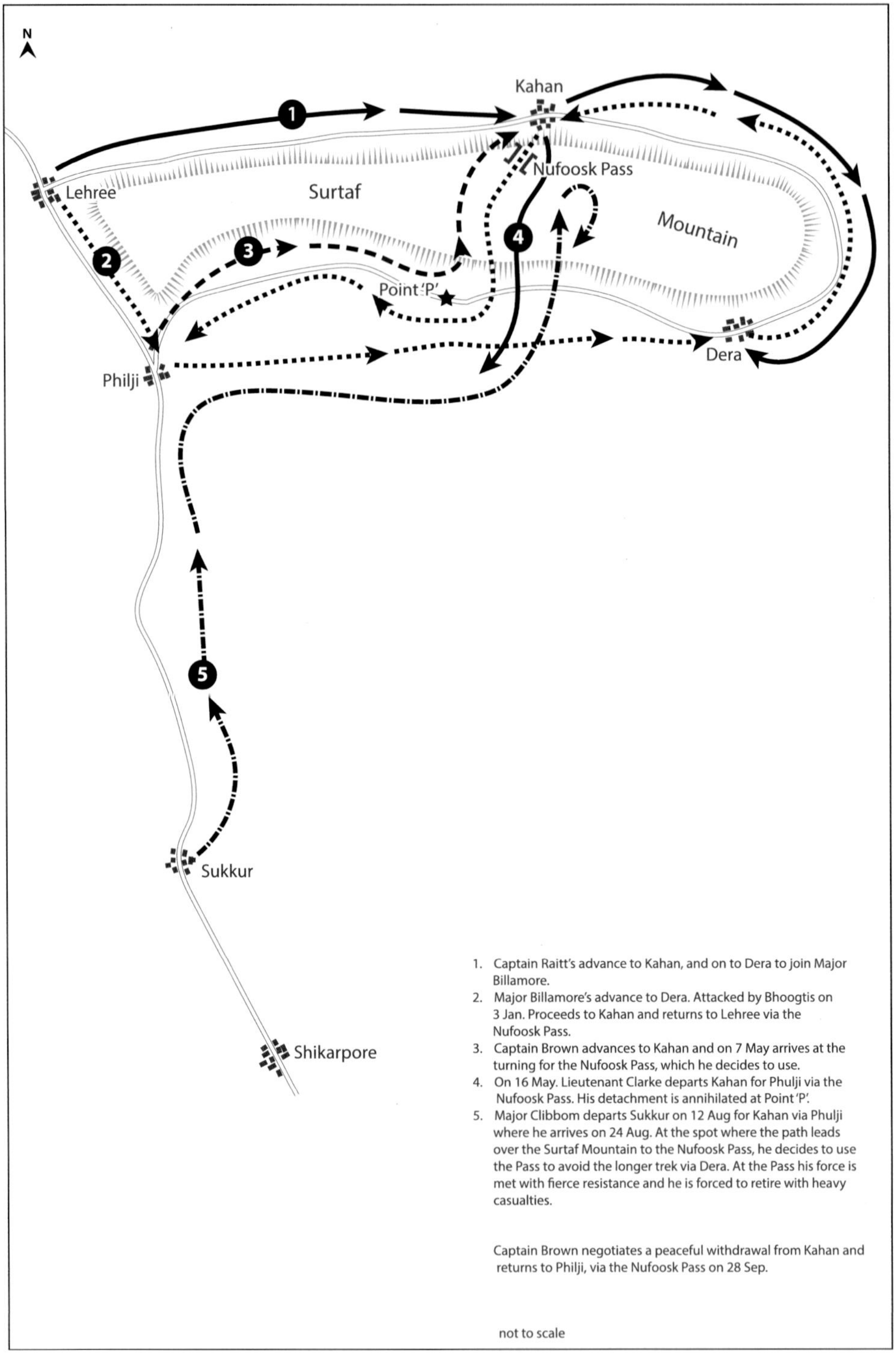

Map 11 Actions around Kahan.

cut down on the number of marches, but also to demonstrate to the Baluchis that the British and their fearsome guns could penetrate their imposing defiles at pleasure, so nowhere was safe. At Phulji Major Billamore was rejoined by Captain Raitt. What this expedition had achieved is debatable, except for making the British acquainted with towns and areas where they had no business, and to collect tributes from tribes who had never paid any, this affair was, on the whole, worthless. Brigadier William Gordon, commanding the garrison at Sukkur, had previously objected to the system of dispersing small detachments up and down the country and had refused to send out Major Billamore's force to isolated places in the mountains simply to satisfy the whims of the politicos; however, he was overruled by the civil authorities, and the Brigadier offered to resign his command.

The scene now switches to the area of Quetta, the country of the Kakur tribe of Baluchis. Soon after the arrival of the British at Quetta, Captain John Bean, of 23rd BNI, was appointed the political agent of the area and when Major General Nott moved to Kandahar his ADC, Lieutenant William Hammersley, remained behind as Captain Bean's assistant. Captain Bean was a most conscientious officer and one of the most gullible, a dangerous combination to put in charge of a sensitive area, however, his selection had more to do with nepotism than his proficiency in Persian, which was nil.[1] Earlier, towards the end of October 1839, this officer took it upon himself, in his role as political agent, to send instructions to Major General Nott ordering him to attack Kelat. What stuck in the General's craw was that this junior officer also had the temerity to suggest the composition of the force required. The General paid no heed to the instructions as he had already received a copy of the orders to Major General Thomas Willshire to make the same attack on his way back to India. Later, full of his self-importance, and without reference to Major General Nott, Captain Bean had sent the main part of the Quetta Garrison, 31st BNI, back to India, leaving a relatively small force of 230 men comprising 200 of the Shah's 6th Infantry Regiment and 30 Baluchi *golandoz*. Based on his acquired local knowledge, Captain Bean also had it made known that the Kakurs were the deadly enemies of the Murrees and that he could persuade them to aggravate the situation with the troublesome Murrees. However, the situation was exacerbated by the behaviour and actions of both Mr Ross Bell and Captain Bean.

The chiefs of the area around Quetta had been invited to come in with proof of the claims to their various *jagirs* and to pay their respects to the Chief Political Officer who, after verifying their claims would sanction them on behalf of the Government. These chiefs made their submission to Ross Bell at Bagh and returned to their *jagirs* on the understanding that they were to hold them under the same tenure as before. Their indignation was not to be surprised at when Captain Bean sent out a mandate that they were to pay rent for their hitherto rent-free *jagirs*. This action greatly incensed the Governor General who heard about it after the event and mischief done. Captain Bean sent out his *munchi* with an escort of 25 *sepoys* to collect the mandated rent from the chief of Mastung, Mohammed Khan Sherwani. The rent collection party was attacked and slaughtered to a man; a barbarous reaction to what these wild tribes saw as a violation of the pledge given at Bagh. The offended Kakars, not expecting any redress, quickly found common cause with their banished chief, Nuseer Khan, to avenge their grievance

1 This reference to 'nepotism' emanates from Captain Ripley's correspondence with Brigadier Roberts. Apparently, Captain Bean was especially selected by Macnaghten to be the political agent at Quetta.

and attack their oppressors. Writing to Brigadier Abraham Roberts, Captain John Ripley, the fort adjutant at Kandahar, had this to say about Captain Bean: 'It really is extraordinary how the Envoy and the Government can have remained so blind to Bean's perfect and total inability to carry on in the duties he is in, unable to speak a word of Persian he is, everyone writes, ludicrously ignorant of everything going on, he has no one about him he can trust and is in short humbugged right and left.'[2] No doubt Captain Ripley's ire was further raised when Captain Bean was awarded the Duranni Medal, at the suggestion of envoy Macnaghten, one of the last to be awarded.

In May 1840 the civil authorities in Baluchistan decided that Kahan was to be occupied once more and that the tribes were to be coerced into paying their tributes. For this purpose a native tax collector accompanied a force commanded by Captain Lewis Brown of 5th BNI. His force comprised 300 *sepoys* under Lieutenant John Taylor, two 12-pdr howitzers under Lieutenant David Erskine and 100 cavalry men of the Sindh Irregular Cavalry under Lieutenant Walpole Clarke. This last named officer had been on Major Billamore's previous expedition and knew the ground well. Captain Brown had been directed to occupy Kahan and was provided with four months supplies carried on 600 camels. Lieutenant Clarke's additional task was to escort the camels back to Lehree once they had been unloaded.

The advance of Captain Brown's force was arduous in the extreme. It was very hot with temperatures reaching 116°, men were dying of heatstroke and both lieutenants Taylor and Erskine became ill and had to fall out with Erskine's guns, except for one, ordered back to Lehree. Lieutenant Erskine soon recovered and re-joined Captain Brown with all his guns. On 7 May, Captain Brown arrived at the spot where he had to make the decision of either proceeding via Dera, a march of 74 miles, or by the shorter route through the Nufoosk Pass. He chose the latter and for the next 24 hours his force toiled its way through the narrow pass and its precipices, ravines and rocks in the 20 miles to Kahan, which they found abandoned and the gates burnt. The selection of routes, at this time, was largely determined by which held the better prospects for water, an essential need for both man and beast in the extreme heat and of which there was a scarcity in the arid terrain of Baluchistan.

On 16 May, Lieutenant Clarke set out with his unladen camels for his return march to Lehree. Finding no opposition through the Nufoosk, Lieutenant Clarke sent back the 100 *sepoys* under a *Subadar*, whom Captain Brown had attached to his party as a precaution, and continued his journey with his original force. The *Subadar* and his men had not got far before they were savagely attacked and totally eliminated except for a *dhooli* bearer who carried the sad news to Captain Brown. Lieutenant Clarke, with his camels in single file stretching two miles, continued through the Nufoosk Pass without being molested. However, on descending the Surtaf Mountain, he was surprised to see a strong body of Baluchis following his force. Fearing a loss of his precious camels, Lieutenant Clarke decided to check the Baluchies and save his force from further annoyance; he backtracked a mile into a good position with 100 men and allowed the camels to proceed under cavalry escort. Along came the Baluchis and a two-hour duel commenced. This rearguard force eventually ran out of ammunition and the Baluchis bounced on their prey slaying every man of Lieutenant Clarke's rearguard; Lieutenant Clarke was brought down by three men while a fourth cut his throat. The cavalrymen, seeing the

2 Edwards-Stuart, *A John Company General*, p.119.

complete rout of the rearguard and the death of their commander, fled leaving all the precious camels to become the property of the Baluchis. Only one *Havildar* and 10 *sepoys* escaped.

The result of this catastrophe meant that Captain Brown was now left in Kahan with 140 bayonets and a single gun to watch over 900 yards of Kahan walls against any assault by the triumphant Baluchis. Although he had provisions for four months, he was in no position to exert British authority or to collect taxes; he was, in effect, besieged. On 21 May, Captain Brown managed to send a *cossid* with a message to Major David Forbes at Sukkur informing him of the disaster and that he would attempt to hold on at Kahan. On 24 May Captain Brown, in a prudent move, put his besieged garrison on half rations. He was to remain besieged in Kahan for the next five months and left to his own devices to sustain his besieged garrison.

The scene now switches back to Quetta where Captain Bean had managed to stir up a hornet's nest with his ill-fated mission to collect taxes from the chief of Mastung. Soon after the disaster that befell Lieutenant Clarke, the Kakars started a series of hostilities which culminated in the loss of Kelat. Their earliest move came on 7 July when they invested the little fort of Mirree, just outside Quetta. The Baluchis, 5,000 strong and led by Guffor Khan, attacked the small garrison which miraculously kept the enemy at bay, and did so for 10 days. On 16 July the besieged garrison was reinforced by the arrival of Lieutenant Hugh Jackson with 150 Afghan Horse who had been sent from the outpost of Killa Abdulah by Major General Nott. This force outflanked the enemy to reach Quetta just in time. Then, surprisingly, the Baluchis raised the siege and retired towards Mastung. Captain Bean, now strong enough to have pursued the enemy and re-establish communications with Lieutenant Loveday failed to do so. Unmolested, the Baluchis proceeded to organise their force and descended on Kelat, led on this occasion by their young chief Nusser Khan. Surrounding the place with 5,000 warriors, they made some ineffective attacks, but were primarily involved in intrigues designed to oust Shah Nawaz Khan.

At Kelat, Lieutenant Loveday had taken up residence in a dwelling outside the town while his 30 *sepoys* found accommodation in the town. Neither Shah Nawaz Khan nor Lieutenant Loveday had made any attempt at repairing the fortifications damaged in the recent British assault; possibly because they were not given the funds to do so. It was here that Charles Masson, masquerading as a Hindu merchant, revealed his true identity to Loveday, who, it would appear, was not entirely convinced, and instead, caught up with the then Russophobia hysteria, reckoned that Masson, a British spy, was in fact a Russian spy, or at least a double agent.

While the attacks on Kelat continued, negotiations were taking place for the restoration of Nusser Khan and the abdication of Shah Nawaz Khan on honourable terms. These negotiations had the full concurrence of the Lieutenant Loveday, who was at the same time being advised by Masson of the precarious situation they were in, advising the young officer to beat a hasty retreat. Eventually, Shah Nawaz Khan left Kelat on acceptable terms.[3] Young Nusser Khan was placed on the *musnad* of his father and both Lieutenant Loveday and Masson were apprehended, the former being stripped of his fineries and hawked around as a trophy of war. Leaving his uncle Azum Khan in charge, Nusser Khan and his warriors, with Masson and Loveday shackled to camels, moved off to Mastung from where the young chief opened up communications with Captain Bean for favourable terms which did not include submission to Shah Shuja and which

3 Shah Nawaz Khan retired to Lankhana on a Government pension of £1,200 (£90,000). Shortly afterwards this was reduced by half and in 1843 it was withdrawn altogether by General Sir Charles Napier.

the political agent was unable to concede. In the last of his communications, Nusser Khan used Masson as his messenger in the hope that the Englishman could better argue the case for him. Just before his departure, Lieutenant Loveday gave Masson a sealed letter for Captain Bean in which he stated his suspicion that Masson was either a Russian spy or a double agent and should be arrested at once. On receipt of this letter Captain Bean placed Masson under arrest. When, some months later, it was established that Masson was not a Russian spy he was released and proceeded to Karachi while Captain Bean remained at Quetta with egg on his face. There is no doubt that the Captain's actions were also influenced by the loathing all officers had of deserters. In mitigation, Captain Bean had acted in accordance with instructions from Macnaghten, who wrote a letter to the confined Masson in which he said, 'I did authorise Captain Bean to detain you at Quetta until the pleasure of the Governor General in Council should be ascertained as to your being permitted to prosecute your travels in countries subject to the Crown of Cabool, since, as far as I know, you are without permission to do so either from the British Government or from His Majesty Shah Shuja.'[4]

The Baluchis were fully expecting their special messenger to return with the British reply and were shocked to discover that he had been arrested; as a result the Baluchis broke up their camp at Mastung and descended down the Bolan Pass onto the plains, taking with them the unfortunate Loveday.

It was in late July 1840 that Brigadier Thomas Stevenson, in command of Upper Sindh, had arranged for a force of 1,000 bayonets with artillery and irregular cavalry to be on stand-by for service in the hills, a sort of 'fire brigade'. Unfortunately, Brigadier Stevenson died of heatstroke on 9 August and Major Forbes, who had arrived in Sukkur only a few days earlier, as the senior officer present found himself the temporary commander of Upper Sindh with the responsibility for the employment of the 'fire brigade'. The first step he took was to recommend that the Kahan garrison should not be relieved but withdrawn. However as Ross Bell had given the most positive orders for the maintenance of the Kahan position, Major Forbes had no alternative but to send out the 'fire brigade'. Major Thomas Clibborn, of 2nd BomNI, was appointed commander of the force which consisted of detachments of 1st and 2nd BomNI, altogether 600 bayonets, a detachment of 300 infantry from HM 40th Foot, 200 irregular cavalry, four 12-pdr howitzers, 1,200 camels and 600 bullocks.

In spite of the intense heat, Major Clibborn and his force left Sukkur on 12 August, marching at night, and were at Phulji by 20 August, a distance of 105 miles. At Phulji he was joined by 200 cavalrymen of the Sindh and Poona Irregular Cavalry under Lieutenant William Loch and Lieutenant George Malcolm respectively. On 24 August this force left Phulji and six marches further on arrived at the scene of Lieutenant Clarke's disaster, clearly marked by the bleached bones of dead *sepoys* scattered around and a heap of stones under which lay the body of the gallant subaltern. Here Major Clibborn made his decision to use the Nufoosk Pass, a decision based on two factors, water and distance; a passage through the Nufoosk instead of proceeding via Dera would shorten his advance by six marches; and he had received a message from Captain Brown to the effect that as it had recently rained water was most likely to be found. A complete day was spent getting the convoy and guns up to the top of the Surtaf feature, the guns being

4 John Ure, *Shooting Leave: Spying Out Central Asia in the Great Game* (London: Constable, 2009), p.103.

dragged up by men already suffering from excessive heat of an August sun. A miserable night was spent on the summit as no water was to be found, the water being at the bottom of the hill and covered by Baluchi fire. At two o'clock next morning, the advance to Kahan was continued. As the force approached the Nufoosk Pass, the heights were seen to be covered with boisterous Baluchis. On arriving at the entrance of the pass, Major Clibborn found that the path, made earlier by Lieutenant Jacob and used by Captain Brown, was now cut and blocked up, thus unfit for use by camels and more so by guns, only admitting men in single file; but worse, there was no water except for a single pool which was covered by Baluchi fire. Major Clibborn had led his force into a 'devil's cauldron'!

The guns were placed in position to enfilade the summit of the pass, and upon the arrival of the rearguard a storming party under the command of Captain Raitt was detailed off and gallantly overcame every difficulty and was about to assail the summit when from all sides the party came under deadly enemy fire with an accompanying shower of boulders hurled down from the precipices. Captain Raitt was severely wounded in the thigh by a *jezail* bullet and three of his officers, Lieutenants Henry Franklin, Fitzherbert Williams and Henry More, were killed in the bitter fighting. Haemorrhaging men, Captain Raitt ordered his party to fall back on the main body, and the Baluchis followed in their relentless attempt to destroy the British force. The firing of the guns at point-blank range eventually overcame them as they fled into the caves in the hills leaving behind 150 comrades dead and wounded.

By now it was midday and instead of battling with Baluchis the *sepoys* were being driven mad by their thirst, tongues swollen, mouths parched with no respite under the pitiless sun. Attempts were made to find water but to no avail and Major Clibborn reckoned that a further attempt on the Nufoosk Pass would prove to be even more hopeless. In the hope of finding water by falling back, the Major ordered the spiking of his guns and the withdrawal of his remaining force. Fortunately, the move back was met with no interruptions, however, once they had arrived at the top, discipline evaporated as the men, frantic with thirst, rushed down the hill, leaping like madmen into the pools of water at the bottom. While the first to arrive at the pools filled their stomachs with the precious liquid, the Baluchis, appearing from nowhere, slaughtered the followers spilling their even more precious liquid. Absolute chaos reigned; while the remaining officers and NCOs sought to re-establish order, the Baluchis made off with the remaining convoy including guns, bullocks and most of the camels. With his remaining camels and men, Major Clibborn led his exhausted and bedraggled force to Phulji 54 miles away where it arrived on 2 September; along the way it lost Captain Critchley Heighington of 1st BomNI to apoplexy. After a short rest at Phulji, Major Clibborn's force made the 50-mile journey to Shikarpore, and on arrival in closing his despatch Major Clibborn solicited a court of inquiry as to his conduct and to the causes leading up to the failure of his mission. This was a customary action by commanders who felt that they were not entirely to blame and sought to be exonerated.

In besieged Kahan, Captain Brown had fully expected Major Clibborn's force to make its appearance from the direction of the Nufoosk Pass, but on 31 August he was to write in his journal:

> A day of great and almost overpowering excitement. It commenced about 3 o'clock last evening when the plains and the hills became alive with Baluchis and at dark signal fires on the top of all the hills. At day-break, large bodies of horse and foot were seen hurrying

> across the plain to the Nufoosk Pass, on the opposite side of which, we soon learnt of the arrival of our convoy.

Then on 1 September, he wrote:

> Not a single Beloochee to be seen on the top of the hills at day light. No sight or sound of enemy all day! Sadly perplexed to know what has become of them, conclude that finding the pass too strongly defended yesterday, that they have fallen back to go round by the Deyrah road, as I first recommended.

Then on 4 September Captain Brown wrote:

> Today some horsemen came and informed us that they had cut up our convoy, taken all the guns and all the stores and supplies, and had killed all the 'sahib log' except three.[5]

Major Clibborn's request for a court of inquiry could not be ignored, nor could the disaster at Nufoosk be swept under the carpet. As this court was essentially to apportion blame, it was of great concern to the political officers that a 'court of inquiry', made up of more sympathetic officers, might well place too high a proportion of the blame on the politicians. Consequently, at the end of October 1840 Major General Brooks was instructed to nominate the officers required to constitute a 'military commission' over which he was to preside without delay. The members selected were Brigadier Thomas Valiant of HM 40th Foot, Lieutenant Colonel George Wymer of 30th BNI, Major Francis Farrell of 6th BomNI and Major Henry Lloyd of Bengal Artillery. The finding of this 'military commission' was to condemn Major Clibborn and all the superior officers who had ordered and provided for his expedition. This wording appeared to totally exonerate any involvement by political officers. As can well be imagined, this finding left a nasty smell in the flared nostrils of the host of condemned officers and a flurry of irate letters to the press; and most mysteriously, the commission's report was in the hands of the *Bombay Courier* before the official date of 20 November given on the report. Clearly a most despicable affair and equally clearly the 'military commission' had been nobbled.

It was to transpire later that Mr Ross Bell had history with Major Clibborn, who had been Brigadier Gordon's brigade major at the time his boss was causing a rumpus about the pointless deployment of small detachments, unsupported, around the countryside, and naturally Major Clibborn had supported his boss to the hilt, thus becoming a target for a vindictive politico. It was also implied that Ross Bell had a dominating influence over the president of the 'military commission.' The upshot was that the commission's findings were upturned by the Bombay Government, which exonerated Major Clibborn, and directed the immediate removal of Major General Brooks from his command and the return of Brigadier Valiant to Bombay. The Bombay Government's actions were in due course approved by the Governor General in Council, the Court of Directors and Horse Guards. Major General Brooks and Brigadier Valiant returned to Bombay in February 1841 and the former left for England in the following May. Brigadier Valiant, being a Queen's Officer, received a reprimand from Horse Guards and remained in

5 Edwards-Stuart, *A John Company General*, p.116.

Bombay as the garrison commander until March 1847. Major General Brookes was replaced by Major General Sir John Fitzgerald and Brigadier Valiant by Brigadier Richard England. The 'politicos' remained where they were.

In the meantime, the political authorities in Upper Sindh, after the destruction of Clarke's detachment and the blaze of Baluchi insurrection, pleaded earnestly for reinforcements from Karachi. Two companies of HM 40th Foot under Major Evelyn Boscawen left Karachi on 10 August followed by further reinforcements consisting of HM 41st Foot.

In the meantime the authorities in Kabul, much disturbed by the extension of problems, had sent an order to Major General Nott for him to retake Kelat. He was to obtain unconditional surrender and assure the people that the son of Mehrab Khan would be recognised by the British Government and His Majesty Shah Shuja as the lawful chief of Baluchistan, on his agreeing to pay personal homage to the Shah in Kabul. The General left Kandahar with a force to comply with his orders, however his personal feelings on the matter were recorded in a letter to his daughters:

> I am disgusted. They most unjustly dethrone Mehrab Khan and place a tool of Shah Shuja in his place. Well, Mehrab Khan's son assembled his father's followers, retook Kalat and the authorities talk big for a day or two, and then send me instructions to offer terms to the boy, declaring that they will place him on his father's throne and thus they disgrace the character of our country. Had they taken this boy by the hand when he was a wanderer in the land of his ancestors, there would have been a generous and honourable feeling, but to bend the knee to him and his bloody chiefs now is disgraceful.[6]

Nusser Khan rejected the proposal, vowing that he would avenge his father's death, set out with 5,000 warriors in the direction of Mastang and was in the vicinity of that town on 29 September. When Major General Nott's force arrived at Quetta, Nusser Khan and his followers fled in the direction of Dadur and attempted to attack the British post there.

Nusser Khan's attack on Dadur was repulsed by 120 cavalrymen of Skinner's Horse under Lieutenant Archibald Macpherson. The Baluchis made a number of further attacks which were also repulsed. As the British reinforcements closed in, the Baluchis withdrew but remained in the area. On 15 October Major Boscawen, with four companies of HM 40th Foot, 38th BNI, guns and a troop of horse artillery, left Shikarpore and directed his march towards Kotra; while the Baluchis continued making a nuisance of themselves plundering villages and towns. Major Boscawen's force arrived at Gundava on 28 October too late to save it from it being sacked and property being demolished by the marauding Baluchis, who now fell back on Kotra, 5,000 strong and led by Nusser Khan; Major Boscawen moved out at once against them. The Baluchis immediately withdrew leaving behind their camp equipment and property worth 10,000 rupees and the still-bleeding body of the murdered Lieutenant Loveday, whom Nusser Khan had been carting around as a war trophy. Apparently Nusser Khan's uncle, Gool Mohammed, had lingered long enough to slit the unfortunate subaltern's throat then galloped off just before the leading bayonets reached the camp.

6 Beveridge, *A Comprehensive History of India*, Vol. 3, p.470.

The narrative now returns to Kahan, where we left Captain Brown and his gallant garrison, seemingly cut off, aggrieved and disappointed. Determined that the fort be maintained, Captain Brown reckoned that he could only do so until 15 October, by which time he would either have to negotiate the best terms possible or fight his way out having destroyed the fort. On 25 September, the chiefs assembled and took a solemn oath on the Koran that if the British force left the fort intact and left within three days, they would protect it to the plains. Finally, although fully aware that some sort of treachery might be played, Captain Brown concluded that these terms were probably the best he could extract and aware that his time in Kahan was fast evaporating, he agreed to the terms. At two o'clock on the morning of 28 September the garrison left Kahan, which had been its home for the past five months. In traversing the Nufoosk Pass, the party came across the bodies of what had been Major Clibborn's relief force, and by 1 October Captain Brown had brought his garrison safely to the plains. The admirable conduct of Captain Brown earned him the thanks of the Government and a promotion to brevet major. Later, he was employed in a political capacity to try to convince his erstwhile besiegers to submit to the new order of governance. Much later the new governor general, Lord Ellenborough, appointed him an honorary ADC.

The setback at Nufoosk does not appear to have had any effect on the policies adopted by the political agents, as they continued to mismanage affairs in Baluchistan. In the area of Kotra, which came under the direct supervision of Ross Bell, *Syud* Mohammed had been selected as the tax collector, another example of the British penchant for selecting traitors to the old order of things in the belief that they would, overnight, become trustworthy adherents to the new. However, as these same politicos were to discover many times over, these appointees, while answering to and being paid by their new masters, remained ever-faithful to their treacherous ways. Such was *Syud* Mohammed. Under the saintly guise of a holy *Syud* he was renowned for being a scoundrel. Much earlier in his career, *Syud* Mohammed had been given the *jagirs* of Hurrund and Dujel by Mehrab Khan, which he then treacherously sold to the Sikhs. Ross Bell could scarcely have found a more accomplished crook to be his tax collector. *Syud* Mohammed was put in control of an area exceeding 5,000 square miles, without the presence of a single British officer to oversee his wicked endeavours.

Earlier Ross Bell had written to *Syud* Mohammed instructing him to inform all the chiefs of *jagirs* in his area that their domains now came under the British and would be restored to them on their making their appearance at Sukkur, showing proof of validity of their claims. Whether all the chiefs were informed is not clear, however a few of the lesser chiefs did show up and their claims were registered and seals applied to their title deeds. The majority, however, stayed away, irritated by their claims being questioned by intruders and annoyed by the insolence of their tax collector. Thus they were to find solace with the growing number of their discontented cousins.

Another area stirred into discontent with a much happier ending was the coastal area of Sonmiani. This province had been governed on a military tenure under the chiefs of Kelat, and for generations had received half the dues collected. Once the British had put Shah Nawaz Khan on the *musnad*, all dues were ordered to be made over to the British in compensation for the handout given to Shah Nawaz Khan. A British officer was duly appointed to make the collections. The chief of Sonmiani, instead of arming his men with bows and arrows, appealed to the Bombay Government and his case came to the notice of Lord Auckland, who censured and reversed all that had been done. This wise and timely action prevented the chief of Sonmiani joining his more warlike cousins.

Meanwhile, Major General Nott moved down from Kandahar with a strong force to recapture Kelat and on the way back to strengthen the garrison at Quetta. His force consisted of 42nd and 43rd BNI, a troop of artillery under Captain William Anderson, a squadron of Shah Shuja's Cavalry under Captain Robert Walker and Shah Shuja's 2nd Infantry Regiment under Captain Clement Macan. Their march took them via Quetta where the General was joined by the political agent, Lieutenant Hammersley, his ex-ADC. This force arrived at Kelat on 3 November to find that the Baluchi garrison had withdrawn, leaving the local non-combatants in situ. These people sent a deputation to the General pleading him not to attack and plunder their homes. Major General Nott agreed and placing four companies in the town issued strict orders that no one was to enter the town without his personal permission. When the political agent attempted to enter in his political capacity, he was stopped. Annoyed at this affront, Lieutenant Hammersley galloped off to remonstrate with the General in an insubordinate manner, who ordered his erstwhile ADC to shut up or be escorted to his tent under arrest. The young officer, not happy with his put-down, complained to Macnaghten who, not surprisingly, asked the General to defend his actions.

On his return to Kandahar Major General Nott left Lieutenant Colonel Lewis Stacy in command of the garrison, with 42nd BNI and some guns, and Lieutenant Hammersley remained there as the political agent. Mr Ross Bell was not exactly enthused by Major General Nott's movements or dispositions, preferring to let matters take their own course. At this time strong feelings were being expressed that it would be more advantageous to make peace with Nusser Khan and Bibi Gunjani, especially as the various charges against Mehrab Khan began to be proved unfounded and it was also quite apparent that the Shah Nawaz Khan experiment had failed to hold the affection of the people. The *Wazir* of Kelat, who had been held prisoner since November 1839, was released and it was made known that both the Governor General and Shah Shuja had decided to restore Kelat to its rightful heir, Nusser Khan. A little later, Colonel Stacy was commissioned to seek out the young chief and to convince him of the generous terms now being offered. The Colonel was to chalk up a great many miles and much frustration before the young chief and his mother-in-law relented. Meanwhile this prudent policy was to be marred by the mismanagement of political agents and the total lack of faith the Baluchis had in the friendly overtures now being made. It was not until 8 September 1841 that Colonel Stacy was able to ride into Quetta with Nusser Khan, and to introduce him as His Highness Mir Nusser Khan, the Chief of Kelat. In the meantime a General Order had been issued, dated 9 August, intimating that Nusser Khan and his followers were no longer enemies of the British.

Consequent to the successful withdrawal of Captain Brown and the elation of the Murree chiefs at getting rid of the British at Kahan, a robber baron by the name of Bejah Khan came in to Shikarpore to make his submission and to negotiate terms with the British authorities, who held him responsible for stealing close to 5,000 camels. Bejah Khan brought with him a renowned *Syud* to ensure his safety. He was received with honour by Ross Bell's assistant, Lieutenant Thomas Postans, and amicable conversations took place over a number of days. However, on the fourth day, when Bejah Khan had come to pay his respects to the political agent, he and his companions were seized and despatched to the prison at Sukkur, and their horses, arms and ornaments were sold at public auction. This action was seen by some to be no less treacherous than any committed by the Baluchis. A few months later, the prisoners were released and compensated for their loss.

In November 1840, Lieutenant Colonel Thomas Marshall was in command of the brigade assembled at Kotra consisting of 25th BomNI, detachments from 2nd BomNI and 21st BNI, two companies of artillery and a squadron of irregular horse. On 26 November Colonel Marshall, on receipt of intelligence that Nusser Khan with a strong force was within eight miles of his position, set off with a strong escort to verify the information. At nine o'clock that morning the Colonel found the Baluchis deployed in a difficult position commanding the entrance to the hills. Marshall then took up a position about 300 yards from the Baluchi outposts. At this juncture a messenger arrived, conveying Nusser Khan's greetings and his desire for a peaceful conclusion. The messenger was sent back with the British commander's reply, that Nusser Khan had one hour to decide whether to surrender or fight. At the same time Marshall also called up his reserve. Before the hour had quite expired the Baluchis started some spasmodic firing to which there was no British reply until the stipulated hour had passed; whereupon Nusser Khan sent forward his *Wazir* with a letter for the British commander stating that in a few days he would disband his followers and proceed to Mr Ross Bell to make his submission. On receipt of this letter, Colonel Marshall withdrew his force and returned to his camp. On 27 November Mohammed Hussain, a Baluchi employed by the British as a spy, reported that Nusser Khan was destitute and needed funds in order to make his journey to Shikarpore to meet Mr Ross Bell. Colonel Marshall, fully aware of the new policy to placate the young chief, sent him 2,000 rupees.

While these peaceful arrangements were being concluded in Kotra, Major General Brookes the military commander, who was 150 miles away oblivious of the proceedings, sent a peremptory order dated 27 November, stating that the Baluchis were to be attacked without delay. This order was brought in by the General's ADC, Captain Thomas Smith of 15th BNI, who had covered the distance in 38 hours and confirmed that the order had the concurrence of Mr Ross Bell and had been written at his house. Apparently Mr Ross Bell was in receipt of intelligence, most probably from a dubious source, that instead of coming in, Nusser Khan had used the respite to strengthen his force. His exact intentions were not given time to mature as Colonel Marshall strapped on his sword and was back in the field with his whole force, and in total bad faith attacked the Baluchis who were taken completely by surprise. After three hours of heavy fighting the Baluchis were totally defeated and retired into the friendly hills leaving 500 of their number dead or wounded. The British casualties amounted to one officer, Lieutenant Charles Lodge, and three *sepoys* killed and 30 wounded. Four of the principal Baluchi chiefs were taken prisoner and escorted to Sukkur by Captain Smith. Once again Nusser Khan managed to escape, ever more suspicious of British intentions.

As mentioned earlier, Captain Brown had been employed in trying to convince the Murrees of the benefits of the new order of things. While tolerably successful, he failed to win over the Kujjuk tribe and persuade it to recognise its obligations to the Government. They had refused to pay the previous year's tribute and shut themselves up in their fort at Sebee, some 40 miles north-west of Dadur. So in early February, at the behest of an irate Mr Ross Bell, Major General Brookes sent a detachment to Sebee under Lieutenant Colonel Peter Wilson of the Bombay Light Cavalry, to give them a specimen of *feringhee* authority. This detachment consisted of a squadron of 2nd Bombay Light Cavalry, four companies each from 2nd and 21st BomNI, a troop of Bombay artillery (six guns) and Lieutenant William Curtis's Irregular Horse. This detachment made a speedy advance to Sebee and after the usual demand to surrender made a frontal attack. But after four hours of combat during which 21st BomNI displayed signs of reluctance, it failed to achieve its objective and Lieutenant Colonel Wilson was forced to order a withdrawal. During the fighting Lieutenant Richard Creed of the artillery and Lieutenant William Falconer of 2nd BomNI were killed. Lieutenant Colonel Wilson had been shot in the thigh and a little while later died of his wound. The total British loss amounted to 11 killed and 40 wounded. On receipt of this shocking news, Major General Brookes moved from Bagh with HM 40th Foot (2nd Somerset), 21st BomNI and other troops to the rescue. However, on arrival at Sebee on 24 February the General found that the fort had been vacated, and having ordered that all property values taken would be distributed as prize money, he and his force moved on to Quetta. It was during this movement that Brookes received the information of his immediate recall for his part in the 'military commission' that had investigated the Nufoosk disaster. Four months later the authorities declared that no part of the property taken at Kujjuk could be considered prize money, it having been found in a town belonging to a friendly power. The monies realised by the sale of the property were returned to the Kujjuks, who were also given money to repair their fort.

17

Events in West Afghanistan

Three hundred miles west of Kabul, in the Zemindawar district, a body of Shah Shuja's force assisting in tax collection had been attacked and dispersed by Ahktar Khan and his followers. A detachment consisting of 2nd BomNI, a troop of horse artillery, a *Rissaldar* of Shah Shuja's 1st Cavalry and a body of *Jan-Baz* (Afghan horsemen), all under the command of Captain Hugh Farrington, was immediately despatched from Kandahar to put down this disturbance before it spread. On 3 January 1841 Captain Farrington encountered the rebels, numbering 1,000 horsemen, in a strong position at the village of Landi Nowah. After a sharp engagement lasting a couple of hours, Farrington's detachment completely defeated and dispersed the rebels, however Ahktar Khan managed to slip away. The startling feature of this uprising was that Ahktar Khan, the rebel chief, was of the Duranni clan, hereditary rivals of the Barkzais and thus ought to have been a strong supporter of the restored monarch. This development certainly had the British authorities scratching their heads.

With the restoration of a Duranni shah, the members of the clan, both in and around Kabul and Kandahar, fully expected the re-establishment of all favours and influence enjoyed during the previous Sadozai regimes and were greatly disappointed that their expectations had not been realised. Shah Shuja, on his entry into Kandahar in April 1839, had promised favourable tax changes and the chieftainship of Zemindawar to Ahktar Khan. But these promises had been swept away by the Shah's appointed agents, and the consequent Duranni discontent reflected the chaotic and corrupt administration of these agents, most of whom had been appointed by the reprobate *Wazir* Mullah Shikore. Many of the new appointees had been hangers-on with the Duranni Court in exile, who had arrived back in Afghanistan poor and were not about to waste time in becoming rich. Unfortunately, the protection provided to these unpopular agents allowed them to operate with impunity, and thus, by association, the British were also viewed with disdain. Macnaghten's immediate reaction to Ahktar Khan's belligerency was to offer a reward of 10,000 rupees for his capture and then to 'hang the villain as high as Haman'. It did not help matters that the treacherous *Wazir* at Herat, Yah Mohammed, using the opportunity of Duranni unrest, had written to urge the chiefs to drive out the British and promised to help them do so.

Captain Elliott Todd, the leader of the British Mission at Herat, had for some time been reporting unfavourably on conditions in Herat and in particular on the perfidy of the *Wazir*, the de facto chief. As at the beginning of 1841 no less than £400,000 (£30 million) had been poured into Herat to strengthen its fortifications, establish stability and to induce the chiefs to forego their trading in slaves. The Governor General had stipulated in the Tripartite Treaty that Herat was a no-go area as far as Shah Shuja's domains were concerned. He viewed a peaceful Herat under Shah Kamran and benign British influence as essential to the success of his Afghan venture, hence he was not as frustrated as envoy Macnaghten and Captain Todd at the manifested perfidy of the scoundrel Yah Mohammed. While the Governor General opted to feed the *Wazir*'s insatiable appetite for British money, the Envoy, taking his cue from Todd's disparaging reports and his continued preoccupations with Russian intrigue, was all for annexing Herat to the domains of Shah Shuja.

The festering situation was brought to bursting point when Yah Mohammed proposed, probably in a move to ingratiate himself with the British Mission, that the Persian-held fortress at Ghorian be retaken and that, with a grant of an extra two *lakhs* of rupees to equip a force, he would do so. Captain Todd, aware of the Government's desire that Persia withdraw a greater distance from Herat, fell for this bold idea but told the *Wazir* that the Government would need some form of guarantee to ensure that this grant would not be squandered; to ensure its correct use he proposed that a detachment of British troops be based in Herat. The *Wazir* agreed, albeit he had no intention of fulfilling his part of the contract. Captain Todd, now well versed in the perfidy of Yah Mohammed, stipulated that the money would be handed over at Girishk to the *Wazir*'s representative at the same time as the agreed detachment of British troops entered Herat. Not surprisingly, Yah Mohammed refused to comply with this too cunning a condition and demanded the money or the withdrawal of the Mission. Rather than have British honour and prestige brought further into disrepute, Captain Todd chose to depart. This was not the reaction that the *Wazir* expected. He was convinced that with trouble brewing in Zemindawar the British authorities would back down and come up with the cash. He was not wrong.

Afghan Foot Soldier, Herat c.1840.

Captain Todd's Mission left Herat on 10 February 1841 and headed for Girishk where it stayed for a while in the hope that the *Wazir*'s want of British money was greater than his fear of their occupation of Herat and so he might request the Mission's return. When Lord Auckland heard about Todd's unauthorised withdrawal he flew into an uncontrollable rage, fuelled by his fear that Todd's action would open up another front of conflict which the authorised vast payments were designed to keep calm. He at once repudiated Todd's actions, removed him from political employment and put him at the disposal of the Commander-in-Chief. On the other hand, Macnaghten's reaction to the news, which he heard before the Governor General, was to muster all available resources for an immediate demonstration against Herat. He wrote to Captain Rawlinson to prepare for a siege and to Mr Ross Bell to send up all the big guns he could spare. Despite his exuberance at now having a good excuse to implement his long-cherished strategy concerning Herat, the Envoy feared, correctly, that the Governor General would do nothing. In answer to Macnaghten's request for more troops and carriage, the Governor General replied:

> I cannot apprehend organised invasion from Herat, there may be a foray on the frontier which will not have the effect of making the advent of Yah Mohammed popular in Zemindawar. I think it, however, more likely that you will have to deal with letters and agents than with troops; and you ask me in what manner you are to receive overtures which may be made to you by Yah Mohammed. I would receive them calmly and coldly, but not repulsively. I would show no impatience to renew a Mission in Herat. I would have to be understood that the stoppage of allowances was unauthorised and the detachment of brigade to the citadel of Herat was not desired, and would not have been acceded to by the British Government, but that the conduct of the Vizier has given great offence, and that we can regard Herat with no confidence or friendly feeling until there shall have been on the side of that state an entire change of policy. I can only repeat, therefore, what I have said very many times within the last two years. That you must be strong in Afghanistan before you can hope to exercise a wholesome influence upon Herat.[1]

While conciliatory letters were sent to Herat, it was still necessary that the disturbance in Zemindawar be resolved if only to ensure that it did not draw in the Heratis into a full-scale rebellion and thus reignite the revolts in Baluchistan. So, instead of a robust response, the British authorities fell back on Plan B.

Plan B was to send a deputation, headed by Lieutenant Edward Elliott, to conciliate with Ahktar Khan to whom Lieutenant Elliott was to offer terms, made more palatable by a generous payment of 'hush money', which the chief was only too pleased to accept. Captain Rawlinson, the political agent at Kandahar, in a letter to Macnaghten, did not see this solution as having much traction:

> I do not anticipate that by this conciliation we gain any other advantage than that of temporary tranquillity, and however prudent, therefore, it may be at present to induce the rebel chief of Zemindawar to abstain from disorder by the hope of obtaining through his influence, substantial personal benefit, I still think that when the danger of foreign aggression is removed, and efficient means are at our disposal, the rights of His Majesty's government should be asserted in that strong and dignified manner which can alone insure a due respect being paid to his authority.[2]

1 Kaye, *History of the War in Afghanistan*, Vol. 2, p.115.
2 Beveridge, *A Comprehensive History of India*, Vol. 3, p.477.

On asking Rawlinson for his views as to the cause of the disturbance, the Envoy was not too happy with Rawlinson's mild suggestion of intrigue implicating Shah Shuja. In acknowledging his letter, Macnaghten told him, 'It will make the consideration of all questions more simple if you will hereafter take for granted that as regards us, the King can do no wrong.'[3] However, he did convince Shah Shuja to terminate the services of his old *Wazir*, Mullah Shikore, and some of the more obnoxious agents. Osman Khan was appointed *Wazir*, a younger, abler and more honest man.

True to form, only a few months were to pass before Ahktar Khan was again at the head of a larger force and was threatening the important town of Girishk, situated on the west bank of the Helmand River 70 miles west of Kandahar. Naturally this development caused a great deal of concern in Kandahar, prompting a force to be sent out on 27 June. Three hundred miles away in Kabul Sir William Macnaghten, basking in the sunshine of Dost Mohammed's recent surrender, pooh-poohed the veracity of the many reports of discontent in the country at large. Again writing to Rawlinson, he observed:

> These idle statements may cause much mischief, and often repeated as they are, they neutralise my protestations to the contrary. I know them to be utterly false as regards this part of the country [Kabul], and I have no reason to believe them to be true as regards your part of the kingdom [Kandahar], merely because the Tukkeer are indulging in their accustomed habit of rebellion or because Ahktar Khan has a parcel of ragamuffins at his heels.[4]

Meantime, the western Ghilzais, never easily suppressed no matter how much they were thrashed or rewarded for their compliance, prompted the British authorities to hold their capital, Khelat-i-Ghilzai, with a force and strengthen its fortifications. The commencement of these works aroused the Ghilzais to anger as a permanent occupation of their capital was viewed as a direct strike against their boasted independence. The situation was fraught with danger needing only a small spark to blow up into open rebellion. This spark was provided by Lieutenant Henry Lynch, who was in charge of political matters in the area. Apparently he had been insulted while passing one of the Ghilzai forts and thought it proper to punish this insolence, so ordered a body of troops to attack and capture the fort. During this unnecessary skirmish, the chief and some of his followers were killed. Needless to say this stupid escapade ignited a Ghilzai revolt. When Lord Auckland heard about Lieutenant Lynch's actions, he had him removed from political service. Major General William Nott had his own caustic take on the behaviour of politicos. Writing to his daughters, he warned:

> The conduct of a thousand and one politicals has ruined our cause and bared the throat of Europeans in this country to the sword and knife of the revengeful Afghan and bloody Beluchi and unless several regiments are quickly sent, not a man will be left to describe the fall of his comrades. Nothing will make the Afghan submit to the hated Shah Shuja who is most certainly as great a scoundrel as ever lived.[5]

3 Archibald Forbes, *The First Afghan War, 1839–42* (London: C. Scribner's Sons, 1892; reprint London: Leonaur, 2007), p.30.
4 Durand, *The First Afghan War and Its Causes*, p.310.
5 Forbes, *The First Afghan War, 1839–42*, p.32.

It now became necessary to send a force out to reinforce the position at Khelat-i-Ghilzai, understandably the prime target for attack by the disgruntled Ghilzais. Lieutenant Colonel George Wymer, with 400 *sepoys* of 38th BNI, a squadron of Christie's Horse and two 6-pdr guns hurried off from Kandahar in the direction of Khelat-i-Ghilzai in mid-April. On 27 May the force had reached Eelme on the banks of the Turnuk and about 30 miles west of Khelat-i-Ghilzai, where it was attacked by a Ghilzai force of 5,000 led by a gentleman named Guddu Khan and known as the 'Gooroo', who was accompanied by Azmal Khan and Akram Khan, the chiefs of Tirin and Derawat. The Ghilzai attacks were relentless, charging the guns repeatedly, but were checked each time by the discharge of grape shot poured in at 50 yards, and after five hours gruelling battle were driven off by the fire discipline of the *sepoys* and the efficiency of the two guns. The Ghilzai casualties were heavy, but Lieutenant Colonel Wymer's force, having lost most of its baggage and carriage, was too weak to attempt any form of pursuit. The force eventually reached Khelat-i-Ghilzai in good order but utterly exhausted, where it joined the force under Captain Clement Macan of Shah Shuja's 2nd Infantry Regiment.

As mentioned earlier, Ahktar Khan in the Zemindawar district had broken his promise to the British and was now at the head of a rebel force 6,000 strong investing Girishk. On 27 June, Major General Nott had sent out Captain John Woodburn with a detachment consisting of 400 *sepoys* of Shah Shuja's 5th Infantry Regiment, 1st and 2nd *Jan-Baz* Cavalry and a troop of Shah Shuja's horse artillery to attack and disperse Ahktar Khan's force at Girishk. At daybreak on 3 July, Captain Woodburn's detachment arrived on the east bank of the Helmand opposite Girishk, at a ford which proved to be impassable and where the rebels had taken up a strong position. At this juncture Captain Woodburn sent Captain Thomas Hart with 2nd *Jan-Baz* Cavalry three miles up the river to a ford at Sumbeeli, which had been reported as crossable by cavalry. Captain Hart's mission was to cross the river at this point then move back along the west bank to the rebel position. It was Captain Woodburn's plan to move the remainder of his detachment further down the river to a ford, reported as only 'knee-deep', cross the river and then for him and Hart to attack the rebels on two fronts. But Murphy's Law now intervened. The ford that Captain Woodburn intended to use was not 'knee-deep', it was uncrossable. The planned coordinated attack unravelled. Fortunately, on his move along the west bank of the river, Captain Hart saw that Captain Woodburn had not moved, and assuming that something had gone wrong, stopped his own advance and returned to the ford at Sumbeeli, where by nightfall Captain Woodburn joined him. Meanwhile, Ahktar Khan had followed Captain Hart, at a distance, and had taken up a position on the west bank opposite the British position.

The next day the rebels, having crossed the river further down, attacked the British detachment. Suddenly the place was swarming with wild Afghans attacking from all sides, chaos reigned and some of the *Jan-Baz* became demoralised. The rebels came on fiercely and repeatedly and were pushed back each time. During this onslaught, Captain Woodburn ordered his rear rank to turn about, so that his force could fire both front and rear at the same time. For a similar action in Egypt, HM 28th Foot was granted permission to wear their regimental badge on both front and rear of their headdress.

Eventually, due to the clever employment of the guns, the tenacity of the *sepoys* and the onset of nightfall, the rebels were driven off just before a lack of ammunition would have been a huge embarrassment. British casualties amounted to 20 dead and 100 wounded; the rebels left 800 dead comrades.

Next morning Captain Woodburn moved his detachment across the river and moved down to Girishk, camping on the high ground to the west of the fort. As stated in Captain Woodburn's report:

> In both a military and political point of view, it would be of the greatest importance to follow up and disperse the rebels, but with reference to their numbers and the notoriously disaffected state of the cavalry, I do not consider that I should be justified in moving after them with a weak regiment of infantry, two guns and cavalry in which every confidence cannot be placed.[6]

General Nott was quick to point out his absolute displeasure at the behaviour of the *Jan-Baz* and his mistrust of them. He was not alone in his feelings. However, as the *Jan-Baz* were reckoned by officialdom to be the elite of the Shah's Afghan army, General Nott's disparagement and censure of them was received by Macnaghten and the Governor General with the greatest displeasure. Writing to Rawlinson on 5 September, the Envoy stated, 'You are unlikely to have Nott with you much longer. His conduct in respect of the *Jan-Baz* has elicited the severest displeasure of government by whom he has been declared disqualified for his present important command.'[7] Of the many engagements in which the *Jan-Baz* were involved, it would appear they behaved well provided the odds were in favour of their paymaster; in the more 'touch-and-go' scenarios, they invariably deserted and joined the enemy, their brothers.

Back in Kandahar city, while there were no overt actions of hostility there prevailed a distinct atmosphere of discontent. The local traders were quite happy with the increase in business and profits but the inhabitants were disgruntled and resentful at the continued presence of the stranger and infidel in their country. On the morning of 25 July Mr Gorman, Captain Rawlinson's writer, was passing through the bazaar when he was suddenly stabbed in the belly with a knife. While there were many bystanders who witnessed the assault, none came to his rescue, in fact they '*shabash*-ed' (gave hearty congratulations) to the assailant. Fortunately, a *sepoy* happened to be in the vicinity and bravely arrested the attacker, and he was taken to Captain Rawlinson. Later that day, Prince Timour ordered the man to be blown away from a gun, which was done at one o'clock that afternoon, about the same time as Gorman departed the land of the living. When news of Gorman's murder was received by Macnaghten, no doubt in terms indicating a deterioration in the state of affairs, the Envoy, while accepting that the fate of Gorman was melancholy, added 'but are there no assassinations in other countries?'[8]

Captain Woodburn's inability to pursue the rebels induced Major General Nott to despatch another force strong enough to finish the task, and he sent out two strong detachments. The first, under the command of Captain John Griffin of Shah Shuja's 1st Infantry Regiment, was sent to Girishk to reinforce Captain Woodburn and then to proceed to thrash Ahktar Khan into submission. The second, under the command of Lieutenant Colonel Robert Chambers of 5th Bengal Light Cavalry, was sent to the Ghilzai country to administer similar retribution on the 'Gooroo'.

6 Stocqueler, *Memorials of Afghanistan*, p.156.
7 Kaye, *History of the War in Afghanistan*, Vol. 2, p.128.
8 Kaye, *History of the War in Afghanistan* Vol. 2, p.127.

Lieutenant Colonel Chambers' detachment came upon the enemy at the Sheea-kotil Pass on 5 August, and even before he could bring up his infantry and guns his cavalry had chased the rebels up the hills and driven them off in all directions, leaving behind a good many dead and wounded. With his force defeated and dispersed, the 'Gooroo' surrendered and made his submission, but Azmal Khan and Akram Khan fled to their respective strongholds. Ten days later at Khawind, the combined forces of Woodburn and Griffin made contact with Ahktar Khan and his followers, numbering 5,000, at seven o'clock on the morning of 17 August. After a few well targeted shots from the guns, the infantry and cavalry advanced to the gardens where the rebels had taken up their position. After a couple of hours of fierce fighting and many of their numbers dead and captured, the rebels took flight. Ahktar Khan was again able to slip away.

The two victories won by Lieutenant Colonel Chambers and Captain Griffin had a calming effect. The Ghilzai power was considered to be broken and Ahktar Khan had fled to the Hindu Kush. Conciliatory terms had been sent to both Azmal Khan and Akram Khan to submit and pay their allegiance to Shah Shuja, but they answered with defiance and started mustering their followers for another struggle. So it was deemed necessary to send a large force, under Lieutenant Colonel Wymer with 38th BNI, to Derawat in the Tezeen Valley. Besides 38th BNI, Wymer's force comprised two 18-pdr guns, two 6-pdr guns, two *Rissaldars* of Shah Shuja's 1st Cavalry Regiment and two companies of 2nd BomNI. In addition, and en route, Wymer's force was to be joined by the force in Zemindawar under Captain Griffin, including the *Jan-Baz*. Lieutenant Colonel Wymer marched out on 11 September and accompanying this force was Lieutenant Elliott, the nominated political agent for this expedition. Many at the time thought that this move in a northerly direction was the expected demonstration against Herat.

A week later Major General Nott decided to join Wymer's force in the Tezeen Valley. He had earlier been expressly forbidden to leave Kandahar; it is not clear whether this was due to Macnaghten's concern for the security of Kandahar, or his greater concern about having a 'loose cannon' upsetting the locals. General Nott appealed against this restriction and was allowed to use his discretion which dictated that, with half his army in the field, he should be there in command.

The size of General Nott's force, some 1,500 strong, had so overawed the disaffected Afghans that the fight in them evaporated as many chiefs appeared in the General's camp to make their submissions. The General, reckoning that his presence was no longer essential, returned to Kandahar. However, Akram Khan had not come into the British camp, instead he vowed to continue his quest to annoy the British into eventual withdrawal. But in Afghanistan a weapon more lethal than a musket bullet or cannon shot was a well-placed bribe and for this, Akram Khan was betrayed by one of his own men. A detachment of *Jan-Baz* was sent out to capture Akram Khan at his lair, under the command of Lieutenant John Conolly and guided by the betrayer. To ensure that this man did not lead them astray, Conolly had his legs tied under his horse's belly to prevent his escape. A rapid advance brought the detachment to a small fort where Akram Khan was surprised, seized and carried back to the British camp. From thence the doomed man was escorted back to Kandahar to await the verdict of Shah Shuja. Apparently Macnaghten persuaded the Shah to make a terrible example of this fugitive chief, and the Shah ordered that Khan be blown away from a gun. The sentence was carried out on 23 October, and witnessed by Captain Thomas Polwhel:

> This morning I was witness to the most disgusting spectacle, such as I never again wish to see. He [Akram Khan] was a good-looking man of about 35 and walked steadily up to

> the gun [9-pdr]. When he arrived at the gun, the gunners commenced loading, putting in a double charge of blank cartridge only. The prisoner was placed with the middle of his back squeezed against the muzzle of the gun, his legs and arms being tightly bound to the wheels and carriage. When the order was given to the kotwal [policeman] the match was applied; the head, upper part of the chest and one arm were thrown upwards, turning over and over in the air, and falling about thirty yards from the gun. One leg remained attached to the wheel, the other was thrown one hundred yards to the right; the centre part of the body was scattered about in all directions, a large piece of flesh and entrails was sent over my head and fell in the citadel yard on the other side of the rampart.[9]

With the execution of Akram Khan and the submission of many chiefs, West Afghanistan was declared to be quiet, and arrangements were put in hand to have a brigade return to India via the Bolan Pass, but due to a sudden change in fortunes this did not happen. In fact, this brigade did not return to India for another year. The reason for this has its origins in the events that were unfolding in Kabul.

9 Anon., *Nott's Brigade in Afghanistan,1838–42; Being the Private Diary of an Officer Who Served in it from First to Last* (Bombay: Times of India Press,1880), p.45. On 10 June 1857 Brigadier John Nicholson, the Hero of Delhi, had 40 *sepoys* of 55th BNI blown from guns as hanging was too good for those who had murdered women and children.

18

Kabul 1841

By the time Shah Shuja's entourage had reached Jalalabad all was *couleur de rose*, and Sir William Macnaghten visualised a period of tranquillity enabling him to shape Shah Shuja's administration to an acceptable form based on western principles of governance. Shah Shuja also felt a sense of relief now that his main opponent, Dost Mohammed Khan, was in safe custody in India and his own position more secure. He felt less dependent on the infidel British and began to show signs of impatience with the Envoy's restraints on the exercise of his despotic authority.

While the atmosphere of calm prevailed in the salubrious climate of Jalalabad, it was a time of much activity with a host of 'welcomes' and 'farewells'. Major General Sir Willoughby Cotton had remained at Jalalabad to welcome and hand over to the new army commander, Major General William Elphinstone, to whom he confidently stated, 'You will have nothing to do here. All is peace.' Not recorded is what Brigadier Abraham Roberts may have said to Brigadier Thomas Anquetil on their exchange of roles. It could well have echoed Sir Willoughby's comment, adding, 'because you will not be allowed to'.

After an honourable tour of duty in Afghanistan, Lieutenant Colonel Joseph Orchard and 1st BER marched out from Jalalabad on their return to India. In their place the Envoy and army commander welcomed Lieutenant Colonel John Shelton and HM 44th Foot. Besides all these military exits and entries, a number of European wives had accompanied the convoys to join their husbands in the English-like climate of peaceful Afghanistan. Sir William Macnaghten, in reflective mood on 27 February, spelt out his vision of the future to Captain Henry Rawlinson at Kandahar:

> All things considered the present tranquillity of this country is to my mind perfectly miraculous long term. Already our presence has been infinitely beneficial in allaying animosities and pointing out abuse; but our proceedings must be guided by extreme caution.
>
> Rome was not built in a day – but I look forward to the time when His Majesty will have an honest and efficient administration of his own, though time must be distant, if ever it should arrive (certainly it cannot arrive during the present generation to whom anarchy is second nature) when we can dispense with the presence of our Hindustanee contingent. Here we are gradually ferreting out abuse and placing matters on firm and satisfactory basis.[1]

1 Durand, *The First Afghan War and Its Causes*, p.308.

However, all was not at peace in Afghanistan. Revolts were to occur in western Afghanistan and there lurked an undercurrent of resentment which was to break out across the far-flung outposts of the country, but, much worse, there was an insidious and ever louder chorus for economy from the baying bean-counters back in London and Calcutta. They had calculated that the Afghan venture was costing £1.2 million (£98 million) per year and the prospect of this continuing and growing caused them great anxiety. Early in the New Year Lord Auckland, writing to Macnaghten, started to apply the brakes:

> Money, money, money, is our first, our second and our last want. How long we can continue to feed you at your present rate of expenditure, I cannot tell. To add to the weight would break us utterly.[2]

His Lordship did not mention that he had already added to the weight of expenditure by launching the Opium War with China; a declaration not objected to by the wily bean-counters back at Leadenhall Street, for the simple reason that this war had been launched to protect their lucrative trade in opium, not some grandiose venture to civilise a wild, impoverished country.

In Calcutta Lord Auckland sat with his immediate advisers to review the correspondence on the situation in Afghanistan. Those reports from his envoy were unfailingly upbeat and invariably contained an assertion of Shah Shuja's popularity. On the other hand every other account, both civil and military, made it clear that the Shah had no influence whatsoever. However, as long as Lord Palmerston remained foreign secretary, the Afghan venture still had merit on the wider geopolitical arena, and as Lord Auckland had always trusted Macnaghten's judgement, this was not the time to withdraw his trust, especially as with the surrender of Dost Mohammed, the prospect of the country settling down to peace was good. Regarding expenses, Lord Auckland applied a band aid by squeezing £460,000 (£34 million) from the *Nawab* of Oudh.

When Macnaghten was last in Jalalabad during the winter of 1840, he had launched 1st BER on its last action in Afghanistan against *Syud* Moosteen of Bajour, and he was now to launch HM 44th Foot on its first action in Afghanistan. On 21 February a force commanded by Lieutenant Colonel Shelton, promoted to temporary brigadier, was sent out to coerce the Sangho Khail, a turbulent tribe in the Nureen valley. The one-armed Brigadier, a Waterloo veteran and strict disciplinarian and thus none too popular, split his force into two columns and in the process of 'coercing' the tribe destroyed over 100 forts suffering only nine fatalities, of which two were officers: Lieutenant Robert Pigou, who had accompanied Colonel Orchard's force the year before, was blown to pieces when endeavouring to force in, with gunpowder, the gates of one of the forts; the other officer was Captain James Douglas of HM 44th Foot, the acting AAG, who was shot dead standing next to his brigadier. On completion of its mission, this 'coercing' force made its way to Kabul, arriving there on 18 March.

In January, back in troubled Punjab, Prince Sher Singh had decided that the time was right to secure power from the disastrous administration of Rani Chand Kaur, known as the 'Mai'. Prior to his move he had approached Mr George Clerk, the British agent at Ludhiana, to seek British approbation for his bid for the sovereignty of the Sikh kingdom. As the Prince had shown his

2 Mount, *The Tears of the Rajas*, p.324.

admiration of the British on many occasions, and as he had the backing of much of the Sikh army including all Ranjit Singh's European officers, his success would not displease the British and would throw open the passage through the Punjab for British convoys. Hence, the Prince was assured of British support despite the fact that a similar bid only a few weeks earlier had been rejected.

Prince Sher Singh arrived at the gates of Lahore on 14 January with a large army to which he had promised an increase in wages. He forced his way into the city and the leading courtiers duly made their submissions. A joint appeal was then sent to the 'Mai' and her officers to lay down their arms. This was rejected and for the next three days the city and fort were subjected to an onslaught of shells resulting in the death of 5,000 souls. On 17 January a negotiated ceasefire was agreed, and the 'Mai' was persuaded to accept a handsome *jagir* worth nine *lakhs* of rupees in exchange for her relinquishing any claim to the throne. Maharaja Sher Singh ascended the *guddi* by the sword of his army which never let him forget it. He remained on the throne for the balance of the British adventure in Afghanistan. British forces on the Sikh frontier were reduced, and passage through the Punjab was no longer disputed.

Shah Shuja's entourage arrived back in Kabul on 15 April 1841 without anything untoward happening along the way. The new army commander, Major General William Elphinstone, accompanied by his ADC, Major William Thain of HM 21st Foot, arrived in a palanquin utterly exhausted. He was at once horrified at the unsecured layout of the cantonment and the ridiculous positioning of its supporting elements. It seemed as if the British had been intent on reproducing the kind of cantonment they had been used to at the peaceful garrison towns in India, where bands played military tunes in the evenings followed by dinner parties and concerts; everyone seemed to be quite oblivious of any imminent or even the remote possibility of danger. The cantonment resembled a 'Butlins' with Afghan forts lurking over it.

Elphinstone addressed his concerns to the Envoy, all of which were vetoed, except the building of a small fort at one end of the cantonment at a cost of £2,400 (£180,000) which was to house the army's reserve ammunition, but in mid June this was also rejected by the authorities in Calcutta. Consequently, from the outset Major General Elphinstone's efforts at assuming command were thwarted at every turn and due to his frailty of health and non-confrontational nature, he was never to impose his will on the situation. In any command this can be calamitous, and in Kabul it was worse because Elphinstone's staff, which could have propped him up, consisted of a collection of egoistical incompetents. His designated second in command was Brigadier Shelton; this martinet smelt the weakness in his commander on their first meeting and held him in utter contempt thereafter. The General's AAG, Captain William Grant, was lazy and arrogant; his DAQMG, Captain Henry Bellew, while a brave officer, was supercilious with it. Brigadier Anquetil was regarded as a 'compliant' colleague and not the 'alarmist' he had replaced. Hence, in the absence of a robust army headquarters, the authority of envoy Macnaghten was ever more omnipotent, and he revelled in it.

Major General Elphinstone's new command consisted of:

1st Infantry Brigade:	Commander: Major General Robert Sale
	HM 13th Foot
	16th Bengal Native Infantry
	35th Bengal Native Infantry
	37th Bengal Native Infantry

2nd Infantry Brigade:	Commander: Major General William Nott
	42nd Bengal Native Infantry
	43rd Bengal Native Infantry
3rd Infantry Brigade:	Commander: Brigadier John Shelton
	HM 44th Foot
	27th Bengal Native Infantry
	54th Bengal Native Infantry

A total of nine regiments of the line plus cavalry, artillery sappers, and the Shah's contingent, an estimated total of 28,000 troops.

In Calcutta, 1,700 miles away, Lord Auckland had received an important epistle from the Secret Committee of the Board of Control, the ultimate authority in all East India Company affairs. The Directors at Leadenhall Street, who had fathered the glorious expedition into Afghanistan, now wished to disassociate themselves because the expense was mounting, and based on the latest intelligence received about the insurrection in Baluchistan, Dost Mohammed's intrigues in Kohistan and the state of anarchy in Punjab, the prospect of an increase in expenses was most likely. The Directors, having spelled out their concerns, instructed their governor general to consider 'with utmost seriousness' the question of his future policy in respect of Afghanistan. In its view, the Secret Committee reckoned that the Governor General had two options, either to quit Afghanistan with honour having restored Shah Shuja to his rightful throne, or to remain in the country to maintain Shah Shuja's authority at whatever cost and for however long this would take.

Lord Auckland received this communication six weeks after it was written, consequently, in the 12 weeks that elapsed between the time of the events on which the Directors' comments were based and the receipt of their instruction, great changes had taken place: Baluchistan was under control, Dost Mohammed Khan was safely locked up in India and an anglophile Maharaja was on the throne in Lahore. In view of all these reversals and the reported tranquillity of the country that these had brought about, the Governor General and his council were presented with an excellent opportunity to opt for the first option which was to quit Afghanistan with credit, honour and the triumphant return of the British Army. To many at the time, including the Commander-in-Chief, this first option was a 'no-brainer'. To Macnaghten, the envoy in Afghanistan, to quit at this juncture would be an act of 'an unparalleled political atrocity', so despite the anticipated increase in expenses, the Governor General and his Council tabled a third option, which was to remain in Afghanistan to firmly secure Shah Shuja's authority until such time as the creation of an efficient national army.

In their serious consideration of the situation, the Governor General and his council reckoned that this was not the time to withdraw from Afghanistan, leaving a discredited void for the Russians to easily fill and by extrapolation endanger the very borders of British domains in India. It is conceivable that Lord Auckland, a devout Christian, was also motivated by Sir Francis Drake's prayer just before he sailed off to sort out the Spanish Armada: *O Lord, when thou givest to Thy servants to endeavour any great matter, grant us also to know it is not the beginning but the continuing of the same until the end, until it be thoroughly finished which yieldeth the true glory.*

The Governor General in Council sent its reply to the Secret Committee on 22 March. The following covering letter indicated the Council's unanimous decision, however it later transpired that the military members of the Council, both the Commander-in-Chief and Colonel William Casement, never great devotees of the Afghan expedition, were not included in the deliberations, but in any event signed the covering letter.[3]

> With reference to your Honourable Committee's despatch of December 31 last, on the subject of our position and policy in Afghanistan, we have the honour to forward, for the information of your Honourable Committee, the accompanying copies of Minutes recorded on the subject by the Governor General and the Honourable Messrs Bird and Prinsep. The perusal of these will most fully explain to your Honourable Committee, our views and sentiments in regard to the important question reviewed in your despatch above referred to.
>
> We have the honour to be, with the greatest respect, Honourable Sirs,
> Your most faithful humble servants.
> Auckland
> J. Nicholls
> W.W. Bird
> William Casement
> H.T. Prinsep

The commander-in-chief, General Sir Jasper Nicholls, while accepting the current tranquillity in Afghanistan, did not feel it would last without the presence of British bayonets and he reckoned that Afghanistan could not be held with less than three of Her Majesty's regiments and 10 native regiments:

> We cannot afford the heavy yet increasing drain upon us. 9,000 troops between Quetta and Kurachee, at least 16,000 of our army and the Shah's to the north of Quetta. The King's expenses to bear in every part, 28 political officers to pay besides Macnaghten, Dost Mohammed's allowances, barracks, a fort or two to build, loss by exchange etc. To me it is alarming.[4]

At the end of May, Captain George Broadfoot arrived in Kabul with his precious convoy of the wives, concubines, children and slaves belonging to the seraglios of both Shah Shuja and his blinded brother, Shah Zaman, plus 1,500 camels and hundreds of camp followers. In recognition of services rendered, Shah Shuja presented the Captain with a horse and a sword, prizes well-earned as the Captain and his Gurkhas had endured a great deal of opposition during their journey of 500 miles from Ludhiana from the obstreperous Sikhs. At Lahore, Sikh soldiery had enticed the Hindustanis of Captain George Broadfoot's command to mutiny. With the assistance of the Gurkhas under his command he was able to bring the mutineers under control, identify the ringleader and award him 50 lashes, which were administered on the spot. At this the abetting Sikhs withdrew. Meanwhile, four regiments of General Avitabile's troops at Peshawar had revolted and were lying in wait for Captain George Broadfoot's convoy. Approaching Attock, Captain George Broadfoot took up a strong position at the Gidargalli Pass and waited for

3 Colvin, *Rulers of India*, p.137.
4 Bruce, *Retreat from Kabul*, p.139.

reinforcements to counter the Sikh threat. Despite General Avitabile's efforts to bring the Sikhs under control, he failed and it was left to Broadfoot's friend Captain Colin Mackenzie, who was at that time the political assistant at Peshawar, to ride up the Khyber Pass to summon help from Brigadier Shelton's brigade. This help only got as far as Jamrud when the obnoxious Sikhs gave up their quest and returned to their barracks in Peshawar. In July, Captain Mackenzie joined his friend in Kabul and was put in charge of the Commissariat, where he developed a strong working relationship with Ali Reza Khan, a Kuzzilbashe.

Captain George Broadfoot's experience with the Sikhs was to leave him with a negative bias, which clearly coloured his dealings with them when he was the British Agent at Ludhiana prior to the First Anglo-Sikh War, 1845–6, which, some say, was brought on by Broadfoot.[5]

In July of that year, the Whig government of Viscount Melbourne (Henry Lamb) lost the election and Sir Robert Peel[6] sought the Queen's approval to form his first Tory administration. It was clear to all, especially to those in India, that this change would herald cutbacks, retrenchments and a big push for economy. To his friend, Sir John Hobhouse, Lord Auckland wrote and asked to be replaced by February 1842; meanwhile he was to live in the hope that the tranquillity in Afghanistan, espoused by his ever-confident lieutenant, was real. By August His Lordship had sought a loan of £5 million (£375 million) from the merchants in Calcutta at the high interest rate of 16 percent. Two months later, back in London, Sir Robert Peel, the Prime Minister, informed Lord Ellenborough (Edward Law), that he had recommended him to Her Majesty the Queen as the next Governor General of India. Lord Ellenborough was at the time the president of the Board of Control, a position he had already held twice before. Of Sir Robert Peel's recommendation, the Duke of Wellington was to comment, 'There is no doubt that Lord Ellenborough is better qualified than any other man in England for the office of Governor General.'

As the summer of 1841 drew to a close and the cool breezes of autumn heralded a freezing winter, it was not the weather that concerned the British in Kabul, but the chilling effect of

5 George Broadfoot had in 1845 replaced Colonel Richmond as the British Resident at Ludhiana: Governor General Sir Henry Hardinge wanted a man of strong moral courage, straightforward and resolute, on the border with a Sikh nation in mounting chaos. There was none better than the 'Hero of Jalalabad', Major George Broadfoot. However, this officer was paranoid about Sikh dispositions and intentions, and when a small party of Sikhs crossed the River Sutlej for legitimate reasons, he read this as a warlike advance by the Sikh nation and informed the Governor General that 'The Sikhs have crossed the river', thus bringing on the First Anglo-Sikh War.

6 Robert Peel (1788–1850). One of Great Britain's better prime ministers. He was born at Bury, the eldest of 10 children. He entered Parliament in 1810 as Member for Cashel in the County of Tipperary, a corrupt Irish borough. He later changed his Parliamentary seat to Tamworth, which he represented for the rest of his life. In 1820 he married Julia, the daughter of General Sir John Floyd, and they had 10 children. Their second son, William, joined the Royal Navy aged 15, and in 1852, then a captain, William was awarded the Victoria Cross. Captain William Peel died of smallpox while serving in India during the Indian Mutiny. Sir Robert Peel was appointed Home Secretary in 1822, and during his tenure he created the modern police force, known colloquially as 'Peelers' or 'Bobbies'. Sir Robert Peel's Tamworth manifesto of 1834 is seen as the basis of enlightened conservatism. In 1841 he and his party won the election and formed the very first Conservative government. His administration repealed the Corn Laws and introduced the concept of income tax. In 1850, while riding in Hyde Park, Sir Robert fell off his horse and died of his injuries on 1 July 1850.

a hostile population. The arrival of the British had been accompanied by an inflow of money, which caused inflation, undermining the position of the city classes and the ensuing resentment gave vent to abuse and even the murder of soldiers who had ventured into the bazaar alone. General Nott's expeditions against the western Ghilzais and Durannis had been worrying, Dost Mohammed's son, Akbar Khan, was stirring up the tribes in the north, and the prospect of Shah Shuja ever being able to control the country without British bayonets was being seen as remote.

In August the Secret Committee of the East India Company, now under the supervision of a Tory government, wrote to the Governor General about its grave concerns at the heavy burden imposed on the Indian finances by the cost of maintaining an army in Afghanistan and instructed him to considered finally abandoning the venture. In turn, the Governor General urged the Envoy to effect some retrenchment and it was decided to withdraw the tributes paid to the eastern Ghilzai chiefs. An annual subsidy (bribe) of £3,000 (£225,000) had been, on the accession of Shah Shuja, paid to the Ghilzai chiefs for their allegiance and the safety of communications with India. This subsidy was ostensibly paid by the Shah, but in reality it was a charge on the Calcutta treasury.[7] Why other expenditures were not considered, such as the reduction of the number of political officers or the tribute made to Herat, can only be attributed to the fact that Lord Auckland was adamant that the time had long passed for the Shah's expenses to be paid by him and for him to adjust his accounts accordingly. No doubt this desired state of affairs could have come about with time, but not to pay *Charon* at this time was not good policy.

At first, Macnaghten appealed against this deduction on the sensible grounds that this subsidy was compensation for the privileges given up of plundering the high roads through the chiefs' respective domains. His appeal was rejected. The chiefs were summoned to a meeting in Kabul at which they were informed of the decision to withdraw their promised subsidies. They received this news without any apparent discontent, but they were no sooner clear of Kabul than they made no secret of their determination to take the remedy into their own hands and issued instructions to invest the passes between Kabul and Jalalabad and to interrupt the lines of communications with India. Shah Shuja, aware that the withdrawal of subsidies would cause much agitation, sent out Hamza Khan to conciliate with the aggrieved chiefs. Why this person was chosen for this very delicate task is a mystery as he was one of the aggrieved, and fostered the revolt instead of suppressing it.

By the beginning of September further evidence of disquiet was reported to the Envoy as the chiefs in the district of Zoormat had resisted payment of taxes. Captain William Hay, the ex-commander of 4th Gurkha Regiment, was appointed to lead a force into Zoormat to coerce the chiefs into payment of their taxes. This force was to discover that it was not strong enough to coerce the tribes and was itself in distress. Macnaghten was not best pleased at this reversal and blamed Captain Hay for needlessly attacking a fort with insufficient means and so being compelled to beat a hasty retreat and sent out a bigger force under Lieutenant Colonel Thomas Oliver, who was to discover that the foe had fled leaving their taxes uncollected.

Shah Shuja, happily united with his family, was nevertheless discontented and complained he had no real authority, that the British managed all affairs leaving him a mere cipher. He had not

7 The editor of Vincent Eyre's journal states in his notes that Lord Auckland never knew, until after the insurrection, that the payment to the Ghilzais had been stopped and that the measure originated with the envoy.

been pleased at the removal of his trusted *Wazir*, Mullah Shikore, and felt that his replacement, Osman Khan, paid more heed to the Envoy's instructions than to his own. Clearly, the Shah was chafing under his close association with his restorers; as an Afghan, he knew that while his chiefs might accept a monarch supported by British money, they would never accept one supported by British bayonets, and he looked forward to the troops' early withdrawal. As the Shah's discomfort increased, so it would appear that the Envoy's confidence in him decreased and by mid-September Macnaghten was of the opinion that Shah Shuja was 'an old woman not fit to rule his people'. Left to himself and able to exercise despotic authority as all rulers in Afghanistan had done, he might have obtained the allegiance of his people by their dread of his power, but this was not possible because of the controlling and superintending power exercised by the British envoy. Then in September Shah Shuja fell very ill, and Macnaghten thought it expedient to have Prince Timour brought to Kabul from Kandahar. Besides the reason he gave Captain Rawlinson in his letter of 21 September, it is conceivable that Macnaghten might also have considered disposal, a manœuvre used by the British in India for unsatisfactory rulers of subsidiary states:

> His Majesty is ill of a fever which has been hanging about him for some time, the issue, to say the least of it, is very doubtful. It seems to be in the highest degree desirable that *Shahzada* Timour should be here in the event of a fatal termination of His Majesty's illness.[8]

Towards the end of September Macnaghten was informed that he was to replace Sir James Carnoc as the governor of the Bombay Presidency. This promotion for stalwart services rendered during the Afghan campaign was to a more lucrative appointment, which could lead to a peerage, and would keep Sir William peripherally involved in Afghan affairs as the Bombay government was the supervising authority for matters in Sindh and Baluchistan. As important as this appointment was, there was no official confirmation as to who was to replace Macnaghten at the much more critical position at Kabul. Sir Alexander Burnes was viewed by many as the automatic choice and the position had been promised to him in the event of Macnaghten's departure. Sir Alexander, refusing other appointments, had been marking time in a totally anomalous position, writing copious memorials on Afghan conditions to which no one gave much attention, least of all the Envoy. In a letter to his brother, Sir Alexander described his status as, 'I am now a highly paid idler, I lead however a very pleasant life, and if rotundity and heartiness be proof of health, I have them.'[9]

Now that the object of his ambition was so near at hand, Burnes had no hesitation in supporting the Envoy's conviction that the country was in stable condition, and to ensure that no reason was given to delay the Envoy's departure, he qualified his congratulatory letter to Macnaghten by adding, 'and at a time of such profound tranquillity'. On the other hand Macnaghten clearly had some reservations about the immediate future, as his letter of 3 October to Captain Rawlinson indicated:

> You will have heard ere now of my appointment to Bombay. I could wish that this most honourable distinction had been withheld a little longer, until I have pronounced our

8 Kaye, *History of the War in Afghanistan*, Vol. 2, p.136.
9 Bruce, *Retreat from Kabul*, p.142.

> relations in this country as being entirely satisfactory, but, thanks in a great measure to your zealous co-operation, I may even now say, that everything is rapidly verging to that happy consummation. No time is fixed for my departure. That will depend on the instructions I receive from Lord Auckland. Should his Lordship direct me to deliver over my charge to Burnes, there is little or nothing that I know to detain me, and I ought to be in Bombay by the middle of December. I am suffering a little anxiety just now, as the Eastern Ghilzai chiefs have turned *yaghe*, in consequence, I believe, of the reduction of their allowances, and their being required to sign an *ittezain* against robberies. We have sent to bring them back to their allegiance, and I think there will be no difficulty about them, unless the root of the *Fussad* lies deeper, and they are, as some assert, in league with Mohammed Akbar. In that case, it will be necessary to undertake operations on a larger scale against Nijrow and Tugao, in the latter of which districts the *Moofsids* [rebels] have taken refuge. They are very kind in breaking out just at the moment opportune for our purpose. The troops will take them *en route* to India and teach them a most salutary lesson.[10]

On 2 October Captain Alured Gray of HM 44 Foot and a friend had ridden out of Kabul for Peshawar, accompanied by an escort of 400 Afghan horsemen headed by Mohammed Azim Khan, who had been recommended by Burnes. This party was attacked by the Ghilzais at the Khurd-Kabul Pass on 4 October and had it not been for the loyalty and experience of Mohammed Azim Khan, Captain Gray and his friend would most definitely have been murdered. This information was given to Sir Alexander Burnes on 7 October and was the first positive indication that communications with India were being actively disputed.

Under normal circumstances the time had come for HM 13th Foot to be relieved and return to India after two years of campaigning. It was also logical that Sir William and Major General Elphinstone should take the opportunity to accompany it. However, the circumstances were not normal, as passage through the Khurd-Kabul Pass was being challenged by the Ghilzais, as reported by Captain Gray. Consequently, it was decided that a vanguard commanded by Lieutenant Colonel Thomas Monteith would first proceed to clear the Khurd-Kabul Pass, 17 miles from Kabul and known as the 'Jaws of Death'; and in the process they were to give the Ghilzai rascals a good trouncing. Prior to the vanguard's departure, Captain George Broadfoot was told that a detachment of sappers was to accompany it. Rather pedantically, Broadfoot sought to establish the role and composition of this detachment. Despite his efforts he was unable to obtain any clear directive from Lieutenant Colonel Monteith, Macnaghten, or Elphinstone, whose only instruction was, 'For God's sake clear the passes quickly, that I may get away, for, if anything were to turn up, I am unfit for it, done by body and mind and I have told Lord Auckland so.'[11]

Lieutenant Colonel Monteith's vanguard, consisting of 800 *sepoys* of 35th BNI, 150 *sowars* of 5th Bengal Light Cavalry, two 6-pdr guns under Captain George Dawes, a detachment of sappers under Captain George Broadfoot, a body of Afghan horsemen and the usual crowd of camp followers, moved out on 9 October and camped that evening at Butkhak a mile from the pass. Here, the chief of the Afghan horsemen was allowed to have some 'friendly' Ghilzais

10 Kaye, *History of the War in Afghanistan*, Vol. 2, p.154.
11 Bruce, *Retreat from Kabul*, p.148.

camp alongside them. The fox was in the coop, as that night the 'friendly' Ghilzais plus their comrades, the Afghan horsemen, attacked the unsuspecting British vanguard. After a harrowing night, the vanguard remained at Butkhak and awaited the arrival of the main body, commanded by Major General Sale, before proceeding through the Khurd-Kabul Pass.

Major General Sale's brigade advanced from Kabul at the crack of dawn on Friday 12 October. It made its way cautiously by occupying the heights on each side with skirmishers through the defiles of the seven-mile–long Khurd-Kabul Pass, at times only 200 feet wide and the track crossing the river 23 times, but in the process, the rearguard was harassed all the way and a good number of camels with their loads of baggage and ammunition were carried away by the raiding Ghilzais. After a laborious 29 miles the brigade reached the valley of Tezeen and preparations were made to attack the fort. Just as the troops were about to attack, the Ghilzai chief, Khoda Bakhsh, sued for peace and General Sale's political agent, Captain George Macgregor, had the General call off the attack while he negotiated with the chief. Macnaghten had great faith in the abilities of this officer and had especially assigned him to accompany Sale's force, confident that his protégé would solve all and any problem. The negotiations were spread over four days and the terms agreed were the restoration of the chief's subsidy and permission for Ghilzais to camp alongside Sale's 'trouncing' force.

This was the General's first error. His mission had been to clear the route to Jalalabad and that would have been better done by seizing the forts and breaking the Ghilzai power; instead, he allowed himself to succumb to political ideals of placating the rapacious and treacherous Ghilzais with 'wads' of money; totally out of character for 'Fighting Bob'.

On the following Tuesday, 26 October, General Sale, confident that the negotiated peace with the Ghilzais would hold, sent back to Kabul a detachment under the command of Major Charles Griffith to escort Macnaghten and his party, which was to include Major General Elphinstone, Captain George Lawrence, Captain Colin Mackenzie and General Sale's wife and pregnant daughter. General Sale then moved his brigade on to Kota Sang, suffering further losses of camels and baggage. At Kota Sang, Sale received information that the Ghilzais were concentrating to block his progress in the Puri-Dera Pass and at Jagdalak; Captain MacGregor gave no credence to this intelligence as he was convinced that his treaty with the Ghilzais would hold. Sale decided to avoid the Puri-Dera Pass and took the route to the south over the hills. Again, this decision was not in keeping with a general who had 'stormed' Ghazni. Had the brigade turned right at the mouth of the defile, it would have caught the Ghilzais in a hopeless position; not exploring this tactical option can only be attributed to lack of ground intelligence, and more probably deference paid to the useless treaty MacGregor had concluded with the Ghilzais.

The brigade reached Jagdalak, halfway to Jalalabad, on 28 October. By now many of the camels were dead-beat and a great deal of baggage had to be destroyed to prevent it falling into the hands of the Ghilzai marauders following on behind like a pack of jackals stalking a wounded prey. The next day the brigade moved through the Kotal-Jagdalak passage where the rearguard was given a very rough time. The brigade eventually reached Gandamak on Saturday 30 October where it halted for two days in order to regroup, reorganise and rest before commencing on the remaining 26 miles to Jalalabad, which it reached on 12 November. While Sale had been struggling through the gauntlet to Gandamak, the garrison at Kabul was enjoying a more pleasant life. Lady Sale's journal entry at the time gives clear evidence of how utterly unconscious they were in Kabul of the storm that was about to break. As late as 24

October Captain George Lawrence, the Envoy's military secretary, was to write in his journal, 'everything in the city then bearing the appearance of complete tranquillity'. That morning Captain Lawrence had had breakfast with Sir Alexander Burnes, who was reported to have been in high spirits and much looking forward to becoming the new envoy. The day before, Lawrence had attended the auction of Macnaghten's goods and chattels in preparation for the latter's departure, the auction of former army commander Cotton's paraphernalia having been held a fortnight earlier. As far as the residents of the cantonments were concerned, the Ghilzai obstruction in the passes was a local difficulty for which they would be thrashed and driven away by General Sale's brigade.

It was at Gandamak that Major General Sale received the news of the revolt at Kabul and the murder of Sir Alexander Burnes. He also received an instruction from the Envoy to return at once with his whole brigade to Kabul. At this point the brigade was 70 miles from Kabul and 26 miles from Jalalabad. To obey, or not to obey, the decision was Sale's. Out of character, the General chose to hold a 'war council' which considered all the factors and with the exception of two dissenting voices, Captains George Broadfoot and Henry Havelock, the decision was made for the General to ignore his superior's instructions and take his brigade to Jalalabad, in the opposite direction. This was not the anticipated reaction of 'Fighting Bob Sale' and one can only imagine the demoralising effect this had on the beleaguered garrison back in Kabul. What made General Sale call a war council in the first place, and on its outcome to disobey an order? There is little doubt that the General's personal inclination might have been to return to Kabul, if only to fetch his wife and daughter; however to do so would have entailed ordering his weak brigade to relive the past 20 days of running the gauntlet of Ghilzai attacks and a further loss of life, a manœuvre which would have totally demoralised his soldiers who were only too anxious to shake off the dusk of Afghanistan as quickly as possible, so rather than make it a command decision he sought a majority decision. In further mitigation it must be stated that a commander's prime responsibility is the efficiency, security and welfare of his own command. On receipt of the message at Gandamak, General Sale and his war council's interpretation of the call to return implied reinforcement not relief, and as the garrison at Kabul had more troops and resources at its disposal than did Sale, he elected to save his command. In fairness to him, General Sale least expected the Kabul garrison to be moribund.

Once safely in Jalalabad, Sale wrote to Elphinstone on 15 November giving his reasons for not complying with the order, which were an acute shortage of equipment and only one day's provisions, the encumbrance of 300 sick and wounded, insufficient camels to carry what he had left, no possibility of provisions on the route back and that the whole country was up in arms. In Jalalabad, the brigade was left unmolested for two weeks thus enabling it to fortify the place before it was invested by a horde of Afghans on 29 November.

As Sir William Macnaghten's departure, originally planned for 3 October, stretched out, there was still no official announcement concerning Sir Alexander Burnes' future and his apprehension is quite evident in the 31 October entry of his journal. 'What will this day bring forth? It will break or make me, I suppose. Before the sun sets I shall know whether I go to Europe or succeed Macnaghten.'[12]

12 Florentia Wynch (Lady Sale), *A Journal of the Disasters in Afghanistan, 1841–42* (London: John Murray, 1843; Uckfield: Naval & Military Press reprint, n.d.), p.43.

Had Sir John Hobhouse, the Whig president of the Board of Control, not been replaced by Lord Ellenborough in September, it is more than likely that Lord Auckland would have sanctioned the appointment of Sir Alexander Burnes to be the next envoy at the Afghan Court. However, with a Tory administration in control, Lord Auckland correctly assumed that it would clamour for total withdrawal from the expensive venture in Afghanistan and in such a scenario a competent military person with political experience would be a more suitable candidate, and Lord Auckland had met such a person during his tour to the North-West Frontier. He was the much admired Colonel John Sutherland, the current resident at the court of Rajputana.[13] Besides, His Lordship, who had initially been awed by Burnes, was beginning to have second thoughts about his young friend due to his imprudence, his instability in his nature and some very unsavoury reports, the likes of which undoubtedly upset His Lordship's sisters. Unfortunately, history was never to know what the long-term future held for Sir Alexander Burnes. Also, His Lordship was undoubtedly aware that a Shah Shuja–Burnes combination was fraught with difficulties as neither had a workable opinion of the other.

According to Sir John Kaye, the immediate cause of the outbreak in Kabul was a seditious letter by Abdullah Khan to several chiefs of influence, stating that it was the intention of Macnaghten to send them all to London. The principal chiefs met on the night of 1 November at the house of Sydat Khan, where, no doubt, they aired their grievances and plotted to challenge the *feringhee* authority; by his outrageous behaviour Sir Alexander Burnes had earned the enmity of leading Afghans and thus became the focus of their plotting. It was rumoured that Burnes had sent for and taken by force a beautiful Kashmiri girl from the house of Abdullah Khan who had intended her to be the wife of his son. Abdullah Khan had complained to Shah Shuja who had taken the matter up with the Envoy, but nothing was done and the girl was not returned. Staying with Burnes at the time were his brother, Lieutenant Charles Burnes, and Lieutenant William Broadfoot, the brother of Captain George Broadfoot whose younger brother James had been killed a year earlier in the Purwandurrah affair. The mansion they lived in was in the city centre, built round a courtyard and with a gallery overlooking the street.

Mohan Lal, who was Sir Alexander Burnes' main source of intelligence and probably his procurer of the stream of local women who were guests at his master's house, warned his master on 1 November that dangerous stirrings in the city were afoot and suggested that it would be prudent for Burnes Sahib to move into the cantonments. To the arrogant Sir Alexander such a step would only encourage the plotters and the concern it would raise would further delay Macnaghten's departure; besides, he was confident that he, 'Sekunder Burnes', could well handle any possible disturbance.

Then, at 3.00 a.m. on 1 November, Taj Mohammed arrived to warn Sir Alexander that the plotters had marked him for death before sunrise, but he still refused to take these warnings seriously. Minutes later, Burnes' *chuprassi*, Bowh Singh, met Osman Khan, the *Wazir*, riding in haste to the mansion, which was about 900 yards from the Bala Hissar. The *Wazir* told Sir Alexander that he and the two officers with him should move into the cantonment immediately, to which warning Sir Alexander replied, '*Wazir* Sahib, do you come here to tell me my duty?' At this juncture, Sir Alexander had a message sent to the Envoy for assistance. The *Wazir*, failing to

13 Colonel John Sutherland was 55 years old in 1843, and the British resident at Ajmere. He was to die of sunstroke five years later.

Death of Sir Alexander Burnes during the outbreak of violence at Kabul.

urge Burnes to withdraw, returned to the Bala Hissar through a small but ugly crowd that had formed up at the gate, led by Abdullah Khan. Very soon more and more rowdy Afghans joined in the disturbance and started to throw stones and sling shots. At the height of the troubles, it was estimated that there were some 300 ruffians clamouring for blood and plunder.

Sir Alexander Burnes, as brave as he was stupid, came out on to the balcony to address the crowd and promised them payment to disperse. Up to now the *sepoy* guard of one *Havildar* and 12 *sepoys* had been ordered to hold their fire. Burnes' pleas for calm were totally drowned out by the yelling of the crowd, which had now set fire to the gate and were storming into the garden. Then a shot rang out and Lieutenant William Broadfoot fell dead at Burnes' side. The *sepoys* immediately returned the fire and chaos reigned; Burnes now tried to offer money for his and his brother's lives. Amidst the firefight and confusion a Kashmiri man, who had somehow gained admittance, approached Burnes assuring him of a safe passage to a friendly Kuzzilbashe fort. Donning local garb, Burnes and his brother hurried after their benefactor, who, once they had exited the building treacherously shouted, 'Here is "Sekunder Burnes"'. In a flash, the brothers were cut down by Afghan daggers; the *sepoy* guard, in fruitless defence, were all murdered along with all the servants, women and children. According to all contemporary and subsequent accounts this was how the 38-year-old Sir Alexander Burnes met his end, however, unless he had been a closet coward, it was totally out of character for this gallant Victorian hero to have contemplated abandoning his post, which he had until then steadfastly refused to vacate, leaving his loyal *sepoy* guard to be butchered. Also, why would the astute know-all Burnes meekly follow a Kashmiri stranger? As there were no creditable witnesses to what actually took place, the circumstances are blurred to say the least. A more plausible and equally distressing account could have been that the gallant brothers and their guard had held out in expectation of relief that never came.

Killing the three British officers did little to diminish the crowd's bloodlust as they turned their fury onto the next-door residence of Captain Hugh Johnson, which also housed the treasury. Here they slaughtered the guard and servants and carried off the treasure. Fortuitously, Captain Johnson was not in residence at the time as, according to numerous accounts, he had spent the night in the cantonment. However, this officer's actual whereabouts and actions during the morning of 2 November were never questioned, and unlike the unfortunate CaptainWilliam Hay, he was never court-martialled for the loss of the treasury, amounting to £17,000 (£1.3 million), more than enough to have paid off the Ghilzais to keep the passes clear, and for not being at his post or attempting to relieve it. The houses of captains Robert Warburton and Colin Troup located on the same street were also attacked.

Back in the cantonments, 5,000 troops were sitting down to breakfast. Officers had taken their early morning rides and some had heard the commotion in the city, which was by now in a roar of wild excitement. At eight o'clock Macnaghten brought in Burnes' urgent plea for help to a gaggle of officers representing the esteemed Army Headquarters. This group of officers were more panic-struck than sparked for action, and their overriding concern seems to have been safety rather than action. Captain George Lawrence, there in his capacity as the Envoy's military secretary, suggested the immediate despatch of a regiment to Burnes' mansion and further detachments to the houses of the known refractory chiefs to immediately apprehend them. Later, Lawrence was to write, 'My proposal was at once set down as one of pure insanity, and under the circumstances utterly unfeasible.'[14]

The only action taken was to increase the guard at the commissariat to a subaltern's command and Ensign Francis Warren of 5th BNI was sent there to take command of 80 *sepoys*. Lieutenant John Sturt was sent to the Seah Sung Camp, two miles to the east of the cantonments, to have Brigadier Shelton move his troops immediately into the Bala Hissar, while Captain George Lawrence was sent to the Shah Shuja to alert him to the situation and the decided moves. The Shah, however, had displayed a lot more dash than his British protectors. His own regiment of 200 men, under the command of Colonel Campbell and accompanied by Prince Fateh Jung, had rushed through the narrow streets to the aid of beleaguered Burnes, but they had been horribly mauled along the way by fire from the rooftops and had been recalled by the Shah to avoid further casualties. On meeting Captain George Lawrence, the Shah exclaimed, 'Is it not just what I always told the Envoy would happen if he would not follow my advice?'[15] His advice had been that all refractory chiefs should be executed.

The Army Commander concluded the morning conference of constipated inaction with the comment, 'We must see what the morning brings and then think what can be done.' Oh for a commander with some dash and vim! As the Duke of Wellington held, when it was necessary to act, it was necessary to act decisively, ruthlessly and above all, immediately. Alas, Burnes and

14 Lawrence, *Reminiscences of Forty-Three Years in India*, p.62.
15 Lawrence, *Reminiscences of Forty-Three Years In India*, p.63.

Afghan Foot soldiers in what was described as 'winter dress'.

his household were left to their fate, while 2,000 yards away 5,000 troops did nothing and were oblivious of Burnes' fate until eight hours later.

A punitive and devastating attack by a vengeful British force had been anticipated by the leaders of the riot, and they had their horses saddled up to make a quick getaway, but as the hours passed and no action came, the apparent impunity fuelled the thirst for blood and plunder and the riot quickly became a headless rebellion. However, Macnaghten had been a little more proactive: he had written to Major General Sale instructing him to return to Kabul with his troops and to Major General Nott with orders to halt the return of Lieutenant Colonel James MacLaren's brigade to India and redirect it to Kabul. Sadly, neither was to happen. The gloom of bleak winter gripped the benighted British cantonment at Kabul, now cut off.

According to Sir John Kaye, Naib Sheriff retrieved the bodies of Burnes and his brother and buried them in the garden of the residence. However, Lady Sale has a different take on this issue. According to her, 'Naib Sheriff had been paid for the interment of Sir A's body, but it was never buried, and part of it, cut into many pieces is still hanging on the trees in his garden.' The events in Kabul were 'breaking news' in all the bazaars around, and the hot topic of conversation in the bazaar of Charikar. The unfolding of events at Charikar are covered in the next chapter.

19

Last Stand of the 4th Gurkha Regiment

The township of Charikar lies 40 miles north of Kabul at the mouth of the Ghorband Valley and the junction of several passes over the Hindu Kush. Roads from Charikar lead to Bamian, Kabul, Jalalabad and north to Turkestan. The town, consisting of a number of fortified dwellings, is watered by a canal which runs through the town south to Istalif, which is located about 20 miles south-west of Charikar. This area of Afghanistan is known as Kohistan. During the reign of Shah Timour many chiefs of Kohistan were exempt from paying compulsory land tax and were inclined to favour Sadozai rule, and as a result did not receive the same generous treatment from Dost Mohammed Khan, and who had put to death many of the chiefs.

At the time of the British 'invasion' of Afghanistan, and with the encouragement of Colonel Claude Wade's agents, the chiefs in Kohistan started an insurrection to paralyse Dost Mohammed. It was thought at the time that the Kohistan chiefs were well disposed towards Shah Shuja, however by the summer of 1840 the Shah's tax collectors and their petty tyrannies changed the mood of these chiefs; in particular that of Mir Musjidi Khan, a much respected chief, who had been offended by the British and who, inflamed by the mullahs, had come out in revolt against the dreaded infidels.

After Major General Robert Sale's campaign in Purwandarrah, some of the Kohistan chiefs were granted small stipends guaranteed by the Shah Shuja and sanctioned by envoy Macnaghten. It was also thought prudent and sufficient to leave a newly raised regiment of locally recruited Kohistanis at Charikar to keep the local population in awe of Shah Shuja's authority. This regiment was placed under the direction of the locally appointed Governor of Kohistan. This was in keeping with the Envoy's ideas of expanding the Afghan National Army, thus reducing reliance on the East India Company-funded military. Reliability of these locally recruited corps, when push came to shove, was not questioned, it was sufficient to get these corps on the ground and so negate the growing criticism of the Envoy's 'Rupee diplomacy'.

The task of raising the Kohistan Rangers and commanding them was assigned to Lieutenant Richard Maule of the Bengal Artillery. To assist him he had Ensign Francis Wheeler and a British sergeant. The site and location of the Kohistan Rangers was on the slope of a hill some 800 yards from the town of Charikar and 100 yards north of the canal, which was the regiment's only source of water. The regiment had wintered there, and during that time Lieutenant Maule was required to build a barracks for his troops with a walled perimeter, and this without causing any alarm in the construction of an impregnable fort. For supplies and provisions, the

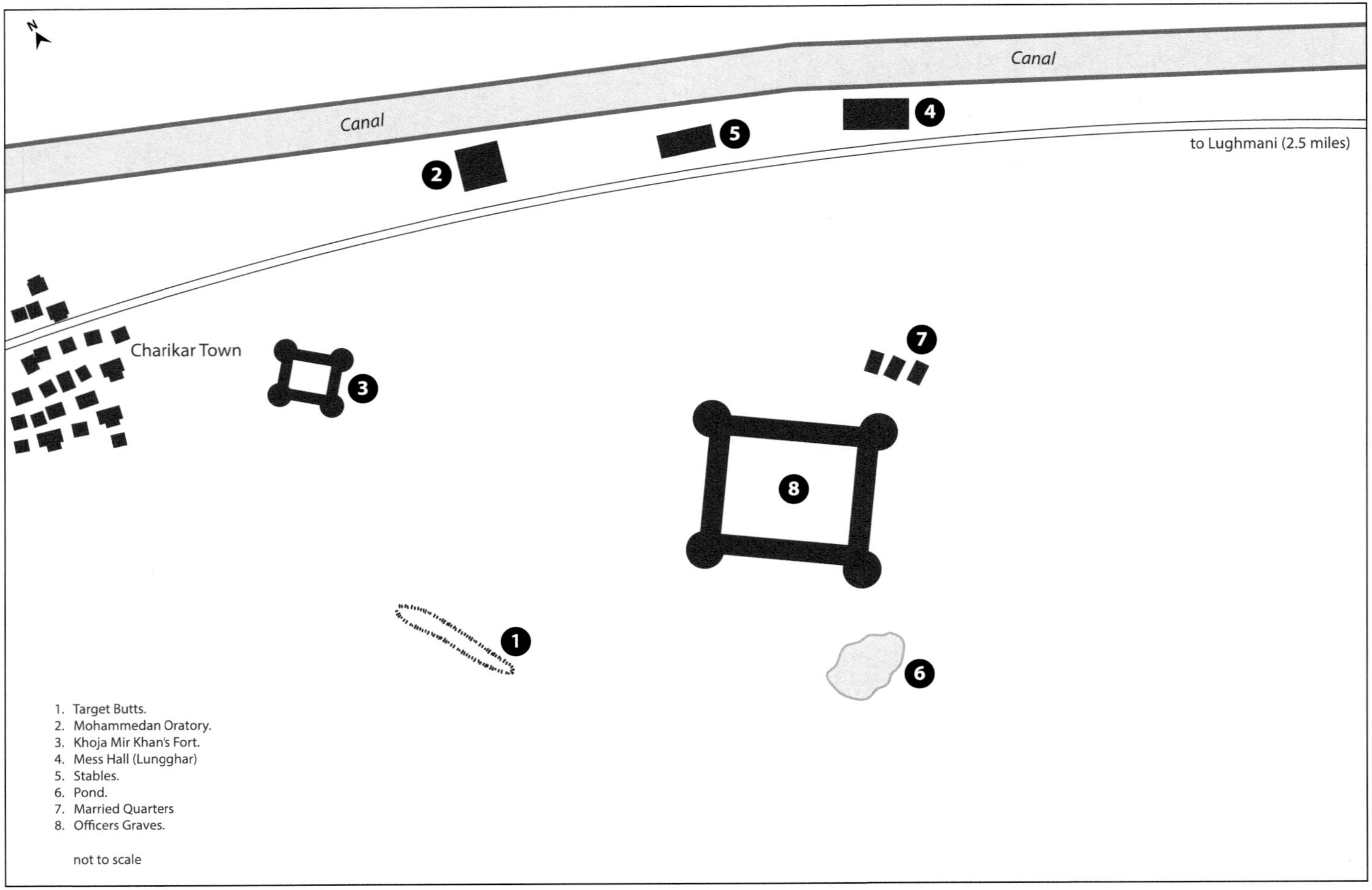

Map 12 Sketch of the 4th Gurkha Regiment position at Charikar.

regiment was dependent on purchases from the local bazaar. Two and a half miles south-west of this site was a cluster of four small mud forts at a place called Lughmani. These forts had been confiscated from Mir Musjidi Khan by Dr Percival Lord and were now occupied by the acting political agent, Lieutenant Charles Rattray, who had with him Dr George Grant and an escort of 150 Afghan horsemen. Bearing in mind that Kohistan already had a native governor appointed by the Shah, it is not clear why it was necessary to keep this outpost instead of handing it back to its aggrieved owner.

In the spring of 1841 the authorities in Kabul, apprehensive of the growing agitation in Kohistan, decided to replace the Kohistan Rangers at Charikar with the 4th Gurkha Regiment of the Shah's contingent and the Rangers were pulled back to Kalakan, about 20 miles from Kabul and 30 miles from Istalif.

On 10 May the 4th Gurkha Regiment marched out of Kabul on its three-day march to Charikar. The column comprised:

Captain Christopher Codrington – commander
Lieutenant William Broadfoot – second in command
Lieutenant John Haughton – adjutant
Lieutenant Edward Salusbury – quartermaster
Dr George Grant – Medical officer
Ensign James Rose
Sergeant Major Byrne
Quartermaster Sergeant Hanrahan
16 Gurkha officers
742 Gurkha rank and file
50 Panjabi Mussulman gunners[1]
240 Wives, children and camp followers

On arrival at Charikar, Captain Codrington was to find that the barracks had not as yet been completed and the regiment was compelled to live in tents for the first four months of their stay. He was also concerned about the indefensibility of the position and wrote to Kabul of his concerns, but to no avail. Instead, he was instructed to complete the building of only the barracks. In some disregard of these instructions, Captain Codrington did have round bastions built, similar to those of Afghan forts. Writing from memory, Lieutenant Haughton had this to say about their new location:

> We had four walls varying from seven to twenty feet in height, pierced by two gateways, east and west, with a row of flat-roofed rooms for the men all round the inside, except atone spot where were the officers' quarters. Unfortunately, as yet we had no gate for the eastern entry, or doors for any of the rooms. The barrack square was built on a slope, so that its interior was commanded by the trees bordering the canal in front, distance about 100 yards. It was also commanded by the high towers of a castle forming the southern

1 These men, all Muslims, were part of the Sikh contingent that had accompanied Colonel Wade from Peshawar to Kabul and were incorporated into the Shah's artillery under Lieutenant Robert Warburton.

> entrance of the town of Char-ee-kar. Its north, south and west faces were commanded by a Mahomedan oratory and a butt erected beyond reach of our muskets. In front, or to the east, the banks of the canal already mentioned, also garden walls, formed abundant shelter for an enemy; but in this direction, what was worse, was a small building, beyond the canal, which we ourselves had erected as a mess house, and a stable on the banks of the canal for our horses. There were also a low range of mud huts for shelter of our married sepoys; but these were built so as to be pretty well commanded from the barracks. Anyone acquainted with military matters will see that our arrangements were as bad as they could be. It is to be observed, however, that the slightly defensive character which our barracks took was in opposition to the intensions of the ruling authorities. The most rigid economy was the order of the day, and had it been possible to select and make defensible a position [which it certainly was], I feel assured the proposition would have been negative, and the proposer would simply have brought himself into disgrace.[2]

In mid-May 1841 the red carpet had been laid out in Kabul to welcome the Hero of Herat, Major Eldred Pottinger.. On being relieved at Herat by Major Elliot Todd, Lieutenant Pottinger had travelled to Calcutta to submit his report to Lord Auckland. Having done so, and instead of being sent back to Bombay, he was retained in Calcutta for nearly a year, no doubt, an advisory capacity and in the process was awarded a CB and promoted to Major, as it was thought inappropriate for such an award to be conferred on a junior officer. In late April, at his own request, Major Pottinger was sent back to Afghanistan in a political capacity to work under Sir William Macnaghten. In Kabul, Pottinger met up with his brother Henry and his friend Dr John Login; he also met with Major Todd, who was on his way back to India in disgrace, and no doubt commiserated with him about Lord Auckland's futile policy of conciliating with the likes of Yar Mohammed Kahn to the detriment of British honour.

At a prearranged appointment, Major Pottinger was ushered into the presence of Macnaghten, who gave his new colleague a much rosier picture of the situation than he had gathered from his friends. The Envoy denied the existence of anything like a national feeling among the Afghan tribes; not necessarily an incorrect assessment, but a common cause could unite even the more feuding of clans. In the Envoy's opinion, those who rebelled were 'ragamuffins' and 'rascals' and the British officers who took an unwarrantably gloomy view of the state of affairs were 'croakers'. Presumably, Pottinger's future role was discussed at this meeting and Macnaghten, loath to have yet another 'star' in Kabul, decided that the best position for Major Pottinger would be to take over the parish of Kohistan, a vacancy created by the death of Dr Lord.

Later, Major Pottinger paid a courtesy call on the army commander, Major General Elphinstone. The General was clearly a sick man, and one who lacked sufficient character to impose his authority on the situation, in fact he was Macnaghten's perfect candidate as military chief with no superfluous opinions to inconvenience the Envoy's conduct of affairs. His next port of call was to the commander of the Shah's contingent, Brigadier Thomas Anquetil, who had replaced Brigadier Abraham Roberts, long since manouevred off the scene. Brigadier Anquetil was a much more pliable character, quite content with bowing to the Envoy's bidding.

2 John Haughton, *Char-Ee-Kar and Service: With the 4th Goorkha Regiment*, p.19.

Naturally, no round of visits in Kabul would have been complete without breakfast with the renowned Sir Alexander Burnes. Here was a man who probably knew Afghanistan and Afghans the best, a man with superior means for local intelligence and best placed to remove the scales from the Envoy's rose-tinted eyes before it was too late. But instead, Major Pottinger found a man resigned to his own anomalous position, totally uncaring as to what was taking place and impatient for the time Sir William Macnaghten would be gazetted elsewhere, leaving him in charge to turn things round for the better. In the meantime Burnes, with good books, good wine and his coterie of admiring young officers, enjoyed a leisurely life. Burnes did admit that the chiefs had grown more openly dissatisfied and that the British were less popular than they had been a year ago. He advised Pottinger to keep his eyes wide open in Kohistan.

Discouraged by what he had seen and heard in Kabul, Pottinger was left with some serious misgivings and he wondered whether his services would make any difference but decided to give it his best shot. On 10 June he received his written orders and with an escort of 50 Afghan horsemen and his friend, Dr James Login, and his bull terrier, Caesar, he marched north to his new home at Lughmani in Kohistan.

At Lughmani, Pottinger met his new assistant, Lieutenant Rattray, and Dr Grant, both of whom gave him a thorough briefing on his new parish and the conditions that prevailed. Essentially the locals were out in their fields and a surface tranquillity prevailed. Pottinger then set upon a series of visits to the main chiefs as a way of introduction and informing them that he was there to discuss their needs and address their complaints. Naturally a visit to the Gurkhas at Charikar was at the top of his itinerary, where he met the commander, Captain Codrington, and discussed the military situation, the role of the garrison and the disparate need for 6-pdr guns. At the time the regiment left Kabul, a troop of Anderson's Horse Artillery was supposed to accompany them, but for some inexplicable reason this did not happen and despite repeated requests, the troop was never sent. Captain Codrington only had two 6-pdr guns and one old 18-pdr, manned by his Punjabi gunners.

In early August, Political Agent Pottinger sent his initial report to Macnaghten. In it he conveyed his views on the status of the countryside, the dangers he foresaw and a list of strong recommendations. Basically he felt that the local Afghans had not been subdued, that Mie Musjidi Khan continued to be a source of trouble in the Nijrao valley and that should any disturbance occur in Kabul, the British outposts in Kohistan would be attacked immediately. To keep the local population in awe, Pottinger recommended that a strong military force be placed in the valley as this would deter any serious attack if the enemy knew they would have to fight through against cavalry and artillery. High on his list, Pottinger recommended that artillery be sent that was capable of destroying forts. However, back in Kabul economic crunch time had arrived and instead of sending guns, Pottinger was instructed to reduce his Afghan escort, Dr Login was ordered back to Kabul and Lieutenant William Broadfoot was assigned to Sir Alexander Burnes as his military secretary. But most disastrous of all, Pottinger was to inform the chiefs that they would no longer receive the promised stipends, which amounted to a mere £3,000 (£225,000), equivalent to the salary Burnes received for doing precious little, this at the expense of alienating the chiefs against Shah Shjua, a monarch who if not totally acceptable in Kohistan was much preferred to Dost Mohammed Khan. Writing to Captain Henry Rawlinson, his agent at Kandahar, Macnaghten gave his reactions to Pottinger's report. 'Pottinger writes as if he is about to be invaded by the Nijraos; but I imagine there is little ground for this alarm'. As the Lughmani position was to lose its

Afghan escort, Captain Codrington agreed to send a company of Ghukhas to Lughmani, which was to rotate on a weekly basis.

As any overt troop movement was discouraged and expenses reduced, a friendly Barakzai chief was sent into the Nijrao valley to open negotiations with the chiefs there and in particular with Mir Musjidi Kahn; but as the days became weeks, the recalcitrant chiefs were further alienated by the petty tyrannies of the Shah's tax collectors and the locals became more daring. By September the mountain robbers became bolder and began to prowl around the half-finished barracks at Charikar, and the chiefs came to see Major Pottinger with many more complex complaints. To the most worthy of these he gave letters of introduction to the Envoy in Kabul, but some were turned away and returned even more resentful. In early October Major Pottinger rode to Kabul for a face to face meeting with Macnaghten to warn him that the situation was far from calm, and to convince him that something had to be done in order to keep onside at least those chiefs who had provided good service and had remained neutral during General Sale's campaign. He also recommended that on the return of General Sale's brigade to India it should be routed via Charikar, as this display of force could quieten things down, but Macnaghten did not cede to any of Pottinger's recommendations.

Instead, the Envoy explained that owing to complaints received from Company authorities, it was mandatory that the gross amount of expenditure had to be reduced by a third. However, Pottinger did get Macnaghten's permission to take hostages to ensure tranquillity. Pottinger returned empty-handed, and to the growing concerns of the officers at Charikar that something very wrong was going on. Captain Codrington was assured by Lieutenant Rattray that he would receive at least 24 to 48 hours warning of any hostilities. To Pottinger, one thing alone was certain: the local chiefs who had not long since revolted against Dost Mohammed Khan, were now ripe for revolt against Shah Shuja and his dreaded puppeteers. Back in Kabul, the Envoy again confiding in Captain Rawlinson, wrote, 'I trust I have at last got Pottinger into a pacific mood, though I tremble whenever I open any of his letters, lest I should find he has got into loggerheads with some of his neighbours.'

On 1 November a gathering of Kohistan chiefs appeared before Major Pottinger's little fort, to make friendly *salaams* to the political agent and to present some Nijrao men, who were said to be men who wished to help in putting down the rebellion in Nijrao. The next day a much larger crowd appeared at the fort and Pottinger urged them to attack the forts of those chiefs who supported Mir Musjidi Khan. On the morning of 3 November there was a gathering of 3,000, ostensibly friendly, Afghans offering their services and clamouring for rewards for their loyalty. But all this, it was to transpire, was a subterfuge as their main purpose was to lull the political agent into a false sense of security.

Later that morning, servants who had been sent on errands to Kabul returned in haste to report that the road was occupied by Nijrao rebels some 18 miles from Charikar. This was the very first indication that these rebels were active in the Shah's territory. As they were to learn later, Mir Musjidi Khan had moved from Nijrao across the plain of Barikat with thousands of followers and on the morning of 3 November had taken up a position at Aksarai, about 16 miles from Lughmani, thus blocking the road to Kabul. On the same day, the Kohistan Regiment at Kalakan rose in revolt, slaughtered their two British officers and sergeant and moved off to swell the ranks of Mir Musjidi Khan's rebels.

On receipt of the servant's information, Captain Codrington rode off along with a Gurkha escort to convey this intelligence to Major Pottinger and to receive his directions as to what action was to be taken in consequence. At Lughmani there was a huge crowd of Kohistanis swarming around the forts in an impatient manner. Leaving Captain Codrington in the fort, Major Pottinger went out with his *munshi* to confer with the leaders of the crowd, while his assistant, Lieutenant Rattray, went out to parley with an armed group of Kohistanis standing apart. Making no headway with the leaders, Pottinger returned to the fort. Regrettably, on withdrawing from the group with whom he had been parleying, Lieutenant Rattray was shot in the back; he still showing signs of life, the Kohistanis discharged a further volley of shots into his body. At this juncture, the Gurkha escort opened fire on the crowd and a firefight ensued. The odds were against the gallant defenders and unless they could be reinforced by the troops at Charikar, they would surely be overrun and massacred.

Back in Charikar, Lieutenant Haughton was anxiously waiting for the return of his commander when, mid-afternoon, he heard the sound of firing coming from the direction of Lughmani. As the intensity of the firing increased Haughton realised that the situation demanded, at least, a reconnaissance in force and that despite the fact that the Charikar position would be left under the command of two young ensigns, he would have to lead it. Haughton detailed his force of two companies of Gurkhas and set off to reconnoitre the cause of the firing and then to provide whatever assistance was required. Consequently, the route he selected was one that allowed his force to approach unobserved. On arrival he found that the attack was coming mainly from a walled garden on the Kabul side. His Gurkhas managed to reach the garden to the great surprise of the rebels, who fled in panic, many losing their lives in the process. Thus, the contingent at Lughmani were saved from inevitable disaster at a loss of a couple of Gurkhas killed and five wounded.

After this affair a decision was made which, with hindsight, would appear to be against all military principles. Instead of concentrating his force in a hostile environment, Captain Codrington agreed to double the Gurkha force at Lughmani to two companies. Clearly this decision was urged on him by Pottinger, who felt that he had to remain accessible to the locals and not discourage their approach by sitting in a fortified fort. On leaving Lughmani for his base at Charikar, accompanied by Lieutenant Haughton, Captain Codrington promised Major Pottinger that he would send a party out with supplies and ammunition from Charikar at dawn the next day and Pottinger undertook to send a party out to meet and guide the group into his fort.

At dawn next morning, 4 November, the promised supply relief left Charikar for Lughmani. In charge was Lieutenant Haughton accompanied by Ensign Salusbury, Quartermaster Sergeant Hanrahan, 200 Gurkhas, several *yaboos* loaded with ammunition and supplies, and one 6-pdr gun. There had been heavy firing during the night and it was clear that the rebels were still active around Lughmani. Lieutenant Haughton had been instructed to convey the supplies to a point where on being seen by the Lughmani lookout, a detachment would be sent out to take over the supplies; he was not, on any account, to comprise his gun or escort. However, on his approach Haughton observed a group of about 800 armed rebels on a hill to his right, which concerned him a great deal. Some years later, Lieutenant Haughton described the situation:

> The high ground passed Lughmanee at a distance of about 500 yards; by a sharp turn to the left, a narrow lane enclosed by mud walls led to the castle. It was foreseen that if we went down this lane, I might lose my gun and possibly not be able to return. I was cautioned against doing so. I halted and sent Ensign Salusbury with two companies, with

> orders to turn up the party who threatened our right, and to draw down to my rear if they appeared too much for him, as, when they came out of the broken ground, I should work on them with the gun. The enemy gave way, and our young soldiers pursued them only too precipitately. Bugles were sounded in vain, and orderlies were sent out without result. At last, seeing no other means of getting the men back, and observing how the enemy were swarming from all quarters, I sent Sergeant Hanrahan with a great number of my remaining men to bring them back.
>
> All this time I had remained within 500 yards of Lughmanee, waiting for the people who were to receive the provisions. They came at last, about ten horsemen, who, however, positively refused to return. Circumstances now rendered it impracticable for me to do anything but fall back on Char-ee-kar. When Salusbury rejoined me, the quarter-master sergeant and several of his party were wounded, and the firing had brought together the enemy from all quarters; the whole country seemed alive with them. When we commenced falling back, the men were disposed to bolt together, and it was with the greatest difficulty I could save my party by sticking up the gun, and with one or two faithful men loading it and firing it. The enemy's cavalry charged us, but as they were compelled to keep to the road, a round from the gun invariably turned them. Before we got over the distance, only three miles, poor Salusbury was mortally wounded, and our numbers much diminished. To wind up, when just within reach of the barracks, the trail of the gun gave way; but the enemy did not venture too close with us.[3]

In view of the developing situation, Captain Codrington put in motion all necessary measures for the defence of the Charikar position. Provisions that were available in the town were brought in and the old 18-pdr gun was placed at the eastern entrance that had no gate; lead from the target butts was dug up and put into little bags, sewn up by the wives, to be used in the guns, and nails and small metal parts were melted into little balls to provide extra ammunition for the muskets. Another concern of Codrington's was the absolute necessity of taking possession of the fort, which commanded the Gurkha position and belonged to a hitherto friendly chief. After discussions with the owner, Khoja Mir Khan, and with his agreement, 50 Gurkhas under the command of a Gurkha officer were moved over to take possession of this fort. Codrington's next big worry was the supply of water, and as it transpired, an enduring one. As much water as could be stored was brought in from the canal. The Afghans realising the importance of this water supply, shut it off by redirecting the water elsewhere; now the Charikar force was entirely dependent on the remaining pools of water in the canal bed and the water in the pit near the barracks from where they had taken the mud to build the walls. Besides all these concerns, a check revealed that the force only had seven days supply of rations and about 200 rounds of ammunition per musket. For the 6-pdr gun they had 120 rounds of shot and eight rounds for the 18-pdr gun. Codrington retained the vain hope that help would soon be sent from Kabul; he was unaware that this source of help was, at this time, in as dire straits as himself.

Meanwhile, back in Lughmani, Major Pottinger had concluded that his position there was no longer tenable and that a second attempt at relief from Charikar would be highly unlikely. While his Gurkhas were putting up a staunch defence under gruelling rebel fire, the rebels had

3 John Haughton. 'Char-Re-Kar and Service: With the 4th Goorkha Regiment', p 24

advanced to the very walls of the fort and the inevitability of the place being overrun was not far off. A moonlight flit to Charikar was the only option and orders were issued to this effect. But sadly, in what must have been an atmosphere of overcharged excitement, noise and anxiety, some of the Gurkhas did not get the word and were left behind in their gallant but worthless defence of their positions. Also left behind was the political agent's treasure chest, of greater value than the saving made in the reduction of his escort. Before his departure, Pottinger sent an urgent message for help to Kabul. With a new moon above, Pottinger's group crept out through the postern gate and with a Gurkha officer leading, made its way, very stealthily, past the investing posts, over the rough terrain of the three miles to Charikar. As Pottinger entered the gate he was greeted by Captain Codrington. 'Thank God you made it!' Then Dr Grant was ushered into the room where Ensign Salusbury, in great pain, lay mortally wounded having been shot in the back and stomach. After his examination, Dr Grant's prognosis was that the wretched subaltern did not have long to live. That night the officers sat around discussing the withdrawal from Lughmani and their situation at Charikar. While not downhearted, they were concerned about the Gurkhas left behind at Lughmani and each expressed a hope that they would, somehow, find their way back. Many did, two nights later.

During their discussion a key decision was made as to who was to assume command of the Charikar position. Major Pottinger outranked them all and could by seniority assume command, but they concluded that by the rules of the service he could not do so as he was there in his capacity of political agent and also of the Bombay Army. While Captain Codrington was still bound to act under Pottinger's instructions in any intercourse with the Afghans, he was the military commander, so all military authority continued with the officers of the regiment. This is an important clarification as quite a number of the campaign's earlier historians erroneously attributed command at Charikar to Major Pottinger. It was Captain Codrington who commanded, and on his death Lieutenant Haughton. It is noteworthy that Pottinger never claimed this distinction for himself, however the good Major did offer his services as an artillery officer, to superintend the small artillery capacity of the force, which was gratefully accepted.

With the abandonment of Lughmani, it was quite clear that the rebels would now concentrate their efforts to take the Gurkha position at Charikar, and Captain Codrington issued the necessary orders for the stronger defence of their position. As expected, on the morning of 5 November thousands of Kohistanis swarmed around their objective and had taken a position on the canal where the stables and mess hut were and from here, with their long *jezails*, caused a great deal of damage. As the remaining puddles of water in the canal were a primary source of water, it was of vital importance that the rebels were driven off and the place retaken. Lieutenant Haughton was ordered to lead a sortie to do just that, which he did and the position was held for most of the day.

As disorganised as the rebels were, their incessant firing began to take its toll. That afternoon, amidst a crackle of musketry, Captain Codrington staggered back shot through the chest, he could hardly speak and was carried to his bunk; and worse, a little later Major Pottinger received a bullet in his thigh. Dr Grant did the best he could for both officers, but in the first case the patient's condition was beyond his medical expertise and in the case of Pottinger, the doctor did not have the appropriate instrument to extract the bullet. So both his patients were left on their bunks in great pain, *hors de combat*. Dr Grant's other officer patient, Ensign Salusbury, died that afternoon and Captain Codrington followed his brave subaltern that evening. News of the commander's death was kept secret for as long as possible as it would definitely affect the morale of the soldiers. So it was in the dark that a pit was dug towards the centre of the square and as Dr Grant read out the Lord's Prayer, the bodies of both officers and that of Sergeant Byrne, who had been shot dead that morning, were laid to rest. By evening the Gurkha numbers were cruelly diminished with more than 200 dead or wounded. In what appeared to be the good Lord's conciliation to the beleaguered garrison, it rained that night and all available utensils were brought out to capture all that they could of this precious liquid.

The next morning the bugler sounded reveille, announcing the beginning of another gruesome day. The Gurkhas manned their posts and Lieutenant Haughton, now the commander, took up his post at the gateless eastern entrance with a keen hope that relief would surely come, but this hope grew fainter as the siege progressed. That night the wounded Major Pottinger sent two armed Gurkhas with a message for the Envoy pleading for immediate help. It was later ascertained that these two men did get through to deliver the message into Macnaghten's hands. At the end of the campaign the two Gurkhas presented themselves to Haughton, and on his strong recommendation they were awarded the Indian Order of Merit.

By the night of 6 November, Haughton decided that it was futile to expend any more ammunition than essential, or yet more precious lives in attempting to hold any outpost other than Khoja Khan's fort. This gave the reduced garrison half the space to protect, and, as the canal was now empty the positions near it had lost their value. As the sun set so the Afghan *jezails* became silent except for the odd shot to let the garrison know that they were still around, albeit many men had returned to their dwellings for breakfast, it being the time of Ramadan.

The next day, the bugler sounded reveille as usual and the remaining combatants readied themselves for the next hail of Afghan bullets. During the course of the day Lieutenant Haughton discovered that from the position of the mess hut the Afghans were causing a great nuisance by firing through the open gate into the square. A most effective and hurried solution was put in place. Using Ensign Salusbury's tent, a screen was erected, thus eliminating targets for the Afghans to aim at. He then discovered that firing was coming from Khoja Mir's fort. This was indeed grave news as it could only mean that the Gurkha detachment placed there had been overrun. What actually happened was that the interpreter, a Muslim who had accompanied the Gurkhas, had convinced the Gurkha officer in charge to surrender, as with only 50 men, already dying of thirst, they would be unable to hold back the Afghans. Instead of abandoning the fort in a fighting retreat back to the barracks, the Gurkha officer surrendered, thus giving the Afghans a huge advantage.

On the morning of 8 November two chiefs approached the position and indicated that they had come to negotiate with the political agent. They were duly ushered in see Major Pottinger, and informed him that they had come with a message from Shah Shuja ordering them to expel the garrison. Pottinger told them that if they could produce the Shah's order, he would evacuate the place immediately. After this, and during the next few days, a number of such deputations came in to negotiate terms of surrender, each time becoming more audacious in their demands. Both Pottinger and Haughton felt that it was utterly futile to treat with these chiefs and in any case with 5,000 troops only three marches away, relief would surely come. That evening they buried 44 Gurkhas in a big pit that had been dug to build a tank. The dead animals were quartered and slung over the wall for further removal, which never took place and the resulting stench was to become unbearable.

As the sun rose the next day, to the great joy of Lieutenant Haughton and the whole garrison, it was reported that in the distance there was a cloud of dust coming from the direction of Kabul which could only mean that a body of horse was galloping to their rescue. But alas, as the cloud of dust drew nearer, all joy and excitement was shattered as the cloud of dust turned out to be nothing more than a herd of cows. At this revelation Lieutenant Haughton gave up all hope of ever being relieved. That evening, a *Synd* from Istalif came in with the news about Kabul, that Sir Alexander Burnes was dead, guns had been captured and there was fighting each day. Major Pottinger conferring with Haughton, decided that they had to hold out for as long as possible thus forcing thousands of Afghans to remain in the area, otherwise they would flock to Kabul and swell the ranks of the rebels there. The next day the last drops of water from the mud pit were brought in and rationed to the fighting men only. While there was a sufficiency of food, any hope of holding on at Charikar for much longer would be impossible without water.

Some desperate Gurkhas had slipped over the wall, and by avoiding the Afghan sentry posts had managed to get around behind the town to where the canal had been cut and there had their fill and returned with some water to share with their families. Based on this intelligence, Haughton organised a party of water carriers and escort to do the same for the benefit of the whole garrison, estimating that they could bring back up to two days supply. Ensign Rose and the best Gurkha officer were put in charge of the sortie and given a detailed briefing of the route, the points to be held until the water carriers returned, and above all, the necessity of maintaining absolute silence. The sortie arrived at its objective without mishap, but once within reach of the water the men became disorganised, rushing to drink until their bellies were full. The containers were filled and now, instead of retracing their silent approach, the men clamoured to make good this opportunity of taking the enemy unawares. Since Ramadan, the Afghans had been less vigilant at night and Ensign Rose's men found a big group of Afghans asleep without any sentry. The Gurkhas fired one volley and followed up with *kukris* to finish the job. Now, fearful of retaliation, the Gurkhas rushed back to the barracks, bringing a variety of battle trophies, but very little water. While the Gurkhas soldiers reckoned they had earned a victory, Lieutenant Haughton assessed the mission a failure.

By now, with no hope of relief and no water there was murmuring in the ranks and morale was at a low ebb. It was also reported that one of the Punjabi Mussulmen had deserted and that the rest of the artillerymen were likely to follow him. Lieutenant Haughton was now to question whether he was serving any real purpose by hanging on to his beleaguered position. He had lost half his number killed or wounded; there remained little more than 350 worn-out men under arms, 150 women and children plus an assortment of camp followers, all thirsting for water. The hard choice was to remain and eventually be overrun, or to attempt a withdrawal to join the garrison at Kabul.

The next day, 13 November, the Afghans were quieter than usual and Lieutenant Haughton saw a man approaching the barracks. He was informed by the *Subardar* of the artillery that the man was a deserter who, no doubt, was being sent back to make terms. Haughton walked out and grabbed the man by the scruff of the neck to bring him in. The man fell to the ground causing Haughton to bend down. At that moment, the *Subardar* had grabbed Ensign Rose's sword and with it struck Haughton a tremendous blow on the back of his neck. With repeated blows, he fractured an arm and almost severed Haughton's right hand. Some Gurkhas rushed to the rescue and with their *kukris* laid low the *Subardar* and the deserter. In the melee the remaining Punjabi artillerymen rushed out of the gate to join the rebels. The Gurkhas brought in the seriously wounded Haughton and placed him on his bunk in great pain. The quiet of 10 minutes ago was now broken by Afghan fire from all sides. It was quite clear that this episode had been pre-planned with the killing of the British commander and in the consequent confusion, the position to be taken by escalade.

On being informed of Haughton's condition and hearing the volume of enemy fire, Major Pottinger had men carry him to the gate, where, with the help of Dr Grant, the old 18-pdr gun was brought into play and effectively halted the rebels' confident advance. The immediate danger was averted, but only for a short while. It was clear to the officers that their position was untenable and a retreat of over 40 miles, outnumbered as they were, was a slightly better alternative than to be slaughtered where they stood.

A council of officers was held in Major Pottinger's room. The two main issues were what was to be done with the non-walking wounded, and the route to be taken. With only one *dhooli* available, it was decided that the non-walking wounded would have to be left behind and take their chances with the Afghans. As both Major Pottinger and Dr Grant had travelled the route to Kabul many times, the route selected by them was a line skirting the mountains as it would give the best chance of escape and a good chance of water along the way.

The decision to withdraw was kept a secret for fear of causing unnecessary panic. Arrangements were made for Quartermaster Sergeant Hanrahan to spike the guns soon after sunset. When all was ready, Dr Grant amputated Haughton's right hand at the wrist and stitched the stump with a needle and thread. In his journal Haughton stated, 'The smell of ether luckily had been too powerful, and a drink of it revived me.' This could be one of the earliest records of anaesthetic being used by the British Army in a battlefield situation.

The force was divided into two groups, one to leave by the main gate and the other by the postern gate. Lieutenant Haughton, mounted on a horse with a man on either side holding him up, was to led through the postern gate. The two groups were then to assemble on what had been the parade ground, to the south of the barracks. Here the advance party, including Pottinger and Haughton, set off in the direction of Istalif, and the main body, which included Dr Grant, Ensign Rose and Quartermaster Sergeant Hanrahan, was to follow. However, in the dark not all of this group had assembled, so Dr Grant went back to fetch them. He never returned. After about four miles the advance party came upon some water and rushed to quench their thirst. As speed and secrecy were essential for any success, Major Pottinger urged the party to move on, but a number of them did not. By now, contact with or evidence of the main body, which was supposed to follow the same route, was lost.

As the sun was about to rise on the first morning of their departure, the wounded bugle major, with much effort, crawled up to the bastion and sounded reveille, a signal to the Afghans that the dreaded infidels were still in occupation and ready for the day's duel. Five days later, two wounded officers on exhausted horses with a Gurkha orderly and Caesar the dog, representing the sole survivors of the Charikar garrison, gave their names to the British sentry at the Kabul cantonment and were hurried to the hospital to be attended to by Dr Alexander Bryce. Their safe arrival was greeted with much joy except by, most probably, Macnaghten, who realised that the belligerent Kabulis would now be joined by the boisterous Kohistanis.

It was later ascertained that on Dr Grant's return to the barracks he found that a group of Gurkhas, mainly families and camp followers, had taken the direct route to Kabul and he was unable to bring them back. He stayed with this group and later when the Afghans realised that the post had been abandoned, the group was surrounded by Afghans and killed or taken prisoner. Dr Grant was hacked to death with an axe.

Ensign Rose, Quartermaster Sergeant Hanrahan and Gurkhas had followed the same route as the advance party as far as Istalif, but then the mistakenly took a pass that was infested with Afghans, who surrounded the group. They put up a good fight and except for about 50 who were taken as prisoners, the rest, including Rose and Hanrahan, were butchered.

During the remainder of the campaign, and after Major General George Pollock had retaken Kabul, many Gurkhas who had escaped came in to Jalalabad and Kabul. At the end of the campaign it was recorded that as many as 165 Gurkhas of the 4th Gurkha Regiment were classified as survivors and awarded the Afghan War Medal.

Mir Musjidi Khan, the Khoistani rebel leader, duly took his followers to Kabul, where later, through the agency of Mohan Lal, an Afghan was bribed to poison the Khan, who to this day is revered as a hero and martyr.

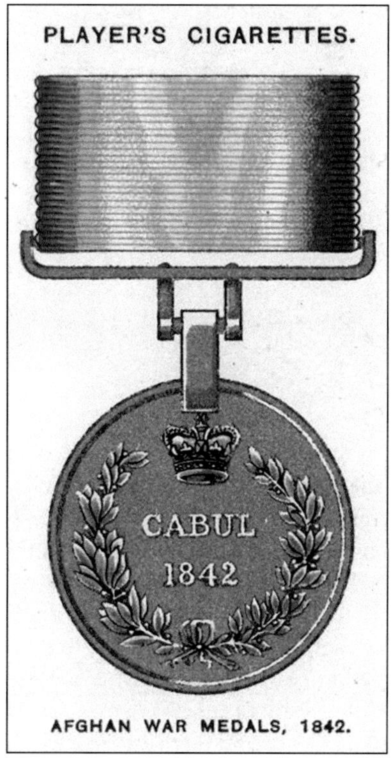

Reserves of Afghan War Campaign Medal (technically The Candahar, Ghuznee, Cabul Medal).

20

Kabul Countdown

The absence of any effective response from the Kabul garrison on that fateful day of 2 November was more than shameful, it bordered on criminality. Heightened tensions in the city had been obvious to all and particularly to those in top positions of responsibility, who had been repeatedly warned, yet, while claiming to be alert to the situation, had deemed it under control, or wished it to be so in order that planned departures and elevation to higher office would not be marred by reality. At the very top was Sir William Macnaghten, the envoy, who had had no hesitation, as recently as six weeks before, in sending out a strong force under Lieutenant Colonel Thomas Oliver, to thrash the refractory chiefs at Zoormat. Yet, as the current crisis gloomed ever darker, the Envoy, who had up to now been resourceful, dictatorial and pugnacious, slumped into political apathy. At this point the situation required the political authority to hand over to the military to nip the disturbance in the bud and to have it handed back once the situation had calmed down, but the hapless army commander, Major General William Elphinstone, who had that day fallen off his horse, seemingly had no desire to accept this authority nor the responsibility. Macnaghten and his wife had already moved into a tent within the cantonment, not many yards from Army Headquarters, and instead of being in the army commander's pocket, he chose to correspond with him in writing, thus allowing any sound advice to be diluted by pointless discussions with officers who clearly lacked British pluck. All appeared to be paralysed by the sudden outbreak and from this day forward the British garrison's stay in Kabul was on countdown.

Wednesday 3 November

The alarm was sounded at 3:00 a.m. as a large body of men were heard to be approaching from the Seah Sung heights. This supposed threat came within artillery range, and to the great joy of the whole garrison the body of men turned out to be Major Charles Griffiths with 37th BNI, who had answered the urgent call to return to Kabul from Khurd-Kabul. The regiment had been harassed all the way back by no fewer than 3,000 Ghilzais and still managed to return with all its baggage and camp followers. While the regiment reinforced the garrison with more bayonets, it also increased the logistical needs. It also meant that this regiment, which had been earmarked to return to India in October, was never to get there.

Afghan's manhandling a gun into position. Kabul is in the background. Beyond is the British cantonment.

During the morning, more guns were sent to the Bala Hissar from where Brigadier John Shelton was ordered to fire on the city, and 'should he find it practical, to send a force into the city'. However while his guns fired aimlessly into the city he made no attempt to enter it. That afternoon Major Stephen Swayne with two companies of 5th BNI, one company of HM 44th Foot and two guns under Lieutenant Thomas Walker was sent out to make a junction at the Lahore gate of the city with a corresponding force sent from the Bala Hissar. Unfortunately Swayne was given the wrong rendezvous and went to the Kohistan gate two miles away. The purpose of this manœuvre was to secure the line of communication between the Bala Hissar and the cantonments, a distance of one and a half miles.

Along the way, Swayne's detachment was opposed by fierce fire from the Kohistan gate and Mohammed Khan's fort, and as there was no sign of any force from the Bala Hissar Swayne retraced his steps, under constant fire, back to the cantonments, with a loss of 20 men. The action proved to be a thorough waste of time and effort, signifying bad staff work. Meanwhile, Macnaghten had sent urgent messages to both major generals Sale and Nott to hurry to the garrison's relief. Unfortunately, the message to Major General William Nott at Kandahar did not arrive until 14 November, and the many messages sent to Major General Robert Sale were not heeded. The Envoy also sent his nephew, Lieutenant John Conolly, to the Bala Hissar in the capacity of liaison officer to Shah Shuja. At this time the all-important Commissariat was located in a rat-infested fort some 400 yards south of the cantonments, and manned by Ensign Francis Warren and 80 men. Between it and the cantonments was the Mohammed Sharif fort, unoccupied and only 150 yards from the cantonment ramparts. One hundred yards beyond the Commissariat was the Mohammed Khan fort. No immediate action was taken to secure either

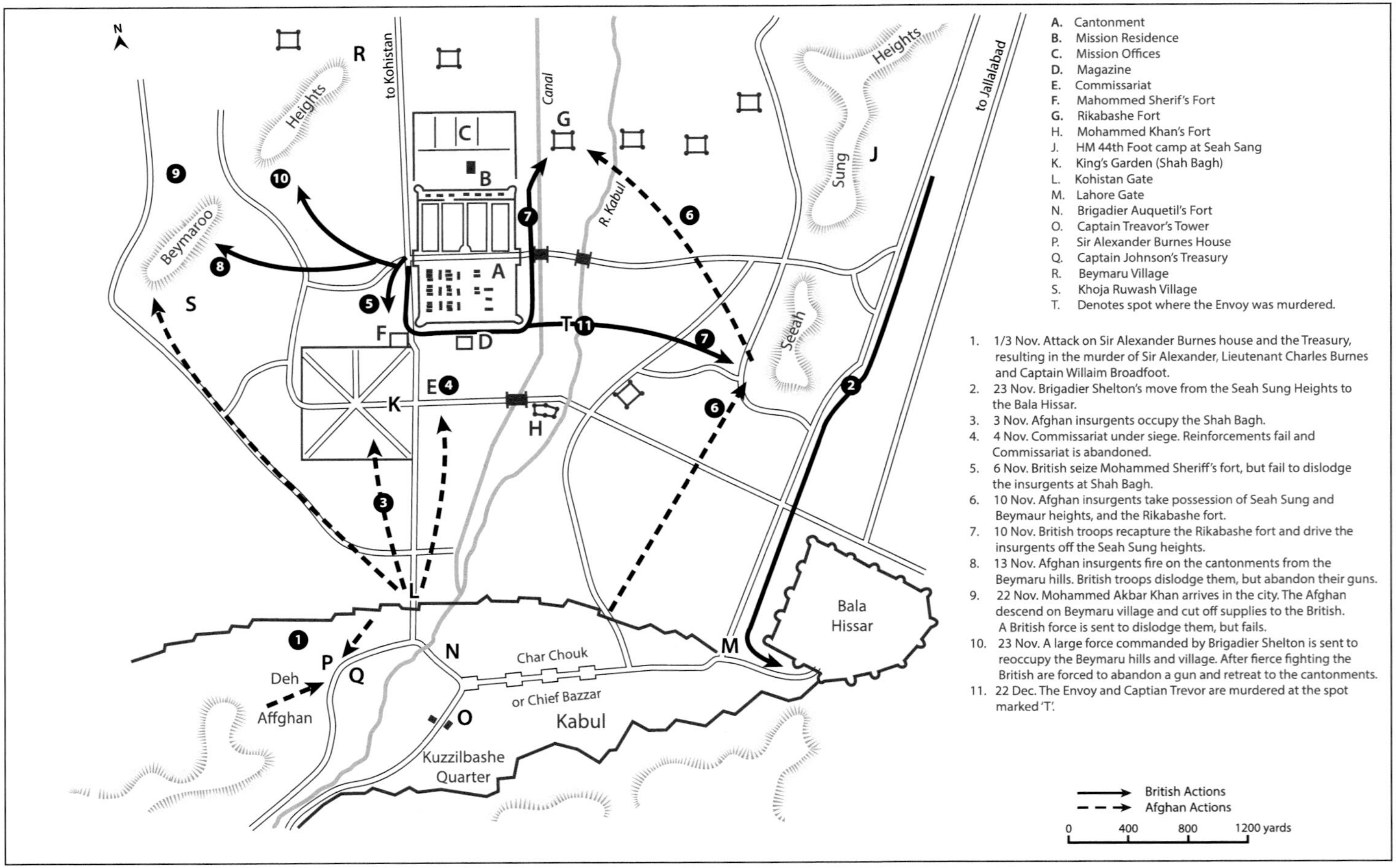

Map 13 Insurrection: Kabul November 1841.

of these potentially dangerous locations. Almost every Afghan fort consisted of a square with a tower at each corner, the walls being built of mud six to eight feet thick at the bottom; the main building varied in height from 12 to 40 feet and all were pierced with numerous loopholes. The day ended with the receipt of the sad news that Lieutenant Richard Maule and Ensign Francis Wheeler had both been slaughtered at Kalakam and that the Kohistan Rangers had defected to the enemy.

Thursday 4 November

By mid-morning,the rebels had taken up a strong position in the Shah Bagh (Shah's Garden), a mass of trees and vegetation, providing excellent cover to sniping rebels who had also manned the Mohammed Sharif fort thus blocking communications between the cantonment and the Commissariat, where Ensign Warren of 5th BNI and 80 *sepoys* had been placed to guard it. The Commissariat being a prime target for the rebels was soon under attack with Warren pleading for reinforcements. Ensign William Gordon with one company of 37th BNI was sent out to reinforce the beleaguered Commissariat. He failed, and in the process was shot and killed. Major General Elphinstone, after some hesitation, now ordered Captain Thomas Swayne of HM 44th Foot to immediately bring off Ensign Warren and his men into the cantonment thus implying that he was quite prepared to abandon a vital supply of provisions.

Swayne, with two companies of HM 44th Foot, on emerging from the cantonment's gate came under fire from the rebel marksmen hiding in the Shah Bagh and the detachment suffered heavy casualties. Both Swayne and Captain Thomas Robinson were killed. The officer left in charge decided to withdraw to the cantonments rather than expose the detachment to complete annihilation. Towards evening, another attempt was made by a troop of 5th Bengal Light Cavalry to save Warren and his men, but this also failed. At this point and to the utter amazement of his Commissariat officers, Major General Elphinstone abandoned any idea of saving the Commissariat. However, after much vacillation, the General was persuaded to send a message to Ensign Warren instructing him to hold his position and that a relief force would be sent out at 2:00 a.m. that night; Ensign Warren later denied ever having received this message. Meanwhile, the essential necessity of capturing the Mohammed Sharif fort in order to secure the Commissariat was impressed on the General and at last it was agreed that a force was to be readied by 4:00 a.m. to carry out this task. By the time the troops were ready it was way past the start time and just as it was about to leave the cantonments, Ensign Warren and his few remaining men sneaked in, having remained at their post for as long as possible.

During the morning of that day, Captain Robert Trevor, Commander of the Shah's bodyguard, who had defended his house in the city until all hope of relief was at an end, came into the cantonments with his wife and seven children escorted by his faithful *Hazir-Bashe* horsemen. His only casualty was Sergeant Smith, who had returned to the house to retrieve some cash he had stored there and was killed in the attempt. In the afternoon, Captain Colin Mackenzie, an officer of the Commissariat, who had held his position in the city until all his ammunition had run out, came into cantonments with his ever faithful *Jezailchees*, headed by *Subadar* Hassan Khan, having had to fight all the way to do so.

Friday 5 November

Dawn evinced the most disheartening scene to the onlookers at the cantonments; hundreds of Afghan ruffians raiding the Commissariat like ants to a sugar bowl. It was far too galling a scene and more so for the men as they saw all their precious rum being taken away and itched to be led out to give the impertinent Afghans a well-deserved thrashing. A number of officers clamoured to lead an attack on the Mohammed Sharif fort especially at this time when the rebels were preoccupied denuding the Commissariat. Poor Elphinstone, wracked with pain and memories of the disasters of the last few days, could not make up his mind as to the correct course of action to adopt. While equally galled at the demolishing of the Commissariat, he was fearful of yet another rebuff, so much time was spent conversing and canvassing for opinions. Eventually the General agreed for a detachment, commanded by Captain Stephen Swayne of 5th BNI, to attack and capture the Mohammed Sharif fort. The General, still wracked with doubt, wrote to the envoy:

> My Dear Sir William. After due consideration, we have determined on attacking the fort this morning with 50 men of 44th and 200 Native Infantry. It behoves us to look to the consequence of failure, in this case I know not how we are to subsist, or from want of provisions to retreat. You should, therefore, consider what chance there is of making terms, if we are driven to this extremity.[1]

At midday the storming party emerged from the western gate of the cantonments, with the guns leading, and when within 100 yards of the fort, started shelling it. At this time Captain Swayne and his storm troops should have moved forward covered by the firing of the guns, but he failed to do so, remaining under cover by the wall on the roadside. The General, watching the proceedings from the ramparts, thought that the guns were running out of ammunition and as the storming party appeared to be pinned down, he feared he was about to witness another disaster, so, succumbing to the advice of his pluckless staff, he recalled the force back into the cantonments. The abandonment of this initiative on top of the loss of the Commissariat had the most demoralising effect on the garrison and caused the General to appear ever more feeble.

Saturday 6 November

It was quite evident that the Mohammed Sharif fort had to be taken, and this time by a regular breach and coordinated attack. In the early morning of the fifth day of the uprising a battery of assorted guns was lined up on the rampart and for two hours battered the fort, resulting in a practicable breach. At which time an assault force comprising one company of HM 44th Foot, under Ensign William Raban, one company of 5th BNI, under Lieutenant Aleck Deas, and one company 37th BNI, under Lieutenant William Steer, all under the command of Major Griffiths, charged forward and speedily carried the fort. Sadly, Ensign Raban was killed while hoisting the flag.

1 Macrory, *The Fierce Pawns*, p.200.

With the Mohammed Sharif fort secured, it was deemed advisable to dislodge the rebels from the Shah Bagh which adjoined the fort. Although a number of additional troops were employed for this task, chances for complete success were missed due to the lack of coordinated action caused by there being no overall commander directing operations. By nighttime many of the rebels had retired to the city and the Shah Bagh had only been neutralised. While this limited success raised morale, it did not diminish the growing anxiety for the supply of provisions and the troops were put on half rations. Despite huge bribes and liberal payments, the Commissariat officers were only able to obtain a scanty quantity of provisions insufficient for a day's consumption. It was quite apparent that the rebel leaders, by coercing the suppliers, planned to starve out the garrison and cut off access to the foraging areas. During the lull over the next few days, the rebels had managed to secure two guns, which they positioned at the Mohammed Khan fort opposite the south-east bastion of the cantonment, and had declared Zeman Shah Khan, a nobleman, as the new King of Afghanistan until the British returned Dost Mohammed Khan.

Macnaghten, whilst entreating the military authorities to exert themselves, engaged in tortuous and dangerous intrigues with the object of sowing discord among the avaricious Afghan chiefs to thus weaken their collective hostility, a tactic still being employed today around the world in the name of democracy and humanity. The agent he used to conduct the intrigues was Mohan Lal, who until Sir Alexander Burnes' death had been his main source of intelligence. This man was commissioned to offer bribes and 'contracts' for the heads of some particularly troublesome chiefs. Involved in these machinations, as a sort of go-between, was Lieutenant John Conolly, who it seems extended the remit given by his uncle. In a letter to Mohan Lal of 5 November Conolly wrote, 'I promise 10,000 rupees for the head of each rebel chief.' This was followed up by another letter of 11 November: 'There is a man called Hadji Ali, who might be induced by a bribe to try and bring in the heads of one or two of the Mufids. Endeavour to let him know that 10,000 rupees will be given for each head, or even 15,000 rupees.'[2]

Tuesday 9 November

During the last two days, the endless meetings resulting in no robust action drew greater attention to the incapacity of the frail General and it was mooted that he should be relieved of his command. Macnaghten was the only person who could possibly authorise this but was loath to do so as the replacement could be none other than Brigadier John Shelton, an officer with whom he shared a mutual detestation. But he recognised that Major General Elphinstone, almost a cripple, needed help, so a compromise was decided. Brigadier Shelton was ordered back to the cantonments in the hope that by heartily co-operating with the Envoy and the General he would strengthen their hands and rouse the sinking confidence of the troops. Basically the Brigadier was to be in command of operations while the General directed them and the Envoy advised on policy. But like all compromises it lacked resolution and cohesion, particularly as the implied co-operation between the General and the Brigadier was nonexistent. In a memorandum written a short time before his death, the General described Shelton's behaviour.

2 Archibald Forbes, *The Afghan Wars, 1839-42 and 1878-80* (London: Seeley, 1892).

> I regret to be obliged to disclose that I did not receive from Brigadier Shelton that cordial co-operation and advice I had a right to expect, on the contrary, his manner was most contumacious; from the day of his arrival he never gave me information or advice, but invariably found fault with all that was done, and canvassed and condemned all orders before officers, frequently preventing and delaying carrying them into effect. He appeared to be actuated by an ill feeling towards me. I did everything in my power to remain on good terms with him.[3]

The Brigadier came into the cantonments bringing with him a company of HM 44th Foot, the Shah's 6th Infantry Regiment, two guns and a supply of *atta*. The very first thing that the Brigadier wanted was to move into the house designated for the Brigade Commander, which was occupied by Lady Sale. The indomitable Florentina Sale refused to move and the Brigadier did himself no favours in continuing to gripe. He also griped about the futility of spending the winter at Kabul and from the very start advocated an immediate retreat to Jalalabad. This sort of despondency did little to raise morale and soon spread amongst officers and men, particularly with the Brigadier's own regiment, and especially in view of the losses the regiment had incurred during the last few days. It is a lamentable fact that these European soldiers, who were expected to exhibit to their native counterparts an example of endurance and fortitude, were among the first to lose confidence and give vent to feelings of discontent.

Wednesday 10 November

At dawn the garrison was awakened by the sharp crackle of *jezail* fire from the Seah Sung hills and from the Rikabashe fort, only 400 yards east of the cantonments, which had also been left unoccupied. At the same time a large body of rebels had crowned the heights to the west of the cantonments. It seemed to those in the garrison that the rebels had engaged in a joint attack. However, the rebels to the west made no further advance while those at the Rikabashe fort had moved down to occupy a line of buildings even closer to the cantonment ramparts where the British gunners were working the guns and did so for a couple of hours.

At this time, only two days' supply of provisions remained within the garrison, and it was quite clear that unless the rebels were driven off the garrison would be hemmed in. Macnaghten, taking the initiative, instructed Major General Elphinstone to send a force to storm the Rikabashe fort. At midday the following troops assembled at the eastern gate under the command of Brigadier Shelton, HM 44th Foot under Lieutenant Colonel Thomas Mackerell, 37th BNI under Major Griffiths, the Shah's 6th Infantry Regiment under Captain Perin Hopkins and two 6-pdr guns under Captain Thomas Walker. Captain Henry Bellew had volunteered to go forward to blow open the gate. However, missing the gate, he blew open a wicket which only allowed two men to enter abreast, a murderous bottleneck where Captains George Westmacott and Robert M'Crae were killed along with a number of soldiers. Lieutenant Colonel Mackerell and Lieutenant Henry Bird with a handful of European soldiers managed to gain entry, and at their appearance the rebels fled out of the gate. Then, to the amazement of the storming troops attempting

3 Kaye, *History of the War in Afghanistan*, Vol. 2, p.209.

'Heroic defence of Lieutenant Bird at Cabul'.

entry, a large body of rebel horsemen charged around the corner of the fort. A cry of 'Cavalry!' was raised and panic ensued. The bugler of the 6th Regiment sounded the retreat and the troops fell back. Major William Scott of HM 44th Foot, realising the fearful predicament that his commanding officer was in, exhorted and beseeched the men to charge forward, but not a soul would follow save a private of his regiment named Steward, who was afterwards promoted.[4] However, Brigadier Shelton, despite being exposed to rebel fire, recalled the troops and brought them together for the assault which proved successful. Meanwhile inside the fort Mackerell had been hacked to pieces, but was still alive. Lieutenant Bird had retreated to a stable where he and one *Sepoy* were discovered having kept up as hot a fire as they could, accounting for at least 30 rebels.

In the fort the troops found 1,400 *maunds* of grain, half of which was removed to the cantonments before nightfall as was the wounded Mackerell, who died that night. Brigadier Shelton stupidly refused to leave a guard at the fort, and the next morning, not surprisingly, the balance of the grain had disappeared. That morning permanent possession was taken of the fort and the line of buildings destroyed. The British loss in this operation was 200 killed and wounded. It had been the first time that any considerable body of troops, 2,000, had been brought into action and

4 Vincent Eyre, *The Military Operations at Cabul Which Ended in the Retreat and Destruction of the British Army, January 1842* (London, John Murray 1843), p.55.

its success caused the rebels to disengage for the next few days. The garrison was not troubled, nor did it take the opportunity of launching a coordinated attack on the city, thus securing the initiative from the rebels and the undoubted support of the Kuzzilbashe. Instead the military command, disunited, sat around at what were imposingly called 'war councils' which resembled the citizens' assemblies during the French Revolution with Brigadier Shelton sitting in the corner knitting his brow. Of these meetings Major General William Hough wrote:

> There were many young officers allowed to join a very extensive Council of War and gave their opinions often unasked, so that the opinions of Brigadier Shelton and other older officers were set aside. Under the peculiar circumstance at Cabul the General would have acted wisely to have adhered to the advice of senior officers and never to have asked the opinion of young officers who had no experience or official position to warrant their giving any advice, as the result proved.[5]

Meantime, Macnaghten, ever hopeful for the return of Sale's brigade, wrote another letter to Captain George Macgregor, the political agent with Major General Sir Robert Sale:

> I have written you several letters, urging you in the strongest manner to come up with Sale's brigade to our relief, but I fear you may not have received them. Our situation is rather a desperate one unless you arrive, because we can neither retreat in any direction, nor leave the cantonments to go to the Bala Hissar, but if we had your force we should be able to hold the city and thus preserve both the cantonments and the Bala Hissar.[6]

Saturday 13 November

Failure to seize the initiative resulted in the rebels, in great strength, occupying the Beymaru Hills, from where the garrison obtained its provisions. They had positioned two guns in commanding positions and had commenced cannonading the cantonments. It was clear to many and especially Macnaghten, that the rebels had to be removed otherwise more would be drawn in to the detriment of the garrison. But General Elphinstone, loath to relinquish command and even more loath to suffer more casualties, hesitated in sanctioning an assault. Instead, he called a meeting and canvassed opinions with his brigadier ever ready with a host of objections; Macnaghten's pleas for action went unheeded until he pointed out that the 'guns must be taken at all costs, and at once, or the loss of the cantonments tomorrow might be the result of our spinelessness today.'[7]

After the Envoy had accepted personal responsibility, a strong force under the command of Brigadier Shelton was ordered out for service. The force comprised six companies of HM 44th Foot under Major William Scott, six companies of 37th BNI under Major Griffiths, four companies of the Shah's 6th Infantry Regiment under Captain Hopkins, two squadrons of 5th Bengal Light Cavalry under Lieutenant Colonel Robert Chambers, one squadron of the

5 Hough, *Narrative*, p.109.
6 Bruce, *Retreat from Kabul*, p.154.
7 Kaye, *History of the War in Afghanistan*, Vol. 2, p.220.

Shah's 2nd Irregular Horse under Lieutenant Robert Le Geyt, one troop of Skinner's Horse under Lieutenant Thomas Walker, one 6-pdr and one 3-pdr gun under Lieutenant Vincent Eyre.

Due to the time lost in meaningless discussions, the force was ready to move at the late hour of 4:00 p.m. and moved out in three columns. Unfortunately, at the very outset, the 6-pdr gun became stuck in a canal and the advance continued without it and consequently the first fusillade of aimless musketry fire, though fired from a distance of only 10 yards, had very little effect. The rebels' answer was a charge of horsemen with irresistible force into the mass of British infantry. For a while there was utter panic and confusion with rebel horsemen charging through the ranks. The infantry retreated down the hill where they rallied and reformed behind the reserve at the foot of the hill. By now the 6-pdr gun had been brought back into action and under cover of its fire plus a timely charge by the 5th Bengal Light Cavalry the rebels were driven back up the hill with the British infantry in close pursuit. The rebels withdrew from the ridge, abandoning their two guns to the victors, which in accordance with the mission's objective were to be brought into the cantonments. One was easily retrievable, the other was covered by deadly *jezail* fire and the soldiers shrank from the perilous task of moving it. Calls by Major Scott to drag away the gun went unheeded. As darkness was fast approaching, the gun was spiked and left. Brigadier Shelton's force was back in the cantonments by 8:00 p.m.

Afghan Foot soldier c.1840.

Monday 15 November

On this day very early in the morning two bedraggled and wounded officers, Major Eldred Pottinger and Lieutenant John Haughton,[8] one Gurkha orderly and the dog 'Caesar' entered the cantonments' gate; this pitiful group represented the remnants of the Charikar garrison. The intelligence that Charikar had been lost and the 4th Gurkha Regiment annihilated was deeply

8 Lieutenant John Haughton. He survived his terrible wounds, and though he received neither reward or thanks for his heroic defence of Charikar, he lived to distinguish himself as governor of the Andaman Islands, and later of Cooch-Behar.

depressing news as the successful Kohistan insurgents would now flock to Kabul. As yet no one rebel chief had emerged as the leader, so Macnaghten continued to use the agency of Mohan Lal to play on the greed of individual chiefs thus causing disunity, but very little progress had been made in this direction. By 17 November the Envoy had confirmation that Sale's brigade had not turned back and that it was now in Jalalabad. As for possible assistance from Kandahar, he had no news.

The lull in rebel activity after 15 November provided an excellent opportunity to move the garrison into the Bala Hissar and abandon the cantonment, which was basically indefensible and required a large number of men to guard the perimeter. While this move was heartily advocated by the Envoy, the military hierarchy pooh-poohed the idea on the grounds that it would be difficult to move the sick and wounded, now numbering 600, and the greater difficulty of obtaining firewood and forage for the cavalry, and above all the psychological boost it would give the rebels in acquiring the cantonments plus the cost of its loss. However, it is more likely that to Brigadier Shelton and officers of similar thought a move to the Bala Hissar presupposed the garrison remaining at Kabul.

There was also much discussion regarding the expediency of taking the Mohammed Khan fort, which was one of the main resorts of the rebels during the day and where they had placed two guns. This fort was only 900 yards from the cantonment ramparts and Macnaghten advised that the effect on morale of capturing it would be more effective than any blow struck to date. The General was initially much taken with the idea, but then vacillated and eventually abandoned the proposal.

Tuesday 23 November

The rebels were back on the Beymaru hills and had descended into the village at the north-eastern end from where the Commissariat officers purchased provisions. As this was an intolerable development, a small detachment under Major Stephen Swayne of 5th BNI was sent out to counter the rebels, but his force was far too small and quickly returned with casualties. The situation called for a more robust response and a much larger force. That evening Major General Elphinstone held another of his interminable war councils at which he tried to obtain a consensus, but there were the usual objections, with the Brigadier and his immediate staff declaring that the troops were exhausted, dispirited and hence physically and morally enfeebled. These objections were eventually overruled. However, based on what transpired, the Brigadier may have been correct in his assessment.

The following morning, a strong force commanded by Brigadier Shelton was sent out to occupy the Beymaru hills. This force comprised five companies of HM 44th Foot under Captain Thomas Leighton, six companies of 5th BNI under Lieutenant Colonel Oliver, six companies of 37th BNI under Captain James Kershaw, a squadron of 5th Bengal Light Cavalry under Captain John Bott, a squadron of irregular horse under Lieutenant Thomas Walker, 100 *sowars* of the Shah's 2nd Cavalry and 100 Sappers under Lieutenant Henry Laing. In support of this force of 2,000 troops, the General and Brigadier, veterans of Waterloo, against all military principles of war, thought fit to send out only one gun under Sergeant Mulhall.

The British force quickly took possession of the hill and positioned itself along the north-eastern extremity and overlooked the village. The one gun was positioned commanding the enclosure of the village and fired a shower of grape into it. Panicked and confused, the rebels fired back with their *jezails* and took up positions in the loopholes and turrets of the houses. With their ammunition exhausted, most of the rebels eventually retreated leaving the more zealous to remain at their posts. It was now determined that the village was to be taken by an assault commanded by Major Stephen Swayne, but he failed to carry the village, and after 40 minutes of fighting Brigadier Shelton recalled his force. Meanwhile the move of the British force to the Beymaru hills had attracted thousands of rebel horsemen and footmen who joined in the fight. This group occupied the hill opposite to that held by the British and they had also reoccupied the village.

The rebel and British positions on the hill were separated by a narrow gorge and the rebel fire from their side became hot and galling. It is worthy of note that the Afghan with his longer-range *jezail* took careful aim with each bullet fired, whereas the British soldier was more inclined to fire his shorter-range musket solely for effect.

Leaving five companies overlooking the village, Brigadier Shelton took the remainder of the force and the one gun over the gorge to the brow of the hill, where he formed the infantry into two squares with his cavalry immediately in the rear. From here the one gun was brought into action and fired away as quickly as it could be loaded, until it became unserviceable due to the vent being so hot that the gunners were unable to serve it. Without the gun, the infantry musket was no match for the longer range *jezails* which poured destructive fire into the infantry squares. Some of the Afghans, making good use of dead ground, crawled from the gorge up the hill and rushed with sudden fury on the squares. This totally unexpected attack caused the troops to panic, turn and run along the ridge. The Brigadier vainly called upon them to rally and charge, but not a man responded, the rebels emboldened by success advanced and rushed the single gun. The cavalry was ordered to charge but the *sowars* declined to follow their officers. The artillerymen stood by their gun and two fell dead beside it. The gun was lost and the disheartened regiments were confused and in disastrous flight. Brigadier Shelton ordered the halt to be sounded, and the troops stopped and started to reform. Meanwhile a body of rebel horsemen took away the horses and limber and abandoned the gun.

In the meantime, the rebel horsemen on the plain had been thrown into confusion by the fall of their leader, Abdullah Khan, whose horse had been shot by a well-aimed cannonball fired by Sergeant Wade from the ramparts and withdrew back to the city. This turn of events provided an excellent opportunity for a body of cavalry to be sent out from the cantonments to pursue the retreating rebel horsemen. Both the General and the Envoy were on the ramparts viewing the unfolding events, and Macnaghten urged Elphinstone to make use of this excellent opportunity, but the timid General thought it a wild scheme and rejected the proposal.

At this juncture, with the enemy in flight and the gun back in British possession, Brigadier Shelton's force could have been brought back to cantonments in good order. Instead, it stayed on the Beymaru hills and the General sent out horses and limber for the gun, but no extra gun. In the absence of any pursuit and an influx of more men, the rebels returned to renew their attack on the Brigadier's force. While the now serviceable gun was in full operation with murderous effect, the Afghan *jezails* played equally murderously on the British infantry and once again, using dead ground judiciously, a group of Ghilzais emerged from the gorge up the hill and burst upon the infantry crouching under a hail of *jezail* fire. Apparently, at this moment Brigadier Shelton, ever at the forefront, fell back to order more men to the front. On this movement to the rear by the commander, the front rank gave way and in a flash the infantry and cavalry ran helter-skelter down the hill. The rebel horsemen were quickly upon the retreating troops and friend and foe were mixed up in inextricable confusion.

The lone gun, bravely guarded to the end, was again lost to the enemy.

In a reversal of the old adage, the best army in the world had gained a 'defeat out of the mouth of victory'. The rout of Brigadier Shelton's force was complete and had the rebels followed up their advantage the cantonments could also have been lost, but the rebel chief, Osman Khan, inexplicably called off the attack, and the rebels moved back to the city with shouts of exultation. The British loss was severe with 300 killed or wounded including Lieutenant Colonel Oliver, captains William Mackintosh and Thomas Walker, and Lieutenant Henry Laing killed, plus other officers wounded. This affair precluded any further offensive action by the British garrison; the initiative now passed to the rebels, who had now been joined by Mohammed Akbar Khan, the second son of the British captive, Dost Mohammed Khan.

The British defeat was the result of weak generalship and a paucity of artillery, the weapon most feared and dreaded by the Afghans, and, one must add, the superiority of the longer-range purposefully aimed *jezail* over the shorter range ill-aimed British musket. Any defeat lowers morale and that of the garrison sank to gloom and doom; the most sanguine now began to despond. The troops were cold, hungry and fatigued, they were broken men and discipline was much shaken, especially amongst the European rank and file. Lady Sale was to insert in her journal, 'Morale had sunk to rock bottom and almost any rumour, no matter how ill-founded, was given credence even among those better able to refute it. It is more than shocking, it is shameful to hear the way that our officers go on croaking before the men. It is sufficient to dispirit them and prevent their fighting for us.' The very next day, salt was rubbed into their wounded pride as they idly witnessed, within musket shot, the rebels destroying the bridge across the Kabul River on the road to Jalalabad.

Now followed a spate of letters between Macnaghten and the military, about the courses open to the doomed garrison. The option of concentrating in the Bala Hissar, a measure favoured by both Shah Shuja and the Envoy, was reviewed and discussed, but the military authorities had long since set their faces against it. On 24 November Major General Elphinstone replied to the Envoy's letter requesting the General's opinion on whether he considered it possible to hold out any longer in the country:

> Sir, I have the honour to acknowledge the receipt of your letter of this day's date, calling for my opinion as to whether, in a military point of view, it is feasible any longer to maintain our position in this country.
>
> In reply, I beg to state, that after having held our position here for upwards of three weeks in a state of siege, from want of provisions and forage, the reduced state of our troops, the large number of wounded and sick, the difficulty of defending the extensive and ill-situated cantonments we occupy, the near approach of winter, our commissariat cut off, no prospect of relief, and the whole country in arms against us, I am of the opinion that it is not feasible any longer to maintain our position in this country, and that you ought to avail yourself of the offer to negotiate which has been made to you.
>
> W.K. Elphinstone.[9]

9 Eyre, *The Military Operations at Cabul*, p.100.

On receipt of the General's reply, the Envoy hesitated no longer. He sent word to the rebel chiefs intimating his willingness to receive a deputation from them to discuss the preliminaries of a treaty. At this juncture, the military cowardly gave up the fight and left the direction of affairs in the hands of the Envoy, for him to obtain the best terms for their retreat.

Saturday 27 November

In the morning, two Afghan deputies were ushered in to present the rebel terms, which were obviously arrogant in the extreme. The British were to deliver up the Shah Shuja and his family, and all British forces in Afghanistan were to surrender unconditionally. Mscnaughten could not possibly accept such terms and informed the deputies that their proposals were too dishonourable to be entertained, sending them on their way with the possibility of continued hostilities the only option.

Back at the Bala Hissar, Shah Shuja's haughtiness had evaporated into fright. Despite his request for the garrison to move into the Bala Hissar the British had decided to negotiate a retreat and by association his own demise. With this dim prospect in view, it is not inconceivable that he may have considered engaging in other options. How else could the wretched man avoid being kicked out of Afghanistan for a third time? According to Lady Sale, the Envoy had written to the Governor General stating that, 'If it really should be proved that His Majesty was acting treacherously against us, then Dost Mohammed Khan should be restored to his country.' However, Shah Shuja, at this stage, was as hopeful as Macnaghten that relief would soon come and that the British would not leave Afghanistan. But as the situation deteriorated, his manœuvring may not have been in concert with his departing allies.

Sunday 5 December

The rebels had commenced mining one of the towers of the Mohammed Sharif fort, so the small detachment there was reinforced by one company of HM 44th Foot under Lieutenant Alured Gray, and one company of 37th BNI under Lieutenant Frederick Hawtrey, who, based on the dire reports of the prior occupants, appealed for the fort defences to be checked out by the chief engineer, Lieutenant John Sturt. No sooner had this officer given the all-clear and returned to the cantonments, when the General received a report that the force at the fort had been seized by panic and taken flight over the walls abandoning the place to the rebels. In her journal, Lady Sale states, 'They ran away as fast as they could. The 44th say that the 37th ran first, and as they were too weak, they went too.' According to Lieutenant Hawtrey, who commanded, 'there was not a pin to choose – all cowards alike.'

While the military did nothing but croak and push for negotiations, the Envoy continued to advocate a move to the Bala Hissar, urging that the sick and wounded could be moved under cover of night and then after destroying all unnecessary ordnance and stores, the garrison could fight its way to the much safer position in the Bala Hissar. Sadly he was unable to convince his military colleagues who were insisting on honourable terms being sought and fearful that to leave the cantonments would negate any possibility of obtaining the desired terms.

Wednesday 8 December

On this day Macnaghten sent an official letter to Major General Elphinstone, requesting he state whether or not it was his opinion that any further attempt to hold out against the enemy would merely have the effect of sacrificing both Shah Shuja and the garrison. The General's reply, countersigned by the various commanders, was as follows:

> Sir, I have the honour to acknowledge the receipt of your letter of this day's date, requesting me to state, for your information, whether or not it be my opinion that any further attempt to hold out against the enemy would merely have the effect of sacrificing both His Majesty and ourselves, and that the only alternative left is to negotiate for our safe retreat out of the country on the most favourable terms possible.
>
> In reply, I beg to state that my opinion is that the present situation of the troops here is such, from want of provisions and the impracticability of procuring more that no time ought to be lost in entering into negotiations for the safe retreat from the country.
>
> As regards the troops in Candahar, and the rumours of their approach, I should be sorry, in the absence of authentic information, to risk the sacrifice of the troops here by waiting for their arrival, when we are ignorant even of their having commenced their march and are reduced to three days' supply of provisions for our sepoys at half-rations, and almost entirely without forage for our horses and cattle.
>
> Our number of sick and wounded in hospital exceeds 600, and our means for their transport is far from adequate, owing to the death by starvation of so many of our camels; from the same cause also we will be obliged at this inclement season to leave tents and bedding behind with such a march before us.
>
> As regards the King, I must be excused entering upon that point, and leave its consideration to your better judgement and knowledge; but I may be allowed to say that it little becomes me, as commanding the British troops in Afghanistan, to regard the necessity of negotiating in any other light than as concerns their honour or welfare, both of which I should be answerable for by a further stay here, after the sudden and universal rebellion which has taken place throughout the domains. The whole of the grain and forage in our vicinity is exhausted, and the defence of this extensive and ill-situated cantonment will not admit to distant expeditions to obtain supplies from the strongly-fortified dwellings of an armed and hostile population, our present numbers being insufficient for its defence, and obliging the whole of the troops to be almost constantly under arms.
>
> In conclusion, I can only repeat my opinion that you should lose no time in entering into negotiations.
>
> W.K. Elphinstone, Major General Commanding in Afghanistan
> I concur in the above opinions
> J. Shelton, Brigadier
> In a military point of view, I concur in the above
> W. Anquetil, Brigadier Commanding Shah Shuja's Forces
> I also concur
> R. Chambers, Lieutenant Colonel Commanding Cavalry[10]

10 Kaye, *History of the War in Afghanistan*, Vol. 2, p.274.

The Envoy's reaction to this reply can be understood from the letter he sent his brother-in-law, the Honourable J.C. Erskine, on 9 December: 'We have now been besieged 38 days by a contemptible enemy. The military authorities have strongly urged me to capitulate. This I will not do till the last moment. We have no energy or spirit here.'[11]

Meanwhile starvation was staring the garrison in the face, and it was essential that measures be taken to obtain further supplies. Lady Sale was to record in her journal, 'They know we are starving, that our horses and cattle have neither grain, bhoosa, nor grass. They have pretty well eaten up the bark of the trees and the tender branches, the horses gnaw at the tent pegs and the artillery horses have eaten the trunnion of a gun.' A meeting was held in the General's quarters which determined that an attack be made on the village of Khoja Ruwash, four miles away, at an early hour the following morning. The morning dawned, but there was no sign of any preparations having been made, no orders had been issued and the garrison just sat around waiting for some divine intervention. For this most extraordinary state of affairs the blame rests solely on Brigadier Shelton.

Later that day, news arrived that Sale's force at Jalalabad had gained a decisive victory (29 November) over a besieging Afghan force. The Envoy, thinking that this news would modify the General's opinion regarding immediate negotiations with the rebels, wrote to him on the matter, but the General demurred, replying that, 'as pleasing as the news was, it could not in the slightest degree influence the expediency of retreating.'[12]

Saturday 11 December

By now, there being no other alternative, Macnaghten sent word to the rebels that the garrison was ready to negotiate a withdrawal from the country. Accompanied by captains George Lawrence, Mackenzie and Trevor, he went out to meet the rebel party at the bottom of the Seah Sung hills, about a mile from the cantonments. The rebel party comprised Mohammed Akbar Khan, Osman Khan, Naib Ameer, Mohammed Shah Khan, Humza Khan, Rhooda Bux Khan, Juayut Oolol Khan and Khan Shereen Khajan, the Kuzzilbashe.

The parties greeted each other amicably and the Envoy proceeded to tell the chiefs that sentiments of goodwill towards the Afghan nation had induced the British Government to lend their aid in restoring to the seat of his ancestors a king, and that this restoration had apparently given utmost satisfaction to all classes. However, he continued, as it was only now made clear that the satisfaction had given way to wholly contrary emotions, it was no longer the British Government's intention to pursue a course displeasing to the chiefs. On this account, the Envoy told them, he was willing to enter into negotiations for the smoothing over of present difficulties, and for the adopting of such measures as were likely to be the most conducive towards the re-establishment of the mutual friendship between the British and Afghan Governments. Macnaghten spoke in fluent Persian and his conciliatory tone was appreciated by the chiefs. He then requested permission to send the chiefs a paper containing the main points on which to base a treaty. These points were as follows:

11 Helen Mackenzie, *Storms and Sunshine of a Soldier's Life: Lt.-General Colin Mackenzie, C.B., 1825–1991*, Vols 1 & 2 (Edinburgh: D. Douglas, 1884; Bibliobazaar reprint, n.d.), p.236.

12 Eyre, *The Military Operations at Cabul*, p.107.

- The British should evacuate Afghanistan, including Kandahar, Ghazni, Kabul and Jalalabad.
- The British should be permitted to return not only unmolested to India, but supplies should be afforded them and that some men of consequence accompany them as hostages.
- Dost Mohammed, his family, and every Afghan currently held by the British, be allowed to return to Afghanistan.
- Shah Shuja and his family be allowed the option of remaining in Kabul or proceeding with the British to Ludhiana; in either case receiving from the Afghan Government a pension of one *lakh* of rupees per annum.
- Means of transport for the conveyance of baggage, stores etc. to be furnished by the Afghan Government.
- An amnesty granted to all those who had made themselves obnoxious on account of their attachment to Shah Shuja and his allies.
- All prisoners to be released.
- No British force should ever again be sent into Afghanistan, unless called for by the Afghan government.
- Perpetual friendship be established between the British and Afghanistan on the sure foundation of mutual good offices.

To all these points the rebels eventually agreed, the only objection coming from Mohammed Akbar Khan, who saw no need in providing provisions as he felt that the British garrison could move out the following day. He was overruled and the British agreed to move out in three days' time. Captain Trevor volunteered to return to the city with the chiefs as hostage for the sincerity of the Envoy. The terms of the proposed treaty were immediately made known to the doomed Shah. As reluctant as he had been to negotiate with the rebels, now by treaty his allies, Macnaghten was pleased with the result and felt satisfied that he had accomplished a parting on friendly terms. But there lurked a dark aspect to this rosy assessment: the Afghans were notoriously avaricious, tricky and vindictive, and there was no guarantee that they would fulfil the treaty terms.

The first step in the fulfilment of the treaty was the withdrawal of the troops at the Bala Hissar into cantonments, and this was to take place on 12 December, but was postponed to allow the troops some time to prepare for the move. In the evening of that day, a deputation of rebel chiefs called on Macnaghten with an unexpected proposition to the effect that Shah Shuja could continue as king on condition of inter-marrying his daughters with the leading Afghan chiefs and abandoning the offensive practice of keeping the noble chiefs waiting for hours at his gate in expectation of an audience. In addition, the rebels demanded that some British officers' families were to be given up as hostages for the fulfilment of the proposed treaty obligations. At first, the Shah reluctantly acquiesced to the chiefs' demand, probably in the hope of forging a more enduring future by forming alliances with some of the chiefs.

Meanwhile, the troops at the Bala Hissar comprising 54th BNI, a troop of horse artillery and a detachment of the mountain train with two howitzers commenced their evacuation from the fortress. Unfortunately, this group was encumbered with an iron 9-pdr gun and a 24-pdr brass howitzer drawn by bullocks, both of which were to be left in situ, but this instruction never got to Major William Ewart, the commander of the group. Much delay ensued as the best part of the day was spent in packing and preparation. Outside the gate, Mohammed Akbar Khan and some followers were assembled to escort the troops to the cantonment. At this juncture, Major Ewart became aware that a crowd of armed Afghans had gathered on the Seah Sung hills, who could well have been there to cause some meditated treachery. While the guns were moving out of the gate, some of Mohammed Akbar Khan's men attempted to enter the fortress but were spotted by the Shah's guard and on his orders the gate was shut. This left Major Ewart and the advance column outside to spend the night on marshy ground without food or firewood.

The next morning the group advanced, unmolested, under the Afghan escort, however, the rearguard which included the big guns became separated and was assaulted by the rebel mob from the Seah Sung hills. A number of the sick, who had been lashed to the guns to carry them, were butchered. Grape-shot from the cantonment and the exertions of Mohammed Akbar Khan eventually drove off the assailants. The whole group was safely in the cantonments by 9:00 a.m. This incident showed that the rebels were not a cohesive or united force.

Thursday 16 December

Shah Shuja for reasons best known to himself withdrew his consent to the arrangement permitting him to remain as king, and the rebels refused to provide provisions and forage until the British proved their sincerity by giving up every fort in the vicinity of the cantonments. The situation in the garrison was such that there really was no option but to concede to this unreasonable demand, even though this would render the cantonments untenable. Thus the forts were given up. The rebels sent in Nusrullah Khan as hostage with 150 *maunds* of *atta*, and a promise to provide 2,000 camels and 400 *yaboos* for the march to Jalalabad.

The delay in furnishing the promised conveyance and Shah Shuja's dilatoriness in deciding his future course of action postponed the eagerly anticipated departure, and the severity of the weather did not help. On 18 December the situation was rendered more desperate by a heavy fall of snow; a new enemy had entered the arena, one which the garrison was destined to find more formidable than the rebels. Some in the doomed garrison were all for striking out for Jalalabad, regardless of any suspect treaty with a people renowned for treachery, but the military heads had resolved to gamble on obtaining the best terms possible, which they thought they now had and for what they, vaingloriously, called an honourable withdrawal.

Meanwhile, Macnaghten had not given up hope of some last minute reversal and this came about on the matter of who was to be Shah Shuja's successor on his abdication provided for in the treaty. Mohammed Akbar Khan and his Barakzai adherents would claim to be restored to their ancient ascendancy, whereas the Ghilzais and the Kuzzilbashe dreaded this prospect and would much prefer to have Shah Shuja remain as king, in the expectation of being able to use him as their tool. The Envoy took this opportunity to profit from the disunity and began to offer bribes to all possible takers. On 20 December he wrote to his ever-obliging agent, Mohan Lal, 'You can tell the Ghilzais and Khan Shereen [Kuzzilbashe] that after they have declared for His Majesty and us and sent in 100 *kurwars* of grain to the cantonments, I shall be glad to give them a bond of five *lakhs* of rupees.' He followed this up with another letter the following day: 'In conversing with anybody, you must say distinctly that I am ready to stand by my engagement with the Barakzais and other chiefs associated with them, but that if any portions of the Afghans wish our troops to remain in the country, I shall think myself at liberty to break the engagement which I have made to go away, which engagement was made believing it to be in accordance with the wishes of the Afghan nation. If the Ghilzais and Kuzzilbashe wish us to stay, let them declare so openly in the course of tomorrow, and we will side with them. The best proof of their wish for us to stay is to send us a large quantity of grain this night. If they do this and make their salaams to the Shah early tomorrow, giving His Majesty to understand that we are along with them, I will write to the Barakzais and tell them that my agreement is at an end.'[13]

It beggars belief that the contents of these communications were not 'breaking news' in the bazaars of Kabul. The Envoy, grabbing at every straw, had blindly entered a contest in the art of trickery in which he was no match with the Afghan to whom trickery was second nature. Macnaghten was disappointed that no grain was brought in that night and no sign that the Ghilzais and Kuzzilbashes had taken the bait. He and the whole garrison were further disappointed to receive news from Colonel Thomas Palmer, commanding at Ghazni, that Lieutenant Colonel James MacLaren's force had returned to Kandahar in consequence of the snow which rendered the passes impracticable, and also the more disastrous news of the massacre of Captain John Woodburn and his escort of 150 men. The Captain had left Kandahar for Kabul on a routine mission when his group was attacked by eastern Ghilzais about 30 miles short of Ghazni. The Chief of Shekabad offered the group safety in his fort, but once the group were in, the gates were shut and the whole group was shot down by fire from the tower. Only three *sepoys* managed to escape.

Tuesday 21 December

In the morning, Macnaghten again met with Mohammed Akbar Khan and his cronies at the foot of the Seah Sung hills. At this meeting the British hostages were agreed, they were Major Pottinger, Captain Robert Warburton, Captain James Airey and Lieutenant John Conolly; captains Trevor and Henry Drummond were returned to the cantonments. Captain Drummond, who had been sent to Afghanistan to survey for iron and coal, had been living in the city. At the time, in the form of inducement, approval was given for the payment of 2,000 rupees per month to officers who agreed to become hostages, but this money was never paid out. It was also agreed that reserves of ammunition and wagons were to be handed over and that the sick and wounded were to be moved into the city to Zeman Shah Khan's house. At Mohammed Akbar Khan's request, the Envoy gifted his carriage to the Afghan chief. He had also asked for a beautiful Arab horse owned by Captain William Grant, the AAG, and on a previous occasion Mohammed Akbar Khan had been given a double-barrelled pistol by Brigadier Shelton for services rendered. Obviously these concessions and other rumoured payments increased the gravitas of Mohammed Akbar Khan among the rebels, many of whom felt that the sooner they got rid of the British the less likelihood there was of a massive counter-force arriving in Afghanistan.

13 Beveridge, *A Comprehensive History of India*, Vol. 3, p.526.

Wednesday 22 December

It was reported that in the morning Mohammed Akbar Khan had gone to the house of Osman Khan for important discussions. That evening Captain James Skinner, who had been living in the city under the protection of Mohammed Akbar Khan, rode into the cantonments accompanied by two Afghans, one of whom was the half-brother of Mohammed Akbar Khan. They had come, bearers of a message of a most 'portentous nature' which the Afghans wished to discuss with the Envoy in private. This message from Mohammed Akbar Khan contained new and staggering proposals ostensibly offering an end to Macnaghten's nightmare. It was proposed that Amenoolah Khan, the ringleader of the initial uprising, was to be handed over to the British as their prisoner, and when a British force was drawn up outside the cantonment as if to start the withdrawal, they were to be joined by Mohammed Akbar Khan and the Ghilzais to attack and capture the Mohammed Sharif fort; the British were to remain in Kabul until the following spring; Shah Shuja was to remain king with Mohammed Akbar Khan as his *Wazir*: and all this was to be guaranteed by the British with a payment of 30 *lakhs* of rupees, plus a pension of four *lakhs* of rupees annually for Mohammed Akbar Khan. The Envoy was utterly blinded by these unexpected proposals which were handing him the object he had been working for during the past six gruelling weeks. He accepted the proposals, assenting to them in writing and agreeing to a conference with Mohammed Akbar Khan the following morning to complete the details of the terms, all of which he kept to himself, in order to avoid further silly objections from his spineless military chiefs.

Sir William Macnaghten must have had a sleepless night as nagging doubt kept him awake. But as dawn came, he had made up his mind to risk all on this single chance rather than prolong the suspense and agony which were making existence intolerable.

Thursday 23 December

After breakfast the Envoy called for captains George Lawrence, Trevor, and Mackenzie to accompany him to the meeting with Mohammed Akbar Khan and disclosed to Mackenzie the nature of the transaction, who warned the Envoy that it could be a plot against him, but Macnaghten was determined to see it through. He then arranged with Elphinstone to have 54th BNI and Shah's 6th Regiment plus two guns on immediate standby for special duties. At the last minute, the envoy remembered the requested horse and sent Captain Mackenzie to acquire it from the owner. Not wishing to part with the horse, Captain Grant demanded a large payment of 5,000 rupees, and under the pressure that he would be facilitating an honourable cause, Grant settled for a payment of 3,000 rupees. Poor Captain Grant; he would have gained more kudos by freely handing over the horse for this honourable cause as the 3,000 rupees were never paid, the Captain being killed 15 days later.

At 12 o'clock Sir William Macnaghten said goodbye to his wife and set off with his three companions and a small escort, for this momentous meeting with Mohammed Akbar Khan. The place of the meeting was about 600 yards east of the cantonments, not far from the banks of the river where it was crossed by a bridge and situated on a slope among some hillocks marked out on the snow by a number of horse blankets. After the usual salutations and profuse thanks from Mohammed Akbar Khan for the beautiful Arab horse, the parties dismounted and sat down on the blankets. Mohammed Akbar Khan opened the meeting by asking the Envoy whether he was ready to carry out the proposals of the previous evening. 'Why not?' replied the Envoy. Captain George Lawrence, who had remained standing at this time, drew attention to the fact that if this was a secret meeting the many onlookers should be removed. At which point Mohammed Akbar Khan said that all of them were in on the secret, and without any warning the three officers were immediately grabbed and dragged away, each being placed behind a mounted rebel chief who rode off at full speed in the direction of Mohammed Khan's fort. Captain Trevor, unfortunately, fell off and was hacked to pieces. Meanwhile, the Envoy had been seized by Mohammed Akbar Khan and was struggling with his assailant. *Jemadar* Ram Singh, of the escort, rushed forward to Macnaghten's assistance and was hacked down for his gallant effort. There are a vast number of accounts as to what happened on this ill-fated day. The two best are those given by the only two British survivors, captains George Lawrence and Mackenzie, and are included in Lieutenant Eyre's journal, *The Military Operations at Cabul*. The only Afghan account comes from an intercepted letter written by Mohammed Sadiq to his uncle in Kandahar:

> The Sirdar [Mohammed Akbar Khan] at last said to the Envoy, 'Come, I must take you to the Nawab's.' The Envoy was alarmed and rose up. Mohammed Akbar seized him by the hands, saying, 'I cannot allow you to return to the cantonments.' The Sirdar wished to carry him off alive but was unable; then he drew a double-barrelled pistol from his belt, and discharged both barrels at the Envoy, after which he struck him two or three blows with his sword, and the Envoy was thus killed on the spot.[14]

There is no doubt that the Envoy had been engaged in a course of tortuous policy and for his misdemeanour he and his friends had been decoyed into an ambush resulting in the murder of himself, Captain Trevor and *Jemadar* Ram Singh. With people capable of such a deed and boasting after it was done, all engagements, however solemn, would normally have been considered useless and null and void, and led to the aggrieved seeking to avenge the wrong, or, at least, trust to Providence and their stout hearts and swords. But the British garrison at Kabul was not made of such stern stuff. Despite the fact that they could see through their telescopes that things were awry and two bodies were lying on the ground, there was no response whatsoever from the garrison. At first the military authorities would not believe that the Envoy had been murdered, and, instead of taking action to dispel all doubt, an officer was sent around to calm the alarm which was generally felt by intimating that the meeting had been interrupted by Ghilzais, the Envoy and his officers had gone to the city, and their return to the cantonments was fully expected. In the words of the brave and departed Envoy, 'Oh for a Wellington!'

Macnaghten was not wrong in his double-dealing, he had only adopted the *modus operandi* of the people he was dealing with, in his sincere desire to achieve ameliorating conditions for the troops and the honour of his country. His only error was in supposing that this was possible with Mohammed Akbar Khan, the most treacherous of the Afghans.

The following day, Major General Elphinstone was handed a letter from one of the captives, Captain George Lawrence, by which he was informed of the true facts of the atrocity, and the

14 Mackenzie, *Storms and Sunshine of a Soldier's Life*, p.247.

brazen request by the murderers to renew negotiations. Instead of revolting at this idea, the proposals were eagerly embraced. These proposals differed very little from Macnaghten's treaty, but when the Afghans discovered that they had only to demand to obtain, they immediately upped the ante. The new demands were, 1. Whatever cash was in the treasury was to be handed over. 2. All guns were to be given up except six. 3. Muskets, in excess of those in use, were to be left behind. 4. General Sale, his wife and daughter, plus other married officers and their children were to be given up as hostages until the return of Dost Mohammed Khan, and 5. All Afghans who had come with the British from India were to remain in Afghanistan. These humiliating proposals, after a fruitless attempt to modify them, were submitted to. For an army to give up its guns was tantamount to a surrender and yet this is what was agreed by the military authorities. On the other hand, the demand for family hostages, clearly indicating Mohammed Akbar Khan's desire to acquire an insurance policy for the return of his father and his own immunity, was inoperable, as the married officers refused to comply, with the exception of Lieutenant Eyre.

Saturday 25 December

A more miserable Christmas could scarcely be imagined. The snow lay heavy on the ground, but not one snowman, no rum, no carols, all hungry, cold and wishing for the good Lord to pluck them up and place them anywhere but Afghanistan. The army commander, feeling the draught of an absent envoy, was even more despondent and appointed Major Pottinger, the senior political officer, to the position of negotiating with the Afghans. From the outset, Major Pottinger made it clear to the General that the Afghans, in their current exuberant mood, could not be trusted and that a retreat to Jalalabad would be a most dangerous undertaking; and that any decision to do so would be a military one to which he would apply his best efforts. On the following day, a message was received from Captain Frederick Matheson, the political agent at Peshawar, announcing the march of strong reinforcements from India. Besides this good news, an offer was received from Mohammed Osman Khan to escort the garrison safely to Peshawar for a fee of five *lakhs* of rupees. Later that day another chief, Naib Ameer, came in with several Hindu *shroofs* for the purpose of negotiating bills to the amount of 14 *lakhs* of rupees, payable to several chiefs on the promise of the late envoy. Major Pottinger baulked at this as he was opposed to any agreement made under duress and demanded that Captain Mackenzie be returned to the cantonments as his presence was necessary in order to prepare bills on India.

Thursday 30 December

On this day, Major General Elphinstone convened the last of his war councils, consisting of himself, Brigadier Shelton, Brigadier Thomas Anquetil, Colonel Chambers, Captain Grant, Captain Bellew and Major Pottinger. Once again Major Pottinger declared his conviction that no confidence could be placed in any treaty formed with the Afghan chiefs, and that the circumstances were such that to bind the hands of the government by promising to evacuate the country and to restore the deposed Dost Mohammed Khan, and to waste vast amounts of public money to save their own lives and property, would be inconsistent with the duty they owed to the government and country they served; and that the only honourable course would be to hold out to the last in Kabul, or to force an immediate advance to Jalalabad. It would have been better for the Major to have saved his breath, as this was not a council of war, but a gaggle of cowards, which pompously declared his suggestion to be impracticable due to the want of provisions and the surrender of the neighbouring forts and therefore deemed it preferable to pay any sums of money rather than sacrifice the whole garrison in hopeless and prolonged hostilities. The council instructed Major Pottinger to renew negotiations immediately and to pay the sums promised to the chiefs, which he reluctantly did. In their deliberations Shah Shuja was to be left to his own devices and not one officer assigned to his force, on a handsome increase in pay, elected to remain behind with the Shah. Shah Shuja, in an effort to retain some meaningful connection with his British protectors, appealed to Lady Macnaghten to join him in the safety of the Bala Hissar. To the commander of his force, Brigadier Anquetil, he wrote, 'if it were well to forsake him in this hour of need, and to deprive him of that aid from that force, which he had hitherto been taught to consider his own'.[15]

As 1841 drew to its end, the garrison was kept in almost hourly expectation of departure. Each day a warning was issued that the retreat would begin next morning and the next morning, at the very last moment, a postponement of 24 hours was announced. All through, the excuses were that the chiefs had been unable either to organise the escort or to collect the stores of food and firewood for the army.

There was a small bazaar near the eastern gate of the cantonments at which local hawkers sold provisions. As the departure date drew near, the bazaar activity increased as these hawkers made the most of a market place about to close, and besides cash bartered provisions for 'not wanted on voyage' paraphernalia. This activity drew the attention of the more aggressive rebels, who plundered the peaceful hawkers and even attempted to force an entrance into the cantonment. Orders to fire on them were repeatedly requested and repeatedly rejected, as on the army commander's strict orders troops were not to get involved. One can well imagine Corporal Jones of *Dad's Army* itching to join the fray with his bayonet. 'They don't like it.'

Wednesday 5 January

On this day the sick and wounded were removed to the city for their medical care. Lots were drawn for two medical officers to remain behind, all under the command of Lieutenant William Evans of HM 44th Foot. The medical officers selected were Dr Archibald Campbell of 54th BNI and Dr George Berwick. Under the circumstances, this was a most heroic gesture on the part of these officers, but one that saved their lives.

15 Eyre, *The Military Operations at Cabul*, p.146.

21

Retreat to Jalalabad

Thursday 6 January, the day of Epiphany, was set for the departure of the garrison from Kabul, starting at 7:00 a.m. The British garrison, after waiting in vain for the promised escort, was to march out without it through an opening in the eastern rampart of the cantonment which had been made the previous evening. It was clear and frosty, and very cold, the thermometer well below freezing point and the snow a foot deep. The total number of those who were eventually to thus quit the cantonments amounted to 4,500 fighting men, of which only 700 were Europeans, with six 6-pdr guns, three 3-pdr guns, 2,000 camels and *yaboos* laden with stores, and a massive crowd of camp followers. Orders were issued for each combat soldier to carry three days' provisions in his haversack and 40 rounds of ammunition in his pouch.

As late as the day before the garrison was scheduled to quit, Newab Zeman Khan, whom the Afghans had set up as king, had written to Major Eldred Pottinger warning him against setting out without the promised escort, but it was too late, everything had been packed up including the minds of the military authorities. For this much desired, retreat to Jalalabad the garrison had been divided into three columns.

Advance column.	Commanded by Brigadier Thomas Anquetil HM 44th Foot Sappers and miners A squadron of cavalry Three 3-pdr guns
Main column.	Commanded by Brigadier John Shelton 37th BNI 5th BNI (baggage guard) Shah's 6th Infantry Regiment Anderson's Irregular Horse Two 6-pdr guns Escort for ladies
Rear column.	Commanded by Colonel Robert Chambers

54th BNI
5th Bengal Light Cavalry
Four 6-pdr guns

While the above organisation neatly packaged the military for the desperate adventure ahead, no provisions had been made for the horde of camp followers, who were simply expected to follow in the normal way. These people had followed the army all the way from India, many with their wives and children. They had made their living by servicing the army and doing so under its protection. Now their benefactors were about to retreat, which in their simple lexicon meant running away, and they meant to run with it, all 12,000 of them.

Prior to the departure, a party of sappers under Lieutenant John Sturt had gone out to make the bridge over the Kabul river, about a mile from the cantonments, practicable for the carriage of guns albeit the river was frozen, not deep and crossable.

Consequently, the start was delayed and the advance column did not cross the start-line until 9:00 a.m. Then, further confusion was caused by an order coming down for the return to the cantonments as the chiefs had written to say that the escort was not yet ready and that the British should not move without it. A short time later this order was countermanded and Brigadier Anquetil was ordered to continue the advance and speedily. All this time the more fanatical of the Afghans were rushing in to the emptying cantonments to plunder and butcher those who had not yet vacated them, mainly the camp followers who naturally rushed forward, in a mass of huge confusion, to join the soldiers in front. As a result, much carefully packed baggage was lost and the rear column became utterly disorganised with frightened camp followers milling around causing formations to break down and discipline with it. It was not until 8:00 p.m. that the rear column was able to extricate itself; leaving behind a cantonment swarming with fanatics who were looting or burning everything. It also left behind the bodies of Lieutenant Charles Handyman and 50 *sepoys* of 54th BNI.

Gathered on the plains between the cantonments and the bridge were bands of Afghan horsemen and it was initially assumed that they were the promised escort, but they soon made it perfectly clear that they were not the escort. These horsemen stalked the column firing shots into the disorganised mass of soldiers and camp followers and the snow was stained with the blood of hundreds of bodies.

The rear column fought continuously, in the dark, all the way to Bagram six miles away, where it arrived at 2:00 a.m. It was here on the open plain that the army commander, against the advice of Brigadier Shelton, had established his first halt. He had originally planned to be at the mouth of the Khurd-Kabul Pass on the first day. It was a miserably cold night with soldiers and camp followers huddled together in the snow with horses, camels and *yaboos*, many to freeze to death. In the morning it was discovered that the bulk of the Shah's 6th Infantry Regiment, with some sappers, had absconded during the night and returned to Kabul. According to Captain Colin Mackenzie, they were disarmed and never trusted by the Afghans.

At 5:00 a.m. that morning the army, less hundreds of *sepoys* who had frozen to death, moved off in reverse order, but in reality there was no order as the army resembled a crowd of football fans rushing to catch the last bus home with soldiers, camp followers and animals mixed up with not even the slightest semblance of order and discipline. The advance proceeded without any rebel intervention although groups of Afghan horsemen could be seen on the flanks. The rearguard was, as always, the prime target for the tribesmen and before it could start it was

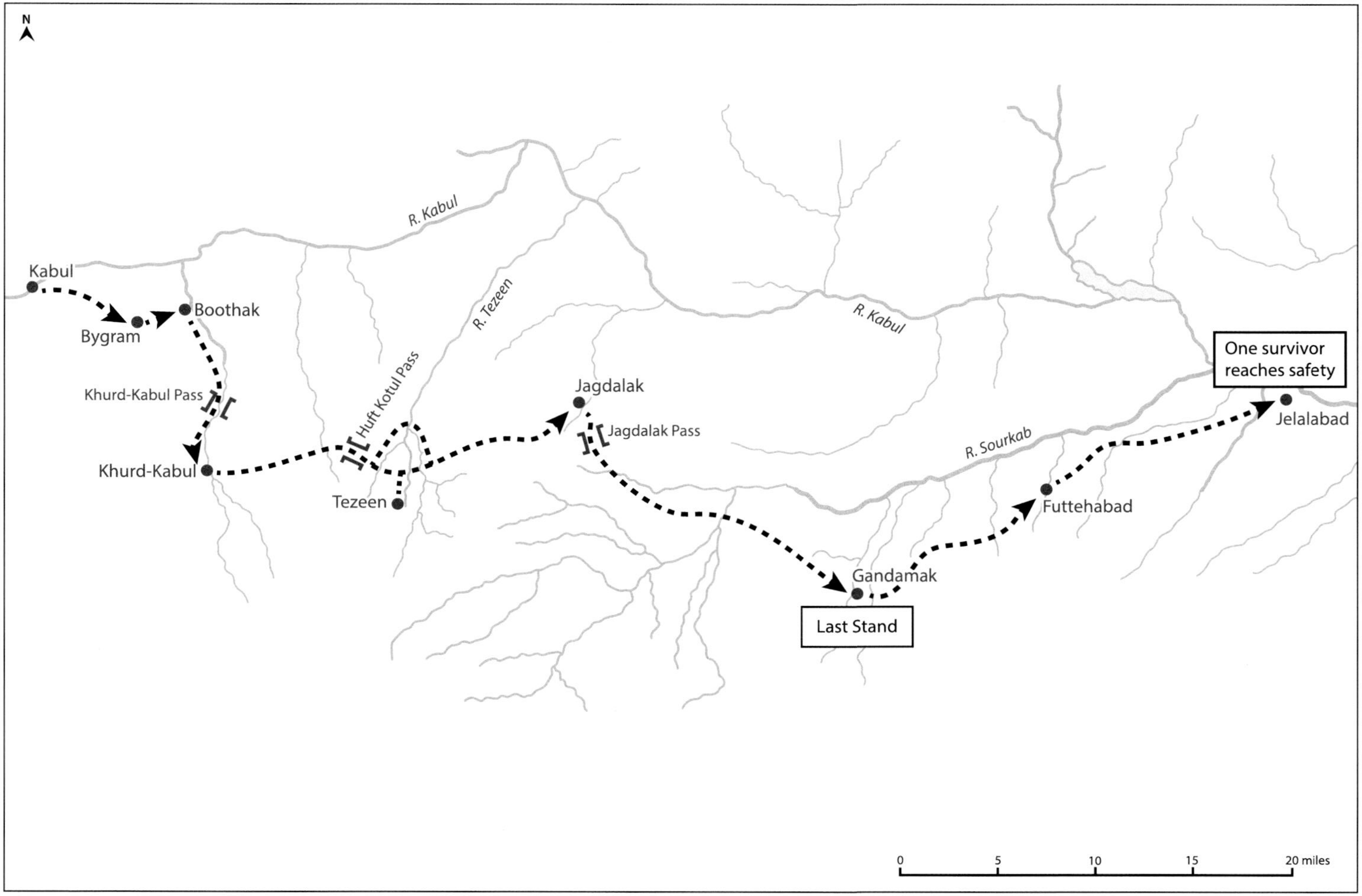

Map 14 Route of fatal Retreat from Kabul, 6–15 January, 1842.

attacked by these flanking horsemen. The rebels were kept in check by troops of HM 44th Foot and the 3-pdr guns, however a great deal of baggage still fell into Afghan hands and two of the 6-pdr guns were spiked and abandoned as the horses did not have sufficient strength to drag them on. Besides, the rearguard's advance was severely hampered by the disorderly crowd that clogged the road in front. At this point the mule-borne 3-pdr guns made a detour to avoid the crowd and got separated from the infantry. In traversing the detour one of the mules fell and the Afghans rushed forward to seize the gun; an attempt was made by the artillery men to recover it, but to no avail as they lacked infantry support. Brigadier Anquetil, who was commanding the rearguard, sent forward for reinforcements, but this proved to be impractical due to the crowded state of the road, and shortly afterwards the Afghans charged into the midst of the column carrying off large quantities of plunder and causing ever more confusion.

On this second day of the retreat, Mohammed Akbar Khan made his presence known by indicating that he had been sent by the chiefs to escort the army and insisted that it halt at Bootkak, 10 miles from Kabul and at the entrance of the Khurd-Kabul Pass, promising to supply food, forage and firewood. Probably in sheer desperation, Elphinstone agreed. But who was to say that this was not a treacherous tactic by Mohammed Akbar Khan to delay the advance, thus assisting the fanatics, who having levelled the cantonments, rushed back to hide behind rocks in the pass, ready for another crack at the dreaded infidels? That night the temperature fell to -10°. No doubt, many felt the same trepidations as Lady Sale when she recorded in her journal:

> Numbers of unfortunates have dropped, benumbed with cold, to be massacred by the enemy, yet so bigoted are our rulers, that we are still told that the *Sirdars* are faithful, that Mohammed Akbar Khan is our friend !!! &c &c &c, and the reason they wish us to delay is, that they may send their troops to clear the passes for us! That they will send them there can be no doubt for everything is occurring just as was foretold to us before we set out.[1]

On 8 January the Ghilzai sharpshooters started firing into the camp. According to Lady Sale, 'At sunrise no order had been issued for the march. The confusion was fearful. The force was perfectly disorganised, nearly every man paralysed with cold, so as to be scarcely able to hold his musket. Many frozen corpses lay on the ground. The ground was strewn with boxes of ammunition, plate and property of various kinds.'[2] Later in the morning, the Ghilzais were gallantly attacked by a company of HM 44th Foot, under the command of Major William Thain, clearly proving that soldiers under brave leadership could overcome these setbacks and redeem their reputation.

Another message was received from Mohammed Akbar Khan insisting that Major Pottinger, Captain George Lawrence and Captain Mackenzie be given up as hostages and an undertaking given by the General that his force would not advance beyond Tezeen until it was confirmed that Major General Sale's force had vacated Jalalabad. The General ordered the three officers to join the chief and they left at 11:00 a.m. to find Mohammed Akbar Khan enjoying his breakfast on the hillside. He gave them breakfast and disarmed them. These three officers were eventually placed in captivity and with the exception of Captain Mackenzie, who was twice used as an envoy to Jalalabad, next appear in this saga when they were rescued on 16 September 1842.

1 Sale, *A Journal of the Disasters in Afghanistan*, p.231.
2 Sale, *A Journal of the Disasters in Afghanistan*, p.232.

Major General Elphinstone, believing that the giving up of the hostages meant that a cease-fire was now in place, ordered his ragged force to prepare to move. However, they first had to take care of a fracas. Apparently some artillerymen had found a case of liquor and drunk the lot to keep warm; now well-oiled and full of drunken bravado, they had mounted their horses and vowed to charge the enemy. The General and his senior officers were aghast at this outbreak of warlike intentions which could only lead to a pitched battle. Captain Thomas Nicholl, commanding the artillerymen, eventually brought them to order. This little spark of aggression, albeit induced by liquor, was the last to emanate from this doomed force.

Only a few hundred fit fighting men now remained as the ragged procession neared the mouth of the pass. While enjoying their breakfast, the three hostages saw the army enter the pass, known as the 'Jaws of Death', a five-mile–long narrow gorge with a mountain torrent dashing down the centre which had to be crossed and recrossed 28 times.

The army commander had decided to march through the pass and to proceed on to Tezeen as fast as possible. The advance started at midday with 54th BNI leading, although the troops were now in a state of disorganisation, baggage mixed up with the remaining camp followers, pushing ahead in precipitate flight. Mohammed Akbar Khan and his followers went through the motions of controlling the fanatical Ghilzais, who poured over the struggling rabble of an army deadly fire from their *jezails*.

Penned in the confining pass, the army fell easy prey to the Ghilzai marksmen, who shot them down from the hillsides like ninepins. There was no time to save anything except one's life; baggage, property and, even in some cases, muskets were abandoned. Three thousand men were reported massacred in this dreadful pass from enemy fire or to have dropped down paralysed and exhausted, to be slaughtered by Afghan knives. It was during the passage of the defile that the indefatigable Lieutenant Sturt was mortally wounded in the stomach and died on 9 January.

The remnant of the force made it to the Khurd-Kabul fort, at the western end of the pass, that evening. Before sunrise the next morning the camp was again in motion as half the *sepoys* and camp followers set off without orders. The remaining troops followed and having marched about a mile another halt was ordered. This time the reason was that Mohammed Akbar Khan had renewed his demand for the surrender, under his guaranteed protection, of all European wives and children. On a previous occasion this proposal had been emphatically rejected, however, under the current circumstances, the proposal had a great deal of merit, as it would remove wives and children, who had already suffered enough, from the probability of continued horrors, to relative safety. There is little doubt that the General acceded to the proposal in the hope of placing the women and children beyond the dangers they currently faced, and also to show the Afghan chief that he was sincere in his wish to negotiate a truce and thus win from him a feeling of similar confidence. However, he realised that the parting of husbands and wives could meet with some resistance, so he allowed the husbands to withdraw with their wives and children, and so the officer-husbands left their soldiers to struggle on. At first the idea was met with a degree of hostility as in the case of Lady Macnaghten, who was horrified at the thought of being protected by her husband's murderer. The fact that Mohammed Akbar Khan's own family was in the hands of the British and that husbands could accompany their wives, swayed the argument in favour of accepting the chief's proposal, so all families became the guests of Mohammed Akbar Khan. As they were led back along the line of retreat they met with harrowing sights of mangled bodies. According to Lady Sale, 'The sights were dreadful, the smell of the bodies sickening and the corpses lay so thick it was impossible to look from them as it required care to guide my horse so as not to tread upon the bodies.'[3] At the time the families were handed over, Captain Aeacas Mackay had been selected to convey a fresh order to Major General Sale at Jalalabad to vacate that place in accordance with the agreed Afghan terms for the provision of protection and supplies, neither of which was ever honoured. However, Mohammed Akbar Khan declined to provide an escort for this officer, who remained with the force to later fall to a *jezail* bullet in his head.

On the morning of 10 January, when the march was resumed, the *sepoys* were almost non-effective and according to Lieutenant Vincent Eyre:

> The European soldiers were now almost the only efficient men left, the Hindustannis having all suffered more or less from the effects of the frost in their hands and feet; few were able even to hold a musket, much less pull a trigger; in fact, the prolonged delay in the snow had paralysed the mental and bodily powers of the strongest men, rendering them incapable of any useful exertion. Hope seemed to have died in every heart; the wildness of terror was exhibited in every countenance.[4]

The advance guard, consisting of what remained of HM 44th Foot, 50 *sowars* of 5th Bengal Light Cavalry and the sole remaining 6-pdr gun, pushed forward through the crowd and proceeded for a couple of miles without opposition to a spot where there was a narrow gorge between precipitous spurs through which a small stream flowed. Here the Ghilzais, securely positioned behind rocks, poured in a destructive avalanche of fire on the crowded column; men falling like flies choked any forward movement. The *sepoys*, seeing no means of escape, flung down their weapons and along with the camp followers fled. The Ghilzais now rushed down on the chaotic mass and a general massacre took place. The last remnants of the native regiments were scattered and destroyed and all remaining baggage fell into enemy hands.

Meanwhile, the advance column had managed to push through to Kubbur-i-Jubbar some five miles ahead where it waited for the rear party to join it, but only a handful of stragglers came in plus camp followers. The garrison that had marched out 4,500 strong was now reduced to 150 cavalrymen, 250 infantrymen and 50 horse artillerymen; counting remaining officers, a total of approximately 450 fighting men and as always a considerable number of camp followers.

At the approach of a body of Afghan horsemen, the ragged band of survivors lined up to meet the expected attack, but none came as, it transpired, the horsemen were Mohammed Akbar Khan and his followers. Major General Elphinstone took the opportunity to send out Captain James Skinner to remonstrate with Mohammed Akbar Khan about the attack on his force in violation of the treaty guaranteeing its safety. Captain Skinner, who had previously enjoyed the chief's protection, had long acted as go-between, between the British and the chief. In reply, Mohammed Akbar Khan expressed his regret at what had happened, adding that the Ghilzais were beyond his control and even of their own chiefs, however if the British were to lay down their arms and surrender to him and he would ensure the force's safe conduct to India. But this proposal did not include the remaining camp followers who were to be left to their own fate. The proposal was rejected by the General; the advance was resumed and came under immediate attack. There was spirit enough

3 Sale, *A Journal of the Disasters in Afghanistan*, p.249.
4 Eyre, *The Military Operations at Cabul*, p.165.

The original title describes this as 'Jugdelluk (Jagdalak) – The last Stand by General Elphinstone's Army in the calamitous retreat'.

remaining for Brigadier Shelton to muster the remaining effective men to launch a counter-attack, thus gaining a short respite. Another appeal came from Mohammed Akbar Khan and it was also rejected. It was now determined that the little force would strike out, by a rapid night march to the fort at Jagdalak, and this was to be done without the camp followers. The advance was resumed with this in view as quietly as possible, but the deception, which dire necessity alone could justify, did not succeed and the fighting men were soon engulfed by the unmanageable rabble of camp followers. The advance party made it to Jagdalak without molestation, while the rear party, commanded by Brigadier Shelton, was much hammered and had to fight all the way.

At Jagdalak, the exhausted and fatigued survivors found shelter behind some ruined walls and were about to settle down for some rest, when, suddenly, a volley of fire poured into their midst from the adjoining heights. They immediately formed up and in a bold effort cleared the ground in front of them and returned to the walls for their rest. In this brave rebuttal of the enemy, Captain William Grant, the AAG who had throughout been a curmudgeon, paid dearly for his display of bravado as he was mortally wounded and died the next morning.

Once again, Major General Elphinstone despatched Captain Skinner to Mohammed Akbar Khan with an appeal for protection. This time this treacherous chief came up with a new ploy to which, probably in sheer desperation, the General agreed, and as usual Brigadier Shelton did not. Mohammed Akbar Khan proposed that a conference be held to discuss all matters and that both the General and the Brigadier were to attend with their interpreter, Captain Hugh Johnson. The main issue for discussion was the proposal to provide protection for the remaining force at the expense of leaving the remaining *sepoys* and camp followers to their fate. The General and Brigadier could not agree to this albeit at the rate of attrition, to date, the inevitability of complete annihilation was staring them in the face. They went and after being received with much friendliness and hospitality, found themselves captives and were to be held as hostages until Jalalabad had been evacuated in accordance with the treaty.

Meanwhile, the minnow British force remained in position awaiting the return of its commander who was in conference with Afghans discussing the maintenance of his tattered honour. It was during this pause that Captain Skinner had ridden out, accompanied by Major Thain, to ascertain the situation and on the way Captain Skinner was shot in the face by Bulund Khan. Skinner fell and was carried back into camp where he died.

At dawn on Wednesday 12 January, the miserable little group of survivors, now reduced to 150 bayonets of HM 44th Foot, 15 dismounted artillerymen and 25 *sowers* of 5th Bengal Light Cavalry, but not one single *sepoy*, correctly assumed that their commanders had been inveigled into a trap and decided to continue the advance. On reaching the pass in front they were stopped by two barricades of prickly hollyoak, twisted together and about six feet high, which the Ghilzais had constructed. In endeavouring to cross this wicked obstacle, nearly all of the sad remnant of the Kabul garrison perished. It was a frightful scene, the survivors tore at the branches with their bare hands and the hidden Ghilzai marksmen poured in volleys of deadly fire then rushed in with their sabres clashing with some still defiant bayonets. Those who were still alive picked up their wounded comrades and somehow struggled through and by sunset were a few miles from Gandamak. After Gandamak, the country opens up without deadly passes and ravines. From here there were two routes to Jalalabad, one over the hills and the other along the valley. Here a dispute occurred as to which route to take and the party split up. One small group, led by Captain Bulstrode Bygrave, took off into the hills; most fell by the wayside leaving only Captain Bygrave, suffering from frostbite, and the Greek merchant, Mr Baness, to struggle on. Eventually, Captain Bygrave was unable to proceed any further and decided to stay under cover to await his fate. He was found by a local tribesman and handed over to Mohammed Akbar Khan. Meanwhile, Mr Baness struggled on and reached Jalalabad on 14 January, but died the next day from tetanus. Most disgracefully, some mounted officers had pushed through without any regard for their troops and not surprisingly some soldiers shot at them. Many of the wounded died during the night and when a count was taken there were 25 officers and 45 men left, The dead included Brigadier Anquetil, Colonel Chambers, Major Thain, Captain Nicholl and Captain William Dodgin.

At daybreak there was a brief respite and the group, on high ground to the left of the track, crouched together in some hovels outside Gandamak. Later in the day an Afghan horseman came in with a message from the local chief to the senior officer suggesting a parley. Captain Charles Griffiths of 37th BNI, accompanied by Mr Blewitt, set off with hope in their hearts. Meanwhile, the little group left at their hovel sanctuary were approached by ostensibly friendly Afghans, but when these fellows tried to relieve the soldiers of their muskets they received not too friendly a reaction resulting in the wretched defenders being picked off one by one by the unerring aim of the Ghilzai *jezails*. Only Captain Thomas Souter and four soldiers of HM 44th Foot survived and were taken prisoners at what was the Army's 'Last Stand'.[5]

5 The annihilation of HM 44th Foot at Gandamak during the retreat was immortalized by Lady (Elizabet) Butler in her painting, 'The Last Stand'. She also painted 'Remnants of an Army', which depicts a lone horseman (Dr Brydon) staggering into the comparative safety of Jelalabad.

Captain Griffiths and Mr Blewitt were taken off as prisoners to a local fort where the chief already had other prisoners with a view to ransoming them. One of these prisoners was Sergeant Major Lisson of 37th BNI, who was sent by the chief to Jalalabad to negotiate the ransom of all the others. Lisson arrived at Jalalabad with a small Afghan escort. The ransom terms were rejected, Lisson remained at Jalalabad and the Afghan escort were paid 20 rupees each and sent on their way. By this time Mohammed Akbar Khan had assembled a large army in the area and the local chief reckoned it more prudent to hand over his prisoners to the Khan.

The mounted group of some 15 officers and men, who had ridden on ahead, were also picked off one by one, and on reaching Futtehabad, 16 miles short of Jalalabad, there were only seven officers alive: Captain Henry Bellew, Frederick Collyer and Perin Hopkins, Lieutenants William Bird and William Steer, and doctors Edmund Harpur and William Brydon, plus the Greek merchant, Baness. They were all so close to safety if only they could urge their exhausted horses to carry them there. Just before Futtehabad, some Afghan peasants offered the group bread and water. While resting their horses and eating the bread, the officers were surrounded by armed Afghans and Captain Bellew and Lieutenant Bird were immediately cut down. The other six managed to gallop off. Dr Brydon, his horse utterly exhausted, fell back, as did Lieutenant Steer and both sought the safety of some rocks while the Afghans gave chase to the others, who were all caught and slaughtered. When the coast was clear, Dr Brydon mounted his exhausted horse and rode on, leaving Lieutenant Steer behind who had collapsed from exhaustion and his horse was in no better condition. An extract from Dr Brydon's journal, covering the rest of his gruelling escape to Jalalabad, is given in George Lawrence's *Forty-Three Years in India*..

On Thursday 13 January at Jalalabad, Ensign George Talbot was the duty officer on the ramparts when one of the sentries pointed to the west where a lone horseman could be seen approaching. Through his telescope, Talbot recognised the horseman as a British officer by his dress and appearance. A squad of sentries led by Captain Jeffrey Sinclair of HM 13th Foot rushed out to bring in the exhausted rider. No sooner had Dr Brydon entered the gate, than his totally jaded steed collapsed and died. From the good doctor, the lone survivor of the infamous retreat, the Jalalabad garrison were to learn the details of the disaster that had befallen the Kabul garrison. Assuming that over the following nine months 40 percent of the original 16,000 souls who marched out of Kabul were either rescued or 'came in' by various routes, would mean that 9,600 people perished, not counting the countless Afghan dead.[6]

6 In 1989 a submission was made by Pamela Magrath, the great-granddaughter of Dr Beauchamp Magrath, that her ancestor also survived the retreat. However, both Lady Sale's and Lieutenant Eyre's accounts of the disaster clearly place Dr Magrath alongside them in captivity, and there is no record of Dr Magrath ever arriving at Jelalabad, an event, which under the circumstances would certainly have solicited some comment. However, the doctor did get as far as Futtehabad where he was captured.

22

Jalalabad Outpost

The force under Major General Robert Sale arrived at Jalalabad on 13 November 1841. It comprised 700 men of HM 13th Foot, 750 men of 35th BNI, 40 men of the Shah's 6th Infantry Regiment, 130 men of 5th Bengal Light Cavalry, 90 men of the Shah's 2nd Cavalry, 60 men of the Mountain Train (artillery), 120 men of a field artillery battery and 80 sappers and miners. Counting staff members, a grand total of 2,100 fighting men plus 5,000 camp followers.

On its arrival the force found the defences of Jalalabad to be in a pitiful condition and as for provisions, the cupboard was bare. This was an extraordinary state of affairs to comprehend, as only eight months previously the place was bristling with troops and it is inconceivable that in the interim Jalalabad, at the head of the Khyber Pass and the Shah's summer capital, would have been left troopless. But such was the case, and this perceived haven was not in any good condition to withstand any determined attack. Clearly, Governor General Lord Auckland and Commander-in-Chief Sir Jasper Nicolls were at great fault for not establishing military posts to keep open communications with India after Lieutenant General Sir John Keane had withdrawn half the Army of the Indus back to India. With the exception of a small force of *Jezailchees* under Captain Joseph Ferris at Pesh Bolak, and a small detachment at Ali Masjid, in the heart of the Khyber Pass, under Mr Mackeson, the brother of Captain Frederick Mackeson, there was no British presence along the route from Ferozepore to Peshawar and then on to Kabul; the first 300 miles through the territory of a turbulent Sikh nation, and the next 195 miles through the territory of treacherous Afghans.

General Sale had left a small detachment of *Jan Baz* and Khyber Rangers under Captain Henry Burns at Gandamak. At Pesh Bolak, Captain Ferris had with him his wife, her sister and his second-in-command, Captain Patrick Gerrard plus Lieutenant John Lukin and Dr David Ritchie. Soon after Sale's force had left Gandamak, the erstwhile friendly chief of the town and the whole countryside rose up in rebellion. The *Jan-Baz* defected to the enemy and joined in the plunder of property, which included a great deal of cash, then they burned the cantonment. On receiving the news of the uprising at Gandamak, Captain Ferris sent Captain Gerrard and 500 *Jezailchees* to bring off the beleaguered Europeans at Gandamak. This mission was accomplished with the assistance of the loyal Khyber Rangers and the whole party retired on Jalalabad. Meanwhile, back at Pesh Bolak with a reduced garrison, Captain Ferris found himself in hot water as on 15 November his post was surrounded by hostile Afghans. With great difficulty he and his remaining *Jezailchees* fought their way to Lalpura where the loyal chief, Tara

Baz Khan, assisted the group to flee across mountain tracks to Peshawar. Major General Sale received the news about Pesh Bolak on 21 November but was in no position to help. Five months later, Captain Ferris and his *Jezailchees* were back in Afghanistan as part of Major General George Pollock's army. Of the Pesh Bolak incident, Major General Sale in a very long letter of 16 April to the Government's political secretary, Mr Herbert Maddock, observed:

> It is to be remarked, that I might in the second week of November have marched on Pesh Bolak, relieved from investment the corps of Jezailchees under Captain Ferris, and with it operated a doubtful retreat upon Peshawar. But I felt it my duty to give support to the last moment to our troops, struggling against their numerous enemies at Cabool, and maintain for them a point on which to retreat and rally if they met with a reverse.[1]

When Sale's Brigade had set off from Kabul, its destination was originally India, then on receipt of Kabul's plea for help, Major General Sale had decided to advance on to Jalalabad and there establish a base from which to assist the Kabul garrison's withdrawal; his brigade was not to touch Indian soil until 10 months later and thus it served in Afghanistan throughout the four years of the First Anglo-Afghan War, and Christmas was spent in the stink-hole of Jalalabad, where the band of HM 13th Foot did not play as all the music was lost and the band master was wounded.

The construction of what defences were to be undertaken at Jalalabad was a major consideration as obviously the defence of the whole city would require a much greater effort and resources than to concentrate the whole force in the citadel. Wisely, the decision was made to defend the whole city and Captain George Broadfoot's sappers and miners commenced the hard work of shoring up the ramparts and clearing the fields of fire, thus transforming Jalalabad into a beleaguered garrison surrounded by 6,000 Afghans. While the construction of the defences continued, a sortie of 35th BNI commanded by Lieutenant Colonel Thomas Monteith was sent out to clear the Afghans and to bring in provisions. On 28 November Lieutenant Colonel William Dennie of HM 13th Foot took out another sortie which cleared the Afghans, resulting in the garrison being unmolested for the following fortnight.

Back in India Mr George Clerk, the political agent at Ludhiana, was the first to hear of the uprising at Kabul and the murder of Sir Alexander Burnes. The news was passed on to the Governor General in Calcutta, and without waiting for a reply Clerk hurried off to Lahore to obtain Maharaja Sher Singh's sanction for British reinforcements to proceed through the Sikh kingdom to Peshawar. The pro-British Maharaja readily agreed and sent instructions to his governor in Peshawar, General Pablo Avitabile, to provide all needed assistance, and another instruction to Raja Gulab Singh of Jummu, to proceed to Peshawar. This gentleman's presence at Peshawar was necessary in order to placate the anti-British sentiments of the Sikh Khalsa (army). Clerk then ordered 64th BNI at Ferozepore and 60th BNI at Ludhiana to advance to Peshawar under the command of Brigadier Charles Wild. Soon afterwards he sent the 30th and 53rd BNI as well. Brigadier Wild's force took a month to travel the 300 miles to Peshawar and did so without any guns, as the commander-in-chief, Lieutenant General Sir Jasper Nicolls, reckoned that guns would be useless in the defiles of Afghanistan.

1 Patrick Macrory, *Fierce Pawns*, p.249.

Lord Auckland did not favour with the knee-jerk reaction of his political agent as is evident by what he was to write at the close of November:

> It is not clear to me how the march of a brigade can by any possibility have any influence upon the events which it is supposed may be passing in Kabul. The difficulty will not be one of fighting and gaining victories, but of supplies, of movement and carriage. The troops in Afghanistan are sufficiently numerous. They would but be encumbered by greater numbers and reinforcements could not arrive before the crisis will have passed. If the end is to be disastrous, they would but increase the extent of the disaster. I fear that safety of the force at Kabul can only come from itself.[2]

Nicolls appeared to be of the same mind and furthermore he was of the opinion that guns were of no use in the passes. So, Brigadier Wild advanced to war with no guns and no European troops, however not long afterwards prestige compelled the Governor General to ensure that the force at Peshawar would be strong enough to guarantee success and troops from various stations were ordered to assemble at Peshawar under the command of Major General George Pollock. Lord Auckland's first choice for commander was the senior Major General of the Company's Army, Major General James Lumley, but this gentleman, then serving as the adjutant general, declined on medical grounds and Lord Auckland, chary of sending yet another sick commander to the Afghan theatre, appointed Pollock, who at the time was in command of Agra Garrison.

The mention of no European troops is significant, as in those days a deep conviction existed that in a fight, the British Tommy was far superior to his *sepoy* counterpart. Consequently, in the formation of battle groups much emphasis was given to ensuring that the group was made up on a ratio of, at least, one European regiment to two native regiments. Of course, as was natural the British officers in native regiments, especially Major General William Nott, held vehemently to the view that his *sepoy* was as good in combat as his European cousin. Young John Neill of HM 40th Foot, in commenting on a later disaster at Khojak Pass in March 1842, touches on this issue saying, 'For the character of the Native soldiery I entertain the greatest admiration, and often I have witnessed their gallant bearing in the field. I trust therefore, that I shall not be accused of uttering anything approaching to disrespect, or in any way derogatory to the fair fame of those who were engaged in what has been described as the most unequal contest at Khojak, if I state my conviction that had a few European infantry been at the storm of that small fort, we should not have to record a disastrous defeat.'[3]

On 2 January, a letter dated 25 December was handed to Captain George Macgregor, the political agent with Sale's force. It was signed by Major Eldred Pottinger, the political agent at Kabul:

> My dear Macgregor,
> We have had a sad Comedy of Errors, or rather tragedy here. Macnaghten was called out to a conference and murdered. We have inter-changed terms on the grounds he was treating on for leaving the country, but things are not finally settled. However, we are to fall back

2 Beveridge, *A Comprehensive History of India*, Vol. 3, p.540.
3 John Martin Neill, *With the Somersets in Afghanistan: the Recollections of an Officer of the 40th … Regiment During the First Afghan War 1838–1842* (n.p.: Leonaur Ltd, 2011),

> on Jalalabad tomorrow or the next day. In the present disturbed state of the country we may expect opposition on the road, and we are likely to suffer much from cold and hunger, as we expect to have no carriage for tents and provisions.

On the following day another letter arrived dated 29 December and signed by both Major General William Elphinstone and Major Pottinger:

> It having been found necessary to conclude an agreement founded on that of the late Sir W.H. Macnaghten, for the evacuation of Afghanistan by our troops, we have the honour to request that you will intimate to the officer commanding at Jalalabad, our wish that the troops now at that place should return to India, commencing their march immediately after receipt of this letter, leaving all guns the property of Dost Mohammed Khan with the new governor, and also such stores and baggage as there may not be the means to carry away and the provisions in store for our use on arrival at Jalalabad. Abdul Ghafur Khan who is the bearer of this letter, will render you all the assistance in his power. He has been appointed governor of Jalalabad on the part of the existing government.[4]

This communication was totally at odds with Major General Sale's staunchly held determination to hold Jalalabad; besides, the letter had not been delivered by the hand of Abdul Ghafur Khan and based on his recent experience of Afghan fidelity to treaty terms, the veracity of the purport of this communication was suspect, especially as Captain Macgregor was privy to a communication from Mohammed Akbar Khan to the local chiefs exhorting them to fight the infidels. Major General Sale assembled a War Council to decide on compliance or rejection. The news that Brigadier Wild was about to advance from Peshawar made the Council's decision a foregone conclusion in regard to the request to withdraw, and this was conveyed in their reply of 9 January:

> Sir,
> We have the honour to acknowledge the receipt of your letter of the 29th ultimo, which you therein state was to be delivered to us by Abdul Ghafur Khan, appointed governor of this place by the existing powers in Caubul. That communication was not delivered to us by him, but by a messenger of his, and though dated 29 December 1841, has only this moment reached us. I have at the same time, positive information that Mohammed Akbar Khan has sent a proclamation to all the chiefs in the neighbourhood, urging them to raise their followers for the purpose of intercepting and destroying the force now at Jalalabad. Under these circumstances we have deemed it our duty to await a further communication from you, which we desire may point out the security which may be given for our safe march to Peshawar.
> We have the honour to be &c
> R. Sale. Major General Commanding.
> G. H. Macgregor. Political Agent[5]

4 Kaye, *History of the War in Afghanistan*, Vol. 2, p.354.
5 Macrory, *Fierce Pawns*, p.296.

There is no record of this reply ever reaching the addressees, who, at the time it was written, were embroiled in the Ghilzai ambush at Khurd-Kabul. At the same time as this reply was despatched, Major General Sale sent a letter to the Commander-in-Chief, stating that in the absence of any instruction from High Command, he considered himself free to refuse Major General Elphinstone's order which was 'forced from our Envoy and Military Commander with knives at their throats', and that he intended to remain at Jalalabad.

On 12 January, Major General Sale was to receive the last message from the Kabul force in which Major General Elphinstone reported that they had left the cantonments and had been held up at Bootlak for two days, and that Mohammed Akbar Khan was escorting them with cavalry, but he believed that the Khan had sent his emissaries ahead to rouse the tribes to attack.

On Thursday 13 January 1842, the sole remnant of the Kabul garrison, Dr Brydon, crawled into Jalalabad, and falling into welcoming arms, he told the fearful tale of the annihilation of the garrison of 4,500 men and thousands of camp followers. It is conceivable that the thought did cross Major General Sale's mind that the Jalalabad garrison could suffer the same fate and that a rapid retreat from Jalalabad would be advantageous. However, with thousands of exuberant Afghans in the vicinity, hell-bent on the destruction of all infidels, the risk would be too great and a strong defence of Jalalabad with the expected relief by Brigadier Wild's force was the more prudent option. Over the next few weeks, *sepoys* and camp follower survivors of the retreat crept into Jalalabad with more horror stories. Then on 31 January, Sergeant Major Lisson of 37th BNI came in; his accompanying Afghan was given 50 rupees and sent away.

Brigadier Wild's chances of success were limited. His task included the replenishment of the treasury and Commissariat at Jalalabad, but he had hardly any carriage and only one troop of irregular cavalry. In addition, his native troops were scared of the Khyber Pass and the Sikh contingent of the Muslim Nujeeb battalion refused to fight against their co-religionists. In Peshawar, the Sikh Khalsa was in a mutinous state and refused to hand over any guns. At the beginning of January the small garrison at Ali Masjid, 15 miles from Peshawar, was in need of immediate help and Brigadier Wild was persuaded to send two of his regiments, commanded by Lieutenant Colonel William Mosley, to its rescue.

Stuck up on a hill, the small garrison at Ali Masjid, commanded by Mr Mackeson, was in dire need of ammunition, provisions and especially water. Mackeson had noticed that the Afghans, after each attack, were remarkably tenacious about recovering the bodies of their dead comrades. So after each assault Mackeson's men would rush out and bring in the dead bodies, which Mackeson bartered with his assailants for two *mussucks* of water per body.

The regiments, under the command of Lieutenant Colonel Mosley, made a successful march, guided by Captain Frederick Mackeson, and arrived at Ali Masjid on 15 January. However, for some inexplicable reason all the essential provisions had been left behind at Peshawar and now the increased garrison at Ali Masjid was in dire straits. With his remaining force Brigadier Wild hurried up to their relief, but the Nujeeb battalion mutinied and marched back to Peshawar. Wild made it to Ali Masjid only to huddle down with his demoralised *sepoys* in total confusion and dismay. The garrison suffered severe losses and the Brigadier was wounded. The garrison at Ali Masjid was starved out and had to fight its way back; the brave venture had been a total failure. Captain Henry Lawrence, who was at Peshawar trying to get the Sikhs to co-operate, had this to say about Brigadier Wild: 'Few officers have been worse treated than the gallant and unfortunate Wild. As brave a soul as ever breathed, he was driven broken-hearted to his grave.' Wild's demoralised force was back in Peshawar on 24 January. On the brigade's return and in a demonstration of their lack of confidence of British success, the 64th BNI refused to accept their pay. This action of refusing to accept the 'salt' of their superiors was viewed as mutiny and was a clear indication of the very low state of morale.[6]

On 21 January Major General Sale, who had been anxiously awaiting arrival of Brigadier Wild's force, received the shattering news that the Brigadier had failed and that Ali Masjid had been abandoned. A few days later he was in receipt of a surprising letter from Shah Shuja, brought in under a flag of truce. The letter informed him that after the success of the initial uprising, feuds and jealousies had wrought much dissension among the Afghans. Among the older chiefs there was growing resentment of the rising power of Mohammed Akbar Khan. There was too a strong feeling that the Shah was the best person able to mitigate the vengeance which the British were expected to mete out. In his letter the Shah stated that while he regretted the grief the British had undergone, he appealed to the British to send him plenty of money and all would be well. 'I shall have the people so much under my control that, if I ordered it, they would carry the shoes of the Sahibs.' The letter concluded by asking the General, referring to the treaty signed by the late Envoy, what his intentions were regarding Jalalabad.

To many at Jalalabad, the situation appeared to be hopeless, especially as the Kabul garrison, the prime reason for holding Jalalabad, had been annihilated and Brigadier Wild's relief force had been ignominiously driven out of the Khyber Pass. The Jalalabad garrison's only contact with India, to date, had been the staunch support of Tara Baz Khan, the chief at Lalpura, who had brought in provisions and 21,000 rupees sent by Captain Frederick Mackeson from Peshawar, and now that Ali Masjid had been abandoned, this slim support would evaporate. Consequently, Major General Sale's mind gave thought to the possibility of negotiating a withdrawal, which his political agent, Captain Macgregor, was confident he could arrange. No one can question his qualities as a brave soldier and as a commander of a regiment there was none better, but the responsibilities that went with commanding a composite force caused 'Fighting Bob' Sale some discomfort, and as in the case of the decision not to return to Kabul the previous November, Sale assembled a war council on 27 January, or, as his ADC Captain Henry Havelock called such meetings, a 'jackdaw parliament', to decide the fate of his force. The members of the council, all commanders of various units, comprised: Major General Sale, Captain Macgregor, political agent, Lieutenant Colonel Monteath commanding 37th BNI, Lieutenant Colonel Dennie commanding HM 13th Foot, Captain James Abbott the artillery commander, Captain Christopher Oldfield commanding the cavalry, Captain Julian Backhouse the Mountain Train commander and Captain George Broadfoot commanding the sappers. Captain Havelock was included as a non-voting member in his capacity as the General's ADC.

The meeting opened with the General and the political agent expressing their conviction that nothing could be hoped for from the Government and that they were resolved to yield and negotiate a safe retreat. At this declaration there was much excitement and Captain George Broadfoot jumped up declaring that he refused to believe that the Government had abandoned the garrison to its fate and he continued in his remonstrations against the proposed action in opposition to the majority of the members. So, in the absence of a unanimous decision the meeting was adjourned. As the members retired to their various quarters with their thoughts, the General was in receipt of a communication to the effect that Major General Pollock had

6 This regiment was to mutiny again at Ferozepore in July 1845, after which it was disbanded.

arrived in Peshawar. Meanwhile, with the support of captains Oldfield and Havelock, Captain George Broadfoot was able to win over more members to his idea of continuing to hold Jalalabad. When the meeting was reconvened, the motion to stay was carried. The great and first military historian, the Honourable John Fortescue, referred to Sale's War Council as 'the most astonishing and perhaps the most disgraceful, recorded in the annals of the Army'.

Thus ended the memorable council of war, whose eleventh hour resolve to hold the fort mainly averted the run of British prestige in India, acquiring for the garrison the designation of the 'Illustrious Garrison'; and credit for its final decision belongs to Captain George Broadfoot, firmly backed by Captain Havelock. The day after the decision, General Sale received a letter from Peshawar informing him that every effort was being made for the relief of his garrison. Consequently, there was no more talk of negotiations or surrender and the garrison's courage was not impaired even when an earthquake on 19 February wrecked the fortifications so laboriously constructed.

The massive earthquake that shook Jalalabad undid in a matter of an hour all the garrison had constructed during the past three months. Undaunted, the garrison, under the guidance of Captain George Broadfoot, set to work the next day to reconstruct the city's defences. After the initial shock, the Afghans felt that the hand of Allah had given them a great advantage with the defences of Jalalabad being levelled to the ground and a high road made for them to walk in, and during the next four weeks Mohammed Akbar Khan made three attacks, all of which were repulsed. Provisions began to fall short and the Commissariat moneybox was near empty. There was no rum, morale low and the troops became ever more suspicious of the local inhabitants, especially of those with dwellings abutting the ramparts. These suspicions gradually extended to include the Afghans who made up the Khyber Rangers and the *Jezailchees*, who had only recently brought off the European officers from the uprising at Gandamak. After much thought, Major General Sale decided not to take a risk on their continued loyalty and had them evicted. On 2 March, Lieutenant Thomas Seaton noted in his journal, 'All our comforts are rapidly disappearing, tea has long been gone, coffee disappeared today; sugar on its last legs; butter gone; there is no grass for the cows, candles not to be had; wine and spirits are matters of memory. In a few days we shall be reduced to our rations of half a pound of salt beef and half a pound of coarse flour and further reductions are in prospect.'[7]

Lord Auckland received the news of Sir William Macnaghten's murder on 31 January and his heart sank with the realisation that his glorious strategy, which only a year earlier had the potential of being a huge success, was now to end in a disastrous retreat. According to his sister, Emily, 'Poor George had aged 10 years in as many hours'. The initial reaction from Calcutta was a boastful proclamation by the Secret Department, which while acknowledging the disaster ends, 'But the Governor General in Council while he deeply laments the loss of brave officers and men, regards this partial reverse only as a new occasion for displaying the stability and valour of the British Indian Army.' On 10 February His Lordship sent instructions to Major General William Nott to act on his own judgement to secure the safety of his troops and to uphold the honour of the British Army. If he resolved to fall back on Quetta, he was to do his best to relieve Khelat-i-Ghilzai. Major General Pollock was instructed to confine himself to extricating Sale's brigade from Jalalabad.

7 Thomas Seaton, *From Cadet to Colonel*, Vol. I (London: Blackett, 1866), p.302.

Only a year earlier the guns at Fort William had roared in celebration, titles and awards showered on the great and lucky, and a settlement in New Zealand was named after His Lordship. In handing over a battered ship of state, it must have occurred to His Lordship, as an eternal regret that he had not chosen to accept the option of an honourable withdrawal offered to him by the Court of Directors (Chapter 18).

As His Lordship was soon to hand over to his successor, he applied all his energies to prepare everything so that his successor could decide for remaining in Afghanistan or for retreating as seemed best. On 19 February, Lord Auckland observed:

> Since we have heard of the misfortunes of the Khyber Pass, and have been convinced that from the difficulties at present opposed to us, and in the actual state of our preparations, we could not expect, at least in this year, to maintain a position in the Jalalabad districts for any effective purpose, we have made our directions in regard to withdrawal from Jalalabad clear and positive, and we shall rejoice to learn that Major General Pollock will have anticipated them than more expressed orders, by confining his efforts to the same objects.[8]

In his final instruction to Major General Pollock of 24 February, Lord Auckland wrote, 'You will consider it one of the first objects of your solicitude to procure the release of all British officers and soldiers and their families, private servants and followers.'[9] Thus did Lord Auckland's administration fall to dust and that of his successor, Lord Ellenborough (Edward Law), start with his arrival in Calcutta on 28 February 1842.

On the 1st and 24th of March and again on the 1st of April, and at the behest of junior commanders, the Jalalabad garrison launched successful sorties to disperse the enemy from the vicinity of the city, and during the last of these sorties 500 sheep were captured to replenish the depleted stocks of the Commissariat. When the distribution of the sheep was made to the various regiments the 35th BNI, in a friendly gesture, gave their allocation to HM 13th Foot as their need for animal food was less than that of the Europeans. One, not too spectacular, event gave the troops something to cheer about. Captain Augustus Abbott of the Bengal Artillery, was renowned for his unerring aim with his guns. One day he took aim at a small hill some 400 yards from the ramparts from which the Afghans frequently annoyed the garrison with their *jezails*, and on this particular day a party of Afghans were making merry on the hill, and in the midst of them was a piper. Captain Abbott loaded a mortar, and taking careful aim, fired. The shell whizzed up into the air and landed directly on the piper. Henceforth, the hill has been known as 'Piper's Hill'.

Major General Pollock had received his appointment on New Year's Day, and with it the news that Lieutenant Colonel Sir Richmond Shakespeare was to be his military secretary. Pollock had not been given any choice in the matter. Shakespeare, now a knight of the realm, had recently returned to India after an acclaim-fuelled visit to England and was now the current glamour-boy of the Company's army. This news was followed by a General Order dated 8 January, which censured Major General Elphinstone's actions with the Government's 'most severe displeasure' directing that a full military inquiry be initiated and that Major General

8 Beveridge, *A Comprehensive History of India*, Vol. 3, p.551.
9 Mackenzie, *Storms and Sunshine of a Soldier's Life*, Vol. 2, p.305.

Pollock replace Major General Elphinstone. At the same time, both major generals Pollock and William Nott at Kandahar were given full power to act according to their discretion, conferring supreme political as well as military authority in Afghanistan on them.

Major General Pollock arrived at Peshawar on 5 February to find 1,800 men in hospital, the troops disheartened, insubordinate and a general atmosphere of unmilitary spirit with some of the officers, which may have prompted Major Pottinger to comment that 'some of the worst officers in the army have been sent with General Pollock'. A captain in the 53rd BNI declared openly at mess, with his colonel and a major being present, that he would do his best to prevent any *sepoy* of his company from ever again entering the Khyber Pass. As in the case of the demoralised 14th Army in Burma 100 years later, Major General Pollock, like Field Marshal Sir William Slim, had first to raise the morale of his army before he could make it fight. Besides the morale of his troops, Pollock's other great problem arose from the desertion of the camel men with their animals, which compelled him, when he did advance, to leave part of his ammunition behind. His first order to his new command was issued on 24 February and distributed for all to read. In part it stipulated that 'his troops will never be called upon by him to make useless sacrifices or undergo unnecessary hardships'.[10]

Another issue with which the General had to contend was the co-operation of the Sikhs. While the Governor of Peshawar could not be more helpful, the Sikh army was decidedly resentful of the British force gathering there. So captains Henry Lawrence and Frederick Mackeson were sent to Attock, to solicit the active involvement of Raja Gulab Singh in providing a significant number of Sikh troops to swell the ranks of Pollock's army and thereby cementing them to the cause.

The wily Raja saw in the aim of the officers' visit a super opportunity to shore up his own future in the turbulent Sikh state and made it quite clear to the British officers that if he helped out, the obligation would be to him and not the Sikh *durbar.* Captain Henry Lawrence assured the Raja that his services would not be forgotten or go unrewarded and guaranteed that the British would see to it that his possessions were secure in the future. Three and a half years later, at the end of the First Anglo-Sikh War, the British sold Kashmir to the Raja for £75,000 (about £5.6 million in modern money). The Raja set off for Peshawar to use all his cunning and skill to persuade the Sikh Khalsa to advance up the Khyber Pass along an alternative route to the British and accompanied by Captain Henry Lawrence. The mutinous conduct of his Sikh allies was the greatest of Major General Pollock's worries and only a combination of promises to Raja Gulab Singh and the offer of Jalalabad eventually brought a change in the Sikh army's attitude.

By the end of March 1842, on receipt of the new governor general's order for the withdrawal of all troops from Afghanistan, Pollock was under grave pressure to complete his task of relieving the Jalalabad garrison. With HM 31st Foot still on its way to join him, Pollock ordered his long awaited advance up the Khyber Pass on 5 April. His force comprised: HM 3rd Light Dragoons, 10th Bengal Light Cavalry, 6th, 26th, 30th, 33rd, 53rd, 60th, and 64th BNIs, 600 *Jezailchees*, plus artillery and a Sikh contingent of 10 regiments.

While Pollock with the British contingent advanced up the normal seven-mile–long route to Ali Masjid, the Sikh contingent of 10 regiments under General Gulab Singh Pohovindia, accompanied by Captain Henry Lawrence, advanced along the 14-mile route known as the Jabla Ka,

10 Stocqueler, *Memorials of Afghanistan*, p.202.

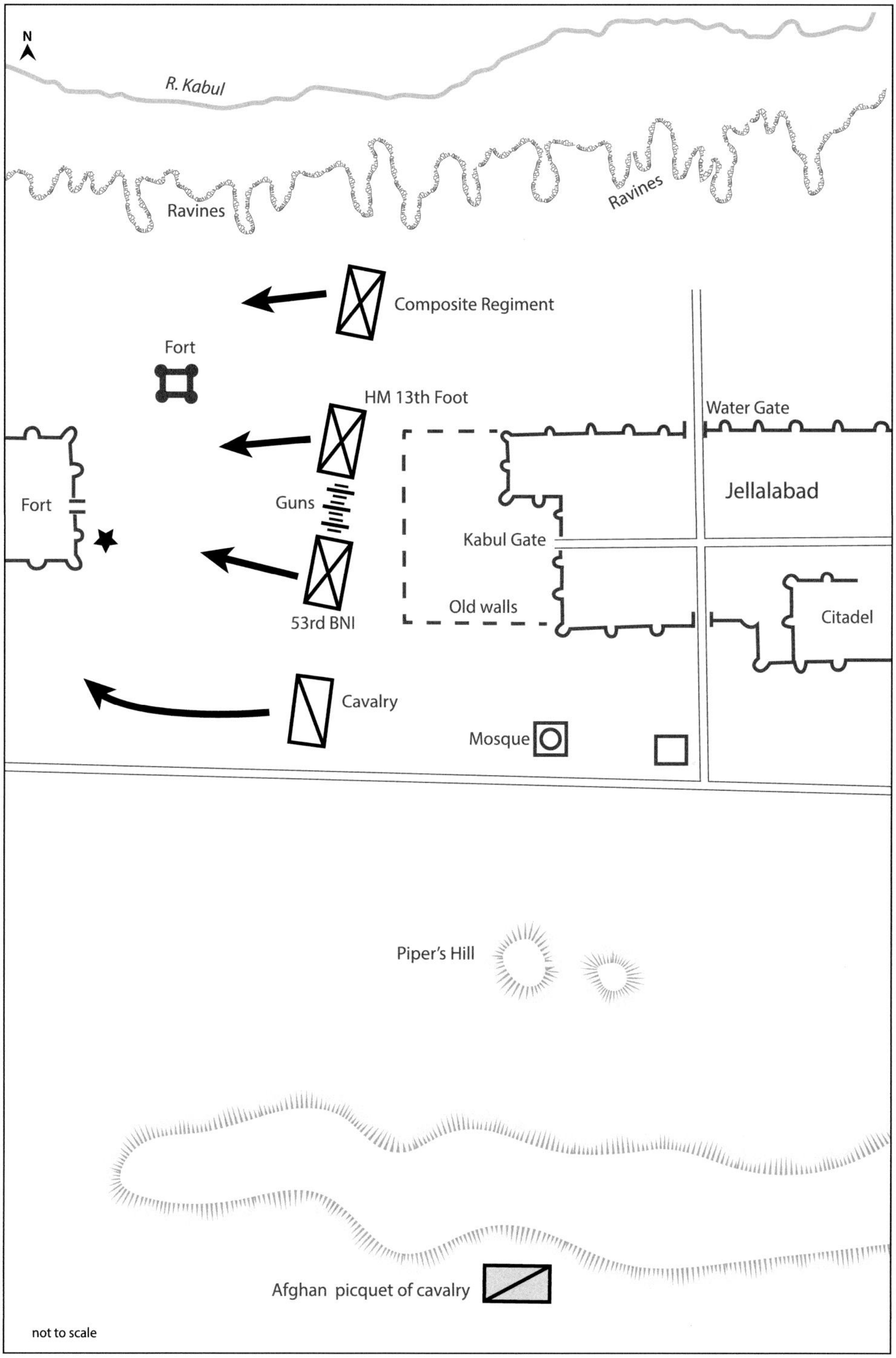

Map 15 Last Action of the 'Illustrious Garrison', Jalalabad, 7 April 1842.

which converged with the route taken by Pollock at Ali Masjid. Both contingents had to fight their way to this first objective, and no doubt with this two-pronged approach the Afridis were put to a great disadvantage. At Ali Masjid, 3,300 Sikh troops were left to garrison the place while the remainder, under their General, followed Pollock's contingent to Jalalabad. In his despatch of 6 April covering the advance to Ali Masjid, Major General Pollock acknowledged the assistance provided by the various elements of his force including that of the *Jezailchees*, of whom he wrote, 'again conspicuous in forcing the enemy to relinquish the stronghold'. He also mentioned both Captains Henry Lawrence and Frederick Mackeson but failed to make any mention of the significant assistance provided by the Sikh contingent. This political slur, probably deliberate, was quickly covered up by the Governor General in his notification of 19 April:

> The Governor General deems it to be due to the troops of Maharaja Shere Singh, to express his entire satisfaction with their conduct as reported to him, and to inform them that the loss sustained by the Sikhs in the assault of the Pass, which was forced by them, is understood to have been equal to that sustained by the Troops of Her Majesty and the Government of India. The Governor General has instructed his Agent at the Court of the Maharaja, to offer his congratulations to His Highness on this occasion so honourable to the Sikh arms.[11]

Back in Jalalabad the garrison had almost given up ever being relieved, and on 6 April information was brought in to the effect that Major General Pollock's force had also suffered a repulse in the Khyber Pass. Urged on by his junior commanders, Major General Sale determined that the salvation of his garrison lay entirely in his own hands and seizing the initiative he attacked the enemy on 7 April in three columns of infantry, the centre column being led by Lieutenant Colonel Dennie while the flanking columns were led by Lieutenant Colonel Monteith and Captain Havelock. The artillery was under the command of Captain Abbott, while the cavalry was commanded by Captain Christopher Oldfield. As the sun peeked over the mountains, the columns sallied forward to execute Sale's simple plan of a direct attack on Mohammed Akbar Khan's camp, to burn it, drive him off into the river and to capture all his guns. The centre column directed its efforts against the fort, which had been selected as the key objective. The struggle was fierce and Lieutenant Colonel Dennie had led his column with his usual gallantry, but after passing the outer walls of the fort and endeavouring to penetrate its interior Dennie fell mortally wounded and died soon after the capture of the fort. The attack was a huge success and was probably the one single most important action that turned the tide of the Afghan insurgency. That evening Major General Sale was delighted to report:

> We have made ourselves masters of two cavalry standards recaptured four guns looted by the Kabul and Ghazni forces, the restoration of which to our Government is a matter of much honest exultation among our troops; seized and destroyed a great quantity of material and ordnance stores, and burnt the whole of the enemy's tents. In short the defeat of Mohammed Akbar Khan in open field, by troops whom he had boasted of blocking, has been complete and signal.[12]

11 Stocqueler, *Memorials of Afghanistan*, p.203.
12 Beveridge, *A Comprehensive History of India*, Vol. 3, p.543.

Immediately after this battle Mohammed Akbar Khan hurried back to Kabul to proclaim himself *Wazir* to Shah Shuja, who had in the meanwhile shut himself up in the security of the Bala Hissar. Disunity among the chiefs was quite apparent and the Shah was viewed as the only person around whom these chiefs could unite in order to face the expected British retribution. On 5 April the Shah was called upon to come out and show his sincerity by leading the Afghans in defence of their country. The Shah, who had been left to his own devices by his erstwhile British ally, had no alternative but to come out and show himself to be the true king of Afghanistan. On his way to the Seah Sung hill to meet with the assembled chiefs, he was shot in the head by Shuja-ud-Daula, the son of Zeman Khan. This mad act was to further disunite the chiefs while the Shah's son, Fateh Jung, safe at the Bala Hissar, declared himself king with Mohammed Akbar Khan his *Wazir*. The situation in Kabul was chaotic and no one knew who actually represented the Afghan nation, albeit the new *Wazir* was very much in charge.

On 16 April, Major General Pollock's army eventually reached Jalalabad, and HM 31st Foot, under the command of Lieutenant Colonel John Bolton, joined him on 6 May. Before this regiment left their barracks in Meerut, it was appealed to by the widows of HM 44th Foot to avenge their slaughtered husbands. Major General Pollock now had an army of 19,000 troops, more than strong enough to march to Kabul, yet his clear order from the supreme Government was to withdraw. However, he had also been tasked by the previous Governor General to secure the release of all the hostages, so the army remained at Jalalabad while negotiations for the release of the hostages were attempted, and it was to stay there in the heat of the summer, with animals and men dying, the stench unbearable, flies everywhere and the men muttering, 'Why are we waiting!'

The Jalalabad garrison had been overjoyed by the arrival of Major General Pollock's forces, and with typical 'Tommy' humour, the soldiers of HM 13th Foot published a fake General Order alluding to Pollock's delay.

> The Governor General has the greatest satisfaction in tendering to General Pollock his best thanks for his gallantry and good conduct in so firmly maintaining his post in General Avitabile's comfortable house at Peshawar in spite of the urgent necessity for leaving it to Advance to the rescue of the British garrison beleaguered in Jalalabad.[13]

If the triumph of forcing the Khyber Pass belongs to Pollock, then the less spectacular achievement of keeping it open for supplies and communications belongs to captains Henry Lawrence and Frederick Matheson, who worked tirelessly to keep Pollock's back door open, for the Khyber Pass was held by the grasping Afridis and truculent Sikhs; at one end Frederick Matheson bribing the Afridis, at the other Henry Lawrence manipulating the disgruntled Sikhs.

On 27 April Captain Colin Mackenzie appeared at the gates of Jalalabad. He had been sent by Mohammed Akbar Khan with proposals for the withdrawal of British forces and the more contentious issue of the hostages. Earlier, Lord Auckland had approved the ransoming of the hostages, whereas the new Governor General was against paying ransom money as this would more likely lead to higher and higher demands and to further delay; besides, it would enrich the very persons who had caused the problem in the first place. As the British held Dost

13 Seaton, *From Cadet to Colonel*, Vol. I, p.327.

Mohammed Khan, his family and that of Mohammed Akbar Khan, the Governor General reckoned that an exchange of prisoners was a much more viable solution.

As was to be expected, Mohammed Akbar Khan's proposals, conveyed by Captain Mackenzie, included a down payment for himself, After a few days of relative comfort, a change of clothing and a debriefing during which the confused state of Afghan affairs and disunity of the chiefs was discussed, Captain Mackenzie returned with Major General Pollock's negative reply. Before he left, Captain Mackenzie borrowed 200 rupees from the Jalalabad treasury. A year later, the Company came knocking on his door for repayment.

23

Kandahar Outpost

Great was the consternation throughout Afghanistan and India of the British predicament at Kabul. The Afghans, alive to the importance of their position, and aware of the likely retribution that would follow, lost not a moment in strengthening their hand to improve on the advantage they had gained. As fast as the call to arms could be carried, insurrections broke out at all British-held posts. A large body of Ghilzais was sent immediately to invest Ghazni, as in the New Year Mohammed Akbar Khan was to do at Jalalabad; while at Kandahar, Prince Suftur Jung defected to join the enemy.

Ghazni was held by 27th BNI and auxiliary troops, all under the command of Colonel Thomas Palmer. They were joined by a small detachment under the command of Lieutenant David Crawford of the Bombay Artillery, which had been escorting some Afghan prisoners from Kandahar to Kabul when it was attacked, forcing it to free the prisoners and fight its way to Ghazni. By 20 November 1841, Colonel Palmer found that his position had been surrounded by the enemy. Earlier, his pleas for money to improve the defences of his post had been rejected, consequently he was not well placed for either a siege or any offensive action. His only option was to hold out until reinforced, particularly with guns, so he was much relieved to learn that the enemy, greatly alarmed at the approach of Lieutenant Colonel James MacLaren's brigade, had suddenly withdrawn to face this threat, thus allowing Colonel Palmer to avail himself of the respite to improve his fortifications and lay in essential supplies. But, equally suddenly, the enemy were back on 7 December encouraged by the retirement of MacLaren's brigade.

An act of humanity, which under the circumstances can only be described as stupidity, caused Colonel Palmer to allow the townspeople to remain in the city instead of turning them out into the bitter weather; and in gratitude for this kindness the townspeople allowed the enemy into the city through a hole in the wall which they had dug on 16 December. The consequence was that the British garrison were compelled to shut themselves in the citadel the next day. There they continued to maintain themselves with the utmost difficulty and with no hope of relief. Then, the infamous letter from Major General William Elphinstone and Major Eldred Pottinger arrived, instructing the Colonel to withdraw under a flag of truce and to hand over the city to Shamshoodeen, who had been appointed Governor of Ghazni. Unlike the responses from Kandahar and Jalalabad to similar instructions, Colonel Palmer's dire circumstances allowed him no choice but to comply, and on 1 March he entered into negotiations to evacuate the place, only to find that instead of being allowed to march out, the whole garrison were made prisoners. On 10 March the *sepoys* of the garrison, disregarding orders, perished to a man in an attempt to force their way across country to Peshawar, which they imagined to be only 50 miles away. Meanwhile, the officers who had surrendered on the futile promise of honourable treatment remained in strict confinement during which period Lieutenant Samuel Davis died of typhus, and Lieutenant David Lumsden and his wife, finding conditions intolerable and fearing the worst, made a fatal attempt to escape and were murdered a few miles into their quest. The British prisoners were eventually taken to Kabul on 18 August and thence to Bamian to join the other hostages.

Colonel Palmer was to report his surrender in a laconic despatch, an extract of which follows:

> Sir, It is with much concern I acquaint you, that from want of water, and by an overpowering force under cover and within 50 yards of us in the city, I have been compelled to enter into terms to evacuate the citadel and fort within six days. In capitulating, I have only acted upon the orders of Major Pottinger and General Elphinstone, who directed me in an official letter to evacuate the citadel and the city.[1]

The Colonel's surrender was criticised by many and was unfavourably compared with major generals Robert Sale and William Nott, who had managed to hold out. In the end he was officially exonerated. His position had been very different. Without water and artillery his beleaguered garrison would have had no success in breaking out, much less fighting its way to safety.

The return, much to the satisfaction of Major General Nott, of Lieutenant Colonel MacLaren's brigade on 8 December after an ineffectual endeavour to reach Kabul where it had been despatched for the purpose of attempting a relief, rendered the force at Kandahar strong enough to resist all opposition provided provisions held out. Nott was well aware that Kandahar would be the next target of Afghan ambitions. 'The good people here', he wrote, 'are anxiously looking for the result of the affairs at Kabul, when they should be against us, they will try their strength.'[2] At this juncture, the Kandahar force totalled 9,000 troops which comprised:

In cantonments under Lieutenant Colonel MacLaren
- HM 40th Foot
- 2nd BomNI
- 16th BNI

In the city under Major General Nott
- 38th BNI
- 42nd BNI
- 43rd BNI

Two regiments of the Shah's force

The detachment at Killa Abdoola had been sent back to Quetta while the force at Khelat-i-Ghilzai was considered safe enough, or the premature withdrawal of it at any rate impolitic.

1 Stocqueler, *Memorials of Afghanistan*, p.174.
2 Beveridge. *A Comprehensive History of India,* Vol. 3, p.546.

The detachment at Ghirishk remained there. Things remained relatively quiet in Major General Nott's parish until mid-December, albeit the General was aware that tribes, both Ghilzai and Durrani, were mustering with no good intentions.

On New Year's Day 1842, Major General Nott wrote to his daughters:

> Many happy returns of the day to you, fair ladies. I suspect it will very troublesome year for me, I hope nothing more than troublesome. The Afghans have not yet assembled in what I call a tangible shape; when they do we shall give them a good licking. I fancy they do not like our state of preparations. Ah well, they are funny fellows, and so I go to tiffin.[3]

On 27 December, the alarm was sounded by a *Havildar* at the Herat gate, who reported that some officers outside had been killed. It transpired that men of the *Jan-Baz* regiment commanded by Captain George Golding, which had earlier been ordered to Ghirishk, had at 4:00 a.m. rushed into Golding's tent and severed his head from his body, then got on their horses and fled to join the Afghan chief at Dahla about 40 miles from Khelat-i-Ghilzai, where the nucleus of the rebellion was gathering. Three *Resildars* of cavalry set off in pursuit of them, caught up with the renegades and killed about 60 of them. Then on 29 December Prince Suftur Jung, the third son of Shah Shuja and one of the most treacherous and ungrateful of that brood, slid out of the city to join the rebel chief, Acktar Khan. Twelve days later, Prince Suftur Jung and Acktar Khan advanced within 15 miles of Kandahar at the head of a force estimated at 20,000and had taken up a strong position on the right bank of the River Urgandab. Major General Nott immediately assembled a force of five regiments of infantry, supported by cavalry and guns and launched it in an attack. After four hours of marching over difficult country, this force came in sight of the enemy, crossed the river and charged at them. The enemy, not waiting for the clash, broke and fled. A limited pursuit caught up with several of them. On recrossing the Urgandab, the British force was faced by a large body of Afghan horsemen led by Mirza Ahmed, a 'sometime' ally, who persuaded the political agent accompanying the force that his disposition towards the British was the most friendly, so his horsemen were not attacked. The next morning, Mirza Ahmed, as proof of his sincerity, joined Acktar Khan. It was not until the close of February that the enemy made their appearance again.

News of Sir William Macnaghten's murder reached Kandahar on 30 January and soon afterwards, on 21 February, Major Henry Rawlinson, the political agent at Kandahar, received instructions from Major Pottinger and Major General Elphinstone directing the immediate evacuation of Kandahar and Khelat-i-Ghilzai. These instructions were similar to the ones sent to Jalalabad. Rawlinson's initial reaction was that under the circumstances, overtures could be made with a view to a negotiated withdrawal. Nott was adamantly against any such treating directed by Kabul. In an official letter to Major Rawlinson, the General wrote, 'I have only to repeat that I will not treat with any person whatever for the retirement of British troops from Afghanistan, until I shall have received instructions from the Supreme Government. The letter signed "Eldred Pottinger" and "W.K. Elphinstone" may or may not be a forgery. I conceive that these officers were not free agents at Kabul, and therefore their letter or order, has no weight with me.'[4]

3 Macrory, *Fierce Pawns*, p.315.
4 Beveridge, *A Comprehensive History of India*, Vol. 3, p.547.

By the end of February Major General Nott received a despatch, signed by Lord Auckland, stating that it was of the highest importance that he should maintain his position in Kandahar in concentrated strength until he received future orders from the Government. He was also instructed that he was no longer to obey orders purporting to come from Major General Elphinstone.

During the period of inclement weather, the rebels remained inactive and the Kandahar garrison remained in barracks consuming its reserve of provisions. Major General Nott, conscious of the potential for problems from an 'enemy within', ordered the expulsion from the city of families of all suspected collaborators. This precautionary measure was started on 3 March and by 6 March 1,000 families had been expelled from the city. On 7 March, leaving 2,500 troops under the command of Major Charles Lane to defend the garrison, Nott marched out with the remainder of his command to give battle to the enemy. Nott's determination to engage with the enemy drew him off 20 miles away from his base, as the enemy kept falling back. On 9 March, his artillery came near enough to open fire with some effect, but once again the enemy broke and fled. This apparent reluctance of the Afghans to fight was part of their ingenious plan to draw the General away from his base, then to make a rapid circuit round his force and attack the lightly garrisoned Kandahar. For once, Major General Nott's tenacity had caused him to be hoodwinked.

During the afternoon of 10 March, large bodies of Afghans both horse and foot were seen assembling and taking up positions in the villages around the city of Kandahar. Precautions were immediately taken by securing all the gates, posting extra sentries and manning the guns. At 8:00 p.m. that night the rebels launched an attack on the Herat gate which was penetrated by a few of them. Then an hour later the Shikarpore gate was attacked, followed by an attack on the Kabul gate. Dense masses of rebels, keeping up an incessant and heavy fire, hurled themselves against the strong defences at the gates while fire from the ramparts cooled their ardour. The battle raged for four hours before the rebels retired with a loss of 1,000 men. Who can tell what might have transpired if the rebels had succeeded, which they nearly did; Nott would certainly have found himself in quite a pickle, and his soldiers in the soup!

In the meantime, Nott fell back from his forward position, along the line of his original advance, back to his beleaguered base, where despite entry into one gate, Major Lane's small force had successfully quashed all efforts by the enemy to capture Kandahar. However, the rebels remained in the vicinity, harassing the surrounding villages. On 20 March Nott sent out a strong battle group under the command of Lieutenant Colonel George Wymer, in the dual role of foraging and to give protection to the numerous villages against the marauding rebels. Three days later Nott was in the happy position of being able to report to Secretary to the Government Mr Herbert Maddock, on the complete success of this operation.

In the latter part of March Nott was in receipt of a letter written by Mr George Clerk, and passed on to the General by Major James Outram. In the letter Clerk had stated that the Jalalabad garrison was to be withdrawn to Peshawar. This shocking news prompted the General to write a long letter dated 24 March to Mr Maddock. In it he declared his perplexity in regard to the Jalalabad withdrawal and to the orders he had recently received to maintain his own position at Kandahar, where he had a considerable body of troops, but was in desperate need for money, medical stores and carriage. His letter continued with his assertion that as long as the Jalalabad and Kandahar positions were maintained, the attention of the insurgents in Afghanistan would be distracted and no combined movement could be made by the Afghans while threatened from both these positions, but if one of these was removed, the undivided force of the people, backed by success and inflamed by religious enthusiasm, would be at liberty to concentrate its energy on Kandahar. His letter went on to state that many people had been prevented from joining the rebels from a feeling that the British were about to retaliate and advance on Kabul, His letter ended by informing Mr Maddock that he was expecting supplies which were being brought up by Major General Richard England, but that he had no real information as to when. This letter clearly had a bearing on what became the ultimate resolution adopted by the Governor General. A month later Nott, writing to his daughters, expressed his utter frustration at the situation.

> The people in power are all mad, or Providence hath blinded them for some wise purpose. I am very tired, tired of this country, and quite tired of the folly of my countrymen, and I long more than ever for my clay-built cottage. My soldiers are four months in arrears, there is not one rupee in the Kandahar treasury and no money can be borrowed. I have no medicine for the sick and wounded, I have no carriage cattle for the troops nor money to buy or hire, and therefore cannot move. I have no good cavalry and but little ammunition. I have been calling for these for six months, but not the least aid has been given me.[5]

At last the political authorities in Sindh took measures to reinforce Kandahar. Major General England's brigade was ordered up from Dadur to convoy nine *lakhs* of rupees, medical stores and 2,000 camels for the garrison. Leaving half his brigade in Dadur to follow, England made his way with little interruption through the Bolan Pass to Quetta. Here he had intended to wait for the balance of his brigade to join him. However on arrival at Quetta he found that forage for the animals was very scarce, and on the advice of the political agent, Lieutenant William Hammersley, he decided to move on to the village of Hykulzye, 30 miles north of Quetta and six miles from the Khojak Pass, where forage was more plentiful, and wait there for the remainder of his brigade. Hammersley had assured the General that the village of Hykulzye was friendly and there was no great cause for concern. England's advance force comprised five companies of HM 41st Foot, three companies each of 21st and 25th BomNI, 50 men of Poona Horse and four guns of horse artillery. This advance force had with it four *lakhs* of rupees, a small amount of ammunition and 500 camels. Apparently the plan was to wait in the friendly area of Hykulzye for the remainder of the brigade, then to proceed through the Khojak Pass and hand over the relief stores to a force sent from Kandahar to Chummun at the northern end of the pass.

England's advance force arrived at Hykulzye on 28 March, all seemed well and the local inhabitants were friendly; there was no indication that for months Mohammed Sadiq, the leader of the insurgents south of Kandahar and an erstwhile ally of the British, had been constructing barricades which completely commanded the road along which England's force was to advance. As it did so it walked into a trap with the rebels on the high ground flanking the British force, a glaring example of the paucity of British intelligence, which relied on questionable local sources and in reality did not extend beyond its own picket lines. England ordered four infantry companies to charge up the hill, in line, to storm the breastworks. The rebels were so well dug-in that despite the detachment reaching the summit, the attack failed. According to some, the failure was due in the main to many *sepoys* of 21st BomNI lagging behind. It was a totally uneven fight

5 Macrory, *Fierce Pawns*, p.316.

and the remnants of the detachment fell back to form squares to meet an audacious rebel cavalry attack. The squares held and the rebels retired. One fifth of England's force had been killed or wounded, with Captains William May and Charles Apthorpe among the dead. He also lost most of his camels but fortunately not his treasury. The next morning, estimating that the enemy were too strong, the Major General withdrew back to Quetta where his force entrenched itself, waiting for the rest of the brigade and further instructions from Major General Nott.

Prior to Major General England's fateful advance, Lieutenant Hammersley had written to Major Rawlinson at Kandahar informing him of the planned advance. When Nott was informed of it, he immediately started a letter in reply, warning England not to undertake the advance into the Pisheen valley with a small force just to hand over some of the supplies. He wanted him to move with the whole of his brigade, with all the badly needed supplies and all the way to Kandahar as he was not in a position to send a force to the head of the pass. Just before this letter was despatched, Nott heard on the local grapevine that England had already advanced, and a little later he received a despatch from England informing him of the repulse at Hykulzye and suggesting that as Quetta was under threat he could only move to the north of the pass on the guarantee that a corresponding force would be sent to the head of the pass at the same time. England's despatch ends: 'I request you have the goodness to apprise me on your views of the subjects I have referred to and I shall do my best to forward them.'[6]

The repulse at Hykulzye was devastating news to Nott at Kandahar, with no money to pay his troops, destitute of medical supplies and ammunition, all of which he had been crying out for the past many months. On 18 April Nott addressed a highly soldier-like letter to his brother officer. The gist of this long despatch was as follows:

- That it was absolutely necessary that a strong brigade of 2,500 men should immediately advance from Quetta, through the pass and on to Kandahar
- That he would send a brigade to Chummun on 25 April to arrive at the rendezvous by 1 May
- That there would be little danger in traversing the pass, providing the heights were properly crowned on either side
- That Quetta could hold out with 500 men provided they moved from the 'wretched' cantonments to the citadel
- That when any difficulties were encountered, it was their first duty to overcome these when national honour and military reputation were concerned
- That had his needs been addressed months earlier he would have been strong enough to have even marched on Ghazni

Major General England did advance as instructed through the Khojak Pass without any problems, probably because the rebels had been subdued into inaction by the presence of a British force at each end of the pass. Lieutenant Colonel Wymer with a brigade left Kandahar on 25 April and a union with England's brigade was duly made at Chummun, with the combined force back in Kandahar on 8 May.

6 Stocqueler, *Memoirs and Correspondence Of Major General Sir William Nott*, Vol. II, p.17.

While these manœuvres were taking place, Governor General Lord Ellenborough, then at Benares, had Mr Maddock pen a letter dated 19 April directly to Major General Nott, ordering him to take immediate measures to draw off the garrison at Khelat-i-Ghilzai, to destroy the guns and the fort, and then to evacuate Kandahar, handing the place over to Prince Timour. On completion of these tasks, he was to withdraw to Quetta and thence to Sukkur when the season allowed.

This communication upset Nott deeply. His duty was to obey, but his every inclination was to challenge this policy as he was convinced it stemmed from unnecessary alarm at the supposed strength of the Afghan opposition, which he knew, from experience, was overrated and would not be a match against his disciplined troops on the field of combat. Had he been given the supplies he had been crying out for, he felt he could have been well on his way to retake Ghazni and on his way to Kabul. He and Major General Pollock had communicated and it was quite apparent that the latter also felt that he was able to advance. In one despatch to Pollock, Nott wrote, 'I believe I shall go mad. I ought to have been on my way to Ghazni to extend my hand to you, instead of which I am obliged to make a movement on the Khojak. As far as cattle are concerned, we are nearly helpless. God knows why such a delay has occurred in sending me money and stores. This is dreadful.'[7] More and more Nott chafed, and baulked at what he described as having to 'sneak away'.

On the arrival of Major General England's brigade at Kandahar, Nott sent an urgent despatch to Quetta to send up all the camels that could possibly be collected under an escort of 800 men and recommended that the fort at Killa Abdoola be garrisoned for the next month. On 19 May he sent Lieutenant Colonel Wymer with a force consisting of four infantry regiments, cavalry and two batteries of Bombay Artillery to bring off the garrison at Khelat-i-Ghilzai. However, before this rescue force could reach Khelat-i-Ghilzai, Captain John Craigie and his gallant garrison of 900 men, which included 40 European artillerymen and 250 men of 43rd BNI left by Lieutenant Colonel MacLaren when he returned to Kandahar, had achieved their own deliverance.

The Shah's 3rd Infantry Regiment, commanded by Captain Craigie, had moved in to garrison Khelat-i-Ghilzai in November 1841, and held out despite the freezing cold, constant rebel attacks and shortage of rations. The garrison was surrounded by rebels who had dug trenches encircling the place and who laid down sustained fire from these protected positions. On the night of 21 May 7,000 Ghilzais made a concerted attack on the garrison. No doubt with news of Wymer's approach, the rebels desired to make sure they had possession of Khelat-i-Ghilzai before he arrived. During this attack the rebels scaled the walls of the ramparts and got dangerously close to some of the guns, but were eventually driven off at the point of the bayonet and retired some 600 yards. The next morning, to the rebels' utter surprise, Captain Craigie launched an attack with some 500 of his men, which resulted in 400 rebels dead with the rest running away as fast as they could. Captain Craigie reckoned that had he had some cavalry the damage inflicted would have been greater. This attack also effectively ended the siege. The next morning Lieutenant Colonel Wymer's force arrived and for the next two days the fort was destroyed under the supervision of Major Edward Saunders. For this gallant defence of

7 Stocqueler, *Memoirs and Correspondence, of Major General Sir William Nott,* Vol. II., p.33.

Khelat-i-Ghilzai, the Shah's 3rd Infantry Regiment was incorporated into the British Indian Army.[8] The combined force was back in Kandahar on 7 June.

In the meantime Nott had received intelligence that Atta Mohammed, chief of the Zamindawar, had joined the forces of Prince Suftur and Acktar Khan on the right bank of the River Urgandab for the purpose of attacking Kandahar in the absence of a good portion of the garrison being away on the expedition to relieve Khelat-i-Ghilzai. The Afghans, under the impression that the garrison was not strong enough to launch an attack, took possession of some hills within a mile of the city's ramparts. On 29 May, leaving Major General England with a small force, Nott sallied forth with a force comprising HM 41st Foot, 42nd BNI, 25th BomNI, three companies of 43rd BNI, a troop of the Shah's Horse Artillery, a detachment of the Poona Horse and a detachment of the Shah's 1st Cavalry. At 1:00 p.m. this force clashed with the enemy and within an hour had driven them off the hills and pursued them across the river and into the mountains at great loss to the enemy. By this action, Nott had cleared western Afghanistan.

On 11 June Prince Suftur Jung, bold as brass, came into Kandahar city to surrender. Nott's attitude towards the Prince can be well imagined, he wanted to hang the rascal from the nearest tree, but good political sense prevailed.

8 In accordance with General Order of 4 October, the Shah's 3rd Infantry Regiment was incorporated into the British Indian Army as the Khelat-i-Ghilzai Regiment and served in numerous campaigns for almost a century. Captain Craigie, who had changed his surname to Halket-Craigie, continued in command of the regiment until 1852. He retired as a major general in 1861 and died nine years later.

24

Retribution

Lord Ellenborough, 'the best man for the job', sailed for India on 6 November 1841 on HMS *Cambrian*. Prior to his departure he had asked the Prime Minister for the title of 'Captain General', last bestowed on Lord Wellesley, a clear indication that the new Governor General intended to rule India 'as if I was its sovereign having nothing to look to but India. I must act like Akbar and not like Auckland.'[1] He had also asked to take with him the secretary of the Board of Control, Mr T.N. Waterfield. Both requests were denied by a Prime Minister who felt that the Home Office was more important than India. Instead Lord Ellenborough took with him as his private secretary Captain Henry Durand, the officer who had blown open the Ghazni gate and a critic of the way the politicos were mismanaging affairs in Afghanistan. Also prior to his departure, Lord Ellenborough had written to Lord Auckland on 14 October, informing him that he had been appointed his successor and requested him to prepare a number of briefs on various subjects, one of which was finance. 'Then your finances! I almost dread to approach the subject, but I must grapple with it.'[2] To replace Lord Ellenborough at the Board of Control, the Prime Minister had appointed Lord FitzGerald and Vesey, a dying man with no inclination to assert any authority. So by 20 February the Prime Minister was writing to Mr Arbuthnot saying, 'The Court [of Directors] is becoming a very troublesome body, mainly from the want of efficient control. They assume on the absence of it and encroach accordingly.'[3] This absence of an assertive head at the Board of Control, with a Prime Minister preoccupied with Home affairs and a governor general determined to rule and not be ruled, was to result in the recall of a governor general who had the potential of being one of the best.

During his long voyage round the Cape, the new governor general's mind was concerned with the expenditure in Afghanistan and more importantly of the proposed expedition to China to safeguard the Company's profits it derived from the opium trade, and the troops being sent on this expedition were of the Madras Presidency. On arrival at Madras on 21 February, his heart sank on being told the news of Sir William Macnaghten's murder and the insurrection at Kabul, plus the unsettled state of the Madras Army. The situation was completely different to what he expected or had been led to believe; he was being handed a time bomb and was expected to

1 Douglas Hurd, *Robert Peel: a Biography* (London: Weidenfeld & Nicolson, 2007), p.291.
2 Law, *India Under Lord Ellenborough*, p.22.
3 Law, *India Under Lord Ellenborough*, p.23.

defuse it. However, none of it was his fault so any measure he introduced to improve the situation would be to his great credit. During the short passage up to Calcutta, Lord Ellenborough must have thought much on the last piece of advice that his friend the Duke of Wellington had given him, which was essentially to take care of the army as without it there would be no British India, adding, 'It is impossible to impress upon you too strongly the notion of the importance of the restoration of our reputation in the East.'

Lord Ellenborough arrived in Calcutta on Monday 29 February 1842. Calcutta was the seat of government and the civil administration that ran it, and this civil administration was the preserve of the East India Company directors, which offered rich provisions for their relatives and those having interest with them. The civil service was therefore the preferred service and remained so. Sir John Kaye said of it, 'It has fattened upon the golden eggs and scattered the feathers among the military. It has not only appropriated all the large salaries and divided almost all the honours of the state, but has on every occasion been permitted to ride roughshod over the military.'[4] The Court of Directors had specially cherished this privileged class and the governor generals had been prone to go along with this exaltation of the civil service at the expense of the military. Upon departing, Lord Auckland told his successor that he would find a lack of 'instruments', but that they were to be got from the army more easily than from the civil service.

After a series of discussions with officials in Calcutta, Lord Ellenborough wrote to the Commander-in-Chief. Reviewing the situation in his letter he concluded that in his opinion the Tripartite Treaty was no longer binding and therefore there was no obligation to imperil the Indian army in its endeavour to carry out its provisions. It was His Lordship's opinion that whatever course of action was decided on, it had to be based solely on military considerations and therefore in the first instance due regard had to be paid to the safety of the troops currently employed in Afghanistan. After that the reputation of the army had to be re-established by the infliction of some signal and decisive blow upon the Afghans. This new policy was perfectly clear and acceptable to all the *Koi Hais* in Calcutta and there was every reason to believe it would be acted on with vigour. Then on 6 April, His Lordship left Calcutta to be nearer the action and in so doing allowed himself to be free of official obstacles. He arrived at Allahabad on 19 April and on being told of the surrender of Ghazni and the repulse of Brigadier General Richard England's advance, Lord Ellenborough directed the commander-in-chief, Lieutenant General Sir Jasper Nicolls, to issue instructions to major generals William Nott and George Pollock, ordering the former to evacuate Khelat-i-Ghilzai and withdraw from Kandahar via Quetta to Sukkur, and the latter to withdraw to Peshawar having relieved the Jalalabad garrison. His sole consideration at this time was to save the army from any further disasters, which it appeared to be prone to. Regarding the status of the hostages, this was considered a highly emotive issue and best resolved by a negotiated exchange. He was hell-bent on securing the safety of the army's communications, and providing abundant transport, supplies, troops and guns, before authorising any advance on Kabul. To do all this the army would first have to withdraw to the right bank of the Indus and there recuperate, regroup and reinvigorate itself.

On 24 April Lord Ellenborough wrote to Major General Pollock informing him that the method of effecting the release of the hostages had been a matter of anxious consideration, that

4 Law, *India Under Lord Ellenborough*, p.57.

the only safe and honourable way was by means of a general exchange, that the redemption by ransom was unacceptable and that failing a general exchange Pollock was authorised to make a partial exchange, but in such a case Dost Mohammed Khan was not to be included without the express authority of the Governor General.[5]

Lord Ellenborough believed that his desired strategic withdrawal was the most potent measure in view of the disasters that had occurred including the near capture of Kandahar. All these reverses were having an adverse effect on the army and also back in India where the potential for trouble was not far below the surface; the Sindh was doubtful and the Punjab threatening. For a man responsible for the whole of India it would have been rash of Lord Ellenborough to have ignored the wider issues, by allowing scattered elements of the army, at the end of stretched lines of communications, dependent on provisions from a hostile people, to continue their worthless endeavour to uphold the honour of a dispirited army. This was not the time to bluster into operations simply to avenge British dignity. This sudden change in the Governor General's opinion to withdraw without first a blow being struck and the hostages released was a shock to all the civilian and military authorities. Faced by a wave of opposition, His Lordship justified his position thus:

> The danger is in the position of the army, almost without communications with India, too far off to return quickly at any season, unable from the season to return now, without adequate supplies of food and carriage. This is the danger which all great statesmen in India would perpetuate if they could, and while they maintain it, destroy the confidence of the *sepoy* and ruin our finances. If I save this country, I shall save it in spite of every man in it who ought to give me support, but I will save it in spite of them all.[6]

However, his apparent disregard for the safety of the British hostages held by the Afghans was to become the Achilles heel of his forthright policy and nibbled away at his intransigent attitude and later at his reputation. Meanwhile the Court of Directors, who had wholeheartedly supported the nomination of Lord Ellenborough as governor general, began to feel that their new man in India was acting as if he was still the president of the Board of Control, during which time he had clearly indicated that he was not too enamoured by their conduct of affairs, and furthermore, as if he was also the commander-in-chief, sidelining General Sir Jasper Nicolls and communicating directly with his frontline generals.

News about the tragic events at Kabul and the destruction of Elphinstone's army eventually reached England at the end of March 1842. On 4 April *The Times* devoted just three leading articles to the matter while being much more expansive about the provisions of Prime Minister Robert Peel's budget, who on 6 April wrote to the new Governor General:

> The events in Cabool are still a horrible mystery. We have read the last act of the tragedy but are at a loss to account for the motives of the actions and for the events which brought the terrible result. The conduct of the political agents, the conduct of the military commanders,

5 Law, *India Under Lord Ellenborough*, p.34.
6 Beveridge, *A Comprehensive History of India*, Vol. 3, p.557.

> the conduct of our ally Shah Shoojoa, the conduct of almost everybody, with one glorious exception – that of a woman, is to us altogether unaccountable.[7]

As the months passed, the Governor General became more irritable as the Indian sun got hotter with the lack of any move being made in accordance with his policy of retrenchment. With his frontline Generals shilly-shallying about their inability to move due to the season and shortage of carriage, His Lordship deplored their lack of tenacity and vim. On 7 June, in a letter to the Prime Minister, his frustration is very evident: 'The Generals Nott and Pollock have not a grain of military talent. The latter has fallen into the hands of two or three young political assistants – he would otherwise have been before this on the left bank of the Indus.'[8]

Meanwhile, the patience of Lord Ellenborough's armies at Jalalabad and Kandahar was being worn out and a feeling of sorrow and disgust had been created by His Lordship's edict to withdraw without marching on Kabul and affecting the release of the hostages.

Ellenborough continued to stubbornly hold to his policy of withdrawal, but by the end of June the unanimous view of both civil and military condemning His Lordship's stance, especially as it made no allowance for the release of the hostages, began to eat away at his determination. The policy was not wrong, but its execution could be massaged; and so, on 4 July, the Governor General wrote to both his frontline generals giving his approval for Nott to advance on Kabul and for Pollock to meet him there, provided they were equipped to do so.

In this way Ellenborough succeeded in squaring his inflexible policy to withdraw with that of the popular demand for some form of retribution and release of the hostages. The Duke of Wellington said of his instruction, 'It is the most handsomest that could be given to a commander', while Sir John Kaye reckoned it to be a 'masterpiece of Jesuitical cunning'.

In his instruction, the Governor General wrote:

> Nothing has occurred to induce me to change my first opinion, that the measure commended by considerations of political and military prudence, is to bring the armies now in Afghanistan at the earliest period at which their retirement can be effected, consistent with the health and efficiency of the troops, into positions where they may have easy and certain communications with India; and to this extent the instructions you have received remain unaltered, but the improved position of your army[ies] with sufficient means of carriage for as large a force as it is necessary to move in Afghanistan, induce me now to leave to your opinion the line by which you shall withdraw your troops from that country.

To Major General Nott, he continued:

> I do not undervalue the aid which our Government in India would receive from the successful execution of a march through Ghazni and Kabul, over the scenes of our late disasters. I know all the effects which it would have on the minds of our soldiers, of our allies, of our enemies in Asia and of our countrymen, and all foreign nations in Europe. It is of just ambition, which no one more than myself would rejoice to see effected; but I

7 British Library, MS 40,471, Peel Papers, Vol. CCXC1.
8 Hurd, *Robert Peel: A Biography*, p.293.

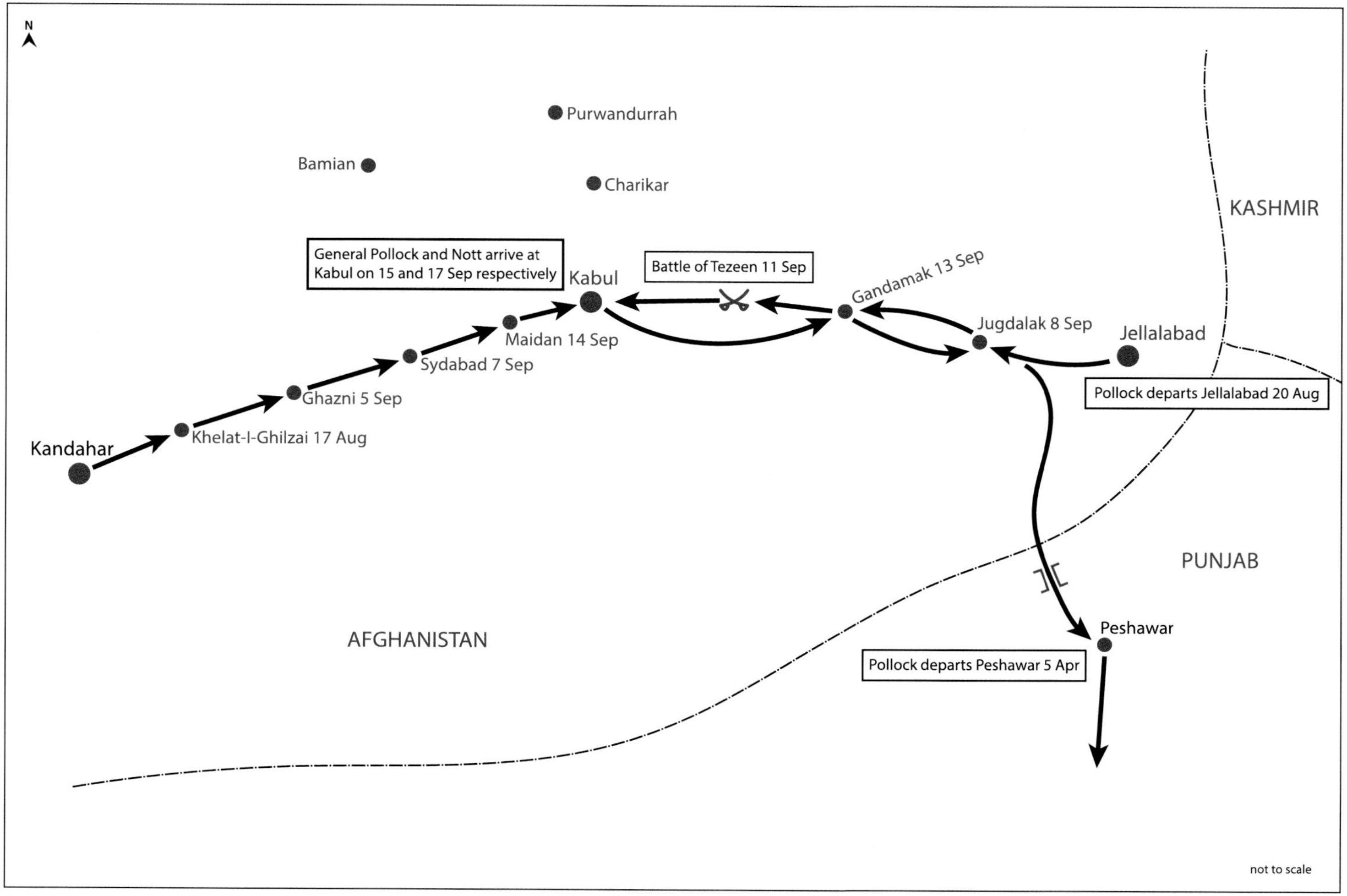

Map 16 Withdrawal via Kabul. The British commenced their departure from Afghanistan on 12 October 1842.

> see that failure in the attempt is certain and irretrievable ruin, and I would inspire you with necessary caution, and make you feel that great as are the objects to be attained by success, the risk is great also. If you should be enabled by a *coup de main* to get possession of Ghazni and Kabul, you will act as you see fit, and leave decisive proof of the power of the British army, without impeaching its humanity. You will bring away from the tomb of Mohmed of Ghazni his club which hangs over it, and you will bring away the gates of his tomb, which are the gates of the Temple of Somnath. These will be just trophies of your successful march.[9]

As the Governor General expected, Major General Nott had no hesitation in selecting his route of withdrawal via Ghazni, Kabul and Jalalabad, what is more the General cherished the hope of getting to Kabul before Pollock, albeit he had much further to march and his progress would be hampered by the dragging of his 18-pdr guns and later the hauling of the demanded Somnath gates, which was no easy task as described in Lieutenant John Hall's journal:

> I may as well mention the great trials and difficulties experienced in dragging along the heavy portions of the baggage, more particularly the celebrated Somnath gates, which it will doubtless be remembered, were taken by the direction of the Governor General, from the tomb of Sultan Mahomed Ghuznee. The General diverted a guard of no less than a wing of a regiment to mount over these gates, which were placed upon two platform carts and driven by six bullocks each. So great was the care taken of them that they were placed next to the main body of the army on the march and nothing was permitted to go before them. The consequence was, that oftentimes, owing to the bullocks growing stubborn, the whole in the rear been delayed and the gates have had to be dragged by fatigue parties of Europeans.[10]

Prior to the withdrawal from Kandahar, all troops had been gradually removed from the city to two camps outside the walls at which point the destruction of the ramparts and unwanted ordnance began. The city was then handed over to Prince Suftur. On 7 August General England's brigade consisting of Bombay troops, 12 guns, the sick and wounded, and families, moved off on their return to India via the Khojak Pass and Quetta. Prince Timour and his family accompanied this brigade, he having elected to return to Ludhiana, where he was joined by his uncle, Shah Zaman, to live the rest of their lives as British pensioners.[11] This march was not opposed apart from the anticipated and habitual marauding. The brigade arrived at Quetta on 26 August.

9 Beveridge, *A Comprehensive History of India*, Vol. 3, p.560.

10 Hall, *Scenes in a Soldier's Life*, p.350.

11 At the start of the First Anglo-Sikh War, when the Raja of Ladwa raided Ludhiana, Prince Timour gave refuge to the Europeans living in the city; and during the Indian Mutiny he remained faithful to the British.

Depiction of the 'Heroic conduct of four privates of H.M 31st Reg. at the Battle of Mazeena'.

On Monday 8 August 1842, Major General William Nott commenced his march to India via Kabul and Jalalabad. His army comprised:

1st Brigade:	Commander: Brigadier George Wymer HM 40th Foot 16th Bengal Native Infantry 38th Bengal Native Infantry Shah's 3rd Regiment Total 2,720
2nd Brigade:	Commander: Brigadier Lewis Stacy HM 41st Foot 2nd Bengal Native Infantry 42nd Bengal Native Infantry 43rd Bengal Native Infantry Total 2,850
Artillery:	Commander: Major Frederick Sotheby Troop of Bombay Horse Artillery Troop of Shah's Horse Artillery Battery of 9-pdr guns and two 18-pdr guns
Cavalry:	Commander: Captain Charles Delamain

By 17 August Nott's army, unmolested, had reached Khelat-i-Ghilzai, which remained a ruin having been destroyed when Captain John Halket-Craigie's garrison was withdrawn in May. Ten days later the army had reached Ghogan where reports came in to the effect that the governor of Ghazni, Shamsuddin Khan, was mustering a force of 5,000 men and two guns at Mukar, 15 miles further on. Earlier Shamsuddin had refused to give up his British hostages to Mohammed Akbar Khan, however when he had departed to confront General Nott's advance his brother, Gool Mohammed, sent the hostages to Kabul.

Soon after leaving their camp at Mukar, the rearguard of Nott's force was attacked by 700 Afghan horse and footmen. Captain Haldane, commanding the 1st Irregular Cavalry, was sent after them and drove the Afghans up the hills killing about 40 of them. Sometime later that day, Captain Charles Delamain of 3rd Bengal Light Cavalry, and being the senior cavalry officer, also the commander of Major General Nott's cavalry brigade, received a report that that the cavalry's 'grass cutters' had been cut up and taken prisoner by the Afghan rebels. Captain Delamain, without reference to his general, ordered out the whole cavalry brigade to give chase and rescue the 'grass cutters'. The cavalry chased the Afghans for about six miles thus being successfully decoyed into a range of hills where about 6,000 Afghans sprung their planned ambush. The cavalry charged the rebels but were met by deadly fire and driven back as every man galloped to the rear for his life. The force lost 50 killed including Captains Henry Bury and George Reeves of 3rd Bombay Light Cavalry, and a few days later Captain George Ravencroft died of his wound.

When Nott was told of this fiasco he immediately sent out a large force of infantry and guns to relieve his cavalry, rescue the 'grass cutters', bring in the casualties and thrash the enemy. This force saw off the rebels, killing about 50 of them, destroyed their fort and rescued the 'grass cutters'. They brought in about 20 mutilated bodies; only the trunk of Captain Reeves was found and Captain Bury's head had been cut off. Nott was in 'a dreadful rage about it'[12] He did not send the customary despatch about this action, instead ordering a court of inquiry to investigate the matter. This Afghan success served to swell the numbers of Shamsuddin's army.

At this juncture, the scene switches to Jalalabad where Major General George Pollock had been detained for the past four months by the indecision of the Government and his inability to move from want of the necessary means. On 18 April Pollock had written, 'My situation at the present moment is a difficult one, and as much as I deprecate any retrograde movement, such a step is by no means improbable, as I have not yet been able to get supplies in sufficient quantities to warrant my remaining here.'[13] Writing a couple of months later, Lieutenant George Chetwynd-Stapylton of HM 13th Foot recorded, 'We are still at Jalalabad without any prospect of going on to Kabul this year, and almost as little of a campaign next spring. At present we have not carriage to move a third of the force with the supplies we should require to go to Kabul.'[14]

This period of apparent stagnation had been used in sending out expeditions against the surrounding tribes and negotiating the release of the hostages. On 2 August, the last of these negotiations took place when Captains Colin Troup and George Lawrence arrived at Jalalabad having been sent on probation by Mohammed Akbar Khan with his terms; none of which were acceptable. The two captains, after being well fed and watered, returned to rejoin the hostages.

On 20 August Major General Pollock commenced his long desired advance to Kabul. His force included 500 Sikhs of the Sikh contingent, the balance of this contingent being left in Jalalabad to keep open the General's back door to India. His army comprised:

1st Infantry Division:	Commander: Major General Robert Sale
1st Brigade:	Commander: Lieutenant Colonel Robert Patterson
	HM 13th Foot
	35th Bengal Native Infantry
	Sappers and *Jehalchees*
2nd Brigade:	Commander: Brigadier Thomas Monteith
	HM 31st Foot
	6th Bengal Native Infantry
	33rd Bengal Native Infantry
	Two companies of sappers
2nd Infantry Division:	Commander: Major General John McCaskill
3rd Brigade:	Commander: Brigadier Charles Wild
	30th Bengal Native Infantry
	53rd Bengal Native Infantry
	64th Bengal Native Infantry
4th Brigade:	Commander: Brigadier Alexander Tulloch

12 Anon., *Nott's Brigade in Afghanistan 1838–1842*, p.93.
13 Law, *India Under Lord Ellenborough*, p.32.
14 Chetwynd-Stapylton, *The First Afghan War: An Ensign's Account*, p.21.

	HM 31st Foot
	6th Bengal Native Infantry
	33rd Bengal Native Infantry
	Sappers and *Jehalchees*
Artillery:	Commander: Captain Augustus Abbott
	Two troops horse artillery
	A light field battery
	Bullock field battery
	Mountain Train (3 guns)
Cavalry:	Commander: Lieutenant Colonel Michael White
	HM 3rd Light Dragoons
	1st Bengal Light Cavalry
	10th Bengal Light Cavalry
	3rd Irregular Cavalry
	5th Bengal Light Cavalry

Sikh Group of 500 under the command of Captain Henry Lawrence

Prior to this move, Major General Robert Sale's garrison with HM 3rd Light Dragoons had advanced to Futtehabad where upon arrival the General had attacked the Afghan forts in the area. By 23 August the whole of Pollock's army was concentrated at Gandamak and intelligence reports indicated that the Afghans were holding the village and fort at Mamoo Khail two miles from the British camp. At four o'clock on the morning of 24 August the army, in two columns, launched its attack. The village was entered without any great resistance and the left column moved on to attack the fort, which was gallantly stormed with the Afghans fleeing, leaving behind great quantities of their tents, provisions, cattle and ammunition, plus large quantities of plunder taken from the doomed Kabul garrison. This victory had immediate effect on the neighbouring tribes who brought in abundant provisions.

On 2 September, while halted at Neemla, a forlorn Afghan in dirty and tattered rags rode into the British camp. He turned out to be none other than Fateh Jung, who, tired of his sham kingship, and the ominous tyranny of Mohammed Akbar Khan, had fled from Kabul in disguise, assisted by Aga Mohammed Khan, a Kuzzilbashe chief. He had come in to beg refuge in the British camp. He later accompanied the army back to India to join the other Afghan Shahs in Ludhiana.

On 8 September General Pollock's army advanced towards Jagdalak where it was rumoured the Afghans were gathering in the passes in great numbers to oppose the British advance. On approaching the heights that commanded the valley, Pollock discovered that the Afghans held strong positions which were difficult to access. Large bodies of Afghans thronged the hilltops, and the position they held formed a sort of amphitheatre inclining towards the left of the road on which the British army was halted. When its guns opened up they had little effect as the Afghans were still able to pour down fire on the British force. At this juncture Pollock sent Captain George Broadfoot and his Gurkhas to the extreme left of the Afghan position and they began ascending the hill on top of which the Afghans were entrenched behind strong breastworks, a most exhausting task. Of this particular action Lieutenant Joseph Greenwood wrote in his journal:

> The little Gurkhas who filled the ranks of Broadfoot's sappers behaved most splendidly. Far in the distance were to be seen small parties of these diminutive warriors, driving strong bodies of the bulky Afghan before them, but the Gurkhas caring no more for their bullets than if they had been so many snowballs, rushed the spot and coolly taking out his knife [kukri] very deliberately hacked the fellows' heads off.[15]

After this successful action Broadfoot was directed to take a party of HM 9th Foot, the sappers now being worn out, except for six men, to attack the hills; the first and second heights were carried at the point of the bayonet, and flanking parties having turned the shoulders of the high range, the main force arrived, and Broadfoot's further progress was stayed, and his separate command now ceased. When Lieutenant Colonel Arthur Taylor saw Broadfoot's report of this action, he was incensed by the insinuation that his HM soldiers had been led in a daring operation by an Indian Army officer. This was to become a long running contretemps, known as the 'Kudi Khel', which went on until both lay dead on the Battlefield of Ferozeshah on 23 December 1845, during the First Anglo-Sikh War.

After this fairly easy victory at Jagdalak the army moved on towards Tezeen, and along the way received a message from Major General Nott announcing his own victory over Shamsuddin Khan and the capture of two guns. At about the same time another message announced the award of the Grand Cross of the Bath to Major General Sale for his services at Jalalabad. One of the more astonishing features of campaigning in those days, particularly in unfriendly country like Afghanistan, was the speed and regularity with which messages, carried by *cossids*, passed through enemy lines.

By 11 September the advance column of the army had reached Tezeen, and during the course of the day it was observed that the Afghans were assembling in large numbers on the hills, and that night they attempted to drive in one of the British pickets. The main body was now ordered up to join the advance column, arriving that night much fatigued. Meanwhile, the Afghan chief of Tezeen, Khoda Buksh Khan, had apparently informed Mohammed Akbar Khan that he had the British army in a trap, and in consequence the latter moved from the Khurd Kabul Pass to the Haft Kothal. The Afghans now had a force of some 16,000 men, in a strong position, opposing the British. Lieutenant Chetwynd-Stapylton recorded the events of the next 48 hours:

> We had repeated skirmishes with the enemy during the day of 12th. That night a strong picket of 200 men was sent up to a high hill overlooking the camp with orders to proceed along the line of hills and flank our march the next morning. At daybreak we commenced our march and had not proceeded far when a heavy fire was commenced on our skirmishers on either flank, and we saw that we had a hard day's work before us. Our column proceeded but slowly the skirmishers having to clear every hill one by one. At last we emerged from the defiles through which we were marching for the first 3 miles and saw the long ascent of Haft Kothal before us covered with the enemy, Mohammed Akbar being there in person with a very large force. Our force was immediately broken into small bodies and detached skirmishing over the hills, it being impossible from the nature of the ground for large

15 Lieutenant John Greenwood, *Narrative of the Late Victorious Campaign in Afghanistan, under General Pollock: with Recollections of Seven Years' Service in India* (London: Colburn, 1844), p.219.

> bodies to move. The enemy fought desperately in some places and every hill was disputed. At last the top of the ascent was gained when the Dragoons were let loose upon them and pursued them to the Khurd Kabul doing considerable execution among them and capturing a couple of guns. The rear guard was closely pressed from Tezeen to the top of Haft Kothal, but through the number of pickets left on the hills and the excellence of the arrangement, no baggage fell into the hands of the enemy and it arrived in camp soon after dark.[16]

In his despatch of the events at Tezeen, Major General Pollock alludes to the Sikhs as the Lahore contingent under the direction of Captain Henry Lawrence, 'who had invariably given the most cheerful assistance dragging the guns, occupying the heights and covering the rear-guard'. This gracious mention of the Sikhs was no doubt included to make up for his total disregard of the valuable assistance they had given at Ali Masjid.

After this victory Mohammed Akbar Khan, a broken reed, fled to Ghorebund leaving his troops to seek safety wherever they could. However, he still remained a potent foe as he held the hostages, an asset much more valuable to him than an army of *jezails*. But this was much dependent on the continued faithfulness of his supporters, who in consideration of their own various agendas could well forsake him.

Pollock's army continued its advance on Kabul, where it arrived on 15 September and encamped on what had been the Kabul racecourse. The next day, the General went to the Bala Hissar and had the British colours planted on its ramparts. As the British approached Kabul with Nott's army moving in from the west, the hostages who had been in a fort some six miles from Kabul were moved in the direction of Bamian. However, as both Mrs Trevor and Mrs Anderson were too ill to move, they, and their combined total of 10 children plus Dr Archibald Campbell and Captain William Anderson of the Bengal Cavalry, were sent in to join Pollock's camp in Kabul. At this point the General estimated that he would be in a position to relieve the other hostages within a matter of eight days, except for Captain Bulstrode Bygrave who remained in the close captivity of Mohammed Akbar Khan.

Upn Pollock's arrival at Kabul there was no shortage of petitions from Afghans in the city of declarations of friendship and faithfulness towards the *Ingrezis*. One such group were the Kuzzilbashes, with whom Mohan Lal, the conduit through whom all previous secret negotiations had been conducted, had sought refuge. Lal reported that the Kuzzilbashes, no doubt in a effort to further ingratiate themselves with the British, had offered to send a group of 700 horsemen to rescue the hostages before they were taken further north into Turkestan to be sold as slaves to the various chiefs, a prospect too horrific to contemplate. While negotiations continued with Mohammed Akbar Khan, this offer to send an Afghan force familiar with the peoples and the country to rescue the hostages had some merit, but to Lieutenant Colonel Sir Richmond Shakespeare it was a God-given opportunity to cement his fame as the 'Great Rescuer of Slaves'; he pleaded with his general to head up the Kuzzilbashe group. Now the scheme had a great deal of merit as it could now be portrayed as a positive British-led action to save the hostages. To ensure the success of this daredevil attempt, Pollock sent a message to Major General Nott, who had just arrived in the vicinity of Kabul, ordering him to send a brigade in Shakespeare's wake. In a long reply, Nott asked to be excused for a number of reasons

16 Chetwynd-Stapylton, *The First Afghan War. An Ensign's Account*, p.28.

British encampment of troops under command of Major General Sir William Nott. The scene depicts the army outside the walls of Kabul at the commencement of the evacuation of Afghanistan.

including the fact that Shamsuddin Khan and other chiefs were still active in the area, and he added, 'I hourly expect to hear that Sir R Shakespeare is added to the number of prisoners.'[17] No doubt after the Captain Delamain affair, Nott was most leery and cautious about sending out small groups without any knowledge of the strength of any opposition, furthermore he was disappointed at not getting to Kabul first and felt that Pollock's troops were more refreshed to be sent on this wild goose chase. His refusal did not endear him to many, especially not to the hostages when they were told of it.

Meantime, Major General Pollock had received a coded letter from Major Eldred Pottinger, who was one of the hostages, informing the General of their whereabouts, so based on this information and Nott's reluctance to move, Pollock ordered Major General Sir Robert Sale to set off with a brigade to rescue the hostages, whose number included his wife and pregnant daughter.

At this point, the scene switches back to the activities of Major General Nott's army. After the slight setback at Mukar, the army continued its advance on Kabul. On 30 August, as the force marched on Ghoaine, Shamsuddin Khan had moved to take up positions parallel to its advance and launched his attack. Despite being bold and gallant the Afghans were no match for Nott's advancing army, and Shamsuddin fled in the direction of Ghazni. On 5 September Nott moved on Ghazni. 'I found the city full of men, and a range of mountains running north-east of the fortress covered by heavy bodies of cavalry and infantry; the gardens and ravines near the town were also occupied. I at once determined to carry the enemy's mountain position before engaging my force.'[18]

The British troops having successfully driven the Afghans off their mountain positions, Nott ordered the occupation of a village, on the spur of a mountain and only 600 yards from the fortress walls where during the night infantry working parties under the direction of Major Edward Sanders erected a battery for the four 18-pdr guns. But before these guns had taken up their positions it was clear that the Afghans had vacated the fortress. Then began the blowing up of the fortifications and setting fire to the principal buildings, plus the total destruction of the 'Zubbir Jang', the massive 64-pdr gun. The General's last task was the removal of the Somnath gates from the tomb of Sultan Mahmoud of Ghazni.

After the capture and destruction of Ghazni Nott continued his advance, taking a short diversion to Sydabad in order to mete out a sharp dose of retribution for the cowardly slaughter of Captain John Woodburn and his escort the previous November. Having cleared the fort of its remaining inhabitants, he had it levelled to the ground. On completion of this satisfying occupation, Nott's army moved on towards Maidan, 20 miles from Kabul, without opposition until 14 September when upon arrival at Maidan the General discovered that Shamsuddin Khan, Sultan Jan and other chiefs were eager to dispute his further progress with a total force of 12,000 men positioned on a series of hills commanding the line of advance. These positions were immediately attacked and in quick order the opposition buckled under. The total success of this engagement prompted the General to report, 'Our troops beat them and dislodged them in gallant style and their conduct affords me the greatest satisfaction.'[19] After this successful affair, Nott's army arrived at Kabul on 17 September and camped about three miles from the city.

17 Beveridge, *A Comprehensive History of India*, Vol. 3, p.563.
18 Beveridge, *A Comprehensive History of India*, Vol. 3, p.566.
19 Stocqueler, *Memoirs and Correspondence, of Major General Sir William Nott,* p.143.

When the news of the reoccupation of Kabul reached Lord Ellenborough he was at Simla, and immediately prepared the necessary declaration document dated 1 October 1843, and signed in the same room as that of Lord Auckland's signing exactly three years earlier. The latter had been written for a British audience to justify a dubious war, whereas the former was written to celebrate a victory, and for an Indian audience dubious about continued British superiority. In any event, as it had come from the pen of Lord Ellenborough, the Whigs and liberal press in England ridiculed it.

On 11 September the hostages were at Bamian under an Afghan escort commanded by Saleh Mohammed, a man not inaccessible to a bribe, who showed Major Eldred Pottinger a letter from Mohammed Akbar Khan instructing him to convey his prisoners to Kulum and deliver them to the *Wali*, which meant slavery. At the same time, Saleh Mohammed made it known to the Major that he had received information coming from Mohan Lal, that if he would release the prisoners, General Pollock would give him 20,000 rupees and guarantee him a pension. The hostages had previously tried to bribe their way out but had failed; this time, with slavery imminent, Major Pottinger and captains George Lawrence, Colin Mackenzie and Hugh Johnson agreed to bind themselves to a pledge promising Saleh Mohammed 20,000 rupees and a pension of 1,000 rupees 'whenever Saleh Mohammed shall free us from the power of Mohammed Akbar Khan'. As Captain Mackenzie was later to write, 'Had Saleh Mohammed proved incorruptible, no effort by any army could have saved us.' It was also agreed amongst the hostages that should the Indian Government baulk at this payment, the officer element of the group would pick up the tab. It is here worthy to assume that General Pollock sanctioned the down payment of 20,000 rupees if only to maintain the integrity aspect of the British secret negotiator, Mohan Lal, however it is doubtful that the pension was ever paid. Thus the hostages were now free and active measures were immediately taken to put their fort in a reasonable defensive footing in case Mohammed Akbar Khan came rushing down to scoop them up back into captivity. Then on 15 September the hostages received the news of the defeat of Mohammed Akbar Khan by General Pollock at Tezeen, and thereupon set off in the direction of Kabul. The freed hostages met Shakespeare's rescue group of Kuzzilbashes on 17 September and a couple of days later Major General Sir Robert Sale's brigade. The hostages and their rescuers were back in Kabul by 21 September, except for Captain Bygrave, still held by Mohammed Akbar Khan. He was eventually released and walked into the British camp on 27 September.

In the meantime Lord Auckland had arrived back in England, where he was subjected to many inquiries as to his policy in Afghanistan. While His Lordship 'behaved well', his Whig party, now in opposition, began a rearguard campaign to cover up its failed policies. Their target was Lord Ellenborough and his policy of not making the release of the prisoners an indispensable condition of the evacuation of Afghanistan. This vendetta was to expand as more and more negative reports came in via the Indian press, fed by disgruntled civil servants and army officers writing scurrilous accounts of various actions, especially about the delay in assertive action. Today these announcements would be referred to as 'fake news' and were to give the gossiping Victorians much to discuss; it would seem that Lord Ellenborough's continued actions and declarations gave these chattering classes in England more and more to gossip about while he continued to swim against the political tide in the conviction that he had the continued confidence of the Prime Minister, Robert Peel, and the major-domo of England, the Duke of Wellington. This situation was encapsulated by Major General Nott in a letter to his daughters, from Kabul:

An artist's glamourised depiction of Lady Florentia Sale reunited wiith her husband Sir Robert Sale.

> The Whig party are attacking Ellenborough with the greatest asperity and doing all they can to divert public attention from the original expedition and its subsequent disaster and to fix the general indignation upon him for the policy he is disposed to adopt. The Government [Tory] have made up their minds to renounce all ideas of permanent conquest and establishment in Afghanistan. The English Public will be satisfied if they get back the prisoners, which is what they think most about, and though they will be dissatisfied and disappointed if some sort of vengeance is not executed upon Akbar Khan, they will on the whole be happy to be extricated from such an embarrassing and expensive scrap.[20]

With the hostages back safe in the British camp, it only remained to fulfil the Governor General's order to leave Kabul with some lasting mark of just retribution of an outraged nation, but to do it in such a way as not to impair its reputation for humanity. What form this should take was much discussed and consequentially political considerations came into play, causing a protracted stay in Kabul resulting in the depletion of provisions. The only thing the soldiers wanted was to leave this mark of retribution and leave the wretched country as soon as possible and not hang about to repeat the ill-fated previous retreat in the snows of Afghanistan. Meanwhile, Fateh Jung had been seated on the throne at a coronation attended by Major General Pollock, which in Afghan eyes stamped the new Shah as another British puppet, and hence the Bala Hissar was off the retribution target list, as was the Kuzzilbashe quarter of the city. It was eventually decided that the mark of 'just retribution' would be the destruction of the Grand Bazaar where the mutilated body of the British envoy had been hung out in a display of Afghan pride.

20 Stocqueler, *Memoirs and Correspondence of Major General Sir William Nott* p.429.

Prior to the British move on Kabul, the refractory chiefs had moved out with their families to Kohistan where, it was reported, Mohammed Akbar Khan was attempting to raise an army, and also where the reputed murderer of Sir Alexander Burnes, Ameenoollah Khan, was hiding. Major General Pollock, the overall commander of British forces, deemed it expedient to send Major General McCaskill with a force of 4,000 troops to Istalif, a place thought by Afghans to be impregnable and a safe asylum, and there to destroy the fort and quash any Afghan will to continue the fight. This expedition was strategically sound as it negated any Afghan effort to deny the British army passage through the passes.

Major General McCaskill moved out on 27 September with a composite force comprising HM 9th Foot, HM 41st Foot, HM 3rd Light Dragoons, 1st Bengal Light Cavalry, 26th BNI, 42nd BNI, 43rd BNI, a battery of 9-pdr guns and two 18-pdr guns.

This force, advancing in two columns, arrived at Istalif on 28 September and met with stiff resistance from the gardens surrounding the city, which was eventually overcome and the force entered the city at midday with the Afghans in full retreat leaving their families behind. The British had 51 men killed in this operation including one officer. Then 'the work of plunder now commenced and every effort was made to save the women and children but several of both were killed and wounded'.[21]

After burning down the city of Istalif and devastating the country around without mercy, Major General McCaskill continued his march northwards to Charikar, the place where the 4th Gurkha Regiment was annihilated and five officers had lost their lives. Charikar was likewise burnt down as a kind of wild revenge for the Gurkhas. By 7 October McCaskill's force was back in Kabul having left the villages of Kohistan marks of retribution long to be remembered.

On Thursday 12 October the British army left Kabul under the commands of generals Pollock and Nott, for its return to India in completion of the policy to withdraw from Afghanistan. Before leaving, the mark of retribution had to be administered and Captain Augustus Abbott was assigned to blow up the Char Chouk Bazaar with gunpowder. As reported in many accounts, very strict orders had been in force prohibiting plunder and looting, however 'the springing of the first fuse, was the signal for all the camp followers to rush into town and commence a work of the most disgraceful plunder'.[22] Apart from the Bala Hissar and the Kuzzilbashe quarter, the whole city was ravaged and destroyed, and looting was not limited to just the camp followers. Even allowing for the exasperation of the troops, the destruction permitted was a little over the top. Significantly, no prize agents were appointed for any of the actions during this phase of the campaign.

Accompanying the British army were 2,000 cripples who had been found in Kabul and who had been *sepoys* or camp followers. They were put on every sort of animal and travelled with Pollock's column along with the rescued hostages. On arrival in India these cripples were pensioned by a large subscription raised among European residents. Later, Lord Ellenborough authorised the grant of a pension to all the *sepoy* element of the group. Also travelling with General Pollock was Fateh Jung, who had calculated that with the departure of the British his days were numbered in single figures, and a better option was to become a pensioner of the

21 This quote is from the diary of an army officer serving with Major General Nott's forces. The contents were first published, in instalments, in *The Times of India.* If the diary is authentic it most probably belonged to Captain Thomas Polwhele of 42nd BNI.

22 Neill, *With the Somersets in Afghanistan*, p.163.

British in Ludhiana; another, much younger son of Shah Shuja was placed on the throne at the Bala Hissar.

The first column, commanded by Major General Pollock, marched through the Khurd-Kabul without real opposition and reached Tezeen on 14 October, where the General ordered the destruction of the fort and the two 18-pdr guns that had accompanied his column. However, the passage through these defiles by the second column, commanded by Major General Nott, was disputed by tribesmen who had assembled in greater numbers and made desperate attacks, no doubt keen to have a last crack at the affluent British convoy. Quite a lot of baggage was taken and at least 20 British soldiers were killed, including Captain Robert Burnett who was mortally wounded and died soon afterwards; he had been a hostage. Pollock reached Jagdalak on 16 October and Nott two days later. Here Nott, due to the exhaustion of many animals, was compelled to destroy the remaining two 18-pdr guns. It was at about this time that he was in receipt of a communication informing him that on arrival in India he was to take up the appointment of British resident at Oudh, a plum job.

By 22 October Pollock had reached Jalalabad, followed by Nott two days later. Here the army spent four days, depleting the place and area of all provisions and any extra carriage that had been sent up from India, and blowing up the bastions that had served them well during the long siege. The army, again in two columns, departed Jalalabad on 26 and 28 October respectively for its last leg through the infamous Khyber Pass; it left Jalalabad completely destroyed.

As the army neared the Khyber, the Afridis and other Khyber chiefs approached Captain Mackeson to know what would be given for a safe passage through the pass. The Captain's answer was 'nothing', as Pollock had decided to force his passage through; so the chiefs returned to their preparations to oppose the army, causing as much damage as possible and taking away as much as they could from the hateful infidels.

The first column was duly subjected to fierce opposition with a loss of about 60 soldiers including Lieutenant Alexander Christie and Ensign Alexander Nicholson, and the loss of lots of baggage and camels. Ensign Nicholson was the younger brother of Lieutenant John Nicolson of 27th BNI who had been taken hostage at Ghazni. He was heartbroken to stumble over the mangled body of his sibling, which he had to leave in a shallow grave for jackals to dig up. The column eventually reached the vicinity of Peshawar on 3 November. Nott's column fared much better, losing not a single camel. On the way he destroyed the important fort at Ali Masjid and arrived at Peshawar on 6 November. The last British officer to leave Afghan soil was Lieutenant John Wakefield. At Peshawar all the British officers were generously entertained by the ever gregarious governor, General Avitabile, who also loaned funds for the army's onward journey to India. Throughout the British affair in Afghanistan, General Avitabile had been a ready banker lending needful funds and all collectable at Calcutta. In this way this genial Italian was able to move a great deal of his vast funds out of the Punjab.

The rest of the journey back to India was through the territories of the friendly Sikh nation. However, the army was now assailed by an enemy more deadly than the Afghans: the press! As John Neill recorded in his journal:

> Scarcely had we cleared the passes when we were assailed by accounts in the Indian press of the horrible excesses we had committed. Enormities unheard unblushingly laid out at our door. Men unprincipled enough had been found to detail the perpetration of crimes which they well knew had never disgraced our army, individuals that were fiendish enough

> to seem loosed out of hell to speak horrors, which had their existence only in their own black malignant hearts.[23]

There were many such accounts written by Company men under the cover of anonymity, representing the recent campaign as a retreat by a disgraced and demoralised force in the course of which all sorts of atrocities had been committed. These reports were eventually to reach England where they were accepted by the opposition as points of fact, so feeding the growing animosity towards Lord Ellenborough. Plundering did take place despite very strict orders against it, but as Major General Nott was to state, 'camp followers were notoriously addicted to plundering', and 'strict orders' did little to suppress this addiction. At a later stage, Nott was asked to report whether his troops had been involved in any atrocities. He replied on 4 April 1843:

> I am desired to state whether unresisting individuals were destroyed in cold blood for mere revenge and whether women were either violated or murdered for their ornaments. I will endeavour to suppress my scorn and indignation while I shortly reply to the charge or suspicion or whatever it may be called by persons from where it emanated.[24]

Meantime, Lord Ellenborough put in motion preparations for a reception at Ferozepore for the 'victorious and glorious' army by an ever more grateful nation. This reception was to be stage managed to impress both friend and foe that, despite recent disasters, British sway in the East never stood on a more secure basis. To this jamboree Ellenborough invited various dignitaries, including the Sikh Maharaja Sher Singh. He also ordered especial silver medals for every officer and other rank that made up the 'Illustrious Garrison' to be handed over to the recipients before they crossed the Sutlej.[25]

The victorious army arrived at Kasur on 14 December, 40 miles from Ferozepore, where it was met by the Governor General's ADCs, Captains Arthur Somerset and Robert Colville, who handed over the Jalalabad medals to the individuals concerned, and briefed the generals of the arrangements in hand for the crossing of the Sutlej into British India and the grand reception at Ferozepore. It is worthy of note that Lord Ellenborough made sure that the widows or families were sent the medal of those men of the 'Illustrious Garrison' who had since died; a procedure followed to this day.

By seven o'clock on the morning of 17 December, the troops of the reserve force at Ferozepore had formed a line some two miles long on both sides of the road from the intended crossing place to the British camp. The Governor General and the Commander-in-Chief and their respective suites took up their positions at the river's edge on the British side of the bridge of boats constructed and decorated by the Sikhs. The first to cross was the 'Illustrious Garrison' led by Major General Sir Robert Sale on his charger, and with him, on an elephant apiece, his wife and daughter. Leading this group was the Flag of HM 13th Foot.

23 Neill, *With the Somersets in Afghanistan*, p.180.
24 Stocqueler, *Memoirs and Correspondence.of Major General Sir William Nott*, Vol. 2, p.218.
25 These medals were later recalled, as they did not bear the image of Queen Victoria and were replaced with ones that did. However not all were returned and these remain in various private collections; no doubt they are now very valuable.

A moth-eaten rag on a worm-eaten pole,
It does not look likely to stir a man's soul.
'T'is the deeds that were done 'neath the moth-eaten rag
When the pole was a staff and the rag was a flag
Rudyard Kipling

Bringing up the rear was Major General Nott's brigade, dragging the Somnath gates into India from where they had been taken some 400 years earlier.

That evening the Governor General hosted a dinner party for all the officers of the 'Illustrious Garrison', all 48 of them. On 26 December a Grand Ball was held to which all officers and wives of the army were invited, and on New Year's Eve a review of the whole army took place before 14-year-old *Kunwar* Pratap Singh, the eldest son of Maharaja Sher Singh, who had sent his son in his place for reasons unspecified: Lord Ellenborough was furious, as the Maharaja's presence had been the key reason for the review, which was to show all what a force the British could bring onto the field. Finally, on 3 January 1843, the process of disbanding the Army of Retribution began and covered the next 10 days as regiments departed for their assigned stations, and the Bombay contingent were sent down the Sutlej to Karachi from where they sailed to Bombay. Thus a venture lasting three years, costing millions of pounds and thousands of lives, came to an end.

25

Epilogue

Now that the Afghan escapade was over, Lord Ellenborough asked the Commander-in-Chief, Sir Jasper Nicolls, to give him a list of the military reasons for the disaster in Afghanistan. This list would, in part, counter the criticism of His Lordship's own policy. Nicolls, who was not much enamoured with His Lordship's antics, submitted the following list:

- Making war with a peace establishment.
- Making war without a safe base of operations.
- Carrying our native army into a strange and cold climate, where they and we were foreigners and both considered infidels.
- Invading a poor country, and one unequal to supply our wants, especially our large establishment of cattle.
- Giving undue power to political agents.
- Want of forethought and undue confidence in Afghans on the part of Sir William Macnaghten.
- Placing our magazines and even treasury, in indefensible positions.
- Great military neglect and mismanagement after the outbreak.[1]

What Sir Jasper failed to include was the important factor of economic restraints. The earlier liberality of Sir William Macnaghten's handouts was the only aspect the Afghans had tolerated of foreign influence and as these became a drain on the Calcutta treasury the parsimonious Court of Directors pushed for economies, and quite stupidly Macnaghten targeted the 'protection money' paid to the Ghilzai chiefs. This gross error is further compounded when one reads that the current National Afghan Army pay the Taliban thousands of dollars not to attack them (*Sunday Telegraph*, 6 September 2015).

As the regiments moved off to their various stations, the Governor General proceeded on the long trek back to the seat of government in Calcutta, elated by the success of his army and in particular its reception back in India, albeit some were to describe this as a 'garish pageant'. The only feature that did not work as planned was the absence of public acclaim for the return

1 Macrory, *The Fierce Pawns*, p.329.

of the Somnath gates. Lord Ellenborough, who had not heard of these gates prior to his arrival in India, was much taken by the knowledge that their return had been a prominent condition in the 1834 treaty between Shah Shuja and the great Maharaja Ranjit Singh, so he latched onto the idea of fulfilling the late Maharaja's desire and thereby reaping the acclaim of a grateful Hindu public, and made their return a key component of his 1 October 1842 declaration. But it was not to be. These gates, reputed to be 800 years old, failed close scrutiny and had been defiled by Muslims; furthermore, for Lord Ellenborough's English Christian audience, the return of these gates was pandering to idolatry. Rather than confront his critics on this botched PR scheme, the gates were taken to the fort in Agra and gradually disappeared into oblivion.

On 20 January Lord Ellenborough ordered the release of his state prisoner, Dost Mohammed Khan. His jailer throughout his time in India, Lieutenant Peter Nicolson,[2] no relation to John, bade a fond farewell to the Dost as he crossed the Sutlej near Ludhiana on his way back to Afghanistan via Lahore, where he signed a secret treaty with Maharaja Sher Singh.

The terms of this treaty remain unknown, however in 1849 the Dost did intervene in support of the Sikhs in the Second Anglo-Sikh War. On his return to Afghanistan he resumed his position as Amir and, it was rumoured, had his obstreperous son, Mohammed Akbar Khan, murdered. Upon a peace treaty being signed with the British in 1852, Dost Mohammed Khan remained faithful to its terms. He died in Kabul in 1863.

Lord Ellenborough has been described as 'a man of ability and businesslike habits, but vain and pompous and abrupt in manner'.[3] He was also very conscious of the dignity of his office. These characteristics were now enhanced by his conviction of the righteousness of his policies despite the growing chorus of criticism back in England, indicated in a letter from his brother-in-law, Sir Henry Hardinge. 'The object of the late Whig Government is to endeavour to throw odium on you and the Government for ordering the troops to retire to the left bank of the Indus, and to justify Lord Auckland's policy and conduct.'[4] It might have been possible for Lord Ellenborough to emerge unscathed by the criticism directed at him had he not imprudently provoked jealousies and animosities between the two main branches of public service, by the way in which his patronage was now distributed. As already mentioned, Lord Auckland had earlier made political agents subordinates to the military commander, which had hitherto been the exception; Lord Ellenborough set about making it the rule. Besides Major General Nott's posting to Oudh as the British resident, Colonel A. Fullarton Richmond was assigned to Ludhiana in place of Mr George Clerk, who replaced the deceased Sir William Macnaghten, and Major George Broadfoot was appointed commissioner at Moulmein;[5] in the Nerbudda

2 After a short break, Lieutenant Peter Nicolson was assigned to the post of assistant political agent at Ferozepore. He was there at the start of the First Anglo-Sikh War and accompanied Major General Littler onto the battlefield. He was killed at the Battle of Ferozeshah on 21 December 1845 and buried at Ferozepore. The plaque in St Andrew's Church wrongly shows his name as Patrick.

3 Nash, *History of the War in Afghanistan*, p.363.

4 Law, *India Under Lord Ellenborough*, p.41.

5 When Sir Henry Hardinge became governor general he assigned George Broadfoot to the important position of agent on the North-West Frontier, the previous holder of this sensitive position having blotted his copybook. In Ludhiana Broadfoot was responsible for British relations with the boisterous Sikh nation. His manner was more stern than diplomatic, and to some he thus provoked the unwanted war with the Sikhs, during which he was shot in the heart and died at the Battle of

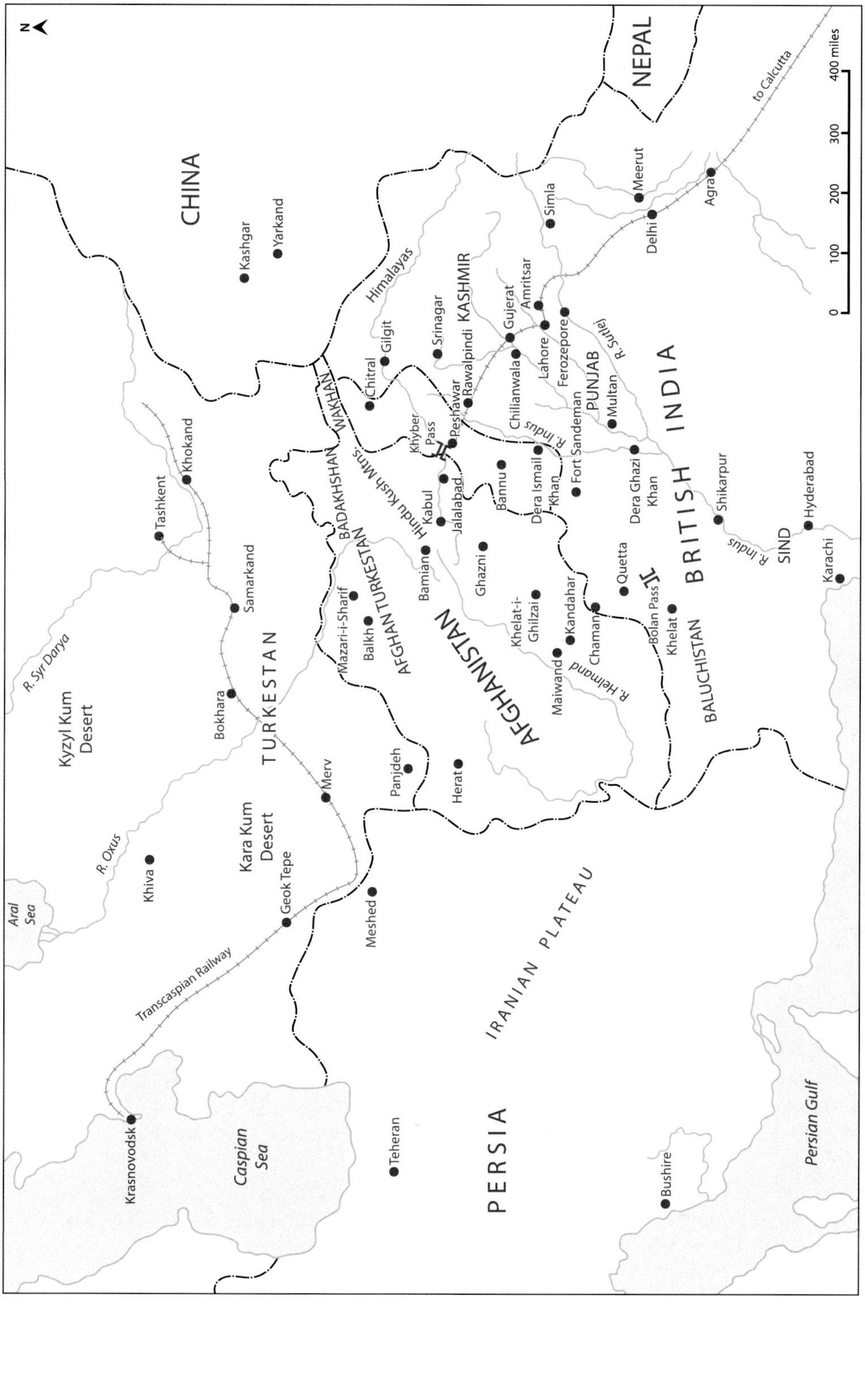

Map 17 Afghanistan and the North-West Frontier in the nineteenth Century.

territories, His Lordship dismissed the entire body of civilians and replaced them with military men. This was naturally much resented by the exasperated civil service. Conversely the army was delighted with its governor general, as is evident in a letter written by Major General Nott: 'I am delighted with him. Some people may laugh at his acts, but he is the keenest Englishman I have ever seen in this country, and just the man to deal with Asiatics.'[6] In consequence His Lordship had arrayed himself against a host of very influential civilian officials in Calcutta, who duly passed on their various gripes to the Court of Directors, thus the matter of exercising their prerogative of recalling a governor general, never used before, was now seriously mooted. However, they held their hand in full expectation of opposition from a strong government and the likes of the Duke of Wellington, the Governor General's friend.

Nearly all the hostages had sailed for England after their ordeal at the hands of the 'barbarous' Afghans, and with them went their jaded opinions of the heartless Governor General, which fuelled the fires of Whig opposition and that of the Court of Directors. Joining this group of returnees was Major James Outram, a Christian soldier who carried a Bible in his scabbard, and who had recently been replaced as the resident at Hyderabad in Sindh. He had fallen out with the Governor General regarding his policy for Sindh; Ellenborough had for some time been looking for an excuse to annex Sindh, thereby extending the sphere of British influence to the banks of the Indus. His excuse was the purported intrigues and unfriendly designs of the Amirs, and in May 1842 he ordered an inquiry to identify the main culprits. He thought that Outram had not been zealous enough, being duped by the Amirs, so he replaced him with General Sir Charles Napier, instructing him, 'It may be convenient that you should at once be informed that if the Amirs, or anyone of them, should act in a hostile manner, or evince hostile designs against the army, it is my strong resolution to penalise such hostility, which shall be a warning to every chief in India.'[7] The penalty was a penal treaty, and the Amirs' disobedience to its terms brought on a war conducted by a willing Napier to the horror of liberal England, where Outram had excited the pitying sentimentality of English people by convincing them that the Amirs had been unjustly accused and cruelly treated, and in a display of moral rectitude, he refused to accept his share of the prize money. By the following March Sindh was annexed to the great satisfaction of the Governor General and the fear of the Court of Directors, who wondered what more and expensive ventures their Governor General would drive them into.

Towards the close of 1843 the situation in the Punjab had worsened. Maharaja Sher Singh along with his son, Pratab Singh, had been assassinated and the fractious *Khalsa* army was in virtual control. Lord Ellenborough's correspondence clearly shows that he fully expected the situation to erupt into all-out war with the Sikh nation. However, he first had to sort out a slight distraction.

Raja Jankaji Rao Scindia of Gwalior had died childless, and brokered by the British Resident, Colonel Alexander Spiers, the 12-year-old widow of Raja Jankaji was made to adopt an eight-year-old boy, the nearest blood relation to the late Raja, and she was to rule as regent during this boy's minority. However the Raja's army disputed this arrangement and chaos reigned. Lord Ellenborough ordered the army into the field under its new commander-in-chief, General Sir

Ferozeshah on 21 December 1845. He was buried at Ferozepore alongside 'Fighting Bob', Major General Sir Robert Sale.

6 Stocqueler, *Memoirs and Correspondence,of Major General Sir William Nott,* p.181.

7 Hall, *Scenes in a Soldier's Life,* p.330.

Hugh Gough, an obedient Irish bloodhound, with but one trick: 'at them with bayonets!' On 22 December the British army marched into Gwalior accompanied by His Lordship and VIP wives, and on 29 December the Raja's mutinous army was beaten at the Battle of Maharajpore.[8] His Lordship's justification for this short war is given in his letter to Queen Victoria:

> The Sikhs no longer friendly, have within three marches of the Sutlej an army of 70,000. It may be expected that no hostile act on the part of the army will occur to produce a war; it would be unpardonable not to take every precaution against it, and no precaution appears to be more necessary than that of rendering our rear and communications secure by the re-establishment of a friendly court in Gwalior.[9]

This letter would not arrive in London before mid-March 1844, by which time Lord Ellenborough was being severely attacked in the House of Commons and his reputation being shredded to bits, thus becoming an embarrassment to the Prime Minister. Thomas Macaulay, the famous humanitarian, historian, essayist and government minister stated in a speech, 'We have sometimes sent them Governors whom they have loved, and sometimes Governors whom they have feared, but never before a Governor whom they have loathed.' Later, Lord John Russell, who was to become the next Prime Minister, added, 'Lord Ellenborough was not a man in whose hands such an empire as India could safely be left.'[10]

In April the first significant crack appeared in Tory defence of Lord Ellenborough. According to Colin Mackenzie, who had returned to England with the other hostages and was in London at the time, the Duke of Wellington while at a soirée was overheard to agree with a condemnation of Lord Ellenborough's policies by some of the guests. This explosive piece of tittle-tattle was immediately passed on to the Court of Directors who, smelling blood, submitted their prerogative for the recall of their prey. Sir Robert Peel, the Prime Minister, in attempting to draw a line under the whole matter, acquiesced. On 21 April the Prime Minister announced in the House of Commons the recall of the Governor General; the Duke of Wellington openly disapproved of it, but the deed was done.

On hearing of this months later, Lord Ellenborough was furious and immediately left Government House for Alipore, like a wounded tiger escaping from a skulk of jackals in Calcutta. He returned some days later to be informed that his replacement was to be his brother-in-law, Sir Henry Hardinge. He left India on 1 August 1844 for England, where he continued his fight to restore his damaged reputation. When in 1852 the Tories were back in power Lord Ellenborough was, for the fourth time, made president of the Board of Control, and was in situ to witness the demise of the East India Company in 1859, and so had the last laugh. Meanwhile the Whigs, who were back in power under Lord John Russell in 1846, appointed Lord Auckland back to his old post of First Lord of the Admiralty, no doubt qualifying as the man who steered the ship of state onto the rocks of Afghanistan.

Major General Nott duly arrived in Lucknow to take up his duties as the British resident at the Court of Oudh from Colonel John Low, who was to retire. Nott's two daughters and

8 Lieutenant Colonel Sanders, who had been Major General Nott's chief engineer, was the only officer to be killed in this battle.

9 Beveridge, *A Comprehensive History of India*, Vol. 3, p.595.

10 Mount, *Tears of the Rajas*, p.345.

son, Robert, joined him there and in June that year he married his second wife, Rosa Dore the daughter of Captain Peter Dore of HM 3rd Foot. Four months later an illness which he had contracted at Kandahar became a whole lot more problematic and he was advised to take a sea voyage to a better climate. He left India for the final time on 20 December on the *Earl of Hardwicke* for the Cape of Good Hope, but despite the better climate his condition became worse and he was forced to proceed to England, where he arrived with his wife and daughters in the summer of 1844. He was received with much acclaim in London where the Court of Directors awarded him a pension of £1,000 (£75,000). After a fairly short stay in London he left for Carmarthen in Wales, where he died on 1 January 1845.

Major General Pollock returned to his command in Agra, but shortly afterwards he was picked to replace the ailing Nott at Lucknow. Shortly thereafter he was selected for the position of military member in the Supreme Council at Calcutta, an appointment he enjoyed, being also a proprietor of the Honourable East India Company. However, in the summer of 1846 he was forced to resign because of serious illness and returned to England. In 1854 he became one of the 12 men who made up the Court of Directors of the East India Company, and by the time he retired from the army in 1870 he had reached the rank of Field Marshal, the first Indian Army officer to do so. Field Marshal Lord Pollock died on 6 October 1872 at Walmer, Kent, and was buried in Westminster Abbey.

Major General Sir Robert and Lady Sale, along with their daughter Alexandrina and her baby, Julia, returned to England for a well-deserved rest. While there, Lady Sale's journal was published and received much acclaim and both she and Sir Robert were presented to Her Majesty Queen Victoria. Also, while in England, Alexandrina married her second husband, Captain James Holmes of the Bengal Cavalry, and returned to India with him. In 1845 Sir Robert accepted the appointment of adjutant general to HM Forces in India, under the command of General Sir Hugh Gough. Regrettably, 'Fighting Bob' was mortally wounded in the first battle of the First Anglo-Sikh War at Mudki, on 18 December 1845. In his time 'Fighting Bob' had fathered 10 children and taken an active part in four wars. At the time of her husband's death, Lady Sale was in Simla and elected to stay there on a pension of £500 (£38,000). In 1853 she sailed to South Africa for health reasons. Unfortunately this indomitable Victorian lady was to die there on 6 July 1853. In 1857 Alexandrina and her second husband, now Lieutenant Colonel Holmes commanding his regiment, were in Segowli, where on 23 July he and his wife were brutally murdered by his own mutinous *sowars*. Alexandrina's daughter Julia Sturt, aged 14, was safely in Devon with her aunt. She died in 1910 and thus was the last survivor of Mohammed Akbar Khan's hostages.

At the end of January a series of courts martial were held at Ludhiana. Those charged included Lieutenant Colonel John Shelton and Major Eldred Pottinger. Such courts martial were customary in the event of any perceived dishonourable action or act. Pottinger was charged for signing the dishonourable treaty with Mohammed Akbar Khan for the evacuation of Kabul. As has already been recorded, Pottinger tried his very best to persuade the military commander not to capitulate, and many witnesses came forward to verify this, including Lieutenant Colonel Shelton. The charge against Pottinger was dropped and instead of joining the other hostages in England, Pottinger chose to join his uncle in Hong Kong, who was then the governor there. Unfortunately, a few months later, Major Pottinger died of typhus on 15 November 1843.

Lieutenant Colonel Shelton faced five charges of dishonourable behaviour. After some deliberation four of the charges were dropped and he was found guilty on the fifth charge of accepting a favour from Mohammed Akbar Khan. This was in fact fodder for his horse, and as he did not, himself, benefit from this act, no sentence was pronounced. He sailed for England and duly reported to his Regimental Depot in Colchester where he was once again appointed commanding officer of the newly raised HM 44th Foot. A while later, on parade with his regiment, the Colonel fell off his horse and died. Not much sorrow was expressed for this Waterloo veteran and difficult man.

The arrogant young politico Lieutenant William Hammersley had remained in Quetta as Major Outram's assistant, but his career was soon to be blighted. His previous actions and advice now came under a barrage of criticism, particularly from Major General Richard England. When Major General Nott was asked for his opinion, he thought the young officer should have been shot. Although Hammersley's defence was taken up by Major Outram, politicos in general were no longer the flavour of the month. The death knell was sounded in Lord Ellenborough's memorandum of 23 April 1843:

> The circumstances detailed in the letters I have received relative to the late disaster of Brigadier England's brigade, satisfies me that Lieutenant Hammersley is of no use in Quetta and I have placed him at the disposal of the Commander-in-Chief.[11]

While the British were busy with celebratory receptions, recriminations and rewards, the Great Game continued; the end of the British venture in Afghanistan was simply the end of a chukka in this game, which Tsar Peter the Great had started some 300 years ago. The game continues to this day with the prime object of gaining or denying influence in the region, with soldiers being replaced by dollars. As Lord Curzon was to write at the end of the nineteenth century, 'We do not want to occupy it, but we also cannot afford to see it occupied by our foes.'[12]

After the Second Anglo-Sikh War the British signed a peace treaty with Afghanistan in 1852, in accordance with which the British undertook not to interfere with Afghanistan's internal affairs, nor to send a representative to its court. Yet in 1878 Britain did exactly that, because she feared that the Amir, Shere Ali, a son of the late Dost Mohammed Khan, was becoming too pally with the Russians and thus launched the Second Anglo-Afghan War. The then commander of British forces, Field Marshal Lord Roberts, noted in his autobiography, 'It is instructive to note how remarkably similar were the circumstances which brought about the first and second Afghan wars, viz, the presence of Russian officers at Kabul.'[13]

Amir Shere Ali's entertainment of Russian officers at his court was understandable in the context of the fact that the Russians had by 1868 occupied Samarkand and six months later had conquered Khiva, then in 1877 Russia had declared war on Turkey. The wretched Amir was doing nothing more than keeping on friendly terms with both the British and the Russians. As the grandson of Dost Mohammed Khan and a later Amir, Abdur Rahman Khan, replied when he was asked what he wanted for Afghanistan, 'My countrymen are unable to struggle with Empires, and we are ruined by want of commerce, and we hope of your friendship that,

11 Mackenzie, *Storms and Sunsets of a Soldier's Life*, Vol. 2, p.6.
12 Curzon, *British Government in India*, Vol. II, p.129.
13 Field Marshal Lord Frederick Sleigh Roberts, *Forty-One Years in India: From Subaltern to Commander-in-Chief* (London: Macmillan and Co., 1901), p.564.

sympathising with and assisting the people of Afghanistan, you will place them under the honourable protection of the two powers.'

After the Third Anglo-Afghan War of 1919, and for the next 30 years, Britain maintained an armed presence on the India–Afghanistan border, a border established in 1893 by Sir Mortimer Durand, the son of Henry Durand, a border agreed by the Russians but not the Afghans, probably because it did not give them Peshawar, the elephant in the room!

Then came the Second World War and on its conclusion the emergence of a more assertive Russia bent on creating Russian soviets throughout the region. This was to cause much consternation in the West and the creation of pacts to stop the expansion of Russian influence. One of the critical areas for concern was the Indian subcontinent, which the British were about to leave with the creation of the two independent states of India and Pakistan. British concern was evident in a report sent to the British cabinet by the British Chiefs of Staff dated 18 April 1946:

> Recent developments makes it appear that Russia is our possible potential enemy. And to meet its threat, areas on which our effort will be based and without which it would not be possible to fight at all, include India.[14]

In July that year the Viceroy of India, Field Marshal Lord Wavell, passed on a note dated 13 July and written by the commander-in-chief, Field Marshal Sir Claude Auchinleck, to the British Government, which observed:

> We ought to consider, should independent India get influenced by hostile powers such as Russia, we could not maintain our power to move freely by sea or air in the northern parts of the Indian Ocean areas, which is of supreme importance to the British Commonwealth.[15]

As the date for the independence of India approached it was quite evident that the British Indian Empire was to split into India, led by the Congress Party, and Pakistan, led by Mohammed Ali Jinnah and his Muslim League. The cause of the split was the Congress Party's desire to shake off the British Raj, and Mr Jinnah feared the establishment of a Hindu Raj instead. Lord Wavell quickly grasped the fact that this split would provide a possible solution for British concerns of Russian expansion after the British left. On the premise that the Congress Party would be more unlikely to co-operate with Britain on military matters and foreign policy, which the Muslim League would be willing to do, this separation of India's strategic north-west from the rest of the country would provide a much-needed buffer to Russian influence.

Immediately after the independence of both India and Pakistan in 1947, Pakistan became a member of a British initiative called the Baghdad Pact, along with Persia, Iraq and Turkey which was set up in 1955. Then in 1971 a new player, the United States, joined in an extended pact called CENTO, which was to be 'the brick wall against Soviet expansion'. But then Persia became Iran with the expulsion of the Shah and Iran and Iraq went to war; CENTO was deemed toothless and the Russians invaded Afghanistan. The only western response to this was President Carter's decision to supply arms to the mujahedin insurgents. The Russian occupation

14 Sarila, Narendra Singh, *The Shadow of the Great Game: the Untold Story of India's Partition* (New Delhi: HarperCollins, 2005), p.21.
15 Sarila, *The Shadow of the Great Game*, p.24.

of Afghanistan lasted 10 years, during which thousands of troops were sent there to be killed on the Afghan rocks and billions of roubles expended. When the mujahedin were given U.S. stinger missiles, the Russians called it quits; bankrupt and broken, they withdrew.

Peace to the Afghans is nothing more than the interval between chukkas, as by 1994 the Taliban emerged under their leader Mullah Omar, and on 11 September 2001 two passenger aircraft crashed into the twin towers of the World Trade Center and President George. W. Bush hauled NATO into Afghanistan. Thirteen years later, after the deaths of thousands of allied troops and billions of dollars up in smoke, the NATO Commander, General John Campbell, announced on 29 December 2014, on the eve of NATO's departure, 'Together we have lifted the Afghan people out of the darkness of despair and given them back their future.' There is not much difference in this rosy appreciation to the one sent by Sir William Macnaghten some 170 years earlier: 'Everything is quiet from Dan to Beersheba. Our prospects are brightening in every direction and everything is *couleur de rose* ...

Appendix I

Tripartite Treaty with Ranjit Singh and Shah Shuja, 1838

WHEREAS a treaty was formerly concluded between Maharaja Ranjit Singh and Shah Shuja-ool-Moolk, consisting of 14 articles, exclusive of the preamble and the conclusion: And whereas the execution of the provisions of the said treaty was suspended for certain reasons: And whereas at this time, Mr Macnaghten having been deputed by the Right Honourable George Lord Auckland, GCB, Governor General of India, to the presence of Maharaja Ranjit Singh, and vested with full powers to form a treaty, in a manner consistent with the friendly engagements subsisting between the two States, treaty foresaid is revived, and concluded with certain modifications, and four new articles have been added thereto, with the approbation of, and in concert with the British Government, the provisions whereof, ascertained in the following eighteen articles, will be duly and faithfully observed:

Article 1. Shah Shuja-ool-Moolk disclaims all title on the part of himself, his heirs and successors and all the Suddozies, to all the territories lying on either bank of the river Indus, that may be possessed by the Maharaja, *viz*, Cashmeer, including its limits, E, W, N, S, together with the fort of Attok, Chuch, Huzara, Khubal, Umb, with its dependencies, on the left bank of the foresaid river, and on the right bank Peshawur, with the Ensufzaee territory, the Khutuks, Husht Nuggur, Mitchnee, Kohat, Hunggoo, and all places dependent on Peshawur, as far as the Khyber pass, Bunnoo, the Vuzeeree territory, Dow-Tank, Gurang, Kalabagh and Khooshalghur, with their dependent districts, Derah Ismaeel Khan, and its dependency, Kot Mithen, Oomur Kot, and their dependent territory; Sunghur, Hurround-Dajul, Hajeepore, Rajenpore, and the three Kutches, as well as Munkehra, with its district, and the province of Mooltan, situated on the left bank. These countries and places are considered to be the property, and to form the estate, of the Maharaja: The Shah neither has nor will have any concern with them; they belong to the Maharaja and his posterity from generation to generation.

Article 2. The people of the country on the other side of Khyber will not be suffered to commit robberies, or aggressions, or any disturbances on this side, If any defaulter of either State, who has embezzled the revenue, take refuge in the territory of the other, each party engages to surrender him, and no person shall obstruct the passage of the stream which issues out of the Khyber defile, and supplies the fort of Futtigurh with water according to ancient usage.

Article 3. As, agreeably to the treaty established between the British Government and the Maharaja, no one can cross from the left bank to the right bank of the Sutlej without a passport from the Maharaja, the same rule shall be observed regarding the passage of the Indus, whose waters join the Sutlej, and no one shall be allowed to cross the Indus without the Maharaja's permission.

Article 4. Regarding Shikarpore and the territory of the Scinde, on the right bank of the Indus, the Shah will agree to abide by whatever may be settled as right and proper, in conformity with the happy relations of friendship subsisting between the British Government and the Maharaja through Captain Wade.

Article 5. When the Shah shall have established his authority in Cabool and Candahar, he will annually send the Maharaja the following articles, 55 high-bred horses of approved colour, and pleasant paces; 11 Persian scimitars, 7 Persian poignards; 25 good mules; fruits of various kinds, both dry and fresh; and Sirdas or Musk melons, of a sweet and delicate flavour (to be sent throughout the year by the way of the Cabool river to Peshawar); grapes, pomegranates, apples, quinces, almonds, raisins, pistahs or chestnuts, an abundant supply of each, as well as pieces of satin of every colour; chogas of fur; kimkhabs wrought with gold and silver; and Persian carpets, altogether to the number of 101 pieces – all these articles the Shah will continue to send every year to the Maharaja.

Article 6. Each party shall address the other on terms of equality.

Article 7. Merchants of Afghanistan who may be desirous of trading to Lahore, Umrutsir, or any other parts of the Maharaja's possessions shall not be stopped or molested on their way; on the contrary, strict orders shall be issued to facilitate their intercourse, and the Maharaja engages to observe the same line of conduct on his part, in respect to traders who may wish to proceed to Afghanistan.

Article 8. The Maharaja will yearly send to the Shah the following articles in the way of friendship: 55 pieces of shawls; 25 pieces of muslin;11 dooputtahs; 5 pieces of kimkhab; 5 scarfs; 5 turbans; 55 loads of Bareh rice [peculiar to Peshawar].

Article 9. Any of the Maharaja's officers, who may be deputed to Afghanistan to purchase horses, or on any other business, as well as those who may be sent by the Shah into the Punjab, for the purpose of purchasing piece goods, or shawls, &c., to the amount of 11,000 rupees, will be treated by both sides with due attention, and every facility will be afforded to them in the execution of their commission.

Article 10. Whenever the armies of the two States may happen to be assembled at the same place, on no account shall the slaughter of kine be permitted to take place.

Article 11. In the event of the Shah taking an auxiliary force from the Maharaja, whatever booty may be acquired from the Barekzais in jewels, horses, arms, great and small, shall be equally divided between the two contracting parties. If the Shah should succeed in obtaining possession of their property, without the assistance of the Maharaja's troops, the Shah agrees to send a portion of it by his own agent to the Maharaja in the way of friendship.

Article 12. An exchange of missions charged with letters and presents shall constantly take place between the two parties.

Article 13. Should the Maharaja require the aid of any of the Shah's troops in furtherance of the objects contemplated by this treaty, the Shah engages to send a force commanded by one of his principal officers; in like manner the Maharaja will furnish the Shah, when required, with an auxiliary force, composed of Mahomedans, and commanded by one of the principal officers, as far as Cabool, in furtherance of the objects contemplated by this treaty. When the Maharaja may go Peshawar, the Shah will depute a Shahzada to visit him, on which occasions the Maharaja will receive and dismiss him with the honor and consideration due to his rank and dignity.

Article 14. The friends and enemies of each of the three high powers, that is to say, the British and Sikh Governments, and Shah Shuja-ool-Moolk, shall be friends and enemies of all.

Article 15. Shah Shuja-ool-Moolk engages, after the attainment of his object, to pay without fail to the Maharaja the sum of two lakhs of rupees, of the Nanukshahee or Kuldar currency, calculating from the date on which the Sikh troops may be despatched for the purpose of reinstating his Majesty in Cabool, in consideration of the Maharaja stationing a force of not less than 5,000 men, cavalry and infantry, of the Mahomedan persuasion, within the limits of the Peshawar territory, for the support of the Shah, and to be sent to the aid of his Majesty, whenever the British Government, in concert and counsel with the Maharaja, shall deem their aid necessary; and when any matter of great importance may arise to the westward, such measures will be adopted with regard it as may seem expedient and proper at the time to the British and Sikh Governments. In the event of the Maharaja's requiring the aid of any of the Shah's troops, a deduction shall be made from the subsidy proportioned to the period for which such aid may be afforded, and the British government holds itself responsible for the punctual payment of the above sum annually to the Maharaja, so long as the provisions of this treaty are duly observed.

Article 16. Shah Shuja-ool-Moolk agrees to relinquish for himself, his heirs, and successors, all claims of supremacy and arrears of tribute over the country now held by the Ameers of Scinde (which will continue to belong to the Ameers and their successors in perpetuity) on condition of the payment to him by the Ameers of such a sum as may be determined under the mediation of the British Government; 1,500,000 of rupees of such payment being made over by him to Maharaja Ranjit Singh. On these payments being completed, article 4 of the treaty of 12 March 1833, will be considered cancelled, and the customary interchange of letters and suitable presents between the Maharaja and the Ameers of the Scinde shall be maintained as heretofore.

Article 17. When Shah Shuja-ool-Moolk shall have succeeded in establishing his authority in Afghanistan, he shall not attack or molest his nephew, the ruler of Herat, in the possession of the territories now subject to his Government.

Article 18. Shah Shuja-ool-Moolk binds himself, his heirs, and successors, to refrain from entering into negotiations with any foreign State without the knowledge and consent of the British and Sikh Governments, and to oppose any power having the design to invade the British and Sikh territories by force of arms, to the utmost of his ability.

The three powers, parties to this treaty, namely, the British Government, Maharaja Ranjit Singh, and Shah Shuja-ool-Moolk, cordially agree to the foregoing articles. There shall be no deviations from them, and in that case the present treaty shall be considered binding for ever, and this treaty shall come into operation from and after the date on which the seals and signatures of the three contracting parties shall have been affixed thereto.

Done at Lahore, this 26th day of June, in the year of our Lord 1838, corresponding with the 15th of the month of Assarh 1895, era of Bikurmajeet.

Ratified by the Right Honorable the Governor General at Simla, on 23rd Day of July, 1838

(Signed) AUCKLAND
RANJIT SINGH

Appendix II

The Governor General's Declaration

Declaration on the Part of the Right Honourable
The Governor General of India
Simla, 1 October 1838

The Right Honourable the Governor General of India having, with the concurrence of the Supreme Council, directed the assemblage of a British force for services across the Indus, his Lordship deems it proper to publish the following exposition of the reasons which have led to this important measure.

It is a matter of notoriety that the treaties entered into by the British Government in the year 1832, with the Amirs of Sindh, the Newab of Bhawalpore, and Maharaja Ranjit Singh, had for their object, by opening the navigation of the Indus, to facilitate the extension of commerce, and to gain for the British nation in Central Asia that legitimate influence which an interchange of benefits would naturally produce.

With a view to invite the aid of the de facto rulers of Afghanistan to the measures necessary for giving full effect to those treaties, Captain Burnes was deputed, towards the close of the year 1836, on a mission to Dost Mohammed, the chief of Caubul. The original objects of that officer's mission were purely of a commercial nature. While Captain Burnes, however, was on his journey to Caubul, information was received by the Governor General that the troops of Dost Mohammed Khan had made a sudden and unprovoked attack on those of our ancient ally, Maharaja Ranjit Singh. It was naturally to be apprehended that his Highness the Maharaja would not be slow to avenge the aggression; and it was to be feared that, the flames of war being once kindled in the very regions into which we were endeavouring to extend our commerce, the peaceful and beneficial purposes of the British Government would be altogether frustrated. In order to avert a result so calamitous, the Governor General resolved on authorising Captain Burnes to intimate to Dost Mohammed Khan, that if he should evince a disposition to just and reasonable terms with the Maharaja, his Lordship would exert his good offices with his Highness for the restoration of an amicable understanding between the two powers. The Maharaja, with the characteristic confidence which he has uniformly placed in the faith and friendship of the British nation, at once assented to the proposition of the Governor General, to the effect that, in the meantime, hostilities on his part should be suspended.

It subsequently came to the knowledge of the Governor General, that a Persian army was besieging Herat; that intrigues were actively prosecuted throughout Afghanistan, for the purpose of extending Persian influence and authority to the banks of, and even beyond, the Indus; and that the Court of Persia had not only commenced a course of injury and insult to the officers of Her Majesty's Mission in the Persian territory, but had afforded evidence of being engaged in designs wholly at variance with principles and objects of its alliance with Great Britain.

After much time spent by Captain Burnes in fruitless negotiations at Caubul, it appeared that Dost Mohammed Khan, chiefly in consequence of his reliance upon Persian encouragement and assistance, persisted, as respected his misunderstanding with the Sikhs, in urging the most unreasonable pretensions, such as the Governor General could not, consistently with justice and his regard for the friendship of Maharaja Ranjit Singh, be the channel of submitting to the consideration of his Highness; that he avowed schemes of aggrandisement and ambition injurious to the security and peace of the frontiers of India; and that he openly threatened, in furtherance of those schemes, to call in every foreign aid which he could command. Ultimately, he gave his undisguised support to the Persian designs in Afghanistan, of the unfriendly and injurious character of which, as concerned the British power in India, he was well apprised, and by his utter disregard of the views and interests of the British Government, compelled Captain Burnes to leave Caubul without having effected any of the objects of his mission.

It is now evident that no further interference could be exercised by the British Government to bring about a good understanding between the Sikh ruler and Dost Mohammed Khan, and the hostile policy of the latter chief showed too plainly that, so long as Caubul remained under his government, we could never hope that the tranquillity of our neighbourhood would be secured, or that the interests of our Indian Empire would be preserved inviolate.

The Governor General deems it in this place necessary to revert to the siege of Herat, and the conduct of the Persian nation. The Siege of that city has now been carried on by the Persian army for many months. The attack upon it was a most unjustifiable and cruel aggression, perpetrated and continued, notwithstanding the solemn and repeated remonstrations of the British Envoy at the Court of Persia, and after every just and becoming offer of accommodation had been made and rejected. The besieged have behaved with a gallantry and fortitude worthy of the justice of their cause; and the Governor General would yet indulge the hope that their heroism may enable them to maintain a successful defence, until succours shall reach them from British India. In the meantime, the ulterior designs of Persia, affecting the interests of the British Government, have been, by a succession of events, more and more openly manifested. The Governor General has recently ascertained by an official despatch from Mr McNeill, her Majesty's Envoy, that his Excellency has been compelled, by refusal of his just demands, and by a systematic course of disrespect adopted towards him by the Persian Government, to quit the Court of the Shah, and to make a public declaration of the cessation of all intercourse between the two Governments. The necessity under which Great Britain is placed of regarding the present advance of the Persian arms into Afghanistan as an act of hostility towards herself, has also been officially communicated to the Shah, under the express order of her Majesty's Government.

The chiefs of Candahar (brothers of Dost Mohammed Khan of Caubul) have avowed their adherence to the Persian policy, with the same full knowledge of its opposition to the rights and interests of the British nation in India and have been openly assisting in the operations against Herat.

In the crisis of affairs consequent upon the retirement of our Envoy from Caubul, the Governor General felt the importance of taking immediate measures for arresting the rapid progress of foreign intrigue and aggression towards our own territories.

His attention was naturally drawn at this conjuncture to the position and claims of Shah Soojah-ool-Moolk, a monarch who, when in power, had cordially acceded to the measures of united resistance to external enmity, which were at that time judged necessary by the British Government, and who, on his empire being usurped by its present rulers, had found an honourable asylum in the British dominions.

It has been clearly ascertained, from the information furnished by the various officers who have visited Afghanistan, that the Barukzye chiefs, from their disunion and unpopularity, were ill fitted, under any circumstances, to be useful allies to the British Government, and to aid us in our just and necessary measures of national defence. Yet so long as they refrained from proceedings injurious to our interests and security, the British Government acknowledged and respected their authority; but a different policy appeared to be now more than justified by the conduct of those chiefs, and to be indispensable to our safety. The welfare of our possessions in the East requires that we should have on our western frontier an ally who is interested in resisting aggression, and establishing tranquillity, in the place of chiefs ranging themselves in subservience to a hostile power and seeking to promote schemes of conquest and aggrandisement.

After serious and mature deliberation, the Governor General was satisfied that a pressing necessity, as well as every consideration of policy and justice, warranted us in espousing the cause of Shah Soojah-ool-Moolk, whose popularity throughout Afghanistan had been proved to His Lordship by the strong and unanimous testimony of the best authorities. Having arrived at this determination, the Governor General was further of opinion that it was just and proper, no less from the position of Maharaja Ranjit Singh, than from his undeviating friendship towards the British Government, that his Highness should have the offer of becoming a party to the contemplated operations.

Mr Macnaghten was accordingly deputed in June last to the Court of his Highness, and the result of his mission has been the conclusion of a triplicate treaty by the British Government, the Maharaja, and Shah Soojah-ool-Moolk, whereby his Highness is guaranteed in his present possessions, and has bound himself to co-operate for the restoration of the Shah to the throne of his ancestors. The friends and enemies of any one of the contracting parties have been declared to be the friends and enemies of all.

Various points have been adjusted, which have been the subjects of discussion between the British Government and his Highness the Maharaja, the identity of whose interests with those of the Honourable Company has now been made apparent to all the surrounding States. A guaranteed independence will, upon favourable conditions, be tendered to the Ameers of Sindh, and the integrity of Herat, in the possession of its present ruler, will be fully respected; while by the measures completed, or in progress, it may reasonably be hoped that the general freedom and security of commerce will be promoted; that the name and just influence of the British Government will gain their proper footing among the nations of Central Asia; that tranquillity will be established upon the most important frontier of India; and that a lasting barrier will be raised against hostile intrigue and encroachment.

His Majesty Shah Soojah-ool-Moolk will enter Afghanistan surrounded by his own troops, and will be supported against foreign interference and factious opposition by a British army. The Governor General confidently hopes that the Shah will be speedily replaced on his throne by his own subjects and adherents, and once when he shall be secured in power, and the independence and integrity of Afghanistan established, the British army will be withdrawn. The Governor General has been led to these measures by the duty which is imposed upon him of providing for the security of the possessions of the British Crown; but he rejoices that, in the discharge of his duty, he will be enabled to assist in restoring the union and prosperity of the Afghan people. Throughout the approaching operations, British influence will be sedulously employed to further every measure of general benefit, to reconcile differences, to secure oblivion of injuries, and to put an end to the distractions by which, for so many years, the welfare and happiness of the Afghans have been impaired. Even to the chiefs, whose hostile proceedings have given just cause of offence to the British Government, it will seek to secure liberal and honourable treatment, on their tendering early submission, and ceasing from opposition to that course of measures which may be judged the most suitable for the general advance of their country.

By order of the Right Honourable Governor General of India
W.H. Macnaghten
Secretary to the Government of India,
with the Governor General

Appendix III

Organisation of Shah Shuja's Force at the Time of Brigadier A. Roberts's Assumption of Command

---

Staff

Brigadier A. Roberts	Commander
Captain C. Troup, 48th BNI	Brigade Major
Captain H. Johnson, 26th BNI	Commissariat Officer and Paymaster
Captain G. Lawrence, 2nd Ben Lt Cav	Auditor and Military Secretary
Captain T. Hutton, 37th BNI	Asst Commander at Kandahar
Lieutenant J. Shaw, 2nd BNI	Asst Commander at Shikarpore
Lieutenant H. Milne, 21st BNI	Asst Commander at Bamian
Lieutenant A. Dallas, 16th BNI	Asst Commander at Kandahar

Horse Artillery

Captain W. Anderson	Commander
Lieutenant G. Cooper	Commander First Troop, at Kandahar
Lieutenant E. Turner	Commander Second Troop, at Kabul
Lieutenant A. Hawkins	Adjutant

Mountain Train (Artillery)

Captain J. Backhouse	Commander
2/Lieutenant C. Green	Second in Command

Engineers

Lieutenant J. Sturt	Surveying Hindu Kush
2/Lieutenant R. Pigou	Surveying Ghilzai country

1st Regiment of Cavalry

Captain J. Christie, 3rd Ben Lt Cav	Commander
Lieutenant P. Nicholson, 28th BNI	Adjutant
Cornet H. Toone, 2nd Ben Lt Cav	Troop Commander

2nd Regiment of Cavalry

Captain W. Anderson, 59th BNI	Commander
Lieutenant Le Geyt, 1st Bom Lt Cav	Adjutant
Lieutenant D. Gaussen, 42nd BNI	Quartermaster

1st Infantry Regiment (at Quetta)

Captain J. Griffin, 24th BNI	Commander
Lieutenant J. Travers, 23rd BomNI	Adjustant

2nd Infantry Regiment (at Kandahar)

Captain C. Macan, 16th BNI	Commander
Lieutenant J. Hope, 16th BNI	Adjutant
Lieutenant A. Podmore, 6th BomNI	Quartermaster

3rd Infantry Regiment (at Kabul)

Captain P. Craigie, 20th BNI	Commander
Lieutenant R. McKean, 17th BNI	Adjutant
Captain MacDonell, 19th BomNI	Quartermaster

4th Gurkha Regiment (at Bamian)

Captain W.E. Hay, 1st BER	Commander
Lieutenant J.B. Conolly, 20 BNI	Adjutant (Envoy's Escort Commander)
Lieutenant W. Broadfoot, 1st BER	Commander of Pioneers
Lieutenant G.W. Golding, 1 BER	Acting Adjutant

5th Regiment Infantry (at Kandahar)

Captain J. Woodburn, 44th BNI	Commander
Lieutenant J.K. Spence, 20th BNI	Adjutant
Lieutenant A.H. Ross, 42nd BNI	Quartermaster

Provisional Battalion (at Shikarpore)

Lieutenant C. Codrington, 49th BNI	Commander[1]

Medical Department

Surgeon J. Forsyth	At Headquarters, Kabul
Asst Surgeon P.F.H. Baddeley	At Kandahar
Asst Surgeon C. McKennon	At Kabul
Asst Surgeon G. Rae	With 2ndRegiment
Asst Surgeon A. Colquhoun	With 5th Regiment

Afghan Levies

Lieutenant R. Warburton, Artillery	Commander King's Guns
Captain A.W. Tayler, 1st BER	Paymaster
Captain R.S. Trevor, 3rd Ben Lt Cav	Mustering Officer for Afghan Mounted Levies
Lieutenant H. Marsh, 3rd Ben Lt Cav	Mustering Officer for Afghan Mounted Levies
Lieutenant R. Maule, Artillery	Commander Khostani Levies

1st Local Corps of Infantry

Captain Perin Hopkins, 27th BNI	Commander

2nd Local Corps of Infantry

Captain H.P. Burn, 1st BNI	Commander
Lieutenant W.R. Hillersdon, 53rd BNI	Adjutant

3rd Local Corps of Infantry

Captain J. Ferris, 20th BNI	Commander
Lieutenant R. Dowson, 5th BNI	Adjutant

4th Local Corps of Infantry

Lieutenant C. Codrington, 49th BNI	Recruiting Officer
Ensign J.C. Haughton, 31st BNI	Adjutant

1 This officer was involved in the recruiting of locals. He was latter to command the 4th Gurkha Regiment.

5th Local Corps of Infantry (at Quetta)

Captain J.D.D. Bean, 23rd BNI	Commander
Lieutenant W. Hammersley, 41st BNI	Adjutant

King's Guards

Captain J. Nash, 43rd BNI	Commander

Abbreviations
BNI = Bengal Native Infantry
BER = Bengal European Regiment
BomNI = Bombay Native Infantry
Bom Lt Cav = Bombay Light Cavalry
Ben Lt Cav = Bengal Light Cavalry

Appendix IV

Lieutenant General Sir John Keane's Despatch After the Storming of Ghazni Headquarters Camp, Ghuznee, 24 July 1839

My Lord,

I have the satisfaction to acquaint your Lordship, that the army under my command has succeeded in performing one of the most brilliant acts it has been my lot to witness, during my service of 45 years, in the four quarters of the globe, in the capture, by storm, of the strong and important fortress and citadel of Ghuznee, yesterday.

It is not only that the Afghan nation, and I understand Asia generally, have looked upon it as impregnable, but it is in reality a place of great strength, both by nature and art, far more so than I had reason to suppose from any description that I have received of it; although some are from officers from our own service, who have seen it in their travels.

I was surprised to find a high rampart in good repair, built on a scarped mound, about 35 feet high, flanked by numerous towers, and surrounded by a 'Fausse-braye' and a wet ditch, whilst the height of the citadel covered the interior from the commanding fire of the hills from the north, rendering it nugatory. In addition to this, screen walls had been built before the gates; the ditch was filled with water and unfordable, and an out-work built on the right bank of the river, so as to command the bed of it.

It is therefore the more honourable to the troops, and must appear to the enemy out of all calculation extraordinary, that a fortress and citadel, to the strength of which, for the last 30 years, they have been adding something each year, and which had a garrison of 3,500 Afghan soldiers, commanded by Prince Mahomed Hyder, the son of Dost Mahomed Khan, the ruler of the country, with a commanding number of guns, and abundance of ammunition and other stores, provisions &c for a regular siege, should be taken by British science and British valour, in less than two hours from the time the attack was made, and the whole, including the Govr and garrison, should fall into our hands.

My despatch of the 20th Inst. From Nannee, will have made known to your Lordship, that the Camp of His Majesty Shah Shoojah-ool-Moolk, and Major General Wilshire, with the Bombay troops, had there joined me in accordance with my desire; and the following morning we made our march of 12 miles to Ghuznee. The line of march being over a fine plain, the troops were disposed in a manner that would have enabled me at any moment, had we been attacked, as was probable from the large bodies of troops moving on each side of us, to have placed them in a position to receive the enemy. They did not however appear, but on our coming within range of the guns of the citadel and fortress of Ghuznee, a smart cannonade was opened on our leading columns, together with a heavy fire of musketry from behind garden walls, and temporary field-works thrown up, as well as the strong out-work I have already alluded to, which commanded the bed of the river. From all but the out-work the enemy were driven in, under the walls of the fort, in a spirited manner by parties thrown forward by Major General Sir Willoughby Cotton, of the 16th and 48th Bengal NI, and HM's 13 Lt Infy under Brigadier Sale. I ordered forward three troops of Horse Arty, the camel-battery and one foot-battery, to open upon the citadel and fortress by throwing shrapnel shells, which was done in a masterly style, under the direction of Brigadier Stevenson. My object in this was to make the enemy show their strength in guns, and other aspects, which completely succeeded and our shells must have done great execution and occasioned great consternation. Being perfectly satisfied on the point of their strength, in the course of half an hour, I ordered the fire to cease, and placed the troops in bivouac. A close reconnaissance of the place all round was then undertaken by Captain Thomson, the chief Engineer, and Captain Peat of the Bombay Engineers, accompanied by Major Garden, the Depy. Qr. Mr. Genl. of the Bengal army, supported by a strong party of 2nd Bengal Light Cavalry and one of HM'13 Lt Infy. On this party, a steady fire was kept up and some casualties occurred. Captain Thomson's report was very clear (he found the fortifications equally strong all round) and as my own opinion coincided with his, I did not hesitate a moment as to the manner in which our approach and attack on the place should be made; notwithstanding the march the troops had performed in the morning, and their having been a considerable time engaged with the enemy, I ordered the whole to move across the river (which runs close under the fort walls) in columns to the right and left of the town, and they were placed in position on the north side, on more commanding ground, and securing the Cabool road. I had information that a night attack upon the camp was intended from without. Mahomed Ufzul Khan, the eldest son of Dost Mahomed Khan, had been sent by his father with a strong body of troops from Cabool to his brother's assistance at Ghuznee, and was camped outside the walls, but abandoned his position on our approach, keeping however at a distance of a few miles from us. The two rebel chiefs of the Gilzie tribe, men of great influence; viz Abdool Rhuman, and Gool Mahomed Khan, had joined him with 1,500 Horse and also a body of 3,000 Ghazees from Zienat under a mixture of chiefs and Moolahs, carrying banners, and who had been assembled on the cry of religious war. In short, we were, in all directions, surrounded by enemies. These last actually came down the hills on 22nd and attacked the part of the camp occupied by His Majesty Shah Shoojah and his troops; but were driven back with considerable loss, and banners taken.

At daylight on 22nd I reconnoitred Ghuznee in company with the chief Engineer, and the Brigadier commanding the Arty, with the Adjt and Qr. Mr. Genl of the Bengal army, for the purpose of making all arrangements for carrying the place by storm, and these were completed in the course of the day. Instead of the tedious process of breaching (for which were ill prepared) Captain Thomson undertook, with the assistance of Captain Peat, of Bombay Engineers, Lieuts. Durand and MacLeod, of the Bengal Engineers, and other officers under him (Captain Thomson) to blow in the Cabool gate (the weakest point) with gunpowder; and so much faith did I place on the success of the operation, that my plans for the assault were immediately laid down and the orders given.

The different troops of Horse Arty, the camel and foot batteries, moved off their ground at 12 o'clock that night, without the slightest noise, as had been directed, and in the most correct manner, took up the position assigned them, about 250 yards from the walls; in like manner and with the same silence, the Infantry soon after moved from their ground, and all were at their post at the proper time. A few minutes before 3 o'clock in the morning, the explosion took place, and proved completely successful. Captain Peat of the Bombay Engineers, was thrown down and stunned by it, but shortly after recovered his senses and feeling. On hearing the advance sounded by the bugles (being the signal for the gate having been blown in) the Artillery, under the able directions of Brigadier Stevenson, consisting of Captain Grant's troop of Bengal Horse Arty, the camel battery under Captain Abbott. Both superintended by Major Pew, Captains Martin's and Cotgrave's troops of Bombay Horse Arty, and Captain Lloyd's battery of Bombay Foot Arty, all opened a terrific fire upon the citadel and ramparts of the Fort, and in a certain degree paralysed the enemy.

Under the guidance of Captain Thomson of the Bengal Engineers, the chief of the Department, Col. Dennie of HM's 13th Light Infy. Comg. the advance, consisting of the light Cos. Of HM's 2nd and 17th Foot, and the Bengal European Regt., with one Coy. Of HM's 13th Lt. Infy., proceeded to the gate, and with great difficulty, from the rubbish thrown down, and the determined opposition offered by the enemy, effected an entrance and established themselves within the gateway, closely followed by the main column, led in a spirit of great gallantry by Brigadier Sale, to whom I had entrusted the important post of Comg. the 'Storming Party,' consisting (with the advance above mentioned) of HM's 2nd Foot under Major Carruthers, the Bengal European Regt. Under Lieut-Col. Orchard, followed by HM's 13th Lt. Infy. Under Major Tronson, and HM's 17th Regt. Under Lieut-Col. Croker. The struggle within the fort was desperate for a considerable time; in addition to the heavy fire kept up, our troops were assailed by the enemy sword in hand, and with daggers, pistols &c, but British courage, perseverance and fortitude overcame all opposition, and the fire of the enemy in the lower area of the fort being nearly silenced, Brigadier Sale turned towards the citadel, from which could now be seen men abandoning their guns, running in all directions, throwing themselves down from immense heights, endeavouring to make their escape, and on reaching the gate, with HM 17th under Lieut-Col. Croker, followed by the 13th, forced it open; at 5 o'clock in the morning, the colours of HM's 13th and17th were planted on the citadel of Ghuznee, amidst the cheers of all ranks. Instant protection was granted to the women found in the citadel (amongst whom were those of Mahomed Hyder, the Governor) and sentries placed over the magazine for its security. Brigadier reports having received much assistance from Captain Kershaw, of HM'13th Light Infy., throughout the whole of the service of the storming.

Major-Gen. Sir W. Cotton executed in a manner much to my satisfaction, the orders he had received. The Major-Gen. followed closely the assaulting party into the fort, with the 'Reserve', namely, Brigadier Roberts with the only available Regt. In his Brigade, the 35th NI under Lieut-Col, Monteath; part of Brigadier Sale's Brigade, the 16th NI under Major McLaren and 48th NI under Lieut-Col. Wheeler; and they immediately occupied the ramparts, putting down opposition wherever they met any, and making prisoners until the place was completely in our possession. A desultory fire was kept up in the town long after the citadel was in our hands, from those who had taken refuge in houses, and in desperation kept firing on all those that approached them. In this way several of our men were wounded and some killed, but the aggressors paid dearly for their bad conduct in not surrendering when the place was completely ours. I must not omit to mention that the three companies of the 35th NI under Captain Hay, ordered to the south side of the fort, to begin with a false attack, to attract attention to that side, performed that service, at the proper time, and greatly to my satisfaction.

As we were threatened with ban attack for the relief of the garrison, I ordered 9th Bombay NI, under command of Lieut-Col. Stalker, to guard the Cabool road, and to be in support of the Cavalry Division. This might have proved an important position to occupy; but as it was, no enemy appeared.

The Cavy. Divn. Under Major-Genl. Thackwell, in addition to watching the approach of an enemy, had directions to surround Ghuznee and to sweep the plain, preventing the escape of run-aways from the garrison. Brigadier Arnold's Brigade (the Brigadier himself I deeply regret to say, was labouring under very severe illness, having shortly before burst a blood-vessel internally, which rendered it wholly impossible for him to mount a horse that day), consisting of HM 16th Lancers, under Lieut-Col. Persse, momentarily Comg. the Brigade, and Major McDowel, the junior Major, the Regt., the senior major of the 16th Lancers, Major Cureton, an officer of great merit, being actively engaged in the execution of his duties as Asst. Adjt. Genl. of the Cavy. Divn., the 2nd Cavy. under Major Salter and the 3rd under Lieut-Col Smyth, were ordered to watch the south and west sides. Brigadier Scott's Brigade were placed on the Cabool road, consisting of 4th Light Drags. under Major Daly and the 1st Bombay Cavy. under Lieut-Col. Sandwith, to watch the north and east sides. This duty was performed in a manner greatly to my satisfaction.

After the storming, and that quiet was in some degree restored within, I conducted His Majesty Shah Shoojah-ool-Moolk, and the British Envoy and Minister, Mr Macnaghten, round the citadel, and a great part of the fortress. The king was perfectly astonished at our having made ourselves masters of a place conceived to be impregnable, when defended, in the short space of two hours, and in less than 48 hours after we came before it. His Majesty was of course greatly delighted at the result. When I afterwards, in the course of the day, took Mahomed Hyder Khan, the Governor, first to the British Minister, and then to the king to make his submission, I informed His Majesty, that I had made a promise that his life should not be touched, and the king in very handsome terms assented, and informed Mahomed Hyder in my presence, that although he and his family had been rebels, yet he was willing to forget and forgive all.

Prince Mahomed Hyder, the Governor of Ghaznee, is a prisoner of war in my camp, and under the surveillance of Sir A. Burnes; an arrangement very agreeable to the former.

From Major-Genl Sir W. Cotton, Comg. the 1st Infy. Divn. (of the Bengal Army) I have invariably received the strongest support, and on this occasion his exertions were manifest in support of the honour of the profession and of our conntry.

I have likewise at all times received able assistance from Major-Genl. Willshire, Comg. 2nd Infy. Divn. (of the Bombay Army) which it was found expedient on that day to break up, some for the storming party, and some for other duties; the Major-Genl., as directed, was in attendance upon myself.

To Brigadier Sale, I feel deeply indebted for the gallant and soldier-like manner in which he conducted the responsible and arduous duty entrusted to him, in command of the storming party, and for the arrangements he made in the citadel immediately after taking possession of it. The sabre wound, which he received in the face, did not prevent his continuing to direct his column until everything was secure; and I am happy in the opportunity of bringing to your Lordship's notice, the excellent conduct of Brigadier Sale on this occasion.

Brigadier Stevenson, in command of the Arty. Was all I could wish; and he reports, that Brigade Majors Backhouse and Coghlan ably assisted him; his arrangements were good, and the execution done by the arm he commands was such as cannot be forgotten by those of the enemy who have witnessed and survived it.

To Brigadier Roberts, to Col. Dennie (who commanded the advance) and to the different officers Comg. Regts. already mentioned, as well as to the officers and gallant soldiers under them, who so nobly maintained the honour and reputation of our country, my best acknowledgements are due.

To Captain Thomson, of the Bengal Engineers, the chief of the Departt. With me, much of the credit of the success of this brilliant 'Coup-de-main' is due;- a place of the same strength, and by such simple means as this highly talented and scientific officer recommended to be tried, has perhaps never before been taken; and I feel I cannot do sufficient justice to Captain Thomson's merits, for his conduct throughout: in the execution he was ably supported by the officers already mentioned, and so eager were the other officers of the Engineers, of both Presidencies, for the honour of carrying the powder bags, that the point could only be decided by seniority, which shows the fine feeling by which they are animated.

I must now inform your Lordship, that since I joined the Bengal Column in the valley of Shawl, I have continued my march with it in the advance, and it has been my good fortune to have had the assistance of two most efficient Staff officers, in Major Craigie, Depy. Adjt. Genl. and Major Garden, Depy. Qr. Mr. Genl. It is but justice to those officers, that I should state to your Lordship, the high satisfaction I have derived from the manner in which all their duties have been performed up to this day; and that I look upon them as promising officers to fill the higher ranks. To the other officers of both Depts. I am also much indebted for the correct performance of all duties appertaining to their situations.

To Major Keith, the Depy. Adjt. Genl., and Major Campbell, the Depy. Qr. Mr. Genl, of the Bombay army, and to all the other offices of both Depts. under them, my acknowledgements are also due, for the manner in which their duties have been performed during this campaign.

Captain Alexander, Comg. 4th Local Horse, and Major Cunningham, Comg. Poonah Auxiliary Horse, with the men under their orders, have been of essential service to the army in this campaign. The arrangements made by Superintending Surgeons, Kennedy and Atkinson, previous to the storming, for affording assistance and comfort to the wounded, met with my approval.

Major Parsons, the Depy. Commissary Genl. in charge of the Dept. in the field, has been unremitting in his attention to keep the troops supplied, although much difficulty is experienced, and he is occasionally thwarted by the nature of the country and its inhabitants.

I have throughout this service, received the utmost assistance I could desire from Lieut. Col. Macdonald my Offg. Sec., and Depy. Adjt. Genl. HM's forces, Bombay; from Captain Powell, my Persian Interpreter, and the other officers of my personal staff. The nature of the country in which we are serving prevents the possibility of my sending a single staff officer to deliver this to your Lordship, otherwise I should have asked my Aide-de-Camp, Lieut. Keane, to proceed to Simla, to deliver this despatch into your hands, and to have forwarded any further information that your Lordship could have desired.

The brilliant triumph we have obtained, the cool courage displayed, and the gallant bearing of the troops I have the honour to command, will have taught such a lesson to our enemies in the Afghan nation, as will make them hereafter respect the name of a British soldier.

Our loss is wonderfully small, considering the occasion; the casualties killed and wounded amounted to about 200.

The loss of the enemy is immense; we have already buried of their dead nearly 500; together with an immense number of horses.

I enclose a list of the killed, wounded and missing. I am happy to say, that although the wounds of some of the officers are severe, they are all doing well.

It is my intention, after selecting a garrison for this place, and establishing a Genl. Hospital, to continue my march to Cabool forthwith.

I have the honour, &c
(Signed) J. Keane
Lieutenant General

Appendix V

General Orders by His Excellency the Commander-in-Chief

GENERAL ORDERS
BY
His Excellency the Commander-in-Chief
Headquarters, Calcutta, 11 February 1841.
By the right Honourable the Governor General of India in Council.
Fort William, 10 February 1841

No. 38 of 1841---With feelings of deep regret, the Right Honourable the Governor General of India in Council announces to the army, the shameful 'misbehaviour before the enemy' of two squadrons of the 2nd regiment Bengal light cavalry, and the ignominious punishment with which, after the fullest consideration, His Lordship in Council feels himself imperatively called upon to visit their disgraceful misconduct.

From the proceedings of courts of inquiry, which have been laid before Government by His Excellency the Commander in Chief, it appears, that on the 2nd of November last, at Purwan Durrah, in the Kohistan of Caubul, the squadrons in question, comprising two-thirds of the whole regiment, while confronting a body of Afghan horse, were ordered to charge, but could not be induced to follow their European officers; and further, that when their manifest cowardice emboldened the enemy to become the assailants, so far from even defending themselves, they turned their horses, and fled in panic and inextricable confusion, and only staid their flight when they had gained the rear of the column from which they had been detached in pursuit.

The noble example set by their European officers, whom they basely allowed to charge unsupported, and of whom Captains Fraser and Ponsonby were severely wounded, and Lieutenant and Adjutant Crispin killed on the spot, renders their dastardly conduct the more inexcusable; and, the disgrace with which they have covered their regiment and themselves, at the close of military operations, during which the most conspicuous bravery had been displayed by their brethren in arms, imposes on Government the necessity of removing them from the gallant army to which they are a reproach, and in which their continuance would doubtless be a source of regret and dissatisfaction.

His Lordship in Council accordingly directs, that the 2nd regiment of light cavalry be struck out of the list of the Bengal army; that the whole of the native commissioned and non-commissioned officers and Troopers, who were present on the 2nd of November with the two squadrons under the command of Captain Fraser, whether borne on the strength of those squadrons, or doing duty with them, be dismissed the service; and that the remaining native commissioned and no-commissioned officers and Troopers of the corps, be drafted into other cavalry regiments, in such proportions as His Excellency the Commander in Chief may be pleased to direct.

The dismissal of the two squadrons is to be carried into effect, in the most impressive manner, as soon as possible, after the return of the regiment to Hindoostan; and none of the dismissed parties are ever to be re-enlisted or employed in any way in the service of the Government.

Should any officers or men of the squadrons ordered to be dismissed, who were present with Captain Fraser's detachment on 2nd November, have been intermediately transferred to the invalid establishment, they are to be forthwith struck off its rolls.

His Excellency the Commander in Chief is requested to issue such subsidiary orders as may be necessary for giving full effect to the intensions of the Government.

Instructions will be issued hereafter for the disposal and employment of the European officers of the 2nd regiment light cavalry.

(Signed) J. Sturt, Lieut. Colonel
Secy. To Govt. of India

Appendix VI

European Officers and Civilians Killed or Died During the Campaign in Afghanistan

Her Majesty's Army

* = Circumstances of death unknown

Armstrong, Archibald	Lieutenant, 44th Foot. Died of cholera at Kabul, 5 Mar 1842.
Arnold, Robert	Lieutenant Colonel, 16th Lancers. Died in Kabul, 20 Aug 1839.
Balfour, William	Asst Surgeon, 44th Foot. Killed in Khyber Pass, 13 Jan 1842.
Bourke, Thomas	Paymaster, 44th Foot. Killed at Jagdalak, 12 Jan 1842.
Bray, Thomas	Lieutenant, 17th Foot. Died of heat exhaustion, 29 Apr 1840.
Cadett, Henry	Lieutenant, 44th Foot. Killed at Soorkab, 12 Jan 1842.
Carey, Robert	Lieutenant, 40th Foot.
Collins, Thomas	Captain, 44th Foot. Killed at Gandamak, 13 Jan 1842.
Corry, Savage	Lieutenant, 17th Foot. Died of cholera, 4 Jun 1839.
Cumberland, Edward	Lieutenant, 44th Foot. Killed at Gandamak, 13 Jan 1842.
Cumming, James	Lieutenant, 9th Foot. Killed at Ali Masjid, 5 Apr 1842.
Dennie, William	Lieutenant Colonel, 13th Foot. Killed at Jalalabad, 7 Apr 1842.
Dodgin, William	Captain, 44th Foot. Killed at Jagdalak, 12 Jan 1842.
Douglas, James	Captain 44th Foot. Killed in Nuseen valley. Feb 1841.
Elphinstone, William	Major General, General Staff. Died in captivity at Tezeen, 23 Apr 1842.
Evans, Thomas	Lieutenant 41st Foot. Killed at Istalif 22 Sep 1842.
Fortye, Francis	Lieutenant, 44th Foot. Killed at Jagdalak 10 Jan 1842.
Fothergill, George	Captain, 13th Foot. Died at Kabul, 5 Sep 1840.

Frere, Richard	Ensign, 13th Foot. Died of liver complaint at Rawalpindi, 10 Dec 42.
Fyers, Francis	Lieutenant, 4th Light Dragoons. Committed suicide, 14 Dec 1838.
Gravatt, Thomas	Lieutenant, 2nd Foot. Killed at Kalat, 13 Nov 1839.
Gray, Alured	Ensign, 44th Foot. Killed at Jagdalak, 10 Jan 1842.
Hackitt, Wellington	Captain, 17th Foot. Died during return to India, 19 Oct 1839.
Halahan, Robert	Quartermaster, 44th Foot. Killed at Jagdalak 12 Jan 1842.
Hamilton, Alexander	Surgeon, 17th Foot. Died at Kandahar 21 Jul 1839.
Harcourt, John	Surgeon, 44th Foot. Killed at Jagdalak 12 Jan 1842.
Hibbert, John	Asst/Surgeon, 2nd Foot. Killed in fire at Jurrak, 30 Jan 1839.
Hilton, William	Captain, 16th Lancers. Drowned in River Jhelum, 12 Dec 1839.
Hobhouse, John	Lieutenant, 13th Foot. Killed at Gandamak, 13 Jan 1842.
Hogg, Arthur	Lieutenant, 44th Foot. Killed at Gandamak 13 Jan 1842.
Inverarity, David	Lieutenant, 16th Lancers. Murdered at Kandahar, 28 May 1839.
Irwin, William	Lieutenant, 40th Foot. Died of apoplexy 25 May 1839.
Janverin, Francis	Lieutenant, 4th Light Dragoons. Died at Sukkur of cholera, 6 Dec 1839.
Keith, Henry	Captain, 2nd Foot. Died of fever at Tatta, 3 Mar 1839.
Kershaw, James	Major, 13th Foot.
King, Edward	Lieutenant, 13th Foot. Killed at Tezeen, 12 Oct 1841.
Leighton, Thomas	Captain, 44th Foot. Killed at Tezeen, 10 Jan 1842.
Mackrell, Thomas	Lieutenant Colonel, 44th Foot. Killed at Kabul, 10 Nov 1841.
Marshall, George	Captain, 31st Foot. Died of heat exhaustion at Pesh Bolak, Aug 1842.
Magnay, Alfred	Lieutenant, 40th Foot. Died of cholera at Karachi, 23 May 1839.
May, William	Captain, 41st Foot. Killed at Khojak Pass, 28 Mar 1842.
McRea, Robert	Captain, 44th Foot. Killed at Rikabashee Fort, 10 Nov 1841.
McIlveen, Dalway	Lieutenant, 31st Foot. Killed at Muraiz on 26 Jul 1842.
Nixon, George	Lieutenant, 2nd Foot. Killed in fire at Jurrak, 30 Jan 1839.
Ogle, Bertrum	Captain, 4th Light Dragoons. Died of cholera at Sukkur, Nov 1839.
Pender, Thomas	Lieutenant, 31st. Died of wounds at Noeshera 1842
Philips, Charles	Quartermaster, 40th Foot. Died of cholera at Kandahar, Jul 1842.
Powell, Thomas	Lieutenant Colonel, 40th Foot. Died of cholera at Karachi, 23 May 1839.
Primrose, William	Asst Surgeon, 44th Foot. Killed at Gandamak, 13 Jan 1842.

Raban, William	Lieutenant, 44th Foot. Killed in Kabul, 6 Nov 1841.
Robinson, Thomas	Captain, 44th Foot. Killed in Kabul, 4 Nov 1841.
Sayers, Henry	Lieutenant, 31st Foot. Died of smallpox at Jalalabad 1842.
Scott, William	Major, 44th Foot. Killed at Tezeen, 10 Jan 1842.
Scott, James	Lieutenant, 13th Foot. Died of sickness in Kabul. 8 Oct 1842.
Skinner	Major 13th Foot. Died of dysentery at Simla.
Sparks, Edward	Lieutenant, 2nd Foot. Killed in fire at Jurrak, 30 Jan 1839.
Spence, James	Captain, 31st Foot. Killed at Pesh Bolak, 1842.
Sutherland, William	Captain, 13th Foot. Died in Kabul Dec 1840.
Swayne, Thomas	Captain, 44th Foot. Killed in Kabul, 4 Nov 1841.
Swinton, Samuel	Lieutenant, 44th Foot. Killed at Gandamak, 13 Jan 1842.
Thain, William	Major, 21st Foot. Killed at Jagdalak, 12 Jan 1842.
Tritton, John	Lieutenant, 3rd Light Dragoons. Died of dysentery at Jalalabad, 1842.
Valiant, Henry	Lieutenant, 40th Foot. Died of dysentery at Quetta Jun 1841.
Wade, Francis	Lieutenant, 44th Foot. Killed at Jagdalak, 12 Jan 1842.
Walker, Henry	Ensign, 44th Foot.*
White, William	Lieutenant, 44th Foot. Died at Junga Fareekee, 10 Jan 1842.

East India Company Army
* = Circumstances of death unknown

Alexander, Robert	Lieutenant, 5th BNI. Killed at Junga Fareekee, 10 Jan 1841.
Anderson, Philip	Major, 64th BNI. Died at Jalalabad, 24 Apr 1842.
Anquetil, Thomas	Lieutenant Colonel, 42nd BNI. Killed at Jagdalak, 12 Jan 1842.
Apthorpe, Charles	Captain, 41st BNI. Killed at Haikalzai, 28 Mar 1842.
Anstruther, Ashford	Captain, 54th BNI. Killed in Kabul, 13 Jan 1842.
Baynes, Edward	Lieutenant, BomNI. Died at Quetta, 12 Aug 1839.
Bazett, Henry	Lieutenant, 5th Bengal Light Cavalry. Killed at Jagdalak, 12 Jan 1842.
Beaufort, Stephen	Ensign, 42nd BNI. Died of cholera at Dadur 31 May 1839.
Bedingfield, Philip	Captain. Died of heat exhaustion.
Bell, Thomas	Captain, 2nd BNI. Died of cholera at Kandahar, 19 Aug 1841.
Bellew, Henry	Captain 56th BNI. Killed at Futtehabad 18 Jan 1842.
Billamore, Thomas	Major, 1st BomNI. Died at Kandahar, 18 Aug 1841.
Bird, William	Lieutenant, 23rd MNI. Killed at Futtehabad, 13 Jan 1842.

Blair, Edward	Captain, 5th Bengal Light Cavalry. Killed at Jagdalak, 12 Jan 1842.[1]
Bott, John	Captain, 5th Bengal Light Cavalry. Killed at Khurd-Kabul, 8 Jan 1842.
Brickwell, James	Asst Surgeon, 20 BomNI. Killed at Bolan Pass Oct 1842.
Broadfoot, James	Lieutenant, Bengal Engineers. Killed at Purwan, 2 Nov 1840
Broadfoot, William	Lieutenant, 1st BER. Murdered in Kabul, 2 Nov 1841.
Brooke, Peter	Lieutenant, 1st Bombay Cavalry. Killed at Ghazni, 23 Sep 1839.
Brown, Lewis	Lieutenant, 5th BomNI.*
Bryce, Alexander	Asst Surgeon, Bengal Horse Artillery. Killed at Tezeen, 10 Jan 1841.
Buist, George	Lieutenant, 10th Bengal Light Cavalry. Killed at Jalalabad, 29 Jul 1842.
Burkinyoung, Frederick	Lieutenant, 5th BNI. Killed at Jagdalak, 13 Jan 1842.
Burnett, Robert	Captain, 54th BNI. Died of wounds sustained at Jagdalak, 29 Oct 1843.
Burnes, Sir Alexander	Murdered in Kabul, 2 Nov 1841.
Burnes, Charles	Lieutenant, 17th BomNI. Murdered in Kabul, 2 Nov 1841.
Bury, Horatio	Captain, 3rd Bombay Light Cavalry. Killed at Mukar 28 Aug 1842.
Campbell, Edmund	Cornet, Bombay Light Cavalry. Died at Sindh 19 Feb 1839.
Cardew, Edward	Asst Surgeon, 27th BNI. Killed at Tezeen, 10 Jan 1842.
Carlyon, Charles	Lieutenant, 37th BNI. Killed in Kabul Jan 1842.
Chalmers, John.	Lieutenant, 43rd BNI. Died of heat exhaustion, 2 Jun 1839.
Chambers, Robert	Lieutenant Colonel, 5th Bengal Light Cavalry. Killed at Jagdalak 12 Jan 42.
Christie, Alexander	Lieutenant, Bengal Artillery. Killed in Khyber Pass. 4 Nov 1842.
Clarke, Walpole	Lieutenant, 2nd BomNI. Killed at Surtoff, 16 May 1840.
Codrington, Christopher	Captain, 4th Gurkha Regiment. Killed at Charikar, 5 Nov 1841.
Collinson, William	Lieutenant, 37th BNI. Killed at Pushoot, 18 Jan 1841.
Collyer, Fredrick	Captain, 5th Bengal Light Cavalry. Murdered at Kudjah, 18 Jan 1841.
Conolly, Arthur	Captain. Executed at Bokhara, Jun 1842.
Conolly, Edward	Captain, 6th Bengal Light Cavalry. Killed at Fort Tutamdara, 29 Sep 1840.

1 His wife Susanna refused to accept that her husband was dead and stayed in India with her two daughters awaiting his return. Regrettably, she and her daughters were massacred in Cawnpore in 1857.

Conolly, John	Lieutenant, 20th BNI. Died of fever at Shewakhe, 7 Aug 1842.
Corrie, Anthony	Captain, 54th BNI. Killed at Kabul, Jan 1842.
Creed, Richard	Lieutenant, Bombay Horse Artillery. Killed at Kajuck, 20 Feb 41.
Crispin, George	Captain, 2nd Bengal Light Cavalry. Killed at Purwan, 2 Nov 1840.
Cunningham, George	Lieutenant, 54th BNI. Killed at Gandamak, 13 Jan 1842.
Cureton, Frederick	Lieutenant 21st BomNI. Died of dysentery at Quetta, Jul 1841.
Davies, Samuel	Lieutenant 51st BNI. Died of typhus at Ghazni, 19 Jun 1842.
Deas, Aleck	Lieutenant, 5th BNI. Killed at Junga Fareekee, 10 Jan 1842.
Douglas, William	Captain, Bombay Engineers. Killed in the Nazian Valley, 20 Feb 1841.
Duff, William	Surgeon General, Bengal Army. Killed at Tezeen, 10 Jan 1842.
Duffin, Adam	Lieutenant Colonel, 2nd Bengal Cavalry. Died at Bahawalpore, 31 Dec 1839.
Ennis Edward	Lieutenant, 21st BomNI. Murdered at Sukkur, 10 Dec 1842.
Erskine, David	Lieutenant, Bombay Artillery.*
Ewart, William	Major, 54th BNI. Killed at Tezeen, 10 Jan 1842.
Falconer, William	Lieutenant, 2nd BomNI.*
Forbes, David	Surgeon, 1st Bombay Light Cavalry. Died at Bagh of cholera, 24 Nov 1839.
Franklin, Henry	Lieutenant, 2nd BomNI. Killed at Kujjuk, 3 Feb 1841.
Gould, William.	Captain, 42nd BNI. Died of cholera at Dadur, 6 Sep 1839.
Golding, George	Lieutenant, 35th BNI. Murdered by *Jan Baz* at Kandahar 26 Dec 1841.
Gordon, William	Ensign, 37th BNI. Killed at Kabul 4 Nov 1841.
Grant, George	Surgeon Bombay Medical Department. Killed near Charikar, 15 Nov 1841.
Grant, William	Captain, 27th BNI. Killed at Gandamak 11 Jan 1842
Greene, Charles	Lieutenant, Bengal Artillery. Killed at Gandamak, 13 Jan 1842.
Haig, Charles	Captain, 5th BNI. Killed at Gandamak, 13 Jan 1842.
Halliday, Thomas	Lieutenant, 45th BNI. Died at Ludhiana 30 Oct 1838.
Halloran, John	Asst/Surgeon, Bombay Artillery. Died of heat exhaustion, 23 May 1839.
Hamilton, Percy	Captain, 5th Bengal Light Cavalry. Killed at Jagdalak, 13 Jan 1842.
Hand, Alexander	Captain, 2nd BomNI. Murdered at Tatta Apr 1839.
Hardiman, Lucius	Lieutenant, 5th Bengal Light Cavalry. Killed at Kabul, 6 Jan 1842.

Harpur, Edmond	Dr, 5th Light Cavalry. Killed at Futtehabad, 13 Jan 42.
Hart, Shepard	Major, 43rd BNI. Died at Kabul 11 Oct 1839.
Hawtrey, Frederick	Lieutenant, 37th BNI. Killed at Gandamak 12 Jan 1842.
Hay, Edward	Captain, 35th BNI. Killed at Gandamak, 13 Jan 1842.
Hay, John	Captain 35th BNI. Died at Kabul 13 Oct 1839.
Heighington, Critchley	Captain, 2nd BomNI. Died of apoplexy.
Herring, John	Lieutenant Colonel, 37th BNI. Murdered at Haidar Khel, 3 Sep 1839.
Hopkins, Perin	Captain, 27th BNI. Killed at Junga Fareekee 13 Jan 1842.
Horsburgh, Charles	Lieutenant, 5th BNI. Killed at Gandamak, 13 Jan 1842.
Hunt, John	Lieutenant, 22nd BNI. Died of heat exhaustion.
Jenkins, Charles	Lieutenant, 35th BNI. Killed at Khurd-Kabul 17 Oct 1841.
Jones, John	Captain, 20th BomNI. Died of dysentery at Quetta, Jul 1841.
Keith, James	Major, 7th BomNI. Died of throat infection. Toba Mountains 19 Oct 1839.
Kewney, Henry	Lieutenant, 50th BNI. Committed suicide at Kurnaul, 5 Nov 1838.
Kirby, John	Captain, 54th BNI. Killed at Kabul, 10 Jan 1842.
Lacing, John	Captain. Died in Sindh, 26 Oct 1839.
Laing, Henry	Lieutenant, 27th BNI. Killed on Beymaru hills (Kabul) 23 Nov 1841.
Le Geyt, Robert	Lieutenant, 1st Bombay Cavalry. Killed at Neemla 13 Jan 1842.
Lewis, Robert	Captain. Died of heat exhaustion.
Liddle, John	Major, 1st BomNI. Died of heat exhaustion.
Liptrap, John	Major. Died of cholera 21 May 1839.
Lock, John	Captain, 5th BNI. Killed in Khyber Pass, 24 Jan 1842.
Lodge, Charles	Quartermaster 25th BomNI. Killed at Kotra, 28 Nov 1840.
Lord, Percival	Surgeon, Bombay Medical Department. Killed at Purwan, 2 Nov 1840.
Loveday, William	Lieutenant, 27th BNI. Murdered at Dadur, 2 Nov 1840.
Lumsden, David	Lieutenant, 27th BNI. Murdered at Ghazni, 9 Mar 1842.
Macartney, John	MNI, Killed at Jagdalak 12 Jan 1842.
Mackintosh, William	Captain, 5th BNI. Killed at Kabul, 29 Nov 1841.
Mackay, Æacas	Captain, 16 BNI. Killed at Jagdalak,12 Jan 1842.
Manning, Francis	Captain 16 BNI. Died of cholera, 31 May 1839.

Marshall, James	Captain, 61st BNI. Killed at Jagdalak, 12 Jan 1842.
Mathias, John	Captain, 33rd BNI. Died at Khota, 14 Jul 1842.
Maule, Richard	Lieutenant, Bengal Artillery. Killed at Kahdarrah, 3 Nov 1841.
Meik, Patrick	Captain, 31st BNI. Died at Quetta, Aug 1839.
Metcalfe, Francis	Asst Surgeon, 5th BNI. Killed at Gandamak, 13 Jan 1842.
Miles, Rawdon	Captain, 5th BNI. Killed at Junga Fareekee, 10 Jan 1842.
Moorhouse, Edgar	Captain, 35th BNI. Killed at Jalalabad 7 Apr 42.
Moore, Henry	Lieutenant, 1st BomNI. Killed at Nuffosh Pass, 31 Aug 1841.
Morrison, William	Lieutenant, 54th BNI. Killed at Gandamak, 13 Jan 1842.
Nicholl, Thomas	Captain, Bengal Horse Artillery. Killed at Jagdalak, 12 Jan 1842.[2]
Nicholson, Alexander	Ensign 30th BNI. Killed in Khyber Pass, 4 Nov 1942.
Nugent, George	Captain, 66th BNI. Killed at Jagdalak, 8 Sep 1842.
Oliver, Thomas	Lieutenant Colonel, 5th BNI. Killed on Beymaru Hills, Kabul 23 Nov 1841.
Oliphant, Robert	Lieutenant, 3rd Bombay Cavalry. Died of heat exhaustion.
Palmer, Nicholas	Captain, 54th BNI. Killed at Kabul, 13 Jan 1842.
Paton, John	Captain, 58th BNI. Killed at Khurd Kabul Pass, 8 Jan 1842.
Patterson, Thomas	Lieutenant, 2nd BNI. Died after amputation of leg, 26 Mar 1842.[3]
Payton, George	Captain, 21st MNI. Killed at Khurd Kabul, 8 Jan 42.
Perry, Henry	Captain 3rd Bom Lt Cav. Killed at Ghazni, 29 Aug 1842.
Pigou, Robert	Lieutenant, Bengal Engineers. Killed at Nazian Valley, 24 Feb 1841.
Pottinger, Thomas	Lieutenant, 5th BNI. Killed at Neemla 13 Jan 1842.
Raban, Robert	Captain, 48th BNI. Died at Kilakaze, 16 Oct 1841.
Raitt, Charles	Captain 1st BomNI. Died of wounds at Surtoff.
Ramsay, David	Lieutenant, 37th BNI. Died at Bolan Pass, 26 Mar 1839.
Rattray, Charles	Lieutenant, 20th BNI. Murdered at Lughmani, 3 Nov 1841.
Ravencroft, George	Lieutenant, 3rd Bengal Light Cavalry. Died of wounds 24 Oct 1842.
Rebenack, Charles	Captain, 21st BomNI. Died of heat exhaustion.

2 Captain Nicholl was a very good friend of Lieutenant Colonel Sir Claude Wade, and on his return to England, Sir Claude married Captain Nicholl's 18-year-old daughter Salina They had one son..

3 This officer was attacked by his *Jan-Baz* troops in the same attack that killed Lieutenant Golding on 26 December 1841. He was badly wounded in the leg but refused to have it amputated. Sadly the leg got worse and the forced amputation failed to save him.

Reeves, George	Lieutenant 3rd Bombay Light Cavalry. Killed at Mukar, 28 Aug 1842.
Revelly, Joseph	Lieutenant, 7th BNI. Died of heat exhaustion.
Rind, James	Captain, 37th BNI. Killed at Gandamak, 13 Jan 1842.
Robinson, Thomas	Captain. Killed at Kabul, 5 Nov 1841.
Rollings, William	Captain, 2nd BomNI. Died of dysentery at Kandahar, 18 Aug 1841.
Rooke, Charles	Lieutenant, 22nd BomNI. Died at Suhkur, 24 Feb 1840.
Rose, James	Ensign, 4th Gurkha Regiment. Killed at Charikar, 23 Nov 1841.
Salisbury, Edward	Ensign, 4th Gurkha Regiment. Killed at Charikar, 23 Nov 1841.
Shaw, David	Captain, 54th BNI. Killed at Kabul Pass, 10 Jan 1842.
Shaw, Robert	Lieutenant, Comm Dept. Killed at Kujjuk Pass 3 Feb 1841.
Shubrick, Thomas	Lieutenant, 7th Bengal Light Cavalry. Died of heat exhaustion.
Skinner, James	Captain, 61st BNI. Killed at Jagdalak, 12 Jan 1842, by Biland Khan.
St George, John	Lieutenant, 37th BNI. Killed at Khurd-Kabul 8 Jan 1842.
Steer, William	Lieutenant, 37th BNI. Killed at Jagdalak 12 Jan 1842.
Stevenson, Thomas	Brigadier. Died of heat stroke at Shirkapore, 9 Aug 40.
Stewart, Charles	Lieutenant, Bengal Horse Artillery. Killed at Gandamak, 13 Jan 1842.
Stoddart, Charles	Lieutenant Colonel. Executed at Bokhara Jun 1842.
Sturt, John	Lieutenant, Bengal Engineers. Killed in Khurd Kabul Pass, 9 Jan 1842.
Sutherland, William	Captain. Died of heat exhaustion.
Swayne, Stephen	Major, 5th BNI. Killed at Junga Fareekee, 10 Jan 1842.
Taylor, John	Ensign, 5th BNI*
Terry, Walter	Lieutenant Bengal Artillery. Died of wound at Jamrud 9 Nov 1842.
Thomson, John	Lieutenant Colonel, 31st BNI. Died of apoplexy at Dadur, 19 April 1840.
Timings, Henry	Captain, Bengal Horse Artillery. Died in Kabul, 12 Sep 1839.
Tombs, William	Lieutenant, 5th BNI. Killed at Kabul 12 Jan 1842.
Trevor, Robert	Captain, 3rd Bombay Light Cavalry. Murdered at Kabul, 23 Dec 1841.
Vanrenen, Augustus	Lieutenant, 37th BNI. Killed at Gandamak 13 Jan 1842.
Walker, Andrew	Surgeon, 42nd BNI. Died at Kandahar, 21 Dec 1840.
Walker, Thomas	Captain, Bengal Cavalry. Killed at Kabul, 25 Nov 1841.
Warren, Francis	Ensign, 5th BNI. Killed at Junga Fareekee, 10 Jan 1842.

Weaver, Henry	Lieutenant, 54th BNI. Killed at Gandamak, 13 Jan 1842.
Westmacott, George	Captain, 37th BNI. Killed at Rikabashee Fort 10 Nov 1841.
Wheeler, Francis	Lieutenant, Kohistan Regiment. Killed at Kahdarrah, 3 Nov 1841.
Williams, David	Captain, 45th BNI*
Williams, Fitzherbert	Ensign 2nd BomNI. Killed at Nuffosh Pass, 31 Aug 1841.
Willis, James	Vet Surgeon, 5th Light Cavalry. Killed at Gandamak 14 Jan 1842.
Wilson, Alexander	Captain, 64th BNI. Killed in Khyber Pass, 24 Jan 1842.
Wilson, Peter	Colonel, Bombay Cavalry. Died of wounds at Kajjuk 10 Feb 1841.
Woodburn, John	Captain, 44th BNI. Murdered at Sydabad, 23 Nov 1841.
Wyndham, Charles	Captain, 35th BNI. Killed at Jagdalak, 17 Oct 1841.

European Civilians

Macnaghten, Sir William	Envoy and Minister. Murdered at Kabul 23 Dec 1841.

Mr Baness	Greek Merchant. Died of tetanus after reaching Jalalabad, 29 Jan 1842.
Mr Fallon	Captain Troup's writer. Killed at Kabul.
Mr Andrew Ross Bell	Political Agent at Quetta. Died of dysentery, 3 Aug 1841.
Mr Jervis	Agent of Firth's Company, Bombay. Died of cholera 3 Jun 39.
Mrs Smith	Wife of Sergeant Smith. Died in captivity.
Son of Sergeant Wade, 16 years old	Died in captivity.
Baby daughter of Mrs Bourne, wife of private in HM 13th Foot	
Mrs Smith	Wife of Conductor Smith. Murdered in Bolan Pass, Sep 1841.
Mrs Stoker	Wife of private in HM 13th Foot. Killed at Khoord Kabul Pass, 9 Jan 1842.
Seymour Stoker, orphaned child	Died during retreat from Kabul, Jan 1842.
Mrs Rosanne Lumsden	Wife of Lieutenant Lumsden. Murdered at Ghazni, 9 Mar 1842.
Mr O'Gorman	Captain Rawlinson's writer. Murdered at Kandahar, 25 Jul 1841.
Mr P.M. Bourke	Died 12 Jan 1842.

European Non-Commissioned Officers in East India Company Service[4]

Sergeant Major Godfrey, 5th BNI	
Quarter Master Sergeant Read, 5 BNI	
Sergeant Douglas, 1st BER	Drowned in Kabul River.
Sergeant MacNee, Bengal Horse Artillery	Died in captivity.
Sergeant Smith. Captain Trevor's Store Sergeant.	Killed at Kabul, 3 Nov 1841.
Sergeant Reynolds	Died of tetanus while in captivity.
Sergeant Mulhall, Bengal Artillery	Killed at Jagdalak.
Conductor Macgregor	Froze to death on road to Tezeen, 7 Jan 1842.
Conductor Haviland	Died at Bagh of heat exhaustion, 3 Mar 1839.
Riding Master Quantrill	
Sergeant Williams	Died of wounds at Kabul 31 Dec 1841.
Sergeant Deane	Killed at Jagdalak 12 Jan 1842.
Sergeant Shannon, 42nd BNI	Died of heat stroke at Dadur 5 Jul 1839.
Sergeant Cameron	Murdered in Khyber Pass.
Sergeant Byrne	Killed at Charikar, 6 Nov 1841.

4 At the time of this campaign it was not customary to list Other Rank casualties by name in official despatches. At regimental level the rank and name of each casualty was listed, but at higher levels it became necessary, due to the numbers involved, to consolidate these casualties by rank only. In only very special circumstances were names of Other Ranks given in the text of the despatch. It is from these and from the journals and letters, written by persons during the campaign, that the following short list of Other Ranks has been compiled. While these lists could claim to be the single most comprehensive, they certainly cannot claim to be complete.

Appendix VII

Annual Salaries of Assigned Political Agents, and in Comparison, their Regular Salaries including Full *Batta*

Political Agent	Political Salary	Regular Salary
Sir William Macnaghten	£311,220 (£841,500)	£4,580 (£343,500)
Mr Andrew Ross Bell	£3,900 (£292,500)	£1,592 (£114,620)
Lt Colonel Sir Alexander Burnes	£3,000 (£225,000)	£1,224 (£91,800)
Major D'Arcy Todd	£1,440 (£108,000)	£936 (£70,200)
Major Eldred Pottinger	£1,440 (£108,000)	£936 (£70,200)
Captain E. Sanders	£1,963 (£147,225)	£496 (£37,200)
Captain Frederick Matheson	£1,800 (£135,000)	£496 (£37,200)
Captain Arthur Conolly	£1,440 (£108,000)	£496 (£37,200)
Captain George Lawrence	£1,440 (£108,000)	£496 (£37,200)
Captain Henry Rawlinson	£1,440 (£108,000)	£496 (£37,200)
Captain John Bean	£1,440 (£108,000)	£496 (£37,200)
Captain P. Lynch	£1,200 (£90,000)	£496 (£37,200)
Captain J. Nash	£960 (£77,200)	£496 (£37,200)
Captain Colin MacKenzie	£840 (£63,000)	£496 (£37,200)
Captain W. Knyvett	£840 (£63,000)	£496 (£37,200)
Captain James Abbott	£840 (£63,000)	£496 (£37,200)
Captain George Macgregor	£1,440 (£108,000)	£496 (£37,000)
Lieutenant Peter Nicholson	£1,080 (£81,000)	£304 (£22,800)
Lieutenant C. Jackson	£1,080 (£81,000)	£304 (£22,800)
Lieutenant Charles Rattray	£840 (£63,000)	£304 (£22,800)
Lieutenant John Conolly	£804 (£63,000)	£304 (£22,800)
Lieutenant William Hammersley	£804 (£63,000)	£304 (£22,800)

Political Agent	Political Salary	Regular Salary
Lieutenant E. Eastwick	£804 (£63,000)	£304 (£22,800)
Lieutenant E. Brown	£804 (£63,000)	£304 (£22,800)
Lieutenant William Broadfoot	£804 (£63,000)	£304 (£22,800)
Lieutenant Robert Leech[1]	£804 (£63,000)	£304 (£22,800)
Lieutenant R. Shakespeare	£804 (£63,000)	£304 (£22,800)
Lieutenant Charles Burnes	£720 (£54,000)	£304 (£22,800)
Lieutenant Sinclair	£720 (£54,000)	£304 (£22,800)
Lieutenant E. Elliot	£720 (£54,000)	£304 (£22,800)
Lieutenant W. Young	£720 (£54,000)	£304 (£22,800)

1 This officer rose in rank to major, but no record could be found of him receiving a larger amount

Bibliography

Archival Sources

British Library
MSS Eur B234. William Bird
MSS Eur C181. Captain James Douglas
MSS Eur C814. Mein
MSS Eur D634. Hutchinson Family
MSS Eur F336. Macnaghten.
Peel Papers. Vol. CCXCI, Ms 40,471. Correspondence with Earl Ellenborough
Essay. Professor Shah Mahmoud Hanifi, 'Shah Shuja, Hidden History'.
Indian Military History Society's Durbar, Vol. 29. No 4
Indian Military History Society's Durbar, Vol. 33, No 3
Records of the Ludhiana Agency, 1808–1815
List of Inscriptions on Christian Tombs or Monuments. By Miles Irving and G.W. Rhe.

Published Sources

Aijazuddin, F.S., *The Resourceful Fakirs: Three Muslim brothers at the Sikh court of Lahore* (New Delhi: Three Rivers Publication, 2014).

Allen, Charles, *Raj: A Scrapbook of British India, 1877–1947* (London: Andre Deutsch Ltd., 1977).

Anon., *Nott's Brigade in Afghanistan,1838–42; Being the Private Diary of an Officer Who Served in it from First to Last* (Bombay: The Times of India Press, 1880).

Archer, Mildred and Toby Falk, *The Passionate Quest: the Fraser Brothers in India* (London: Alfalak/Scorpion Publishing, 1989).

Atkinson, James, *The Expedition into Afghanistan* (London: W.H. Allen, 1841).

Ayde, General Sir John, *Indian Frontier Policy: An Historical Sketch* (London: Smith, Elder & Co., 1897. Kessinger Publishing reprint, n.d.).

Barfield, Thomas J., *Afghanistan: A Cultural and Political History* (Princeton: Princeton University Press, 2010).

Barr, Pat and Ray Desmond, *Simla: A Hill Station in British India* (London: Scolar Press Ltd, 1978).

Barr, William, *Journal of a March from Delhi to Peshawar and thence to Cabul* (London: J. Madden, 1844).

Beveridge, Henry, *A Comprehensive History of India*, Vol. 3 (Delhi: Atlantic Publishers, Reprint 2003).

Biddulph, Major H., *Early Indian Campaigns and the Decorations Awarded for Them* (Chatham: Royal Engineers Institute, 1914[?]).

Broadfoot, W., *The Career of Major Broadfoot* (London: John Murray, 1888).

Brown, David, *Palmerston: A Biography* (New Haven: Yale University Press, 2010).

Bruce, George, *Retreat from Kabul* (London: Mayflower-Dell, 1967).

Buist, George, *Outline of the Operations of British Troops in Scinde and Afghanistan, betwixt Nov. 1838 and Nov. 1841; with remarks on the policy of war* (Bombay: Times Office, 1843. ULAN Press reprint n.d.).

Burnes, Alexander, ed. Kathleen Hopkirk, *Travels into Bokhara: Being the Account of a Journey from India to Cabool, Tartary and Persia* (London: Eland, 2012).

Callahan, Raymond, *The East India Company and Army Reform, 1783–1798* (Cambridge, Mass.: Harvard Historical Monographs, 1972).

Chetwynd-Stapylton, Ensign Granville, *The First Afghan War. An Ensign's Account.* Pamphlet.

Churchill, Winston, *A History of the English Speaking Peoples* (London: Cassell & Co. Ltd, 1956).

Coates, Tim. *British War in Afghanistan: The Dreadful Retreat from Kabul in 1842* (London, New York: Tim Coates Books, 2006).

Colvin, Auckland, *Rulers of India. John Russell Colvin, the Last Lieutenant Governor of the North West Under the Company* (n.p.: Kessinger Publishing, 2007).

Cunningham, J.D., *A History of the Sikhs, from the origin of the nation to the battles of the Sutlej* (Calcutta: N. Roy, 1904).

Curzon, Lord, *British Government in India: the Story of the Viceroys and Government Houses*, Vol. I & II (London: Cassell & Co., 1925).

Dalrymple, William, *Return of a King: The Battle for Afghanistan, 1839–42* (London, Bloomsbury, 2013).

Dennie, William H, &William Steele, *Personal Narrative of the Campaigns in Afghanistan, Since Beloochistan, etc.: Detailed in a Series of Letters of the Late Colonel William H. Dennie* (London: Longman, Brown, 1843; n.p.: K L reprint, n.d.).

Diver, Maud, *The Judgement of the Sword* (London: Constable, 1913).

Docherty, Paddy, *The Khyber Pass. A History of Empire and Invasion* (London: Faber, 2007).

Drummond, Emma, *Beyond All Frontiers* (London: Corgi Paperback, 1984).

Dunbar, Janet, *Golden Interlude: the Edens in India, 1836–1842* (London: John Murray, 1955).

Durand, Major General Sir Henry, *The First Afghan War and Its Causes* (London: Longman Green, 1879).

Edwardes, Michael, *Playing the Great Game* (London: Hamish Hamilton, 1975).

Edwardes, Michael, *The Necessary Hell* (London: Cassels & Co, 1958).

Edwards-Stuart, Lieutenant Colonel Ivor, *A John Company General* (Bognor Regis: New Horizon, 1883).

Eyre, Vincent, *The Military Operations at Cabul Which Ended in the Retreat and Destruction of the British Army, January 1842* (London, John Murray 1843).

Eyre, Lieutenant Vincent, *Journal of an Afghanistan Prisoner* (London: Routledge & Kegan Paul, 1976).

Fane, H.E., *Five Years in India: Comprising a Narrative of Travels in the Presidency of Bengal: A Visit to the Court of Runjeet Sing, etc.* (London, Henry Colburn, 1842).

Farwell, Byron, *Queen Victoria's Little Wars* (Ware: Wordsworth Editions, 1999).

Fermont-Barnes, Gregory, *The Anglo-Afghan Wars, 1839–1919* (Oxford: Osprey Publishing, 2009).

Forbes, Archibald, *The Afghan Wars, 1839–42 and 1878–80* (London: Seeley, 1892).

Forbes, Archibald, *The First Afghan War, 1839–42* (London: C. Scribner's Sons, 1892. Reprint London: Leonaur, 2007)..

Forrest, Sir G.W., *Life of Field-Marshal Sir Neville Chamberlain* (Edinburgh: Blackwood, 1909).

Fraser, Antonia, *Perilous Question: the Drama of the Great Reform Bill 1832* (London: Phoenix, 2014).

Fraser, George MacDonald, *Flashman* (London: Harper, 2005).

Fraser, James Baillie, *The Persian Adventurer: Being the Sequel of 'The Kuzzilbash'* (London: H. Colburn and R. Bentley, 1830).

Greenwood, Lieutenant John, *Narrative of the Late Victorious Campaign in Afghanistan, under General Pollock: with Recollections of Seven Years' Service in India* (London: Colburn, 1844).

Greville, Charles, *The Greville Memoirs: 1814–1860* (London: Longmans, 1874).

Hall, J.H,W., *Scenes in a Soldier's Life: Being a Connected Narrative of the Principal Military Events in Scinde, Beeloochistan and Affghanistan, during 1839, 1840, 1841, 1842 and 1843, under Generals Lord Keane, Brooks, Sir R. Sale, Wiltshire, Pollock, Nott, England, M'Caskill and Sir C. Napier* (Montreal: R. and C. Chalmers, New York: Berford, 1848. Facsimile Publishers reprint, n.d.).

Haughton, John, C., *Char-ee-Kar and Service There with the 4th Goorkha Regiment* (London: Provost 1879; n.p.: ULAN Press reprint, n.d.).

Haughton, John, and Eden Vansittart, *With the Gurkhas in Afghanistan: the Defence of Char-Ee-Kar During the First Afghan War, 1841* (n.p.: Leonaur reprint, 2010)..

Havelock, Henry, *Narrative of the War in Afghanistan in 1838–1839* (London: Colburn, 1840; n.p.: Kissenger Legacy reprint, n.d.).

Heathcote, T.A., *The Afghan Wars 1839–1919* (Staplehurst: Spellmount, 2007).

Henty, G.A., *To Herat and Cabul: A Story of the First Afghan War* (London: Blackie, 1902; n.p.: Forgotten Books reprint, n.d.).

Hensher, Philip, *The Mulberry Empire* (New York: Alfred A. Knopf, 2002).

Hilton, Boyd, *A Mad, Bad and Dangerous People? England, 1783–1846* (Oxford: Oxford University Press, 2007).

Holdsworth, Thomas, *The Campaign of the Indus in A Series of Letters from an Officer of the Bombay Division* (London: 1840).. Reprinted as *Experiences of a British Officer of the 2nd (Queen's Royal). Regiment in the Campaign to Place Shah Shuja on the throne of Afghanistan 1838–1840* (Driffield: Leonaur Ltd reprint, 2007).

Hopkirk, Peter, *The Great Game* (London: John Murray, 2006).

Hough, William, *A Narrative of the March and Operations of the Army of the Indus* (n.p.: Elibron Classics Reprint 2006).

Hügel, Charles Von, *Travels in Kashmir and the Punjab: Containing a Particular Account of the Government and Character of the Sikhs* (Oxford: Oxford University Press, 2003).

Hunt, Tristram, *Ten Cities that Made an Empire* (London: Penguin Books, 2015).

Hurd, Douglas, *Robert Peel: a Biography* (London: Weidenfeld & Nicolson, 2007).

Irvine, Andrew Alexander, *Land of No Regrets* (London: Collins 1938).

James, Lawrence, *Raj: The Making and Unmaking of British India* (London: Abacus, 2009).

Kaye, Sir John, *History of the War in Afghanistan*, Vols. 1 & 2 (n.p.: Forgotten Books, 2012).

Kaye, Sir John, *The Life and Correspondence of Charles, Lord Metcalfe*, vols 1 & 2 (London: Richard Bentley, 1854).

Kennedy, Richard, *Narrative of the Campaign of the Army of the Indus in Sind and Kaubool in 1838–9* (London: Bentley, 1840. ULAN Press reprint, n.d.).

Keay, John, *When Men and Mountains Meet: the Explorers of the Western Himalayas, 1820–75* (Oxford: Oxford University Press, 1997).

Keay, John, *The Honourable Company: A History of the East India Company* (London:. Harper Collins, 1991).

Kekewich, Margaret, *Retreat & Retribution in Afghanistan 1842: Two Journals of the First Afghan War* (Barnsley: Pen and Sword, 2011).

Lal, Mohan, *Travels in the Punjab, Afghanistan and Turkistan to Balk, Bokhara and Herat, and a Visit to Great Britain and Germany* (Calcutta: K.P. Bagchi, 1977; n.p.: Elibron Classics reprint, 2005).

Latif, Syed Mohammed, *History of the Punjab from the Remotest Antiquity to the Present Time* (London: Sampson Low Marston & Co., 1889; n.p.: Sang-e-Meel Publications reprint, n.d.).

Law, Sir Algernon, *India Under Lord Ellenborough, March 1842–June 1844* (London: John Murray, 1926).

Lawrence, Sir George, *Reminiscences of Forty-Three Years in India* (London: J. Murray 1874; Sang-i-Meel Publications reprint, 1969).

Lawson, Philip, *The East India Company: A History* (London: Longman Group, 1993).

Macintyre, Ben, *The Man Who Would Be King: The First American in Afghanistan* (New York: Farrar Straus & Giroux, 2004).

Mackenzie, Helen, Lieutenant General Colin, *Storms and Sunshine of a Soldier's Life: Lt.-General Colin Mackenzie, C.B., 1825–1991*, Vols. 1 & 2 (Edinburgh: D. Douglas, 1884. Bibliobazaar reprint, n.d.).

Mackenzie, Colin, *The Crisis in India: Its Causes and Proposed Remedies* (London: Richard Bentley, 1857; n.p.: Nabu reprint, n.d.).

Mackinnon, Daniel H., *Military Service and Adventures in the Far East, Including Sketches of the Campaigns Against the Afghans in 1839, and the Sikhs in 1845–62* (London: C. Ollier, 1847; n.p.: Oakpost Ltd, Leonaur reprint 2012).

MacLean, Fitzroy. *A Person from England and Other Travellers* (London: Jonathan Cape, 1958).

Macrory, Patrick, *The Fierce Pawns.* (the U.S. title of *Signal Catastrophe*). (Philadelphia: J.B. Lippincott Co., 1966).

Macrory, Richard, *The First Afghan War 1839–42* (London: Osprey, 2016).

Mason, Philip. *A Matter of Honour: An Account of the Indian Army, its Officers and Men* (Harmondsworth: Penguin, 1974).

Malcolm, John. *Malcolm: Soldier, Diplomat, Idealogue of British India: The Life of Sir John Malcolm* (Edinburgh: Jon Donald 2014).

Masters, John, *Bugles and a Tiger* (London: Cassels Military, 1956).

Meyer, Karl and Blair Shareen, *Tournament of Shadows* (London: ABACUS, 1999).

Michener, James, *Caravans: A Novel* (New York: Random House, 1963).

Moore, Geoffrey, *Vincent of the 41st: a Soldier's Battles in the First Afghan and Crimean Wars* (Huntingdon: author's publication, 1979. Bedford: Jaycopy Ltd, n.d.).

Morris, Mowbray, *The First Afghan War* (London: Low, Marston, Searle, & Rivington, 1878; n.p.: Leonaur Reprint, 2010).

Mount, Ferdinand, *The Tears of The Rajas: Mutiny, Money and Marriage in India 1805–1905* (London: Simon & Schuster, 2015).

Nash, Charles, *History of the War in Afghanistan, from its Commencement to its Close* (London: Thomas Brooks, 1843; Kessinger Legacy reprint)..

Newby, Eric, *A Short Walk in the Hindu Kush* (London: Harper Press, 2010).

Neill, John Martin, *With the Somersets in Afghanistan: the Recollections of an Officer of the 40th … Regiment During the First Afghan War 1838–1842* (n.p.: Leonaur Ltd, 2011)..

Northey, Major W.P., *The Land of the Gurkhas: the Himalayan Kingdom of Nepal* (Cambridge: W. Heffer & Sons, 1937).

Osborne, W.G., *Ranjit Singh: The Lion of the Punjab* (Calcutta: Susil Gupta, 1952. New Delhi: Rupa & Co, reprint n.d.).

Palit, D.K., *Musings and Memories* (New Delhi: Palit & Palit in association with Lancer Publishers, 2004).

Preston, Diana, *The Dark Defile: Britain's Catastrophic Invasion of Afghanistan, 1838–1842* (New York: Waller & Co., 2012).

Prinsep, H.T., *The Gurkha War:* The *Anglo-Nepalese Conflict in North East India, 1814–1816* [1825?]; n.p.: Leonaur Ltd, reprint 2007).

Reid, Walter, *Empire of Sand: How Britain Shaped the Middle East* (Edinburgh: Birlinn, 2013).

Richards, D.S., *The Savage Frontier: A History of the Anglo-Afghan Wars* (London: Macmillan, 1990).

Roberts, Field Marshal Lord Frederick Sleigh, *Forty-One Years in India: From Subaltern to Commander-in-Chief* (London: Macmillan and Co., 1901).

Roberts, P.E., *British Rule in India*, Vols. 1 & 2 (Dehradun, India: reprint, 2006).

Sale, Florentia Wynch (Lady Sale)., *A Journal of the Disasters in Afghanistan, 1841–42* (London: John Murray, 1843. Uckfield: Naval & Military Press reprint, n.d.).

Sarila, Narendra Singh, *The Shadow of the Great Game: the Untold Story of India's Partition* (New Delhi: HarperCollins, 2005).

Seaton, Thomas, *From Cadet to Colonel*, Vol. I (London: Blackett, 1866).

Shahamat Ali, *The Sikhs and Afghans, in Connexion with India and Persia, Immediately Before and After the Death … of Ranjeet Singh* (London: J. Murray, 1846. Elibron Classics reprint, 2005).

Sleeman, Sir W.H., *Rambles and Recollections of An Indian Official* (London: J. Hatchard, 1844. New Delhi: Rupa Co., reprint 2003).

Singh, Khushwant, *A History of the Sikhs*, Vols. 1 & 2 (Oxford: Oxford University Press,1999).

Smith, Vincent A., *The Oxford History of India* (Oxford: Oxford University Press, 1919).

Stewart, Jules, *Crimson Snow: Britain's First Disaster in Afghanistan* (New York: History Press, 2011).

Stewart, Jules, *On Afghanistan's Plains: the Story of Britain's Afghan Wars* (London: I.B. Tauris, 2011).

Stewart, Rory, *The Places in Between* (London: Picador, 2014).

Stocqueler, J.H., *Memorials of Afghanistan: Being state papers, official documents, dispatches, authentic narratives, etc.* (Calcutta: Ostell & Lepage, 1843. Bishop's College Press reprint, 2010)., p.21.

Stocqueler, J H., *Memoirs and Correspondence of Major General Sir William Nott Vol 2* (London: Hurst and Blackett, 1854; Elibron Classics).

Strawson, John, *Beggars in Red: The British Army 1789–1889* (Barnsley: Pen & Sword, 2003).

Tanner, Stephen, *Afghanistan: A Military History from Alexander the Great to the War Against the Taliban* (Philadelphia: Da Capo Press, 2002).

Taylor, William, *Scenes and Adventures in Afghanistan* (London: T.C. Newby, 1842. Naval & Military Press reprint, n.d.).

Tytler, Harriet (ed.)., Anthony Sattin, *An Englishwoman in India: the Memoirs of Harriet Tytler, 1828–1858* (Oxford: Oxford University Press, 1986).

Ure, John, *Shooting Leave: Spying Out Central Asia in the Great Game* (London: Constable, 2009).

Vigne, G.T. *Personal Narrative of a Visit to Ghuzni, Kabul, and Afghanistan* (London: Whittaker, 1840. Cambridge: Cambridge University Press reprint, 2012).

Waller, John H., *Beyond the Khyber Pass: the Road to British Disaster in the First Afghan War* (New York: Random House, 1990).

Warburton, Sir Robert, *Eighteen Years in the Khyber, 1879–1898* (Oxford: Oxford University Press, 1900. Memphis: General Books, reprint 2011).

Whitteridge, Gordon, *Charles Masson of Afghanistan: Explorer, Archaeologist, Numismatist and Intelligence Agent* (Bangkok: Orchid Press, 2002).

Woodruff, Philip, *The Men Who Ruled India 1: The Founders* (London: Jonathan Cape, 1953).

Wylly, H.C., *The Military Memoirs of Lieut.-General Sir Joseph Thackwell* (London: John Murray, 1908).

Yorke, Edmund, *Playing the Great Game: Britain, War and Politics in Afghanistan Since 1839* (London: Robert Hale, 2012).

Index

The period 1815-1914 is sometimes called the long century of peace. It was in reality very far from that. It was a century of civil wars, popular uprisings, and struggles for Independence. An era of colonial expansion, wars of Empire, and colonial campaigning, much of which was unconventional in nature. It was also an age of major conventional wars, in Europe that would see the Crimea campaign and the wars of German unification. Such conflicts, along with the American Civil War, foreshadowed the total war of the 20th century.

It was also a period of great technological advancement, which in time impacted the military and warfare in general. Steam power, electricity, the telegraph, the radio, the railway, all became tools of war. The century was one of dramatic change. Tactics altered, sometimes slowly, to meet the challenges of the new technology. The dramatic change in the technology of war in this period is reflected in the new title of this series: From Musket to Maxim.

The new title better reflects the fact that the series covers all nations and all conflict of the period between 1815-1914. Already the series has commissioned books that deal with matters outside the British experience. This is something that the series will endeavour to do more of in the future. At the same time there still remains an important place for the study of the British military during this period. It is one of fascination, with campaigns that capture the imagination, in which Britain although the world's predominant power, continues to field a relatively small army.

The aim of the series is to throw the spotlight on the conflicts of that century, which can often get overlooked, sandwiched as they are between two major conflicts, the French/Revolutionary/Napoleonic Wars and the First World War. The series will produced a variety of books and styles. Some will look simply at campaigns or battles. Others will concentrate on particular aspects of a war or campaign. There will also be books that look at wider concepts of warfare during this era. It is the intention that this series will present a platform for historians to present their work on an important but often overlooked century of warfare.

Submissions

The publishers would be pleased to receive submissions for this series. Please contact series editor Dr Christopher Brice via email (christopherbrice@helion.co.uk), or in writing to Helion & Company Limited, Unit 8, Amherst Business Centre, Budbrooke Road, Warwick, Warwickshire, CV34 5WE.

Books in this series:

1. *The Battle of Majuba Hill: The Transvaal Campaign 1880-1881* John Laband (ISBN 978-1-911512-38-7)
2. *For Queen and Company: Vignettes of the Irish Soldier in the Indian Mutiny* David Truesdale (ISBN 978-1-911512-79-0)
3. *The Furthest Garrison: Imperial Regiments in New Zealand 1840-1870* Adam Davis (ISBN 978-1-911628-29-3)
4. *Victory over Disease: Resolving The Medical Crisis In The Crimean War, 1854-1856* Michael Hinton (ISBN 978-1-911628-31-6)
5. *Journey Through the Wilderness: Garnet Wolseley's Canadian Red River Expedition of 1870* Paul McNicholls (ISBN 978-1-911628-30-9)
6. *Kitchener: The Man Not the Myth* Anne Samson (ISBN 978-1-912866-45-8)
7. *The British and the Sikhs: Discovery, Warfare and Friendship (c.1700–1900)* Gurinder Singh Mann (ISBN 978-1-911628-24-8)
8. *Bazaine 1870: Scapegoat for a Nation* Quintin Barry (ISBN 978-1-913336-08-0)
9. *Redcoats in the Classroom: The British Army's School for Soldiers and Their Children During the 19th Century* Howard R. Clarke (ISBN 978-1-912866-47-2)
10. *The Rescue They Called A Raid: The Jameson Raid 1895-96* David Snape (ISBN 978-1-913118-77-8)
11. *Hungary 1848: The Winter Campaign* Johann Nobili (ISBN 978-1-913118-78-5)
12. *The War of Two Brothers: The Portuguese Civil War 1828-1834* Sérgio Veludo Coelho (ISBN 978-1-914059-26-1)

14. *Forgotten Victorian Generals* Christopher Brice (editor) (ISBN 978-1-910777-20-6)
15. *The German War of 1866: The Bohemian and Moravian Campaign Theodor Fontane* (ISBN 978-1-914059-29-2)
16. *Dust of Glory: The First Anglo-Afghan War 1839-1842, its Causes and Course* (ISBN 978-1-914059-33-9)